9/11
AND THE
WORLD
TODAY

DAVID WAKEEN

Truth Be Told Publishers
2803 Gulf to Bay Blvd. #166
Clearwater, Fl 33759
911andtheworldtoday.com

10 9 8 7 6 5 4 3 2 1
Printed in the United States of America

Library of Congress Control Number: 2017913299
ISBN: 978-0-9634911-0-7

To the fallen of that infamous day and their heartbroken families and friends, to the heroic rescue workers who sacrificed themselves with honor and dignity, to all who have since suffered inestimable loss, and to people of goodwill and kind deeds—this book is lovingly dedicated to you.

David Wakeen

Table of Contents

Acknowledgments

UNBOUNDED THANKS TO MY WIFE for your help in creating a better life for everyone. You are invaluable to me, your friendship is irreplaceable, and your kindness is overly abundant. You are a treasure beyond compare, and your heart shines brighter than the sun.

My dear parents, thank you for everything you have provided through the years that contributes to making me the man I am today. Your love, kindness, and sacrifice are felt in every breath I take. To my brothers and sisters, your love is appreciated more that you will ever know.

Great homage is extended to the various freedom fighters I have admired over the years, who have at their own peril fought for the evolution of humanity; thank you for your sacrifices and efforts. To the authors and video contributors whose works are included and cited in this book, I thank you from the bottom of my heart for your great work that exposes evil and helps humanity to right its wrongs.

A special thanks to my too few friends for their support and patience during the writing of this book; I have missed you all.

Finally, the reader is highly commended, for you obviously stand against oppression and injustice and instinctively possess the intent of bringing peace to the world. You are deeply thanked, appreciated, and heavenly blessed.

Note to the Reader

E ACH OF US HAS A UNIQUE GIFT of talent, bestowed upon us, that we are called to share with humanity. We that choose the side of good and righteousness possess a helpful intention, coupled with a unique ability to assist and improve the surroundings, the well-being of others, and the world in general, and by doing so, we improve and uplift our own lives.

It has been demonstrated throughout the ages that as a society, humanity functions at its zenith when individual members of society focus their intentions and actions in a manner that improves the lives of others, rather than focusing on what will improve their own lives. The former is how the world becomes a better place for all involved, and the latter is the reason we are in this individual and collective predicament—selfishness.

It is imperative to incorporate kindness as our foundational philosophy and use it to principally guide our decisions and corresponding actions as individuals and as a nation. This change in philosophy alone would immediately contribute to calming down and cleansing the world of the thoroughly infested criminality that is responsible for the denigration of man.

The only way this ship or this world, which we are all an inextricable part of, gets righted is if we all stand to one side and use our might to overcome the stormiest and deadliest of seas. Against all odds, we must pull the ropes and levers that need to be pulled while all the time effectively adjusting our course of direction to successfully navigate our way through the unflinching storm to calm and safer waters.

The belly of the sea often mercilessly digests any fledglings that show the slightest doubt or reservation to do what is right for the crew. For the storm does not relent with our pleas for calmness and mercy. It is an inescapable storm of such size and power that it will challenge us to our limits and come back again and again trying to steal more and more till there is nothing left to take.

Ferocious beatings from the waves can never take our dignity, for it can only be forfeited from the depths of our souls and with our personal consent.

Those who survive the gauntlet and fury of the seas, which has taken many greater men than we, honor their duty to fellow crew above personal concern. Under unfathomable duress, they cling and pull the ropes and levers with all their gumption and grit, knowing that personal failure is mutiny. Those that live to tell their story have fearlessly fought on behalf of their noble and blessed crews to upright the ship or die in the attempt.

Wave after wave claims the weak and faint of heart. Those that gave up were never seen again. They were swallowed by the hungry and insatiable sea.

The rocks approach with great speed and fright. Still we do our jobs and hope like hell the Almighty will keep us from violently crashing into rocky graves that lie just ahead and have taken too many good lives.

It is only with great courage and working together that the crew can survive the thunderous fury of the tireless sea.

Welcome aboard to our human crew. Your assistance is not requested; it is required. If we stand shoulder to shoulder, we can defeat the storm that unnecessarily harms humanity, a storm that humankind must survive.

Our actions are the only thing that will contribute to improving this world towards a condition suitable for inheritance by future generations as a gift, rather than a nightmare beyond compare.

A ship's crew, and not its sails, directs the course of the vessel into the future. Let's do our part and make it through the storm that is battering the ship of humanity. Billions of people are counting on us! We can do it. We can make this world a better place.

I love you and good luck.

Study Note

In this book, every word was specifically chosen to convey a complete concept for the reader. Each sentence is a complete and examinable concept in itself, worthy of due consideration. To fully grasp the concepts put forth in this book, please liberally use a dictionary whenever there is a word that you do not entirely understand. Before schools became places of state indoctrination and mass medication, our grandparents were taught to liberally use dictionaries whenever they were confused about the meaning of a word or a symbol.

Fully duplicating and understanding what one is reading raises the comprehension, the intelligence, and the performance levels of the individual. With this in mind, we in turn can then raise the comprehension, intelligence, and performance levels of our society.

Without adequate education, there is a disintegration of the culture.

In reading this book, for a more thorough understanding of the topics covered, please verify all the data for yourself on the websites provided and feel free to further research any of the topics covered throughout this book.

In order to derive the most benefit from this book, it is advised that the reader take the time to study the recommended videos in the order they appear throughout this book. The information in the videos complements the enclosed information and reinforces and substantiates the claims made in this book and should be viewed as an integral part of the educational information presented within this book.

Since the subject matter contained herein could be considered vast and extremely encompassing, each chapter contains a multitude of subject matters, which are included to give the reader an expanded viewpoint of the overall theme of the chapter. The information contained herein and the interrelations of that information are presented in each chapter to expand the reader's knowledge and understanding of the subject matter.

If the information presented within this book and the associated videos are fully and correctly studied, it would be somewhat comparable to receiving advanced degrees in several subjects.

The purpose of this book is to enlighten and assist the reader to gain better understanding and control over his or her life and the direction this world is taking. This book was written to help humanity to better identify, understand, and eliminate from society those individuals, forces, and organizations that act contrary to the interests of us all and prevent humanity from evolving to a higher plateau or level of existence.

If we are going to make any difference at all in the way things are, your help in improving our government and our world is required. When we consider our mission as human beings, if our life is to have any purpose whatsoever, we must foster a basic agreement that our actions make the world a better place.

There are organized counterforces hard at work with intentions to disrupt and destroy the natural harmony of this planet; they are evident from their actions. Evil lurks in government hallways and back offices in every federal building; it breeds an organized effort to bend and reshape our planet using whatever force is necessary, regardless of the cost in human lives and tragedy.

Enough is enough, and those who perished at Ground Zero and beyond deserve much better. This writing is my attempt to honor the lives of our friends that were lost on and after September 11, 2001, and to assist the world by doing my part to make a better, safer, more caring civilization for us all. Let us all do our special part in order to ensure that all who perished and breathed their last breath under circumstances of such horror and fright have not died in vain. For the sake of humanity and all those yet to be born, we must change the course of this world, wrestle it from the hands of evil, and return it to kind and caring people that can govern the world sanely.

Thank you in advance for giving a damn. Now it is up to us to do our part to reverse the direction of this planet, where the greatness of humanity will once again thrive over evil. Future generations thank you, and I am sure our friends of Ground Zero do as well.

The President and the Press

P RESIDENT JOHN F. KENNEDY'S ADDRESS, "The President and the Press," was spoken to the American Newspapers Publishers Association at the Waldorf Astoria Hotel, New York City, April 27, 1961. I recommend listening to the full speech as you read along with John Fitzgerald Kennedy, one of the brightest and greatest men in American history (jfklibrary.org/Research/Research-Aids/JFK-Speeches/American-Newspaper-Publishers-Association_19610427.aspx).

Kennedy's words are more applicable today than ever; his concern for his fellow man, incredible wisdom, and intelligence were obvious and abundant to all that listened. The challenges of the Cuban Missile Crisis threatened the nation, as do the challenges we face today, which threaten also the existence of our American way of life.

Kennedy gave his life attempting to unlock the shackles of oppression and enslavement that weigh heavy on the shoulders of every American. He is an American hero and is in our prayers and in our hearts.

Mr. Chairman, ladies and gentlemen:

I appreciate very much your generous invitation to be here tonight.

You bear heavy responsibilities these days and an article I read some time ago reminded me of how particularly heavily the burdens of present day events bear upon your profession.

You may remember that in 1851 the New York Herald Tribune under the sponsorship and publishing of Horace Greeley, employed as its London correspondent an obscure journalist by the name of Karl Marx.

We are told that foreign correspondent Marx, stone broke, and with a family ill and undernourished, constantly appealed to

Greeley and managing editor Charles Dana for an increase in his munificent salary of $5 per installment, a salary which he and Engels ungratefully labeled as the "lousiest petty bourgeois cheating."

But when all his financial appeals were refused, Marx looked around for other means of livelihood and fame, eventually terminating his relationship with the Tribune and devoting his talents full time to the cause that would bequeath the world the seeds of Leninism, Stalinism, revolution and the cold war.

If only this capitalistic New York newspaper had treated him more kindly; if only Marx had remained a foreign correspondent, history might have been different. And I hope all publishers will bear this lesson in mind the next time they receive a poverty-stricken appeal for a small increase in the expense account from an obscure newspaper man.

I have selected as the title of my remarks tonight "The President and the Press." Some may suggest that this would be more naturally worded "The President Versus the Press." But those are not my sentiments tonight.

It is true, however, that when a well-known diplomat from another country demanded recently that our State Department repudiate certain newspaper attacks on his colleague it was unnecessary for us to reply that this Administration was not responsible for the press, for the press had already made it clear that it was not responsible for this Administration.

Nevertheless, my purpose here tonight is not to deliver the usual assault on the so-called one party press. On the contrary, in recent months I have rarely heard any complaints about political bias in the press except from a few Republicans. Nor is it my purpose tonight to discuss or defend the televising of Presidential press conferences. I think it is highly beneficial to have some 20,000,000 Americans regularly sit in on these conferences to ob-

serve, if I may say so, the incisive, the intelligent and the courteous qualities displayed by your Washington correspondents.

Nor, finally, are these remarks intended to examine the proper degree of privacy which the press should allow to any President and his family.

If in the last few months your White House reporters and photographers have been attending church services with regularity, that has surely done them no harm.

On the other hand, I realize that your staff and wire service photographers may be complaining that they do not enjoy the same green privileges at the local golf courses that they once did.

It is true that my predecessor did not object as I do to pictures of one's golfing skill in action. But neither on the other hand, did he ever bean a Secret Service man.

My topic tonight is a more sober one of concern to publishers as well as editors.

I want to talk about our common responsibilities in the face of a common danger. The events of recent weeks may have helped to illuminate that challenge for some; but the dimensions of its threat have loomed large on the horizon for many years. Whatever our hopes may be for the future—for reducing this threat or living with it—there is no escaping either the gravity or the totality of its challenge to our survival and to our security—a challenge that confronts us in unaccustomed ways in every sphere of human activity.

This deadly challenge imposes upon our society two requirements of direct concern both to the press and to the President—two requirements that may seem almost contradictory in tone, but which must be reconciled and fulfilled if we are to meet this national peril. I refer, first, to the need for a far greater public information; and, second, to the need for far greater official secrecy.

I

The very word "secrecy" is repugnant in a free and open society; and we are as a people inherently and historically opposed to secret societies, to secret oaths and to secret proceedings. We decided long ago that the dangers of excessive and unwarranted concealment of pertinent facts far outweighed the dangers which are cited to justify it. Even today, there is little value in opposing the threat of a closed society by imitating its arbitrary restrictions. Even today, there is little value in insuring the survival of our nation if our traditions do not survive with it. And there is very grave danger that an announced need for increased security will be seized upon by those anxious to expand its meaning to the very limits of official censorship and concealment. That I do not intend to permit to the extent that it is in my control. And no official of my Administration, whether his rank is high or low, civilian or military, should interpret my words here tonight as an excuse to censor the news, to stifle dissent, to cover up our mistakes or to withhold from the press and the public the facts they deserve to know.

But I do ask every publisher, every editor, and every newsman in the nation to reexamine his own standards, and to recognize the nature of our country's peril. In time of war, the government and the press have customarily joined in an effort based largely on self-discipline, to prevent unauthorized disclosures to the enemy. In time of "clear and present danger," the courts have held that even the privileged rights of the First Amendment must yield to the public's need for national security.

Today no war has been declared—and however fierce the struggle may be, it may never be declared in the traditional fashion. Our way of life is under attack. Those who make themselves our enemy are advancing around the globe. The survival of our friends is in danger. And yet no war has been declared, no borders have been crossed by marching troops, no missiles have been fired.

If the press is awaiting a declaration of war before it imposes the self-discipline of combat conditions, then I can only say that no war ever posed a greater threat to our security. If you are awaiting a finding of "clear and present danger," then I can only say that the danger has never been more clear and its presence has never been more imminent.

It requires a change in outlook, a change in tactics, a change in missions—by the government, by the people, by every businessman or labor leader, and by every newspaper. For we are opposed around the world by a monolithic and ruthless conspiracy that relies primarily on covert means for expanding its sphere of influence—on infiltration instead of invasion, on subversion instead of elections, on intimidation instead of free choice, on guerrillas by night instead of armies by day. It is a system which has conscripted vast human and material resources into the building of a tightly knit, highly efficient machine that combines military, diplomatic, intelligence, economic, scientific and political operations.

Its preparations are concealed, not published. Its mistakes are buried, not headlined. Its dissenters are silenced, not praised. No expenditure is questioned, no rumor is printed, no secret is revealed. It conducts the Cold War, in short, with a war-time discipline no democracy would ever hope or wish to match.

Nevertheless, every democracy recognizes the necessary restraints of national security—and the question remains whether those restraints need to be more strictly observed if we are to oppose this kind of attack as well as outright invasion.

For the facts of the matter are that this nation's foes have openly boasted of acquiring through our newspapers information they would otherwise hire agents to acquire through theft, bribery or espionage; that details of this nation's covert preparations to counter the enemy's covert operations have been available to every newspaper reader, friend and foe alike; that the size, the strength, the location and the nature of our forces and weapons, and our plans and strategy for their use, have all been pin-pointed in the press and other news media to a degree sufficient to satisfy any foreign power; and that, in at least in one case, the publication of details concerning a secret mechanism whereby satellites were followed required its alteration at the expense of considerable time and money.

The newspapers which printed these stories were loyal, patriotic, responsible and well-meaning. Had we been engaged in open warfare, they undoubtedly would not have published such items. But in the absence of open warfare, they recognized only the tests of journalism and not the tests of national security. And my question tonight is whether additional tests should not now be adopted.

The question is for you alone to answer. No public official should answer it for you. No governmental plan should impose its restraints against your will. But I would be failing in my duty to the nation, in considering all of the responsibilities that we now bear and all of the means at hand to meet those responsibilities, if I did not commend this problem to your attention, and urge its thoughtful consideration.

On many earlier occasions, I have said—and your newspapers have constantly said—that these are times that appeal to every citizen's sense of sacrifice and self-discipline. They call out to every citizen to weigh his rights and comforts against his obligations to the common good. I cannot now believe that those citizens who serve in the newspaper business consider themselves exempt from that appeal.

I have no intention of establishing a new Office of War Information to govern the flow of news. I am not suggesting any new forms of censorship or any new types of security classifications. I have no easy answer to the dilemma that I have posed, and would not seek to impose it if I had one. But I am asking the members of the newspaper profession and the industry in this country to reexamine their own responsibilities, to consider the degree and the nature of the present danger, and to heed the duty of self-restraint which that danger imposes upon us all.

Every newspaper now asks itself, with respect to every story: "Is it news?" All I suggest is that you add the question: "Is it in the interest of the national security?" And I hope that every group in America—unions and businessmen and public officials at every level— will ask the same question of their endeavors, and subject their actions to the same exacting tests.

And should the press of America consider and recommend the voluntary assumption of specific new steps or machinery, I can assure you that we will cooperate whole-heartedly with those recommendations.

Perhaps there will be no recommendations. Perhaps there is no answer to the dilemma faced by a free and open society in a cold and secret war. In times of peace, any discussion of this subject, and any action that results, are both painful and without precedent. But this is a time of peace and peril which knows no precedent in history.

II

It is the unprecedented nature of this challenge that also gives rise to your second obligation—an obligation which I share. And that is our obligation to inform and alert the American people—to make certain that they possess all the facts that they need, and understand them as well—the perils, the prospects, the purposes of our program and the choices that we face.

No President should fear public scrutiny of his program. For from that scrutiny comes understanding; and from that understanding comes support or opposition. And both are necessary. I am not asking your newspapers to support the Administration, but I am asking your help in the tremendous task of informing and alerting the American people. For I have complete confi-

dence in the response and dedication of our citizens whenever they are fully informed.

I not only could not stifle controversy among your readers—I welcome it. This Administration intends to be candid about its errors; for as a wise man once said: "An error does not become a mistake until you refuse to correct it." We intend to accept full responsibility for our errors; and we expect you to point them out when we miss them.

Without debate, without criticism, no Administration and no country can succeed—and no republic can survive. That is why the Athenian lawmaker Solon decreed it a crime for any citizen to shrink from controversy. And that is why our press was protected by the First Amendment—the only business in America specifically protected by the Constitution—not primarily to amuse and entertain, not to emphasize the trivial and the sentimental, not to simply "give the public what it wants"—but to inform, to arouse, to reflect, to state our dangers and our opportunities, to indicate our crises and our choices, to lead, mold, educate and sometimes even anger public opinion.

This means greater coverage and analysis of international news —for it is no longer far away and foreign but close at hand and local. It means greater attention to improved understanding of the news as well as improved transmission. And it means, finally, that government at all levels, must meet its obligation to provide you with the fullest possible information outside the narrowest limits of national security—and we intend to do it.

III

It was early in the Seventeenth Century that Francis Bacon remarked on three recent inventions already transforming the world: the compass, gunpowder and the printing press. Now the links between the nations first forged by the compass have made us all citizens of the world, the hopes and threats of one becoming the hopes and threats of us all. In that one world's ef-

forts to live together, the evolution of gunpowder to its ultimate limit has warned mankind of the terrible consequences of failure.

And so it is to the printing press—to the recorder of man's deeds, the keeper of his conscience, the courier of his news—that we look for strength and assistance, confident that with your help man will be what he was born to be: free and independent.

Introduction

SAME PLANET, DIFFERENT WORLD. The events of 9/11 changed the lives of virtually every member of the human race. Whether we live in New York or New Delhi, our lives and the world we live in changed drastically when the World Trade Center towers were demolished. On that day, the most heinous day of modern infamy, 2,976 people perished in the attacks that occurred in New York City, Washington, DC, and Shanksville, Pennsylvania, leaving families and friends devastated and a nation reeling in the after-effects of the worst terrorist attack on the United States since Pearl Harbor on December 7, 1941.

The country and the world were shocked when the media informed us that nineteen hijackers of Saudi Arabian descent were responsible for the deadliest attack on the soil of the continental United States.

Many find it impossible to fathom that the planes, full of many tough Bostonians and New Yorkers, did not subdue or kill the supposed hijackers armed with a box cutter and its one-inch blade.

We watched in fright as the media broadcast the towers crumbling to the ground, along with the hopes and dreams of the people inside. As the World Trade Center towers were being destroyed, an amalgamation of toxic dust bellowed and spread for miles in every direction, scattering onlookers as they fled for their lives. The mass grave of the victims murdered at the World Trade Center smoldered as the dust and its toxic fumes wafted in the air.

The press quickly classified those that died as heroes, which they are, and their spirits should be memorialized as such. Their families and friends will never fill the void in their broken hearts left by those who were needlessly and tragically taken. Every man, woman, and child whose heart stopped beating that fateful day was a victim of an evil of the most horrific type. Those who were buried in the wasteland of twisted steel and burning debris left survivors who will never fully recover from the unexpected departure of their loved ones.

One can only imagine the horror and suffering of the people who leaped from the towers to their death, rather than withstanding the excruciating pain of burning to death. The wonderful people that perished at the hands of the unconscionable perpetrators of 9/11 need to have closure and need to have justice.

Far too many children were orphaned as billions around the world cried at the inhumanity orchestrated by one of the most evil slivers of society. People around the world could only imagine what kind of depraved persons were responsible for such heinous attacks.

Politicians filled the airwaves with conjecture and fabrications of what occurred to bring the once glorious World Trade Center towers, and those who were in them, to their ultimate demise. Within two minutes, the blame was laid at the feet of Osama bin Laden, whose family, oddly enough, just happened to vacation with the Bush family.

The Saudi Arabian hijackers were decisively portrayed by the media as the party responsible for executing one of the largest terrorist attacks in world history. Unfortunately, the media never showed video evidence of any of the purported attackers boarding a single plane on September 11, 2001. This turned out to be one of the many lies told to hide the true identities of the orchestrators of the largest mass murder in America's history.

The pre-fabricated story was told, and a mourning world listened as President George W. Bush rallied Americans into a frenzy where war and war alone would be conducted to mend the broken hearts of Americans.

The world changed more than any of us realized in those devastating and tumultuous days of September 2001. Politicians took every opportunity to use the airwaves, preparing the population for the New World Order that was being ushered in under the noses of unsuspecting and good-hearted people of the world. A new world was promoted where America was no longer safe, and the government immediately seized further power over the people by passing laws that eviscerated the Constitution and the laws of the land.

The Patriot Act, which provides the government with the ability to detain suspects indefinitely and conduct warrantless searches, disregards the protections and freedoms once enjoyed by every American under the US Constitution. The act was quickly passed by Congress and signed into law by President George W. Bush.

Many of the freedoms and liberties we enjoyed as Americans were now going to be restricted and illegitimately taken from the people by the US federal government, supposedly to provide the people with security and safety from terrorists around the world, terrorists who now suddenly wanted to kill all Americans indiscriminately.

Politicians were incessantly being paraded in the media, talking about how Americans had to sacrifice their liberties for their safety, their freedom for their security. Such sacrifice has always been incompatible with the American way of life.

The snowball effect of hate and retribution, driven by the politicians and the media, continued with America somehow choosing to bomb Afghanistan and Iraq while ignoring Saudi Arabia, where a majority of the alleged hijackers allegedly originated. US foreign policy immediately shifted toward war, and the United States, under the direction of George W. Bush's administration, quickly became responsible for creating World War III.

America, a once peace-loving nation, was transformed by the actions and decisions of President Bush into a warmongering nation, a status and repute that continues today.

Humankind is traveling at an accelerating pace down a road of destruction toward extinction because of the political decisions made by a small and evil group of people, decisions that came to fruition in the fall of 2001. Over the past fifteen years since 9/11, the nation, once a beacon of love and hope, has disintegrated into a military bully, terrorizing, threatening, and killing millions of people around the world. The United States is a misdirected and out-of-control nation.

For fifteen years, the lives of those lost at Ground Zero have been used as an excuse for the United States to proliferate unnecessary wars that are destroying the human race. The quality of all our lives has been lowered by policies crafted to profit the rich while maiming and killing millions upon millions of people. There is a lot of blood on US hands.

The efforts undertaken to write this book were conducted to investigate the actions that have occurred as a result of political decisions made in the days preceding and following the events of 9/11. This book reveals the actual perpetrators of international terrorism and how and why terror is being used to control the masses.

The 9/11 Commission Report and the many other fanciful stories told in the media to justify US military actions around the planet are basically filled with lies. Millions upon millions of people are being slaughtered to perpetuate and cover up the lies of the Bush and Obama administrations, told and sold by the media to the American people.

This book attempts to explain the truth regarding the change of direction that has occurred on this planet where one religious group is in direct opposition to another religious group—where the Christians are killing the Muslims and the Muslims are killing the Christians. Wars have been blamed on religious beliefs since the dawn of religion, and very little has changed over the years. How convenient it is to blame all acts of international terrorism on ISIS, the Taliban, and al-Qaeda or some other fabricated and manufactured terror group while the true perpetrators of military malice and warfare walk the corridors of Washington, DC, wearing two-thousand-dollar suits.

Many people are usually quite busy working at their highly taxed jobs in order to pay their rent and feed their families. They believe they don't have time to make a difference. Nothing is further from the truth. A small group of hateful and vile individuals benefits from Americans' ignorance regarding why the World Trade Center towers were demolished and who demolished them. They want to keep the masses in the dark and therefore in a controllable and exploitable state.

This book aims to explain who the bad actors really are and who is ultimately responsible for bringing down the towers. These same criminals are wholly responsible for bringing the world into a never-ending state of war. This book reveals the corrupt motives and desires of those who created the events of 9/11 and changed the direction of this world for their own advantage and profit at the expense of mankind.

Your assistance is required to bring the truth to light and to banish from the face of the Earth the distorted principles and policies implemented by the Bush and Obama administrations, which are destroying international relations and international tranquility. Never has your help been needed more urgently than now. Never has humanity been in such dire straits where inaction will equate to an irreversible direction being taken by world leaders, costing billions of lives and in the process removing all the freedoms Americans are accustomed to enjoying.

What each and every one of us does in this very moment of history will affect the quality of each and every person's life on this planet. We do not have the liberty to allow bought-and-sold politicians to stumble about and betray the American people because they are the ones who created the current predicament and turmoil we now experience.

To do nothing to improve our world is to let it die. Moreover, to do nothing is to turn our backs on the future of this planet and the generations to come. To do nothing is hardly ever the right course of action required to solve a problem. America and the world at large need your help. To do nothing is to give our approval to the oppression and tyranny we live under and deprive future generations of the freedoms and liberties that Americans see slipping away right before our very eyes. To do nothing in a decaying world is essentially condemning our posterity to a horrible future of slavery and misery.

Please do something. Billions are counting on you! The 911truthbe told.com website was built by the author for those of us interested in actually building a better world. Through this site, we can build a better world and simultaneously honor our friends that perished on September 11, 2001.

CHAPTER 1

A New Yorker's Perspective

The best way to predict the future is to invent it.

           – ALAN KAY

Truth is incontrovertible. Malice may attack it, ignorance may deride it, but in the end, there it is.

           – WINSTON CHURCHILL

Facts are stubborn things; and whatever may be our wishes, our inclinations, or the dictates of our passion, they cannot alter the state of facts and evidence.

           – JOHN ADAMS

By doubting we are led to question, by questioning we arrive at the truth.

           – PETER ABELARD

All truth goes through three stages. First it is ridiculed. Then it is violently opposed. Finally it is accepted as self-evident.

           – ARTHUR SCHOPENHAUER

It is to be regretted that the rich and powerful too often bend the acts of government to their own selfish purposes.

           – ANDREW JACKSON

Three things that cannot be hidden: the sun, the moon, and the truth.

           – BUDDHA

J UST AFTER AN HOUR INTO THE REPUBLICAN DEBATE of January 14, 2016, when asked to respond to Senator Cruz's disparaging and insulting remarks regarding New York values and his limited and short-sighted observation that "Not a lot of conservatives come out of New York," Donald J. Trump retorted the following, with an abundance of integrity and justness:

> *So conservatives actually do come out of Manhattan, including William F. Buckley and others, just so you [Cruz] understand.*
>
> *And just so—if I could, because he insulted a lot of people. I've had more calls on that statement that Ted made—New York is a great place. It's got great people, it's got loving people, wonderful people.*
>
> *When the World Trade Center came down, I saw something that no place on Earth, could have handled more beautifully, more humanely than New York. You had two one hundred [outburst of applause interrupts Trump] you had two 110-story buildings come crashing down. I saw them come down. Thousands of people killed, and the cleanup started the next day, and it was the most horrific cleanup, probably in the history of doing this, and in construction. I was down there, and I've never seen anything like it.*
>
> *And the people in New York fought and fought and fought, and we saw more death, and even the smell of death—nobody understood it. And it was with us for months, the smell, the air. And we rebuilt downtown Manhattan, and everybody in the world watched and everybody in the world loved New York and loved New Yorkers.*

Trump finished stating,

> *And I have to tell you, that was a very insulting statement that Ted made.*

During Trump's last sentence, he was pointing at Cruz with authority and in an ethical and moral manner, as though he spoke on behalf of the people of New York and the people of the world. Trump encapsulated the hurt and suffering of millions, but moreover, he encapsulated the pride and the greatness that can only be found in the City of Heroes.

The audience, with great approval and appreciation of Trump's heart-felt defense of the people of New York, applauded in admiration.

CHAPTER 2

The Author's 9/11 Experience

It always seems impossible until its done.

– NELSON MANDELA

Everything we hear is an opinion, not a fact. Everything we see is a perspective, not the truth.

– MARCUS AURELIUS

A slave is one who waits for someone to come and free him.

– EZRA POUND

It does not require a majority to prevail, but rather an irate, tireless minority keen to set brushfires in people's minds.

– SAMUEL ADAMS

Those who expect to be ignorant and free expect what never was and never will be.

– THOMAS JEFFERSON

Human progress is neither automatic nor inevitable... Every step toward the goal of justice requires sacrifice, suffering , and struggle; the tireless exertions and passionate concern of dedicated individuals.

– MARTIN LUTHER KING JR.

Condemnation without investigation is the height of ignorance.

– ALBERT EINSTEIN

The truest service private man may hope to do his country is, by unbiasing his mind as much as possible.

– JONATHON SWIFT

The great and mighty only appear so because we are on our knees. Let us rise.

> – JAMES CONNOLLY

Start where you are. Use what you have. Do what you can.

> – ARTHUR ASHE

The best and most beautiful things in the world cannot be seen or even touched—they must be felt with the heart.

> – HELEN KELLER

ARRIVING AT GROUND ZERO at four in the morning on September 13, 2001, was an experience that changed me to the core, to the essence of my spirit. The Stuyvesant High School on Chambers Street was about three-quarters of a mile away from what was called the "hole" or the "pile," which was where the World Trade Center towers previously stood and shone brightly above the city.

Inside the school, the volunteers endlessly swept the floors, yet they were losing the ongoing battle to clean and remove the relentless toxic dust that continuously wafted from the demolished towers. Soon, another forty-five foot tractor-trailer arrived, packed by volunteers from the Jacob Javits Convention Center with donations from the good and caring people of New York and from across the nation.

One after another, forty-five-foot tractor-trailers pulled in front of the Stuyvesant school with all kinds of donated supplies, and a small group of us worked as fast as we could to unload them. More supplies were on the way, and we hurriedly worked, knowing that another truck was just around the corner, waiting to be unloaded. The work never stopped, the pace was frantic, and the job got done.

Local restaurants donated thousands of meals to feed the more than four thousand rescue workers who were searching for loved ones, buried under acres of entangled metal, devastation, and heartbreak.

The outpouring of donations was nothing less than you would expect from a land of such great people. Trailer after trailer arrived full of clothes, boots, gloves, and eventually even breathing or respiratory masks. Anything that the rescue workers needed was donated, and my four friends and I, who had traveled from Florida to volunteer, unloaded the trucks and organized the supplies in the school as best we could.

There were about twenty volunteers working in and around the school; everyone pitched in. It was an all-out effort that I will remember forever. As we worked, we were breathing the deplorable dust-filled air. The toxic dust from the towers loomed over lower Manhattan like a sorrow or sadness that would not leave. The taste of death will haunt me forever. The rain, as hard as it tried, could not dampen the plumes of billowing smoke pouring off the massive pile of twisted steel.

A John Deere Gator, a green, four-wheel-drive machine with bright yellow seats, pulled up to the Stuyvesant school, and I went to work with its driver, Tim Mullally. Tim was a John Deere dealer from a small town about a hundred miles north of New York City called Jeffersonville, New York. Tim has a fantastic story regarding the generosity of the John Deere Company's donations of equipment that really helped the people of New York and the rescue workers of Ground Zero. (His story, "A Day in September," is a must-read article detailing and demonstrating the greatness of ordinary people and humanity in such dire and extraordinary times. See thrnewmedia.com/adayinseptember/mullally.htm.)

I jumped in the John Deere Gator, and we continued on our quest and headed to the hole. Tim and I became immediate friends, as often happens when two people depend on one another in catastrophic disasters.

There were ominous signs pointing the way to the hole from the Stuyvesant school. My mind was attempting to predict what I could never have imagined in a million years and what I was about to see in any moment.

The streets from the school to the hole were covered with a four-inch blanket of gray dust that made the area seem a little like outer space, as if we were driving on a different planet. I initially thought every car had been abandoned by its driver as each ran to save his or her life, but soon I realized some of the drivers remained buried in the smoldering, colossal pile of steel that lay just around the bend.

On the way to the hole, we traveled south to a plaza, which was silenced by dust and guarded by stairs on every side. Papers were scattered in the toxic landscape of dust for what seemed like miles. It was eerie; it was a different world. Sound did not travel with its ordinary vibrations but became absorbed by the gray blanket of hazardous dust that had billowed out of the towers as they raced towards the Earth taking with them life after precious life.

The environment was in a horrific turbulence, yet everything seemed to pass in a slower motion and on a slightly different wavelength. It seemed almost like the way a person would view the world shortly after being knocked out—constant confusion permeated the air.

Speeding along in the Gator, we twisted and turned, and with an uneasy feeling in my mind, we finally rounded the corner, and there stood the entrance to the hole. The devastation of the towers was the eeriest scene that I have ever witnessed in my life, and it totally entranced me. The destruction was beyond comprehension and exceeded imagination.

Remnants of steel beams reached for the sky, barely perceivable through the ever-present toxic dust that snowed down on everything. The gray dust was indiscriminant and covered everything. We had no respiratory masks. The toxic dust had suspended shards of glass floating in it, as it sliced and shredded the skin much like a cheese grater but on a smaller scale. The deadly dust pierced our lungs as we were breathing the remnants of the Twin Towers and those that tragically perished. The dust completely invaded our bodies. I wondered if the taste of the dust, the taste of death, would ever leave me or if it would last forever.

The all-encompassing dust changed the biology of everyone that breathed it, as we searched for survivors. Years later, it was to become sadly obvious that those who had breathed the deadly dust had been destroying their lungs with every breath. Once you breathed the dust, you were never the same. Today when I cough, it serves as a reminder that I am honored to have been part of one of the greatest teams in the history of humanity, the recovery effort at Ground Zero.

Tim and I pulled our shirts up to cover our faces and fight off the choking and toxic dust. The blanket of dust silenced the echoes of the Gator's engine as we drove through the hole. Not knowing where exactly to start, we began surveying the operation to discover whom to help first in order to be as effective as possible.

The hole was a massive mountain of destruction that seemed to sprawl endlessly in every direction. The gray dust and black smoke poisonously cohered as they wafted off the pile and headed toward the heavens. The smoldering remnants were all that remained of the once beautiful 110-story buildings that laid claim to New York's majestic skyline.

Everywhere you looked there were rescue workers, thousands of firefighters, police officers, and construction workers, sacrificing their bodies and their health to recover anyone fortunate enough to have survived the demolition of the towers.

The hole was a bustling effort of dedicated men and woman that cared more for their lost friends and family members than for themselves. Blessed is he who lays down his life for his brother.

Since the twelfth of September, rescue workers were on the job in full force, searching for proof of life, swarming the smoldering steel, like ants defending their mound. The exhaustive search for survivors was well underway before I set foot upon the wreckage of twisted steel, which represented in my mind an uncountable number of destroyed lives.

The pile was the monolithic altar of destruction that laid waste to so many lives, so many dreams, and symbolized a tragic world of broken promises unto itself. Many of the rescue workers believed the souls of the recently departed, the spiritual presence of the deceased, seemed to congregate in and emanate from the sky above the pile of twisted steal and shattered lives. Through the never-extinguishing plumes of smoke that spewed from the beast of destruction, many of the souls of the recently departed could be tangibly felt, as though they were not ready to leave and rest in peace. It seemed they had unfinished business, mostly unfinished family business.

The pile had a life of its own. Those that labored to find any sign of life tried to make sense out of an unfathomable environment, comprised of annihilation and death. In searching for signs of life, the positive actions and attitude of the rescue workers, who displayed vast bravery in the face of what appeared to be insurmountable adversity, brought a special kind of life to the area. With death all around, the element and abundance of human compassion uplifted the area and the rescue workers. The entire disaster site and all that were in it soon became larger than life, larger than anything evil could contrive. As a rescue worker, you had to be bigger than the destruction, or else you could not function.

K9 handlers and their dogs cautiously searched the monstrous pile of debris hoping to hear the voice of a missing friend, a whiff of a loved one, or any positive sign of life in an otherwise deadly and horrific place. The smoke and dust were blamed for the deaths of many canines after the first few days. Other search-and-rescue canine teams, which came from around the country and around the world to help in the recovery efforts, tragically replaced the rescue canines who breathed their last breath searching the pile for signs of life in service to mankind.

Firefighters and other volunteers came from as far as California and Florida. A continuous flow of love and concern was steadily overcoming the evil and destruction that seemed everywhere. It was incredible to see the outpouring of human decency and love replace the hatred that was responsible for the slaughter of thousands of innocent lives.

Time passed in the most unusual manner. It was often difficult to discern how quickly or slowly time was actually passing. The entire area seemed as if it was in its own twilight zone. The entirety of Ground Zero was unfathomable. The days sped by in a most erratic fashion; hours seemed like minutes, and seconds could seem like days. Time was being altered by the spiritual experience that was becoming Ground Zero.

There was something mystical about the area, as though the recently departed decided not to go to their next destination but to stay and moan and lament the losses of their families, their loves, and their lives. It seemed like the victims were trying to make sense of it all, just as we were, as we searched for proof of physical life and did all we could to help.

With all the randomness that was occurring in the hole and all the disorientation we continually fought, we knew there was no relenting in this massive rescue effort. There were no coffee breaks, no sit-downs. Pretty much a "work till you drop" attitude pervaded the scene, as there was an inordinate amount of things to do. Everyone there stood up to the challenge and got the job done!

The John Deere Gator is a powerful, rugged, and impressive golf cart–sized machine that climbed and overcame every obstacle in its way, often while carrying a payload of well over a ton. Tim and I used the Gator to bring heavy acetylene and oxygen tanks to the welders who were busy cutting huge steel beams, which were removed by massive cranes and extra-long flatbed trucks. The acetylene tanks weighed about 250 pounds, making them almost twice as heavy as the oxygen tanks. We punishingly piled ten of the oxygen and acetylene tanks in a triangle pattern in the bed of the powerful Gator. What a machine!

If you were not there, you likely could never envision what a horrific environment remained after the towers were demolished. Could you imagine if the concrete had remained behind in the cleanup site and had not vaporized into toxic dust? There would have been concrete slabs in the Hudson River; the slabs would have been piled four hundred feet high. Every other building in the world that has ever been demolished always leaves huge concrete slabs in and around the building's footprint. When the individual floors of a building pancake and crash onto the floor below, the concrete from every floor of the building does not vaporize but instead ends piled up in and around the foundation of the building.

Another interesting phenomenon of a building that pancakes is that the steel erection almost always remains standing in place. Just the concrete and everything between floors comes crashing down. Why and, more importantly, how did the erected steel of the World Trade Center towers structurally fail and come tumbling down?

This was the first time in history that a skyscraper came down because of fire. But more importantly, this was the first time in demolition history that there were no slabs to be found, specifically 220 slabs of concrete, one for each floor, that should have remained in the debris pile after the towers were demolished. If the buildings came down due to fire, why then would the lower floors, unaffected by fire, collapse? The majority of the steel beams in the building were never exposed to fire; therefore, it becomes difficult to explain within the bounds of logic the twin towers' total collapse and the total disintegration of the buildings' steel I-beam structural supports.

There was very little in the way of transportation, and we used the Gator to supply whatever was needed on the monstrous site. My new buddy Tim and I moved plywood, welding supplies, food, water, and most importantly, people. Whenever someone or something was requested, he floored the pedal on that Gator and got it! We picked up exhausted workers that needed to be moved back to civilization for much-needed sleep breaks. Whatever was needed, we found it, usually back almost a mile at the Stuyvesant school, and delivered it to the hole in order to keep the search-and-rescue efforts going. We raced frantically back and forth between the school and the hole for what seemed like hundreds of round trips a day, keeping supplied the massive rescue effort that was being conducted under some of the worst conditions imaginable.

Supplies are a vital and integral part, contributing and bolstering the sustainment of any search-and-rescue initiative, especially in a disaster of this magnitude. Consider that in the hole four thousand rescue workers consumed about eighteen thousand meals during a long day of demanding and unending work.

Volunteers constructed a makeshift café out of plywood and dubbed it the Freedom Café. A new warehouse and distribution station were quickly established in the nearby St. John's Chapel. It housed almost anything you could imagine. There were stacks of drinks, canned goods, filters for respirators, and gas masks, the kind used in battle. There were towels, clothes, sheets, and blankets. There were lots of little hidden treasures intermixed and buried among the heaps of clothes.

Virtually everywhere you looked, people were hustling with an urgency and a professionalism seldom seen outside a battlefield, and Ground Zero was a battlefield.

There were public notice boards near the chapel covered with photos of missing loved ones. It was somewhat overwhelming to see all the death and suffering first-hand; it changed us to the core. I remember seeing a fireman place a picture of his son on the board. Tears uncontrollably ran down his dust-covered face. As I was walking past, he wiped his eyes and started to talk. During our heart-wrenching conversation, it became obvious and yet remained unspoken that in the back of our minds we just knew we would rather have been anywhere but there.

People were glad to help, but it was horrific; the amount of death in the air was unfathomable. However, this job needed to be done. The overflowing professionalism and human character that were portrayed by all the rescue workers in the hole were stellar examples of humanity at its best, under conditions that were the worst.

After providing the welders with the oxygen and acetylene tanks, Tim and I concentrated on moving food, clothing, and supplies from the Stuyvesant school to St. John's Chapel just outside the hole. Surprisingly, socks were in exceptionally high demand, as the rain drenched everyone and the worker's feet got soaking wet.

Tim and I made countless trips around the hole and back and forth to the Stuyvesant school, helping anyone who flagged us down and was living through an emergency of one type or another. It was amazing how many supplies were needed to support four thousand rescue workers. As you can imagine, it was no small feat to keep the rescue operation up and functioning and to supply the demands of the harrowing rescue effort.

The Gator was continually overloaded with plywood and lumber, food, clothes, and whatever supplies we thought would be useful in the recovery effort. We just made the best decisions we could and loaded the Gator to the hilt, trip after trip.

That first afternoon, as I wrestled with one heavy tank, there was a body part on a body board or a rescue stretcher being carried out of the hole. As the firefighters—suddenly turned pallbearers—approached me carrying the body board, I did not know exactly what to do. I felt numb and naturally showed as much reverence and respect as possible as the situation became more real to me by the second.

One of the fireman and I shared a moment as our eyes sorrowfully met, and we understood that because there was so much wrong with Ground Zero—the hatred and the death—that we would have preferred to have been doing anything, anything in the world, but this. It was as though a common thread of sorrow and loss ran through all the workers in the hole and we were there not as much for the unfortunate people that lost their lives but for their families and loved ones. All our atten-tion focused upon finding survivors, but I regrettably realized that finding anyone became more and more unlikely as time marched on.

Over and over you could feel them, the souls of the recently departed. They never quit. They occupied the space and the sky over the smol-dering remains of the towers; they floated above it. They communicated to anyone that would listen. They were angry, confused, and heart-broken, wanting one more moment of quality with a loved one. They were pissed! They were taken too soon.

Those who rode the crashing towers to a world beyond this one per-vaded the space of Ground Zero; you could feel their spirits and thoughts. Many, if not most of the rescue workers, reported that they heard their friends' voices call out to them from in and around the pile. The presence of their spirits was palpable in the deepest recesses of my soul. The spiritual presence of thousands of the victims was obvious to many of the rescue workers, and many people had revelations concerning life and the continuation of the spirit after the body dies. It was plainly obvious that those who physically perished on September 11 were still in the vicinity and were spiritually communicating with those working in the hole.

Among all the sadness and sorrow, there was a feeling that pervaded the area that somehow we were fortunate and privileged to have the unique opportunity to see not only the worst of man—the disaster made this abundantly clear—but also the best of man, a side seen far too seldom. The camaraderie, the esprit de corps of America, was never higher than it was in and around the hole. Rescue workers feverishly labored for countless hours, searching for any possible survivors, any proof of life, any sign of the recently departed: a finger, a possession, anything.

Everyone worked ferociously around the clock. Many of the people I brought back to civilization from the hole had worked for days on end and well deserved a few hours of much-needed sleep, only to awake and do it all over again. Day after day, the exhausted workers were fueled by the intention and purpose of helping humanity. Everyone worked in the most deplorable of conditions, and through it all, their valor and honor made America proud!

The personal sacrifice of the rescue workers and all the volunteers was done as part of our American duty; we were there to serve the country, the people that died and their families they left behind.

Tim Mullally and I were tiring that first long and busy day. As we checked out, about twenty hours after my arrival, I reflected on the situation, of what I had seen and felt. After pondering the situation repeatedly in my mind, I still could not reckon with the insanity of it all.

When my friends and I exited the perimeter where the public could not pass, the streets were lined with people, five to ten deep. There were hundreds hoping to better understand what lay just around the corner but worlds away. It was two in the morning, and New Yorkers applauded us; good-hearted people clapped in appreciation as we passed by, thanking us for our rescue efforts and the sacrifices made by each of us. I had not thought of my actions as being worthy of applause, or anything else, and this deeply touched me.

On September 14, my second day working in the hole, my friends and I woke at dawn, had a quick breakfast, and left the mansion in New Rochelle, which was about an hour north of the city. Through friends of friends, my friends somehow had managed to secure a mansion where we would stay with a busload of other volunteers.

This day, our daily commute from New Rochelle to Ground Zero was through a sad and dreary rain. As we headed into the city, it became apparent that a surreal feeling permeated the entire city, a city eerily quiet and visibly shaken. New Yorkers seemed overly polite. No horns were honking. New York drivers were allowing others the right of way in a most pleasant and unusual manner.

Like tears from heaven, raindrops fell on the streets as our gang from Florida headed back into the war zone. Not knowing exactly what route we should take, we headed for the columns of billowing smoke that blackened the gray sky of Lower Manhattan.

After making it through security, we arrived as the sun was breaking through the ominous and overcast sky. We started organizing the school and the massive amount of donated supplies that were pouring in from around the country. Classrooms were filled with all kinds of clothing and some very cherished items as well.

I got an autographed T-shirt from a class of grade school children who wished us all well in our rescue efforts. As I read what each child had written from the bottom of his or her little heart, I felt filled with the realization that America, as exemplified by the children's thoughts of kindness written on that T-shirt, was a great and loving nation filled with great and loving people.

A lively group of volunteers, who were now responsible for feeding the four thousand rescue workers, commandeered the Stuyvesant school's kitchen and started cooking. The school kitchen was alive, and tinfoil tray after tinfoil tray filled with fantastic food was frantically shuttled from the school to the hole. Local restaurants from around Manhattan also donated thousands of incredibly delicious meals. There were countless trays of pasta dished from Dominic's Restaurant and other fine eating establishments, too many to recall. The food just magically appeared as it was needed. The outpouring of charity and kindness from the people of New York and even from across America was magnificent.

Earlier that morning, the Gators arrived at the Stuyvesant school on a car-carrier trailer. My new friend Tim somehow managed to get thirteen more Gators, compliments of the John Deere US organization. The previous day, Tim had promised that I would get one of the John Deere Gators. These machines were so vital in handling and transporting all the desperately needed supplies used in the massive rescue effort that was well over four thousand strong and growing.

The police now had taken five Gators with permission and were trying to commandeer a sixth one, which was the only one left. Seven had already gone to the fire department. I arrived in the very nick of time and fervently requested or demanded that last Gator because it was desperately needed to shuttle water, food, and other essential supplies to the hole. No Gator meant that there would be no food or water delivered to the hole for the workers. Thankfully, Tim took control of the situation and saw to it that the last Gator was given to me. What a relief.

Sergeant Churchill, one of NYPD's finest, was posted to oversee the Stuyvesant school and made sure all in the area were safe. He was a terrific guy and reflected all the good qualities one would expect to see in a peace officer. He commanded the area with the pride and competence one would hope to find in law enforcement officers across the country. He treated people with decency and earned the respect he deserved and garnered from all who had the opportunity to interact with him. Churchill and the other NYPD officers kept the area in front of the Stuyvesant school very well organized as there were many trucks delivering all kinds of things day and night.

For the next several days, the crew at the school worked furiously filling my new Gator as fast as possible, and then I would fly down the roads filled with toxic dust toward the hole. As I sped to the hole, the Gator left a wake of gray dust that refused to be washed away by the rain.

Like a maniac, I drove the Gator pedal to the metal and would drop the food off as fast as possible at the Freedom Café, which was set up just outside the hole. There were about twenty people who worked in shifts at the café to serve the food and drinks to the rescue workers. One thing was for certain, anytime during the day or night, there were always hungry rescue workers being served delicious food at the Freedom Café.

We tried not to eat too much of the dust, as it constantly fell from the sky. The café workers covered the food with foil as best they could, but in the end, the dust ended up in our food, in our bellies, and eventually in our blood.

I delivered other badly needed supplies to St. John's Chapel. Everything happened at a frantic pace, as though we were short on time. Each time I returned to the school to refill the Gator with supplies, it was as if I was pulling into a pit stop at the Daytona 500. People were flying!

On one of my first visits to the hole, I was trying to calculate the amount of damage and destruction created by the evildoers responsible for those who perished when the buildings were demolished.

The hole was hard to fathom, as was the entirety of the disaster. It was an almost overwhelming amount of destruction, more by far than I had ever seen or even dared to imagine. The hole had a magnitude of destruction that was beyond compare with any catastrophe that had occurred in the United States.

With all the people combining, like a collective organism working in unison for a common, achievable objective, the hole seemed to take on a life of its own. The organism breathed, it moved, it evolved over time. Bucket brigades consisting of thousands of men and women worked tirelessly and with great purpose and intention to find any sign of life.

In the air you could feel a concern that is felt only in circumstances involving the gravest of conditions, which challenge an individual's character to the very core and to the essence of his or her very soul. Times of challenge define the character of a person, and there was an abundance of character in the hole and throughout the entire city of New York.

As the search for life continued, an overall sense of caring and kindness was replacing the craziness and the insanity that was responsible for the destruction of 9/11 and the loss of human life. Alongside one of the most devastating scenes ever to darken America's door was the greatness emitted by all the rescue workers who went about their business looking for signs of life in a landscape full of death.

When you wrap your wits around the situation and realize that there are thousands of broken families as a result of the wickedness and evilness committed by those who orchestrated the events of that infamous day, you soon realize those responsible for 9/11 should not go unidentified, unindicted, and unpunished. It became abundantly clear to me that the American people needed justice for the outright murder of so many innocent people.

Around the hole, there were many rumors being passed around. One was of a woman who was in a stairway in one of the towers. She rode the building down from the fifty-seventh floor and was subsequently recovered by some fine men and women of the New York Fire Department. One worker commented, "She rode the building down in the hand of God." Another worker with tears welling in his eyes said, "They all did; they all rode down in the hand of God."

It was incredible how fortunate some were, while the majority of people, people with lives and families, with dreams and futures, were never seen again. The woman who rode the building down fifty-seven floors got to share more moments with her loved ones while thousands of others passed like butterflies, leaving their cocoons and embarking upon another journey, another glorious part of life that we all will experience in the ultimate commonality of our earthly existence—passing from this world to the next.

When I looked over the hole and really duplicated in my mind the amount of destruction that faced us all, I could feel with certainty the life force of the hole. The hole was emanating a vibration declaring that it was the ultimate form and shape of evil and destruction. It prayed to be worshipped; it begged to be admired as it emanated its ultimate wavelength, one filled with evil and destruction.

Never before or since being at Ground Zero have I experienced such strange wavelengths and harmonics as the ones that emanated from the hole. The hole radiated everyone in the area with its presence and was emblematic of the state or reality where humankind had arrived, a state or reality filled with hatred and consequences, a reality undreamed of in our childhoods.

It was reassuring to see the thousands of beautiful people who cared enough to jeopardize themselves and their health to help their fellow brothers and sisters in humanity. The rescue effort was emblematic of the goodness and decency inherent in the human race and the goodness and decency that reside in the hearts of all of us.

As the search through the rubble continued, we were all doing our best to desperately help find someone, anyone, or anything. Every action was devoted to the goal of recovering survivors or even signs of a survivor. Stories and rumors were bantered about, as we grasped whatever hope we could that someone would be pulled from the wreckage, thereby rewarding all the combined efforts of the rescue workers.

In the exhaustion that ran rampant, everyone carried his or her personal hurt and emotional suffering inside as best he or she could. Hurt and suffering were quickly replaced with the eagerness to recover a breathing body and the hopes of finding a missing friend or, worse, a family member. Fathers were searching for their sons and daughters; others searched for their brothers and sisters. Everyone there was searching for someone dear. It was very sad; it broke my heart.

Every time I gave a lift to the rescue workers, I was updated as to the latest finds of body parts or what different things were going on in different parts of the hole. Rescue workers and I shared stories and information as they loaded themselves onto the Gator and I took them back to the city. Workers would pile on the Gator, sometimes ten at a time, to get away from the disaster and get some well-deserved rest. I chauffeured firefighters, police officers, welders, and whoever else managed to jump into the indestructible Gator or just pig pile on top of it when it was already overstuffed with exhausted rescue workers.

Return trips from the hole were always filled with workers that jumped onto the Gator, and I would sometimes give them a ride all over Lower Manhattan. We discussed our harrowing and sorrowful experiences. The rescue workers often stood for hours on the pile, as bucket after bucket of debris was strategically removed to gain a better vantage point to recover someone or something that belonged to the victims.

As the days passed, it became apparent, or at least very unlikely, that no one else was going be rescued. The hole had offered up all the living survivors that it would. Now the debris was being taken away, piece by piece, in the hopes of a miracle.

At one point, a small group of firefighters, who had managed to survive the building's demolition, were recovered in a spectacular rescue from over forty feet below the surface of the steel. Details of such rumors were never exact. With ten different people telling me the same story, each had his or her own twist as to what had actually happened. Later I found out that there was a movie directed by Oliver Stone and starring Nicolas Cage called World Trade Center, which detailed the heroic rescue and survival of those trapped firefighters.

Hundreds of thousands of Americans gave blood to the American Red Cross in hope of being helpful, but that blood would not be used at Ground Zero.

Ground Zero was appropriately named because it gave back nothing; it just took. There were very few survivors, and little was recovered in the way of human remains.

Tiny body parts were the only things recovered after the firefighters and the lady from the stairwell were carried out from the monster of twisted and smoldering steel. A finger and an indiscernible part of a torso were found. I witnessed the removal of several body bags containing a piece of a person with the hope that a family would know through DNA and obtain confirmation that their loved one had been found.

I remember one firefighter I gave a ride to who discussed with me his recent shift in the hole. He had the thousand-yard stare we all shared and was visibly rattled and eager to speak. I asked if he had found anyone or anything, and he said, "Yeah. I found a heart today."

I said, "A heart?"

He responded as his eyes began to tear, "We found a heart all by itself. There was a heart. It was all alone. There was no torso, no nothing. Just a heart; it was unreal." At that moment, we silently and tacitly agreed that the hole was unnatural; it was a mass grave, created by a vile and hateful group that has festered far too long.

As I drove my passengers from the hole back to civilization, we discussed the events of the previous days and realized the importance of understanding what really happened to bring the World Trade Center towers down. We could only speculate about what had happened to America.

One hundred ten stories of buildings imploded from 1,362 feet high and crashed to the ground. The force was horrific, and sadly, there was very little left but twisted steel and underground fires that smoked for weeks on end. Some say the fires were from the jet fuel, but the jet fuel would not have accumulated in one place if a plane travelling five hundred miles per hour smashed into the towers. In such a ferocious impact, the plane's fuel would have scattered into the sky and not puddled in the towers for almost an hour.

Years later, others speculated that the smoke and molten lava were from the steel that was cut with thermite during the demolition of the buildings that fateful day.

There was nothing else in the hole but tons of twisted steel and clouds of smoke and dust. There was no concrete bigger than the smallest pebble; it was all vaporized into the dust that blanketed the city's landscape. There were no plane parts, no office equipment, no chairs, and no filing cabinets anywhere to be found. There was nothing except the dust and the tiny glass shards that cut the skin like a razor. There was a lot of steel in the pile, but it seemed as though there should have been a whole lot more, especially when you consider the towers had 110 floors with something like 330 support columns. The debris pile looked as though it was from a ten-story building, not a 110-story one!

Oh, yes, there was a lot of paper everywhere, waving like little white and yellow flags, polka-dotting the gray landscape. Post-it Notes were everywhere with lists of things to do that never got done.

I thought of my work in Nicaragua assisting the government with the recovery efforts of Hurricane Mitch. I remembered that in Nicaragua's capital, Managua, there were remnants of a ten-story building that had pancaked during an earthquake in 1972. It killed almost everyone that was inside the building at the time of the earthquake. Unlike the people that vanished in the towers on 9/11, the bodies of the office workers in Nicaragua were recovered.

In Nicaragua, the erected steel of a pancaked building was still standing, mostly undamaged. The concrete floors that had collapsed one onto the next one below it remained in large slabs in and around the foundation of the structure. At Ground Zero, there was nowhere near the amount of concrete one would expect to find from the collapse of two 110-story buildings; literally all the concrete and a majority of the steel had mysteriously vaporized.

As I surveyed the overwhelming damage that formed the pile at Ground Zero, I wondered why the steel erected in the World Trade Center towers crumbled to the ground like spaghetti, and I further pondered how everything else had vaporized. The actual building components of the towers, much of their concrete and steel, along with all the office equipment and other miscellaneous incidentals one would expect to find in an office building of this sort, had inexplicably vanished. Where were the huge concrete slabs that one would expect to see at any demolition site? Why and how did all the concrete and glass vaporize into the toxic dust that filled the air? In the minds of millions, these questions were never adequately answered.

There was only a fraction of the half a million tons of steel used to build the towers ever salvaged. A certain way to ascertain the reliability factor of the previous statement pertaining to the missing steel is to calculate the amount of steel that was used in the construction of the World Trade Center towers and subtract the total amount that was salvaged. There should be little discrepancy, perhaps less than 5 percent missing. I estimate that 80-90 percent of the steel was never recovered and sold as salvage.

Despite the deplorable conditions, bucket brigades with lines of hundreds of fearless workers covered the pile like a spider web. The pile was being removed bucket by bucket in the hopes of recovering proof or signs of life in any form. The bucket line stretched and wound over the piles of twisted and bent steel until it reached the road where the trucks were loaded.

The smoke poured through the gaping holes in the pile, making it impossible to breathe in many places. The dust swirled everywhere, but the darkness that loomed over the hole could not tarnish the spirits of those who searched steadfastly for loved ones.

Once we got respirator masks, the glass and dust suspended in the air soon filled the respirators to a much higher concentration than the amount of glass that was wafting through the air at Ground Zero. It was as bad, if not worse, to use the respirators as it was to breathe the glass-filled air directly. Imagine my amazement when I soon discovered the respirators were insufficient for the breathing conditions we found ourselves in, as we, detrimentally to our own health, worked tirelessly in the hole. All the workers were breathing the dust, a dust filled with shards of microscopic glass and mixed with the taste of death.

Those who were there knew the truth when news from Kathy Sibelius, secretary of the US Health and Human Services, decreed that the air at Ground Zero posed no health problems for the rescue workers and residents of lower Manhattan. It was pure propaganda. It was a pure lie. The air was deplorable as it seared the lungs, attacked the eyes, and tore the skin.

One time when I was driving through the hole, I saw an exhausted fireman sweating and in desperate need of a break. As he drank a swig of water and rested in his eighty-pound fire gear—often called turn-out gear by the firefighters—he wiped his forehead with his finger to get the sweat off his brow. By simply wiping his forehead, the glass cut his skin, and he started to bleed. The glass on his skin was causing micro holes that allowed only a little blood to escape at a time. It looked like a bruise, but it was blood. The glass in the air tore our skin. Imagine what it did to our lungs.

A similar thing happened to me. My wrist bled from repeatedly scraping against the top edge of my left pocket each time I placed the Gator's key in and out of my pants' pocket. It was funny how much I had to guard the key to the Gator. On a few occasions, I had people trying to commandeer the Gator from me. The Gator was in such high demand and an integral tool that greatly assisted the entire rescue effort.

A big thank-you goes out to the wonderful folks at John Deere for its incredible support during America's worst hour. John Deere is one of America's greatest companies, truly a national treasure.

Transportation establishes an entirely new level of power in emergency situations, including both natural and manmade disasters. Having the Gator allowed me to take people all over the twenty-square-acre disaster site for whatever minor emergency was occurring. I transported countless people.

I helped the fire chiefs who coordinated the rescue efforts from the command tents that were set up in the nearby perimeter. The public officials would congregate in these areas. People like Mayor Rudi Giuliani and his entourage huddled under the tents to get out of the rain and for quick coffee breaks to discuss the massive rescue effort under the direction of the chiefs and commanders who ran the entire operation as best they could.

President Bush spoke a block or two from the chief's tent. He stood on a pile of rubble and incited the crowd to cheer, "U-S-A! U-S-A! U-S-A!" I sat nearby on top of a destroyed fire truck overlooking the entire scene, forty feet from the cheerleading president—after all, he had been a cheerleader at Yale.

His words echoed with more revenge than intelligence. He incited the crowd with promises and threats of retribution to those who had committed this atrocity, when all the while I thought those who had committed this atrocity were already dead. The more he spoke, the less sense he made, which is often the case with liars.

As I did my part to help, I wondered how many years or even decades were being knocked off my life and the lives of everyone who worked, breathed the dust, and endured such hazardous conditions.

I can't shake the tragic image of a rescue dog that lay dead on the pile, overcome by smoke and toxins while sniffing and searching for human life. One owner who loved and trained one of these magnificent animals could not hold back his emotion as he told me the story of how his faithful dog had breathed its last breath, searching for someone else's loved ones.

The Gator carried the dogs and their exhausted owners back to civilization after days and days on the pile. I remember one day when a rescue dog and his handler jumped in my overstuffed Gator; all the guys started patting, hugging, and kissing the dog. It is amazing; no matter how bad people feel, patting a dog will usually make them feel a lot better. It definitely makes the dog feel better.

The schedule was crazy. There was supposed to be a regulation to work only eight-hour shifts at a time, but that did not happen. We all dug in and searched and worked as hard as we could for as long as we could.

Sleep happened in the Stuyvesant school. Classrooms were converted to makeshift sleeping quarters, thanks to the abundance of blankets and cots donated by thoughtful New Yorkers. Many firefighters would take a ride back to their firehouse for a quick nap.

As I continued driving the Gator around the entirety of the site, I probably saw more of the site than most anyone did. I drove as fast as I could, all the time making sure everyone had what he or she needed. If something were needed, someone would stop me, and I would pick the person up and somehow miraculously get whatever was needed.

Heroes told me their versions of the events of 9/11 and how they lost brother FDNY firefighters they had worked with for one year, ten years, even more than twenty years. One such hero tried to cleanse his soul as we discussed how fourteen of his closest friends exited an elevator and entered a smoke-filled floor of WTC Building 7. All fourteen took a right out of the elevator while he, for some unknown reason, went left. The fourteen fell to their deaths through a seven-story hole in the floor. He survived with a vacancy in his heart that will never be filled and the voices of his friends that will never be heard again outside the confines of his mind.

I remember one man I spoke with who was troubleshooting a phone system from outside the Twin Towers. His brother was inside handling the other end of the phone system's problem from a floor just above where the planes hit. He shook and sobbed as he told me that the instant the phone went dead, he immediately knew he would never talk to his brother again.

The amount of devastation and emotional suffering that the heroes carried with them did not slow them for a minute. When people broke down, they would quickly recover and return to work. Searching and crawling on the pile was more than an exercise in brotherly love; it was therapy for everyone there, for it seemed far better to do something rather than nothing. It seemed better to look and not find than to not look.

Everyone working in the hole was there to do his or her best and to make a difference, if that was possible. One's effort never seemed enough, as the lives of those who perished mystically drove the workers' coordinated rescue effort, and the hopes of hearing good news and finding someone, something, anything, motivated everyone.

The sorrow and horror we all absorbed and experienced by being in a place so dark and so calamitous was forced back into the far recesses of our minds with the hope that the visions, the sounds, the memories we all shared would somehow remain tranquil in those dark places of our minds that we hopefully seldom visit.

For me, the rescue efforts in the hole ended on September 18, 2001. That was the day the authorities limited access to the site to the fire-fighters, police, and specific construction workers. Welders were in high demand as there was a lot of steel being cut and hauled from the site on a regular basis. First to be cut by the welders was a pathway that allowed access, and then the pile was strategically addressed to maximize the pos-sibility of pulling someone alive from the hole.

My friends and I were volunteers, and we were suddenly, without no-tice, barred from assisting in the hole. This was shocking news. I had to do something. I had to help to offset the evil committed in the heart of New York and in the heart of America.

First, I had to recover a bit because, like everyone working there, I was beyond exhausted. I needed sleep, like the kind you dream about.

The next day, my friends and I treated ourselves to some prosciutto and melon in Little Italy before heading home in our rented van. As we headed back to Florida, I remember looking out the window at the set-ting sun while we drove through the Virginia countryside. I snapped a picture of the sunset and wondered what would be next.

Finally, I got home and got some more well-deserved sleep. The next day, we headed down to Clearwater Beach to relax and unwind. It was the first day I spent at the beach since moving to Clearwater six years earlier. I like to go boating or jet skiing, but I never just go to the beach and bask in the sun. But this time, it was unbelievably great for my psyche. Florida beaches on a sunny day with people everywhere the eye could see—what else could you ask for? The water was a perfect relax-ation medium, and the waves seemed to cleanse my soul.

After a few days, we could not bear to be away from the city. It was calling. There was nothing for me to do in Clearwater but be haunted by my experiences at Ground Zero.

My friends Mark, Chris, Rex, Lisa, and her two daughters got hold of me, and before I knew it, we were headed back to NYC to see if there were some way we could help the firefighters. This time as we drove back to Ground Zero, Mark's Crown Victoria was stuffed to the gills with clothes and people. We stopped at a McDonald's in Jacksonville, Florida, and Mark told me that starting now it was my shift to drive the car. It was close to midnight, and he wanted me to drive for as long as I could.

I luckily remember at least three or four occasions when, despite two cups of coffee, my eyes became too heavy while I was driving. As the sun came up and my eyes were closing down and getting heavier and heavier, I caught myself and responsibly pulled over at the next rest stop a few miles up the road. I realized we were in Virginia and I had made good time. Someone else took charge of the wheel. I was too tired to notice who replaced me, as I passed out in record time in the overcrowded back seat of the Crown Victoria.

There was still a lot to do when we arrived back in New York. We pulled up to that mansion in New Rochelle, unpacked our suitcases, and headed into the city during a congested commute. This continued every day from the end of September until just before Thanksgiving.

We visited firehouses all around Manhattan. Originally, we were going to set up a workshop where the firefighters could organize and decide what kind of assistance those most affected needed, and then that service would somehow materialize and be provided to help the firefighters and their families and friends. In theory, this sounded good, but there was an unanticipated factor that would make getting many firefighters together for a simple seminar impossible. They were too busy working the hole or attending the funerals of their fallen friends.

For the next five or six weeks, I went from firehouse to firehouse, meeting some of the greatest people I have had the privilege to meet. The hospitality extended was beyond anything that I had anticipated. The charity, the kindness, the love, and the friendship provided in abundance by the FDNY made us all appreciate life a little more than perhaps we deserve. The stories were absolutely nothing short of incredible, and so was the food.

It is almost impossible to find a better home-cooked meal than the ones we shared in New York with the generous and hospitable firefighters. Firefighters can cook!

As we visited the firehouses, the firefighters there were very welcoming and open in sharing their horrific 9/11 stories. They are a unique breed, one with a slightly better DNA structure or some other unknown, innate quality that allows them to run into, instead of out of, buildings that are on fire. Each of the heroes of the New York Fire Department that we had the privilege to meet had unique stories of what they saw, what they experienced, and whom they lost on September 11, 2001.

The amount of loss and emotional suffering was colossal. Grief and torment filled the air of our discussions. The stories could not have been sadder or more eye opening.

Funerals happened every day. They were conducted on coordinated schedules in order that the firefighters could attend without conflict the funerals of those they knew like brothers and sisters. Too often fire-fighters would attend multiple funerals in a single day. The grief was ev-erywhere. It was all consuming. Each firefighter's story that was relayed to me was sadder than the last one I had just heard.

The public outflow of the great people of New York was amazing. People were still coming by the firehouses, bringing flowers, cakes, and pies. Beautiful New York girls would stop by and flirt with the fire-fighters as they dropped off small gifts to assuage the losses that every firefighter was experiencing. The people of the city and their support were remarkable.

The firefighters at one firehouse in south Manhattan who had lost a lot of men told me of the detonations and explosions they had heard when they were fleeing one of the towers for their lives. Many firefighters reported that, while in the World Trade Center towers, they heard con-cussive explosions that were going off in the basements of the building, as well as on many higher floors.

Several firefighters from different firehouses indicated they ran for their lives in WTC Building 7 as explosions were going off everywhere around them. Many other firefighters corroborated there were explosions on several floors and in the basement of the North and South Towers—the 110-story towers.

I talked with a fireman who had lost a friend, a chaplain crushed by a falling body as he attended to another who was in need. As he told the story to me, I could feel the upset that he suppressed as he conveyed this ghastly and horrific tale. The misery of those on the top floors must have been terrible—they had to make the most horrific decision to leap to their certain death a hundred stories below or remain and burn. In hor-rific dismay, we witnessed people—fathers and mothers, brothers and sis-ters, daughters and sons—plunging to earth in a last desperate attempt to escape the agony of the outrageous heat and the overly abundant sufferings of this world.

Behind every story was a veil of disbelief that we as Americans had to endure during this unimaginable human tragedy, all because someone thought it was a good idea to attack the World Trade Center towers. Who could have such an idea? Who would profit?

One of the most poignant things I remember, one that will haunt me forever, is when a four-year-old came in a firehouse with his mother and approached a firefighter with whom I was talking. The firefighter went down on one knee so he could look eye to eye with the young child. With a negligible trace of hope in his voice, the child asked the firefighter, "Did you find my daddy today?" The firefighter was shocked, and the little boy repeated the question. It was by far the most terribly sad question I have ever heard. The firefighter managed to choke out, "We're still looking for him." The child's mother looked desperately into my eyes and into the depths of my soul for an answer that she already regrettably knew.

The level of grief and tragedy was overwhelming and incomprehensible. Those who lost a loved one lost everything. Thousands upon thousands of widows, widowers, and orphans were created that day. Far too many people died and for what?

A child will never play catch with his dad; a mom will never teach junior to read and write; husbands and wives forever forfeited the love of their lives. Loss was experienced so profoundly, so substantially throughout the city that it truly demonstrates the incredible and resilient character of New Yorkers. Those inflicted with such dreadful loss may feel there are no limits to their pain and there are no bounds to the depths of sorrow.

So many lives crumbled as the towers came down. Too many loved ones went to work and were never seen or heard from again. As the dust fanned out through the city, thousands of lives were suddenly and inexplicably thrown into tragedy and turmoil.

How does one tell a child that his mother or father is not coming home from work today or ever? How does anyone manage to pick up the shattered pieces of his or her life and move forward? New Yorkers do it with dignity and resolve.

The events of September 11, 2001 changed everyone, some much more than others, but it changed us all. It changed America; it changed the world. Life changed that day for every man, woman, and child on this planet and not for the better.

My work in New York affected me in several ways, spiritually, mentally, and physically. I was honored to have the opportunity to work alongside and be a small part of the greatest rescue effort ever conducted on American soil. As I visited the many firehouses, I was privileged to be invited as a guest for dinner and to break bread with American heroes, who put the lives of others ahead of their own.

I was proud to assist the heroes that subjected themselves to deplorable conditions while tirelessly searching among the strewn, smoldering pieces of twisted steel that stole the lives of so many Americans and others from around the world.

America has many good people. Those who worked in the hole are the best of the best. The families most affected on that infamous day crave for resolution, and they crave for justice.

If we are to ever live in a world where peace is the norm, then we must come together and rise as a species or be doomed to a world where insanity and stupidity reign.

The decision is ours. Imagine what kind of world you would like to live in, and without further delay, start creating it!

Chapter 3
Present-Day Orientation

The price of apathy toward public affairs is to be ruled by evil men.

– PLATO

Rise up! Like lions after slumber. In unvanquishable number. Shake your chains to earth like dew, which in your sleep had fallen on you. Ye are many—they are few!

– PERCY SHELLEY

Heaven knows how to put a proper price upon its goods; and it would be strange indeed if so celestial an article as freedom should not be highly rated.

– THOMAS PAINE

Whenever I hear anyone arguing for slavery, I feel a strong impulse to see it tried on him personally.

– ABRAHAM LINCOLN

Is life so dear or peace so sweet as to be purchased at the price of chains and slavery? Forbid it, Almighty God! I know not what course others may take, but as for me, give me liberty, or give me death!

– PATRICK HENRY

Government's first duty is to protect the people, not run their lives.

– RONALD REAGAN

Let us never forget that government is ourselves and not an alien power over us. The ultimate rulers of our democracy are not a President and senators and congressmen and government officials, but the voters of this country.

– FRANKLIN D. ROOSEVELT

The most terrifying words in the English language are: I'm from the government and I'm here to help.

– RONALD REAGAN

THE HEIGHT OF OUR FATHERS' and grandfathers' neglect of duty and responsibility for monitoring the government's functioning and performance is dwarfed only by our generation's treasonous abandonment of those same duties and responsibilities, which has resulted in the enslavement of the American people and people across the globe. The responsibility of monitoring the government's functioning falls squarely upon the shoulders of its citizens. The people get the government they not only deserve but also, more importantly, the government they demand.

We have been neglectful in exercising our duties to uphold the federal government described in the US Constitution. The government, if we are even correct in still calling it that, is no longer a government of the people, by the people, and for the people. Rather, it has become a government for a small group of criminals that profit at the expense of the masses. This is called a kleptocracy, a government ruled by thieves that steal from the rest of us.

According to Wikipedia, "Kleptocracy is a form of political and government corruption, where the government exists to increase the personal wealth and political power of its officials and the ruling class, at the expense of the wider population, often with pretense of honest service" (en.wikipedia.org/wiki/Kleptocracy).

Wikipedia further defines kleptocracy as a term applied to a government seen as having a particularly severe and systemic problem with officials or a ruling class (collectively, kleptocrats) taking advantage of corruption to extend their personal wealth and political power. Typically this system involves the embezzlement of state funds at the expense of the wider population, sometimes without even the pretense of honest service.

Beyond the aspect of reelection, no longer are the interests of the American citizenry a concern for the so-called representatives in Washington. Those elected to represent the American populace have failed miserably and are concerned only with their own profits and entitlements. Treason is the standard operating procedure most politicians exhibit in American politics.

Lining their own pockets with funds from the special interests that finance their campaigns, politicians seem unconcerned about the people and ignore their constituents. In Washington, DC, politicians implement the agenda of the corporations that finance their elections while not caring about the people that elected them.

When was the last time that ordinary citizens were proud of the actions undertaken by their government? With political public opinion polls being at all-time lows, the American people have had enough of the betrayal regularly committed by their elected officials.

America's infrastructure is falling apart. American industry and its exports are still suffering as the United States spends trillions fighting wars.

How often are disgust and disdain bantered about in conversations relating to our elected officials and political system? Is it time that we the people wrestle control of this nation back into the hands of the people and return it to its proper constitutional form? Its original form was designed to provide freedom and liberty to those who can responsibly utilize those vanishing concepts. Instead, the government and our elected officials have deteriorated the government into a group of self-serving hedonists, depriving the population of even the most fundamental necessities, including employment.

For those who are currently wiping the sand from their eyes as they wake from their hypnotic sleep, the corporately privatized government serves a master other than the American people. The government has plundered the treasury and wealth of the country by adhering to an agenda dictated by the special interests. As outrageous as this plundering has been, Americans remain apathetic and silently condone those federal politicians who are financially raping the people of this country.

America is not alone; an ongoing financial raping is occurring in virtually every country of the world. Those countries that do not cooperate with the financial raping get bombed.

The special interests' agenda is blatantly perilous for the average American and is designed to keep the wealthiest of this planet in power by any means and at any cost, a tragic cost measured both in dollars and in human lives. Citizens who fail to take action against the transgressors of their liberties not only condone those transgressions but also encourage them. While the populace sleeps and dreams of freedom and liberty, the politicians are busy eviscerating and destroying the people's God-given rights.

People need to educate themselves about the incredible damage both Democratic and Republican representatives are committing against citizens while furthering the financial elite's agenda. People need to take action to extricate the special interest groups from the various levels of government in order to preserve and guarantee all that is great about America.

The primary reason these thieves, kleptocrats, or special interests are allowed to continue with their profitable extractions from the government and the people's wealth and riches is the people's lack of understanding, caring, and organizing to do something about it! Without understanding, caring, and organizing, we are damned to a life in which the screams of injustice and contempt for our government will be bellowing from sea to shining sea.

Thousands of different groups of Americans voice their grievances regarding the actions undertaken by government charlatans, and yet there never seems to be any resolution that consoles the disgruntled public and gets the country back on its proper track and headed in the right direction. The country is not on its proper track because a group of people like to profit by keeping our country, and the world, on the wrong track.

This world is headed toward death and destruction rather than evolving in a direction toward life and creation. The current world system is disempowering the people when we should be uplifting and empowering the people, not the politicians who are supposed to serve us.

The wealthiest of the wealthy, with evil intentions and using virtually the same methods of oppression utilized throughout the ages, have embezzled magnificent fortunes from the unsuspecting remainder of the population. Pharaohs and kings have a history of enslaving their subjects to the point of poverty and inevitable revolution. Suppressed cultures have undergone untold duress at the hands of political criminals. With their evil intentions, they focus on reallocating all the wealth of society from the masses, or the common people, to the same tiny group who has captured control of the world's governments for the past several centuries.

Regardless of whether it is a despotic dictator, a "freely elected" president, or a prime minister, upon the attainment of power, campaign promises are quickly forgotten and abandoned. The head of state's interests and loyalties are no longer to those who elected him or her into office but to the unseen handlers who pull the politicians' puppet strings.

Political betrayal of the American people is highly rewarded. Politicians who control the destiny of the nation never earnestly value the well-being of their constituents; the political criminals simply concentrate on fattening their secret Swiss and Cayman Island trust accounts, quite hidden from public scrutiny.

If one considers any recent US president's tenure, it is obvious that public campaign promises are quickly broken and replaced by prior private promises pledged to those who have overtaken control of the government.

Why is it so difficult to get politicians to act on the people's behalf, as they promised they would when they were begging and pandering for our votes?

In the old days, all the votes in an American election were actually counted. Now votes are programmed by machines in accordance with the whims of the managers of the elections. Voting software programs are designed to criminally manipulate the tally of the votes. The public's votes can be remotely programmed and changed. The one who controls the voting machines controls the outcome of the elections in which they are used.

There should be paper ballots used in all elections to limit cyber-election fraud that is occurring on a massive scale. Your vote means nothing if it is not honestly counted. It's as Joseph Stalin said, "It is enough that people know there was an election. The people who cast the votes decide nothing. The people who count the votes decide everything."

Politicians do not campaign for the US presidency, the Senate, or the Congress; instead, handlers appoint them well in advance. Many might find this point contentious, discreditable, or incredulous, but this conclusion is logically reached when one looks at the choices presented to the American people.

In Bloodlines of the Illuminati by Fritz Springmeier, genealogical relations are shown to be shared by most of the US presidents. As a matter of fact, virtually all the presidents are related to one another, and this is substantiated by the work of the remarkable twelve-year-old BridgeAnne d'Avignon of Salinas, California, who created a groundbreaking family tree that connects forty-two of forty-three US presidents to one common and rather unexpected ancestor: King John of England. Her fascinating story and achievements can be read at the Daily Mail website (dailymail.co.uk/news/article-2183858/All-presidents-bar-directly-descended-medieval-English-king.html). King John of England signed the Magna Carta in 1215 and was the king from whom the legendary Robin Hood stole in order to aid the poor. What are the chances that these ancestral bloodlines are coincidently the same and all are related back to one King John of England? To more readily understand the similarities in the appointed nominees of US president, one only needs to look at the Bush-Kerry election.

Is it merely coincidental that both Bush and Kerry graduated from Yale University with mediocre grades? Both Clintons and Bush Sr. also graduated from Yale.

Another of many, more fundamentally disturbing coincidences is the fact that George Herbert Walker, George Walker Bush, and John Kerry are all members of the fraternal Skull and Bones. Skull and Bones is a secret society exclusively for a select group of Yale students that usually wind up with influential positions in politics, industry, finance, and media and at the helm of most other industries. Key political bodies, large corporations, and financial institutions are controlled by former members of the Skull and Bones who are exclusively appointed to high positions in many important organizations. Your own study of this group should provide you with some interesting revelations. You ought to research the list of Skull and Bones members on Wikipedia's awesome site at en.wikipedia.org/wiki/List_of_Skull_and_Bones_members.

Many people who belong to special interest groups continually classify this sort of information as conspiracy theory jargon and the people that spout such information as conspiracy nuts or worse. That is not happening as much as it previously did because people are getting smarter and are starting to see right through the deception that is being manufactured by the controlled media.

There is no conspiracy theory. Instead, there is simply conspiracy. How long are we going to fall for the same tricks over and over again?

The conspiracy is quite hidden; it is kept from Americans' view and inspection. Its actions are instrumental in the deaths of many millions, and its heart, where one would expect to find decency and kindness, has long died and is no longer extant. The defense contracting conspirators thrive financially when the world is at war and rejoice in the bloodbaths they ritually create, which deprive the population of peace and tranquility and all the higher virtues that seem to be vanishing from humanity and society.

To learn of some of the crimes committed on September 11, 2001, watch the documentary Loose Change9/11: A Film About September 11, which portrays an interesting viewpoint of the structural failures that occurred on 9/11; more specifically, Loose Change delves into and conveys interesting perspectives regarding the demolition of the World Trade Center towers. You can buy a fantastic compilation of videos at loose change911.com.

The video September Clues 9/11 gives incredible insight into the media conspiracy that manufactured much of the footage seen that blood-soaked day. Some will say maybe all this evidence is just a big coincidence, as any evidence contrary to the official story is purportedly to be part of a conspiratorial network of subversives who want people to be free and not enslaved.

For some interesting revelations concerning the demolition of Building 7, you should watch the video Incontrovertible—New 9/11 Documentary by Tony Rooke.

David Ike's book Alice in Wonderland and the World Trade Center Disaster indicts some of the obvious US government officials responsible for the slaughter of thousands of Americans on 9/11. Ike's book deals with terrorism on a much grander scale hidden within our government and exposes the traitors that directed every action needed to accomplish the largest and most horrific mass murder in the history of this country. It is inexcusable that we share the same world and breathe the same air as those politicians and ex-politicians who are guilty of killing thousands of Americans on September 11, 2001.

Is it okay to kill Americans just because one is a member of a perverted fraternity like Skull and Bones?

Thus far, official government-led investigations into appalling and horrendous American tragedies, whether it be the sinking of the USS Maine, the Kennedy assassinations, the demolition of Oklahoma City's

Federal Building, the demolition of the World Trade Center, or even the economic crisis of 2008, have yielded nothing conclusively and have held no individuals or groups liable for such nefarious crimes. Most reports issued by the government on these matters are nothing short of farcical and fanciful.

When was the last time a government official was prosecuted and thrown in jail? We are not talking about a patsy here. When was the last time a government official did some hard time? The only politicians that ever do time are the ones that are acting contrary to the intentions of the elite who own and control the government. Independent investigations conducted by the government do nothing but placate the population while the perpetrators of seriously felonious crimes go unpunished. After horrible crimes are committed and the nation weeps, there is usually a long, lame, and bogus report provided by an independent investigator who is actually not independent at all. This is done to keep up the appearance that our great government is on the case, ensuring fairness and equity in order that we can have justice and the American way.

It never happens. Americans have not gotten justice for the crimes that are committed by politicians within the halls of government, crimes that greatly affect and harm the American people. The US Justice Department appoints an independent investigator, and then there is a corollary and laughable independent investigation, which takes years to conduct. The independent investigator, who is handpicked for the job because of his or her allegiance to the criminal government network, is hampered and controlled by the same government criminal network that is purportedly being investigated.

The promulgation and artful dissemination of the latest disaster are controlled through the media, and as usual, not a soul will be brought to justice for heinous and unforgivable crimes.

More than that, many of these politically created tragedies have led to the shredding of the Constitution, the stripping of Americans' liberties, and the loss of far too many precious American and non-American lives.

In 2008, in a Wall Street Journal interview, "Shaping the New Agenda," Rahm Emanuel, Obama's White House chief of staff stated, "You never want a serious crisis to go to waste. And what I mean by that is that it's an opportunity to do things that you think you could not do before." That type of statement is one found in the mind of an opportunistic psychopathic government criminal. It is no wonder that under the direction of Mayor Rahm Emanuel, Chicago has turned into a hell-hole with a super-high murder rate and, sadly, a sickening and disturbing number of black-on-black killings.

Politicians, with the purpose of creating a society that has fewer freedoms and much higher levels of government control and oppression over the population, legislate policies that are incredibly destructive to many segments of society and affect none more negatively than the blacks of America's inner cities.

The deplorable and violent acts we see thrust across the television news are simply a method of conditioning the public to more readily accept lives of increased servitude without the hope of liberty. These horrific media stories are broadcast to indoctrinate and influence the world's population. Each horrific story that is broadcast by the media is carefully programmed and sensationalized in order to create the biggest effect possible on the population. The news stations relay the stories to the public through repetitive news blitzes, hypnotizing the docile masses into further accepting their subservience and slavery.

Consider the televised events of 9/11. Within minutes, the fabricated news stories were being propagated all over the world's televisions, and impressions were being implanted into the minds of the population in a coordinated campaign devised to manipulate public opinion regarding the World Trade Center's demolition. There never has been anything that rivals the yarns spun by the media regarding the events of 9/11; these incredibly fabricated stories tarnish the annals of American history and are desperately in need of correction.

The media is at liberty to disseminate anything with or without veracity, often fabricating stories that do not even resemble the truth. The stories the media present are absorbed by the American people like water in desert sand and often with about as much evaluation and speculation.

Unanalyzed, many terroristic stories highly promulgated by the media are traumatizing and horrifying in nature. These slanted and often fabricated news stories lead the public to unite, usually with the purpose of invading with the intention to destroy a falsely created enemy that is being repeatedly and with great frequency broadcast over the networks to appropriately influence public opinion. Does anyone remember reading 1984?

Do we really know anything that is happening halfway across the planet? One day, Osama bin Laden was a US freedom-fighting asset of the CIA, fighting with US backing and support against the Soviets. In just one minute and forty-eight seconds after the second plane allegedly hit the second tower, the media claimed it was the work of Osama bin Laden.

Then one day in September, when it was convenient for the George W. Bush administration, Americans were told by the media to no longer believe in the "lone gunman" theory that was responsible for the death of the great President Kennedy; now Americans were told to start believing in the "Muslim box cutter" theory and vanishing planes.

Americans are supposed to believe that nineteen or so mostly Saudi Arabian terrorists, using box cutters, are solely responsible for the killing of nearly three thousand Americans by acrobatically flying massive jetliners into the World Trade Center towers.

This book is intentionally limited in scope to the mass murder committed at the World Trade Center on September 11, 2001, and does not incorporate the just-as-malicious and villainously calculated events that occurred at the Pentagon and in Shanksville, Pennsylvania.

These parallel incidents were committed by the same religious, ethnic, political, entertainment, military, financial, and industrial criminal network.

The events of 9/11 were planned to incite war as corroborated in the video, Uncovered: the Whole Truth About the Iraq War. It comes as no surprise that the Bush family and other defense contractors unconscionably profited from American and Iraqi soldiers and civilians. Also watch youtube.com/watch?v=FJIijKM8O4A$spfreload=1#t=642.379672 for more insight into the events of 9/11.

Upon deeper reflection and consideration of the story that the media continue to promote, it becomes apparent, often slowly at first, that the stories broadcast are not only inaccurate but also intentionally and uniformly misleading. Piece by piece, diligent public investigation has been undertaken by those not so easily duped into believing the prevailing chatter propagated via the airwaves, and very soon, more accurate accounts began to appear, contradicting the conventional media's lies and inaccuracies one by one.

Documentaries and so-called conspiracy theories popped up on the Internet, exposing the truth of what actually occurred on 9/11 and by their very honest nature contradicted the fabricated and alleged terrorist lies spewed forth by the media.

As we know, investigations by the government, such as the Warren Commission and the 9/11 Commission, are conducted and orchestrated by the government's appointees, and when the officially manufactured and fabricated story is released to the public, with only minimal inspection, the official reports are found filled and riddled with lies and impossibilities.

Are we as Americans still supposed to believe that President Kennedy was actually shot by the crazed lone assassin, Lee Harvey Oswald? Many, or rather most, Americans believe not. Do you believe JFK's brother Robert F. Kennedy was shot by another crazed and lone gunman? How about Dr. Martin Luther King Jr. and Malcolm X?

And what about our musical friends John Lennon, John Denver, Michael Jackson, and Prince? In Michael Jackson's case, we are led to believe that the doctor was the lone gunman who pulled the trigger. Many contemplate that Jackson's secret message to the Illuminati had something to do with his death. Watch his incredible video, They Don't Care About Us (vimeo.com/85532489). He also left as part of his musical legacy Michael's Secret Message to the Illuminati at youtube.com/watch?v=agiDbehnlXc.

Great men and women are assassinated each year because they pose a threat to those in power and control of nearly every national government; still there is no justice.

It is as though the fox is in charge of investigating the missing chickens from the henhouse. We Americans need to conduct our own private investigations of the purported and falsely reported terrorist and criminal activities that have occurred over the years. We need to hold the true criminals accountable for their blatant crimes committed against humanity. Either they pay for their war crimes and the world gets justice, or the world gets injustice and we all pay a million times over by choosing to live in a society strewn with endless war and continual terror. That is the goal of Obama and the European leaders when they let millions of Middle Eastern refugees into Christian lands and Christian culture.

The families of 9/11, who suffered catastrophic losses, are unable to get justice or to hold accountable those who are truly responsible for the murder of their loved ones because the government is allowed the privilege to solely investigate itself. In atrocities that various governments of the world commit to further the ends of the special interests, the government-led investigations are slanted away from the truth and directed to cover up the identities and motives of the guilty parties.

Look at the Warren Commission that declared Lee Harvey Oswald as the lone assassin of President John F. Kennedy, despite this conclusion contradicting the laws of physics. Any slanted findings of a government-sponsored investigation that disagree with the laws of physics should be fundamentally challenged and dismissed when proven to be hogwash.

Vice President Dick Chaney and President George W. Bush should have been forced to individually testify before Congress under sworn oath regarding the events of 9/11. Instead, the two answered questions together in a closed-door session before a federal commission, the transcripts of which have never been made available to the American people. Bush wanted the testimony to be limited to only one hour. Imagine, the president of the United States wanting to limit his testimony to less than an hour regarding the death of close to three thousand citizens. That equates to almost a whole 1.2 seconds per victim. I guess Bush was a busy guy with his painting and all. Was he that busy, or did he have full knowledge and forewarning of the government's performing an inside job on 9/11?

We Americans need to conduct our own investigation and hold the real terrorists, the government criminal network, responsible for the carnage of September 11. We really need to form an impartial, independent investigative committee to determine and punish the criminals within the government who are responsible for any and all false-flag occurrences, from the past and in the future. There is no statute of limitations on mass murder. Americans need justice; it is all part of that Superman tradition, which consists of truth, justice, and the American way!

Wikipedia defines a "false flag" as "covert operations designed to deceive in such a way that the operations appear as though they are being carried out by entities, groups, or nations other than those who actually planned and executed them."

The 1993 attack on the World Trade Center, the Oklahoma City bombing of the Alfred P. Murrah Federal Building, and the demolition of the World Trade Center towers are only three of the hundreds of false-flag operations committed by the covert criminal network hidden within the US government, its intelligence agencies, and intelligence agencies around the world.

One would expect that those whose family members were slain at the World Trade Center would be allowed to obtain justice by prosecuting the government traitors who orchestrated the events of 9/11. However, we soon come to realize, in a country where justice does not exist, neither does appropriate redress nor remedy.

A main and distinguishing characteristic of a moral and ethical society is that punishment and justice tools are equally implemented by that society, in a manner that applies fairly to all members of that society. In a fair and just society, no one is above the law. When we have a society in which there is a select class of people to whom the law does not apply, then we have a society where the criminals control the justice department.

In such a society unable or unwilling to enforce equal application of the law, the pool of inmates incarcerated is comprised of the remaining members of the society who are not part of the criminal element that runs the government and controls its privately functioning for-profit justice system.

When there is tyranny within a government that is operated by a conspiring network of criminals, in order for such a corrupt system to continue, the criminal network within the government needs to be legally protected and kept hidden from the light of scrutiny and public exposure.

That is why our press is failing in the performance of its constitutional duties; it fails to protect and keep the public safe and informed of any government actions that are conducted contrary to the interests of the American people. Just the opposite, the press intentionally obfuscates the truth from the public.

With every right comes responsibility and corresponding obligation. The press is the only business protected by the US Constitution, but still the press fails to do its investigative duties to protect the people and simply reports what it is told to report by its owners.

Most of the media are comprised of a bunch of bought-and-paid-for talking heads. The press continually fails to report the important stories that really affect civilization, an example being the enslavement of nearly all of the world's population.

One of the main deficiencies of the US Constitution is that it was constructed for a government whose members possess a sliver of decency and believe and uphold to the best of their ability the ideals of a kind and loving Christian God. It was the Founding Fathers' belief that a God-fearing Christian would not even consider operating treasonously toward the interests of his or her constituents.

Today, those traitors who have usurped and silently overthrown the government, without a shot being fired, need to be vanquished and held accountable for the countless lives they have damaged and destroyed.

A group of federal workers who have run amuck with the government cannot possibly accomplish effective in-house investigations and ethical monitoring of itself. Are we to believe that a criminal group that commits such incredibly heinous acts and atrocities is capable of morally disciplining itself? There needs to be accountability by those who, through deception and maneuvering, have changed the face of this planet into a human slaughterhouse. Every day, people are dying atrocious deaths at the hands of a military that is used by a vast criminal network to protect and enforce its demented desires and visions.

Throughout civilized society, it has come to be expected that investigations are conducted by outside police agencies and not by the actual perpetrators of a crime. This ensures that fairness, impartiality, and thoroughness apply in the investigation, allowing and rendering justice to be achievable for the benefit and empowering of society. Imagine if we allowed criminals to conduct their own investigations into the crimes they have committed. Our society does not have gang members investigating their own drive-by shootings, yet this is occurring within the government. It appoints its own special commissions to investigate its own special crimes.

In a fair and moral society, people need to have justice for the criminal acts committed by politicians, federal workers, and anyone else doing business with the US government who kill our brothers and sisters and face no penalties. War crimes are responsible for a majority of the insanity that is occurring on the international scene. As long as the US military is used to enforce the dictates of the governmental criminal network, we will have an unstable and hateful world, instead of a tranquil and peaceful world. We the people decide by silence or protest which world we will live in and pass to our offspring.

Impunity for war crimes should not be camouflaged behind the same flag that drapes the coffins of countless fallen heroes, who died unwittingly enforcing the special interests of a small group of insidious men and women that plague and pillage our world.

Who has paid for the mass murder that happened at the World Trade Center on September 11, 2001? Follow the money, as they say, and watch 9/11 Trillions: Follow the Money at youtube.com/watch?v=eB-SObbExwaI.

All Americans will either pursue justice or succumb to the tyrannical government operatives who have created and continue to create these terroristic types of calamities—these terroristic types of false flags. As a society, we will reap what we have sown. Devastation and peril will continue to describe the plight of the American scene and the worldwide scene unless there is truly an evolution of thought in the minds of the people. We have been walking down a road of destruction; it's time to change the course of this world toward a more attractive world.

Today's US government has been replaced with a shadow government that serves only its master and could not care less about the American people. That is the major problem—citizens are no more the masters of the government; they are its slaves.

The present US government, which was created to be a sovereign republic, is far removed from its original intent and operation as directed and outlined in the US Constitution and conceived by the Founding Fathers. Today, America would sadly be unrecognizable to the signers of our nation's founding documents.

It would behoove all of us to read again the US Declaration of Independence, the US Constitution, and its Bill of Rights. These documents are essential to understand the amount of tyranny and suppression the colonialists faced under the wrath of King George III of England and his henchmen, the Redcoats. There is not much difference today, as we still have oppressive taxation without representation!

When you understand the concepts conveyed in the founding documents and the protections they provide, you begin to understand how America has slipped from a free republic to an America operated by a despotic regime serving its own interests and agenda.

Our personal actions should lead us to attain a higher and more abundant moral and ethical character as a nation. As the United States gets its own house in order, we can begin to focus on making the rest of the planet a safer, more trustworthy place for the human race. Not for an instant should the human race allow a small, morally derelict criminal network to destroy the world for its so-called profit and debauched enjoyment.

Criminals have an inability to think sequentially. Therefore, policies and behaviors of criminal politicians will lead the governed to unexpected and unpredicted future difficulties, making the past of this country seem like a fairy tale and the future like an unimaginable nightmare.

There is no telling if we can avoid reaching the bottom or how far down the United States can go as a country, but those in power are driving America there with wild acceleration and abandonment. The goals of the world's ruling families are horrific and calamitous in scope, and as you can imagine, their actions are just as vile.

Now is the time for all of us to stand up for ourselves, for our fellow citizens, and for every man, woman, and child in this world who is counting on us because the future of America is the future of the world.

Organizations of like-minded citizens need to come together in matters regarding civil liberties and return this country to the image the Founding Fathers had in mind when they wrote the Constitution.

We need to stop contributing to a political system designed to monetarily deprive, subjugate, and enslave its citizens. We Americans must make our voices heard and stand up for ourselves and for mankind!

There is an ever-growing awareness that something is terribly wrong with the operation of the federal government and in the operation of its foreign affairs. The politicians are the ones responsible for creating and implementing the policies and operation of the federal government, its foreign affairs, and international relations. They are failing the people miserably.

Many Americans now believe that the government is covering up the truth of the events of 9/11 and that it was an inside job. The time has come for an evolution to improve and return the US government to its original form of a republic by removing the hogs from the trough of special interests (no offense to hogs). It is in the citizens' best interest to remove from our government the wretched criminals who stop at nothing to implement insane policies that are leading to the deaths of millions and perhaps even billions of people, as they futilely attempt to achieve their twisted and demented goal of world domination.

The international government criminal network has infiltrated virtually every government of the world at its highest levels. However, it has underestimated the tenacity and resolve of the American people, and people from around the world, who will not surrender our liberties in exchange for shackles of enslavement.

We, as a people and nation, must no longer surrender our future or the future of our children, our children's children, and their grandchildren to a maniacal regime responsible for ushering in World War III right under our noses.

America kills at an unrivaled rate, and there is no worldly improvement as a result, but there are a lot of rebuilding contracts given to companies like Halliburton, Bechtel, and other firms that are politically connected.

False profit is why we kill, why we murder, and why we war.

Some of the most brutal upheavals in history have occurred as a result of the elite's believing that they possessed the ability to dominate the entire population without recourse. The elite have never fully succeeded in enslaving the entire population of the planet.

Throughout history, the people have rebelled and executed a portion of the oppressive ruling elite as the citizens eventually revolt and regain their freedom. Today, some might conclude that the American people appear ready to start stringing up those responsible for creating the international havoc and chaos of this world; the funny thing is, they might be right.

Let us hope cooler heads prevail and our society can forego all that typical bloodshed and unnecessary killing we historically witness time and again.

In this book the enemies of humanity are revealed and identified; their cover is blown. As far as cleaning up this degraded world, the rest is up to us, and by us, I mean you.

Many of us work towards an ethical reformation of our government and an evolution of our society with hopes that we will make the needed changes to raise the role and functioning of government to a more humane and acceptable level, without the need of resorting to physical violence and revolution. Many others believe either way—violent or peaceful—change is coming. Let's fix this broken country like adults, please. Let's fix the people-problems of this world for a nice change without creating even more problems. That is what politicians do—they cut off the foot because of an ingrown toenail.

The solution to war is the acquisition and creation of peace through implementing creative, constructive, and sane international policies that invite harmonious global agreement and cooperation, as opposed to implementing insane and destructive militaristic actions that breed global hatred and revenge.

The billions of people who want to claim their freedoms have more combined force and power than the few suppressors who want to maintain their stranglehold on the populace. Once it is discovered who exactly holds the keys to our shackles, in a short period, we can return the keys to their rightful owners. Once the key holders are discovered and methods of enslavement understood, it is only a matter of time, coupled with the population's demand to evolve the human species to a higher level, until the slaves are freed.

Once the leadership of the world is forced to cease its military actions, the world will rise and elevate to a higher plane, reflective of the true image of humanity. Most people deplore military action and realize that it is created only to enrich the undeserving merchants who thrive and profit from military conflicts.

Many ask how it is possible that those who delve in the financial enslavement of humankind could ever make peace with their conscience. It is impossible, for they are a species with no conscience; they are a different breed than the rest of us. They are a sick, psychopathic, and deprived breed of creatures who cannot emotionally reflect on the harm they continuously commit against humanity and the security of the world's nations. Young men and women are irresponsibly used to unleash the mightiest military force in the world against helpless people around the globe.

A good friend of mine is a veteran. He told me that he was not a warrior filled with pride and honor as a result of his military service to our country. It was only after he returned that he realized upon vast reflection that his military title should include the words "corporate mercenary." He felt this way because, as he confessed, he had harmed wrongly, and he realized that he and his brothers-in-arms were put into deadly conflict to protect the special interests of US corporations. He contrasted and compared the great Native American warriors, who fought the technically superiorly armed white men, to the services he provided as a member of the US Army. The Native Americans fought battles because of their threatened survival. It saddened me as he lamented and he remorsefully explained to me the actual reasons he killed during his tours of duty. He is a great man, and I am honored to know him and call him a friend.

The American spirit still resides in the good people of America. I earnestly hope that Americans innately have the integrity and bravery our ancestors displayed in providing and protecting our freedoms throughout history. I thank and appreciate greatly all the fine men and women of the military for their indispensable and honorable service to this country and pray that the United States stops making any more wounded warriors.

One life lost in war is too many. It has been demonstrated throughout history that war is never a viable solution to the problem that preceded the conflict. Remember the US military has never started a war; it is always ordered to conduct military actions and war by the commander-in-chief.

It is important that we pay homage to those that have militarily protected the great nation of America and for the countless sacrifices made to safeguard the freedoms and liberties only found in America. Members of the military, possessing volumes of integrity and love for the United States, are upset with the direction and mismanagement of the US military and want nothing more than for America to revert to its roots and follow the US Constitution, instead of doing what it is today.

Please take the time to watch Fort McHenry & Francis Scott Key's Star Spangled Banner at youtube.com/watch?v=6UprqxlIuwg and appreciate the great sacrifices others have made to provide Americans with the freedoms we share as a nation. Our deepest and most heartfelt thank-you goes out to every loyal American military man and woman of this nation. Your service is commendable and highly appreciated.

The help of all Americans is desperately needed to regain the freedoms that have been taken by our nation's enemies hidden deep within the US government. What Americans do in the next days and years of our lives will determine whether we live in freedom and liberty or cast aside those most awesome of gifts for shackles of servitude and depravity.

The choice is ours. The writing is on the wall. We need to ensure that we do not waste this brief moment in humankind's history and that we immediately divert from the destructive course we as a species are traveling. Our extinction is imminent should we fail at our task to adjust and correct the direction of this staggering nation and this decaying world. If you have any concern for the future of this planet and the continuation of humanity, then you are definitely on the crew and responsible for fixing it. Welcome to the crew; it happens at birth, whether you like it or not.

Our actions determine if good will prevail over evil, and what we do to contribute to humanity's improvement determines in some way whether there will be heaven on Earth or hell. Right now, this world is going to hell in the proverbial handbasket; now is the time to intercede and take a stand. Now is the time for good-willed men and women to stand and choose the light over the darkness and take back our God-given freedoms that have been stripped from us by politicians and satanic special interests.

Let us start discovering the truth of this world and its operation, its mechanics, and its tendencies. Let us look with questioning, open eyes at what really exists and what is really happening all around us. Let us look at how global affairs are conducted to destroy our fellow brothers and sisters, vastly affecting the quality of our lives, our society, and our planet. Let us fearlessly and relentlessly hunt down and rid the earth of the enemies of humankind, whose intentions are evil and actions are destructive and deliberate.

In failing to stand up for ourselves, we are choosing to tighten the chains of restraint and enslavement around our throats and the throats of our posterity. The choices we make and the challenges we face, for ourselves and future generations, are not to be considered lightly. What we do today determines our tomorrows and shapes our destiny as individuals and as a nation. More importantly, what we do and every action we perform either contributes to or detracts from humanity's continuation and survival as a species.

Do we strive for freedom or lick the boot on our brother's throat? Do we accept the challenges of reforming this nation and the nations of the world or suffer the consequences of cowardice, apathy, and ignorance?

We stand at the brink of obliteration as a nation, morally, financially, and culturally. Popular actions and revolts have been amply demonstrated ineffective, while inaction has led only to further degradation and debasement of humanity and civilization. Nevertheless, we can do better and create more effective and competent oversight and management of our government and foreign affairs.

To do nothing is to acquiesce and leave the country in the hands of tyrannical despots. To do nothing is to deny our posterity the chance to live in the greatest country the world has ever seen or ever will.

Let it be said that the light of liberty was neither diminished nor extinguished on our watch. Let it be said that on our watch the light of liberty shone into the darkness of suppression and lifted man to a higher, more evolved species, making the world a place of peace and prosperity.

Unifying our intent to cease supporting a corrupt and failing government is the first step in unchaining the shackles of humankind's oppression. For it is far better to die, tearing off one's shackles of oppression, than to live another moment as a slave.

We have been remiss in our duty as stewards to improve the world and negligent in our common responsibility to raise humanity to a higher realm. It is time we do our duty for the sake and future of humankind. Let us make the world a better place, where people can live in peace and trust one another, and then there will be heaven on Earth.

CHAPTER 4

The Government's Fleecing of the People

We are free not because we claim freedom, but because we practice it.

> – WILLIAM FAULKNER

It does not require a majority to prevail, but rather an irate, tireless minority keen to set brushfires in people's minds.

> – SAMUEL ADAMS

And the LORD said unto me, "A conspiracy is found among the men of Judah, and among the inhabitants of Jerusalem."

> – KING JAMES BIBLE, JEREMIAH 11:9

America is a land of taxation that was founded to avoid taxation.

> – LAURENCE J. PETER

Inflation is taxation without legislation.

> – MILTON FRIEDMAN

If taxation without consent is robbery, the United States government has never had, has not now, and is never likely to have, a single honest dollar in its treasury. If taxation without consent is not robbery, then any band of robbers has only to declare themselves a government, and all their robberies are legalized.

> – LYSANDER SPOONER

Taxation is the price we pay for failing to build a civilized society. The higher the tax level, the greater the failure. A centrally planned totalitarian state represents a complete defeat for the civilized world, while a totally voluntary society represents its ultimate success.

– MARK SKOUSEN

Money is time made tangible—the time invested in the earning of it. Taxation is the confiscation of the earner's time. Although some taxation is necessary, all taxation diminishes freedom.

– GEORGE WILL

The way to crush the bourgeoisie is to grind them between the millstones of taxation and inflation.

– VLADIMIR LENIN

The cardinal rule of taxation is that, whatever you put a levy on, you'll inevitably get less of. Taxing corporate activity means less investing, less hiring, fewer jobs and a smaller economy, which hurts the rich, the poor and the middle class alike.

– ADAM DAVIDSON

I don't want to remember 2005 as a year that the government heaped unnecessary burdens upon American families. Stealing from the poor and middle class and giving to the rich, while increasing the deficit, is hardly responsible.

– MARTY MEEHAN

I think coercive taxation is theft, and government has a moral duty to keep it to a minimum.

– WILLIAM WELD

MANY PEOPLE BELIEVE things on planet Earth are moving along just swell and there is no need for any action or impetus on their part to correct anything that happens, specifically regarding the actions of the governments of the world, towards the people of the world. Some believe there is no need to correct anything that is happening in Washington, DC, Europe, or the Middle East. Further, they believe there is no need for people to voice their objections to the pathway that humanity is blindly strolling down, a pathway designed and crafted to lead inevitably towards the extinction of our species.

This perilous course of humanity, continuing because of the people's unwillingness to intercede in political and worldly matters, is unaddressed by the apathetic, incompetent, and shortsighted. There are continual distractions designed to keep the population's attention diverted from the truth of what is really occurring in this society. All the differences of the classes, races, and religions are broadcast to keep the masses from discovering who the real enslavers of humanity truly are. The good thing is that there are not that many enslavers!

A curtain obfuscates and hides the truth of international events, cleverly disguised and wrapped in a nice box, called the status quo. The status quo is broadcast internationally. In this box, society appears a little frightening, and there is no action required on our part to correct anything. Everything will be taken care of by the heroes, the state, and its concerned politicians. The media brainwash the masses and infer that the people should just keep playing video games and watching television day and night.

We are led to believe that all wrongs will right themselves under the watchful hands of our elected politicians in Washington, DC. This justifies the creation of a superstate that will take care of everything and the people will have to do nothing but pay exorbitant taxes.

There are a few problems associated with the super-state scenario. First, there is a vast range of interests among the people of Washington, DC. The least agreed-upon concept is that politicians in Washington, DC, are there to fix the problems of this world, a world whose problems are entirely created, legislated, and regulated by virtually the same politicians.

The entire political system is bankrupt financially, ethically, and morally. The soul, once tarnished, is tougher to clean; this applies to you, me, and everyone in between. It would also apply especially to the government.

The federal government has intentions to regulate or tax everything that occurs in this society, and presently, it appears that it does regulate pretty much everything. Regulations come in different forms including licensing, prohibiting, and permitting; all are basically different ways of controlling the masses and extracting wealth from the citizens.

Can people imagine having a neighbor that acts like the US government? Imagine that this neighbor is continually flying a military flag outside his house. His only source of income is beating up the neighborhood kids and taking ("taxing") their money. He spends virtually all his "borrowed" funds on guns and weapons and armament to fight off imaginary enemies in a land far, far away. He taps the neighbors' phones. Surveillance of the neighborhood is never higher, and people feel more afraid than ever. Does this sound familiar?

This kind and amount of insanity felt globally affects everyone on this planet. People live in a world being run by psychotics. As a result of inbreeding, the psychos that run this planet happen to be morally, ethically, and financially bankrupt, as well as emotionally corrupt and evil beyond the imagination.

Citizens have inalienable rights from God, yet these have been usurped in concert under the federal and state governments' control and taxing of the nation for the private benefit of a select few.

Taxation is one of the greatest tools used to control the masses by oppressive international criminals. Controlling the taxation of a nation gives these criminals control over the economic health of the nation. Famous statesman Daniel Webster once said, "The power to tax is the power to destroy." Never has Webster's statement been more true than today.

There are various methods of taxation used to fleece Americans of their wealth. The United States is the land of unjust taxation, which cripples and stagnates the economy, making it tougher for all Americans to find and retain gainful employment. Hundreds of millions of taxpayers begrudgingly pay the different taxes listed below.

None of these taxes existed a hundred years ago when the United States of America was the most prosperous country in the world. These taxes are un-American and exact the life and vibrancy out of our nation's economy and, most importantly, the people. Here is a partial list of the actions or activities that the government unscrupulously taxes:

- For money not yet received in a business: accounts receivable tax
- For holding one's money in a corporation: accumulated earnings tax
- For claiming exemptions: alternative minimum tax

• For bullets and cartridges for a firearm: ammunition tax
• For opening an IRA for a minor: annual custodian fees
• For buying, selling, processing, or handling blueberries in Maine: state blueberry tax
• For building a house or renovating a bathroom: building permit fee
• For making a lot of money selling one's home (heaven forbid): capital gains tax
• For buying or selling a deck of playing cards in Alabama: playing card tax
• For driving a big truck or limo: commercial driver's license tax
• For smoking: tobacco tax
• For starting a company to employ people: corporate income tax
• For speeding: court costs and fines (indirect tax)
• For a puppy: dog license tax
• For buying a car: excise taxes
• For getting a job: federal income tax and federal unemployment tax (FUTA)
• For fishing: fishing license tax
• For fishing specifically for rainbow trout: trout stamp tax (in some states)
• For hunting ducks in a boat: watercraft registration tax and waterfowl stamp tax
• For selling food: Pennsylvania (and other states) food license tax
• For operating a trucking company that travels interstate: international fuel tax agreement license and tax
• For going to the dump or putting one's barrel on the curb for removal: garbage tax
• For diesel fuel: diesel tax (approximately fifty cents per gallon in 2015)
• For a corporation selling goods: gross receipts tax
• For eating foods over five hundred calories: hamburger tax
• For killing wild game: hunting license tax
• For smoking weed in North Carolina: illegal drug possession tax

- For the death of one's parents: inheritance tax
- For being late paying taxes: IRS and State Taxing Authorities' interest and penalties tax (a tax on tax)
- For owning an oil or natural gas well: lease severance tax
- For buying a house in Louisiana or North Carolina: local income tax—parish or county tax
- For buying a car, boat, watch, purse, or airplane: luxury tax
- For settling down: marriage license tax
- For wining and dining: meal tax
- For being hired: Medicare tax
- For visiting a strip club in Utah: nudity tax
- For getting a professional license (doctor, insurance agent, hairstylist, etc.): occupation tax
- For striking it big in Texas wildcatting: oil and gas assessment tax (after you fork over for a well permit tax)
- For moving to a state, county, parish, city, or town: personal property tax
- For selling illegal drugs: sales tax
- For buying a house: property tax (or the sheriff will sell the house)
- For living in Maryland and other states: rain water tax
- For buying or selling a house: real estate tax
- For buying an RV to get away from it all: recreational vehicle tax
- For driving in many states: road usage tax
- For taking a shortcut on a toll road: toll road tax, toll bridge tax, and a toll tunnel tax.
- For hauling stuff around in a trailer: trailer registration tax.
- For staying at a hotel: room tax
- For buying something: state, county, or parish sales tax
- For education: school tax
- For seeing a show: service charge tax
- For having a business: self-employment tax.
- For being employed: Social Security tax (and state franchise tax in some states)
- For turning on the lights: utility tax

- For being employed: unemployment tax
- For a new car and driver's license: vehicle license, registration tax, and vehicle sales tax
- For hiring American workers: workers' compensation tax
- For buying a bottle of wine to forget about taxes: liquor tax

Many people live in states that also assess an income tax for the privilege of working in those particular states. When employers can no longer afford to pay the state taxes, they up and move. Then the unemployed people depend, at least for a little while until they lose their homes, on the state unemployment tax (SUTA) for their meager survival.

Regarding the phone, we pay the Telephone Federal Excise Tax, Telephone Federal Universal Service Fee Tax, Telephone Federal Surcharge Taxes, Telephone State Surcharge Taxes, Telephone Local Surcharge Taxes, Telephone Minimum Usage Surcharge Tax, Telephone Recurring Charges Tax, Telephone Non-Recurring Charges Tax, Telephone State Usage Charge Tax, and Telephone Local Usage Charge Tax. That's a lot of telephone tax!

The above-listed taxes seriously challenge the financial ability of the lower and middle classes to survive. Paying these taxes also financially challenges the corporations that employ everyone. The United States has the highest rate of taxation of any country in the world.

Taxation is the modern-day shackles of slavery that all races in America wear and share equally. Every race and class within the society is being pinned against the others to prevent people of all colors and classes from collectively focusing and discovering who has been responsible for the injustice, taxation, and enslavement we all shared for the past thousands of years.

Is it any wonder that in the US economy, with its over-burdensome taxes, almost half of all American businesses fail in the first couple of years? Taxation handicaps the starting and fledgling businesses and the people that dare strike out as entrepreneurs. Entrepreneurs drive the US economy and therefore the world economies with creativeness, productiveness, and ingenuity while battling an oppressive monetary and taxation system enforced by the government against the interest of the people and specifically against the growth and sustainability of start-up companies.

Many people are unaware of where their money goes while they live paycheck to paycheck. It is easy to see that the government, in one form or another, does not just have its fingers in our pies; the government is taking most of the pie and leaving us the crumbs.

When a company has a bad year and loses money, does the government or the Internal Revenue Service average out the loss with the previous good year(s) the company had and reimburse the company to offset the loss and help the company stay in business? No. The IRS has its hands out or guns out when one is doing great, but where is the IRS when the bankers dry up the money supply and there is not ample credit available to sustain one's business in a slumping economy?

If you have a great year, the IRS takes a big chunk of your money. If you have a bad year and lose money, why doesn't the IRS give you back some of your money that you paid in the year(s) before the loss? The IRS is the small businessperson's partner in good times, but when the small business loses money, the IRS is not returning one cent to help the business survive. It seems as though the IRS is not pro-business; it is just pro-taxing of businesses to the point where the government is cannibalizing American productivity and making it almost impossible for a fledgling business to survive. A partner is there in good times as well as bad. Again, where is the IRS when a company stumbles and loses money?

The extraction of taxes in America makes it much more difficult for many families to scratch out a living and provide for their families. The strife and difficulties many undergo, due to these burdensome taxes, could simply be resolved if many of these unconstitutional taxes were eliminated. Yes, we should eliminate unconstitutional taxes for the benefit of the people!

The only reason the United States has income tax is that the government has forfeited the country's constitutional right and control of its own money into the hands of the Federal Reserve. America has given control of the nation's money supply to the private international banking families—a cabal comprised of charlatans and war criminals —who control the Federal Reserve System.

The US Constitution reads:

Article 1, Section 10. No State shall enter into any Treaty, Alliance, or Confederation; grant Letters of Marque and Reprisal; coin Money; emit Bills of Credit; **make any Thing but gold and silver Coin a Tender in Payment of Debts;** pass any Bill of Attainder, ex post facto Law, or **Law**

impairing the Obligation of Contracts, or grant any Title of Nobility [emphasis added].

Article 1, Section 8: Powers of Congress. The Congress shall have Power to lay and collect Taxes, Duties, Imposts and Excises, to pay the Debts and provide for the common Defense and general Welfare of the United States; but all Duties, Imposts and Excises shall be uniform throughout the United States.

All of the above-listed taxes are a direct violation of the taxing methods provided under the Constitution. The taxing methods written in the Constitution were created to keep the federal government small, non-intrusive, and out of the lives of the American people. The purpose was to limit the federal government's power and keep citizens free from governmental abuses and interaction.

Violations of the above constitutional sections have enabled the government to surpass its constitutional limits and allowed for government intrusion into virtually every aspect of our lives. The ability to tax its citizenry was intentionally limited by the Constitution to minimize the federal government's ability to implement enslaving taxation schemes that are more favorable to one class of citizens than the rest of the citizens.

These constitutional limitations imposed upon the taxing power of the federal government were incorporated to keep the federal government within the ten square miles of operation called Washington, DC. These taxation restrictions limit the federal government to providing the essentials needed to honor, maintain, and uphold those items listed in the Preamble of the US Constitution, which reads as follows:

We the People of the United States, in Order to form a more perfect Union, establish Justice, insure Tranquility, provide for the common defense, promote the general Welfare, and secure the Blessings of Liberty to ourselves and our Posterity, do ordain and establish this Constitution for the Unites States of America.

With everything going on today in America, does it sound as if the country is behaving in accordance with the Preamble of the Constitution? Do you feel tranquility? How is your general welfare these days? Are you satisfied with our antiquated and usurped justice system that provides anything but justice?

Is the government behaving in accordance with the will and desires of the people? If one says, "Yes, the government is reflecting the will and desires of the people," then the will and desires of the people must include insane taxation.

Reflection pools are found in virtually every national capital around the globe. When we stand and look in the reflection pool of our government, the government that reflects back to us—good or bad in quality and nature—is the government that we the people demand and deserve.

If one disagrees and says, "No, the government is not reflecting the will and desires of the people," then the government must align with the will and desires of the people by stopping unjust taxation, warring, and criminal actions against the American people and the world's population. If we would like to have a better government, we must improve as individuals, stop acting apathetically towards our world, and take responsibility for our government.

Furthermore, one of the main reasons for international instability is that the federal government is supposed to be bound to operate only within the ten-square-mile area designated as Washington, DC, and not be the policing power of the world.

Article 1, Section 8, clause 17 of the US Constitution states:

To exercise exclusive Legislation in all Cases whatsoever, over such District (not exceeding ten Miles square) as may, by Cession of particular States, and the acceptance of Congress, become the Seat of the Government of the United States, and to exercise like Authority over all Places purchased by the Consent of the Legislature of the State in which the Same shall be, for the Erection of Forts, Magazines, Arsenals, dock-Yards, and other needful Buildings.

Through chicanery and other deviously underhanded deception and tricks, the government has exceeded its constitutional boundaries to beyond the ten square miles of Washington, DC, and its authorized area of operation. The federal government has extended its scope of taxation throughout the continental United States and beyond, thereby inappropriately entangling American citizens in the unconstitutional, pseudo federal government currently operating as a private corporation, responsible only to its private shareholders and all the while being grossly mismanaged by Congress. More details are presented further in this book regarding the federal government's transmutation from a bona fide government into a private corporation.

Article 1, Section 8 of the US Constitution essentially limits the US Congress to creating and applying laws to the ten-square-mile jurisdiction of Washington, DC, and the different ports of entry and other very limited places. One can just imagine if Congress were completely relegated to making tax laws that pertained only to its authorized jurisdiction limited to inside the Beltway, or the ten-square-mile jurisdiction detailed above in Article 1, Section 8, Clause 17.

Further restraint was attached to US legislative powers in the following clause of the Constitution at Article 1, Section 8, Clause 18:

To make all Laws which shall be necessary and proper for carrying into Execution the foregoing Powers, and all other Powers vested by this Constitution **in the Government of the United States, or in any Department or Officer thereof** [emphasis added].

What a different world it would be if the politicians in Washington, DC, abided by these two clauses.

How free from oppressive taxation would we be if the federal government responsibly exercised its powers as intended, described, and limited under the Constitution? How free would we be if the different departments of the government operated as intended? What if the IRS regulated itself, rather than continually exceeding its jurisdiction by applying its bogus regulations to all Americans that do not even live in Washington, DC, but rather live outside the above mentioned "ten Mile square" area?

What if the government supported the economy and did not enforce a graduated income tax in accordance with the planks of the Communist Manifesto? The US government's modern kleptocracy would make Karl Marx and other Communists extremely proud.

By overstepping the bounds and the limitations placed on the federal government by the Constitution, the federal government has been allowed to intrude into its citizens' lives to the point where the Founding Fathers would not even recognize what we have allowed to become of our country, our freedom, and our liberty. Taxation is running rampart and destroying the US economy.

Citizens have been remiss in watching the store, and the thieves who stole it aim to make us penniless. There should be no doubt that rampant and extravagant taxation results in nothing but poverty for the masses and the creation of a superclass; the superclass are the ones stealing our wealth in the form of taxes. All IRS income tax is reallocated —or simply stolen from the taxpayer—to pay twelve foreign banking families that own the Federal Reserve, the US federal debt, and its unpayable interest.

The Comprehensive Annual Financial Report (CAFR) is reported, compiled, submitted, and annually made available to the public by every level of government—federal, state, county, city, town, municipal—and the different corporate departments: police, fire, school, sheriff, water, etc. All levels of corporate governments are required to compile and have these financial documents available for citizens' review. Every corporate independent faction of government, such as a local school board, county sheriff, even local municipality sports activities, have a CAFR report annually compiled, documenting its overall financial affairs. It is a very accurate and exacting report.

There is a level of deception, crafted into these documents, which tends to mislead the novice accountant. One of the most telling tricks performed is to not carry forward all surplus monies or profits from one year to the next. Many cities and counties having surpluses measuring in the billions perform this accounting magic trick of not carrying forward the annual profits from one year to the next. As an example, many municipalities' books show figures like one billion dollars reported on December 31, 2014, and zero dollars reported on January 1, 2015. The funny thing about their books is that usually there is no mention of where the one billion dollars went. This should raise the brow of any forensic accountant, as it makes this dog's ears stand straight.

Inquiring minds would want to know, where does the money go?

To whom is the money from a parking ticket disbursed and in what amounts? The answer is nebulously described in the state statutes.

Many Americans will be amazed to discover that the US government is one of the richest corporations in the world. It appears that surplus funds reported within the CAFR migrate from the different levels of government until they reach the coffers of the federal government.

For example, if one receives a speeding ticket in any US city, to whom does the money go? A portion of it will go to the local municipal services, as outlined in the traffic code statutes of that state. Other monies will go to the judges' and other municipal employees' retirement funds. In essence, here we have a small section of the population stealing from the rest of society for their retirements—great work if you can get it. In other words, there is a slush fund for judges and other municipal employees in America's kleptocracy that is fit for a king. A small section of the people steals from the rest of the people and tells us, "It's just the way it is." In actuality, an even smaller group of criminals steals a lot more from the people and tells us, "It's just the government, and that's just the way it is!"

It is the most efficient legalized system of theft that there is in the world. Money buys everyone in the system. How can one expect tax court judges, or any judge for that matter, to be unbiased and fair if their retirement funds profit from the adjudications they determine? How can the police not give tickets if every ticket they give is funding their own retirements? These days tickets are expensive!

A portion of the speeding ticket fine ends up supporting and expanding the community's budget to new heights year after year. This creates and expands the governments' yearly budgets year after year as standard operating procedure, and it guarantees larger, more intrusive government year after year. This is because the additional funds injected into the system must be mandatorily spent in that given year.

This repeating pattern of municipal government growth occurs as a major percentage of the total value of traffic tickets, as well as other fees charged for the variety of government services, are added to the city's budget in the current year. This increase to the budget is automatically added to next year's budget, and in order to pay for the next year's larger budget, there is an associated increase in property taxes the following year.

Many of the government costs, fines, and fees collected are allocated in a similar fashion. Collected government funds directly increase the municipality's budget and automatically increase the municipality's budget for the following year. This outdated accounting model is one of the contributing factors that gives the different governments the financial incentive to grow, increase the number of regulations, and further restrict our liberties.

Having a bigger government is an incentive for additional taxes in the form of government costs, fees, and fines. There are additional incentives for government workers to raise costs for their services that they provide to the private sector, which often ends in draining the public dry at the hands of corrupt and abusive government.

Today, much of the adversarial position between the police and the private sector stems from this system of growing the government through the issuance of tickets and infractions that generate more revenue and higher taxes. This ever-increasing system of taxation is often unseen and unnoticed in its relationship to bigger and bigger government. Moreover, much of the anti-police rhetoric and vitriol we see in a small segment of society, as is the case within organizations such as Black Lives Matters, results from this too-often adversarial position created between the police and the private sector.

In order to spend that larger budget, the government expands and hires more people, and it becomes a vicious cycle. The government takes in more money, adds it to its budget—or, more accurately, adds it to its expenses. It hires more people. It increases the city's or town's property taxes to pay for the budget increases, and then it all starts over again the next year.

This government-only accounting cycle is responsible for the propagation of bigger and bigger local, state, and federal governments and the outrageous taxes needed to support such largess and waste.

This government system pits the city workers—including the police, prosecutors, judges, and officers of the court—against the city's taxpaying civilians. These defunct accounting procedures and philosophies create a built-in incentive to grow the various governmental departments. We especially see exponential growth in those departments that collect fees and fines such as judges, police, and meter maids.

A good percentage of all revenues generated eventually ends up in the coffers of the federal government or is reallocated to private parties. This is evident in the privatization of certain segments of the various governments where private parties, in many cases who are friends of the active or past politicians, receive lavish contracts and profits.

The federal government takes its money from the people and invests it in stock markets throughout the world. In fact, the corporation called the US government is the largest stockholder in the entire world. The United States or, better yet, the families that own the United States own large stock positions in a majority of the companies listed in all the world's stock markets.

International thieves use blind trusts in the Cayman Islands or other countries to provide tax shelters that aid and abet political criminality, enabling politicians and bankers to hide their enormous wealth that they stole from the American people.

While investigating cafr1.com and cafrman.com, I quickly realized that legislators are continually stealing from unsuspecting American citizens. In the future, CAFR funds and all funds tendered to the government should be allocated to people and projects that are designed to improve the quality of life and that of humankind.

This information regarding CAFR needs to be exposed and understood because this is one of the largest reallocations of funds in the history of the world or, better yet, the largest theft in the history of the world.

Under a vicious criminal taxation system levied against virtually every American, theft through taxation is an example of class warfare between the superrich and everyone else. This great theft impacts the overall society with incalculable damage and devastation. The constant and continual robbery and fleecing of the American citizenry specifically benefits and rewards with incredible riches and wealth a few parasitical families of society while bringing poverty and incredible economic struggle to virtually every remaining member of society.

If one really wants to monitor criminal behavior, it is necessary only to trace the government's funds and to shine the light of truth into the shadows of political deception, criminality, and continual theft through taxation.

The CAFRs tell the true story of the ongoing theft of this nation's wealth by an oppressive taxation system that benefits only the superrich.

Informing our fellow Americans is the first step in changing our current government from a criminal kleptocracy back to an ethical republic —in accordance with the Founding Fathers' intentions at the time this country was established.

Enslavement of the population through taxation has not dramatically changed since the days of the feudal system. The feudal system was very similar to the financial oppression and taxation we silently experience and endure today. As far as slavery is concerned, there is little difference between the feudal and taxation systems; both contribute to form intricate parts to our nation's oppression. According to Robert Plant and Jimmy Page, "It's the same old song and dance, my friend." There have been slight modifications to the oppressive methods employed in order to continue the seldom-discussed human enslavement that has existed for more than the past few centuries.

Comparing our overreaching government interaction, taxation systems, and related financial structures with those of the feudal period may reveal many appalling similarities. Enslavement during the feudal period consisted of the landlord's leasing the lands and fields to the peasant serfs who worked and farmed the land. The serfs were contracted to meet the agricultural production demands of the landlord, or the serfs would be evicted from their homes and property.

The serfs' lease was paid by the labor they were required to perform in the tending of crops and livestock. A serf and his family could never really get ahead and flourish under the feudal system, beyond the meager lifestyle permitted by the landlord. Often the serfs lived in abject poverty; it was similar to the conditions observed in the American share-croppers' lifestyle, which existed on many American farms from the late 1800s to the early 1900s.

Unproductive serfs were blackballed and exiled from the land and the local vicinity. These blackballed serfs needed to travel far to find food and work that would sustain them and their families.

The landlord owned everything, and serfs, not able to honor and fulfill the landlord's contract, were in grave danger of facing death by starvation should they fail to produce enough to satisfy the landlord. It was highly perilous not to obey the orders and desires of the lord.

Feudal concepts are well dramatized and conveyed in the Mel Gibson movie, Braveheart (1995).

The feudal form of oppression and slavery was more obvious and apparent than today's corporate slavery. In today's slavery, one may think there are no landlords leasing lands to serfs, and that is because today we have free-range slavery.

Instead of chains and whips used in the past to enforce slavery, in today's slavery, on April 15, most Americans reluctantly hand their money over to the twelve international private banking families that own and control the IRS and the United States.

The US Congress, under the direction of the banking families, is the legislator of the enslavement, the IRS is the enforcer, and the people are the suckers or, rather, the slaves. Today's citizens work and give their share to the government under fear, duress, and coercion. One needs to look a little more closely to discover the mechanisms implemented to replace the slave master's whip of yesteryear with the so-called volunteer tax system of today.

Today's slavery is created through the implementation of crooked and unfair tax laws. This is a field most politicians are very familiar with since a majority of them are lawyers. Some tax experts believe American

workers are entrapped wrongly by providing their signature to new employers when starting a job by completing IRS W4s and 1099s. Very few
if any employers have ever read the burdensome tax code, and too often,
corporations wrongly demand that newly hired workers fill out IRS
forms agreeing to their own self-imposed taxation of their labor. Most
companies robotically have new employees sign IRS forms when they are
hired; whether the employee or employer is obligated to fill out IRS
forms is subject to interpretation of the Internal Revenue Code.

Many of us are completely unaware that every signature we fasten to a
contract obligates us to certain activities, duties, and obligations. How
many of us actually read and understand the contract we sign when we
open a bank account or start a business? How many of us actually receive
a copy and research the laws that we just agreed to be bound by upon
opening a bank account or starting a business? A person signs many important and binding legal contracts during the term of his or her life, yet
many of us just sign here and sign there, oblivious to the personal ramifications contractually binding us under such specific contracts.

These contracts, as well as all tax contracts with the IRS, are invisible
and unintelligible to most people, yet many gladly sign their lives and
freedoms away. These include many contracts in which one receives a
privilege or benefit from the government. Usually we have rights that are
granted by God and protected by the Constitution, but many rights are
stolen by the government and returned for profit to Americans as a privilege or benefit that is licensed and penalized by federal, state, and local
government employees and officers.

Any type of contract—driving or occupational, food stamps, a traffic
ticket, Social Security benefits, school registrations, virtually any piece of
paper one signs, which is received from a government worker—binds us
in more ways than most will ever imagine or realize. Through the
binding aspects of these contracts—or, better phrased, obligations—citizens agree to fulfill these contracts, which provide the government jurisdiction over the citizenry. People give their permission and sign up to
voluntarily be the slaves of the government.

Excluding governmental presumptions, the chains of voluntary servitude are for the most part fastened and constructed with a pen and our
own signatures. Therefore, to reverse the slavery and obtain our freedom,
we must first use a pen and sign our way out of this legally constructed
prison to which we have all submitted ourselves.

Consider that the federal government is supposedly limited to exercise its power in the ten square miles of Washington, DC, and the other territories and enclaves afforded it under the US Constitution. What mechanism does the government employ to ensnare one within its nexus of governmental control and jurisdiction when most of us live outside the ten square miles of Washington, DC? How does the government contract with us as though we live within its jurisdiction?

The government does not force people to join it. It persuades them to volunteer by offering benefits and concealing the entirety of the contract that we are agreeing to participate in when we provide a signature on a government-issued form and accept their offer and paltry benefits. When dealing with a government that has abolished involuntary servitude, one must agree, either through writing or by consent in action, to become a state-controlled slave.

In the US Army, a soldier has to step over the yellow line in order to show his consent to enlist in the armed forces and become United States property. The ceremonial volunteering method of stepping over the yellow line is covered in detail in a fascinating article "How To Avoid the Draft Or National Service" at 100777.com/node/1154.

These are all contracts, just as the IRS 1040 form is a contract we sign, seal, and are requested to deliver by April 15 of each year.

The nation is being fleeced in every aspect of our society through unethical government taxation. The government pretty much regulates and taxes nearly everything, except for the things it should be regulating and taxing.

The ultimate fleecing is when the government takes control of a person's body in order to profit. If there were no money in the prison business, there would be no prisons.

Prisoners are not supplied with the content of the contract that they agreed to when providing their signature during the booking and intake process. One's property, including one's body, is assigned to the county jail or state prison with the tendering of the prisoner's signature. This fact is hidden from the soon-to-be inmate while being booked; he or she signs an electronic blank screen containing only a signature line and is subjected to great duress from a jailer's demand to "sign here!" The electronic screen is the type one signs when using a credit or debit card, except it is just a blank screen containing a signature line. There is no contract for the new inmate to read; he or she just signs his or her life away—literally.

Many of those who have lost their jobs and need to support their families volunteer to accept unemployment benefits. However, as we know from economics, there is no such thing as a free lunch.

Silence, compliance, and invisible contracts are the mechanisms used to fleece Americans who unsuspectingly participate in the various government schemes and systems, therein forfeiting their sovereign rights as they unwittingly agree to be bound as US citizens.

George Mercier wrote a great book titled, Invisible Contracts, which is available at constitution.org/mercier/incon.htm. It provides information regarding the subject of invisible government contracts, which we continually sign during the course of everyday business; therein, some claim, we forfeit and throw away our rights, as one would discard valueless trinkets.

It is interesting to examine how the government has gained control over nearly everyone. The people originally created the government, and now the government dictates and controls the people! The slave has conquered its master. This government creation has grown like a monster insatiably feeding off the wealth and production of the nation.

Americans are not subjects of imperial rule, wherein a king has dominion over our lives, yet we are compelled by the government to bow down and be its slaves and pay unfair taxes without any personal representation. As a nation, we have important decisions made without our concern or best interest in mind by neglectful and treasonous criminal politicians representing only the interests of the banking families.

The United States, the most taxing government in the world, is not ruled by stupid and bumbling politicians as the press would have us believe; it is ruled by cunning, competent, and highly treasonous individuals hell-bent on passing the special interests' agenda, regardless of its impact on the country and its citizens.

Contrary to common lore, former secretary of state John Kerry is not an idiot. He is one of the many politicians whose bread is buttered by the lobbyists and bankers who order the politicians around and tell them how to vote in Washington, DC.

Americans, while the government's pillage of the people through outrageous taxation continues to burden us, lost our government representation long ago, which is why legislation in Washington, DC, is never passed for the benefit of the American people. The people pay for all that is legislated in Washington, DC, and still practically nothing gets done for the benefit of the American people.

The IRS and the rule of accounting have replaced imperial rule of days past. We live under a taxation system of free-range slavery without the expenses or the upkeep and the maintenance of the slaves being paid by the masters. Free-range slavery is slavery, absent the plantation. The masters' chains and whips of the past are replaced by the forms and filings of the enforcement agents of the IRS and biased federal judges that benefit from the fraudulent taxing scheme imposed upon Americans from the cradle to the grave.

Under modern slavery, we can pick the job or occupation that we favor. There are no obvious chains and whips keeping us slaving away on a plantation as in the 1800s. Modern slavery is highly exemplified by our working for the government for about half the year to pay our taxes without fail.

Should we dare express ourselves as more than mere slaves and question our tax obligations to our usurped government, we might receive a computer-generated correspondence from the IRS demanding a payment. Only a relatively small number of inquisitive citizens, or tax protesters as they are usually called, experience the weight and pressure of the mighty, unthinking, and uncaring government-endorsed debt collectors of the IRS. Such fate befalls a small percentage of those not properly and promptly volunteering for slavery by submitting the appropriate federal tax form or forms on April 15 each and every year. Paying taxes is a very arduous and confusing task; it takes a long time, and tax forms are virtually impossible to fill out correctly.

By allowing the various oppressive forms of taxation, the world operates as a global plantation where human farming, human ownership, and human trafficking are the standard operating procedures of the day. We live under a system of free-range human enslavement where we enjoy the freedom to pick our jobs or start a business.

Individually, we choose which plantation we are going to work on and in which capacity; however, under this system of free-range slavery, the slaves need to feed, clothe, and take care of themselves. Free-range slaves provide their own shelter, as well as all necessary maintenance and upkeep. This is a far better deal for slave owners than the conditions of plantation-style slavery that use whips and chains to enhance the slaves' motivation.

The Founding Fathers created the US experiment whereby citizens of the various states, in essence, were kings and the federal government became established to serve the kings by providing services including national defense. The federal government was better equipped to administer the national defense than the individual states.

The federal government formed the US Navy to ensure the safety, general welfare, and protection of the nation from foreign enemies. Additionally, the citizens' militia formed to protect the people and the land from foreign invasion, as well as invasion from the federal government itself, should it fail to keep itself within the limits explicitly expressed in the US Constitution.

Now citizens believe national welfare is in the form of checks and food stamps. This is not what the founders had in mind when they discussed welfare; they meant the protection and safeguarding of the people. Benefits such as those listed above are offered to expand government intervention into people's lives in order to establish the parameters necessary to form a taxable relationship between the federal government and the people.

I once read a definition in an old edition of a dictionary for the word "federal." "Federal" used to mean "contract," so federal government in the 1700s meant contract or compact government because that is how the relationship was formed between the several states and the government, via contract. It is not much different today; we contract with the federal government just as the word "federal" indicates.

Remember, citizens are forfeiting their sovereign status, their status as kings, for Social Security benefits that will probably not even be available when many of us are ready to retire into a life of meagerness and poverty.

As we have discussed, the government creates government expansion and employment at a substantial cost to the remainder of the population, the non-government employee. According to New York University Professor Paul C. Light, the author of The New True Size of Government, "the 'true size' of the federal government stands at 14.6 million employees."

When the complexity and size of the government are examined, with all the different departments and subdivisions, one can start to grasp the managerial nightmare inherent in the daily operations of such a behemoth enterprise. The US government is the largest corporation in the world, and there is not a team capable of effectively managing and controlling it in its current condition. Or is there?

Just imagine the complexity of managing almost fifteen million people. When the intricacies of the different departments of government are considered, it appears nearly impossible to monitor the functioning of this organizational behemoth and to direct its operations in a manner consistent with the survival of the planet and its population.

Organizational inefficiencies, compounded by a lack of independent citizens diligently and faithfully monitoring the government, have allowed selective groups to infiltrate and utilize government resources for their own private gains and purposes. This lack of independent monitoring of the government by the citizens has allowed a shadow government to exist within the operational confines of the public government. This shadow government is a different form of government from the one that voters erroneously believe they elect. This shadow government hides deep within the colossal halls of government and continues to exist from one presidential administration to the next, regardless if the administration is Democratic or Republican.

The three-hundred-dollar hammer, six-hundred-dollar toilet seat, and the gas station the US built in Sheberghan, Afghanistan, which should have cost five hundred thousand dollars but ended up costing forty-three million dollars, are huge red flags indicating an inefficiently and criminally operated government. It cost forty-three million dollars to build a gas station because forty-two million dollars of taxpayers' money were stolen and given to friends of the administration.

The Pentagon cannot find trillions of dollars of tax funds that are simply labeled as "unaccountable" per the video 9/10/2001: Rumsfeld says $2.3 TRILLION Missing from Pentagon (youtube.com/watch?v=xU4GdHLUHwU). Where is the Internal Revenue Service that is supposed to be hunting down the crooks who stole the missing trillions?

That is where the Internal Revenue Service is supposed to operate, within or internal to the government, and not be messing around with civilians. The Internal Revenue Service's jurisdiction is not to exceed the ten square miles of Washington, DC, and its sole responsibility is to account for the funds and assets of the United States and, more important, the taxes of federal employees and federal employees only!

Where is the Justice Department and why is it not prosecuting those that cannot account for the loss of trillions of dollars? That is a huge crime, or business as usual, which was swept under the rug to protect those members of the shadow government that are responsible for the most massive theft imaginable against the American people.

Where these funds went is no mystery; they were stolen. Any forensic accountant worth his weigh in salt would easily be able to identify those responsible for this astronomical theft. It should be the first priority of the IRS to find and recover the stolen trillions and to prosecute the thieves to the fullest extent of the law. The IRS should do its job and get back the trillions of dollars of America's money that was stolen. Surely, anyone but the government would spend a billion dollars to recover a few trillion! For only a 1 percent finder's fee, I will tell the government who stole the still missing and supposedly unaccountable trillions.

There was not even an investigation conducted to find the funds or expose the protected culprits responsible for this massive theft against the US government and the American people.

Let us demand that the IRS find those who stole these trillions of dollars and get it back. If I know who stole it, I am sure the government does as well. The exact details regarding this government-sanctioned theft are revealed later in this book.

It is nearly impossible to believe that Donald Rumsfeld does not know exactly where the military's missing trillions of dollars are and to whom it was specifically given. Rumsfeld should be personally held accountable for this massive loss. How are trillions in government funds not traceable or not even worth chasing when stolen by government-sanctioned insiders and yet the IRS comes knocking on our doors if we earn a couple of extra bucks?

It would really help every American if the "Internal" as in "Internal Revenue Service" was interpreted as it should, to mean internal to the government and its operation. Imagine what a relief this would be to every working American! The IRS has a patriotic duty to identify and recover any internal government theft or fraud, and this especially and most importantly includes the Pentagon's missing trillions.

The IRS is supposed to enforce, internal to the federal government, US revenue laws. The IRS, as well as the rest of the federal government, is not supposed to enforce internal government policies and revenue laws against the American people. The IRS is supposed to apply their rules and regulations to employees of the federal government in order to ensure that proper accounting is occurring within the US government.

When trillions of dollars go missing by anyone in the government, it falls upon the IRS to find and prosecute those who embezzled the money. If trillions are missing and there is no recovery action or investigation, one has to wonder, at what point does the government take action? When does the government's red flag go up? Does the theft from the government have to exceed the trillion-dollar mark before anyone gets off his or her bureaucratically fattened ass and recovers the missing taxpayer funds?

Most businesses have built-in safeguards to prevent embezzlement, but the government tolerates government-sanctioned theft and enrichment policies that favor a small, select group of thieves.

How long can three trillion dollars be ignored by the Pentagon? Why aren't the IRS and all its enforcement officers getting to the bottom of this and returning that money to American taxpayers? The missing trillions is a criminal matter, which, in an ethical government, would be immediately investigated and the perpetrators of this huge crime would be prosecuted and rightly incarcerated. But no . . . the criminals walk.

A crime like the missing Pentagon's trillions could only have been perpetrated, to this day protected, and surviving from one presidential term to the next by the work of a group of conspirators, hidden deep within the various administrations. This evil cabal's survival has been based never on the voice of the electorate but on the whispers of the plutocrats.

Today, more than ever, people believe there is a deep state, a sinister power base that exists in Washington, DC, which actually runs the administrations from behind the scenes, no matter who the president happens to be. Although most sense there is something very wrong, many have a hard time identifying exactly who are the puppet masters that are actually pulling the politicians' strings and making the planet so crazy.

There has been an infiltration of a dedicated and treasonous group that controls the course of our government's philosophical ship and is intentionally crashing it into the rocks as a true enemy would. This surreptitious group profits by controlling not only the government but also the military, medial, entertainment, and industrial corporations that profit from the decisions, policies, and actions that the hijacked federal government implements.

Woodrow Wilson wrote—I believe in a personal letter, although the origin of the quote and the content has been subject to an abundance of speculation:

I am a most unhappy man. I have unwittingly ruined my country. A great industrial nation is controlled by its system of credit. Our system of credit is concentrated. The growth of the nation, therefore, and all our activities are in the hands of a few men. We have come to be one of the worst ruled, one of the most completely controlled and dominated governments in the civilized world. No longer a government by free opinion, no longer a government by conviction and the vote of the majority, but a government by the opinion and duress of a small group of dominant men.

Wilson wrote this despondent statement after he treasonously approved and signed the Federal Reserve Act in 1913. Wilson's tears of regret can never compensate and relieve the burdens born by the American people because of his treasonous decision to subvert the US Constitution and betray the American people by adopting a privately controlled fiat money system. Wilson's approval of the Federal Reserve Act privatized the issuance and control of the currency of the United States into the hands of an international cabal, consisting of twelve families, inviting tyranny and suffering upon generations of Americans. The Federal Reserve Act is the single-most heinous enslavement mechanism created by criminal politicians through legislated laws, which abrogate the American Dream and the freedoms and liberties protected under the US Constitution.

Who is this small group of dominant and treasonous men and women of whom Wilson speaks? How did they wrest such controlling economic influence over the people of the United States? How can this private, international, and evil group, which controls and holds the nation financially hostage, avoid and resist detection and reformation by the public for more than a century since Wilson's sorrowful lament?

The American people seem quite tolerant or ignorant of their own slavery—take your pick; it is hard to tell which one is the worse of the two evils, although most agree on this occasion that tolerance is more indulgently reprehensible in these matters than one's correctable ignorance.

The people who have stolen this country to satisfy their own private greed need to be prosecuted to the full extent of the law. The political agents of the internationalists have caused great pain and duress for the American people; they are the worst types of duplicitous traitors.

For the sake of the nation, we need to protect and defend the interests of the American people and not the interests of the taxing politicians and bankers. We need to ensure that all politicians who have acted against the interests of the people are held accountable for their treasonous actions; for without justice, freedom will perish.

CHAPTER 5

Bank or Bust

I believe that banking institutions are more dangerous to our liberties than standing armies. If the American people ever allow private banks to control the issue of their currency, first by inflation, then by deflation, the banks and corporations that will grow up around them will deprive the people of all property until their children wake-up homeless on the continent their Fathers conquered. . . The issuing power should be taken from the banks and restored to the people, to whom it properly belongs.

– THOMAS JEFFERSON

The modern theory of the perpetuation of debt has drenched the earth with blood, and crushed its inhabitants under burdens ever accumulating.

– THOMAS JEFFERSON

I helped purify Nicaragua for the international banking house of Brown Brothers in 1909–1912. I brought light to the Dominican Republic for American sugar interests in 1916. In China I helped to see to it that Standard Oil went its way unmolested.

– SMEDLEY BUTLER

The banks—hard to believe in a time when we're facing a banking crisis that many of the banks created—are still the most powerful lobby on Capitol Hill. And they frankly own the place.

– RICHARD DURBIN

History records that the money changers have used every form of abuse, intrigue, deceit, and violent means possible to maintain their control over governments by controlling money and its issuance.

– JAMES MADISON

If congress has the right under the Constitution to issue paper money, it was given them to use themselves, not to be delegated to individuals or corporations.

– ANDREW JACKSON

The Government should create, issue, and circulate all the currency and credits needed to satisfy the spending power of the Government and the buying power of consumers. By the adoption of these principles, the taxpayers will be saved immense sums of interest. Money will cease to be master and become the servant of humanity.

– ABRAHAM LINCOLN

Issue of currency should be lodged with the government and be protected from domination by Wall Street. We are opposed to . . . provisions [which] would place our currency and credit system in private hands.

– THEODORE ROOSEVELT

It is well enough that people of the nation do not understand our banking and monetary system, for if they did, I believe there would be a revolution before tomorrow morning.

– HENRY FORD

WE DID NOT LISTEN. Jefferson was an incredibly insightful politician who actually cared for this country and the citizens he represented. He identified banks as the primary evil in society that need to be diligently regulated to prevent their usurping the United States by privately issuing money to the government for profit; this is the primary reason why we, as a nation, are in the shape we are in today.

Money itself has changed since the days of ethical politicians. Money was something of substance, gold or silver, and the United States is now using the vestiges of money called fiat currency. "Fiat" means "decree." Under a fiat money system, if a king or a politician decrees it's money—well . . . then it's money!

Fiat or magic money is created from debt. Federal Reserve Notes are fiat money. Real money has real metal or other commodities backing it. Fiat money has nothing backing it.

In economic systems that use real money, the paper money is backed by and redeemable for metals that have intrinsic value. Gold is worth something; it has value.

In a metal-backed money system, one dollar of paper is redeemable for one dollar of metal, usually either gold or silver.

In the current fiat monetary system, paper money is not backed by a metal or commodity and is only redeemable for another piece of paper money. If we bring a Federal Reserve Note to the bank and ask for it to be redeemed, the banker will take our Federal Reserve Note and give us a different one.

The redemption of a fiat note is an intrinsically worthless redemption. All your hard work boils down to nothing, to a worthless redemption in an economy that conducts transactions using fiat currency. With real money, we go to the bank and redeem our real dollar. We get a dollar's worth of gold; that makes our labor intrinsically worth something.

Regarding our labor, a quantity of gold represents a quantity of production. A quantity of silver represents a quantity of production. When money is backed by production or metal and is representative of a quantity of production, the real dollar is redeemable for the amount of metal written upon the specific denomination.

Under the Federal Reserve System the one-, five-, ten-, twenty-, fifty-, and one-hundred-dollar notes in use are not backed by an equivalent amount of metal. The US dollar in use today, better known as the Federal Reserve Note, is a typical form and example of fiat currency. There is no ability to redeem such worthless paper for any stable commodity that backs it, since it is backed by nothing but misplaced confidence.

A true and real dollar of money is backed by a redeemable and corresponding amount of metal that intrinsically contains value, and that is what differentiates fiat currency from actual or real money. Real money is redeemable for metal; fiat paper money is redeemable for another piece of fiat paper.

The fiat currency used in the US economy is controlled by foreigners who own the Federal Reserve System—the devious and unscrupulous private bank that controls the issue of America's currency. Unfortunately, this financial usurpation of the US government's banking and monetary system is exactly what Jefferson warned us would happen should we fail to be diligent in protecting our nation's monetary system with its exclusive control being by and under the Congress.

The twelve families (some suggest there are eight) that own the Federal Reserve System create fiat currency using special powers, unconstitutionally granted and chartered surreptitiously by Congress. The anointed bankers have special powers to print worthless money, which totally enslaves the people. Bankers were given these destructive powers with the blessings of the US House of Representatives and the US Senate via the Federal Reserve Act signed into law by the treacherous and traitorous President Wilson.

Intellectually grasping the built-in enslavement mechanism of private banking requires understanding the fundamentals of banking in order to form an accurate realization necessary to comprehend the amount of peril and suffering that waltzes hand in hand under the oppressive Federal Reserve's so-called banking system.

The Rothschilds are the primary creators of the private central banks of the world. In a communication to their associates in New York, the Rothschild brothers of London wrote of the private central banking system:

The few who understand the system, will either be so interested in its profits, or so dependent on its favors that there will be no opposition from that class, while on the other hand, the great body of people, mentally incapable of comprehending the tremendous advantage that capital derives from the system, will bear its burden without complaint, and perhaps without suspecting that the system is inimical to their interests.

The banking interests believe that the general public is too stupid to understand the complexities of their private banking system that was built to deceive and confuse the masses. Deceit and confusion are the bankers' tools of trade, used to keep the masses in the dark about the ruthless banking monopoly.

Disclosure of these banking secrets and an understanding of the facts surrounding the horrendous fiat banking system that we sweat and labor under can assist in bringing to an end the bankers' international stranglehold over the people. This will motivate people to return control of the banking system into the hands of the government where it truly belongs. This will remove incredible amounts of oppression from the lives of the people and lift every American's personal economic station in life. Government control of the banking system will greatly remove the most destabilizing influences from the world economy.

The history of banking is quite remarkable, very important, and tragically not taught in public schools. The mechanisms of money and banking are constantly obfuscated from the public and are only divulged to the few, who use fiat currencies to enslave the world's entire population.

A good story concerning money is thoroughly told in The Money Masters by John Train (themoneymasters.com). Another more concise explanation of money is Money as Debt (youtube.com/watch?v=2nBPN-MKefA). For further reading, I recommend The Creature from Jekyll Island by G. Edward Griffin, as well as one of my favorites, The Coming Battle: A Complete History of the National Banking Money Power in the United States by M.W. Walbert; these are classic books describing the financial oppression and the enslavement of the American people, created 100 percent by the Federal Reserve System.

In most historical textbooks, little has been written telling the true and hidden story of money and its relation to international conflict and controversies. Although instrumental in every international conflict, money and the financing of military conflicts are never mentioned in the textbooks used in the public school system today. I wonder why we are seldom told the truth.

The Unseen Hand by A. Ralph Epperson discusses money as the mechanism used to create, propagate, and select the victors of all international conflicts since 1776. The international private bankers have been applying the same enslaving mechanisms for many centuries. Their financial interests underlie every military conflict we see among nations. Our finest young men and women are sent to kill and die for the insatiable greed of the private bankers.

Private bankers will concoct a foreign enemy or even instigate a civil war to overthrow a functioning government or dictatorship not receptive to the aims and interests of the international private bankers. History has shown that countries that are militarily invaded are often delinquent in paying their interest payments to the private bankers. Many borrowing countries eventually understand that the interest payment amount, demanded by the private bankers, exceeds the ability of their country to pay. The ever-burdening and increasing amount of interest that a country owes to a central bank is incredibly oppressive to the borrowing country's economy, and at some point the borrowing or debtor country is unable to, or refuses to, any longer participate in the bankers' heavy-handed loan-sharking schemes.

The banks operate just like the Mafia, but the bankers have a better public relations division; they publish their lies with the aid of complying news personnel of the mass media, which they just so happen to own.

Muslims and Arabs do not believe in accepting or creating loans where there is interest associated with the loan. Usury is highly frowned upon in the Muslim religion, and it is even against the Christian beliefs as dictated in the Holy Bible.

Jesus Christ became furious in the temple and overturned the tables of the moneychangers and drove them from the temple according to Matthew 21:12. The significance and function of the moneychanger of Christ's day were similar to those of the private banker of today.

People would come from faraway lands to the temple. The various currencies from the different lands were not allowed to be directly exchanged in or around the temple; all foreign currencies were exchanged for a fee charged by the unscrupulous moneychangers. Only the moneychanger's coins could be used in the temple. All non-moneychangers' coins had to be exchanged into the moneychangers' coins; this was the only permitted currency that could be used to purchase goods and services in the temple market or bazaar.

It is comparable to traveling from the US to Canada and exchanging US dollars for Canadian dollars. The bank that makes the exchange or conversion from US to Canadian dollars charges a fee for this service, as did the moneychangers of the temple. This charge, in essence, was a tax created by the moneychangers who siphoned their profits by taxing everyone who needed to purchase the moneychangers' coins in order to conduct business in the temple bazaar.

According to Matthew 21:12, Jesus told the moneychangers, "My house will be a house of prayer, but you are making it a den of robbers." Jesus's words appear even more true today when one considers the world's oppressively interwoven banking and taxation systems.

Although simple in style, the following story should enlighten the reader of the historical perspective money has played and its evolution through the centuries.

Many centuries ago, people became frustrated with the shortcomings of the barter system. People then started using many different things that were considered valuable as money. All types of items were used as money, therein replacing the burdensome barter system, which was originally created to trade one good directly for another, such as exchanging a chicken for three sacks of wheat.

This was the way in which the early farmers' markets functioned before the adoption and use of money. People would meet in the town square and exchange goods at their discretion. You can imagine that it might be difficult to locate just the right buyer for whatever goods you were selling.

Problems with the barter system arise when, for example, a chicken farmer wants a beer but the drinking establishment does not want a chicken. The chicken farmer would have to find someone to accept his chicken for something that the bartender would take for his beer, such as beef jerky. The chicken farmer could get a beer after trading his chicken for jerky and then trading his jerky for beer. This is cumbersome because no single item is universally acceptable in a barter economy.

There was no storage of wealth available to allow the chicken farmer to exchange his chicken for an acceptable and universal medium of exchange that he could use to later purchase any desired goods he wanted.

The barter method of trade was replaced by a more convenient means of exchange. This led to the use of a standard commodity, usually gold, as a means of exchange, or what we commonly call money. Since gold was available and easy to form into different sizes and shapes, people agreed to use it for money, for storage of wealth, and as a means of exchange. People liked and valued gold, and it was soon accepted and coined as money.

Our chicken farmer in the above example could now go to the market and exchange his chickens for gold pieces as a storage of his wealth. On his way home from the market, he could stop by and have a few too many beers at the tavern and pay his bar tab with the shiny gold coins he had traded for chickens earlier in the day.

What a great society. The farmer's drinking problem was solved.

The community goldsmith soon acquired storage vaults to warehouse his gold and protect it from theft. Other people soon requested that the goldsmith protect their gold by placing it in his vault. The goldsmith agreed to store the people's gold in his vault, but for a small price.

When the customers that had their gold stored in the goldsmith's vault wanted some of their gold, they would withdraw their gold from the goldsmith's vault. This worked out well until the people got annoyed with carrying heavy amounts of gold to the market in order to buy their needed provisions.

People soon discovered that the goldsmith could easily furnish them with a receipt for their gold, and the people would take the goldsmith's receipts and trade them in the market place, just like money. This was much more convenient than lugging around heavy gold coins, and in no time this became common practice. The goldsmith's receipts were being used as a means of exchange, or what we call money.

The goldsmith's receipts were convenient, and everyone seemed happy to use the goldsmith's paper, rather than carry around heavy gold coins. However, the goldsmith soon discovered an interesting phenomenon that allowed him to realize even greater profits from storing customers' gold in his vaults.

People left their gold in the vaults, and the goldsmiths started issuing receipts to customers for their gold stored in the goldsmiths' vault. These receipts were used as currency. To make additional profits, the goldsmiths started issuing loans on the gold that was kept in his vaults, and he collected interest from his borrowers at the same time. The interest and the principal were paid back to the goldsmith in gold. What a deal! The goldsmiths would loan paper and receive in return payments of the principal and the interest in gold! What a scheme!

This was great for the goldsmith, who started making record profits and grew fond of loaning paper based on the gold that was stored in his vault. Soon thereafter, the goldsmith discovered he could issue even more paper loans, not only on the existing gold in his vault but also on whatever value of gold that he claimed was in his vault, and no one would ever be the wiser. The goldsmith started to make profits beyond his wildest dreams and soon became the richest man in town. Everyone owed him money, and he accepted only gold for the paper he issued, thereby continually adding to his gold reserves and his wealth by criminally capitalizing and unjustly enriching himself at the cost of the people.

All the townspeople were indebted to the goldsmith, and soon word got around that some people who received loans were having a hard time finding enough gold to pay back the goldsmith. People got anxious about their gold and started demanding the return of their gold in exchange for the goldsmith's receipts, which were already collected by vendors in the marketplace in exchange for goods sold in the marketplace.

The jig was up. The goldsmith didn't have enough gold to cover all the paper receipts he had leveraged from the gold in his vault, and that was, what is known today as, the first bank run. Receipts of paper loans exceeded the value of the gold stored in the goldsmith's vaults that were supposed to be used to collateralize the paper loans. When the people returned to the goldsmith to redeem their receipts, he did not have enough gold to pay all the paper receipts he fraudulently issued to his customers.

This was more than embarrassing to the many goldsmiths who had to deal with the wrath of angry customers taking their revenge by inducing medieval torture and punishment against the devious goldsmiths. The public hangings of the local goldsmiths were usually conducted with the same frequency as bank runs.

To prevent future bank runs from happening, the goldsmiths, who were not hanged, agreed to pay customers interest for leaving their gold in the goldsmith's vault. The customers thought this was a great idea, getting paid interest for placing their gold in the goldsmith's vault while still being able to spend some of the paper that the goldsmith issued based on the amount of the gold the customers had in his vault. This new policy of the goldsmiths gave birth to what is known as depository accounts.

Even after this type of primitive banking system was in place, many goldsmiths still experienced bank runs when many of their customers panicked and decided to take their money out of the goldsmiths' vaults at the same time. To protect against bank runs, goldsmiths formed alliances with other goldsmiths. These alliances assisted the goldsmiths in cases where, if one goldsmith was having difficulty, he could depend on the other goldsmiths to lend him additional gold reserves to avoid a bank run. This seemed to assuage the fears of many of the goldsmiths' customers.

As Europe expanded, demands for credit grew by leaps and bounds. The goldsmiths formed stronger alliances and started to loan to various countries to fund the many wars that occurred between nations. The goldsmiths soon discovered that financing war was by far the most lucrative of all business models and would be aggressively followed at any price.

In the 1600s, there was one family of goldsmiths and bankers known as the Rothschilds who were cleverer than the rest when it came to financing wars between nations. The Rothschilds formed allegiances with European countries and started lending several countries massive amounts of money to wage wars with their neighbors.

After increasing his wealth twenty times in one shady bond deal during the Battle of Waterloo, Nathan Rothschild had the government of England in so much debt that England gave the Rothschilds control of the Bank of England. When the English government wanted to print money, it was forced to borrow it from Rothschilds' private bank. An interesting article is "Who Owns the Bank of England?" (darkpolitricks.com/?s=Who+Owns+the+Bank+of+England%3F&submit_button=Search) and is suggested for your reading pleasure.

Although the Bank of England sounded like a legitimate bank owned by the country of England, it was not. The Rothschild family owned the Bank of England from 1694 until 1946. The Bank of England's name was a very clever device to confuse people into believing that the Bank of England was actually owned by the country of England, when in essence the Bank of England is a private corporation, operated to enslave humankind through the act of loaning fiat money at interest.

The Bank of England was operated and owned by one of the same families that is an owner of the Federal Reserve System. Without doubt, the Federal Reserve System has taken control of the United States by taking control of its currency. Today, more than ever before in the history of the world, there is an international private banking cabal more sinister and deviously positioned to enslave the nations of the earth through financing war and chaos.

People may find this enslavement of humanity implausible and hard to believe, but the evidence of this enslavement is ubiquitous and currently affects virtually every aspect of our lives.

All calamitous war crimes and human suffering result from, and are traceable back to, the greedy and insatiable private bankers. All tragedies of war, chaos in the world, and the unjustifiable starvation of billions of people demonstrate the depth of evil and viciousness that those who control the private central banks create and employ to satiate their avarice.

Banks are no longer involved with nuisances like having gold or lending their depositors' actual money to borrowing customers.

Fraud occurs whenever one receives a loan from a bank. The bank never actually lends any funds that its customers deposited in the bank. The banker loans no money, as there is no money to lend. Bankers make profits in an unfair and criminal manner by deceiving and duping their customers. Talk about bank robbery!

Here is an example of how today's money is magically created during the loan process. A customer walks into a bank and requests a loan. After completing a huge loan application, the bank agrees to make a loan and the customer signs a promissory note for one hundred thousand dollars to buy a house. The promissory note is considered a negotiable instrument by member banks of the private Federal Reserve System. The bank receives the borrowing customer's promissory note and places it into an account that it creates in the borrower's name, just as it would if a new customer tenders a check for deposit into the bank.

These facts are thoroughly documented in Tom Schauf's enlightening book, Top Secret Banker's Manual for Bankers Only. Schauf is a CPA court expert witness who systematically testifies to the actual generally accepted accounting principles (GAAP) that occur when a bank loans money. Schauf's information is imperative to understanding the true depths of banking corruption. I also recommend you Google and read his other fascinating books, America's Hope: How to Cancel Bank Debt without Going to Court and American Voters vs. the Banking System.

Banks intentionally fail to disclose that the promissory note is actually considered money in today's banking system. Thus, the banks commit fraud every day. They have people sign promissory notes and then mortgage agreements. In fact, the only one bringing anything of any value to the bank closing, the promissory note, is the borrower who eventually receives the mortgage.

Upon the borrower signing a promissory note to initiate a bank loan, the bank lodges that promissory note as a deposit in the bank, almost exactly as if you came in off the street and deposited one hundred dollars in the bank. The bank then returns that deposit in the form a check to the borrower and places it in an account under the borrower's name. The borrower then writes a check off the newly created account to buy the house.

The bank never lends its own funds to the borrower; under the law, banks are forbidden to lend their own assets or their customers' bank deposits in the course of creating a mortgage. The bank never really lends any actual money to the borrower, yet the borrower must work for the next twenty or thirty years to pay off the mortgage that the bank duped him into acquiring.

Realize, of course, the bank also places a lien on the property in the event that the borrower becomes unable to make the monthly mortgage payments promptly and without interruption over the next twenty to thirty years.

During the next few decades, the banks usually constrict the money supply of the economy, causing a housing and employment crisis sometime during the term of the mortgage and foreclose on the houses that people have been paying on and maintaining for years. In essence, the bank tricks the borrower into signing a mortgage while never actually providing a loan to the borrower. When the borrower cannot make the monthly payments and meet the terms of the mortgage agreement, the bank forecloses on the home and kicks the tenants to the street. Then after foreclosing on the house, the bank resells the house and receives all the funds from the sale, in addition to all the money paid for the mortgage while the tenant was living in the house. Banks clean up when they foreclose on a home.

Under today's banking system, if a borrower never signs the promissory note, then there can never be a loan processed. It is impossible for one to receive a loan from a bank without signing a promissory note; therefore, the promissory note is the negotiable instrument that is fundamental to underwriting the mortgage and necessary in the bank's issuance of loans. Without the promissory note, there cannot be a so-called loan and its accompanying and enslaving mortgage.

Here's a quick summary of the theft bankers commit when saddling a customer with a bank mortgage. The bank never actually loans any money to the so-called borrower. Instead the bank monetizes the promissory note, and unknown to the borrower, it is deposited in a transaction account under the borrower's name. The bank then writes a check off the borrower's newly created transaction account and gives the borrower back his own so-called money; under today's banking system, money is derived and created as a result of the required endorsement of the promissory note. Finally the bank fraudulently induces the customer into paying a mortgage for the next two or three decades.

The bank never loans the borrower anything, not one cent. Under today's banking system, loans are a mere illusion.

A mortgage is a unilateral contract, a one-party contract, an unfair and unequal contract. There is nothing fair and equitable in the world of banking.

The bank takes the signatures on the promissory notes and monetizes them with the Federal Reserve. The bank does not lend its customers' money, which has been deposited in the bank; that is against the law. We can only conclude that if banks are unable under the law to lend the money of their depositors, then the banks must create electronic digits that represent money for the loan using the promissory note as collateral. There is no other way to generate the so-called money for the so-called loan and the so-called corresponding mortgage.

This is the magical power legislated to banks to create money out of thin air. Bankers are special people under the law with magical powers. It is an abomination against all Americans that under federal law the banking class has the magical privilege and financial advantage over the remaining citizenry to create money out of nothing.

The borrower, in fact, does not borrow anything at all from the bank. In today's banking system, the promissory note is the magical instrument that creates magical money out of thin air. Although it is not really money that the bank creates, the bank creates an electronic representation of magical money.

It is as though the borrower deposited the amount of the promissory note into a transaction account and the bank wants the customer to pay back the total amount of the deposited promissory note, plus interest. It is almost identical to going into a bank and depositing a hundred thousand dollars and then the bank lending you back your own one hundred thousand dollars. Now you have to pay the one hundred thousand dollars that you deposited in the bank, back to the bank, plus interest! We have to work to pay off our mortgages and car payments while the bankers enslave us in debt with only a tender of our signature.

Because of the lien that the bank places on your property, if you get sick or unemployed and miss a mortgage payment, the bank can foreclose on your house and kick you to the street. This is the rip-off that the banks conduct against all its customers.

In this system, money is created with the signature of the customer endorsing the promissory note and the lodging of it with the Federal Reserve. Without the borrower's signature, the promissory note is valueless and worthless.

So how can the deceived loan customer be responsible and required to work for thirty years and pay the bankers who never actually lent, not even a cent? This is the construct of commercial slavery that is imposed by the bankers upon the rest of society.

Think of it. The bank puts none of its money into your loan to purchase the house but instead creates the money using magical financial instruments. The bank places a lien on the house and, at its first opportunity, forecloses after the so-called borrower allegedly dishonors the mortgage agreement.

In summary, the bankers are granted special powers that enable them to make money out of thin air—they are financial magicians, if you will. Under the law, bankers are treated as a separate and special class of people with a special advantage to magically create fiat money; all the while, the rest of society needs to work and sweat for its measly paychecks to service and pay their illicit mortgages, courtesy of your neighborhood criminal banking conglomerate.

It would be great if all the people possessed this magical power to create money out of thin air. We could buy anything we wanted—land, houses, planes, cars, and all the things our little hearts ever desired.

Criminal banking is the most inequitable and enslaving financial mechanism that is in use today and has plagued humanity throughout history.

To make things even more interesting and profitable for the banks, consider a loan of one hundred thousand dollars that is made in today's fraudulent banking system. The banks, as a collective network, can now take that promissory note of one hundred thousand dollars and lend up to approximately nine hundred thousand dollars, based solely on the borrower's so-called promise to pay as outlined in the promissory note and its accompanying mortgage agreement. All of this is occurring without one's knowledge or permission while the bank leverages the note for nine times the profit of the original promissory note.

The above banking rip-off, and all its details, is commonly referred to as the Mandrake Mechanism in the suppressive world of banking. The Mandrake Mechanism was devised to provide the bankers with the special privilege of creating money out of thin air while, most importantly, enslaving the masses through this financial deception.

Additionally, the banks fail to notify the unsuspecting borrower that the promissory note is packaged and sold on the open financial markets for further banking profits. This specific practice led to the subprime housing crisis the United States experienced in 2008.

Modern Money Mechanics (rayservers.com/images/ModernMoney Mechanics.pdf) from the Public Information Center of the Federal Reserve Bank of Chicago explains in great detail how today's money is created from thin air to the benefit of the bankers and the detriment of the nation. It is recommend that all Americans read this informative booklet at the above website and discover the continual fraud perpetrated daily against the American people.

Below are some interesting perspectives regarding money and the Federal Reserve System's substantiation of the above information:

> *Of course, they do not really pay out loans from the money they receive as deposits. If they did this, no additional money would be created. What they do when they make loans is to accept promissory notes in exchange for credits to the borrowers' transaction accounts.*
>
> – Modern Money Mechanics Workbook
> Federal Reserve Bank of Chicago, 1975

> *When you or I write a check there must be sufficient funds in our account to cover the check, but when the Federal Reserve writes a check there is no bank deposit on which that check is drawn. When the Federal Reserve writes a check, it is creating money.*
>
> – "Putting It Simply"
> Boston Federal Reserve Bank

> *We are completely dependant [sic] on the commercial banks. Someone has to borrow every dollar we have in circulation, cash or credit. If the banks create ample synthetic money we are prosperous; if not, we starve. We are absolutely without a permanent money system. . . . It is the most important subject intelligent persons can investigate and reflect upon. It is so*

important that our present civilization may collapse unless it becomes widely understood and the defects remedied very soon.
– ROBERT H. HAMPHILL ATLANTA FEDERAL RESERVE BANK

Neither paper currency nor deposits have value as commodities, intrinsically, a "dollar bill" is just a piece of paper. Deposits are merely book entries.
– MODERN MONEY MECHANICS WORKSHOP
FEDERAL RESERVE BANK OF CHICAGO, 1975

The Federal Reserve System pays the U.S. Treasury 020.60 per thousand notes—a little over 2 cents each—without regard to the face value of the note. Federal Reserve Notes, incidentally, are the only type of currency now produced for circulation. They are printed exclusively by the Treasury's Bureau of Engraving and Printing, and the $20.60 per thousand price reflects the Bureau's full cost of production. Federal Reserve Notes are printed in 01, 02, 05, 10, 20, 50, and 100 dollar denominations only; notes of 500, 1000, 5000, and 10,000 denominations were last printed in 1945.
– DONALD J. WINN
ASSISTANT TO THE BOARD OF GOVERNORS
FEDERAL RESERVE SYSTEM

Many Americans believe the Federal Reserve System is a government corporation. Don't take my word for it; read what the Supreme Court has decreed on this matter.

The Federal Reserve Banks are not federal instrumentalities.
–LEWIS V. UNITED STATES 9TH CIRCUIT 1992

The regional Federal Reserve Banks are not government agencies . . . but are independent, privately owned and locally controlled corporations.
– LEWIS V. UNITED STATES, 680 F. 2D.1239 9TH CIRCUIT 1982

The private banking cabal of the Federal Reserve System, under the control of the Bank for International Settlements and the International Monetary Fund, forms a nexus so vast and powerful that it embodies the evils Jefferson and others spoke of in this chapter's opening quotations.

The Federal Reserve System has stockholders who have never been forced to reveal or disclose themselves to the public, have never been subject to audit, and have focused on profit indiscriminately and at a cost of millions of lives. The total amount of evil done by the international private bankers is incalculable. Their actions, which are solely responsible for the international turmoil reported nightly on the news, are continued with the overriding intention of enslaving everyone else who is not a banker.

Banks affiliated with the Federal Reserve System must pay homage in the form of interest for the benefit of creating money out of thin air. That means that every auto, business, and house loan and every credit card issued ultimately profits the Federal Reserve System.

Imagine that such a powerful private banking corporation exists and that it controls the governments of the world, the world economy, and the destiny of the United States. Americans are allowing the international private bankers to rape and pillage the wealth from our nation by foreclosing on thousands of houses per day and allowing the most unfair of all banking systems to be implemented to the detriment of the citizens of our country, our freedom, and our liberties.

The bankers loan nothing of value when they magically create mortgages, which every homeowner labors most nearly a lifetime to pay. We are all slaves to the banks.

To recap, after lending not a cent, the banks place a lien on the property, which allows the bankers to foreclose on that same property at a later date. It is as if the bankers get a sucker, Joe Homeowner, to move into a house, pay the mortgage to the bankers, and fix the house up. Most new homeowners paint a room or two, plant bushes, and fix up the place. A few years later, the banks constrict the money supply, which devastates the stock market, which increases unemployment, which causes Joe Homeowner to lose his job. Next comes the foreclosure, and the bank receives the following in profits: a fixed-up house, plus Joe Homeowner's down payment on the property, plus the mortgage payments Joe and his family made during the time they were living in the property. The bank gets all this profit, and it never lent a penny of its own money! Then the bank sells the foreclosed house and makes a phenomenal profit while Joe Homeowner, none the wiser, licks his financial wounds caused by the predatory bankers.

This corrupt banking cycle of financially raping Joe Homeowner repeatedly happens, and it is time we put an end to it.

Banks make the rules that politicians follow. They dictate to politicians what types of regulations are to confine and not confine the banking industry from running amuck and profiting while financially destroying the lives of millions of unsuspecting Americans. The regulations that the government places on the banks are regulations that the banks dictate to Congress and Congress passes. Having the US Congress regulate the banks is like having the world's fattest man writing a diet book for everyone else to follow.

The banks carefully controlled the crafting of all legislation that allowed them to create and profit from the subprime mortgage crisis of 2008. They profited in the trillions.

When banks' profits are high, all is well, and when the banks' financing game explodes, they come crying to the government and eventually to the taxpayers to bail them out. This is what occurred, and instead of letting the banks that were very much over-extended fail, the government transferred the wealth of this nation into the hands of the international bankers. This move is comparable to liquidating a corporation's assets under a bankruptcy.

The corporation called the United States, or if you prefer, the federal government or US or USA (all trade names), was created to solve the fundamental problem of the original government of United States, which was its bankruptcy and insolvency. We as a nation, or more precisely, a national private corporation, have been allowing the private international bankers to run amuck as was the case in the sub-prime debacle under the Bush-Paulson regime.

Unfortunately and expectedly, no one was held accountable for the largest banking debacle in the history of America. No additional regulations have yet been adopted to prevent similar future banking calamities from occurring. Currently, regulations are more lax since the financial meltdown of 2008. This can be empirically verified, as the banks are now bigger than ever.

One thing is for certain—there are many more, and even worse, financial debacles just ahead for America and the world if we are not willing to correct our defunct and debased private banking system.

Where is the legislation preventing the pending and ever-looming derivative crisis, which will be measured in the quadrillions, compared to the 2008 housing debacle that was measured in the trillions? There is no form of legislation written that will prevent the obliteration of the US monetary system or, better yet, the collapse of the Federal Reserve System. When it arrives, the derivative crisis is going to be more impactful than the housing crisis by a huge factor.

Why have the banking parties, who are responsible for the criminal actions that caused the financial collapse of 2008, never been jailed for their blatant crimes against the American taxpayers? It is theft when one group of people, belonging to a special class called bankers, is able to transfer wealth, without authorization from another group of people called taxpayers or suckers (take your pick). This is how those that committed that particular banking theft view the American people—as suckers at best and more likely as contemptible people not worth as much as the gum that sticks to the bottom of their shoes.

The international bankers stripped Americans of three trillion dollars with the assistance of the elected officials in Washington, DC, as the media did its job and covered it up. To this day, no one has been held accountable; yet the bankers made fortunes. At every turn, the bankers continue to profit at the taxpayers' expense.

The financial fiasco of 2008 is very brilliantly explained by Joan Veon, executive director of the Women's Institute of Media Group in Maryland, in her eye-opening video, When Central Banks Rule the World (youtube.com/watch?v=wn2eBcpdsDo). The central banks created the international economic chaos to further their goal of world domination through enslaving monetary control over the people.

Remember the old saying, "He who has the gold makes the rules."

One of the more interesting aspects of the control, implemented as a result of the created financial crises of 2008, is that the Federal Reserve System and US Treasury have virtually eliminated congressional oversight of the country's banking and monetary affairs. This is the final plundering of America, done to such an extent that citizens should be ashamed for allowing the overall takeover of the treasury, a true coup d'état. The 2008 crisis was a blatant and unconstitutional overthrow of the government, and it eliminated the government's ability to handle its own financial affairs.

The private bankers' plans to control the masses have been in the works for many centuries. We must realize that the economic meltdown of 2008 was a cold and calculated expanded seizure of the US monetary system by the foreign banks and the beginning of the international banks' ongoing liquidation of the bankrupted assets and cash of the United States, as well as the liquidation of any remaining wealth possessed by the American people.

The cards have been dealt, the horse has been shot, and the party is over.

Considering the economic and mathematical implications of the manufactured banking crisis, it seems impossible to continue with the existing debt system of monetary and fiscal policy and expect any real recovery of the economy. An economic recovery in the long term is impossible with an economy built on unsustainable monetary policies and philosophies that are starting to crumble around us at the time of this writing.

Mathematically, it is impossible for US taxpayers to service the interest of the Federal Reserve System's debt because the amount of interest due is spiraling out of control at an exponential rate. When factors like unemployment, depreciating housing prices, and potential hyperinflation are considered, it becomes apparent that we should take drastic action to replace the failed monetary system imposed upon our government by the families of the Federal Reserve.

Inaction has been the swan song of many civilizations perched on the brink of financial disaster. The recent recession—or depression, depending on how you decide to measure the economy—is but a slight inconvenience compared to what is in store should citizens fail to replace the fiat currency being manipulated and controlled by private banking families at the expense of us all.

How long should we continue to let ourselves be robbed by the bankers? The bankers are nothing more than an organized pack of criminals like the mob, providing incompetent financial solutions to problems that they create.

If Americans do not solve their ongoing financial crisis with the Federal Reserve and its antiquated enslavement and banking practices by a total restructuring of the banking system, the economy and civilization as we know them are doomed to tragedy and ruin. It is best to prepare for the upcoming financial catastrophe in a proactive manner before the inevitable economic collapse of the Federal Reserve's fiat currency and the American and world economies.

Instead of being the greatest nation ever created and the land of the free, America, because of the Federal Reserve System, is becoming the home of the slave. Today America is nothing more than a colony, territory, or possession of the Federal Reserve System and its foreign stockholders. America has sadly become one big plantation—and in case you haven't noticed, all of us are slaves.

People are shackled by the international bankers and are whipped by their hoodlum collection arm, the Internal Revenue Service. The interrelation between the international bankers and the IRS is the biggest of all the government's swindles and rackets. The amount of money paid by the IRS to the twelve families that control the international banking and taxing cartel could rid the world of poverty and starvation forever. That fortune, stolen yearly from Americans, could rebuild America's infrastructure and still have an abundance of funds to create new technologies and methods to improve civilization through projects that are humanitarian in purpose and intent.

It is horrific that 100 percent of all the taxes the IRS collects each year are paid to the twelve families that own the Federal Reserve System. The annual theft, in the form of taxes stolen from every American taxpayer, does not even quite cover the interest due on the national debt. Not a penny goes to paying down the principal. This leads to perpetual and total enslavement of the American people, who find themselves working close to half the year just to pay taxes to twelve foreign families who do not even need the money!

Not a penny paid by the US taxpayer to the IRS is used to run or support the government or any programs that help the American people. All the money paid yearly to the IRS could be used to improve America and the world; instead, it is being stolen from the American people and given to foreigners because a few congressional flunkies way back around Christmas 1913 signed the Federal Reserve Act. To all the slaves, we wish you a Merry Christmas!

Should you doubt that all money collected through federal income taxes is given to the international private bankers, read The Private Sector Survey on Cost Control Grace Report commonly called the Grace

Commission Report or the Grace Report, ordered by Ronald Reagan. You can find the Grace Report at the incredibly informative website thetruthnews.info/GraceCommissionReport.pdf. A special thanks to the good people at thetruthnews.info for their incredible information.

Federal tax dollars should be used for productive projects designed to better society, rather than to fatten the coffers of the already filthy rich. Many programs could be initiated that would create jobs and industry, thereby bolstering America to become the economic power it once was.

The money people pay to the government for taxes should be kept in the hands of the person who actually earned it and spent as the earner sees fit and proper, no matter what that may be. Many men spend their time and money buying fast cars and chasing faster women. The rest of their money they squander and waste; but that should be the prerogative of the earner, not the prerogative of the government.

Not only has the Federal Reserve System taken over the US Treasury; also the twelve family members of this cabal have infiltrated and over-taken the treasuries of virtually every nation in the world. In conjunction and partnership with the Federal Reserve System, the International Monetary Fund and the Bank for International Settlements have seized control of the world's monetary markets.

By financially enslaving the people of every nation on earth, these corrupt banking organizations are allowed to control puppet govern-ments, their populations, and the United States military to produce in-ternational retribution, comprised of war and strife, to any country that attempts to free itself from the bondage of the private international bankers. These bankers, incidentally, also control all the world's curren-cies, as well as all the major taxation organizations of the world's nations, including the IRS.

What a wonderful world it would be wherein the United States used sane approaches to handle its disagreements. Most Americans are getting tired of seeing their government officials acting like incompetent little children fighting over oil. Is this the best America and Americans can do?

There is a way to obtain peace, and that is to be peaceful.

In order to enforce the fiendish methods of the private international bankers, threats are made to cajole the heads of countries to accept the usurpation and forfeiture of their nation's currency and replace real money with the bankers' fiat money. This condemns the people and the nation to monetary slavery.

If the president of a country were to disagree with the international bankers' control of the nation's currency and/or the lending terms proposed to that nation, the president would shortly be threatened that devastating and vicious attacks would soon befall him, his family, and even his country.

The book and video Confessions of an Economic Hit Man by John Perkins (johnperkins.org) recount the methods of persuasion implemented by world bankers to enslave people of all countries. The world bankers take control of a nation's currency by inevitably providing loans to countries, which they can never afford to repay.

Perkins explains his activities and the persuasive and ruthless actions undertaken to ensure that all countries play ball with the international bankers. His work explains the devious methods employed by bankers to take control of different nations' currencies by providing huge loans used to build infrastructures and massive construction projects, such as power plants and hydroelectric dams. These projects are intentionally designed from conception to ensure that the borrowing nation is unable to generate enough electricity and ultimately cash to pay for the loans it received in order to build the massive and very much needed humanitarian projects.

Loans are the financial mechanisms used to enslave the borrowing nation and its people through debt that quickly becomes unaffordable and impossible to pay. The offer to any resistive head of state is an offer that cannot be refused.

Perkins or an associate would make the threatening offer to uncooperative presidents and heads of state. In one hand was a bullet; in the other, a bank account with three hundred million dollars for the president's cooperation in turning the country over to the sinister international bankers. The president of the country would have two choices: accept the bank account with the three hundred million dollars and sign loan agreements to sell out the country into huge debt that can never be extinguished, or watch beloved family members suffer brutal deaths at the hands of the bankers' assassins.

Should the president fail to cooperate swiftly with the demands of the international bankers, his assassination or that of a beloved family member was virtually guaranteed. After the assassination of a president, the succeeding president would be more amicable in his country's negotiations. Often, to avoid future problems, the bankers would handpick a more agreeable replacement president, as was the case in Iraq and many other nations plagued by American-initiated regime change.

Such fates usually guarantee that the heads of state will be reasonable when it comes to the financial matters of the international bankers and their respective countries. However, there is yet another method applied to uncooperative heads of state.

What happens when a country's leader simply fails to accept the relinquishment of the country's monetary policy into the hands of the international bankers, thereby placing the people into the financial slavery created by the World Bank's debt? If assassination attempts are unsuccessful, then a coalition of armed forces will unite to overthrow the uncooperative government officials and replace them with more cooperative government officials under the guise of regime change.

We have witnessed this all over the world when the US military, the enforcement arm of the banking mob, initiates a military assault and overthrows the current foreign political leadership. Then the bankers select a political appointment or conduct a trumped-up election to install a new president, more amicable and agreeable to the desires of the international banking community.

These methods of puppet government control through banking can be fully verified by examining the debt that most countries have. Countries that do not placate the demands of the World Bank are viciously attacked by the United States under the dictates of the private international bankers.

Look at what is happening in the Middle East. ISIS is trying to become an Islamic nation and is coining its own money out of gold. No wonder the international bankers hate them!

Notice how Iraq was attacked for failing to comply with the United States' demands, or essentially the demands of the World Bank, resulting in the killing of over two million civilians. The United States demanded that Iraq and Saddam Hussein use only the almighty US dollar to conduct oil transactions. Saddam refused to capitulate and continued to sell his oil for euros, which he believed to be more stable than the US dollar.

Another desired political result occurred in post-Saddam Iraq. After Iraq was attacked and destroyed by a US-led international military coalition, Iraq forfeited its sovereignty and capitulated to the international bankers. Iraq has now become a member of the Bank for International Settlements, and it no longer prints its own currency. Any country printing its own currency is automatically subject to attack by the international banking community's military, or at least subject to vilification, like North Korea, Iran, Syria, Libya, and any other sovereign nations.

Oil is a secondary booty. Control of a country's money is the primary booty in any military action. Control of the country's currency is always the primary and most profitable objective that the military assists to accomplish. If you own and control a country's money, you own everything. Remember what the father of the international banking system famously said:

> *Give me control of a nation's money and I care not who makes it's [sic] laws.*
>
> – MAYER AMSCHEL BAUER ROTHSCHILD

International bankers are not nice people. They, along with their practice, need to be immediately exterminated from the face of the earth. What a wonderful world it will be.

CHAPTER 6

Media's Hidden Agenda

Because today we live in a society in which spurious realities are manufactured by the media, by governments, by big corporations, by religious groups, political groups. . . . So I ask, in my writing, "What is real?" Because unceasingly we are bombarded with pseudo-realities manufactured by very sophisticated people, using very sophisticated electronic mechanisms. I do not distrust their motives; I distrust their power. They have a lot of it. And it is an astonishing power: that of creating whole universes, universes of the mind. I ought to know. I do the same thing.

– PHILLIP K. DICK

If the people in the media cannot decide whether they are in the business of reporting news or manufacturing propaganda, it is all the more important that the public understand that difference and choose their news sources accordingly.

– THOMAS SOWELL

Just because something isn't a lie does not mean that it isn't deceptive. A liar knows that he is a liar, but one who speaks mere portions of truth in order to deceive, is a craftsman of destruction.

– CRISS JAMI

All I know is just what I read in the papers, and that's an alibi for my ignorance.

– WILL ROGERS

If you believe that your thoughts originate inside your brain, do you also believe that television shows are made inside your television set?

– WARREN ELLIS

We are not afraid to entrust the American people with un-pleasant facts, foreign ideas, alien philosophies and competitive values. For as a nation that is afraid to let its people judge the truth and falsehoods in an open market is a nation that is afraid of its people.

– JOHN F. KENNEDY

P LEASE REREAD "THE PRESIDENT AND THE PRESS" and appreciate the admonition and foresight of John F. Kennedy, one of America's and humanity's greatest leaders. Since the delivery of that powerful speech, those who control the media, and are intentionally ignoring Kennedy's warning against sabotaging the freedoms of their fellow citizens, have had over fifty years to increase the quality of their technology and their stranglehold over the minds of the population.

For those who doubt that a group of men exists to gain power over the population of the world by moving toward and maintaining global domination, President Kennedy's words accurately illuminate the way things were organized and functioned in the 1960s.

The treasonous press of today has the added advantage of utilizing more sophisticated high technology to assist in achieving its aims. Mind-control technology has aided the media's objectives and assisted the private bankers' plans of acquiring control over the population, not only of America but the rest of the world as well.

It would be nice if the media actually did their job and communicated the truth of what is occurring in the world. There is nothing of substance discussed in the media that lessens the oppression humankind is currently enduring. Instead, the media focus on the sensational activities of the day, week after week, year after year. People are inundated with repetitive, overwhelming coverage of news that is designed to leave an individual in a fearful state.

Watching the news can change people's opinions regarding their fellow man and the conditions of the human race. After watching thousands of broadcasts of bad news showing people at their worst, one might conclude that the human race is more vile in character than it actually is.

The degradation of the world is mostly accomplished with television programming. It is vital to those who control the media that the human race's opinion of itself is debased and demoralized. Brainwashing is performed with the objective of killing the people's hope and aspirations to fix or better the environment. The media would like everyone to become highly apathetic and mindless, unable to care or even think to question our surroundings with the intention of elevating humankind from this degraded version of ourselves.

The human race is actually great and should be assisted and preserved. The last thing the media would like is for the people of the world to wake up and unite with great compassion to effectively correct the wrongs of society. Those who control the media do not want anyone to realize how magnificent each and every person actually is. As a united race, the people of Earth are an international union of humanity, which is a magnificent and powerful force. This force, of the combined intention of the world's population, should have the largest input into world affairs, yet our potentially thunderous voice is silent and never heard by the world's governments.

The politicians have betrayed the people to such an extent that many might find it almost impossible to forgive the political traitors, for they know exactly what they do!

Should foreign affairs be privatized, removed from the control of psychotic politicians, and put into the hands of the people of the world? Surely the people could not do any worse than the politicians in world affairs.

I never met anyone I did not like, and I surely never met anyone I wanted to bomb. No normal and decent person would ever bomb another. That is what psychos and terrorists do. That is the number one good or service that the US government exports. Does anyone see a problem?

Why isn't this covered in the national news? Why don't we export anything that builds a better planet? The media are complacent and neglectful of their duties and responsibilities in reporting the infiltration of the government by special interests and an ever-present nexus of betrayal and treason that lurk within the halls of government, wreaking havoc, misery, and injustice on Americans and foreigners alike.

The media should actually analyze the situations they report on and give constructive solutions to solve world problems. Military conflict is never a solution to world problems; it is the world's primary problem. If the people universally decide to abolish military conflict, humanity will automatically evolve into higher states of existence—where life will be more enjoyable, sustainable, and survivable for all.

It would be a refreshing change if the media informed their audience of what is actually occurring in the world and stopped doing the bidding of the defense contractors by disseminating lies regarding international affairs. Instead, we get the constant barrage of news stories that are used to shape and modify public opinion and to lessen any opposition by the masses to the plans of the special interests that are running the government without detection, right under the noses of the American people. It is outrageous!

The American kleptocracy that everyone lives under and shares is hidden and obfuscated from examination by the media in their biased reporting of fabricated news. Today, nearly all the news is fabricated. It has to be when one looks at the purpose of news and what it is used to achieve, a docile non-argumentative public. It does not matter one bit to our oppressors if the news is telling the truth or blatantly lying. The news is designed to captivate and control your thoughts and your mind, not educate and inform the public. Veracity and truth have no place in media or in the mind-control experiments conducted on the pubic.

There are billions and trillions and quadrillions of things that happen every second of every day. When these events happen, they are not news. Events become news when a person in the media determines an event to be newsworthy. Each news story is specially selected for the viewers. The logical question after, "Who selected it?" is, "Why was it selected out of the trillions of events that happened that very instant of that day?" Selection is made for the benefit of the advertisers whose revenue supports the news stations and for the stockholders of the news corporations that serve humanity's earthly oppressors.

The abandonment of the fundamental principles of media, including remaining unsponsored and immune to being monetarily persuadable, is largely responsible for the condition of society.

The mendacious media are designed to prevent the masses from ever discovering those vile people who are enslaving the public in order to financially benefit themselves and their ilk. Either you are on the side of the people or you are not, and the press is not on the side of the people. It is on the side of the corporations that pay their salaries.

It is simply contrary to any business model of the media to be in favor of educating the public. The entire mission of the media is to misinform the masses and to form and persuade public opinion, allowing the oppressive members of government and industry to remain in power and undetected by the average person.

As an example, the press continually promotes how free Americans are, while the government incarcerates Americans at an alarming rate and taxes Americans at an even more alarming rate. American freedom is an illusion sold to the people by the media.

There is both a monetary cost of enslavement and a corresponding emotional cost, which is measured not in dollars but in lives. The destructive results of a media-induced, emotionally apathetic population is a society that is not thriving and expanding in peace and harmony but a society that is contracting and suffering in constant pain and discord.

The media need to report on the ultimate fight between good and evil that exists today and choose to side with the good, well-intentioned people of the world. The good people have little representation in the media, while bloodthirsty villains and their agendas are publicly promoted and lionized.

True reporting of the causes of military conflict and of its benefactors is replaced with sensationalized news stories, which are designed to disturb the audience's mental equilibrium and to create agitation and disdain in the minds of the television audience. This brainwashing prevents the improvement of the individual, as well as the collective improvement of humanity. And therefore it follows that it is the collective improvement of humanity that a majority of the media is working to prevent.

The media's inability to assist in the correcting and uplifting of society, and their abandoning all responsibility regarding the repair and improvement of society, makes for a recipe of disaster. Evidence of this is seen on the nightly news. News is an electronic bombardment of what is wrong with society and not a hint of what is right.

By the media abandoning their prime purpose of being the public's watchdog, to ensure the government does not abuse its power against the American people, they have failed miserably in their jobs. The media control the news and ultimately the perceptions and minds of their viewers. The media ignore the horrific crimes committed against the people by those that have infiltrated the US government and are currently operating a private agenda on behalf of special interests.

Controlling the populace through education deprivation and thought control results in emotionally apathetic individuals who are less capable of generating effective actions to improve their immediate situations. This hampered emotional state is more detrimental to individual freedoms than physical shackles could ever be.

People have fallen victim to mind control and the various mechanisms programmed and broadcast throughout the world. "Couch potatoes," as they were called in the 1980s, were blobs of protoplasm resembling men and women who plopped down on their couch and watched television for endless hours. Couch potatoes were armed with pillows and blankets, sandwiches and shakes, potato chips and most importantly, the highly prized television remote. Witnesses claim that the limited activities of a couch potato mainly consist of migrations from one end of the couch to the other.

The most insidious aspect of prolonged television watching is that life passes by the couch potato, who completely fixates on television for years on end. Retarded levels of action by couch potatoes ensure they will hardly muster enough energy to improve not only their own lives but also the lives of those unfortunately associated with them.

The only guaranteed salvation in life is to improve the condition and quality of the lives of the people around us. Much of television is aimed at preventing personal growth, which becomes abundantly evident, once and for all, when a couch potato decides to unplug the television for good.

Our spiritual development is indicative of the quality of life we experience and enjoy. More important, our spiritual development dictates how creatively and valuably we may serve our fellow man. Without service to our fellows, we cannot improve our own conditions, and the quality of life on this planet will continue to deteriorate.

Instead of being mesmerized by the media, our actions need to garner and support activities that provide spiritual and intellectual growth, leading to more competent humans who can help change the world for the better. Millions are already striving for a better planet and better living conditions for everyone, but this number has to increase in magnitude. As this number accelerates and creates momentum, the overall IQ of the planet will increase, and as a species, humankind will evolve to a higher level and exemplify and reflect a higher and saner image of humanity. This is how society solves problems, by bringing the intelligence level of the entire society to a higher plateau, where it will be unacceptable for the population to tolerate debased and other destructive international policies.

Without continual emotional upset and strife, our society will naturally elevate itself and solve its problems, not continue and stupidly prolong them. Humankind keeps mentally getting pulled down and degraded day after day by the media; story after story is filled with objectionable lies and deceit.

The media's contribution to the American people and to the people of the world has been void of substance and sincerity. The media are loyal to shareholders while forfeiting the opportunity and responsibility that we all share to improve the conditions of society; thus, they broadcast to negatively influence and impact the world.

The media fail people and society at large because they fail to point out the truth of what is occurring around the world. Media are funded by those companies with special defense contracting interests that outrageously profit from initiating and continuing wars.

The media are barred from speaking the truth against the special interests that pay their salaries. For if ever they should be so bold as to speak their minds and tell the truth against their master, their employment and careers would be terminated, followed by, perhaps, the termination of their lives.

Consider for a moment the media's methods of covering a story. First, let us examine the actual content of the news and consider the following perspective. If a news story is neither relevant nor valuable and does not assist in leading to a better, more productive world, then why is it broadcast at all?

If the information that is programmed, designed with a purpose, and broadcast to virtually every household around the globe does not raise the quality of life for all, or at least a majority, then it must be programmed to lower the quality of life. Why would anyone promote only bad news, intended to diminish the quality of life and contribute to the degradation of society?

How can something as blatant as the actions of members of the intelligence communities be overlooked and elude the eye of the media, while the media points the finger of misdirection at patriots and patsies, leaving the most heinous criminals hidden from lights, cameras, and prosecution?

Think of the many false-flag operations recorded in the annals of history and the correlating blind eyes of the media. There is nothing more suicidal in this universe than to wreak havoc and destruction. Karma is not always kind; as we have learned, self-execution is the most punishing and painful of forces that this universe offers to darken the lives of evil-intentioned people.

The news media regularly deliver the most catastrophic and calamitous stories they can find. They concentrate on bad, upsetting news in both film and print. We are often compelled to ask ourselves, why is the media's coverage so slanted toward death and destruction on the domestic and international fronts?

What is the purpose of reporting to the American audience that a busload of schoolchildren in Brazil was driven over a cliff into the Amazon basin? It does not affect American lives, but it surely makes the environment sound scary. "More news at eleven" is the theme of fear. Be afraid; be very, very afraid.

Why are the most significant and important aspects of the economy ignored so greatly by the news and even the business channels? Bankers, genetically modified foods, pollution, and the extinction of man are topics the media need to expose. The media need to report on important topics and stop reporting stories about one politician who is disagreeing with another politician. News reports should discuss humanitarian topics of how people are working to create a better world, the programs that contribute to doing that, and the effectiveness and results of those programs. That is real human news, not the fabricated news we get today. Today we get news that is not fit for a family of reptiles and other lower species.

The media constantly promote distraction. "Look over there! Look over there! There is danger everywhere! The environment is not safe! The environment is dangerous and full of peril! And for heaven's sake, don't look at the environment, or you'll be bitten!" These are the types of messages that the media promote, so turn off the news and let's start thinking for ourselves!

In reality, there is something more alarming than what is continuously reported, and that is the amount and quality of news that the media are intentionally trying to hide and fail to ever report. Where are the real journalists who should be breaking open the big stories of the corrupt and unethical politicians and Wall Street corporations that are stealing from the American people 24/7, 365 days per year? Where is the reporting of the actual activities that the government is undertaking that throws our freedoms and liberties down the toilet? Where are the stories that matter?

The media, for the most part, is a shameful and despicable group.

TELEVISION AND EDUCATION

Failure to turn off the television and turn on one's self-determinism leads to a self-constructed prison from which there is no escape.

Television operates on frequencies that are particularly harmonious with and influential upon the human brain. Cartoons are especially designed and broadcast to effectively impinge on a child's brain-wave frequencies. The format of news broadcasts with those distracting tickers at the bottom of the screen, can confuse the viewer and increase his or her level of hypnotic suggestibility.

One can calculate and correlate the relationship between the amount of television watching and the rate of the viewer being placed into a hypnotic state. Varying from person to person, there is a correlation between the amount of television watched and the achievement of this induced suggestibility and hypnotic state, which improves advertisers' ability to sell an increased amount of anything from soap to snake oil.

The more television that people watch, the more comfortably and quickly they relax and enter into this suggestive state, thereby sacrificing their self-determinism for a state of suggestibility that can lead to a higher percent of market share for the companies sponsoring the networks. This mesmerizing state assists in selling more of everything—soap, pharmaceuticals, and the fabricated stories broadcast by the nightly news.

Before continuing this discussion of the evils associated with television, we should examine some demographic facts regarding and its habits. This can shed some light on the importance of effective time management in the conduct and evolution of our lives.

In "American Time Use Survey Summary," the Bureau of Labor Statistics (2008) reports: "On an average day, nearly everyone age 15 and older (96 percent) engages in some sort of leisure activity, such as watching TV, socializing or exercising. Of those engaged in leisure activity, men spent more time in these activities (5.7 hours) than did women (5.1 hours)" (bls.gov/tus).

The destruction of the American Dream relates directly to the amount of time that people spend idly wasting their days. What happened to educating oneself and striving to do, become, and produce something great?

Did the Founding Fathers spend their time so idly? America is built upon the hard work and the dedication of its members to improve the lot of humanity and that of society.

The Bureau of Labor Statistics (BLS) survey further explains, "Time spent reading for personal interest and playing games or using a computer for leisure varied greatly by age. Individuals age 75 and over averaged 1.2 hours of reading per weekend day and 0.3 hour, 17 minutes, playing games or using a computer for leisure.

"Conversely, individuals ages 15 to 19 read for an average of 0.2 hour, 10 minutes, per weekend day while spending 1.0 hour playing games or using a computer for leisure" (bls.gov/tus).

The younger demographic spent five times as many hours playing computer games as reading. How much life experience or benefit do individuals who play hours upon endless hours of video games receive? Are the populations of other countries like China spending as much of their free time watching television and lounging around instead of working hard and educating themselves?

How is endlessly playing video games contributing to society or even the players' own physical and mental development? It appears that perhaps this may simply be the result of bad parenting and poor leadership qualities. Dr. Nicholas Kardaras's book, Glow Kids: How Screen Addiction Is Hijacking Our Kids and How to Break the Trance, explains the brain damage and additional harm that occurs when children under the age of ten spend too much time playing video games.

History has shown that nations progress in relation to the education level of their citizens. This explains the public's inculcation and indoctrination received via the public school system and the deterioration of American society.

When one considers the state of education in the United States, it becomes evident that it is up to the individual American to educate himself or herself. We cannot rely on a national educational system administrated from Washington, DC, through the Department of Education.

The Department of Education and its blaring inefficiencies are discussed in depth in Vicky E. Alger's book, Failure: The Federal Miseducation of America's Children. Alger's solution to a defunct Department of Education is to return the functions of the Department of Education to the states, giving more localized control to the parents and local school boards across America, where the control rightfully belongs. Alger discusses in depth the strategic dismantling of the Department of Education as a first step in correcting America's crumbling national educational system.

Around the world, people want to develop themselves and take full responsibility to educate themselves. In an age of information, there is no excuse for ignorance. The Internet provides unlimited information to anyone with the desire to gain knowledge. There is a world of information today at one's fingertips. Many schools, even the prestigious Massachusetts Institute of Technology, offer free online courses. See MIT's online offerings (ocw.mit.edu/index.htm).

We must educate ourselves; no one else can. No one can sit us down and force us to study; knowledge is voluntarily acquired. There is a hunger, a thirst for knowledge, which we alone can attempt to quench. Realize as you endeavor to intellectually enhance yourself that the more one drinks from the fountain of knowledge, the thirstier one gets. Have fun and Google away, and when in doubt, break out and use your dictionaries!

It behooves us all to further our education and improve our intelligence as lifelong endeavors. In order to get ahead, we need to work very hard and sit down with our texts and dictionaries and burn the midnight oil educating ourselves and improving our skill sets. Life without education not only leads to a dismal state of affairs for an individual but also contributes to the denigration of the entirety of society in general.

We should also turn off the television, develop an industrial attitude in our endeavors, and drastically increase the time spent working to achieve our goals. We accomplish nothing without effort, and typically, the more effort one exerts over the environment turning dreams into reality, the greater the reward that is received. For every endeavor, one's work ethic substantially contributes to the level of one's success. Hard work is the lubricant in the machinery of success.

Culture is a collective reflection and composition of the qualities contained within each member of society. By enhancing ourselves, we essentially and positively influence and enhance the state of our collective society. Our culture is dying because our educational system is failing our families, and still too many Americans fail to crack a book on their own initiative.

In order to bring American culture and, equally important, American values back to health and life, individuals within our society need to strive for and obtain continually higher education and personal enhancement. If we all work to become better images of ourselves, our society will automatically reflect that improved version of ourselves and we will start to see improvements in our society.

The opposite is true as well. The media, by bombarding our senses with despicable and inhumane acts of terror, are conditioning the viewing audience to form a disgusting opinion of human nature and our culture. This degraded view of humanity makes it acceptable for people to pick up a gun and kill our brothers and sisters.

Since culture is an accumulated series of agreements and traditions, raising the essence and education level of individuals is the way to raise the essence and education level of society and its culture. The reverse is true as well, as substantiated by the poor educations provided across America in too many inner-city and black communities. Look at the dismal education levels in America's inner cities, like Chicago, with its tragic and ever-increasing rate of black-on-black murders. This is no accident; this is designed chaos and death.

Upon noticing the correlation between high crime areas and the lack of education in those areas, we begin to understand that education assists in uplifting the individual and the overall society to a more peaceful, tranquil, and acceptable state where humankind is proud to assist our fellow man. For only by helping others can we, in any way, help ourselves. To think otherwise is to be deluded.

According to the Bureau of Labor Statistics (BLS) survey, Americans' education fared far worse than many would imagine. "About 10 percent of the population engaged in educational activities, such as attending class or doing homework, on an average weekday. Those who attended class on a weekday spent an average of 5.3 hours doing so, and those who did homework and research on a weekday spent 2.7 hours in such activities" (bls.gov/tus).

Our nation's education has diminished to the level that only 10 percent of the population is even engaged in education. By extrapolating and averaging these educational figures to include the entire US population, this equates to only about .53 hours of weekly education per person.

It is apparent and disheartening to imagine that there is a dumbing down of the American population to the point of making the American people more ignorant, apathetic, and capable of being subject to enslavement and servitude under a more intelligent controlling class.

A more compelling survey regarding television statistics comes from the godfather of television statistics, A. C. Nielson, which reports that the average American watches more than four hours of television each day, or twenty hours per week, or two months of nonstop television watching per year.

In a lifespan of sixty-five years, the average person will spend 10.83 years of his or her life glued to the television, becoming more brainwashed and sold more products that he or she does not need.

Sleeping eight hours per day over a sixty-five year long life, equates to having slept for a period of 21.6 years. With our employment time of working eight hours per day, 239 days per year, allowing for weekends, fourteen days of vacation, and the eight federal holidays, one has spent another 14.81 years at the job. If we add our total sleep time and our total employment time, over a sixty-five-year lifespan, we have spent 36.41 years of our lives sweating on the job and sleeping in our beds.

Cumulatively, in accord with the above examples, sleeping, working, and television watching account for over forty-seven years of a sixty-five-year life. This gives us eighteen years to accomplish something worthwhile besides bathing, eating, and grooming.

It is our duty to ourselves, to our country, and to our Creator that we develop intelligently and spiritually into the best image of ourselves, thereby improving ourselves and our culture and performing our rightful part to assist, enlighten, and contribute to the brotherhood of humanity. If everyone used his or her time more productively, it would lead to a better, more competent, and more productive individual; a better, more competent, and more productive nation; and ultimately a happier, more harmonious, and more productive world.

Spending an hour per day on any activity equates to 2.7 years over a sixty-five-year period. Successful people examine their activities and discover where they are dawdling and wasting time; they implement corrective actions to utilize their time more constructively to achieve their goals. This provides happiness and contentment in their lives and the lives of their loved ones.

Reflecting on episodes of one's time poorly spent, wasted, and never recoverable conjures up the greatest of life's remorse. Television does not contribute to people achieving their goals in any meaningful manner. Turn it off and get busy building a better world for your sake and the sake of the world.

Time is an illusion and all we ever have. Use it wisely.

TELEVISION AND BRAINWASHING

Television is used as an electronic device to control the minds of its audience. If one were to construct a method of brainwashing to achieve mental compliance over the entire population, what other electronic device, found in virtually every household around the world, would be better to use than the television? The answer is not a blender, although television seems to scramble the mind as a blender scrambles a dozen or two eggs.

Pictures and sounds influence humans in many ways. Motion pictures and television programs can pull at the heartstrings of the most mighty and stoic; images can make us elicit very sorrowful and heartfelt emotions. One becomes emotionally controlled and engrossed in characters on the screen as one vicariously experiences emotions that range from sorrow to exhilaration. Movies are produced to elicit our deepest and most personal emotions and to make us feel as though we have become one with the characters on the screen.

Hypnosis and brainwashing are achieved by causing the subject to enter into a relaxed mental state, therein increasing the subject's suggestibility. Some may argue that television is a harmless activity, but any single activity that accounts for such a big part of one's life needs to be thoroughly examined and put in its proper perspective.

Watching television is a spectator sport. To change the world, one needs to be a participant and not simply a spectator. To accomplish anything involves activity and dedication; life is a game to play, not watch.

One can hardly imagine any more sinister intentions than those possessed by the executives who control television programming to influence and control the masses. Is there a better method of mind control than hypnotizing and brainwashing the population without the people even suspecting this is occurring?

When hypnotists perform their craft, the first thing they command is the attention of the subject to be hypnotized. Known as the father of hypnotism, Franz Mesmer realized when a hypnotist implants a command into the subject's mind, the hypnotist needs to have the subject's attention focused on a specific thing, such as the hypnotist's voice or a shiny pocket watch or the rotating black-on-white cardboard spiral we can recall in episodes of the Twilight Zone.

Next, the hypnotist commands and suggests the subject to relax and block out all outside influences, except for the sound of the hypnotist's voice.

The attention of the hypnotist's subject is focused only on the voice of the hypnotist or that shiny watch or whatever. The hypnotist repeats, "You are becoming very sleepy, and you will only hear the sound of my voice, calming you, soothing you; you are very, very sleepy."

Television hypnotizes us automatically. Television captures one's attention to the point that people are unconsciously being placed into a suggestible trance and implanted with commands at a subconscious level. How many times do we fall asleep watching golf and enter a state between consciousness and unconsciousness? Have you ever dreamed along with the television, as you slept on the couch watching an action movie? When a person's dreams correlate with the show playing on the television, this demonstrates the control that television has over our minds.

If you doubt people have been implanted with hypnotic suggestions while watching television, simply start a discussion regarding foreign affairs and listen to what they say. Usually, there is not a single, independent thought. Instead, we can ask ourselves, "Does this person sound more like Fox News or CNN?"

Many people believe without analysis or consideration the news stories of the day. Unfortunately, there is seldom an adequate evaluation of the subject of the news, and the true purpose and intentions of those who create and present the news often remain hidden beyond the purview and evaluation of the public. The media deliver the news in a fashion to gain agreement among the masses, and the media's opinions and viewpoints solidly settle into the mind of the masses, like a heavy snow falling upon the grass.

Television operates on a massive scale and affects the minds of billions of people much more than we realize. With only a cursory look, it is plain to see that television is an electronic device designed to capture the full attention of the viewer to the point of blocking out the surrounding environment. Television watching induces and increases the relaxation, suggestibility, and implant-ability level of the viewer.

Hypnotism continues with the objective of relaxing the subject to a point where the hypnotist can directly command and implant the mind of the subject with instructions to operate as directed by the hypnotist. This allows for great humor when conducted as a parlor trick but has other implications when subjects receive hypnotic commands via the television or, worse yet, by a retired commando of the Psychological Operations division of the armed services who now works as a news consultant, plying one of the military's most dangerous and deceptive trades, mind control.

If the hypnotist installs any potentially dangerous post-hypnotic suggestions that obfuscate and compartmentalize various sections of the subject's mind, at a later date an implanted trigger could involuntarily be stimulated, causing actions to be performed by the hypnotized subject that are beyond his or her control and volition. With the presentation and receipt of a triggering stimulus, such as a specific phrase, hypnotized and programmed subjects can be brainwashed to perform many different tasks, including murdering others and/or blowing themselves up. This is the method used in the formulation and creation of Manchurian candidates and the suicide bombers that are regularly manufactured by intelligence agencies around the globe.

Today, a very important role of the hypnotist is in psychological operations and mind-control research at the world's militaries and intelligence communities. Television is the tool of the oppressive groups that control and influence the minds of the masses. The US military states, "Psychological Operations are a vital part of the broad range of US political, military, economic, and ideological activities used by the US government to secure national objectives. PSYOP disseminates truthful information to foreign audiences in support of US policy and national objectives" (military.com/ContentFiles/techtv_update_PSYOPS.htm).

Some will inevitably doubt the validity of the inclusion of the word "truthful" in the government's above statement. The veracity and trustworthiness of the US government has never been viewed as more questionable than it is today. When we ask people to list their opinions of the US government, it is likely that the words "untruthful" and "dishonest" are towards the top of their list.

It just seems obvious and apparent that the US government would use television as a ubiquitous tool to secure national objectives. After all, the FCC not only regulates interstate communications; it also regulates international communications by radio, television, wire, satellite, cable, and practically all media companies.

Media use television's artificially induced hypnotic state to introduce suggestive commands to a worldwide audience, to have their audiences think in a certain way, and to have them buy advertised products. This is the purpose of television—to make us want to buy the products that are continuously sold to the audience in the form of commercials.

Interestingly, the television corporations induce the television audience to believe all the lies they are told and, most importantly, to go out and buy the products being advertised every few minutes. Watching television over extended periods produces such a high level of suggestibility that the advertisers find it beneficial to continually advertise their products via the television, even though a majority of the audience changes the channel or fast-forwards at the first glimpse of a commercial.

The book Propaganda by Edward L. Bernays, the "Father of Public Opinion" and a relative of Sigmund Freud, explains in great detail the methods the media use to inculcate, indoctrinate, and ultimately shape public opinion and beliefs. Television is the primary tool to reach the masses and to control the actions and the thoughts of the people. CNN, Fox News, One America News Network, Sky News, and other networks can reach an audience of billions internationally with the flick of a switch.

From politics to one's clothing, from the house one buys to the car one drives, virtually every aspect of American life has been influenced and inculcated by the repetitive brainwashing provided via television. The masses regularly regurgitate the opinions put forth by the media regarding politicians and their political stances. Those who watch the nightly news, without the least bit of critical analysis, are highly suggestible and controllable. Many times these suggestible subjects hear the news and repeat it almost verbatim, as though it were gospel.

Our only hope as a nation is that enough people inform themselves and decide to make a positive difference in the world. This is done by turning off the boob tube and doing what you were born to do. Start now!

Most Americans fail to read to any significant degree, thereby denying their brains the opportunity to actually cogitate, ponder, and reflect on the information they receive. Television provides information at such a fast rate that it relentlessly inundates a person's psyche and may prevent effective evaluation of the data that is received, as there is very little time to process the information and its implications. Information that we do not evaluate, before we accept and assimilate with our preexisting base or reservoir of knowledge, can lead us to having incorrect and often unusable data detrimentally recorded in our minds.

Today one might say that the news programs' and news stations' anchors are the nation's hypnotists or agents of mind control.

Using present-day technology, there are implants of both the mind and the body that are being transmitted via the television and computers. Some investigators even speculate that the technology is quite advanced and makes the transmission of disease possible via the airwaves and cables of the networks.

Recently, a news channel showed a firefighter falling through a roof into a fierce fire. The news channel was nice enough to include the audio of the man's horrific, blood-curdling screams as he burnt. We have to ask for what purpose did the news channel show this brave firefighter falling to his death into a burning building and horrifically screaming as he perished?

The media continually strive to adjust their viewers' psyche and teach viewers that the world's environment is very dangerous. The media continually propagate this attitude of fear via television; look at the race wars, police shootings, and civil protests that are being broadcast and incited by the media.

Repetition is vital to mind control. Creating a relaxing environment conducive to suggestibility and then repetitively commanding a specific action with an accompanying emotion are necessary in controlling others' psyches. The television news stations often mimic one another by running the same story with only slightly different slants. The propaganda has become so effective that the news stations make it acceptable for mothers and fathers to even send their babies off to war and sacrifice them for what they believe to be the good of the country.

A guaranteed way to find a sad woman is to speak with an American Gold Star Mother, who has lost a son or daughter in war. There will be a hole of sorrow, reaching into the aching depths of her soul; such emptiness is easy to spot but impossible to fill. It is apparent when we speak with such a woman, hurting because of the passing of her son or daughter, that there appears no scarcity of regret and little chance of comforting the overwhelming sorrow in her heart. Her despondency is deeply magnified when the mother realizes she has been lied to by the government and by the media.

The amount of force and destruction during war is horrific, and yet war is continually being promoted as something citizens should get behind and support by showing their patriotism.

The war campaigns are aptly named, "Shock and Awe," "Operation Iraqi Freedom," or whatever campaign they are selling, to inspire and provoke the highest emotional response from the television public; this spurs military recruitment. At the same time, the media are quick to disparage and label anyone and everyone who disagrees with war as unpatriotic dissenters.

For years, military and intelligence agencies have conducted special psychological operations utilizing hypnotic techniques and have diligently incorporated the addition of drugs and pain to facilitate long-term suggestibility and heightened mind control of their subjects. With the addition of pain, drugs, and implanting post-hypnotic commands that demand certain actions of the hypnotized subjects, the creation of military assassins and suicide bombers is standardly achieved with great precision and uniformity.

Many theorize that several assassins, including most of the suicide bombers of the Middle East, have undergone similar treatments as those designed by the CIA during the 1970s in projects such as MK-Ultra. Often the patsy that is sacrificed, such as Sirhan Sirhan in the assassination of Robert F. Kennedy, has little recollection of his actions after he is falsely accused of acting alone in quite an incredibly heinous crime. To this day, Sirhan Sirhan cannot recollect shooting RFK.

Adding alcohol, medicine, or street drugs to viewers' minds only increases their suggestibility to the media's brainwashing programs and campaigns. The media understand this more than the public does and have departments in place that control the overall programming of the audience to keep the viewers as addicted as possible to specific television shows. Combine this with continual advertising inducing one to imbibe large amounts of alcohol, and one has the makings of potential zombies unable to direct their own lives, sadly appearing to be little more than Pavlov's dogs salivating for a bone.

Marx may have been right in that "Religion is the opiate of the masses." More recently, Edward R. Murrow's statement seems more accurate, "Television is the opiate of the people."

Executives in charge of television programming are trained to implement those programs that influence the viewers with the aim and objective that viewers become a most malleable and controllable populace.

Bankers and their production dollars dominate showbiz, making it terribly difficult for an outsider to get their big break. The bankers heavily guard the television domain. The purpose of those who control the airwaves is to control the minds of the audience.

Control over people's minds particularly benefits a select group of special financial interests. Special financial interests therefore determine what information they broadcast to create a diminution in the mind of the viewer who will readily accept not only the products being advertised but also the often far-fetched perspectives and opinions being transmitted through the many news outlets.

News is crucial to those deluding the majority of the population into not thinking for themselves. The media no longer report the news; they opine on it. On the screen in bright lights, there is a quick presentation of the news events that occurred, and then the anchor's interpretation quickly follows, biasing the audience to what the anchor repeatedly conveys. Today the news channels discuss the day's events among panels of hired consultants, rather than just honestly reporting the news.

There is an opinion that accompanies whatever seems to be happening in the news. The "news soap opera" continues day after day, reporting some of the most repugnant stories not fit for human or intellectual consumption. CNN slants the news in favor of the Democratic Party, while Fox news is loyal to the Republicans. Diametrically opposed media companies, like CNN and Fox News, are created to give the appearance that there is actually a significant difference between the Democratic and Republican Parties. There is no difference between the parties; both are controlled by the Establishment.

News conglomerates are intending not to improve the conditions of the planet but to improve the financial conditions of the special interests that provide billions in revenue to the unconscionable media industry.

By continually broadcasting political content that is argumentative and fearful, the news industry is attempting to shape the viewer's world to conform and agree to the never-ending political propaganda that the media are busy disseminating. By continually broadcasting conflicting political viewpoints, the news industry promotes the government as a congress of baboons, incapable of solving the problems of the day.

In actuality, the "television government" aims solely to camouflage the fact that bankers have taken over the world's governments and are using media, the world's governments, and war to destroy anyone that disagrees with their financial policies and agenda.

When some networks are pushing an agenda of the Democrats and others the Republicans, they delude the public about the actual underlying problems that enslave the world. The media obfuscate the fact that the government is completely under the control of outside forces and special interests.

The media withhold the fact that all politicians legislate for the special interests; the special interests are what we commonly refer to as "US national security interests."

Should a politician dare stand up to the special interests, during that brave politician's next election, the special interests will finance the renegade politician's political opponent, ensuring that political compliance with the special interests' wishes is restored within the government.

Another favorite of media agents is to create a scandal, ruining the reputation of any rambunctious and unruly politicians who dare to care about their constituents and the planet's needs over the needs of special interests.

Should all other attempts of controlling politicians fail, the special interests, along with the conspiring media and politicians, will dispose of any rebels, such as John F. Kennedy, Martin Luther King Jr., Robert F. Kennedy, Malcolm X, and anyone else who dares to stands up to the special interests who have infiltrated and control virtually every government on this planet.

The media continuously create two or more opposing camps. In order to keep the discussion and the flames of turmoil stoked, the media use diversionary or simply divide-and-conquer tactics to keep the audience from discovering the true cause of the real problems in their lives. One thing is for certain—the masses must never discover the identity and intentions of the media's "man behind the curtain." For the past several centuries, the people have allowed criminals to rule the world and to control, manipulate, and oppress the general population. Control and rule over the population is mostly acquired with the assistance of a strong propaganda campaign conducted on behalf of the world's oppressors for their own profit and even entertainment.

The press is protected under the Constitution in order that it may properly, and without interference from the government, report to the people any actions of the government that may curtail or actually infringe on the freedoms and rights of the American people. The press is supposed to be the watchdog on behalf of the American people, barking loudly whenever the government oversteps its power or acts in a manner that is the least bit harmful to its citizenry.

Instead, the press is doing the bidding of the special interests. Should a news agency fail to report the news in accordance with the special interests' agenda, then the various corporations will pull their advertising dollars until compliance is garnered or the news agency quickly becomes bankrupt.

Where is the reporting by the press regarding the four great Americans that lost their lives in Benghazi, while Washington, DC, did nothing to help? These great men were sacrificed in order that President Obama and the parasitical Secretary of State Clinton would fare better in the next election, only fifty-six days away. Where was the coverage of this crime by the democratically biased media? Where is the outrage from the liberal press and its investigation on who exactly called off the military personnel that were ready to rescue Ambassador Stevens, information Officer Sean Smith and CIA operatives Glen Doherty and Tyrone Woods who were unnecessarily sacrificed? They departed this life as true heroes, saving American lives. Watch the informative and revealing movie, 13 Hours: The Secret Soldiers of Benghazi.

Incredible information regarding the deaths of the above four heroes can be gathered from the thorough report conducted by the following honorable US representatives: Trey Gowdy of Texas, Susan Brooks of Indiana, Jim Jordan of Ohio, Mike Pompeo of Kansas, Martha Roby of Alabama, Peter Roskam of Illinois, and Lynn Westmoreland of Georgia. All honorably served as members of the Select Committee on Benghazi and worked tirelessly to bring justice to the fallen in Benghazi. The above fine and upstanding representatives who conducted this painstaking investigation, breathed hope once again into America's representative process by restoring the people's faith in our government. Americans are very proud of the ethical investigation conducted by this fine committee. Their outstanding work—"Report of the Select Committee on the Events Surrounding the 2012 Terrorist Attack in Benghazi"—can be read at the bottom of the following page, benghazi.house.gov/reports. Now the families just need to get justice.

As long as news stations do not mention the real problems that are stripping Americans of their freedom, the people will need to look elsewhere to find their news and the truth. The constant barrage of bad news is designed to keep the masses distracted and unable to discover the culprits responsible for most every calamity that plagues this world.

The next time you see the media reporting on a story, realize that it is slanted, biased, and distorted in order to mold your mind into thinking exactly as you are being programmed to think. Take some time and realize just how hell-bent on destroying the world these lunatics truly are. Whenever we see atrocities perpetrated, such as the deplorable mass killings in Paris on November 13, 2015, "Friday the Thirteenth," do not believe the story that is transmitted via the news. Investigate the matter for yourself and find the truth and those intelligence agencies responsible for such false-flag operations and the horrific slaughter of innocent lives; after all, it's just another sacrifice in accordance with one heinously corrupt and hate-filled agenda. Check out the insightful article "Paris Shooting: 10 Ways It Looks Like a Hallmark False Flag Op" at activist post.com/2015/11/and you will be amazed at what is not reported on the nightly news.

Most if not all so-called terrorist acts are conducted by the CIA, Mossad, and other intelligence agencies around the world.

This is one of the big secrets that the media keep hidden from the world's populace. Once the world realizes how morally corrupt the media truly are, countries and their citizens will realize how pressing, necessary, and beneficial it will be to demand truth and veracity from the media.

The press standardly fails to report the true enemies of our nation in their broadcasts. The press fails to report and expose to the masses that the enemy is deeply entrenched within and controls our national government. We need to have the press working for the American people and exposing the criminals that exist hidden within the government. This cabal directs every important government action in coordinated step with the agenda of the special interests. Their agenda is enforced by the minions that work tirelessly to achieve the aims of the shadow government.

Reporting of the financial meltdown of the US economy in 2008 is one in a long list of examples in which the press failed miserably in its duty to protect the people. When important matters like the world of international finance is shanghaied right before the eyes of the American people and the press focuses on events like the death of a celebrity, one starts to see that the press is diverting the attention of the American people away from what is truly important. Incredibly, the media would rather focus on the funeral of a single celebrity than the death of the world's economy.

On many occasions, usually to save the hide of a favored politician or bury a serious crime committed against the people, the media are adept at using celebrity scandals to divert the population's attention away from events that more importantly affect our freedoms. The press often tries to focus attention on more trivial matters when the survivability of the country ought to be the number one priority of the press, especially at this crucial time in history.

Unsubstantiated and fabricated theories are broadcast over the news channels, culminating in the Sunday morning shows where insults between opposing political parties are designed to give a false air of honesty and a platform for the politicians to tell it like it is or isn't. These Sunday morning shows lull the populace into accepting the most absurd explanations imaginable as to why our world is in such deplorably bad condition.

It is always the other party's fault; the Democrats blame the Republicans, and the Republicans blame the Democrats, when in actuality they are both to blame.

Instead of the media allowing the politicians to answer questions vaguely, the people want journalists who actually care about accurately informing the public. The public wants journalists that ask the tough questions and insist on receiving specific answers to their specific questions! The press usually fails to report and expose the responsible parties for whatever the calamity of the day is and plies deception as the guiding principle of broadcast journalism.

Remember the financial devastation created by the banks. Why were the bad actors involved in creating the financial debacle of 2008 never indicted and incarcerated for their part in collapsing the US economy?

It would be refreshing to return to the journalistic honesty of yesteryear, when America had a press and reporters who actually observed and investigated any corrupt governmental acts and exposed the guilty federal employees that committed those acts against the best interests of the people.

Where was the press investigating and writing stories exposing all the bad guys, the guys that made billions in bonuses as they tanked the economy? Where are the next Bernstein and Woodward? Wikipedia defines "investigative journalism" as "a form of journalism in which reporters deeply investigate a single topic of interest, such as serious crimes, political corruption, or corporate wrongdoing. An investigative journalist may spend months or years researching and preparing a report [emphasis added]."

Hell, "investigative journalism" even has the word "investigate" right at the beginning; it could be no plainer. There sure are a lot of crimes to investigate and report to the public; after all, that's the media's damn job! To the media, have a shred of decency and start doing your jobs.

The people have left the investigation of major stories to the incompetent and untrustworthy personnel of a dishonest and corrupt media. The stories told on the nightly news indoctrinate the masses to think, believe, and behave exactly as the controllers of the media desire. Further conditioning and brainwashing by the media are underway, using advanced technological tools to morph the people into sheep who are too frightened to think for themselves.

Another interesting activity of major media is the methods they use to control information that is placed in the various types of media whether it be print, radio, or television. Organizations like the Associated Press (AP) and the United Press International (UPI) consistently monitor and control the information they allow disseminated to newspapers and media outlets across the globe. By controlling the AP and UPI, which edit, limit, and filter the news before its international dissemination, it is easy to control what news is printed, what news is altered, and what news is censored. This allows for the promotion of propaganda, rather than news, in accordance with the outlined objectives of those who control and oppress the world.

At the 1991 Bilderberg Group's annual meeting in Baden, Germany, David Rockefeller thanked the press for their contributions in building a New World Order in alliance with the Nazi's Third Reich. He stated:

> We are grateful to the Washington Post, the New York Times, Time Magazine and other great publications whose directors have attended our meetings and respected their promises of discretion for almost forty years. . . .

> It would have been impossible for us to develop our plan for the world if we had been subjected to the lights of publicity during those years. But, the world is more sophisticated and prepared to march towards a world government. The supranational sovereignty of an intellectual elite and world bankers is surely preferable to the national auto-determination practiced in past centuries.

Among the attendees of this meeting were Bill Clinton, then-governor of Arkansas, and Dan Quayle, the vice president in George Bush Sr.'s administration.

The Bill of Rights guarantees a free press. The First Amendment states:

Congress shall make no law respecting an establishment of religion, or prohibiting the free exercise thereof; or abridging the freedom of speech, or of the press; or the right of the people peaceably to assemble, and to petition the Government for a redress of grievances.

The Founding Fathers ensured these rights in order that the press could be the citizens' watchdog, perpetually on guard, should any criminals try to trespass against our liberties. The rich, who purchased the media to conceal their ongoing criminal trespass against the people of this nation and the world, are attacking the freedoms of every American at every opportunity they have. There is an ongoing international war for the minds of the people, conducted by the filthy rich against the people of the world.

People need to fully understand the duplicitous nature of the charlatans who pass for journalists and fabricate news, created and promulgated to further the aims of the ruling class. The media's betrayal of the

American people is instrumental in allowing politicians to engage freely in the deliberate destruction of this country in accord with the directives of the special interests, who control the purse strings of corporations, the media, and ultimately the government.

There was an experiment conducted by a man who did not care much for frogs. In 1872, A. Heinzmann reported that, if you place a frog in a boiling pot of water, it immediately jumps out to save itself. However, if you place the same frog in a pot of room-temperature water and slowly heat the water to a boil, the frog does not jump out; the poor fellow boils to death.

When will the American people realize that the United States is in hot water and has been for years? Will we jump out of the water and save our nation's future, or will we ignore our responsibility to our friends and ourselves? Do we fight for freedom and liberty or let them fly to the wayside, like an unsecured manuscript escaping from a speeding convertible?

When will the American people wake up and smell the burning remnants of our country, our freedoms, and our future? There is not an abundance of time before this beloved country becomes unrecognizable; it would already be unrecognizable to the Founding Fathers. They would roll over in their graves if they knew what has become of their glorious land. They would be appalled, but not surprised, to realize that the media are not only compliant but also complicit in the destruction of this great nation, while robbing the rights of the people.

Can you imagine the disgust on Thomas Jefferson's face if he surveyed America's population and pondered what kind of people could let themselves go from the freest country in the world to the slave state we are now calling America? Can you imagine the Founding Fathers' thoughts as they reminisced about their numerous friends, better people than most of us, who died to ensure that we could be free?

What have we the people done to that inestimable gift of freedom, for which many great soldiers laid down their lives, so that the future of America and the ideals it represents could lead the world to new heights and glory for humankind?

In John F. Kennedy's Presidential Inauguration Speech on January 20, 1961, he proclaimed, "Let every nation know, whether it wishes us well or ill, that we shall pay any price, bear any burden, meet any hardship, support any friend, oppose any foe to assure the survival and the success of liberty" (jfklibrary.org/Research/Research-Aids/Ready-Reference/JFK-Fast-Facts/Inaugural-Address.aspx). Today, too many Americans couldn't care less about their rights and freedoms; if you don't care about your rights, be assured that shortly you will have none.

Doing one's part to reform the world does not magically happen watching television and letting someone else do it. Instead of being spectators, we need to participate by taking action to educate and motivate ourselves to be able to do something about the nation's current state of affairs. Americans must not wait for a traitorous press to report honestly but must reach for a higher level of freedom and liberty for everyone by first understanding those conspiratorial members of society who are suppressing Americans and stealing our wealth, our freedoms, and our liberties.

Can one sincerely feel that the great men and women who sacrificed their lives for this nation would be proud of the way Americans are repaying their sacrifice and their honor? Have the great sacrifices of our beloved veterans, who died ensuring Americans' freedoms and liberties would always reign free, been for naught, or will we take back the power of the people from the tyrants?

Let us honor our friends of Ground Zero who lost their lives that fateful September morning by creating a freer and more ethical civilization in their honor and memory, or heaven forbid, will we turn a blind eye and go on with our lives, letting tyranny reign for all the days to come.

Have we led lives of any importance? Have we displayed any commitment to our brothers and sisters by ensuring our nation's future is free from tyranny? On the other hand, have we sadly shirked our American duty, leaving it for the next person to fix, damning our nation and the next generations of Americans to a future filled with despair and oppression?

Our American ancestors battled Great Britain's oppressive imperial rule during the American Revolution. Great men died to preserve the ideals of American freedom and liberty and not to have their sacrifices go tainted, unappreciated, and cast to the wind like dust. They died carrying the torch of freedom, and it is up to us to reinvigorate its fire.

You will not find the answers to life's important and tough questions on the nightly news; you will find them in your heart.

CHAPTER 7

Healthcare Socialism

Back in 1927, an American socialist, Norman Thomas, six times candidate for President on the Socialist Party ticket, said that the American people would never vote for socialism but he said under the name of liberalism the American people would adopt every fragment of the socialist program.

– RONALD REAGAN

And one day we must ask the question, "Why are there forty million poor people in America?" And when you begin to ask that question, you are raising questions about the economic system, about a broader distribution of wealth. When you ask that question, you begin to question the capitalist economy.

– DR. MARTIN LUTHER KING JR.

We are Socialists, we are enemies of the capitalistic economic system for the exploitation of the economically weak, with its unfair salaries, with its unseemly evaluation of a human being according to his wealth and property instead of responsibility and performance and we are all determined to destroy this system under all conditions.

– ADOLF HITLER

There is no difference between communism and socialism, except in the means of achieving the same ultimate end: communism proposes to enslave men by force, socialism—by vote. It is merely the difference between murder and suicide.

– AYN RAND

Socialism only works in two places: Heaven where they don't need it, and hell where they already have it.

– RONALD REAGAN

Socialist governments traditionally do make a financial mess. They always run out of other people's money.

– MARGARET THATCHER

Compassion is not weakness, and concern for the unfortunate is not socialism.

– HUBERT HUMPHREY

Socialism is a philosophy of failure, the creed of ignorance, and the gospel of envy, its inherent virtue is the equal sharing of misery.

– WINSTON CHURCHILL

Poverty is not an accident. Like slavery and apartheid, it is man-made and can be removed by the actions of human beings.

– NELSON MANDELA

Socialism is one of the oldest and most often expounded delusions and fallacies which this world has ever been afflicted by. It consists not merely in a general leveling of mankind, but in keeping them level once they have been beaten down.

– WINSTON CHURCHILL

To be a socialist is to submit the I to the thou; socialism is sacrificing the individual to the whole.

– JOSEPH GOEBBELS

A S YOU CAN IMAGINE, the press never reports the actual stories to inform and protect the interests and traditions of America. One such failure is exemplified in the Patient Protection and Affordable Care Act, also called the Affordable Care Act or Obamacare, which is drastically incorporating socialism into the healthcare and insurance industries of America. The American people now subsidize the medical and insurance industries in this so-called capitalistic country. The Affordable Care Act is a form of welfare for the medical-related industries.

When one penalizes individuals for failing to obtain medical insurance and mandates that every taxpayer in America must comply by obtaining health insurance or pay fines and penalties, one sees the government expanding and overstepping its constitutional limitations to a point that would make the most silly Socialists and committed Communists proud.

The medical and health insurance industries are operating according to a business model of a subsidized industry, which provides government welfare to the rich by demanding all Americans purchase insurance, whether they want to or not. Having medical insurance is now mandatory in the United States. That sounds more than socialistic; that sounds quite communistic and rather unconstitutional, as it places an involuntary financial demand, dictated by the government, onto the citizens under threat of penalty.

By forcing Americans to buy medical insurance, the government is creating an artificial demand for insurance with the intention of increasing profits for the politicians and their cronies, who one would imagine own interests in several insurance companies. This gravy train of welfare for the rich was designed to allow absurd amounts of money to be siphoned from the American population by the government and given to the special interests who own the insurance companies. This is similar to the criminal welfare gravy-train spending we witness within the defense budget and the doling out of military contracts to close friends of heartless politicians.

The only problem with Obamacare was that the financial model that the elite used to approximate the public's enrollment into government-enforced healthcare was faulty. Evidently, the insurance elite did not calculate that mostly lower-class people would sign up for health insurance, and now many insurance companies are losing their shirts and abandoning their positions as insurance providers under the failing Obamacare.

The cost of medical insurance is skyrocketing, making the Affordable Care Act anything but affordable. The insurance companies are hemorrhaging money and running for the hills.

One problem with a subsidized healthcare system is that the insurance industry and government allow inflated price fixing by the medical and pharmaceutical industries, making the costs of medical care and medications unaffordable for average Americans. When the government subsidizes the medical and pharmaceutical industries, it prevents the market from naturally determining the supply and demand relative to medical goods and services. Instead, the prices that the medical and pharmaceutical industries charge do not reflect the natural supply and demand that consumers are willing and able to pay for these goods and services, as we find in most other industries.

To demonstrate the insurance industry's influence on the cost of medical goods and services, consider the following analogy explaining legislative influences upon a simple and hypothetical business model for the ditch-digging industry. With no outside government oversight, the hypothetical cost to dig a three-foot-deep, two-foot-wide, and fifty-foot-long ditch is five hundred dollars, or ten dollars per foot. When the legislators discover the ditch-digging industry is quite profitable and in their opinion under-regulated, the legislators make sure the opposite becomes true.

The legislators need the help of the media to get people to believe there are problems, dangers, and abuses in the ditch-digging industry and that the government must step in and change that before someone gets hurt. Meanwhile, the media start running stories attacking and declaring the ditch-digging industry unsafe and in need of regulatory reform.

The government steps in, and soon the ditch-digging business is subsidized and insured. The insurance costs unfortunately exceed the revenue generated from ditch digging; therefore, ditch-digging prices increase to cover the new government oversight, insurance costs, and other regulation costs affecting the ditch-digging industry.

Next, in our Communist or Socialist society, the politicians pass legislation demanding that not only ditch diggers but also all Americans must carry ditch-digging insurance; whether they want to or not is irrelevant. The media blast the airwaves, telling us repeatedly, "You must obtain ditch-digging insurance or pay penalties and extra fees that the IRS will be happy to collect."

The ditch-digging lobbyists infiltrate Washington, DC. They give billions of dollars to politicians through Cayman Island private trusts and corporate sweetheart deals. They buy many politicians and control them like the whores they are.

Years later, there is a long-standing pattern of corrupt hiring practices exposed in one ditch-digging scandal after another, including lavish perks and outrageous salaries for politicians. They retire rich from Congress after legislating on behalf of the ditch-digging lobbies and special interests. This sweetheart of a relationship is often referred to behind Washington's closed doors as the "ditch-digging triangle."

The legislators say that the ditch digging industry needs more regulations, and so US ditch diggers are charged additional fees to ensure that the posh jobs of the politicians' families and friends are well protected in the ditch-digging and its new insurance industry.

A year later, the same ditch, three-foot-deep, two-foot-wide, and fifty-foot-long, dug under the government's oversight and overbearing regulations now costs five thousand dollars, or one hundred dollars per foot, instead of ten dollars per foot. Ditch-digging permits cost five times more and are subject to price fluctuations at the whims of the government. Inflated costs now put the services of ditch digging out of the reach of many Americans; the government then provides subsidies to all the companies that can no longer turn a profit. Schools sprout up and charge thousands of dollars to teach the now licensed occupation of ditch digging.

Can you dig it?

Politicians, aided and abetted by the media, are key players that shape society, endorsing legislation that seems unconstitutional at best and treasonous at worst, always chipping away at the people's rights and freedoms.

Many in the media fully support and promote the Affordable Care Act as the best way to handle the healthcare demands and needs of Americans. The media report the issue as a political story, using it as an opportunity to discover finally which political party, the Democrats or the Republicans, supports the firmly established ideals and traditions of America—and which party is more demonic.

Americans are finally figuring it out. Many understand that the Democratic and Republican Parties are controlled by the same corrupt money that is provided by the same special interests. Therefore, both parties' only concerns, in essence, are the special interests of those who fund the entire political game.

The media fail to mention that when politicians pass a bill—often without even having had an opportunity to read it before voting on it—

the politicians will usually stuff the bill with as much pork as they can. The politicians often seem to be fattening their own future pockets by passing such pork-rich legislation, including adjuncts to the mandated healthcare system and other socialistic programs.

As an aside, Hillary Clinton was one of the first champions of a socialistic national healthcare plan. She can afford to pay for useless insurance as her net worth is reportedly at over $250,000,000, but she has that great health insurance that the Congress legislated for itself. Exactly what business does Hillary Clinton do in order to accumulate such wealth? She is, after all, supposed to be a public servant. Many Americas believe that Hillary has sold her soul, the US government, and ultimately the American people's interests to the highest foreign bidders.

What has happened to this country? It has deteriorated to the point where making easy access to above-top-secret information that compromises national security is tolerated and accepted by the US government and the American people as standard operating procedure.

The moral and ethical deterioration of the United States that has occurred during our watch is shameful. We are failing our children by our inaction and apathy.

Getting back to Obamacare, the medical and pharmaceutical industries are allowed by government legislation and other cumbersome regulations and guidelines to charge ridiculous prices for products and services, knowing that the insurance companies will pay the cost. The pharmaceutical lobbyists persuade enough politicians with lucrative bribes and conspiratorial largess to ensure that the US government, the largest buyer of pharmaceuticals in the world, will be paying close to retail prices for pharmaceuticals and the American public will pay even higher prices.

One might think that the insurance industry overall is going to lose money when it suffers substantial losses. However, quarter after quarter and year after year, this is one of the most profitable sectors of the financial industry. The different states regulate the insurance industry and are responsible for adequately auditing the insurance companies that sell insurance within their state. The insurance companies that apply to provide insurance in the different states have their financial stability evaluated by each state to ensure the insurance company's financial sustainability and its ability to pay all claims and losses the company may experience in that state.

The practice of subsidization allows little opportunity for the free economy to establish an equitable supply and demand within the medical and pharmaceutical industries that are needed to correct inflated market prices that are far beyond the reach of the average consumer. The healthcare market is artificially inflated by endless subsidies and guaranteed payments in order that certain companies will continue making billions of dollars off the people. This is really a reallocation of income, a tax if you will, from the people to the insurance and pharmaceutical industries. The government has essentially provided the insurance, medical, and pharmaceutical industries with the ability and right to tax Americans, or at least hold them over a barrel, medically speaking.

It's too bad for the insurance companies that their plans to financially clean up at the people's expense backfired under Obamacare, which caused the insurance companies to lose billions of dollars. It is unfortunate that the states that monitor and audit the insurance companies did not evaluate the flaws in Obamacare sufficiently to detect its unrealistic projections and inefficiencies.

If citizens want to correct the unfair prices charged by professionals such as doctors and dentists, they should eliminate the special financial treatments these professions are receiving because of their ability to lobby politicians unfairly and unethically, thus ensuring favorable government legislation that unjustly enriches those that control the medical profession. Obamacare tried to divide the insurance pies into slices that were favorable and especially profitable to the insurance industry.

Subsidized and mandatory health insurance acts as a monetary reallocation mechanism that transfers wealth from the general population to those who insure and control the medical industry. Obamacare was promoted to help stabilize costs for American citizens.

In essence, every American family is still exposed to the threat of bankruptcy due to the medical profession, as is the case with virtually all who fall catastrophically ill. Catastrophic illness means requiring prolonged hospitalization or recovery. If a person undergoes hospitalization for a prolonged period, that patient is almost certainly guaranteed to be financially broke after paying the hospital and associated doctors' bills. Patient by patient, the medical community strips the life savings and fortunes of most all Americans who seek medical treatment in the last days, months, and even years of their lives.

Any industry that has guaranteed government payments can artificially inflate its prices to the point where the prices for its services become unaffordable to the public. Think of it. Americans are forced to carry insurance on our vehicles, our houses, and our bodies; there is little choice in the matter.

Dentists can charge over one thousand dollars per hour, and doctors and surgeons can charge thousands per hour, while most Americans make significantly less than those wages. Much of this massive amount of money charged by these professionals eventually ends up in the coffers of the insurance companies in the form of outrageously expensive malpractice insurance premiums.

We need to examine the government and the insurance companies' financial domination over the highly trained medical professionals and the general population. Today it is almost impossible to be a small independent doctor; Obamacare makes it necessary for independent physicians to join massive conglomerations in order to dilute costs and expenses created by Obamacare's burdensome paperwork demands. Most doctors now have to hire more accountants and bookkeepers than they do nurses and assistants because the demands of the insurance forms are arduous and complicated.

Certain medical trades do better than others under the Obamacare bureaucracy. Chiropractors are becoming bankrupt under Obamacare, while massage therapists are not even covered under most plans. It appears as though how much money is made in the healthcare system depends on how well each specific segment of the medical industry is represented by lobbyists in Washington, DC.

The truly unconstitutional aspect of Obamacare is the demand made by the government for Americans to enroll in a crooked and broken system. It's throwing good money after bad. If you fail to obtain insurance, the IRS will come to collect penalties; therefore, if you refuse to comply, you should be prepared to deal with your friendly local IRS agents.

How is it fair and not un-American for the government to subsidize the medical industry at the expense of all other businesses and the rest of the population?

The American people should have the option to manage and pool their money for their insurance needs. This pool could be run in a similar manner as a mutual insurance company and eliminate much of the extravagant spending that typically occurs at many insurance companies.

Americans should start our own mutual insurance company that watches the interest of the people, above the interests of the insurance companies' shareholders and the government's cronies. In our fanciful mutual insurance company, all profits will be shared exclusively among the policyholders.

Other countries have better and more affordable medical services than the United States. In fact, according to Forbes magazine, the United States is ranked tenth among the world's countries in providing quality healthcare services.

People understand that exorbitant healthcare costs are the direct result of the government subsidizing medical programs, guaranteeing payment, and artificially inflating prices so that the politicians, assisting the special interests that own the AMA and the hospitals, can extract the life savings from every American as he or she approaches death. In many cases, it will be a death attributable to the direct treatments provided by the medical community.

We must remove government and the insurance industry's financial interference in order for the healthcare industry to economically function like every other unsubsidized business. Eventually the medical industry would have to set its equilibrium price points at a level where the American people could afford to pay for their family's healthcare without mortgaging the farm and without needing insurance.

We do not pay for insurance to fix our automobiles. Why should we pay for insurance to fix our bodies? Why should it cost so much to be sick in America? The insurance industry, which controls the healthcare professionals' incomes through legislative decree, is financially crippling not just the healthcare professionals but every American as well. Obamacare is impoverishing healthcare providers, and they need to wake up before their hopes for the American Dream are fractured into a million pieces. If one looks objectively at Obamacare, one soon understands that the people are financially being negatively impacted by healthcare professionals, the healthcare professionals are financially being negatively impacted by the insurance industry, and the insurance industry is financially being negatively impacted by the government and its destructive policies!

Who then is winning under Obama's abominable care? When we think about it and cut out the middlemen, Obamacare is such a disaster because the people are essentially being damaged by the government. We need to create a healthcare system where, instead of everyone losing, everyone wins!

Perhaps, if we are going to provide a national healthcare system, it is important that we first fix this broken industry before demanding the participation of every American. Otherwise, it becomes a futile and dangerous exercise to participate in such a frightening system.

Many aspects of the medical community, including oncology with its barbaric treatments of cancer, approved by the FDA and applied by the AMA, are all just a big rip-off considering the statistics regarding the ineffectiveness of these treatments. Chemotherapy comes to mind with its very dismal record of success.

Another area in dire need of evaluation and reformation is the American Psychiatric Association, or the APA. The APA has some of the worst treatments imaginable for mental disorders. Psychiatrists provide little if any psychological benefit to their patients. Most psychiatric patients walk around like zombies ingesting mind-altering drugs that can too often lead to suicide or worse. Psychiatrists hardly cure anyone. Just sit in a psychiatrist's waiting room, and you'll certainly see a number of basket cases waiting for their anointments with their shrink.

It was discovered that most mass shootings are done by people that are under the care of a psychiatrist, and almost 100 percent of those looking down the scope of a rifle and robotically pulling the trigger are on mind-altering drugs prescribed by their psychiatrist.

There are unfair advantages given to the medical community over the remainder of the population. A simplistic solution is to bar the federal government and insurance companies from interfering with the medical industry in any shape or manner. Soon afterwards, the healthcare industry would eventually find itself having to adapt to the free market economy like all other industries. Why should the medical industry be specially guaranteed that inordinate charges will be paid by the federal government?

Medical services are affordable in other parts of the world. Why is the medical industry in such a frightening condition here in America? If an elderly man spends three days in a hospital having a triple bypass and three stents placed in his heart's arteries, and eats delicacies like pea soup, can someone explain why the cost of that procedure should be eighty-seven thousand dollars? This is not an exaggerated example; it is an actual case, and things like this happen every day in the American healthcare system.

If the medical industry was not subsidized in the above example and could charge only what an average family could afford for a triple bypass —in essence, what the market will bear—the hospital would have to survive by charging affordable prices for their healthcare goods and services. A three-day hospital stay should cost less than ten thousand dollars, and this should include the cardiologist's and the anesthesiologist's time of six hours to perform the operation.

According to health.costhelper.com/heart-surgery.html, "For patients not covered by health insurance, the cost of the most common types of heart surgery can range from less than $30,000 to almost $200,000 or more, depending on the facility, the doctor and the type of surgery."

To allow the medical industry guaranteed subsidies is evidence that special interests are at work conspiring to steal the people's money and line the medicos' pockets with exorbitant profits. Some reports indicate that Americans spend close to 90 percent of all healthcare dollars in the last year(s) of their life. The medical system is designed to reallocate the average American's wealth into the hands of the medical community. This occurs every day.

The government is attempting to assist the insurance companies to profit by taxing Americans under the pretext of a universal health insurance plan that is good for the country. Greedy executives and shareholders should have been happy with making billions from the public on existing medical, home, and auto insurance policies; but billions are not enough. As long as people attempt to fix America's broken healthcare system, they are acting like imbeciles trying to fix a flat on a moving vehicle. America needs a whole new healthcare system.

There is nothing special about the healthcare industry. It is simply another industry, and like all big industries, it is only concerned with profits. The medical industry varies somewhat from other industries in that most everyone in America is eventually treated by the medical industry.

It is a shame that most patients' life savings, which they planned to leave to their families and rightful heirs, are tendered to the medical community to pay for exorbitant medical bills. Medical treatments can cost millions of dollars. As anyone having a catastrophic illness can testify, the medical industry can very quickly gobble up virtually all of a patient's life savings. In effect, the medical industry steals the patients' children's inheritance without having the slightest remorse or second thought. This is particularly unconscionable when the patient dies from the toxic treatments delivered by incompetent medical professionals.

Why do pharmaceuticals cost multiple times more in the United States than in Canada or Europe? Why is it so difficult to find proper treatment that does not inflict terrible pain and discomfort when a person has cancer? Moreover, why on earth, after spending billions and billions of dollars, is the medical community unable or unwilling to produce a cure for cancer, instead of poisoning patients and calling it treatment?

Other countries offer holistic cures for cancer that improve the function of the body and allow the body to rid itself of its cancer or disease. The AMA administers poisonous treatments because the AMA understands it is more profitable to treat cancer than to cure it. Why are the people and the press not all over this? Where is the outrage that after billions and billions are given to different charities—for cancer, AIDS, muscular dystrophy, and others—still today there are no cures?

An entire investigation, evaluation, and overhaul of the medical industry and the treatments it administers to the public ought to be conducted in order to analyze the effectiveness of the AMA's treatments. This would assist to direct the future of medical research toward the discovery and creation of more humane and successful treatments and ultimately cures. It is time that citizens demand more from the medical community and better understand the healthcare issues that affect every American.

The AMA provides no cures for cancer because curing cancer would diminish profits. It is not difficult to figure this out. Cancer simply metastasizes throughout the body. Are we supposed to believe that, after spending countless billions, the medical research community cannot find an economical method to prevent unwanted fungi-cancerous cells (cancer is a fungus) from spreading throughout the body? Give me a break.

At the very least, healthcare should be affordable for the masses—if not a right for every citizen. The AMA and America's healthcare system are very ill and in need of treatment. Let us fix America's very corrupt and ailing healthcare system in order that all of us may lead happier and healthier lives.

CHAPTER 8

Stock Market Misconceptions

An investment in knowledge pays the best interest.
– BENJAMIN FRANKLIN

Invest in yourself. Your career is the engine of your wealth.
– PAUL CLITHEROE

I never attempt to make money on the stock market. I buy on the premise that they could close the market the next day and not reopen it for five years.
– WARREN BUFFETT

The stock market is filled with individuals who know the price of everything, but the value of nothing.
– PHILLIP FISHER

If stock market experts were so expert, they would be buying stock, not selling advice.
– NORMAN RALPH AUGUSTINE

I will tell you how to become rich. Close the doors. Be fearful when others are greedy. Be greedy when others are fearful.
– WARREN BUFFETT

One of the funny things about the stock market is that every time one person buys, another sells, and both think they are astute.
– WILLIAM FEATHER

It's not how much money you make, but how much money you keep, how hard it works for you, and how many generations you keep it for.

– ROBERT KIYOSAKI

Know what you own and why you own it.

–PETER LYNCH

The difference between betting the stock market and the horses is that one of the horses must win.

– JOEY ADAMS

W HEN THE VALUE INVESTED in speculative financial markets exceeds investment in the production and manufacturing segment of the economy, those who control the financial markets control a majority of the wealth of the economy and therefore the financial destiny of the people.

Many Americans are fond of placing their money in the stock market to have it, as they say, "work for them." There are interesting mechanisms at work in the New York Stock Exchange and virtually all the other financial markets of the world, which many would shy away from as they become more aware.

Wall Street is like gambling—but gambling at a casino where the house can change the rules any time it pleases. Just think of it. You get dealt twenty-one, and the dealer decides this hand we're stopping at twenty. Instead of winning black jack and collecting double on your bet, with this change of house rules, you lose your wager! That's how the stock market works for most people that place their bets on Wall Street.

In Las Vegas, there is at least a semblance of agreement that you should get something for your hard-earned dollars—whether it is free drinks or a complimentary dinner at one of the many rather opulent restaurants. Everyone that visits Vegas understands that the odds are in favor of the house and that gambling is for the entertainment of the customers and mostly at the customers' expense.

If you hit the jackpot, you are one of the few that do and congratulations. Nearly every gambler goes home losing the money he or she brought, and some lose a great deal more. If there were more winners than losers, there would not be so many gazillion-dollar hotels lining the Las Vegas Strip.

There are odds-setting parameters and state-sanctioned guidelines that require Las Vegas casinos to notify gamblers of the odds of winning and losing when they play slots, craps, and other games. Las Vegas goes as far as printing the odds of every slot machine right on the machine itself, informing the gambler of the chances of success and failure every time the arm of the one-armed bandit is pulled or, nowadays, every time the slot machines' buttons are pushed. Those familiar with playing slots will recall the machines are preprogrammed, and you can read the payback percentage and the hit-to-win ratios in plain sight. Perhaps it is the casino's way of giving notice that gamblers are going to lose money.

There are volumes written regarding the basic strategy of blackjack, as well as the house favorite, roulette. These odds are no big secret to the experienced gambler.

To one driving down the Strip, it should come as no great mystery that the colossal temples of Vegas are built on the forfeitures of the masses. It is obvious that the odds are in favor of the house, and if you are going there, chances are you are going to leave a donation in exchange for having a great time gambling and drinking free booze and a chance or two at love. This is what the great city of Las Vegas is known for: gambling and good times! You want it, you expect it, and by golly, they provide it. I hope that when you visit Las Vegas you have a great time and tell them I sent you!

However, Wall Street is a very different story. Many are lured to the mighty street of dreams with the notion of hitting it big. The old lyrics, "If I can make it there, I'll make it anywhere," is as true today as the day it was crooned by the bigger-than-life Frank Sinatra.

Stock promoters proclaim that fantastic opportunities for the accumulation of extravagant wealth exist on Wall Street. Many Americans feel confident about the stock market, as demonstrated by tendering their hard-earned cash over to whom they believe is a conscientious broker, one who is going to watch their hard-earned money and, with any luck, make it grow. Unfortunately, this seldom occurs over the long term. More often than not, the conscientious brokers watch their clients' hard-earned nest eggs fly out of their accounts in the form of devastating losses.

The mantra on Wall Street is "your money needs to be working for you." Most investors are willing to risk their life savings, believing that their money needs to grow in order that they can become rich and secure in their old age. That is the idea most Main Street investors believe when they send a check to an investment firm on Wall Street. Instead of Wall Street's being the street of financial dreams, millions have come to know it as the boulevard of broken dreams. It all depends on what kind of return on investment the investor receives.

Often people fail to consider the long-term effects that the markets can wreak on their investments. Examination of the stock market can lead to some interesting revelations. The overall premise most people believe is that the market is uninfluenced by human conspirators and that the market moves at the whims of uncertainty or as a result of the latest traumatic news story. Even more absurd, some believe that the stock price is a true reflection of the company's actual value, function, and performance.

The market does fluctuate in relation to the latest stories broadly disseminated by the media. The overall management of a company, as well as its value and its performance, is usually important in evaluating a company's stock price, but few companies are immune to massive stock price fluctuations in markets that are subject to outside control and manipulation.

There is an unseen hand controlling the market—a direct technological influence on the movements of the overall markets and a controlling of various segments of the financial markets without disclosure to or knowledge of the general investing public.

The following example incontrovertibly illustrates that financial markets are, and can be, controlled by a few corporations that lurk in the shadows, unbeknownst to the masses. In the seventeenth century, the Rothschild family was able to manipulate England's stock exchange, and the family has been manipulating the world's financial markets ever since.

During the Battle of Waterloo, the Rothschilds controlled the protected messenger service. The messengers wore red caps to distinguish them from the fighting forces and were granted safe passage to and from the various battlefields. The red-capped messengers were comparable to today's news media. Their purpose was to inform the non-fighting population of the status of the war, which side was winning the most recent battles and things like that. Most people of that time relied on the news provided by the messengers to plan activities in order to live their lives, but the Rothschilds relied on the messengers' news to boost investments.

Nathan Rothschild was England's chief financial agent. For this greedy and unscrupulous man, the Battle of Waterloo presented a marvelous opportunity. Rothschild understood that news received from his messengers telling of the defeat of Napoleon at Waterloo would be good for the financial markets of England. When the news arrived in London that Napoleon had been defeated in the Battle of Waterloo, Rothschild was the only person to get the news for some time ahead of the masses. He decided that duplicity and deception were potentially the most profitable courses of action.

Consols were England's government-backed securities or bonds in the form of basic annuities. Great Britain sold the consols to the public at their face value, and interest was paid to the holder when Great Britain purchased them back at a later date, say, five years after the purchase date.

If Napoleon won the Battle of Waterloo, then the people believed that England and the rest of Europe would likely be placed under the rule of France and, more frighteningly, under the demented despotic rule of Napoleon. Conversely, his defeat meant that England would continue to be the hegemony and ruling faction of Europe. Regardless, Rothschild had a plan that could yield him millions if he could manipulate the news in his favor and strongly influence the price of the consol market.

When Rothschild got the news of Napoleon's defeat at the Battle of Waterloo, he conspicuously positioned himself outside the stock exchange and began selling his consols. Rumors started. Since "everybody knew" Rothschild owned the messengers and was an authority in these matters, people figured Napoleon must have been victorious and therefore England was done for.

Rothschild sold more and more of his consols; this soon was responsible for creating a crash in the consol market. There was a fever to unload consols as the price began to fall to practically nothing. At the opportune time when the market bottomed out, Rothschild reversed his position and bought the largest amount of consols ever purchased, and at bargain-basement prices.

Moments later, Rothschild broke the news regarding England's victorious and crushing defeat of Napoleon, and the price of consols soared.

Notorious and phenomenal profits gave the Rothschilds control over the consol market and therein control over England's stock exchange.

This swindle eventually led to Great Britain transferring ownership of the Bank of England to the Rothschild family.

We should learn a grand lesson from Rothschild's corrupt speculation on that fateful day in June of 1815. Imagine how many other markets the Rothschilds control today; they control and manipulate virtually every market at their will and discretion.

Today, fabricated information disseminated by the media can be manipulated to control and influence those who are invested in the financial markets to behave in a certain and predictable manner.

Market-manipulating computer technologies are utilized to control today's financial markets with lightning precision and profit-churning algorithms.

Controlling the media greatly assists in influencing the minds of the masses to act in specific ways, such as buying or selling stock based on alarming information generated by media outlets.

Consider the financial meltdown of September 2008 and the announcement by President Bush declaring that the United States was suddenly experiencing the worst financial crises since the Great Depression. That is how Bush Jr. worded the announcement, and it initiated the largest crash of the stock market in its history. If one had this privileged information days, weeks, or months before the disastrous financial news statement was announced to the public, one could profit just the way Rothschild did with the consols of 1815.

Imagine the stock positions of those in the know, including members of the US government, the Bush family, Henry Paulson, Goldman Sachs, and many others privy to this information, weeks and even months before Bush Jr. made his announcement. How difficult would it be to place one's bets that the stock market was going to drop significantly, almost immediately after that depressing announcement was made public?

This resulted in huge profits for those insiders that were privy to this inside information, far before the general investing public was notified. Why is it legal for politicians and their families and cohorts to profit from economic circumstances and collapses, which the same criminal politicians create and orchestrate from behind the scenes?

As many know, a similar opportunity occurred preceding the World Trade Center disaster. The largest short bets ever placed in the history of

American and United Airlines stock were placed on September 10, 2001. However, the proceeds were never claimed, thereby keeping undisclosed the identity of the visionary investors who profited using inside information as discussed above in 9/11 Trillions: Follow the Money.

It would be interesting to examine the stock trades of the Bush family in relation to the incidents of 9/11, as well as the incidents of the economic meltdown of 2008. The American people need to examine the Bush family's balance sheets and stock portfolios; only then will we truly discover what some speculate and allege to be vast improprieties that occurred under Bush's militant reign as president.

As an aside, is it equitable or criminal that Bush Sr. actively worked with one of the largest, if not the largest, defense contracting companies in the world, the Carlyle Group, while his son was busy starting WWIII?

How difficult would it be for Bush Sr. to order George W. to invade a country like Iraq for example and yield huge profits for Bush Sr. and his friends? A situation like this, where the Bush family profits potentially billions of dollars, makes Hillary and Bill Clinton look like a bunch of bush-league hillbilly amateurs when it comes to stealing from this nation. The real money, the Bush money, is from controlling and financing military conflicts, military defense contracts, and the initiation and proliferation of war.

Independent investigation regarding the Chicago Commodity Exchange, which remained open during and after 9/11, may shed some light on who exactly knew ahead of time that the World Trade Center buildings were going to be taken down, as well as the identities of the cold-blooded villains who profited from these blood-soaked trades.

Over and again, Wall Street induces the public to invest their funds with the intention of providing a better life for themselves and their families by acquiring oodles of financial profit and gain. This inducement is largely influenced by the legislature and bank regulators that allow the banks to offer paltry rates of interest on savings accounts. Typically, in order to keep up with the rate of inflation, the elderly and others on a fixed income are easily persuaded to put their life savings into the stock market and/or mutual funds in the hopes of being able to garner a better return than the insignificant interest paid by the banks on savings accounts.

The stock markets are working exactly as designed—to extract the wealth of the unsuspecting middle class and transfer it to the wealthy class. The stock market is engineered to reallocate the funds from the middle class to the rich, and this can occur in a matter of seconds, days, weeks, and even years.

Some may find the notion that the rich have privileged access to the markets to be based upon some nebulous conspiracy theory. However, examination of simple phenomena will prove it is standard operating procedure that the rich bankers control the world's financial markets and exchanges, guaranteeing incredible profits for the wealthy class as a result of this unfair market access, control, and manipulation.

Every few years, there is a stock market cycle that virtually guarantees the bankers an unbelievable profit by stealing trillions of dollars from the 401(k) retirement plans of the general public. Let us examine how this theft is repeatedly committed in order to fleece the American people of their savings.

First, the bankers crash the markets in coordination with the media. After the markets crash, the bankers, who have access to unlimited money, buy huge percentages of the stock, commodity, and currency markets. When the markets crash, there is ample time for the bankers to reinvest their cash because there is no great rush or panic, like that experienced when the market is in freefall.

Soon thereafter, in concert with an expansion of the money supply, economic indicators improve, and the stock, commodity, and currency markets begin to soar. This naturally occurs once reinvestment is initiated by the banks. Cyclically, this fleecing operation occurs at the discretion of the wealthy class and demonstrates the preferred pattern that the bankers use to rob the public.

In reality, many bankers will change their long positions in the market for short positions just before the market crashes. This ensures that the banks capitalize and profit when the markets go down, as well as when the markets are driven back up to a higher range.

Another unjust and ruinous practice is to have a separate, special class of people with legislated rights and privileges that do not extend to the whole of society. The private banking class that runs the Federal Reserve System meets privately and discusses plans regarding the economy and national interest rates. The decisions made in the Fed's secretive meetings are disclosed to the public days and even weeks after these important and impactful decisions are initially concluded by the international private bankers. After the disclosure of the Fed's imminent actions regarding the economy, certain predictable financial events are performed by the public that specifically affect the financial markets of the world. If a small group is allowed to obtain the Federal Reserve's inside information prior to the public, that group's members would have the opportunity to place incredibly favorable bets in the stock markets, taking advantage of this valuable and timely inside information.

Now, some may find it difficult to think that these events are utilized or even predictable by those who disclose the information regarding the secretive Federal Reserve System meetings. I highly recommend William Cooper's classic book exposing government conspiracies, Behold a Pale Horse. This book illustrates the lengths that those in control of the financial markets of the world undertake in order to monitor the various changes of the different financial variables of the economy. Cooper explains in great detail how the government and major financial institutions use computer systems or computerized financial weapons against the general population to control and predict various aspects and fluctuations of the world markets. This area should be thoroughly understood by all Americans before investing in such controllable and manipulatable financial markets.

These computerized financial weapons create predictable massive fluctuations in stock and commodity prices in conjunction with many other profitable financial schemes. For example, the bankers can accurately predict what the price of lumber is going to do when gas prices drop by ten cents. They can estimate this and a whole lot more.

Additionally, Cooper's book details how credit card data, sales tax revenues, and other indexes are all examinable via computers by those who control the US economy. By having the advantage of insider financial information prior to and exclusive from the general public, those with this timely information advantage can unjustly enrich themselves at our expense.

Cooper believed in and fought for America. Unfortunately for us, this brilliant man's heroic life tragically ended when he was murdered by a sheriff deputy's bullet, fighting for his freedom and our rights.

These types of covert financial activities should be considered insider trading on a massive scale. If a stockbroker or investor buys stock based on an inside tip, that person has broken federal law and is going to federal prison.

Bankers have special privileges and advantages that other investors are prosecuted for if they partake in such schemes of insider trading. Bankers control and manipulate the markets on a daily basis with unparalleled speed and ferocity profiting hundreds of millions if not billions per day.

Wall Street is complicit and greatly profits from the predictable US military agenda. We fight wars in which hundreds of millions have died throughout history, all because the bankers value profit over people.

On behalf of the Federal Reserve, the US government starts many military conflicts that generate profits for weapons manufacturers and defense contractors, which can exponentially increase their corporate stocks' value on Wall Street. Very unacceptable is the fact that Wall Street, the Federal Reserve, and the US Treasury have enjoyed a revolving door of hiring and taking care of one another for several decades.

Government officials from the US Treasury who retire from public service receive fantastically well-paying jobs on Wall Street working for corrupt banks. To discover which of your favorite politicians have benefited from potentially corrupt hiring practices after retiring from Congress, visit opensecrets.org/revolving. This site lists the sweetheart deals crooked politicians receive after a tenure of supposedly serving our country as federal employees.

The media also fail to report the corporate revolving-door hiring practices for politicians who legislate and fund the wars that benefit military armament manufacturers and other corporations that are waiting in the wings to hire corrupt, compromised, and unethical politicians.

Wall Street has many other programs that make it difficult for the average investor to compete when gambling in the stock markets. There are many benefits given to companies that enjoy privileged computerized information, even if that privileged information is exclusive and lasts only for a few fractions of a second.

Massive banks, which receive market information fractions of a second or even several seconds before everyone else, enjoy a significant advantage over other Wall Street investors. This time advantage is literally worth trillions of dollars to those that can capitalize on it by accessing and manipulating the markets fractions of a second before the remainder of the market is even allowed access to the aging financial information.

Theoretically, this microscopic time advantage should be of such importance and significance that crashes and recoveries of the markets could be systematically programmed into an algorithm designed to manipulate market fluctuations, thereby enabling bankers to align their stock positions and holdings with the foreseeable and predictable market fluctuations that they themselves create.

Automated trading is comprised of computer programs that decide which stocks to buy, hold, and sell; all this and so much more are performed in nanoseconds. Automated trading eliminates human intervention or delay. Having special purchasing, technological, and timing advantages, companies such as Goldman Sachs can purchase blocks of shares of stocks in fractions of a second and create a shortage of the stock, which leads to an immediate higher demand and price for the manipulated stock.

Automated trading creates incredible profits for Goldman Sachs and other companies that are members of this privileged banking class. This is but one of the fundamental electronic profit-generating schemes applied and used daily to generate fortunes that are beyond one's ability to count.

These advantages are for only a privileged and select few to enjoy by profiting directly from the rest of the unwitting stock market investors. It is like belonging to a secret private segment of a club that profits by drowning the other duped members of the club in losses. Certain companies utilizing this microscopic time advantage cannot help but wildly profit. These privileged companies profit by electronically driving the price of stock up or down before the other investors are even allowed access to the stock information. This allows those select companies to accurately predict the market response once the information is received by the remainder of the investors. In essence, this special class of bankers can manipulate the price of stocks before the rest of the market can even access the market data.

As an example, one of the advantages of buying stocks utilizing algorithmic trading software is the ability to make thousands and even millions of micro-transactions in a matter of seconds. Instead of buying, say, a million shares, the privileged buyer's computers can buy the shares in tiny batches, thereby increasing the value of the stock as it is becomes amassed and guaranteeing an automatic profit on the shares that it systematically buys. Automated trading software has algorithms in which organized purchasing of varying amounts of stocks, in fractions of a second, can artificially drive the prices of those specific stocks up, thereby creating astronomical profits from using computerized purchasing protocols.

As an example, the purchase of ten thousand shares of a single stock is conducted in increments of one thousand shares or much smaller lots. Let's say the price starts at one dollar per share and predictably increases as the stock is purchased and becomes more scarce. After the entire ten thousand shares are purchased, the price during this process has risen to ten dollars per share. That means that all the stock that was purchased for less than ten dollars per share is immediately profitable. This is a crude example of automated trading, but hopefully you understand the process. With a fraction-of-a-second advantage to access stock markets, the yields are unlimited; it is one of Wall Street's versions of printing its own money out of thin air.

An ethical and moral financial oversight board like the SEC should outlaw such unfair time advantages, and every investor should be allowed access to the same financial information at the same time. Technological trading advantages used only by a select class of bankers are just another way for the rich to get richer at the expense of the rest of the suckers in the market.

In the August 23, 2009, New York Times, the article "Arrest over Software Illuminates Wall St. Secret" by Alex Berenson describes the story of an alleged software thief, Sergey Aleynikov. He was arrested for allegedly stealing software code from Goldman Sachs, his former employer. At a bail hearing three days later, a federal prosecutor asked that Aleynikov be held without bond because the software code he allegedly stole could be used to "unfairly manipulate" stock prices.

Goldman Sachs might be one of the most unethical banking corporations in the world, yet it was upset that someone might have stolen some software from their company, which could be used to "unfairly manipulate" stock prices. Does anyone else sense the irony in this statement? The US government prosecuted an individual who allegedly stole software from a corporation that developed it; the software can unfairly influence the prices of stock, but the government does not prosecute Goldman Sachs; the government only goes after the non-influential individual.

It helps to know that the US government and Goldman Sachs are completely in bed and together form integral parts of the golden, financial triangle, comprised by the US Department of Treasury, Goldman

Sachs and other Wall Street banks, and the Federal Reserve System. Therefore, because such nefarious relations exist, it is legal for Goldman Sachs to build and use software that can unfairly manipulate stock prices and generate incredible profits with the government's blessing, approval, and assistance.

We have to decide for ourselves at what point the unethical actions of politicians are classified as illegal and at what point they are classified as treason. The American people should consider these unethical posh jobs and other lavish perks minimally as conflicts of interest and maximally as treason whenever a federal employee obtains a benefit as a result of selling out the country.

Any government employees who provide or receive special perks and privileges to or from the Federal Reserve and/or the Wall Street banks should be prosecuted for acts of self-dealing, conflicts of interest, and basically hijacking and literally privatizing the US government for personal financial benefit.

We, as citizens, need to address the cronyism and thievery that we see in Washington, DC, which allows elected officials to receive billions by betraying the people of this nation. To keep politicians honest and to ensure they serve the people and not the special interests, we must implement term limits and remove those politicians who betray their constituents and essentially all Americans. The citizenry should not allow an incumbent politician to remain in office for multiple terms, no matter how popular. We must insist and demand that all Washington politicians actually represent their constituents and not the corporations they have been pandering to for at least the past century.

Notwithstanding the Washington–Wall Street unethical relationship, an overall examination of the stock market during a ten-year period can yield some interesting perspectives. This is especially pertinent as many investors claim that the best way to grow money in the stock market is to keep it there for the long term. Let us consider investing over a ten-year term.

If one were randomly to select several ten-year periods of the stock markets indexes and draw a graph of the starting price of the market index to an end point ten years later, it would be apparent that there would be very little gain in actual money for many typical investors. Subtract any adjustments for inflation, broker's fees, and forfeiture of capital use, taxation, etc., and it appears that there is barely a winning wager in the markets.

There are winners and losers in the market, but when the day ends, many realize they have built nothing and have received someone else's forfeited monetary gain as a result of their speculation. The stockbrokers and hedge fund managers siphon money from the masses in the form of management fees, trading fees, and other expenses; they are smart enough to know better than to invest their own funds in the markets. They make money on commissions and fees, regardless of market fluctuations. It is common knowledge that less than one-third of stockbrokers trade their own money in the markets.

Even more interesting, the average Main Street investor does not simply invest in the market at one time and leave it in the market for ten years. Many smaller investors will invest at different times. Most people invest as the market is going up because there is usually more money in the economy and people usually have extra money available for investment when times are good. Most investors will also sell their stocks and investments as the economy and the markets start to go down because, with a crashing market and economy, the investors may desperately need their money and there is less money available in the economy.

Not many investors are farsighted enough to sell their stocks while the stock market bubble is still inflating. The phenomenon of buying and selling stock as one can afford to adjusts the success curve of the small investor, making it significantly less likely for the small investors to succeed against the conglomerates that invest billions of dollars and understand the market and its controlled and predictable movements.

Instead of simply plotting a ten-year period and drawing a graph, people can examine the investors' buy-and-sell patterns to see in whose pocket most smaller investors' losses end up, namely, the Wall Street bankers'. If you ran the Wall Street casino, would you like the odds to be stacked in favor of the house or the gamblers? Compare the overall structure of the gaming industry in Las Vegas with the theft of Wall Street, and you soon realize that the longer you gamble at each place, the more you inevitably lose.

A realistic improvement of the average investor's yield could happen if the person were to control his or her funds, invest, and withdraw in a timely manner, thereby appreciating the gains and eliminating devastating losses. Brokers very often keep investors' money moving in the markets because brokers usually earn commissions on every trade they make. Investors' funds are busy working to increase the brokers' commissions, regardless of the investors' yields or losses.

More commonly on Wall Street, there are catastrophic collapses or artificially created market adjustments that benefit the banking class because of its inside information.

A good example of one of these artificially created market adjustments is 9/11. The tragic events of that day allowed the rich to profit, and today they continue to profit, never satisfying their unquenchable blood thirst for profit. There needs to be competent auditing and analysis of the financial markets in the days, weeks, and months preceding the World Trade towers' demolition and discover who exactly had the inside stock positions, who knew what, and when they knew it. An interesting perspective is given by author Michael C. Ruppert in his fascinating article "Suppressed Details of Criminal Insider Trading Lead Directly into the CIA's Highest Ranks," available at globalresearch.ca/articles/RUP110A.html

Another example of the stock market's artificially created adjustments, which ultimately reallocated the wealth from the small investors to the pockets of the wealthy, is what occurred in the financial markets from 1998 to 2002, commonly referred to as the "dot-com era," or as others consider this debacle of the high-tech industry more appropriately named, the "dot-bomb era."

Many investors' funds were in high-tech stocks that the media had been touting for years as the way for the average investor to spectacularly grow his or her money. At least on its surface, the stock market appeared to be a better investment than the banks. During this time, the banks were offering pathetic returns on deposit accounts—half a percent, almost nothing.

There were trillions of dollars invested in the high-tech market from 1995 to 1999, which created and expanded the dot-com, high-tech segment of the market. Eventually this led to a high-tech bubble with inflated and over-valued stock prices that were calculated and derived without considering stock valuation fundamentals, such as price/earnings ratios, daily volume traded, profit and loss statements, balance sheets, annual reports, etc.

The money invested prior to the dot-com debacle came in torrents from many American and international investors. It became readily apparent that many of the stock evaluations of high-tech companies that exploded in value were unfortunately based on faulty methods used to estimate the value of these companies and their public stock offerings.

Many high-tech companies had valuations making them worth hundreds of millions, even billions of dollars, while having virtually no revenue. Outrageous corporate valuations, wrongly based on the amount of Internet traffic or the number of visitors to a particular website or other such unreliable statistics, meant that the investors were paying quite a premium for corporate shares while barely considering the fact that most of these companies had zero dollars in revenue, never mind profit. This invested wealth was converted into corporate shares in accordance with the shares' overinflated market values.

The high-tech companies, many established by technical renegades, were not under the control of the powers-that-be enough to satisfy the greedy desires of the planetary oppressors. The entrepreneurs had honestly created an industry outside the control of the traditional investment bankers. Many traditional investment bankers did not participate in the creation of these companies or their technologies; they were late in the game and came in after the initial formation and development of many startup companies and their technologies.

For the most part, bankers survive and thrive in a parasitic capacity by profiting off the labor and intelligence of many gifted high-tech entrepreneurs.

What happened next? The bankers, who control the financial markets, withdrew any money they had in high-tech stocks and announced loudly through the media that all high-tech companies and their stocks were very much overvalued. This sent high-tech stock prices plummeting to all-time lows.

The media reported that the entire high-tech market crash was due to overinflated high-tech stock prices. The media's portrayal of the dot-com market collapse was just an uncontrollable popping of the high-tech bubble that affected all investors the same. That is what the media want the investors who lost their life savings to believe. As well, the special interests prefer a duped public to believe there are no evil forces behind and creating catastrophic stock market losses and collapses that financially drain the masses, as we have witnessed repeatedly the past several decades.

Herein lies the simplicity of how the high-tech reallocation of wealth and technology occurred during the dot-com era, which financially injured most investors and high-tech companies while profiting the few bankers with the power to orchestrate such events.

Many different venture capital funds invested in the high-tech industry with investors believing that the evaluations placed upon high-tech companies' stocks and futures were indicative of the value that the high-tech companies would be worth as the company created, developed, and commercialized its proprietary technology.

As discussed, many high-tech companies had corporate valuations based upon the number of visitors to a website, rather than revenue, earnings, and profit generated. Investors understood that the stock valuations of many companies were based on the potential and future expected revenue of the company and not the actual revenue companies were generating at the time of investment.

Google, for example, might have been losing money or making only a fraction of what it makes today, but its stock prices of the dot-com years reflected the future potential revenue, which was promised to come as soon as a proper revenue model for the company could be imagined and implemented.

Then one day in 1999, things started to drastically change. The powers-that-be desired to take control and buy ownership of the high-tech companies, but the price of these companies' stock was too high. Along came today's equivalent of the Rothschilds' messengers—the wonderfully controlled media.

The media, which for many years had been touting the great opportunities of investing in high-tech stocks, one day suddenly and without notice or warning, loudly reversed their opinion and position. They filled the airwaves, wildly decreeing the overvaluation of the same high-tech stocks it had praised only days before. The high-tech stocks predictably crashed, and the people on Main Street lost trillions while the rulers of Wall Street profited by virtually the same amount.

Day after day, week after week, and month after month, the media pounded the high-tech stocks until the prices had dropped to cost investors most everything they had invested. After the stock markets bottomed out, many of the bankers then capitalized and swooped in and purchased incredible technology companies at bargain-basement prices.

The plan was to purchase the high-tech companies and their technologies at a steal and then several months later have the media, once again, tout the great value and opportunity of the high-technology sector, causing stock prices to rebound and stabilize with predictability. The public relations strategy employed by the media caused a predictable increase of the high-tech stock prices, and that recently worthless stock, acquired at bargain-basement rates by the bankers, was now worth a fortune.

This was all just a repeat of the same method used in Rothschild's swindle of England's consol market in 1815. It's the same thing time and again, my friend; criminality in the financial markets has been going on for centuries.

The media crushed the confidence of a majority of high-tech investors who sold on the way down. As new management and ownership of the high-tech companies was acquired by the bankers, the ones directly responsible for orchestrating the high-tech stock market crash, the markets stabilized and began rebuilding.

Bankers, in concert with the media, gained ownership of high-tech dot-com companies without knowing the difference between a bit or a byte.

Control, however, is the main craving of those who hold the world's power. Control is exerted over the masses not for riches, for they have all the money and wealth of this planet; control is exerted over the masses to dominate and enslave the people. Power and domination are the ultimate concerns of humankind's never-satisfied financial oppressors.

Jefferson's ominous admonishment regarding the tricks and mechanisms of the private bankers comes to mind:

> *If the American people ever allow private banks to control the issue of their currency, first by inflation, then by deflation, the banks and corporations that will grow up around them will deprive the people of all property until their children wake up homeless on the continent their Fathers conquered. . . . I believe that banking institutions are more dangerous to our liberties than standing armies. The issuing power should be taken from the banks and restored to the people, to whom it properly belongs.*

Jefferson's insight and perspective ring as true today as when he wrote. Moreover, his warnings specifically apply to the bankers' influence and control of the world's stock exchanges, as well as the international currency and commodity markets.

Bankers inflate and then deflate the value not only of the high-tech companies but also of nearly all companies in the various financial markets. When the prices bottom out, the bankers swoop in and purchase the stock, taking control of the vulnerable companies. This is the traditional process of transferring ownership of the stock markets' public companies from the entrepreneurs who built the companies into the hands of the world's bankers. Since bankers put next to none of their own money into creating and developing startup companies, they avoid most of the risk by buying these incredible companies after they are established and at bargain-basement prices.

The avaricious banking crowd of Wall Street stifled the high-tech bonanza, and who knows how many great technologies fell by the wayside during those turbulent days. Many investors feel that these examples are unfathomable because most people are unaware of the constant conspiratorial activities perpetrated by Wall Street.

Do not feel dismayed if you have not noticed the activities of the oppressive market manipulators. Many people believe they should have known of the unethical manipulators, but this knowledge is buried deeply from society's view under many layers of confusion provided by the all-too-eager-to-assist media.

The people who control the economy operate with trillions of dollars at their disposal. When people have unlimited funds, eventually they buy everything and everyone who will assist them in their accumulation of even more power. Bankers debase the rest of the populace to the position of serfs and unwitting slaves.

Do people really think that powerful banking families want to relinquish any of their power after centuries of domination? They have devised the stock markets in particular, and the economy in general, to operate in such a manner that no matter what happens, at the end of the day, the bankers take all the money and rule all the people.

The stock market is an integral tool used to extract the wealth from the middle class and place it into the hands of the wealthiest members of society.

He who has the gold makes the rules, and the financial rules are far from fair.

CHAPTER 9

Government-Imposed Economic Slavery

No taxation without representation.
– SLOGAN OF THE US REVOLUTIONARY WAR

He, who passively accepts evil, is as much involved in it as he who helps to perpetrate it. He who accepts evil without protesting against it is really cooperating with it.
– DR. MARTIN LUTHER KING JR.

The individual is handicapped by coming face-to-face with a conspiracy so monstrous he cannot believe it exists.
– J. EDGAR HOOVER

Those who expect to reap the blessings of freedom, must, like men, undergo the fatigue of supporting it.
– THOMAS PAINE

We can easily forgive a child who is afraid of the dark; the real tragedy of life is when men are afraid of the light.
– PLATO

The injustices endured by black Americans at the hands of their government have no parallel in our history, not only during the period of slavery but also in the Jim Crow era that followed.
– JIM WEBB

Freedom means you are unobstructed in living your life as you choose. Anything less is a form of slavery.
– WAYNE DYER

For in reason, all government without the consent of the governed is the very definition of slavery.

– JONATHON SWIFT

If that form of government, that system of social order is not wrong—if those laws of the Southern States, by virtue of which slavery exists there, and is what it is, are not wrong—nothing is wrong.

– LEONARD BACON

L ET'S CONTINUE WITH THE THEME of government-imposed economic slavery and oppression. Imagine a group of people whose sole activities contribute to the deprivation of the public's financial stability. Now look at the Internal Revenue Service. Horrific abuses needlessly occur between the IRS and millions of Americans over the collection of alleged taxes that may or may not be owed.

A startling revelation to many taxpayers is that all the federal income taxes are used solely to pay the interest on the national debt. As you read earlier, this was the finding of the Grace Commission Report, requested in 1982 by President Reagan and delivered to him in 1984. The Grace Commission's conclusions were definitive. All federal income taxes are paid to the owners of the Federal Reserve to satisfy the fraudulent interest payments of the fraudulent national debt, which politicians created to enslave their constituents.

None of the tax revenue collected by the IRS is used for anything Americans commonly think of when they think of taxes; not a cent goes to building bridges and highways, repairing roads, paying for schools, or funding a myriad of social betterment programs.

In fact, without the Federal Reserve there would be no need for its private collection arm, known as the IRS, to harass the American people enforcing a very suppressive graduated income tax system. The IRS was exclusively created in order that the Federal Reserve System could covertly pillage Americans. Most people consider the IRS and the Federal Reserve System as separate entities when, in truth, they are one and the same; they are two suppressive entities simply operating in unison under different names to enforce the enslavement of virtually every American. The IRS's only loyalty is to the foreign banking families who own the Federal Reserve System and basically everything else in the world.

It is up to the people to keep the government honest. According to the Supreme Court, the government and the IRS can misinform the public through publications, documentation, and verbal communication. If citizens ask questions of the IRS or the federal government, the government and the IRS have the approval of the Supreme Court to lie openly and directly to the public. It is up to the populace to keep the government from erring and to keep the government functioning as intended. It is the duty of the citizenry to monitor and keep the government in check to ensure our freedoms and liberties are preserved. If we do not fulfill our obligations and protect our rights, ultimately we will have none.

A fantastic video exposing the methods employed by the IRS to dupe Americans into paying taxes, which in many cases they do not owe, is called Code Breaker Key to the Tax Code / One True Master of American Tax Law by David R. Myrland and can be watched at youtube.com/watch?v=bey0EfpKeiQ&nohtml15=False. For more of Myrland's incredible tax and other legal information, you can visit his site at takefromcaesar.us/TFC_FILES/PAGE_83/tutorial.htm. This is highly recommended for anyone wanting comprehensive data about the fraudulent shenanigans employed by the IRS to trap Americans into a corrupt and enslaving taxation system.

A society's freedoms are equal to the people's demand for freedom. Without a true desire and demand for freedom, man will eventually invite and accept slavery as a way of life.

The Supreme Court has directly bolstered the responsibility to keep the government honest and acting with integrity squarely upon the shoulders of its citizenry. It is up to every American to do our part to ensure we have a government that serves rather than enslaves.

You can visit freedom-school.com/tax-matters/debunking-irs-lies.html for addition and enlightening tax information.

Nothing in this chapter, or for that matter in this book, should be construed as legal or tax advice. The author is not an attorney, thank God, or a tax expert—despite having spent over two years reading the tax code for an average of fifteen hours per day.

One problem with understanding our rights under the Internal Revenue Code (IRC) is the complexity of the code, which consists of over seventy thousand pages. This makes it virtually impossible to find a bona fide tax expert that is familiar with all aspects of the code.

Many of the IRS agents operate oblivious to the IRC and simply follow their training, which consists of IRS procedures, regulations, and in-house manuals not based on the IRC but simply the application of collection activities that often disregard the laws of the land under Title 26 and the rights of the citizenry. See Ex IRS agent tells it like it is at youtube.com/watch?v=meRpmFuk4rE.

If one is interested in reading and exposing the fraud and abuses that are commonly undertaken by IRS agents, read the IRS's own book titled Criminal Investigation: Handbook for Special Agents. This is a fantastically revealing look into the deception the IRS uses to oppress Americans into paying taxes, which many believe, most Americans do not owe.

There is a warning or notice to agents on the cover of Criminal Investigation: Handbook for Special Agents, which reads "AGENTS . . . Our tax system is based on individual self-assessment and voluntary compliance . . . the material contained in this handbook is confidential in character. It must not under any circumstance be made available to persons outside the Service. Signed Mr. Mortimer Caplin, Internal Revenue Service Commissioner."

The above quote is astonishing proof that the IRS is intentionally misleading the American public in order to steal from and further bankrupt Americans and the nation.

Freedom Law School (livefreenow.org) and the Family Guardian (famguardian.org) have been challenging the IRS's activities for years and have accumulated volumes of information regarding a multitude of different tax issues and scenarios.

Many Americans find it horrifying that IRS agents feel that the US Constitution is irrelevant in their daily activities, and nowhere does this important national document allow for the implementation of a direct tax on the incomes of Americans.

Most of America's disdain for the IRS is because there seems to be little accountability for the revenue agents who regularly misapply the law. This is so blatant that a quick survey of the population reveals that far too many Americans have outright animosity and hatred for this group and those federal agents who regularly misapply the law.

Joe Stack had enough of the IRS wrecking his life and retaliated by flying his plane into an IRS building in Austin, Texas, killing himself and another person and causing a massive fire in the building. You might be surprised that the IRS building did not collapse and pancake to the ground, as the World Trade Center towers purportedly did.

What level of frustration does a man undergo that makes flying his plane into an IRS building seem like an appropriate solution to a tax problem? The IRS torments the lives of millions of Americans. The IRS progressive taxing scheme is more detrimental to the US economy than nearly any other financial device created to enslave humanity.

There must be more accountability in monitoring this out-of-control organization from the outside, as well as from within the government. One solution for America to recover economically is the total dissolution of the IRS and its Communist taxing policies. All taxation to support the federal government should comport with the Founding Fathers' writings in the US Constitution.

There should be no partial corrective actions employed when dealing with an organization that is destroying the fabric and liberties of American life. The continual fear that the IRS instills in the American population needs to be replaced by facts and the recognition that those who work for the IRS are in violation of their constitutional oaths of office and are enemies of the people, as well as the freedoms and liberties that were guaranteed in the founding of America.

Joe Stack is not a hero but a man at the end of his rope, put there by a ruthless and criminal conspiracy that extorts earnings from virtually every American. Joe Stack and his sentiments toward the IRS are symptomatic of a problem that has festered in America for far too long and to the detriment of the populace and for the benefit of the Federal Reserve. The Internal Revenue Service, right alongside with the Federal Reserve, should be dismantled to restore the economic freedoms America was built upon.

The IRS is a cancer to the American economy and the American way of life. As long as the IRS reigns, the prognosis for the United States is far from good. The IRS is a foreign agency and tool of the international bankers that must be removed from America, as it is treasonous and un-American in so many ways.

Several groups and organizations believe there is no obligation or law requiring ordinary Americans to file income taxes. Further, many Americans who have researched the tax code believe there is no law requiring them to file any tax forms annually.

Aaron Russo's America: Freedom to Fascism (youtube.com/watch? v=ZKeaw7HPG04) shows previous IRS Commissioner Sheldon Cohen being pressed by Russo with the question, "Is there a law requiring the average person to pay taxes?" Cohen did everything except provide an answer to that question because he knows there is no law requiring the American people to mandatorily pay federal income tax. That would be involuntary servitude, which is really a nice couple of words that essentially mean slavery.

It is interesting to discover that the following private corporations were designed to mislead and delude the American public; the government is no longer acting on behalf of the people, but is actually a government comprised of private corporations acting on behalf of their shareholders.

The state of Delaware's website at icis.corp.delaware.gov lists the following corporations as privately owned corporations:

Internal Revenue Tax and Audit Service (IRS)
For Profit General Delaware Corporation
Incorporation Date 7/12/33
File No. 0325720

Federal Reserve Association (Federal Reserve)
Non-profit Delaware Corporation
Incorporation Date 9/13/14
File No. 0042817

Central Intelligence Authority Inc. (CIA)
For Profit General Delaware Corporation
Incorporation Date 3/9/83
File No. 2004409

Since we nationalized the automobile and banking industries under Obama's rule, why not just nationalize the above corporations and save everyone a lot of grief? The economic stimulus and recovery would be sped up incredibly.

Here are some more interesting private corporations:

Federal Land Acquisition Corp.
For-profit General Delaware Corporation
Incorporation Date 8/22/80

File No. 0897960
RTC Commercial Assets Trust 1995-NP3-2
For-profit Delaware Statutory Trust
Incorporation Date 10/24/95
File No. 2554768
Social Security Corp., Dept. of Health, Education and Welfare
For-profit General Delaware Corporation
Incorporation Date: 11/13/89
File No. 2213135
United States of America, Inc.
Non-profit or religious Delaware Corporation
Incorporation Date 4/19/89 File No. 2193946

You can visit Colonel Wilson's coppermoonshinestills.com/id71.html, and we thank the colonel for allowing the use of the above information. According to Wilson, you can become a state rather than a US citizen. As a bonus, if you are into the whole moonshine thing, check out the artfully crafted distilling products on Wilson's website.

Most people might find it quite a revelation that what we thought of as the US government is actually a nexus of for-profit private corporations. We should realize that these are corporations pretending to be the US government and not the actual government.

The United States has become a de facto government that was originally created as a de jure government. A de jure government is a government created by and for the people and their interests; a de jure government is a government by right and legitimate claim. A de facto government is a corporation posing as a government, a government by fact only, not right or claim. A de facto government is the kind of government that presently exists in the United States.

Most people have an insufficient view of history to be able to understand the environment in which they live. It is imperative that we the people discover the true history of this country and not some romantic version, blindly taught and indoctrinated in the nation's public schools.

Without a historical understanding, a person has no foundation with which to understand the present-day environment. It is of the utmost importance for every American to fully understand the morphing of the de jure US government, a true government of, by, and for the people, into a private corporation or de facto government, designed to benefit only its criminal stockholders and not every American.

Returning to the IRS, some rightfully believe this is one of the most despicable and detrimental private corporation whose mere existence and its enslaving policies are destroying the nation's economy. There are some interesting mathematical facts associated with taxation that need to be examined to fully understand the damage perpetuated by the Communist, graduated-income taxing scheme implemented today across America.

Let it be perfectly clear that the IRS is not the problem. The IRS is the necessary collection arm of the private bankers of the Federal Reserve System, which is one of the organizations that is destroying America and the world.

If it were not for the IRS stripping and plundering trillions of dollars annually from the US economy and its citizens, the United States and the entire world would suffer incredible hyperinflation.

As long as citizens permit a private class of people, mainly the private international banking families of the Federal Reserve, to print money out of thin air and charge the United States interest on that money, the enslavement of the American people will endure. In order for such a debilitating enslavement system to survive and to continue to rob the American people of their wealth, the American people simply need to remain silent as we are.

America's economy uses fiat money; therefore, it needs a suppressive tax system to remove excess funds from the economy in an attempt to stifle hyperinflation and protect whatever perceived value remains of the Federal Reserve Note. In order to avoid hyperinflation using a fiat money system, the Federal Reserve must manipulate and constrict the money supply in the short term by raising interest rates. As one would imagine, this old economic trick is neither as dependable nor as reliable when applied to affect a national economy that has a gigantic national debt like the United States.

Our nation's economic stability is getting exponentially harder to control using the available tools of the Federal Reserve. The true solution is for the United States to regain its ability to regulate and issue its own real money that is backed by gold and silver.

Controlling and adjusting the US economy forty years ago compared to today is like holding a little kitten's tail compared to holding the tail of a six-hundred-pound Bengal tiger. You can make a couple of mistakes holding a little kitten's tail and live to see tomorrow.

The problem we face is that people focus on the IRS as the bad guys when, in essence, they are a necessary evil to assist the criminal, bought-and-paid-for politicians, who allow private bankers to usurp America's economic and monetary systems.

When examining the taxing methods of state and local taxing organizations, one soon learns some interesting aspects regarding our economy as a whole. When we mandatorily tax the entire population of a nation, the taxing organization responsible for collecting these taxes will eventually control all the money in any given economy.

The Founding Fathers understood that control of the economy would be overtaken by the taxing agencies should an all-encompassing tax scheme be allowed in America. They only allowed taxes for a small section of the economy as enumerated in the Constitution:

ARTICLE 1 SECTION 2 CLAUSE 3— LIMITS ON CONGRESS

Direct Taxes shall be apportioned among the several States which may be included within this Union, according to their respective Numbers, which shall be determined by adding to the whole Number of free Persons, including those bound to Service for a Term of Years, and excluding Indians not taxed, three fifths of all other Persons.

ARTICLE 1 SECTION 8 CLAUSE 1— POWERS OF CONGRESS

The Congress shall have Power To lay and collect Taxes, Duties, Impost and Excises, to pay the Debts and provide for the common Defense and general Welfare of the United States; but all Duties, Imposts and Excises shall be uniform throughout the United States; Article 1, Section 8, Clause 17 expounds further, outlining the geographical limits of the power of Congress as follows:

To exercise exclusive Legislation in all Cases whatsoever, over such District (not exceeding ten Miles square) as may, by Cession of particular

States, and the acceptance of Congress, become the Seat of the Government of the United States, and to exercise like Authority over all Places purchased by the Consent of the Legislature of the State in which the Same shall be, for the Erection of Forts, Magazines, Arsenals, dock-Yards, and other needful Buildings;

ARTICLE 1 SECTION 9 CLAUSE 4— LIMITS ON CONGRESS

No capitation, or other direct, Tax shall be laid, unless in Proportion to the Census or Enumeration herein before directed to be taken.

Many believe that they are paying their fair share when it comes to taxes but what is all that tax being used for? As mentioned above, all money that Americans pay to the IRS is exclusively going to pay the interest of the national debt to the foreign families that own the Federal Reserve, period.

In essence, everyone who pays tax in the United States is working a good portion of the year for a handful of suppressive families who own the Federal Reserve. Americans allow a miniscule group of people to enslave our entire nation. It is utterly ridiculous and totally irresponsible for the people to allow this tiny criminal group to enslave the cowed and frightened people of the United States. Stand up, Americans. No one else will do it for us.

Unfortunately, under the current taxation system thrust upon Americans, there are no remaining funds that are used to pay for the schools, for paving roads, or for the other infrastructure and social programs that we need to invest in as a nation. The local property tax pays for the schools, and the gas tax handles the road repairs, etc.

After paying the interest to the international bankers, there is no remainder of federal income tax funds going toward the improvement of society or making America a greater nation. All tax funds leave the country and are used exclusively for servicing only the interest of the federal government's debt.

If the government needs more money to pay for programs, it prints it. Instead of printing national dollar bills backed by metal, the Congress sorely chooses to allow the Federal Reserve to lend the US money at exorbitant and devastating prices. It would be much better for the United States if we just printed real money and told the Federal Reserve to take a hike. Why are we paying trillions to criminal bankers that simply do fancy accounting to deceive and enslave the people? Time to wake up, America!

Tax money removed from the national economy, contrary to the advice and writings of the Founding Fathers, is a detriment to each American and his or her posterity. Americans are going to be complete slaves, unduly bearing a greater and greater tax burden, unless we decide to start acting like Americans. We need to replace the corrupt fiat banking and taxation systems with a monetary system that uses real, redeemable money and a taxation system limited to tariffs, imposts, and other custom-inspection services and the like.

The United States needs to print its own money, as Lincoln and Kennedy mandated just prior to their assassinations. The Federal Reserve System and the Internal Revenue Service are treasonous organizations that we need to extricate and forever ban from the United States.

Please review the above resources regarding the IRS to discover additional reading, specifically for the handling of individual tax situations. It is time to stand against the tyranny that we all face, but first we may have to take our heads out of the sand.

There are many interesting discussions based on whether or not taxes are owed by any Americans to a foreign group of banking oppressors who have circumvented the nation's prescribed form of money as described in the US Constitution, government-issued money that is backed by substantive metals and not created out of thin air.

It remains easy to understand that the Founding Fathers had a very limited perspective of the federal government's taxing privileges. Today, those taxing privileges have expanded to the detriment of America's economy and its standing in the world economy.

The Founding Fathers agreed to allow apportioned taxes, as well as avoidable or indirect taxes: imposts and tariffs. These methods of taxation were intentionally designed to keep the federal government small and under the thumb of the individual states and their populace. Today's behemoth federal government is the direct result of allowing the taxing methods of the IRS to fundamentally rob and pillage every working-class American.

Under the Constitution, there is no universal taxing authority given to Congress to directly tax individual citizens' labor. The Founding Fathers believed that the power to tax is the power to destroy. What fools we have become to fall for the chicanery and the deceptive legislation that has led to hundreds of millions of people paying taxes that, many believe, they are not obligated to pay. The tax code is a very large and intentionally unintelligible document, written to prevent the average citizens from discovering the extent of the criminality and the swindle perpetrated against every American annually on April 15.

Unexamined myths are often more dangerous to humanity than enforced brutality. Americans have fallen for the lies that the government is constantly disseminating because we fail to conduct adequate due diligence of our government, which is the duty of every citizen of this great land.

The venerable John F. Kennedy stated, "The great enemy of truth is very often not the lie—deliberate, contrived and dishonest—but the myth—persistent, persuasive and unrealistic. Too often we hold fast to the clichés of our forebears. We subject all facts to a prefabricated set of interpretations. We enjoy the comfort of opinion without the discomfort of thought."

Most Americans never bother to read the tax code simply because it is mostly confusing, incomprehensible, somewhat challenging, and above all, incredibly boring. How are taxpayers supposed to comply with a tax code that they cannot understand? How is the government supposed to comply with and enforce a tax code that it does not understand?

Many of us do not understand the incomprehensible IRS tax code, yet most Americans believe they are somehow bound to obey whatever the IRS tells them to do, even if it means handing over their life savings to such a rogue organization. Why do Americans pay taxes to a rogue, highly corrupt, and incompetent government when many people believe they are not even obligated or required to pay taxes under law? Could it be fear that motivates us away from standing against tyranny? We have to ask, what kind of government are we afraid of and why?

The United States outlawed involuntary slavery, but voluntary slavery lives in the hearts, minds, and lives of the ignorant and uninformed.

The drudgery and burden encountered by having our labor taxed is only a small reason why we should not allow the government to institute a universal and graduated income tax. The government was not created, neither is it entitled, to rule the lives of Americans. The US government was originally created to serve the people. Now with its behemoth size, it has become the enemy of every freedom-loving American.

We have allowed a usurped and infiltrated government to abuse Americans and to impose tyrannical and unconstitutional policies that benefit the few, while enslaving the masses of good-hearted and unsuspecting people.

The constitutionally imposed limitations on the federal government —restricting the activities that the government may partake in—were crafted to protect the people. Any powers not enumerated in the Constitution and delineated directly to the federal government are reserved for the states or the people.

The US Constitution's Tenth Amendment stipulates:

The powers not delegated to the United States by the Constitution, nor prohibited by it to the States, are reserved to the States respectively, or to the people.

This is the Constitution's limiting caveat meant to ensure that the federal government remains under the control of the people and is never allowed to expand its power to tyrannize the states and their citizens.

The IRS taxation scheme that is employed today gives a magnitude of power to the federal government that the Constitution does not authorize it to possess. When the government incorporates an unconstitutional taxation scheme, which taxes every American without apportionment or authority, it has obtained control over the economy in order to enslave the people.

Many find this claim to be an exaggeration, but a mathematical model demonstrates that, when a limited or fixed taxation rate is applied against the working class, all the money of the economy will eventually end up in the hands of those who are imposing the tax.

Today's graduated income and sales taxes are literally government-sanctioned forms of theft. The US federal tax rate is the highest of any country in the world, and it becomes shocking how much money the IRS steals every year from American workers.

Below, we can see what happens to an economy that has a total money supply of $1,000 when a 10 percent tax is applied to each transaction. This system works similarly for any size economy at any tax rate. The same end result is total theft from the nation; it just takes a longer time to steal all the money using a lower tax rate. Here is an example of the pillage and plunder that occurs in our economy.

Economy	Total Tax Taken (10 percent of economy)
$1,000	$100
$900	$100 + $90 = $190
$810	$190 + $81 = $271
$729	$271 + $72 = $343
$656	$343 + $65 = $408
$590	$408 + $59 = $467
$531	$467 + $53 = $520
$478	$520 + $47 = $567

One thousand dollars are taxed, and $100 are removed from the overall economy and placed into the hands of the taxing agency. Then $900 are spent, and $90 additional money is extracted from the economy. This continues, and soon it becomes apparent what a massive and parasitic theft is occurring. This unjust taxation method simply transfers the wealth of the people to the privileged and special class that does nothing but enrich itself from taxing our labor and transactions.

How deep does the rabbit hole go? In the above simplified example, one sees what will eventually occur as the government removes 10 percent from the economy every time money is spent. It takes seven cycles of taxation in this example before more than half the economy's money is under the control of the taxing agency.

This system will eventually lead to having virtually no money in the economy, except for that possessed by the taxing agencies, unless the bankers and/or the government re-injects additional fiat currency into the economy. The return of fiat money back into the US economy occurs primarily through the country's fiscal policy, in accordance with the spending dictates of the Congress.

Federal Reserve Notes, printed by the US Bureau of Engraving and Printing, are sold to the Federal Reserve System at bargain-basement prices; it pays 2.6 cents each to cover the printing cost, no matter if the denomination is a one-, five-, ten-, twenty-, fifty-, or one-hundred-dollar bill. That being the case, each hundred-dollar bill that the Federal Reserve buys for 2.6 cents equates to an instant profit, a little over $99.97; and it has the audacity to charge the United States interest as well. If I could buy an unlimited amount of one-dollar bills for 2.6 cents each, I would be an incredibly wealthy guy!

The United States has transferred its most important right and duty to the Federal Reserve, leaving its people paupers and penniless.

If the United States simply took back control, regulating and issuing the US money in accordance with its inherent responsibilities and obligations under the Constitution, the US government would immediately emancipate all Americans from financial tyranny and slavery imposed by the Federal Reserve. For the preservation of freedom, the power to print, regulate, and control our nation's money supply rightfully belongs to the US government and not the Federal Reserve.

Getting back to the above example, the taxing authority actually retains the majority of money and the controlling interest in the economy after only seven taxation cycles. This example applies to all economies that have tax collection agencies, similar to or under the international umbrella of the Internal Revenue Service.

When you factor in the yearly removal of 30–35 percent of America's money supply by means of the federal income tax, you can easily see the vast reallocation of funds and wealth from the entirety of the working class into the hands of thieves.

As time marches forward and the federal deficit increases to exponentially higher amounts, the tax rate of 30–35 percent of earned income may necessarily increase under the graduated income tax scheme in order for the United States to even have the slightest chance of keeping current in paying only the interest on the national debt.

It really is not our debt; it is the government's debt. The big trick was to get the people to believe that it's theirs and not the politicians' debt. This is financial enslavement.

If the above taxation example were to continue, the taxing authorities would eventually receive virtually all the money within the economy. The way that this economy perpetuates and continues to have any money at all is that the government decides how much money it is going to spend back into the economy on programs that some say are unfairly accessed and used by different segments of the population.

The control of the economy and its money system is predicated upon conspiring and treasonous government officials who allow, protect, and dedicate themselves to ensure the continuation of the privately owned, fantastically corrupted, and viciously controlled monetary system that enslaves this world. This system of financial enslavement continues to batter and bludgeon humanity in concert with the dictates of some of the world's most depraved, deceitful, and duplicitous betrayers of humankind.

Keynesian economics is based on the theories of John Maynard Keynes, a British economist of the twentieth century. One of the basic philosophies of Keynesian economics is that free enterprise is a wild and unruly system, which leads to instability in the overall economy, resulting in and characterized by fluctuating periods of inflation and deflation.

According to Keynes, these money supply fluctuations of inflation and deflation are the result of the private sector's inability to control the economy without government or third-party intervention. Therefore, the active participation of a third-party economic managerial agency is necessary to control the perceived value of money and to ensure the stability of the US and world's economies.

The federal government by itself can monitor and avoid fluctuations of inflation and deflation without the outside impetus or assistance of an outside third party. To Americans, there is no advantage in having an outside entity control the monetary system of the United States, only disadvantage and enslavement.

The active participation of the federal government in any part of the economic affairs of the citizens is not granted by the Constitution.

Instead of minding its financial business, the government has allowed the privatization of its money system in direct violation of the US Constitution. The federal government should assume its rightful duties to the American people, retake control, and issue a US, interest-free, value-backed dollar.

To remove international financial suppression, Presidents Lincoln and Kennedy printed US Notes interest free, and the economy immediately flourished. In retaliation, the bankers found it fitting to assassinate these great American heroes.

Every day of our lives, the government is committing treason against the American people, and the politicians are in violation of their oaths to uphold the US Constitution by the continuation of a private, foreign-controlled, monetary and banking system. Politicians' abandonment of their duty by allowing private banks to control the US economy makes it necessary for the federal government to devise unconstitutional methods of taxation to extract ever-increasing amounts of money by continually siphoning America's wealth into the pockets of the twelve foreign, private banking families.

After selling out America and the American Dream to the bankers, we are reminded again of Woodrow Wilson's solemn confession where he stated, "I am a very unhappy man. I have unwittingly ruined my country. A great industrial nation is now controlled by its system of credit. We are no longer a government by free opinion, no longer a government by conviction and the vote of the majority, but a government by the opinion and duress of a small group of dominant men."

By the way, I feel Americans should pay every penny they truly owe to the IRS and not a penny more or less. There are a lot of opinions and contradictory information regarding the IRS, or Aunt Iris, as a couple of my country boys say, so be careful as you tread in unfamiliar and shark-infested waters.

For interesting historical information pertaining to the IRS, the Citizens for Better Government (afn.org/~govern/IRSkinny.html) describe the clandestine history of the IRS and its supposed legitimacy or illegitimacy.

Those having tax difficulties might enjoy and benefit from reading Chris Hansen's The Great Income Tax Hoax: Why We Don't Owe Income Tax. If you have the opportunity to study Hanson's work, it is quite informative and useful to understanding the duplicitous operation of the Internal Revenue Service. It gives a hundred questions you might want the IRS to answer to clarify any confusion you may have.

As mentioned, the simplest approach for understanding our obligations under the tax code that I have found is discussed in the hour-and-a-half video Key to the Code by David Myrland.

There are millions of different points of view regarding the IRS's tax policies and procedures. America taxpayers must have their own reasons for believing why they should or should not file taxes every year. Most people's tax beliefs are usually based upon misinformation and ignorance. Most people who pay taxes have never read one paragraph of the Internal Revenue Code, nor have they bothered to discover whether or not they meet the parameters that define who and what a taxpayer is under the Internal Revenue Code.

Ignorance to a larger degree is exemplified when hundreds of millions of people volunteer to pay their taxes, unaware of their rights, obligations, and responsibilities to themselves, their families, and their fellow Americans.

The United States of America was conceived, created, and preserved by the spilled blood of patriots to prevent the enslavement of Americans through burdensome and oppressive taxation schemes. The Founding Fathers worked to ensure future generations would be free from enslavement through unjust taxation. This was a principal reason countless patriots fought and died—in order that the celestial ideals of America would live on and pass to the next generation.

With minor study of the subject, the American public will become much more informed of their actual duties under federal tax law and hopefully act accordingly to preserve the great ideals of America for generations to come.

Informed opinions regarding the IRS develop after the examination of facts, not on the hearsay of others or the malarkey heard on daily news stories. The old platitude proclaims two things are unavoidable in life, death and taxes. One must wonder who started this rumor in order to gain the citizens' compliance to pay taxes.

Whether Americans owe taxes or not seems somewhat immaterial to many but is vastly important to all. The IRS's history, along with our relation to this monolithic corporation, needs to be understood by asking more questions and getting exact answers from the government. Some government workers hate to answer our questions because they fully understand and know, deep in their hearts, the fraud they are committing against the American people.

What type of opportunities are the majority of Americans losing by just robotically paying federal taxes without examination of the mountains of information contained within the Internal Revenue Code? Aside from a quick consulting with an accountant—a person who makes a living off other people's taxes—most people never even question their tax status and responsibilities under the tax code. Imagine if a majority of Americans have no liability to the IRS and yet are duped into paying taxes they do not even owe!

People should ask their accountant several questions to raise their understanding of the tax code before writing a check to the IRS.

Where in the code does it specify who or what class of individuals are liable to pay federal tax? Where is the agreement between you and the IRS that states that every year you will hand over a small fortune to the

IRS? Where is the IRS's definition for income in the tax code? Where is the law requiring one to file a 1040 form? What is the jurisdiction and definition of the United States in the Internal Revenue Code? What is the geographical location and definition of the United States under the code? Why does the IRS always fail to include paragraph A and only includes from paragraph B forward when it is levying property or wages in direct conflict to section 6331 of the IRS code (26 USC 6331)?

Every American should pay any money legitimately owed to the government and not a penny more or less. It behooves us to ask questions until we understand our exact obligation, if any, to pay taxes.

It makes little sense to operate on a lack of information, no matter the field of study or endeavor. Success sides with the intelligent and knowledgeable more plentifully and frequently than with the obtuse. Can one imagine a person attempting to wire a house without studying electricity? That would be an undoubtedly shocking and hazardous experience.

The validity of the tax code and the legality of the IRS to enforce it are personal judgments and decisions everyone must make for his or her own well-being and the well-being of this nation.

If you ever receive a letter from the IRS, it is actually a test to see what you know and what you are made of as a person. Will you blindly fail or pass the test? Will you demand to know the legitimacy of the claims levied against you by demanding proof of the IRS's claim? Will you pay without learning a thing or two about the fairness or absence of it in America's enslaving tax system?

We should support our government only when it is responsible, is held accountable, and represents the interests of the population it serves. To support and fund a tyrannical government, which serves only the needs of the rich and those eviscerating the liberties of the masses, is suicidal for the masses. Financially supporting an unethical and tyrannical government is equivalent to financing our own enslavement and demise.

The American population is continuing to finance its own destruction through the taxes it pays into a non-representative form of government. Watch the incredible seminar by Mark Passio, Natural Law: the Real Law of Attraction, at youtube.com/watch?v=C1pkJaNbzLU This is one of the most important videos in this book, as well as on the entire Internet; it's well worth your time to study natural law.

To ignore the demands of the masses has been and will always be the cause of political revolt. There is a line that kleptocracies cross that makes it blatantly evident that those wielding power are destroying the lives of the masses while enriching themselves and their friends. We already crossed that line in America and unfortunately realize the depths of destruction thrust upon Americans through unfair, government-imposed taxation and economic slavery.

Unfair taxation is hardly the American Dream for which our ancestors sacrificed and died. We have ignored our responsibilities and have squandered the American Dream. We are as unappreciative and undeserving as a generation can be for allowing politicians to steal the liberties and freedoms of all Americans.

Americans need to get off their knees and stand up for the American Dream. Too many of our military men and woman have ultimately sacrificed, fighting to preserve America's unparalleled glory, until their last breath. To abandon one's duties as an American stains the memories of the great men and women who sacrificed and died upholding the glory and ideals of this great nation.

Let it be said that America's torch of liberty burnt brighter because of the commitment and courage of our generation. Let it be said that we stomped evil and tyranny from the land. Let it be written that Americans have not turned their backs on themselves, their families, and the future of all humankind. Let it be written that Americans joined and stood in the face of seemingly unconquerable odds and prevailed against a wickedness that breathes no more.

CHAPTER 10

The FDA Passes Poison;
Politicians Get Rich

If you can't feed a hundred people, then just feed one.
                                        – MOTHER THERESA

You don't need a silver fork to eat good food.
                                        – PAUL PRUDHOMME

People remember two things on their deathbed, the great meals they've eaten and the friends they've shared them with.
                                        – MARY NELL

If people let the Government decide what foods to eat and what medicines to take, their bodies will soon be in as sorry a state as the souls who live under tyranny.
                                        – THOMAS JEFFERSON

Life expectancy would grow by leaps and bounds if green vegetables smelled as good as bacon.
                                        – DOUG LARSON

There is no sincerer love than the love of food.
                                        – GEORGE BERNARD SHAW

Food is our common ground, a universal experience.
                                        – JAMES BEARD

One cannot think well, love well, sleep well, if one has not dined well.
                                        – VIRGINIA WOOLF

Tell me what you eat, and I'll tell you who you are.

        – JEAN ANTHELME BRILLAT-SAVARIN

Let's keep the chemists over here and the food over here, that's my feeling. What do I know? But a big aspect of fast food is their ability to artificially taint the colors and the smells and stuff to stimulate appetite.

        – GREG KINNEAR

Open your refrigerator, your freezer, your kitchen cupboards, and look at the labels on the food. You'll find "natural flavor" or "artificial flavor" in just about every list of ingredients. The similarities between these two broad categories are far more significant than the differences.

        – DAVID CHANG

On Christmas Day 1859, the Victorian Acclimatization Society released 24 rabbits into the Australian countryside so that settlers could hunt them for sport and feel more "at home." The rabbits multiplied to well over 200 million, spreading out over 4 million square kilometers. That Christmas present now costs Australian agriculture about $600 million per year.

        – JEFFREY SMITH

Food compulsion isn't a character disorder, it's a chemical disorder.

        – ROBERT ATKINS

Research has shown that even in small amounts, processed food alters the chemical balance in our brain and cause [sic] negative mood swings along with noticeable dips in energy.

        – MARILU HENNER

I know how hard it is for you to put food on your family.

        – GEORGE W. BUSH

I know human being and fish can coexist peacefully.

        – GEORGE W. BUSH

Life's just much too hard today, I hear every mother say, the pursuit of happiness just seems a bore, and if you take more of those, you will get an overdose, no more running to the shelter of a mother's littler helper, they just helped you on your way, through your busy dying day.

— MICK JAGGER AND KEITH RICHARDS

IT IS TIME FOR THE PSYCHOTIC GOVERNMENT'S CONTROL over people's lives and their bodies to end. Now is the time for people to question and challenge the authorities that are injecting poisons into the world's food supply and ecological systems. Irreparable harm to the ecology of the planet is created when scientists play God and introduce bastardized genetic mutations into the natural environment.

The mission statement of the US Food and Drug Administration (FDA) states:

> FDA is responsible for protecting the public health by assuring the safety, efficacy and security of human and veterinary drugs, biological products, medical devices, our nation's food supply, cosmetics, and products that emit radiation.

> FDA is also responsible for advancing the public health by helping to speed innovations that make medicines more effective, safer, and more affordable and by helping the public get the accurate, science-based information they need to use medicines and foods to maintain and improve their health. FDA also has responsibility for regulating the manufacturing, marketing and distribution of tobacco products to protect the public health and to reduce tobacco use by minors.

> FDA also plays a significant role in the Nation's counterterrorism capability. FDA fulfills this responsibility by ensuring the security of the food supply and by fostering development of medical products to respond to deliberate and naturally emerging public health threats.

The FDA is in charge of adjudicating what is allowed to be consumed by and placed on Americans' bodies. An interesting fact is that Congress has classified Americans' bodies as government property, subject to laws the FDA enforces.

The FDA supposedly has the responsibility and purpose of ensuring that the food and medicines produced are beneficial and not harmful for human consumption and use. Consumers ingest and suffer FDA-approved foods, medicines and treatments in the hope that these often-poisonous concoctions will cure what ails them.

The FDA is supposed to operate independently of the corporations that it oversees in order to perform its duties in a just and ethical manner, on behalf of and for the protection of the health of the American people. If morally administrated, the FDA would assure all Americans that the medicines and treatments delivered by the medical community are safe and cause no damage to the patient.

The FDA is incredibly negligent in the performance of its duties to the detriment of virtually every American. It is a horrible fact that a corrupt FDA contributes to shortening Americans' lives. It is unforgivable for the FDA to rob us of our most precious gifts of health and life. The unconscionable actions of the FDA are exceeded only by the boundless pain and suffering inflicted upon millions of patients in America's healthcare system. It is vital that we demand better service and performance from this incredibly broken bureaucratic institution.

FDA approval of dangerous medicines and treatments that it knows will kill and shorten the lives of those consuming such products is gravely unacceptable and is a direct violation of the people's health and their trust. Investigation of this agency is urgently needed in order to remove those persons responsible for allowing deadly medicines, food additives, and genetically modified organisms (GMOs) into people's lives and bodies without properly informing US consumers of the related risks and dangers to our bodies, our environment, and our species.

It should be illegal for a person to work at the FDA approving products for the pharmaceutical, chemical, or any other industries that develop harmful medicines or genetically modified foods and then later be given private employment with the very same companies whose products were given the FDA's seal of approval for human consumption.

The revolving-door policy of government employment and the quid pro quo financial opportunities, which are always tempting corrupt politicians who assist the massive food and drug companies, are responsible for the ethical disintegration of the FDA and the poor quality of artificial foods, deadly medicines, and barbaric treatments inflicted upon American society. This revolving-door policy between the corporations and the government is evident to anyone who would like to investigate the subject at rense.com/general33/fd.htm.

I would like to thank Jeff Rense for his outstanding humanitarian efforts to inform and educate people on topics commonly missing from the nightly news. He is a true American patriot and a great person. You can visit Rense.com for many interesting perspectives and maybe discover just how deep the rabbit hole goes.

It happens far too often that a person in authority at the FDA will retire and quickly land a fantastic job at a food or pharmaceutical company, often a company for which he or she oversaw, assisted, and ensured FDA approval of the company's harmful products. Many former employees of the FDA obtain outlandishly lavish employment with those same companies, for favors performed while employed by the FDA. At best, a highly questionable kickback occurs between the FDA and many large corporations, which happen to need FDA approval of their products.

Is it right, ethical, or even legal for a former FDA executive, upon leaving public office, to receive a huge salary with extravagant bonuses as payback for favors done while under the employment of the US government?

The other direction of the revolving door pays just as well. Many food and pharmaceutical company corporate executives land jobs in strategic government positions in order to draft FDA policy and regulations that conform to the needs and wants of the behemoth food and drug companies.

Donald Rumsfeld, as duplicitous as they come, while serving as the point man for Searle Pharmaceutical, received the blessing of the FDA and obtained approval for aspartame to be added to Americans' foods and drinks. Aspartame is a sweetening additive found in thousands of products on supermarket shelves across America.

Although aspartame had encountered severe opposition from the FDA for over a decade, Rumsfeld utilizing his connections, got aspartame approved by the FDA. Aspartame became the FDA-approved additive of choice for many massive food and beverage producers. For further insight, I recommend How Aspartame Became Legal: The Timeline by Rich Murray (rense.com/general33/legal.htm).

Aspartame is often described as the most deadly food additive ever passed by the FDA. Research indicates that aspartame turns into formaldehyde as it warms shortly after it contacts the acids of the stomach. According to Holistic Med, there has been an increase in aspartame users claiming severe toxic reactions, including seizures, confusion, severe migraine headaches, eye damage, and vision loss. Only studies funded by Monsanto, the manufacturer and owner of aspartame at the time, showed no health problems, according to Ralph Walton, MD, chairman of the Center for Behavioral Medicine. Monsanto has since sold the NutraSweet Company to J. W. Childs.

Holistic Med provides an analytical breakdown of NutraSweet—a brand name for aspartame—as it enters the body. According to Holistic Med, NutraSweet initially breaks down into methanol, commonly known as wood alcohol. Methanol is quickly converted by the body into formaldehyde, the same chemical used for the preservation of corpses during the embalming process.

Could it be that giant chemical companies are suddenly interested in the preservation of people's bodies?

Some believe there exists a correlation between ingesting aspartame and developing the highly incapacitating and debilitating multiple sclerosis. If one sees someone ingesting three or more diet drinks a day, there is a possibility one is looking at a future candidate of multiple sclerosis. Many highly acclaimed professionals assert such dangerous claims regarding aspartame. See fda.gov/ohrms/DOCKETS/dailys/03/Jan03/012203/02P-03 17_emc-000196.txt.

Can one imagine the damage that is occurring to millions of Americans who are drinking diet soft drinks as their bodies are inundated with formaldehyde and other deadly toxins that the FDA approved? Is it any wonder that men have a 50 percent chance of dying of cancer and women have over a 33 percent chance of dying the same miserable death? Today's cancer rates greatly exceed the cancer rates of a generation ago.

Aspartame is one of thousands of products approved by the FDA that may be harmful to humans. The poisoning of America really took shape when Bush Sr. was in power. Bush Sr.'s administration had a unique relationship with Monsanto and many other companies, including pharmaceutical giant, Eli Lilly, the manufacturer of Prozac. (Additional information regarding Prozac comes later in this chapter.)

Food, Inc. (2008) is a fantastic documentary discussing Monsanto's genetically modified foods. It is available for purchase on Amazon and is well worth the price.

As mentioned before, it is no secret that there is, and has been for many years, a revolving door of hiring between many of the departments established by the federal government and the corporations that the government has the responsibility to oversee and regulate. Consider the golden triangle of the FDA, which includes the giant pharmaceutical, chemical, and food companies.

Conflict of interest, corruption, and kickbacks are commonplace inside Washington's Beltway. For any true representation to occur on behalf of the American people, criminality of this magnitude needs to discontinue immediately. If this corruption continues, we need to indict the bad actors for the crime of treason against the United States. The utmost integrity concerning government positions is paramount if the American people are to obtain proper and healthy representation by the federal government.

An interesting story is that of Michael Taylor, an attorney and former FDA deputy commissioner of policy. This position develops the governing policy on topics such as food and drug-warning labels. Monsanto, the leader in genetically modified organisms employed Taylor. His resume can be read at Wikipedia's website at en.wikipedia.org/wiki/Michael_R._Taylor. He allegedly assisted in implementing policy that was beneficial for Monsanto and detrimental to the diet of natural food-eating members of the human species.

Much controversy exists about allowing Monsanto and other companies to sell their GMOs and DNA-modified food products, including GMO soybeans, GMO corn, GMO apples, GMO salmon, and GMO high-fructose corn syrup, which we find in thousands of processed foods. For more information, visit foodandwaterwatch.org and see how difficult it is to avoid ingesting GMOs. Food and Water Watch claims, "In 2014, 93% of corn and 94% of soybean acres in the U.S. were GMO, and these crops sneak into your food in places you might not expect, from high-fructose corn syrup to sugar (made from sugar beets) to chemicals made from soybeans are used as additives in processed foods."

There is no federal labeling requirement in America warning or informing the end consumer, the one ingesting the food, that most food products in America's supermarkets contain GMOs. GMO high-fructose corn syrup is in a majority of processed foods that are commonly found in supermarket chains and in our bellies. GMO corn is often a substitute for other staples, such as wheat and flour. The GMO corn industry is massive and manufactures a vast array of ingredients used throughout the food industry. These GMO-laced foods are purchased without any declaration or notification to the unwitting consumers, who unknowingly feed DNA-modified organisms to themselves and their families.

Genetically modified plants are designed to withstand poisons that would ordinarily kill natural or non-GMO plants. GMOs, including plants that can tolerate high levels of toxins, may act as impelling agents and absorb toxins from the soil and fertilizer. Consuming GMOs allegedly contributes to the population's ingestion of certain toxins not found in natural foods.

If given the choice to eat GMO corn or natural non-GMO corn, pigs choose the natural corn every time. Still the FDA does not demand that GMO manufacturers label their foods as being or containing GMOs. If pigs chose the natural food over GMOs, humans should at least be given the same choice. We need notice and labels describing what kind of food we are buying and ingesting.

America needs to start demanding and requiring proper GMO labeling of its food. It is unethical and immoral to an incalculable degree that American consumers do not have the opportunity to make an informed decision to either ingest GMOs or not. It is beyond reckless and completely unjustifiable that the FDA fails to demand that GMOs are accordingly labeled for the benefit of the people. However, the government does not work for the people; it works for the corporations.

What if we were to discover, years from the date of introduction of GMOs into the food chain, that consumers of GMOs died at an alarming rate from DNA-related malfunctions? What if these human DNA-related malfunctions suddenly were discovered to affect the health and prematurely terminate the lives of hundreds of millions of Americans without notice or warning?

The problem with humans' senses of taste and smell is that we are not as perceptive as pigs. Evidently, pigs have a better nose for these things.

This is especially true when it comes to recognizing and differentiating natural foods from GMOs created in a laboratory, unsanctioned by God.

That is why we need labels. If GMO foods are not labeled to inform the consumer, then Americans are being subjects of a massive GMO experiment without our knowledge and consent. Many believe changing the DNA of the food supply is agricultural terrorism and should be accordingly investigated and punished.

A multitude of the health consequences result from the proliferation of GMOs and their introduction into nature, which are incalculable and beyond frightening. The "corn" that Monsanto makes is not natural corn, but it may look and taste even better than natural corn. Some GMOs may have a different cellular or recombinant DNA structure and be detrimental in ways that are currently unknown in science and medicine or, more frightening, in ways that are already known. Scientists may discover in the future that GMOs are very dangerous to the human race. Only time will tell to what extent the introduction of GMOs will have upon the world's environment and the food supply. Humanity should probably err on the side of caution over recklessness.

GMOs are in the feed of livestock, as well as human beings. Some remnants of GMO feed, given to livestock, is eventually consumed by humans when we eat beef, chicken, and pork. The damage caused by eating GMO is, for the most part, presently incalculable and will become more obviously observable over the next generations. Does eating GMO foods contribute to or cause an increase in disease? Who can really say? Will eating GMOs shorten the lifespan of Americans? Will the cancer rates of Americans increase? What do you think?

One could assume there is a higher human rate of malady and disease found in those who consume GMOs and GMO-fed livestock, but the GMO companies will likely never tell. Is it even possible to demonstrate that eating GMO food leads to a higher level of illness than eating organically raised livestock?

People simply do not know all the facts about GMOs. Instead of erring on the side of caution, is the world's population throwing caution, as well as humankind's future, to the wind in the shape and form of GMO foods and seeds?

The least that the FDA could do is demand labeling by the manufacturers of all foods that contain GMOs. This would provide Americans the same food labeling notifications that the Europeans have had for years in supermarket products across Europe. Europeans rioted and demonstrated in the streets and demanded that their foods include GMO labels. The European governments soon sided with the angry public, and the politicians laid down the law—European food labels must inform consumers whether a food contains GMOs or not.

It is a most regrettable sentiment to state that in America politicians do not hear the pleas of the American people but hear only the demands of the corporations. The FDA knows that if it were to mandate the labeling of GMO foods, no consumer in his or her right mind would buy GMO foods over natural foods, and GMO producers would have to focus on providing natural, non-GMO food to its customers. This all seems like the elementary economic theory of supply and demand.

The FDA has classified GMO foods under the GRAS designation, thereby not requiring any GMO labels for the consumer's benefit. "GRAS" means "generally recognized as safe."

Currently, the FDA's position on labeling is covered under the Food, Drug and Cosmetic Act, which concerns only the labeling of food additives and not food products that are classified as GRAS. The FDA in its never-erring omniscience has decreed that GMOs are substantially equivalent to natural, non-genetically modified foods. Therefore, the FDA's position is that there is no need to inform the American consumer or give the American consumer a choice in the matter by stringently requiring the labeling of genetically modified foods, which would make it simple to identify GMO and non-GMO foods.

The 2003 New York Times story, "Monsanto Sues Dairy in Maine Over Label's Remarks on Hormones," demonstrates Monsanto's propensity for litigation, as it sued the Oakhurst Dairy of Portland, Maine, a company that stood up to legislative tyranny, bravely fought a behemoth corporation and prevailed. The interesting article is at nytimes.com/2003/07/12/business/monsanto-sues-dairy-in-maine-over-label-s-remarks-on-hormones.html. This article makes us reflect on the depths that some greedy corporations will undertake to ensure shareholders' profit.

In the agricultural arena, Monsanto has been even more litigious when it comes to protecting its patented GMO corn products. Monsanto sued non-GMO corn farmers for patent infringement when innocent farmers were growing natural corn on their farms and Monsanto's genetically modified corn planted nearby went airborne and freely pollinated the farmers' natural, non-GMO corn, mutating it into Monsanto's patented GMO corn.

It is rumored that Monsanto's GMO corn can pollinate up to approximately a two-thousand-foot radius and will dominantly force pollination and mutation of natural, non-GMO corn into Monsanto's GMO version of corn. Therefore, Monsanto can plant its GMO corn in a small section of farmland next to a large field of natural non-GMO corn, and the natural corn will usually become pollinated and mutate into Monsanto's laboratory version of GMO corn. Still, Monsanto's lawyers have the audacity to file suits against small farmers for patent infringement when Monsanto's GMO corn is genetically designed to be a dominant gene.

The small farmer in most cases does not have the ability or money to litigate against a huge conglomerate like Monsanto, a company that makes untold billions of dollars. Many say the litigation practices of Monsanto are without scruples, but many also say that about most lawyers. One can read about the onslaught of cases brought to the courts by Monsanto. If you want to keep busy, just Google "Monsanto suing farmers" and read away till the cows come home.

Corporations do whatever is necessary to prevent the American consumer from discovering the truth, and the FDA lets GMOs pass as food —GRAS, generally recognized as safe. I guess there is nothing to worry about . . . quick, look over there!

It kind of reminds me of what George W. Bush succinctly stated, "There's an old saying in Tennessee, I know it's in Texas, probably in Tennessee, that says, fool me once, shame on . . . shame on you; fool me . . . you can't get fooled again."

Americans need to do what the Europeans did. As a first step, we must demand that the FDA provide proper labeling on every food item that contains GMOs, providing the American consumer a choice either to consume GMOs or to eat natural food with DNA created by a higher power than Monsanto.

A total ban and destruction of GMOs, if it is not already too late, is needed to ensure that the farms of the world and their crops suffer none of the adverse effects that often are witnessed only years after unnatural activities are undertaken in the agricultural and biological realms. Remember the example from the 1800s when two dozen rabbits were introduced to Australia to make foreign hunters feel more at home. Not surprisingly, those little bunnies grew up and bred like rabbits, and now their offspring costs the Australian farm industry six hundred million dollars in crop damages per year.

Congress needs to go even further to enact a complete overhaul of the labeling regulations and policies that surround the GMO controversy. Consumers should have the right to inform themselves as to what they are buying, whether it is natural food or GMOs. Why is Monsanto so afraid of labeling its GMOs? Is it afraid that if consumers knew they had a choice of eating natural food or GMOs they would pick natural non-GMO food?

Until Congress cares about the American people, we can take effective action by eating organic foods as much as possible and sending a message to the GMO companies. As a species, we cannot forfeit our right to God's food, which is essentially a gift from nature, meant to be protected and not genetically altered by scientists whose intentions are less pure than the fruits of their labor.

There are similar positions adopted in the creation of genetically modified fish and animals as well. So the next time you sit down for supper to enjoy a great steak, realize that the DNA of the meat of this animal you are about to eat may have been internally modified by the GMOs the cow ingested over its lifetime.

I recommend the informative article called "GMO Facts" for astounding information pertaining to what we are actually eating. Visit nongmoproject.org/gmo-facts/

We can only imagine the long-term detrimental human, environmental, and ecological effects associated with growing and consuming so-called food, regardless of whether the FDA classifies GMOs to be GRAS or otherwise. The food humans were eating before Monsanto decided to make GMOs has been just fine for the past thousands upon thousands of years.

It used to be, "If it ain't broke, don't fix it." Our food was not "broke." Nevertheless, food corporations now believe they can out-think and out-design nature without consideration or concern regarding any possible impact to the environment or even the extinction of the human race. More frighteningly, perhaps Monsanto does have in mind the potentially devastating effects GMOs may have on the human race leading or at least contributing to its extinction.

Imagine if we find out when it's too late that GMO plants killed all the bees. Einstein said, "If the bee disappeared off the surface of the globe then man would only have four years of life left. No more bees, no more pollination, no more plants, no more animals, no more man."

Why would a company be interested in manufacturing and selling seeds that were unnaturally created and risk injuring the health of every person who eats its products? Do corporations have any interests in the preservation of the human species or only consider their bottom lines?

Consider the competition between the different species of corn, the natural corn versus the GMO corn, in their fight for survival. GMOs, in order to survive, are unique in design as they wipe out and remove natural crops from the face of the planet. This occurs because the domination of the GMO's pollination ability is superior to the natural crop's ability to reproduce. The GMOs are designed through pollination to mutate natural crops into GMO crops. Think of the abominations and implications of having man intercede with the natural pollination and direction of nature and our food supply. Think of the consequences and the possible ramifications.

By allowing GMOs into the ecological and agricultural systems, politicians have allowed corporations and the government to decide what types of so-called food organisms can enter and affect our bodies. Since there is virtually no testing on humans regarding the long-term effects, one must ask, "Is there a safe way to conclude that GMO foods are not killing or harming the population as we blindly continue to consume them?"

The quality of the food that the FDA allows America's supermarkets to sell is likely the major contributor to the ongoing obesity problems we are experiencing in America. A generation ago, there was a much smaller percentage of obese Americans, compared to today.

Obesity is the result of the quantity and, more importantly, the quality of the food individuals ingest. When we consume GMOs, we cannot accurately predict if the long-term effects may be detrimental to our health and the health of the species as a whole.

The American population is far more obese and is less healthy than it was only a few decades ago. This is true across all ages. In our classrooms, where there used to be only a few obese children per class, now the obese students are approaching the majority of the class.

Natural News reports the correlation between GMOs and obesity (naturalnews.com/045247_GMOs_weight_gain_obesity.html).

Upon investigation of FDA-approved medications and treatments, it becomes apparent that there are other toxins and substances that the FDA approves and allows companies to market that are far more dangerous than GMOs. These products can severely damage and often kill those people who regularly ingest FDA-approved mind-altering medications and other forms of barbaric treatments.

There is a plethora of pharmaceuticals that contain warnings of side effects that one wouldn't wish on one's worst enemy. Side effects include everything from a sudden loss in eyesight to anal leakage. In addition, there are many undisclosed side effects, which an unsuspecting patient may not even anticipate. This is especially true when the patient starts mixing a variety of medications. Who knows what the side effects will be when a person ingests a veritable pharmacological cocktail?

Today, pharmaceutical commercials often list "death" as a possible side effect. "Death is not a side effect," the great comedian Robin Williams used to say. "It's not a side effect, it's an effect!"

The number of people routinely taking prescription drugs has exponentially increased, making America the largest bio-chemical society in the world.

Years ago, it was commonly understood that people would occasionally have a tough day here and there. Rough days are the part of life that tests the mettle of each of us. People stoically bore the tribulations life presented as best they could without resorting to taking toxic, psychologically altering, and destructive medicines.

Today, we inundate people with invented diseases created by the psychiatric community and television ads that encourage viewers to speak to their doctor for many newly concocted symptoms and ailments. For several decades there has been a noticeable increase in the creation of new diseases and disorders, fabricated by the psychiatric community and promoted through television commercials, with the purpose of selling more pharmaceuticals.

"Shift work disorder" is an example that leads one to examine exactly what so-called diseases the psychiatrists are concocting to further medicate the American population. People that have worked their entire lives on a standard work schedule and suddenly have their schedule switched to the graveyard shift will undoubtedly have their sleep patterns adversely affected. Obviously, it takes time to adjust one's sleep schedule under such conditions, and it may be necessary to undertake other nutritional programs to ensure a good night's sleep for the rescheduled worker. Many workers may have to block out the sunlight from windows so they can sleep during the light of day. One of the points to consider is that one may want to address some environmental factors and even physiological factors to help one adapt to a new sleep schedule.

Additionally, it may take several days or even weeks to adjust to the graveyard schedule. At first, it may seem difficult, if not next to impossible, to fall asleep during daylight hours. This seems normal, and most people might consider medication in these circumstances unnecessary, but there are those who have an interest in the pharmaceutical industry, share in its profits, and would like to see everyone taking a pill or two every couple of hours.

In America, when did it become normal to live a life medicated like a pseudo-zombie because a person has a problem that should be discussed with a friend? The American population has accepted the notion that when dealing with a mental situation it is perfectly acceptable to take prescription drugs, which in many cases are designed to destroy the human mind and are manufactured to be as addictive as possible.

For a list of the side effects of many drugs, visit drugs.com/sfx. This website mentions a large number of drugs and their side effects, although it may not be complete because not all side effects are reported to the FDA. The same website warns, "Please note—many side effects of medications may not be reported. Always consult your doctor or healthcare specialist for medical advice. People may also report side effects of drugs to the FDA at fda.gov/medwatch/ or 1-800-FDA-1088 (1-800-332-1088)."

When a pharmaceutical company spends hundreds of millions and even billions of dollars conceiving, creating, designing, manufacturing, and marketing a new drug, is it financially prudent to design that new drug to have terrible withdrawal symptoms experienced by users that attempt to quit such dangerous medications? Do pharmaceutical companies have an interest in keeping a customer for the entirety of the customer's life? You bet they do!

Most drugs, especially the "feeling good" psychotropic drugs, were created specifically to keep customers hooked for life. Customer retention is an extremely important aspect of any successful business. What better way is there to ensure having a customer for life than by creating a customer who is addicted to the pharmaceutical products we are discussing? When "an elevation of suicidal thoughts" is a side effect, it may be time to reevaluate one's healthcare provider's intentions in prescribing medicine that makes a patient think of chewing on the end of a gun barrel and taking one's own life.

Knowing that the pharmaceutical companies' primary concern is to their stockholders, one can only imagine the lengths these conglomerates endure to ensure their customer base is as addicted as possible to and uses as much of their company's specific brand of pharmaceutical products for as long as humanly—or inhumanely—possible.

People need to consider the controlling influence of the American Medical Association (AMA), the American Psychiatric Association (APA), and their guidelines defining acceptable medicine and treatment. Reports indicate that during the 1930s and 1940s the Rockefeller family and the Carnegie Foundation took control of a significant percentage of the pharmaceutical industry and quickly established control over the AMA and APA. "The Truth about the Rockefeller Drug Empire: The Drug Story" by Hans Ruesch (whale.to/b/ruesch.html) discusses the House of Rockefeller's sinister motives and interest in drugging the world's population for profit.

The House of Rockefeller utilizes front groups and politicians to successfully accomplish its mass medicating objectives and goals. Upon leaving the CIA, Bush Sr. ran Eli Lilly Corporation, the manufacturer of Prozac. As told in George Bush: The Unauthorized Biography, Dan Quayle's father was the largest stockholder of Eli Lilly when Quayle was selected as Bush's vice president (tarpley.net/online-books/george-bush-the-unauthorized-biography/). Incidentally, Tarpley's book is a great read. It is no wonder that there was a huge proliferation of Prozac consumption during the Bush-Quayle administration. This massive increase of Prozac consumption was not by happenstance but a contrived drugging of the American population.

One quite illuminating article from drugs.com/prozac.html brilliantly discusses the pharmaceutically engineered antidepressant Prozac and its possible dangers. Some side effects of Prozac listed in the article include:

> sleep problems (insomnia, strange dreams);
> headaches, dizziness, vision changes;
> tremors or shaking, feeling anxious or nervous;

pain, weakness, yawning, tired feeling;

upset stomach, loss of appetite, nausea, vomiting, diarrhea;

dry mouth, sweating, hot flashes;

changes in weight or appetite;

stuffy nose, sinus pain, sore throat, flu symptoms; or

decreased sex drive, impotence, or difficulty having an orgasm.

Many claim Prozac is not alone; many of the selective serotonin reuptake inhibitors (SSRI) present horrible withdrawal symptoms for the person prescribed such so-called medicine.

Funny enough, there is no mention of "suicidal thoughts" in the above side effects, yet many users of SSRIs complain about a substantial increase in such thoughts.

Any discussion of psychotic mass murderers ought to include gunman Charles Whitman, a University of Texas engineering student and America's first mass murderer, who climbed the school's clock tower and cold-bloodedly shot forty-nine people. It should be mentioned that Whitman, like most mass murders, was heavily medicated by his psychiatrist at the time of his horrific shooting. Analysis of the medical histories and state of mind of mass shooters indicates almost all shooters are on mind-altering psychiatric drugs when they murder their innocent victims. Often the reports on the news indicate that the shooters were under the care of a psychiatrist but fail to report the shooter was consuming incredibly dangerous, mind-altering medications.

It would be interesting to discover if the National Rifle Association has done any research on the medications taken by mass shooters when they lose it and take their imagined revenge against society.

Before anyone decides to take medications, the informative articles found on drugs.com should definitely be consulted prior to undertaking such a potentially damaging course of action. Look at the number of people that are hooked on OxyContin and oxycodone and other synthetic opioid pharmacological derivatives.

OxyContin and oxycodone are opiate pain medications (heroin is an opiate as well), commonly prescribed after surgery or sustainment of an injury. Doctors often initially prescribe up to one hundred pills for their patients. Taking one hundred pills of highly addictive opioid medications sounds like the prescription to a lifetime of addiction. The problem is heroin is much cheaper than OxyContin and oxycodone, and the medical patient, because of the price, more often than not turns to heroin to satisfy an addiction created by the medical community and its immoral practice of prescribing incredibly addictive drugs to its customers.

Many thanks to drugs.com for its wonderful articles and it is hoped that our readers are more educated regarding antidepressants and pain killers, their accompanying health warnings, and the potentially devastating side effects far too often experienced by unwitting and uneducated pharmaceutical consumers.

There still is great controversy regarding Prozac. There are many claims that patients taking Prozac have experienced a magnification of suicidal thoughts and other violent tendencies. There is allegedly unprecedented and higher rates of suicide among Prozac users than there are among differently classified pharmaceutical drugs that are ultimately sanctioned and approved by the FDA.

Regardless of the brand name of a drug, it seems difficult to engineer a drug that has the same exact effect on millions of people. That is why the prescription of pharmaceuticals to stabilize a chemical imbalance in a person's brain is often more detrimental to the well-being of the person than the symptoms the patient is attempting to alleviate. See Pubmed.gov for extensive details regarding pharmaceuticals and their effectiveness; Google and read the real-life stories of victims claiming their lives were ruined by taking pharmaceuticals.

For most people who suffer from mood swings and other so-called psychological problems, many nutritionists claim that for every mental disorder, there exists an underlying physical or nutritional problem that is contributing to the unwanted cognitive behaviors and mental difficulties experienced by the person.

It seems appropriate that in order to eliminate irregularities in mental cognizance, the first course of action would involve eliminating from the affected person's diet anything that is non-optimal. Some might suggest that the next likely course of action is discovering how the person's life is going. What are the sleep and exercise patterns of the person? What does the person do throughout the day? Finally, the person could have discussions with people in his or her life that are creating stress for the person and about different ways to sufficiently resolve such matters.

Obviously, not all drugs are destructive to a person. Many drugs are used to actually correct a patient's acute condition and assist in the recovery of a person back to health. One must educate oneself in the field of pharmaceuticals and beware of the snake-oil sales campaigns we see on the television every ten minutes while watching a football game.

There were congressional hearings that included heart-wrenching testimony from family members describing relatives who were on Prozac and killed their own children and often followed that deplorable act by ending their own lives. You can read "Congressional Hearings On Antidepressant-Induced Suicide In The Military" in the Huffington Post (huffingtonpost.com/dr-peter-breggin/congressional-hearings-on_b_480613.html).

Dr. Peter Breggin is an Ithaca, New York, psychiatrist and author of Medication Madness: The Role of Psychiatric Drugs in Violence, Suicide and Crime, which can be found at breggin.com. This book tells the dark side of pharmaceuticals, which we should all be made aware of before taking any addictive medications.

What legal processes are in place to regulate and hold members of federal agencies responsible for practices that are self-serving, illegal, or at least considered highly improper and unethical in the private sector? We jeopardize the safety of the private sector when those making FDA adjudications, regarding potentially lethal medicines, own the very stocks and financially benefit from the companies upon which they sit in judgment.

Double-dealing and self-dealing are long-time practices in Washington, DC, and nowhere are they more rampant than in the relationship between the federal government and the pharmaceutical industry. Legislators, in particular, have a neat way of profiting from the laws they pass. Through the ownership of trusts and other legal entities used for the protection of assets, a politician acquires stocks as a gift or at a steep discount from the same corporations he or she is often responsible to regulate and legislate.

I hate mentioning Hillary again, but she is incredibly scandalous. You can read about her criminal adventures as a pork-bellies trader at en.wikipedia.org/wiki/Hillary_Rodham_cattle_futures_controversy.

A prudent person would wonder why Clinton never reinvested her reportedly ill-gotten pork-belly profits back into the pork-belly market that she evidently knew so well. If she could turn one thousand dollars into over one hundred thousand dollars in record time, I am certain that she could allegedly turn that one hundred thousand dollars into an even larger fortune.

Perhaps her stock-market wizardry vanished as quickly as the commodity gods bestowed it upon her. Evidently, genius in the pork bellies market has a short shelf life and a vanishing quality associated with it.

Further instances of the all-too typical political self-dealing are examined in the humorous 1998 movie Bulworth starring the incomparable Warren Beatty and Halle Berry.

For a classic example of political self-dealing, imagine that politicians' trusts each receives a gift of shares from the pharmaceutical industry. Then the legislature passes a law positively affecting the profits of the pharmaceutical industry; this positively affects the ill-gotten stock, which is held in the politicians' trusts. The legislators benefit from the approved legislation that was passed to profit the pharmaceutical companies. If corrupt congressional representatives and senators do not get enough compensation and stock, the legislation fails to even get to the floor and becomes buried in one of the controlled political committees until the politicians become generously rewarded for their purchased votes.

These types of stock deals happen all the time in all the various industries, including insurance, pharmaceutical, oil, banking, you name it; any industry that is being legislated under the authority of Congress has to pay to play. Politicians should have to disclose all interests and holdings they possess before, during, and after serving in office.

It is amazing when we see lifetime politicians, like the Clintons, that leave public office with what appears to be very little wealth, yet within a few years, they have somehow managed to accumulate a fortune from speaking engagements or other alleged covert criminality that appear to endanger the very existence of the nation and its defenses. The Clintons amassed a fortune, and it appears that much of the money was received as an unethical form of remuneration for services performed while Hillary held office as the US secretary of state.

This book was written before the email scandal has been resolved, and the author reserves the right to write another book specifically dealing with criminality within the pre-Trump government and the social implications and ramifications created by such a criminal government. It appears President Trump is not sticking to his word and not locking her up.

In a nutshell, a government that is operated under the direction of criminals will always injure the citizenry and the world at large. Just look at what happened under Obama. The obliteration of America's health-care system was nearly completed, the financing of terrorism to the tune of 150 billion dollars was successfully accomplished, and the delivery of 1.7 billion dollars of cash to Iran, the number one state sponsor of terrorism, was achieved. The 1.7 billion dollars in cash can finance quite a bit of mischief, never mind what devious acts can be accomplished with the 150 billion dollars Obama gave to Iran.

Some of the many crimes committed by the Clintons are discussed in Peter Schweitzer's Clinton Cash: The Untold Story of How and Why Foreign Governments and Businesses Helped Make Bill and Hillary Rich and Dinesh D'Souza's Hillary's America: The Secret History of the Democratic Party. The above works discuss the Clintons' and the Democrats' duplicitous crimes against the United States and the American people, with extra highlights drawn from the Civil Rights Movement illustrating the plight of African-Americans and their incredible struggle against Democrats for their freedom.

With such blatant criminality and largess available, it becomes understandable why people are spending billions of dollars running to be the next president of the United States, a position with an annual salary of 400 thousand dollars and 169 thousand dollars for travel, expenses, and entertainment.

This practice of a select group of federal employees ripping off the public has been going on for years, and there is hardly ever a conflict of interest or criminal charge brought against the dirty scoundrels, unless the politician gets way out of line and bucks the system, as Congressman James Traficant, the distinguished gentleman from Ohio bravely did. Later there is more discussion to come about this great American hero.

Few in Congress possess the purpose of being altruistic and working for the betterment of the planet by doing what is right and in the best interest of their constituents. Politicians typically quit caring about their constituents' needs years before arriving in Washington.

Faults within the government and especially the FDA are not only in the kickbacks to politicians but also in the approval processes that can favor one drug company over another. The FDA also errs in approving some drugs that should never have been approved for the market, never mind human consumption. Fen-phen is an outrageous example of the FDA being extremely incompetent in its evaluation, decision, and approval processes. It wrongly granted this dangerous drug access to the market at the expense and eventual demise of many moderately over-weight and very obese Americans.

Fen-phen was a combination of two weight-loss drugs; in hindsight, this deadly combination of medications should never have been combined and sold to the public. Several deaths resulted, and damages from resulting lawsuits totaled over thirteen billion dollars (en.wikipedia.org/wiki/Fenfluramine/phentermine).

It is ironic that people who were concerned about their health, particularly about their heart and cardiovascular system, were attempting to lose weight using fen-phen and many died of heart problems linked and attributed to the same drug. The testing of fen-phen should have demonstrated the dangers associated with the drug, but somehow the approval line of the FDA was unable to detect, from thorough medical studies, the associated detrimental cardiac damage, inextricably linked and attributed to the ingestion of fen-phen.

We must have better control of our government and its agencies that were created to safeguard the health and lives of the American people and the people of the world. One might find it entertaining to consider the different government agencies, which were created to perform certain activities but which now perform contrary and opposite actions that devastate the populace.

To get a better understanding of the functioning of the different government agencies, one could adopt and apply to each agency a reverse viewpoint where black is white and right is wrong. The FDA is now literally in charge of poisoning Americans' foods and drugging us from birth until death. The Department of Public Welfare creates poverty instead of assisting with skills and job creation. The Department of Children and Families separates and destroys families. The IRS is not internal, does not re-venue the society's funds, and is not a service for the people; it is a collection agency for the private international bankers. The Department of Defense starts and propagates wars. Foreign aid does not aid the populations of any foreign countries but enriches criminal dictators and organizations posing as governments.

The list goes on and on, but do not argue with this assertion; substantiate it one way or the other for yourself; draw your own conclusions.

Where is the press reporting the atrocities citizens face at the hands of the FDA? Where are the fearless news correspondents speaking out for the health of the American people? If it does not involve the murder of a pregnant mother, maybe it simply is not newsworthy. Still, is the killing of millions and even billions of people enough to mention when discussing the current state of affairs and the quality of what passes now as food, pharmaceuticals, and healthcare treatments?

There needs to be accountability of government officials for the crimes that they are continually committing against the population at large. Politically favored professional occupations should not continue to be equated as licenses to steal from, rape, and kill the population at large. Those who pass laws that are unconstitutional and unconscionable or fail to uphold their oaths of office need to be removed from office on the first offense and without mercy. The punishment for federal employees that abuse their office for personal profit should be extremely harsh and act as a deterrent to other government workers. Government criminals should be made such an example of that no one else dares to betray the trust of the American people.

For centuries, governments conducted public hangings for more than simple entertainment. Public hangings were a deterrent to all future probable criminals, especially deplorable murderers and traitors. Many onlookers saw the murderous souls hanging in the gallows and realized that hanging was not the best way to leave this life and meet one's maker.

Government workers swear to uphold the US Constitution; failure to do so means they have committed treason and should appropriately be prosecuted in a court of law. The zealous prosecution of only a few corrupt politicians will quickly motivate the rest of the less criminal politicians to fall in line and start doing their jobs with enthusiasm and in alignment with their oaths of office and the best interests of the American people.

The nation has passed the point of civility and decency. The amount of political criminality, combined with the slavery of the American citizenry, is unparalleled in the history of the world. Those lunatics, the criminal politicians who are destroying this great land, need to be legally held accountable for their crimes.

A nation cannot tolerate its government's usurpation by a few at the costs of the many. The United States was not conceived to enslave its citizenry at the hands of the few, yet that is exactly what has occurred. This nation was not conceived so that corrupt parts of federal agencies could conspire and contribute towards humanity's extinction using the dirty hands of unhealthy food, pharmaceuticals, and the barbaric medical treatments for America's terminally ill. People must become informed and make a difference. Dangerous foods and medicines have no place on our table or anywhere else in our country.

America was once the bastion of almost everything good. Now we are getting the country we deserve and, more importantly, the country we are silently inviting and accepting. We must start speaking up and demanding more from our government, for our sake and the sake of future generations. To do nothing to fight oppression is to agree and, ultimately, perish.

Thomas Jefferson acutely foretold,

> God forbid we should ever be twenty years without such a rebellion. The people cannot be all, and always, well informed. The part which is wrong will be discontented, in proportion to the importance of the facts they misconceive. If they remain quiet under such misconceptions, it is lethargy, the forerunner of death to the public liberty. . . . And what country can preserve its liberties, if its rulers are not warned from time to time, that their people preserve the spirit of resistance? Let them take arms. The remedy is to set them right as to the facts, pardon and pacify them. What signify a few lives lost in a century or two? The tree of liberty must be refreshed from time to time, with the blood of patriots and tyrants. It is its natural manure.

Chapter 11

The Medical Mafia

We can cure physical diseases with medicine, but the only cure for loneliness, despair, and hopelessness is love. There are many in the world who are dying for a piece of bread but there are many more dying for a little love. The poverty in the West is a different kind of poverty—it is not only a poverty of loneliness but also of spirituality. There's a hunger for love, as there is a hunger for God.

– MOTHER THERESA

Let us be the ones who say we do not accept that a child dies every three seconds simply because he does not have the drugs you and I have. Let us be the ones to say we are not satisfied that your place of birth determines your right for life. Let us be outraged, let us be loud, let us be bold.

– BRAD PITT

Wherever the art of Medicine is loved, there is also a love of Humanity.

– HIPPOCRATES

Treatment without prevention is simply unsustainable.

– BILL GATES

Isn't it a bit unnerving that doctors call what they do "practice"?
– GEORGE CARLIN

Though the doctors treated him, let his blood, and gave him medications to drink, he nevertheless recovered.

– LEO TOLSTOY

As to diseases, make a habit of two things—to help, or at least, to do no harm.

– HIPPOCRATES

The doctor of the future will give no medicine, but will interest his patients in the care of the human frame, in a proper diet and the cause and prevention of dis-ease.

– THOMAS A. EDISON

It is very expensive to give bad medical care to poor people in a rich country.

– PAUL FARMER

Be skeptical, ask questions, demand proof. Demand evidence. Don't take anything for granted. But here's the thing: When you get proof, you need to accept the proof. And we're not that good at doing that.

– MICHAEL SPECTER

Doctors are just the same as lawyers; the only difference is that lawyers merely rob you, whereas doctors rob you and kill you too.

– ANTON CHEKHOV

It is much more important to know what sort of a patient has a disease than what sort of a disease a patient has.

– WILLIAM OSLER

Surgeons can cut out everything except cause.

– HERBERT M. SHELTON

THE FEDERAL GOVERNMENT is monopolizing healthcare—as if Americans already didn't have enough problems. Now, allowing the federal government to take control of over 15 percent of the nation's economy can only lead to disaster.

During the Clinton administration's first term, as Hillary Clinton rushed around the country to implement socialized healthcare, former Senator John D. Rockefeller (Democrat from Virginia) said on Larry

King Live, "The American people are going to get healthcare, whether they want it or not." Talk like that substantiates that there is an organization that has an agenda and orders around the puppet politicians, mandating their compliance in order to ensure reelection.

Rockefeller was wrong, and the Clintons were not able to pass healthcare reform. It took until President Obama's approval of the Affordable Care Act, or Obamacare, before socialized healthcare became a reality in America and Rockefeller's intention for America's healthcare system was actualized.

The American Medical Association utilizes some interesting techniques in treating its patients, which warrant inspection and consideration. Some may consider the field of medicine to still be in its nascent stage of development, as only 150 years ago it was commonplace to leech blood to cure ailments. Today there are magic pills that are supposed to fix whatever ails the patient.

Shane "The People's Chemist" Ellison wrote a very interesting exposé regarding the AMA called "How the AMA Hooks You on Drugs, Harms Your Health and Hurts the Earth." Ellison's incredible article is available at thepeopleschemist.com/how-the-ama-hooks-you-on-drugs-harms-your-health-and-hurts-the-earth/ and ecohearth.com. Ellison and EcoHearth editor Rick Theis are leaders in environmental protection. Visit their websites to learn how a person can contribute in the global fight to save the planet. Much appreciation and thanks are extended to Shane Ellison for permission to include his informative article, presented here in its entirety for the reader's benefit.

How the AMA Hooks You on Drugs, Harms Your Health and Hurts the Earth

Founded in 1847, the American Medical Association (AMA) set out to "promote the art and science of medicine for the betterment of public health." But the benevolent veil is wafer thin. The AMA has relentlessly hounded alternative medicines and therapies, forcing them out of business or keeping them at the margins. It has ignored good health and prevention in favor of pushing less safe and less effective— though more profitable—treatments, primarily surgery and drugs. And some startling facts show that it has done all of this at the expense of our health and that of the environment.

The Rise of AMA Tyranny

In the beginning, there was natural healing—botanical, Chinese, eclectic, homeopathic, nutritional and Native American medicine, as well as chiropractic, to name just a few. But in the eyes of the AMA, that was too much competition. It had to be minimized, which meant removing the glut of choices so that only AMA-approved treatments could be positioned as the cure-alls that they are considered today.

Early on there were skeptics. In 1833, the New York Evening Star wrote: "Medicine [allopathic], like every useful science, should be thrown open to the observation and study of all.... We should at once explode the whole machinery of mystification and concealment—wigs, gold canes and the gibberish of prescriptions—which serves but as a cloak to ignorance and legalized murder." But over time, the AMA mystification proved too complex, while the public ultimately relinquished control and became guinea pigs, which AMA doctors could use to "practice" allopathic medicine.

From their early vision of a one-size-fits-all medicine, in 1904 the AMA established the Committee on Medical Education (which later became the Council on Medical Education). Without government intervention, they singlehandedly used this branch to standardize medical education in America under their belief system, which was hailed as a "scientific breakthrough" with all others labeled "quackery, charlatanism or, at best, alternative medicine."

In 1910, with support from John D. Rockefeller and the Carnegie Foundation for the Advancement of Teaching, the AMA funded Abraham Flexner with a grant to travel with the secretary of the AMA Council on Medical Education to medical schools then in existence. This pushed medical education to the forefront of America's public health agenda. The project resulted in Flexner's famous report, "Medical Education in the United States and Canada," which became a catalyst for a historic shift in thinking, which ultimately positioned their medical ideals as scientifically superior to all others. The birth of the AMA tyranny, known technically as "allopathic medicine," was officially born—and surgery, vaccines and drugs became the primary health option for Americans.

Medical schools were forced to comply with the new standards—by removing other modes of healing from their curriculum—or lose AMA support. Under these restrictions, their numbers dwindled from more than 400 US medical schools in the 19th century to 148 by 1910 and just 76 by 1930.

This was defended by the AMA in a phone interview with Robert Mills, who showed that, "The medical education system churned out an overproduction of uneducated and ill-trained medical practitioners, who in general practiced with 'an absolute disregard for the public welfare and without any serious thought of the interests of the public.' Flexner noted that there were five times as many U.S. physicians in proportion to population than in European nations such as Germany. What drove this oversupply was commercial exploitation by a large number of schools whose mission was profit, not education. For these diploma mills, the expense of setting up a laboratory to aid didactic instruction took away from the bottom line, and the quality of education suffered as a result."

The Allopathic Occult

With all competition weakened or removed starting in 1910, the AMA quickly established a "knowledge monopoly" in medicine, primarily with the intentional use of Latin bio-babble. The AMA Council on Medical Education published the first edition of Essentials of an Acceptable Medical College, revised eight times over the next 41 years from 1910, to be superseded by the Functions and Structure of a Modern Medical School. This successfully gave rise to a gap in scientific literacy, which removed health education from the reach of the layman and placed it into the self-serving hands of the AMA, and their "approved" medical schools. It paved the way for the allopathic, drug model of healing, which was to benefit AMA supporters John D. Rockefeller and the Carnegie Foundation via their interests in chemical manufacturer IG Farben—infamous for its manufacture of Zyklon B, a pesticide used for human extermination in the gas chambers of Nazi death camps during the Holocaust.

Attacks on Chiropractic

With the dwindling of all other forms of medicine, only chiropractic remained a challenge. In an effort to suffocate the profits of that industry, AMA secretary Morris Fishbein led an anti-chiropractic campaign in medical journals and public media. He portrayed them as members of an unscientific cult—caring about nothing but money—despite chiropractic's proven health benefits. The war against chiropractic continued into 1987 when, in the case of Wilk v. American Medical Association, the AMA was found guilty under the Sherman Antitrust Act of conspiring to destroy the profession of chiropractic. But the AMA's propaganda campaign has had staying power. Chiropractic is still reeling from bad press and is seen by many as quackery.

As of 1992, AMA's official stance on chiropractic is that, "It is ethical for a physician to associate professionally with chiropractors provided that the physician believes that such association is in the best interests of his or her patient. A physician may refer a patient for diagnostic or therapeutic services to a chiropractor permitted by law to furnish such services whenever the physician believes that this may benefit his or her patient. Physicians may also ethically teach in recognized schools of chiropractic."

To this day, there is no opposition to the allopathic occult. The Journal of the American Medical Association admitted as much when it published a 2004 article by Andrew Beck, which stated that "all accredited US medical schools strive to apply Flexner's 'uniformly arduous and expensive' brand of medical education…" And the monopoly is fully supported by the Food and Drug Administration (FDA), the Federal Trade Commission (FTC) and even mandated by the US court system, as seen by the myriad charges against parents who opt out of vaccines, psychiatric meds, surgery or traditional chemotherapy for their children. "As long as science shows these to have public health value," the AMA insisted that they, "endorse mandating certain medical treatments."

A Drug-Addicted Nation

Prescription drugs have become more popular than McDonald's hamburgers. In 2008, there were 3.9 billion prescriptions written—about 14 per American—compared to 560 million Big Macs sold—just two per American. Drug spending is projected to top $445.9 billion by the year 2012. This drug addiction is the result of two tactics designed to spread AMA's beloved allopathic "scientific breakthroughs" to hundreds of millions.

The first tactic is the creation of mini-sagas culminating in a miracle answer: drugs. This is direct-to-consumer (DTC)

advertising and one of the most potent ways to get unsuspecting patients to ask their doctor if a drug is "right for
them". Whether you're reading a magazine, watching television or listening to the radio, it is guaranteed that you'll be
bombarded by these types of slick drug ads. No surprise, the
concept of DTC ads was created by the AMA, FDA and the
Pharmaceutical Manufacturers Association. Officially, this
was done as a means of "promoting health awareness among
consumers to ensure their health and safety." Unofficially, it
was done to sell more drugs under the medical umbrella of
allopathic medicine. In a 2010 American Association of Retired Persons (AARP) survey, 90 percent of respondents said
they had seen a drug ad, 10 percent asked their doctor for
the drug, of which two-thirds received either a prescription
or a sample. Former US Senate Majority Leader, Bill Frist
(R-Tennessee), is seen in the film, Big Bucks, Big Pharma,
clearly identifying the DTC advertising threat: "Let there be
no mistake: drug advertisements fuel America's skyrocketing
prescription drug costs. They influence consumer behavior.
And they influence physician behavior. They cause more
people to take prescription drugs. They create an artificial
demand."

In defense of my claim, the AMA insisted that they are
strictly against today's rampant DTC advertising, but that
they do support it when the ads satisfy AMA accepted policies, which ultimately help to, "improve the communication
of health information; enhance the patient-physician relationship; and contain accurate and reasonable information
on risks, precautions, adverse reactions, and costs."

Billing Code Extortion

The second tactic, standardized billing codes, is much more
clandestine. The AMA isn't dependent on membership to
flex their allopathic muscles among doctors. Members or
not, physicians who accept insurance or Medicare are forced

to prescribe drugs for payment via billing codes—known as Current Procedural Terminology (CPT)—established by the AMA as a "universal language" to help practitioners communicate to insurers. A matrix of slick computer technology, CPT codes are matched to AMA-approved treatments—generally prescription drugs—and thus don't allow for payment toward preventive, complementary or alternative medicine. Though, the AMA insists that any organization can begin "providing their own codes."

CPT codes are the result of a covert agreement between the AMA and the US government's Health Care Financing Administration (HCFA). The long-secret agreement was exposed in 1997. The US Court of Appeals, Ninth Circuit, ruled that the AMA's exclusivity agreement with HCFA for using CPT code "gave the AMA a substantial and unfair advantage over its competitors" and "constituted a misuse of the copyright by the AMA." But the codes are still in full force. In 2009, the AMA made $70 million in revenue courtesy of physicians using their payment codes.

Payment codes coupled with DTC advertising ensures that the masses are hypnotized into a prescription drug addiction, in the name of health. But it's health in name only. Americans are sick, sick, sick. The United States ranks 12th among the top 13 countries in the ill health of its citizens—at least 80 percent of seniors have at least one chronic disease and 50 percent have at least two. Relative to children in other industrialized countries, the health of US children is worse in virtually every category. But more worrisome than declining health is the overt toxicity of using drugs as prescribed by doctors. And until the AMA puts a stop to it, they are just as much an accomplice as the industry making the drugs.

Doctors of Death

You don't have to dig deep to know that allopathic medicine has become risky as hell. A Levitra ad recently discussed that a drug-induced erection may be accompanied by blindness. That's serious. My college roommate used party drugs that were more fun—with half the side effects—and he had to buy them illegally. Yet following doctor's orders has become synonymous with danger.

Legal drugs prescribed through the wisdom of allopathic medicine kill an estimated 105,000 people per year. That equates to one individual dying about every five minutes from an "approved" drug—almost 300 deaths daily—that is, twice as many fatalities in a single year from approved drugs as the total number of US deaths (58,000) from the nine-year Vietnam War. And this does not include the 98,000 killed every year by physician medical error.

Illicit drugs, on the other hand, directly and indirectly kill an estimated 17,000 people annually. Paradoxically, the US government spends nearly $50 billion every year to "fight a war" against illicit drugs in an effort to ameliorate this death toll. Yet America's more deadly allopathic drug problem continues to be ignored.

If not killed, an estimated two million people are victims of prescription-drug-induced illnesses, according to the New England Journal of Medicine. These include drug-induced obesity, diabetes, cancer, kidney disease, autism, depression and heart failure, as well as the super-bug phenomena that is sweeping the nation due to overuse of antibiotics. This troubling trend is ignored by lazy thinking and myopic physicians who dismiss the symptoms as "worsening health."

Then there are the staggering hospital-death numbers. Even the AMA's own, probably conservative, statistics paint a bleak picture. They show that more than 12,000 people are killed every year by unnecessary surgeries. About 7,000 die from hospital medication errors. And 20,000 more lose their lives thanks to non-medication-related hospital-staff mistakes.

Environmental Evils

Besides often making people sicker, allopathic medicine, with its reliance on chemical drugs also, harms the ecology. Realizing that prevention in most cases can eliminate the need for prescription drugs and that many are counterproductive to our overall health, the negative environmental impact of their widespread use is even more troubling.

Pharmaceutical manufacturing plants expend energy and release toxic wastewater. Their global shipments create a large carbon footprint. Vast quantities of their products pass through our bodies, are flushed down toilets, and end up in our rivers, lakes, and groundwater. Health facilities alone flush an estimated 250 million pounds of drugs annually. A 2008 Associated Press investigation discovered "a vast array of pharmaceuticals including antibiotics, anti-convulsants, mood stabilizers and sex hormones . . . in the drinking-water supplies of at least 41 million Americans."

While allopathic medicine has become a disaster for both the environment and many individuals, the AMA, US government, and drug-giant descendants that have grown from IG Farben continue to amass huge sums of wealth at the people's expense. As long as the AMA holds the medical monopoly and refuses to act against the atrocity, this holocaustic trend will continue. Every man, woman, and child will become enslaved by surgery, vaccines, drugs, more drugs, and whatever else the AMA chooses to label a "scientific breakthrough." And ecosystems, waterways, and aquifers worldwide will continue to be fouled by the chemical pollutants flowing from both the manufacture and the use of pharmaceuticals.

Shane Ellison holds a master's degree in organic chemistry and is the author of Over-the-Counter Natural Cures Expanded Edition (Sourcebooks). He has been quoted by USA Today, Shape, Woman's World, US News and World Report, as well as Women's Health, and appeared on Fox and NBC as a medicine and health expert. You can start protecting yourselves and your loved ones with Ellison's free report, The 5 Deadly Pills Checklist: How to Protect Your Family at thepeopleschemist.com/chemist-exposes-5-deadly-pills/.

I also recommend the documentary video Big Bucks, Big Pharma—Marketing Disease & Pushing Drugs (2006) available at youtube.com/watch?v=D1uARFrI9U4. Incredible information can be gathered in The World without Cancer by G. Edward Griffin. In depth, Griffin's video discusses the suppression of vitamin B-17 by the government, denying cancer patients this often lifesaving medicine and can be seen at youtube.com/watch?v=QeYMduufa-E.

A great video series to better understand cancer and patients' options for treatment can be watched in Ty Bollinger's fantastic work, The Quest for the Cure, available at youtube.com/watch?v=gR8SQzCJK0Q. Bollinger's hard-hitting and super-informative video, The Truth About Cancer: A Global Quest—The True History of Chemo & The Pharmaceutical Monopoly, is available at youtube.com/watch?v=KqJAzQe7_0g. These are must-see videos for anyone that is personally or has a friend or family member suffering from cancer.

The great folks at thetruthaboutcancer.com website have volumes of information regarding the cancer industry, purportedly effective methodologies, and helpful tips for people with cancer. They also explain some of the dirtiest secrets of the cancer industry and discuss some of the most acclaimed cancer treatments available anywhere on the planet. If you know anyone with cancer or have it yourself, you need to watch Bollinger's videos. Learn more about cancer and its conventional and nonconventional treatments and expose yourself to a life of possibilities. These are some of the most informative videos ever made regarding cancer. Do yourself a favor and watch all the videos. They really expand one's scope of knowledge.

Wikipedia defines "allopathic medicine" as "an expression commonly used by homeopaths and proponents of other forms of alternative medicine to refer to mainstream medical use of pharmacologically active agents or physical interventions to treat or suppress symptoms or patho-physiologic processes of diseases or conditions."

WebMD defines "homeopathy," or "homeopathic medicine," as a medical philosophy and practice based on the idea that the body has the ability to heal itself. Homeopathy was founded in the late 1700s in Germany and has been widely practiced throughout Europe.

Allopathic medicine is comprised of medical treatment in which the physician will administer foreign agents called medicine; medicine often treats the symptoms and not the causes of diseases that are affecting patients. In allopathic medicine, one would expect that a doctor would administer aspirin to treat the symptoms of a headache.

Homeopathic medicine incorporates the body's inherent defense mechanisms to allow the body to address and handle the causes of disease, instead of simply treating the symptoms of disease. In homeopathic medicine, patients consume herbs and other natural agents to assist the body in curing itself. In homeopathic medicine, patients might take salt and potassium immediately to treat headaches that are the result of dehydration; headache sufferers may undergo weekly massage therapy treatments as well.

Founders of the AMA, in order to control and maximize profits in the field of medicine, demanded that allopathic treatments would be the only type of treatments allowed to be taught in all medical institutions and indoctrinated into the intellectual bowels of every medical student. This ensured hospitals and medical practitioners would exclusively deliver the most profitable treatments available, regardless if they resulted in harm and, far too often, the death of patients.

As a matter of fact, there were financially rewarding policies implemented that required the medical schools and universities to concentrate only on those medical practices, approved by the AMA, which yielded the most profit per treatment, medication, and procedure. The medical industry today utilizes barbaric treatments developed strictly with this profit model in mind.

Consider the treatments for cancer. Should one be so unfortunate to be diagnosed with cancer, such as melanoma in this example, one would ordinarily seek information regarding the available treatments and weigh the options. It is very difficult to find the actual statistics, which the medical community should be required to publish, that discuss the success rates for the different melanoma treatments. Good luck finding it on the Internet or having one's doctor provide these vital statistics.

For some reason, cancer-treatment statistics are almost impossible to find and, if found, to understand. One might think statistics regarding the effectiveness of different treatments would be readily available, but when an organization such as the AMA is attempting to hide its crimes, correct and accessible data are either seldom available or not easily found.

One would assume that there would be a medical site indicating which treatments were most successful in treating stage 4 melanoma, but this information, hidden from the public, is virtually impossible to locate. The AMA has years of experience treating this devastating disease and does not care to assist or educate the melanoma patient in choosing a specific treatment based on national statistics and facts.

It is bad enough being diagnosed with cancer, but not having intelligent data from which to choose a type of treatment is an abomination and speaks volumes regarding the AMA's philosophy and its unwillingness to inform patients of the risks associated with receiving today's often fatal medicines and treatments. Many times the medicine prescribed for patients hurts the suffering patients more than the disease does; many die from the toxins that are in the medicine provided by the AMA and not from the disease itself.

If the AMA's treatments had any measure of success, there would be surveys compiled, easily accessible websites, and information demonstrating its members' competence in curing this and other cancers. The AMA does not promote the success and failure rates of the different treatments because the medical field in general is quite unsuccessful when it comes to treating cancers.

Dr. Glidden, author of The MD Emperor Has No Clothes, claims that, according to a twelve-year study published in the Journal of Oncology in 1994, "Chemotherapy is ineffective 97 percent of the time." For a very enlightening discussion, listen as he blows the whistle regarding the profits and kickbacks that doctors receive as a result of prescribing chemotherapy in the short video Chemotherapy Doesn't Work 97% of the Time at youtube.com/watch?v=WF_14hSs4z8.

According to Glidden, "A doctor prescribes chemotherapy and here's how it goes more or less. The doctor buys it from the pharmaceutical company for $5,000, sells it to the patient for $12,000, insurance pays only $9,000 and the doctor pockets the remaining $4,000." Glidden claims the only reason chemotherapy is used is because the doctors make money from it, period. According to Glidden, chemotherapy is successful 3 percent of the time.

Glidden's website has developed a self-help recovery program for anyone that is sick, which can be found at his site, glidden.healthcare.

People do not usually die as a result of their cancer; they die as a result of the chemo, which is a horrific and perhaps the most ghastly, pain-filled death one could imagine. The toxins in chemotherapy invade and destroy the cells of the human body. How is chemotherapy an acceptable form of cancer treatment in the twenty-first century? Chemotherapy is more barbaric than the most macabre and medieval torture known to humanity.

Visit the Chemo-Free Survivors' Health Blog at chrisbeatcancer.com/how-effective-is-chemotherapy/ to learn fascinating data regarding chemo-free treatments of cancer and other interesting perspectives.

Understand this is not medical advice, and as a further disclaimer to the reader, use your best judgment. Always consult a competent physician before starting any health regimen or treatment for disease.

Decision making by cancer patients and their families is hampered when one cannot easily examine statistics of the various cancer treatments available for specific diseases. The medical community intentionally obfuscates and outright hides the true statistics of its cancer and other medical treatments; this helps motivate a number of patients to consent to the appalling and barbaric treatments offered by the AMA, especially chemotherapy.

Chemo, with accompanying radiation treatment, more often than not kills the patient in the timespan that the doctor's initial prognosis estimated that the patient had left to live. If a doctor gives the patient eight to nine months to live, more than likely, the doctor's cancer treatments will kill the patient in eight to nine months!

What is going on with the billions of dollars raised by the cancer charities? One could ask, "Why hasn't there been a cure for cancer developed and made available to everyone?" Better yet, one could ask, "Is the cure being suppressed so that trillions of dollars can be made fighting the ever-losing battle of cancer?" Millions of men and women run wearing pink clothing to raise money for breast cancer research, but virtually not one penny of that money goes into holistic medicine research for fighting the ever too-prolific breast cancer.

Dr. Glidden claims that the daily ingestion of the right amount of selenium could reduce breast cancer by 80 percent in one generation. Think of the implications of saving millions of women that are needlessly suffering from breast cancer and destined for early death because of the corrupted and controlled medical mafia.

There is more money to be made by not curing cancer than by curing cancer. By focusing on and delivering only the most profitable treatments, it is easy to see that the AMA is more concerned with monetary profits than with curing disease. This is a pathetic commentary on the effectiveness of allopathic medicine specifically and the healthcare and pharmaceutical industries in general.

Some may find this difficult to believe, but one only needs to look at the overall results of these deadly treatments to understand the AMA's sweeping and sinister philosophy and modus operandi. Obviously, not every doctor is evil and concerned only with profit. Many doctors become dismayed and disgusted by losing patients after prescribing one of only a few treatments that doctors are allowed to prescribe to their cancer patients. Hospitals are restricted from prescribing treatments that are not covered by insurance companies, which is a method of control crafted by the legislature and the insurance industry under the blessing and direction of the AMA.

Quality homeopathic research and its widespread publication need to occur, ensuring that the public understands the effectiveness of the various types of cancer treatments that are not offered by the AMA. This information helps cancer patients to better understand and locate the most effective treatments available for their specific cancer.

Holistic treatments are not nearly as destructive as those treatments and medicines provided by the AMA, including, but certainly not limited to, chemotherapy and pharmacology.

The media, with a majority of its profit coming from mammoth pharmaceutical companies' advertising budgets, are not going to inform the public of the actual effectiveness—or, rather, the ineffectiveness—of the AMA's cancer treatments.

Anything that results in curing cancer must be suppressed in order to control the monopoly of the AMA, which dictates and limits the current treatments available to the public. It is incredible and even outrageous to imagine how radiation and chemotherapy were sold to the public as treatments for cancer. Radiation, chemotherapy, and certain medications are highly toxic to the cells of the body. How are toxic elements being sold to the public as treatments for disease?

Do you remember stories of Grandpa Rockefeller, the snake-oil salesman, who worked beside a doctor, wore a white coat, and traveled around selling elixirs that were filled with oil to uneducated customers who wanted to prolong their lives and become disease free? These elixirs were promoted to cure anything from rashes to arthritis and anything else that might be eating away at a person. Snake oil of that time was fraudulently sold to the public, just as chemotherapy and radiation are fraudulently and unconscionably sold today.

There are many who complain that cures for cancer, AIDS, and many other diseases are intentionally being suppressed from the market; they are 100 percent correct.

Many doctors have discovered much less harmful and more effective treatments for cancer than those used by the AMA's minions. Across Europe, doctors are using food-grade hydrogen peroxide to treat cancer patients. The One Minute Cure: The Secret to Healing Virtually All Diseases by Madison Cavanaugh, which has sold over a million copies, has a great discussion of the medical industry and its suppression of alternative cancer treatments.

There are many other treatments for cancer that claim to change the pH and oxygen levels of the body making it virtually impossible for cancers to live in such modified environments. This is a promising area for cancer research that is not being conducted or supported by the AMA.

Why would the US government ban treatments, including the many cancer treatments being practiced in Tijuana, Mexico, which are located beyond the reach of the AMA? Many holistic treatments are not nearly as dangerous and do very little harm to patients, compared to devastating chemotherapy and radiation treatments prescribed by American doctors.

Purportedly created to destroy cancerous cells, chemotherapy and radiation treatments unfortunately and simultaneously kill the body's healthy cells as well. These treatments do not differentiate between the cancerous cells and the body's healthy cells; they kill all types of cells, effectively, efficiently, and indiscriminately..

These allopathic treatments are so dangerous that, if one were to practice these treatments without obtaining a license by the state and the patient died, the practitioner would be arrested and indicted for murder. Therefore, you could say treatment with a medical license legalizes murder.

Can you imagine bringing your car to an auto mechanic who destroyed 97 percent of his clients' cars? How long would he be in business? The mechanic would be sued. Why are the doctors who apply chemotherapy not prosecuted and sued for giving chemotherapy to patients when it is 97 percent ineffective?

There is another interesting phenomenon to consider regarding Americans' health, and that is the massive increase in the number of people dying of cancer. These statistics have sharply increased and are growing at an alarming rate. The statistics are somewhat diluted by the AMA as a result of the methodology implemented in the gathering of the data and the corollary statistics from which they are derived.

Patients whose cancer is in remission and survive for five years are no longer considered by the medical community to have cancer. If they die one day after five years of the first date of remission, then they are not counted as having died of cancer. The number of cancer deaths is staggering, and the statistics, although doctored, speak for themselves: 50 percent of men and over 33 percent of women currently die of cancer.

Perhaps the reason that so many more people are dying of cancer today than only a few decades ago has something to do with the foods we eat, the air we breathe, and the water we drink.

Many blame the high rates of cancer on cigarette smoking, but people have smoked for centuries. Granted, there were far fewer toxic chemicals intentionally placed in the cigarettes of yesteryear than there are today, but people have been puffing for a while. It is interesting to investigate the intentional poisoning of smokers, as discussed in the 1999 movie *The Insider* starring the acclaimed Al Pacino and Russell Crowe. Behemoth cigarette companies purposely add ammonia-based complex chemicals to make cigarettes as addictive as possible. The cigarette industry shares the same modus operandi as the pharmaceutical industry; when cigarette companies obtain a customer, they try to keep him or her till death.

It is simply misinformation and redirection to blame cancer totally on cigarettes when the food that people are eating only looks like food and has little to no nutritional value or sustenance. Our air is full of toxins, and our water is unfit for a dog to drink. Without eating real food and drinking clean water, it is virtually impossible for the body to overcome many diseases it may develop in order to reacquire good health.

Years ago, I read that the nutrient depletion of the soil from American farms has become so significant as a result of the use of petroleum-based fertilizers that in 1975 one would have to eat twenty-eight heads of lettuce to receive the same nutritional value as eating one head of lettuce in 1920. When we walk into a modern supermarket, much of what we see looks like food, tastes like food, but is void of nutritional value. When food lacks nutritional value, a person overeats until the body has received the level of nutrition that it needs. No wonder obesity is everywhere; people are overeating because their food contains little in the way of nutrients.

At least people are aware and given notice of the dangers of smoking. It says it right on the package—"SURGEON GENERAL'S WARNING: Smoking Causes Lung Cancer, Heart Disease, Emphysema and May Complicate Pregnancy."

One of the sad statistics regarding the healthcare industry is that millions of people have undergone chemotherapy and radiation only to have the last months of their lives become a living—or better yet, a dying— hell. Chemotherapy utilizes a similar concoction of chemicals as those found in mustard gas. Under the guise of fighting cancer, physicians harmfully inject these damaging biohazardous chemicals into patients as a treatment to save their lives. Those who undergo this trauma are appalled at the devastating effects it has on the body.

When a doctor injects potentially lethal biohazards and noxious toxicities into a person's body, the patient often becomes violently ill as the body attempts to ferociously expel the foreign toxins. As chemotherapy patients cling to life, they regularly report overwhelming side effects with unspeakable discomfort, nausea, and vomiting spells; chemo patients' hair often falls out by the handful.

Cancer.gov/cancertopics/coping/physicaleffects/chemo-side-effects is recommended to learn about the side effects from chemotherapy, the steps to take, problems to call the doctor about, and questions to ask before agreeing to the AMA's barbaric treatments. It lists the following as some of the side effects of chemotherapy:

- Anemia
- Appetite changes
- Bleeding problems
- Constipation
- Diarrhea
- Fatigue
- Hair loss
- Infection
- Memory changes
- Mouth and throat changes
- Nausea
- Vomiting
- Nerve changes
- Pain
- Sexual and fertility changes
- Skin and nail changes
- Swelling
- Urination changes

There are downloadable PDF files at the above link describing these debilitating side effects in detail. It behooves the reader to learn the options before you or a loved one begins chemotherapy as a so-called treatment for cancer.

Radiation is simply a method of burning a person using a more targeted approach than an open flame, killing both healthy and unhealthy cells. Many patients hope the radiation kills the cancerous cells before it inevitably kills the body. It can be compared to hitting a person over the head with a hammer in the hopes of treating a headache!

There must be a more humane method of treating cancers than the largely ineffective treatments used today. In the twenty-first century, there should be more effective treatments that simply prevent cancer from growing in the body.

We would think that before treating patients with cancer, doctors would determine what cancer actually is. Many people are perplexed and amazed to discover that most doctors do not even know the actual composition of cancer and that it is simply a fungus, which selectively grows exclusively within an unhealthy body.

According to oncologists, cancer can exist and flourish only within an environment that has an acidic pH level, as opposed to an alkaline pH level. Dr. Tullio Simoncini, a leading Italian oncologist, has devised a simple and cost-effective method of treating cancerous tumors with baking soda injections. There are numerous videos on the Internet discussing the sodium bicarbonate treatments that he employs to make cancerous tumors vanish in a matter of days. Simoncini can be reached at the contact page of curenaturalicancro.com/en/.

An informative video that is highly recommended is How to Treat Cancer—Cancer is Fungus, which may be difficult to find, as it's constantly being banned and taken down from the Internet by the technocratic authorities. There is an extraordinarily interesting interview of Dr. Tullio Simoncini, Chemo Kills You. Cancer Is Fungus & Can Be Treated With Sodium Bicarbonate! available at youtube.com/watch?v=RXHaZJ 0Y6Xc.

Get these videos while you can. Many of the links provided within this book are constantly being censored; you might have to hunt a bit on the Internet. In case the video and other links within this book become censored and removed from the Internet, it might be advisable to download the videos and other information in order to preserve the information in a library on your computer for later retrieval and sharing with others.

One of the main objectives for controlling high-tech companies is to enable the censorship of information that exposes the truth, sometimes the deadly truth, regarding our society. Truth is the replication and conveyance of reality; the world needs more truth. Truth is the building block of culture. Truth is feared, yet the most chased-after treasure. Truth is yelled from the rooftops yet ignored by the majority!

According to Simoncini, after receiving an injection of a mixture of baking soda and water into the arteries servicing malignant tumors, within days the cancerous fungus begins to shrivel and die. Amazingly, Simoncini's treatment has an incredibly effective rate of ridding the body of cancerous tumors, which is virtually unheard of under the AMA's treatments. Many proclaim that the sodium bicarbonate treatments are far more effective than chemotherapy and have none of the horrific side effects.

Simoncini's treatment methods are being strongly opposed in Italy and internationally simply because the treatment eradicates cancers with greater success than virtually any chemotherapy treatment and it is very inexpensive. The problem is that sodium bicarbonate treatments cost only a few cents, whereas the cost of American treatments can exceed hundreds of thousands of dollars before the patient dies from cancer or more likely the toxic treatment.

It appears to make more sense, when seeking competent health care, to undergo a method of healing that aligns with the tenets of the Hippocratic oath: "I will remember that there is art to medicine as well as science, and that warmth, sympathy, and understanding may outweigh the surgeon's knife or the chemist's drug . . . I will not be ashamed to say 'I know not,' nor will I fail to call in my colleagues when the skills of another are needed for a patient's recovery" (en.wikipedia.org/wiki/Hippocratic_Oath).

This is often more briefly stated as the following: "As to diseases, make a habit of two things—to help, or at least, to do no harm."

One should implore the medical community, which has such a dismal record of accomplishment in the handling and curing of cancer, to investigate experimental and new treatments and procedures that deliver better results and more optimistic prognoses for the patient. There needs to be a revolution of thought in the medical field that would allow doctors and medical practitioners the freedom to implement more reliable and humane treatments, without the debilitating side effects experienced by undergoing chemotherapy and radiation treatments.

There is a nexus of collaboration among the FDA, AMA, pharmaceutical industry, and mega-corporate hospital chains that depend financially on the delivery of ineffective yet highly profitable treatments. Quickly analyzing the hospital industry, it becomes quite apparent that there is an overall commonality of control, a medical Mafia if you will, that prizes profit above patients.

A few mammoth corporations control a majority of the hospital chains nationwide, which results in a reallocation of society's wealth from the patients to the owners of these hospitals and the entire medical community.

When this data is coupled with the pharmaceutical companies' lavish endowments to medical schools, we are left with the understanding that medical schools, by design, merely serve and contribute to the profit desires of the mega healthcare and pharmaceutical industries.

Doctors suffer through the regimen of medical school and are required to perform a residency with shifts that can last over seventy-two hours at a time, three long grueling days, nearly without sleep. Participating residents often experience insomnia and exhaustion. A resulting level of indoctrination and even brainwashing occurs in conjunction with the sleep deprivation most residents regularly endure. Many residents turn to stimulants and other addictive amphetamines to cope with working demandingly long shifts.

Further analysis of the medical industry yields some interesting bits of information. Approximately 35 percent (although many believe the number to be much higher, even reaching over 90 percent) of all health-care funds generated occur in the last year of a patient's life. Believe it or not, 1 percent of the population is responsible for approximately 30 percent of the nation's medical expenses relating to end-of-life care, as cited in thirteen.org/bid/sb-howmuch.html.

Most people are relatively healthy until something catastrophic occurs, such as cancer. Cancer patients placed in America's massive medical machine usually endure about a year of treatment, at which time many patients' lives end with a most miserable and agonizing death. The value of medical treatments during the last year of a patient's life can tally in the millions of dollars, but only if the doctors and the hospitals handle things correctly. These catastrophic illnesses, and their associated treatments, bankrupt nearly every family unfortunate enough to fall prey to unconscionable medical practitioners.

Being at the hospital greatly improves a person's chances of dying. There is no more common way to die than to check into a hospital for treatment. Hospitals do not provide cures; they provide only FDA-approved treatments.

As many of us have witnessed a friend or family member die of cancer, we realize that often the treatment is more damaging than the actual disease. Many patients rightly wonder whether they may have a better quality of life and live longer by never going to the hospital in the first place.

Patients choosing conventional medical treatment entering their last year of life soon realize this is going to be their most agonizing and painful year yet. Being tested, prodded, and poked at irregular intervals often causes sleep deprivation in patients who are trying to heal. Being placed in a hospital is often the beginning of a healthcare disaster, consisting of sometimes dreadful medical treatments that far too often culminate in the patient's worsening and even death.

Radiation and chemotherapy can cause even the strongest of people to become feeble shells of their healthy selves, wanting nothing more than to end their persistent and prolonged pain and misery, caused by incompetent practitioners delivering substandard treatment and operating in an unethical healthcare system.

A prudent person could conclude there is a special financial interest in treating patients during the last year of their lives since that is when a lot of money reallocates from the pockets of the patients and their families into the bulging bank accounts of the medical community. This transference of wealth negatively affects far too many families and causes money that would otherwise be the rightful inheritance of a patient's family to transfer to the medical community through costly tests, treatments, and outrageously expensive hospital stays.

There are experimental injections for heart attack patients, delivered in many medical evacuation helicopters, which can exceed fifty thousand dollars per injection. A person just suffering a heart attack might find it almost impossible to refuse an offer by the paramedics for this high-cost, experimental drug "that could help save ya!" The injection cost is on top of the incredibly overpriced helicopter flight, which can easily cost over ten thousand dollars for even the shortest distances.

Heart problems kill more people in America than any other malady; almost half a million people die from cardio-related problems per year. Many medical professionals believe heart problems are the result of continually eating poor-quality food and a lack of exercise.

Often people with heart problems and clogged arteries report benefits from chelation therapy, which can be consumed orally or taken by injections. Chelation therapy works by introducing a liquid chelating substance into the blood system that helps to rid the veins and arteries of plaque buildup that has occurred over the years. This is sort of like a Liquid-Plumr method of cleaning one's arteries.

The medical community rarely prescribes chelation, although many believe chelation is a very effective preventive measure against heart and coronary disease.

Angioprim is one of the world's leading providers of oral chelation and is very affordable. You can research more information at angioprim.com. According to its website:

> Angioprim is a safe, fast and cost effective way to clean your veins and arteries. Many believe that no matter what your age or health condition, you can extend your life and add life to your years beginning right now! You can improve your overall health and vitality and increase your energy levels. You can truly look and feel younger than your years. Angioprim can help promote a healthy cardiovascular system.

This product is often highly recommended by competent physicians to those who want to clean and remove plaque from their arteries and improve cardio function. One cannot say enough regarding the benefits of chelation.

Here is another disclaimer: always consult a competent physician before undergoing any type of chelation program. Please consult a competent medical professional to evaluate and diagnose your individual medical case, whatever it may be.

None of the comments or claims made in this book has been evaluated by the FDA, and any actions taken by the reader are the sole responsibility of the reader.

For cancer, as well as the treatment of most other diseases, logic dictates that in a body in which cancer is able to develop, there needs to be changes made in order to retard the growth and eventually reduce the number of cancerous cells that the body is supporting. This is how a patient recovers; the constitution of the body changes, and these changes allow the patient to begin to truly recover. While initially treating cancer, it makes sense to attempt an approach that does little or no long-term damage to the existing condition and functioning of the body.

If one were to consider the actual healing process, it becomes interesting to note the various methods utilized to bring about the return of good health.

Let us first take a look at how a body becomes ill. It proceeds through a number of diminishing conditions, which affect the various systems of the body, leading step by step down the path toward deterioration and sickness and arriving finally at death.

It becomes obvious healthcare treatments that attempt to reverse the actions that have led to the patient's diminished state of well-being may contribute to the body's improvement and well-being. If one were able to reverse the steps that lead to sickness, would that person regain his or her health? Can the human body reverse the effects of sickness by reversing the actions that led one to become sick?

Many believe that the most fundamental improvement and change a person with cancer can undergo are to raise the alkalinity level of his or her body. As mentioned earlier, scientists claim that cancer can only live in an acidic environment on the pH scale. Many reports indicate that changing the body from an acidic environment to an alkaline environment prevents cancer from living and flourishing in the body. Many believe raising the alkalinity level of the body prevents or deters the development of cancerous cells, as an alkaline environment is supposedly hostile to the development of cancerous cells.

Ozone therapy is a promising technology for treating cancer by changing the body from an oxygen-deprived environment to an oxygen-rich one. Some believe that increases in ozone levels may assist in causing shifts in the pH level of cancerous patients from an acidic to an alkaline pH level, thus making it theoretically impossible for cancer to grow.

The North Carolina Institute of Technology in Ashville, although heavily attacked as quackery on the Internet, offers ozone treatments that may have better results treating cancerous patients than the conventional chemotherapy route. Ozone treatments have some very positive and promising results in the treating of leukemia, along with other maladies, and are quite popular south of the border in Tijuana, Mexico.

Others claim that a diet of organic fruits and vegetables in combination with ozone therapy is even more effective in killing cancer.

There are probably as many theories on the treatment of cancer in the underground medical community as there are renegade members. Oasis of Hope (oasisofhope.com) has several alternative treatments for cancer, and there are many other alternative clinics in Tijuana, Mexico, that provide unconventional treatments for cancer, AIDS, and other diseases.

The above information regarding the medical community and the treatment options for various diseases, both conventional and nonconventional, is in no way to be inferred as medical advice or as a medical suggestion, diagnosis, or evaluation. People who have cancer, other diseases, or symptoms should do their own research and seek competent medical advice before starting any treatment plan or regimen. Good luck with whatever treatment, if any, you choose to undergo.

Medical treatments that are prescribed that do not pass a minimum standard of effectiveness should not be covered under insurance policies and should be barred by medical professionals, the AMA, and the FDA. Foremost, this would include chemotherapy and radiation therapies.

Should a doctor who prescribes a medical treatment that damages and kills a patient be made to refund all money he or she received to the patient's family and heirs? Should such doctors face murder, manslaughter, or similar charges? Why should the American people pay to have their loved ones killed by dangerous pharmaceuticals and barbaric treatments at the hands of the medical community?

In Chinese medicine, to correct the non-optimum functioning of the body, natural doctors have been prescribing herbs for centuries without the dangerous side effects associated with pharmaceutical concoctions.

The first course of action in treating cancer or any illness should be to promote the patient's quality of life, even if the patient's death is imminent. It makes sense to most of us that in the case of a suffering patient the primary action should be to lessen the patient's level of suffering.

What the medical profession is currently delivering in the area of cancer treatments are barbaric and incredibly unsuccessful types of treatments that increase the pain and discomfort levels of the person receiving the treatment. Replacing these highly unsuccessful treatments with more effective, less damaging treatments that aim to cure an unhealthy body, and not kill it, will vastly improve the quality of care that cancer patients receive in the United States.

It is time that cancer research foundations aim their research on experimental holistic treatments and procedures that make sense. Effective and competent research should develop a number of better methods to assist patients suffering from cancer and AIDS.

One area in which the AMA and the FDA might concentrate their efforts in discovering a cure for cancer is to develop medicine with ingredients that are consumable by patients and have no side effects. The ingredients of a potential cure will likely be a mixture of herbs, foods, and food components that change the body's innate characteristics to an environment that no longer sustains cancerous growths. A primary objective is to assist the body to reduce its acidic level and provide alkaline agents that can contribute to the continuation of an internally abundant alkaline environment, safeguarding the body from future disease.

Researchers predict that cures for cancer will result from microbiology adjustments, rather than damaging chemical and pharmaceutical adjustments. Microbiological adjustments aim to correct the body's internal environment into one where it is impossible for cancer to grow or even survive. If the focus of medical research is concentrated on transforming the body into an environment that does not support cancer, the body will automatically expel the cancer.

There is another aspect of health not given its just due by the medical community—the circulatory system. If one considers that most Americans are sedentary and do not get much exercise, it is not difficult to deduce why heart-related deaths are the number one killer in America. Consider the relationship between obesity and heart failures; then you will soon realize the importance of doing vigorous exercise and its contribution to one's overall health.

How much longer are people going to tolerate the American Cancer Society not developing and bringing to market a cure for cancer? The same thing applies to all the other associations that have telethons or 10K walks or simply raise endless amounts of money without developing any decent treatments or cures. Virtually all those billions in raised funds go to programs that are allopathic in nature in order that pharmaceutical corporations can develop medications, patent them, and sell them for wild profits.

Charity is one thing, but when a majority of the money raised goes to executive salaries and operation costs, one starts to reconsider where and for what purpose one's charitable donations are being used. Raising charitable funds for organizations in which only a fraction of a penny of every dollar donated is actually spent on research and finding a cure will not solve the health problems that face the world. Many medical and charitable associations make some administrative personnel very wealthy without providing any substantial treatment breakthroughs for decades. It is more profitable to continually research cancer and other such chronic diseases than it is to cure them once and for all.

When was the last time we heard of an amazing and revolutionary cure or breakthrough from the American Cancer Association or the American Diabetes Association or the Muscular Dystrophy Association? Apparently, it is as though some people would rather see the populations perish through disease, instead of flourish in health.

This lack of medical progression is just another indication of the amount of oppression affecting the medical industry and its patients. We live in a society that hides medical breakthroughs in the darkest recesses of the shadows of evil. Addressing health problems with a different approach can make a difference in the lives of millions of people. The time-tested pharmaceutical methods have proven themselves to be unsuccessful, and to continue down this research road leads only to further destructive procedures and treatments for humankind.

Another topic worthy of discussion is the different vaccinations the government is encouraging or, in some cases, forcing the population to take.

One may find it difficult to comprehend that the H1N1 virus precariously spread starting only days after Obama's visit to Mexico. Most influenza types of flu originate in the Far East, but H1N1 suddenly sprang up in the Western Hemisphere in Mexico. The H1N1 virus was most likely created in a military laboratory, just as AIDS and many other diseases were conceived.

I recommend Alan Cantwell's article, "The Man-Made Origin of AIDS: Are Human and Viral Experiments Responsible for Unleashing the HIV Holocaust?" (rense.com/general45/cant.htm). Many thanks are extended to Rense.com for its accurate and informative reporting documenting the truth. Jeff Rense and his associates provide research that explains many of the ills and important topics that affect millions and even billions of people worldwide.

As mentioned above, many of the various governmental departments function in a manner opposite to their name, which leads one to imagine the true intent of the World Health Organization (WHO). The folks who control the WHO and implement its global policies are responsible for internationally unleashing some of the most catastrophic diseases over the past decades. The WHO's diabolic interests are nothing short of the total decimation and annihilation of the human race. The WHO has implemented policies that have proven to be detrimental to the human race.

Although reported as a hoax, Russia disclosed that people infected with the AIDS virus should thank the WHO for creating the virus at the Fort Detrick Air Force Base in Maryland. According to numerous reports, the WHO was instrumental in allowing the wide-scale testing of HIV on many tens of thousands of Africans during the Kennedy and

Johnson administrations under the auspices of vaccinating for measles and mumps.

The battle cry of the sadistic eugenicist is often, "Oh, the poor children! We have to help the poor unfortunate children!"

Some may find it difficult to face the facts. However, there is no way that the spread of AIDS throughout the continent of Africa could have occurred so quickly and devastatingly if it had originated from one airline pilot being bitten by a green monkey in the early 1980s or at a central starting point, a ground zero point of origin, if you will.

Should one use calculus to determine the transmission rates of AIDS throughout Africa, one quickly discovers that the calculations based on the "one man, one monkey theory" are incorrect by a magnitude of over a thousand. There is no way that the disease could have had a single origination point in the early 1980s and then have seventy-five million AIDS cases infecting and devastating the African population by the late 1980s. If there were a single origination point, scientists calculate there would have been an estimated seventy-five thousand cases, not seventy-five million!

The American AIDS epidemic spread in a similarly covert fashion by delivering HIV-laced hepatitis B vaccinations into the US homosexual population in the early 1980s. There was a media-manufactured hepatitis B scare aimed at the homosexual population throughout various cities. Gay men lined up on the streets of Boston, New York, Miami, Chicago, and San Francisco, desperate to receive the hepatitis B vaccination to protect themselves and their partners from contracting such a horrible and debilitating disease. The only problem was that the hepatitis B vaccination they received was secretly infected with the HIV-AIDS virus, and shortly thereafter, there was an epidemic infection rate of AIDS among the same homosexual population. The massive and sudden AIDS infection of America's homosexual population was attributed to the reported promiscuity that was rampant in the 1980s among the gay population, especially in some of San Francisco's and other major cities' bathhouses.

Later, the homosexual population decreased its number of AIDS cases by taking sexual precautions but only after thousands upon thousands of unsuspecting men perished from the disease that was supplied courtesy and compliments of the US government. Just Google "US gov spread AIDS," and there is endless documentation and substantiation available regarding the tragic spread of AIDS throughout America's homosexual community. For additional information, you can also read "The Gay Experiment that Started AIDS in America" at rense.com/general68/gayex.htm.

Everyone needs to be wary when he or she hears of the government's wanting to help its citizens by controlling healthcare. Is there anything the government can do that the private sector cannot do better?

When one considers the takeover of the Centers for Disease Control and Prevention (CDC) by the vaccination companies, it is easy to comprehend that there are strong and powerful special interests in the medical field that dictate the heath quality for the entire planet. New York Times bestselling author Robert F. Kennedy Jr. details the reckless vaccination companies that develop intentionally harmful vaccinations and are indemnified by the government for any damages caused by injecting their poisonous vaccinations into unsuspecting children and uninformed adults.

Kennedy's Thimerosal: Let the Science Speak: The Evidence Supporting the Immediate Removal of Mercury—a Known Neurotoxin—from Vaccines discusses the destruction caused by vaccinations that include mercury as an ingredient, which is a harmful neurotoxin. Every parent and parent-to-be should research the dangers associated with most vaccinations and the government's collusion with and indemnification of the entire vaccination industry.

Kennedy explains the relationship of thimerosal and the sharp rise of developmental disorders, including autism, resulting from receiving vaccinations that contain mercury toxins, which attack the neurological system of its recipients. The European Union banned thimerosal according to Wikipedia.

According to "In These Times," by Annette Fuentes, the Indianapolis-based pharmaceutical giant Eli Lilly developed and registered thimerosal under the trade name Merthiolate in 1929. Eli Lilly began marketing Merthiolate as an antibacterial and antifungal preservative in vaccines (inthesetimes.com/article/649/eli_lilly_and_timerosal).

At traceamounts.com, Kennedy promotes a banner on his website that reads "Trace Amounts, Autism, Mercury and the Hidden Truth." This is a very educational site. It details the relationship between mercury, which is contained in many vaccinations, and the many unfortunately immunized infants and toddlers who suddenly develop autism right before their parents' eyes. It is frightening to realize that today the percentage of autism within the United States is at an all-time high; see articles.latimes.com/2013/mar/20/science/la-sci-autism-20130321.

Everywhere one looks in the medical community, one sees madness. America deserves a higher level of competence in its healthcare treatments and system.

Concerning the infringement of the US government into the lives of the American people through the Affordable Care Act, citizens must ask themselves, "What interest does the government have in dictating, controlling, and regulating Americans' health issues? Who benefits from this act, and to which insurance companies will go the reallocated healthcare dollars that are taken from the wallets of unwitting Americans?"

Today we can all agree that far too many patients under the care of the American healthcare industry unnecessarily die from ineffective treatments. In conclusion, with all the above evidence taken into consideration, we must regrettably ask, "Is the healthcare industry a vehicle of population control implemented by the elite? Is Obamacare, which was signed into law against the will of the American people, the driver of such a corrupt and debased plan for exterminating the human race?"

Every reader needs to grasp the wickedness of the vision held by those in power, which includes detailed views and plans of the massive reduction of the world's population. It seems as though a majority of legislation, which comes out of Washington, DC, is filled with death.

What do the healthcare industry and the military industry have in common? One answer is obvious: they both kill too many people!

As a nation, America's healthcare prognosis must improve. Is it too much to ask that medicine evolve to a higher level and finally provide effective and humane treatments for disease? The world deserves better medical treatment; get on it, science boys and girls.

CHAPTER 12

Unsustainable Economics

Unsustainable economics is assured when one class is profiting from the remainder.

– GEOFFREY BELFRY

A chicken in every pot and a car in every garage.

– HUEY P. LONG

Every gun that is made, every warship launched, every rocket fired, signifies in the final sense a theft from those who hunger and are not fed, those who are cold and not clothed.

– DWIGHT D. EISENHOWER

As a member of Congress, I believe it is the responsibility of those elected to represent the people at every level of government to ensure that our government works to ensure that every person who wants gainful employment has it.

– LEONARD BOSWELL

It turns out that advancing equal opportunity and economic empowerment is both morally right and good economics because discrimination, poverty and ignorance restrict growth while investments in education, infrastructure and scientific and technological research increase it, creating more good jobs and new wealth for all of us.

– BILL CLINTON

The best way to appreciate your job is to imagine yourself without one.

– OSCAR WILDER

Economics is extremely useful as a form of employment for econo-mists.

         – JOHN KENNETH GALBRAITH

The first lesson of economics is scarcity: there is never enough of anything to fully satisfy all those who want it. The first lesson of politics is to disregard the first lesson of economics.

         – THOMAS SOWELL

The only place where success comes before work is in the dictionary.

         – DONALD KENDALL

Geography has made us neighbors. History has made us friends. Economics has made us partners, and necessity has made us allies. Those who, God has so joined together, let no man put asunder.

         – JOHN F. KENNEDY

When a management with a reputation for brilliance tackles a business with a reputation for bad economics, it is the reputation of the business that remains intact.

         – WARREN BUFFET

Economics is all about consumption. People either spend money now or they use financial instruments—like bonds, stocks and savings accounts—so they can spend more later.

         – ADAM DAVIDSON

In economics, the majority is always wrong.

         – JOHN KENNETH GALBRAITH

Commercial institutions, proud of their achievements, do not see that healthy living systems—clean air and water, healthy soil, stable climates—are integral to a functioning economy. As our living systems deteriorate, traditional forecasting and business eco-nomics become the equivalent of house rules on a sinking ship."

         – PAUL HAWKEN

IF THE GOVERNMENT WANTS TO ENSURE continual and viable employment, it needs to stop constructing barriers made up of regulations that impede employment, start protecting its borders from illegal immigration, and enforce protectionist tariffs to create American manufacturing opportunities.

Two of the most pernicious agreements the United States entered were the General Agreement on Tariffs and Trade (GATT) and North American Free Trade Agreement (NAFTA). These destructive agreements have been legislatively concocted to intentionally destroy America's standard of living until it becomes on par with that of a third-world country. Instead of raising the world's standard of living, those that treasonously legislated GATT and NAFTA thought it was easier to decimate America's standard of living and bring the American economy down to the level of Russia's economy.

The United States is now experiencing the consequences of an economy void of border protection. Illegal immigration is a significant problem that lowers employment opportunities and the standard of living in the United States. More important to improving the US economy, the concurrent obliteration of US tariffs and unfair trade protections need to end. It would greatly improve the US economy and protect the American way of life if these protective mechanisms were reestablished.

By opening America's borders and failing to control our international trade positions and tariffs, politicians have intentionally forfeited control of the economic destiny of the United States into the hands of the international trade organizations and illegal immigrants. Any acts, tariffs, or legislation that turns over the inherent economic rights or lessens the sovereignty of the United States is a destructive act, tariff, or piece of legislation designed against the best interest of the United States.

To improve and sustain a vibrant US economy and world economy, we should remove severe fluctuations within the economy as a result of money-supply constrictions and expansions. These constrictions and expansions create shortages and abundances of money in the economy and operate at the whims of the biggest and most powerful special interest—the banks.

When there is a contraction or constriction of the money supply, there is a shortage of money in the economy, times become tough, and unemployment becomes high. When there is an expansion of the money supply, there is an abundance of money in the economy, unemployment lowers, and times tend to improve.

The Federal Reserve is the private company that independently dictates the levels and amounts of the money supply. The Fed conducts private meetings and then announces to the public the monetary decisions it has concluded. Knowing what the Federal Reserve will do in the near future is incredibly valuable information, which unfairly is made available only to a select group of people.

When the economy is recessed or depressed, many people optimistically believe that its recovery will naturally occur in an unassisted and timely manner. Nothing is further from the truth. Recessions and depressions are intentionally created and caused by the Federal Reserve and the monetary expansion and contraction policies it implements that positively or negatively affect the money supply.

The direct actions and economic tools available to the Federal Reserve are the most powerful mechanisms used to influence and determine the vibrancy, quality, and performance of the US economy. The Federal Reserve creates recessions and depressions by constricting the money supply until there is very little money in the economy, which is needed to lubricate the wheels of commerce. In order to create an economic recovery, the Federal Reserve simply expands the money supply, and the economy predictably recovers.

The simplicity of this pattern of economic manipulation, control, and ultimately oppression is getting more difficult to ensure, as the overall world economy heads perilously into oblivion, propelled by overburdensome debt and wicked criminality.

Employment is an important function to understand in its relationship to the money supply. Simply stated, if there is an abundant money supply, there are jobs available and unemployment is low. If there is a constriction of the money supply, there is a shortage of money available and commensurately, there is high unemployment. Underemployment, unemployment, as well as abundant employment are the result of the direct actions of the Federal Reserve and its monetary policies pertaining to constriction and expansion of the economy's money supply.

Today's corrupt monetary policies ensure that the economy is controlled by a few bankers and at the expense of the rest of the people. With special private banking interests being granted special privileges under the law, it is only a matter of time before the greed of those controlling the policies and actions of the economy destroy it.

Currently, Americans are witnessing the destruction of the US economy and the US dollar (the Federal Reserve Note) right before our very eyes. As discussed above, the Federal Reserve Note is not redeemable for any metal of value, like gold and silver, but is based on a corrupt, privately owned, fiat banking system. Every economy that has ever used a fiat currency has calamitously failed, and the mighty US economy will also soon collapse, you can rest assured, with mathematical certainty.

Without intervention, it is highly unlikely that the Federal Reserve Note will outperform the previous two thousand fiat currencies that were used by various countries and empires throughout history and which inevitably came crashing down to the ground.

The United States needs competent economic intervention and reform, including readjustment or cancellation of the national debt. Additionally, it is imperative for the United States to demand and start using stable and redeemable money that is controlled by the nation under the direction of the US Congress. Only by an ethical government retaking control of its nation's money are its citizens freed.

When one calculates the interest that the private bankers charge, it becomes apparent that the United States has already passed the point of no return. Negotiation and reduction of a substantial amount, if not all, of the national debt is necessary in order to maintain a properly functioning economy, free from oppressive banking influences that we stupidly and needlessly tolerate. Interest payments that increase exponentially become unserviceable by a nation when those payments interfere with its citizens' ability to purchase staples, such as food and water. Depriving economic situations, as those just mentioned, are the seeds of revolt and revolution, as witnessed in Syria.

As a nation's tax rate increases to service loan payments, which cover only the interest on the national debt, the population will often find revolution as a viable course of action, rather than spending their lives working as slaves to pay unfair and overly burdensome taxes.

Look at the 2016 presidential election and the large number of citizens that were dissatisfied with their government and rallied behind Donald Trump—the great hope of the people and the American way of life. Trump was the only candidate who paid his own way and stood up to the special interests, and look what's happening.

The people are finally just beginning to demand that criminality is extricated from the US government, that national tyranny is removed from the lives of every American, and that all people of the world are treated with dignity.

As food prices increase and economic pressures mount, there is an increase in the number of government revolutions and rebellions. "The Math That Predicted the Revolutions Sweeping the Globe Right Now" by Brian Merchant at motherboard.vice.com/en_us/article/539b55/a-complex-systems-model-predicted-the-revolutions-sweeping-the-globe-right discusses how increases in food prices urge and incentivize a population to resort to revolution.

This is happening all over the world. One after another, countries are failing due to financial impossibilities imposed by the international bankers, requiring the citizens to turn almost all their earnings and savings over to the bankers just to pay the interest on the failing country's debt. For evidence of recently bankrupted and/or financially distressed and revolting countries, simply consider Greece, Iceland, Venezuela, Ukraine, Thailand, Bosnia, Syria, and many others; this list keeps growing at a frightening rate. Many African as well as Latin and South American countries have financially bitten the dust in the last few years. All countries inevitably suffer a similar fate of enslavement to the loan-sharking banks.

One of the major differences in today's economy compared to economies of the past is that the media can disseminate the special interests' propaganda across the planet in a matter of seconds. Today we can cause and calculate financial changes internationally in fractions of a second. Earlier, when technology was less advanced, there was no ability of the media to destroy consumer confidence on an international scale in only a matter of seconds. Today, international economic impressions of America and its actions are created and promoted with the flip of a switch, while the public is never truly informed of those who are actually controlling the economy. One of the media's main responsibilities is to distract the population from discovering the truth regarding who is calling the financial shots in this country and throughout the world.

Previously, we citizens held a false confidence that the government was working for the people to create an environment of economic hope and prosperity, an environment in which people could obtain employment that paid well enough to feed and provide for a family of six, eight, or even ten people on one income. What happened to America's wealth and the dollar's buying power?

There was the Great Depression, supposedly a random occurrence resulting from people playing the stock market with leveraged money that, in case of loss, they could not afford to pay back. That is exactly what those in charge would like people to believe; such hogwash is even written in the history books we find in public schools.

Those that control the economy fear the people will discover that massive fluctuations of the economy do not occur by happenstance but are monetarily engineered to profit those that have repeatedly ransacked the economy of the once-free markets of the world. Years later, it was proven that the Federal Reserve System and its constrictive money supply policies intentionally created the Great Depression in order to transfer much of the wealth of the nation into the bankers' greedy hands. Prior to the depression, the Federal Reserve had actually contracted the money supply twenty-seven times, shrinking it by 35 percent, and continued this constrictive policy until the country began eagerly ramping up for WWII. See federalreservehistory.org/essays/great_depression

President Roosevelt approved and signed the New Deal to revert the effects of the Great Depression, but many people do not adequately understand what actually occurred as a result of the creation of the New Deal at en.wikipedia.org/wiki/Great_Depression#Keynesian.

The New Deal changed the operation of the US financial system to ensure that the American people were commoditized, monetized, and enslaved at birth through the birth certificate system and in cahoots with the Social Security Act. This is elementarily explained in the YouTube video called Truth about Your Birth Certificate at youtube.com/watch?v=N_sEXpAXxgg.

The New Deal gave the government control over people's lives in a manner that is unprecedented in American history. The big trick was to get the people to go along with the changes surrounding the economy and federal government without explaining the details of the New Deal, its implications, and its impact on every American.

The incentive or benefit offered to Americans to participate in the New Deal was and still is the Social Security Insurance Program. By signing up for Social Security, one receives a benefit. This makes a tacit agreement with the person accepting the benefit to become an employee and/or the property of the United States. These insurance benefits allow the government to gain control over citizens' lives to the point where the government can infringe upon and remove our constitutional rights and other freedoms.

The birth certificate registers the person's birth event as a financial instrument, or a security interest, that the government uses to create money. Money is no longer backed by gold. Under the birth certificate system, money is backed by the future labor represented by the birth of an individual. The birth certificate is evidence of the collateralization of the individual, which is proof that the government uses the birth certificate to print debt instruments called Federal Reserve Notes and makes Americans liable for the government's debt that is owed to the international banking shysters.

During a private meeting between President Woodrow Wilson and Colonel Edward Mandell House, the colonel conveyed the following foreboding remarks just prior to the creation of the Federal Reserve System and the implementation of the birth certificate system of the United States:

> Very soon, every American will be required to register their biological property in a national system designed to keep track of the people and that will operate under the ancient system of pledging. By such methodology, we can compel people to submit to our agenda, which will effect our security as a chargeback for our fiat paper currency.

> Every American will be forced to register or suffer being unable to work and earn a living. They will be our chattel, and we will hold the security interest over them forever, by operation of the law merchant under the scheme of secured transactions.

> Americans, by unknowingly or unwittingly delivering the bills of lading to us will be rendered bankrupt and insolvent, forever to remain economic slaves through taxation, secured by their pledges.

They will be stripped of their rights and given a commercial value designed to make us a profit and they will be none the wiser, for not one man in a million could ever figure our plans and, if by accident one or two should figure it out, we have in our arsenal plausible deniability.

After all, this is the only logical way to fund government, by floating liens and debt to the registrants in the form of bene- fits and privileges. This will inevitably reap to us huge profits beyond our wildest expectations and leave every American a contributor to this fraud which we will call "So- cial Insurance."

Without realizing it, every American will insure us for any loss we may incur and in this manner, every American will unknowingly be our servant, however begrudgingly. The people will become helpless and without any hope for their redemption and, we will employ the high office of the Presi- dent of our dummy corporation to foment this plot against America.

That's quite a mouthful, and it lays out the gist of the New Deal in half a dozen paragraphs. At the birth of an individual, the birth certifi- cate system that funds the national debt collateralizes and pledges the fu- ture labor of the individual infant, thereby guaranteeing and comprising the full faith and credit of the United States. The birth certificate is evi- dence that the United States is monetizing the labor of the people to pay the twenty trillion dollars of the national debt.

Unless you were a US senator or US representative, chances are you actually had nothing to do with the mismanagement of the government or the creation of its debt!

Even though they were infants at the time of the birth certificate con- tract, people agree to become collateral, chattel, and property of the US government.

The United States actually owns citizens and their bodies, as the birth certificate appears to be the actual certificate of title, demonstrating bodily ownership, similar to the certificate of title for a motor vehicle. Citizens continually agree to allow the government to control their bodies as property by entering into legal agreements, even though most citizens never even considered the inherent existence and implications of such agreements.

Citizens forfeit their rights when they enter invisible contracts, beyond their understanding, with the federal government. Many unsuspecting people are completely unaware of the legal implications initiated when they place their signature on what appears to be a simple piece of paper. For example, when people sign a signature card at the local bank, they unwittingly agree, without receiving full disclosure, to the terms and conditions of a whole slew of laws and regulations, hardly understanding the many legal implications associated with opening a bank account. Do citizens actually concern themselves with the details in the fine print of the banking agreement they have signed? Do citizens ever stop and think of the implications such agreements may have over their lives and their individual sovereignty? Do we even bother to read the laws we agree to abide by when signing any piece of paper that eventually winds up in the hands of the federal government?

Traps of governmental oppression are constructed through the law and the legal contracts that many of us unknowingly enter. In order to free ourselves from the legally constructed and contracted restraints on our liberties, we need to start familiarizing ourselves with the actual agreements that we agree to abide by with all federal, state, and municipal government agencies.

It is quite enlightening to read the US codes and statutes contained in the banking agreements that we sign when we open a bank account. These can be found under United States Code, Title 12.

I support and highly recommend Cornell Law for its informative and resourceful website, law.cornell.edu. Cornell Law is a great free resource to use when studying the different areas of law.

As we know, the government continually places the interests of corporations over the interests of the voters. The banking elites rule over virtually all corporations, including the US government. They do this by loaning money at interest but also by funding corporate mergers and acquiring positions as board members in the newly merged companies.

Let us take a situation where one company purchases or merges with another company. Many merges requires bank loans, which are used to pay the shareholders for the stock of the company that is being acquired; this amount can be as high as several billion dollars. Barbarians at the

Gate (1989), starring James Garner, is an entertaining movie regarding the merger of R. J. Reynolds and Nabisco companies. The movie shows the amount of financing needed to acquire and merge mammoth corporations. In the RJR Nabisco merger, the amount of financing needed to transact the merger exceeded twenty-five billion dollars in 1988.

In return for the billions of dollars loaned to acquire a specific corporation, the bank insists that the board of directors of the borrowing corporation is stacked with lifetime appointees of the bank. These board appointees, handpicked by the bank, allow the lending bank to control the new board of directors. Since the lending bank now controls a majority of the company's board of directors, the bank virtually controls the company.

Corporations and bankers do not run for Congress or the Senate; they find it much easier to buy congressmen and senators who, when compromised, provide the corporations and bankers with preferred status over the very constituents who elect them. Politicians never demonstrate more disloyalty to their constituents than when they pass a bill or law in direct opposition to the desires and interests of their constituents.

The silent cries of the American people go unnoticed, but the whispers of the special interests deafen many crooked politicians' ears.

Lack of loyalty to the American people was quite apparent when Bill "Slick Willie" Clinton ran for president of the United States. Clinton campaigned wildly against NAFTA, while Bush Sr. campaigned mightily for it.

Clinton won the election, and his first act as president was to betray the American people and throw all his support behind NAFTA and ensured that it got passed. This was the exact opposite of what he had promised to the American people during his presidential campaign. This proves that Clinton was acting on behalf of those that had a hidden agenda to pass NAFTA against the will and interests of the American people. This duplicity stained the oval office for the next eight years.

It has not mattered for decades whether a Republican or a Democrat was elected president. What matters is that the puppet masters' agenda is protected by the president at all costs. These puppet masters control the president and the entire US government and pass laws that shape and mold society as the controlling dark forces dictate. The agenda was to pass NAFTA—no matter if Republican Bush or Democrat Clinton won the election. NAFTA was going to be implemented, and its implementation by Slick Willie was very much a betrayal of the American people!

NAFTA is devastating to the US economy and its trade balance, as was its forefather GATT when it passed in 1947. GATT virtually wiped out the borders and sovereignty of all the nations that participated in this agreement, and NAFTA has taken almost half of all American manufacturing jobs.

GATT and the Bretton Woods Agreement are the governing agreements that regulate and place the post-WWII world monetary and financial systems into the hands of the international banking cartel. These agreements in essence did as they were intended to do and relinquished the economic control of the United Stated into the private hands of the international bankers (en.wikipedia.org/wiki/Bretton_Woods_Conference) and under the control of the World Trade Organization.

For more financial insight, the very illuminating article regarding the systemic collapse of the world's economy and how to counteract it is found in the "Shiller Institute Call For New Bretton Woods" at rense.com/general77/schill.htm. We should all become well versed in what has resulted from the implementation of NAFTA, GATT, and the Bretton Woods Agreement, as the control of world finance and international trade has developed into the financial and monetary arms or tentacles of the New World Order.

In 1994, GATT was placed under the control of the World Trade Organization, where it remains today. Placing control of US tariffs and trade policies into the hands of a foreign-controlled international group weakens the American economy and relinquishes America's control of its own destiny.

GATT has allowed other internationally minded organizations to control and monitor America's economy simply by determining the level of tariffs that pertain to specific imported goods. By allowing GATT to become law, the manufacturing of products in third-world countries became fortified by removing the power of the US government to regulate its own tariffs; as a result, the United States has weakened its international manufacturing position and strength.

Under GATT and NAFTA, the United States has essentially destroyed its own economy and is murdering its own manufacturing base.

Whenever a country does not have the power to regulate and determine its own tariffs, that country's economy, particularly its employment rate and manufacturing capabilities, is at the mercy of those regulating that country's tariffs.

Before GATT, there were tariffs that prevented Americans from losing their jobs to foreign countries that had lower labor costs and produced similar or substitutable goods. This protected America's manufacturing industries and prevented US salaries and jobs from being undercut and exported to third-world countries that employ slave labor.

Countries implement tariffs and trade agreements to safeguard against the destruction of their economies by the remainder of the world. Forfeiting control of tariffs and creating disastrous trade agreements are two of the primary reasons that countries economically fail.

A fascinating book, Handbook for American Citizens is an enlightening read of the political climate of the late 1800s. That book discusses the different political parties' platforms regarding US tariffs and various other interesting topics and perspectives (it is available for free at archive.org/details/handbookforamer00mann). It is quite fascinating to compare the political parties of the late 1800s to those of today and examine how America's political system has denigrated over the centuries and its trade policies have been compromised against the direct interests of the people.

Having the World Trade Organization in control of US tariffs and trade guarantees that America is on its way to becoming a third-world country. The implications of sacrificing one's tariff and trade powers to a third party are treasonous and more destructive than almost anything else—except, of course, transferring a country's ability to regulate and produce its own money interest free.

Perhaps one of the greatest conspiracy books ever written is Gary Allen's The Rockefeller File (amazon.com/Rockefeller-File-Gary-Allen/dp/1568493681). It presents an ominous look at the illuminati's plans to unite the countries of the world into a global state. Allen exposes the purposes and intentions of internationally focused globalists to destroy the economies of the world in order to bring about a single world order. Every so-called wacko conspiracy theory and plan for world domination exposed by Allen in his prophetic book has already come to fruition.

Globalists believe that bringing the US standard of living down to the level of Russian peasants will allow for the unification of both countries into a new world government. This is just another example of the continuous and uniform systematic processes that are being conducted to usher in a New World Order under the noses of billions of unsuspecting people.

Americans no longer have to wonder why their economy is being downsized. We now know that the New World Order globalists are to be blamed for the exportation of millions of American jobs.

In order to accomplish the globalists' objectives, most legislative actions undertaken on a worldwide scale are designed to bring the rich nations' economies down to the level of the poorest nations. Destroying the American economy is paramount to leveling the playing fields between the nations of the world and has been achieved quite nicely under the Bush Sr., Clinton, George W. Bush, and Obama administrations.

Those intent on orchestrating and ushering in the New World Order are hell-bent on implementing unrestricted terror around the globe in order that the people of the world not only will welcome the New World Order but also will beg and fight for its implementation.

Creators of the New World Order have abrogated America's ability to control its own financial destiny and, in doing so, have placed control of America into foreign greedy hands, void of any governmental regulations or oversight.

As one explores the real dangers of the Federal Reserve System, the mathematical impossibility of the system to sustain itself indicates that the system is doomed to catastrophic economic collapse, unless prudent action is undertaken to avoid such calamity. Because the national debt can never be paid—it is a mathematical impossibility—it behooves the people to examine the current economic condition of the nation and devise plans to restore the nation's monetary system, along with the people's freedoms.

If we view politics with a critical eye, we can see that legislation is being passed to fortify our own slavery. The Federal Reserve, the New Deal, GATT, and NAFTA are all examples of legislation aimed to further denigrate the American economy and way of life.

NAFTA necessitates that US jobs will be shipped overseas to a third-world country in order for corporations to remain profitable and competitive in world markets. Since all economies are interrelated, it appears inevitable that we should expect fallout of the value of many world currencies in the near future.

A major and pending threat to the US economy is that the Federal Reserve Note is no more insulated from destruction than any other fiat monetary system used throughout history. Those that believe they are in control of the drowning world economy spend their lives attempting to keep the economy's nose just above constantly rising water. There are so many holes in America's economic boat that it's a miracle it still floats at all.

Those in control of the monetary policies and economic systems of the world know above all else that the financial system is very broken and is in need of a total overhaul. The current unsustainable monetary and fiscal systems cannot be fixed but must be replaced with a system in which one class of people does not parasitically enslave all the remainder of humanity.

Fair and equitable banking and monetary policies need to be implemented to protect the American worker and economy. Each job shipped overseas brings us one step closer to the level of a third-world country. The American Dream, which millions have fought and died for, is now becoming the American Nightmare.

America is at the point where the economy and the banking systems are no longer sustainable and are on the brink of collapse. The US economy is unsustainable without a major intervention and restructuring. Without a manufacturing base, artificially inflating the money supply becomes a less useful monetary tool, which makes short-term economic recovery sometimes possible, sometimes not.

Inflating and deflating the money supply is simply a form of kicking the economic can down the road. As the American monetary system is falling apart at the seams, it is ever more pressing that we address its faulty and collapsing monetary system and replace it with a system designed for stability that will lead to the expansion of the nation's manufacturing base.

Expanding America's manufacturing base is done by demanding banks lend to promising small industrial and manufacturing-based businesses, thereby expanding economic growth. This national banking practice, implemented under Hitler in the 1930s, was responsible for making Germany economically flourish and become a global threat to the world's power structure. See one of the most incredible videos of your life at thegreateststorynevertold.tv, and attempt to comprehend the magnitude of the lies that we are being taught to this day.

Once upon a time, there was a beacon of light illuminating the world with hope and opportunity, and its name was America. The chance to come to America burned in the hearts and imaginations of people from around the globe, along with economic dreams and hopes that this great land of opportunity would welcome them with open arms. From every corner of the world, immigrants sailed the oceans blue for their shot at a better life and the American Dream.

The American Dream was shipped overseas because of treasonous trade legislation, along with millions of US jobs, as the American people rolled over in their hypnotic sleep. People have allowed the politicians and corporations to destroy the fabric of this great land by allowing foreign powers to dictate domestic economic policies in direct opposition to the US Constitution. By handing the keys of America's banking castle to foreign powers, we have destroyed the nation. America's greatness has become dissolved and unrecognizable. Our livelihoods were stolen and exported to a foreign land, and our homes foreclosed upon by vicious banking predators.

If citizens continue to stand by idle, America will become completely unrecognizable as a nation and its concept of freedom will no longer be available in a world overflowing with tyranny and terrorists.

Various sectors of humankind are being antagonized through the creation of terror and racism to hate and kill one another.

The United States of America was once a nation that controlled its own economic destiny and was free from tyranny. It has now been conquered from within, and unless we intercede, the country will only become worse and even more tyrannical. Foreign banking and political terrorists have infiltrated the United States over the past centuries without much notice or disruption by the people. Any nation that allows a foreign master to rule its people is simply an example of present-day feudalism and financial slavery.

In order to create a great national power, a nation must both be self-determined and control its own money. To allow foreigners to control and dictate the future of the US government through the exercise of foreign monetary control is a recipe for disaster that is responsible today for America's perilous economic instability, which deeply affects every sector of this society.

No foreign power values the economic interests of America over its own, so how can we the people expect a foreign power to govern the United States better than we would? At the very minimum, we must govern ourselves. For economic stability and sustainability, we must wrestle control of the regulation and creation of money back from the lecherous hands of the Federal Reserve and return it to the rightful and prudent hands of the American people and the US government.

As a nation, America cannot continue to participate in such unsustainable economic and monetary systems, which are mathematically destined to collapse. To ignore the warnings of a worldwide economic collapse is to participate in and adhere to an economic system that can result only in the additional suffering of billions of people.

We the people need to get control of our country and its money and use a redeemable dollar that it is worth something. After that, the next course of action necessary to restore this nation is to regain our powers over trade and tariff regulation. The United States was born free, but for centuries, the bankers have continually implemented monetary treachery and slavery to enslave and control the lives of Americans.

The American Revolution accomplished nothing. America still suffers under British-imposed imperial rule. Today, there's just a different king, and he's a banker.

CHAPTER 13

The Constitution and the State of Banking

If in the opinion of the People, the distribution or modification of the Constitutional powers be in any particular wrong, let it be corrected by an amendment in the way the Constitution designates. But let there be no change by usurpation; for though this, in one instance, may be the instrument of good, it is the customary weapon by which free governments are destroyed.

– GEORGE WASHINGTON

The two enemies of the people are criminals and government, so let us tie the second down with the chains of the Constitution, so the second will not become the legalized version of the first.

– THOMAS JEFFERSON

A Constitution of Government, once changed from Freedom, can never be restored. Liberty, once lost, is lost forever.

– JOHN ADAMS

Our Constitution was made only for a moral and religious people. It is wholly inadequate to the government of any other.

– JOHN ADAMS

But whether the Constitution really be one thing, or another, this much is certain—that it has either authorized such a government as we have had, or has been powerless to prevent it. In either case, it is unfit to exist.

– LYSANDER SPOONER

Do not separate text from historical background. If you do, you will have perverted and subverted the Constitution, which can only end in a distorted, bastardized form of illegitimate government.

– JAMES MADISON

Those who served, and those who continue to serve in the Army, Navy, Air Force, Marines, and Coast Guard took an oath to uphold and protect the Constitution against all enemies foreign and domestic, and we can never forget the importance of their commitment to our Nation.

– ROBIN HAYES

We the people are the rightful masters of both Congress and the courts, not to overthrow the Constitution, but to overthrow the men who pervert the Constitution.

– ABRAHAM LINCOLN

Every generation gets the Constitution that it deserves. As the central preoccupation of an era make their way into the legal system, the Supreme Court eventually weighs in, and nine lawyers in robes become oracles of our national identity.

– NOAH FELDMAN

The aim of constitutional government is to preserve the Republic; that of revolutionary government is to lay its foundation.

– MAXIMILIEN ROBESPIERRE

The ultimate tragedy is not the oppression and cruelty by the bad people, but the silence over that by the good people.

– MARTIN LUTHER KING JR.

THE UNITED STATES has monumentally deviated from the original ideals this great country was founded upon, which guaranteed and helped secure the liberty of the people. The unconstitutional policies President Lincoln set in motion, when Jefferson Davis and the Southern senators protested the unjust taxation policies of the North and walked out of Congress never to return, still affect the American way of life today. The US Senate can only operate with a quorum or a majority vote under the Constitution, and with the South's abandonment of the US Senate, a quorum could not and still can no longer be reached. Therefore, under the Lincoln administration, the United States began the process of transforming itself from a government into a corporation right before the eyes and under the noses of the American people. Lincoln declared a state of emergency and imposed a state of martial law that is still in existence today.

Marti Oakley has given permission for her article below to be reprinted here in its entirety at ppjg.me/2008/09/05/the-occupation-of-the-united-states-orhow-lincoln-made-slaves-out-of-all-of-us/ and discusses these implications and more. Sincere thanks to Marti for her great writings and her contributions that inform and empower humanity.

The Occupation of the United States, Or How Lincoln Made Slaves Out of All of Us

In 1871, the District of Columbia (D.C.) was created and at the same time a new constitution was adopted by the 41st congress which, without authority or authorization granted itself the status of a corporation to operate within the ten dedicated miles of Washington (District of Columbia) D.C. The UNITED STATES Corporation exists only within the District under this new constitution of 1871. As a corporation, it is bound and ruled by commercial contract law, not by the common law of the people. [1]

Lincoln suspended the constitution (the one we think we operate under) during the Civil War and established martial law. That order has never been retracted or rescinded as required under the Lieber Code [2]. There has been no declaration of peace, nor any treaties between the newly adopted constitution and the occupied people of the formerly sovereign states, to retract the order. We have effectively been in a state of occupation perpetrated by the corporation operating in the District of Columbia known as THE UNITED STATES or as, UNITED STATES OF AMERICA (a corporation).[3] This as opposed to the collection of sovereign states known as the United States of America.

Capitalization is an important point to take note of here. Capitis Diminutio Maxim means a maximum loss of status or "civil death" for the individual. Through the use of capitalization, e.g. JOHN DOE or DOE JOHN, the individual (with rights) is reduced to slave status with no rights or in this case to a corporate trust as an entity who can own nothing. This is why any correspondence from federal agencies which have to do with taxes or legal issues with the government will have your name capitalized. This capitalization is a notice to you that:

a) You are a corporately held trust no different than any other commodity and have no human status.

b) You will appear in an administrative court rather than a judicial court and cannot use the constitution to defend yourself because the Uniform Commercial Code will be administrated as per contract commercial law, not the common law.

There have not been any judges in America since 1789. There are only Administrators. This is why so-called "judges" are appointed and not elected. Administrators, not judges, are appointed by federal and state officials to administer commercial contract law using the Uniform Commercial Code (UCC). Which I guess would explain how people with no law background become "judges." Judges administer law, while administrators administer codes and statutes. [4]

Commercial contract law (UCC) is used to override the common law that we believe we are living under via the constitution. Our court systems are nothing more than a web of administrative courts which administer the law of contracts. In order for the law of contracts to apply to you, you must first enter into a contract with the corporation: in this case, THE UNITED STATES (a corporation). To enter into this contract you simply have to register to vote, file a birth certificate, apply for government provided benefits of any kind, get a driver license, apply for a business license, pay a fee for permission to use or access government owned properties (parks, etc.) or waterways. There is no instance when your interaction with what we know as THE UNITED STATES (a corporation) does not result in you automatically being entered into contract with said corporation. Once done, you have ceased to be a human individual in the eyes of the government and now are reduced to a corporate trust (an entity) and vulnerable and subject to the law of contracts.

How does this happen? Ever hear of something called an "adhesion contract"? These are contracts with irrevocable terms which never change. Each and every time you sign your name for taxes, licenses or government benefits you are in effect renewing the contract. This renewal or even first time signing is a statement to the effect that you agree to the control of the federal government (a corporation controlled by contract law) and have forfeited your rights to constitutional protections. In the case of taxes unless you sign the w-2 or the Form 1040 or any of the other forms, in essence agreeing to the contract you are not obliged to pay.

The one advantage to all of this is that under the laws of contracts, you the signatory must be informed in advance of all provisions of the contract. In lieu of this you can revoke your signature and be repaid all funds paid into Social Security and taxes going back to the original and first time you entered into the contract unknowingly.

You should also be made aware that "citizens of the UNITED STATES" includes only those people living within the corporate ten mile boundary of the District of Columbia. Using this basis for defining who was and was not a citizen enabled the changes to the original "Trading with the Enemy Act" of 1917. Under the original law it described "enemies of the state" as "other than citizens of the United States."

Section 2 subdivision (c) Chapter 106

Trading with the Enemy Act of Oct. 6, 1917 (40 Stat. L. 411) amended March 9, 1933, Chapter 106, Section 5, subdivision (b "...any person within the United States."

H.R. 1491 Public No. 1."

Notice in both cases that United States is not capitalized, so neither version of this act is applied to the corporation known as THE UNITED STATES, or THE UNITED STATES OF AMERICA. It applies to the common citizen of the occupied collective states, or the United States.

So all this time, I, who prided myself on actually reading the Constitution, assuring myself that I knew what my rights were, what the laws were, and thoroughly convinced that a return to the Constitution would reverse all the devastation heaped on us by one corrupt administration after another; one spineless congress after another have had to admit that we have no options left to us. All of us who are here now and those to come have and will exist in servitude to the corporation known as THE UNITED STATES.

Some days it's good to be old.

References:

[1]With no constitutional authority to do so, Congress creates a separate form of government for the District of Columbia, a ten mile square parcel of land (see, Acts of the Forty-first Congress, Section 34, Session III, chapters 61 and 62). Act 1871 allows the "Corp US" to control the country in the place of the natural Government teamlaw.net/History-Outline.htm

[2]Instructions for the Government of Armies of the United States in the Field (Lieber Code). 24 April 1863.

icrc.org/ihl.nsf/73cb71d18dc4372741256739003e6372/a25aa5871a049 19bc12563cd002d65c5?OpenDocument

[3] Google US Code Chapter 28 section 3002 subsection 15 which states the following:

(15) "United States" means—

    (A) a Federal corporation;

    (B) an agency, department, commission, board, or other entity of the United States; or

    (C) an instrumentality of the United States.

[4] FRC v. GE 281 US 464, Keller v PE 261 US 428 1Stat.138-178

From SourceWatch—sourcewatch.org

The Trading With the Enemy Act, Title 12, §95(a) and §95(b) of the United States Code, is considered by many to constitute a declaration of war made in 1917 against the people of the United States and was further modified by President Franklin D. Roosevelt.[1]

sourcewatch.org/index.php?title=Trading_With_the_ Enemy_Act

© 2008 Marti Oakley

It is obvious that the government of the United States no longer exists and has been replaced by a corporation occupying the ten-square-mile area known as Washington, DC.

Lincoln eloquently wrote in the Gettysburg Address that a "government of the people, by the people, for the people, shall not perish from the earth." Nevertheless, it did. And citizens are now under the domain of a corporate fascist group of pseudo-politicians overseeing the bankrupt proceedings of the United States. Further liquidation of the bankrupt United States in 2008–2009 transferred trillions of dollars of assets from the United States to the private international bankers. Too big to fail!

For your reading pleasure, additional information can be gained from Lisa Guliani's "The United States Isn't a Country—It's a Corporation." See serendipity.li/jsmill/us_corporation.htm.

There is no longer true adherence or loyalty to the original US Constitution since "it is just a goddamned piece of paper," according to George W. Bush. There is no sense in following that old piece of paper since the US Corporation, acting as the made-for-television US government, is not a party to the old Constitution.

An interesting decision was made in Padelford, Fay & Co. v. Mayor and Alderman of City of Savannah, 14 Ga.438, 1854 WL 1492, (Ga., Jan Term 1854) (NO.64). The judge concluded, "No private person has a right to complain by suit in court on the ground of a breach of the United States constitution; though the constitution is a compact, he is not a party to it." Today we have no constitutional rights in courtrooms across the United States.

The US Constitution provides protection to the people indirectly by theoretically limiting the actions of the federal government. Americans do not have constitutional rights; in the fifty United States, we have God-given rights.

People enjoyed protection from the federal government because of the US Constitution, that glorious document for which many a great man has died in order to protect and preserve our freedoms. However, the Constitution, concurrent with the federal government, has been tarnished and disabused without a word from the populace. The actions of the people really determine, enforce, and uphold any rights we may still have, whether stated or omitted in the Constitution.

The Constitution explicitly outlines the powers given to the government; any extension of those powers is considered unconstitutional. The Constitution appears to be from where the people's protection from an obtrusive federal government is derived. In the verbiage of the Constitution, there are limitations placed upon the powers and acts that the federal government and the states may undertake.

Many become frustrated with the unconstitutional actions that the US corporation conducts daily. Consider the passing of the Affordable Care Act. Is it constitutional for the government to demand that every American obtain health insurance, or is this another example of the overextension and overreach of the federal government's power? One must be the judge and jury while always remembering that the Affordable Care Act does not apply to every American; it applies "only to taxpayers," according to the Supreme Court.

In defending our rights under the Constitution, Jack and Margy Flynn have extensive experience standing against tyranny in America and are two of America's leading constitutionalists. They teach people about federal and state constitutions, how to apply them in real life, and how constitutional methods have helped their group and others win court cases against unlawful governmental actions and have successfully resolved situations of corporate abuse. The Flynns favorably resolved many other issues outside of court.

The Flynns' methods have also been instrumental in removing errant and criminal public officers, up to and including judges. They also demonstrate how we can hold public servants accountable, pursuant to their oaths as public officers, to do what is right and uphold the Constitution for the United States of America, circa 1787, as amended in 1791 by the Bill of Rights. Although the Flynns announced their retirement over five years ago, from time to time, they hold seminars, workshops, and lectures; make radio appearances; and present material on their website, CitizensoftheAmericanConstitution.net. Watch their incredible videos!

It is amazing what happens when citizens hold public servants accountable for their actions or inactions. Imagine if everyone said, "Enough is enough."

The Flynns gave permission to use the following poignant article describing the current state of America, the constitutional implications, and the criminal overrun of the government. The Flynns are true patriots, and I am proud to include them among my good friends.

America's Beginning and Our Need for Our Constitution

The Dalai Lama was once asked by an interviewer what he thought of Western Civilization. That holy man looked directly at the questioner, smiled, and said: "I think that would be a good idea."

The history of Western Civilization has been written in blood, as has been the known history of this entire world. If the astute, rational, reasonable, objective observer were to thoroughly analyze the rule of nations upon this Earth, beginning with the earliest known history, that research would indicate that virtually all nations have been led by tyrants, despots, warlords, maniacal kings and emperors, and even those who were less barbaric treated their people like slaves. The rulers, the "elite" and the money-men had supreme authority and did whatever they wanted. Nobody dared question them, if they wanted to remain intact and alive. It sounds just like now, doesn't it?

This ruthless, barbaric ruling practice continued unabated and unstoppable throughout history, until one bright concept took hold in America and permeated the consciousness of many of the people living there. This beginning showed the way to the rest of the world. At that point, some very courageous individuals and a citizenry that had been abused, misused and treated like scum by their own government decided that enough was enough. These people were the British Citizens in America during the 1760's and 1770's. Their so-called "Mother Country", England, up to that time was the most barbaric, cruel, unjust, tyrannical powerful nation that ever existed on this Earth. England ruled the seas and many other countries, which they deemed "primitive", beneath them, and considered their people nothing more than slaves to serve the glutinous greed of the "glorious" Empire.

The American Colonists had had enough of it, but they fully realized that, in order to stop this unjust, barbaric treatment of them, a herculean effort had to be made to reach their objectives. That effort included the unifying of many different peoples and belief systems throughout the Colonies and taking an actual offensive posture against "Mother England". These early Americans realized that freedom is not free. In fact, nothing is free on this planet, because someone or something must pay, in one way or another, for that freedom. Independence cannot be achieved if tyrannical government controls exerted on the people prevent and prohibit the very freedom that the people seek. Although many different people, who were involved in this planning, had various objectives, they were unified in one position, and that was the defeat of England and the thrusting out of that diabolical power from America, forever.

Since most know the overall story of the American Revolution, we will not repeat it here, but rather jump forward to the time when independence had been won from England and the task ahead for the Colonists was how to best put together a free nation of individual states that would never infringe upon the inherent rights of its people. The people were adamant that they did not want a tyrannical government that would abuse them as England had, and they did not want to have their efforts spent in fighting a bloody revolutionary war, striving for freedom, wasted by the creation of another tyrannical central government.

Naturally, there was much debate over how to do this and, initially, the Colonists had decided that a loose confederation of independent states would be the best way to proceed. They drafted the Articles of Confederation to assure the common good and the common defense, which essentially was our nation's first "Constitution". The Articles had some deficiencies that could have been worked out, but, unfortunately, they were not. One must wonder whether the deficits in the Articles were put into place so that the document would have to be replaced by one which provided for strong centralized power over the states. The "leaders" and representatives of the people, most of whom were wealthy business owners and lawyers, would create the opportunity to draft another document which would give power to a more centralized form of government. There was grave concern among the people about forming a stronger centralized federal government, since the individual states and people still feared that they would lose power to the central government and be subject to its dictates. Does this sound familiar?

A conference was convened in Philadelphia in which delegates from the Colonies came under the guise of a trade conference and positions to be discussed regarding western lands. There was also some talk about adding to or amending some of the Articles, and most of the delegates from the states were instructed by their states to perform only additions and amendments to the Articles, and nothing else. George Washington was elected president of this conference and he maintained and demanded strict secrecy as to what the delegates were doing. Nothing could be discussed outside of the conference room and no papers could be left anywhere regarding the subject matter of the conference. No discussions were to take place with the people and the press, under any circumstances. Despite the shameful fact that what turned out to be the Constitutional Convention was held in secrecy, what emerged from this convention was the Constitution for the united states of America, without the Bill of Rights. The common people had no input in the writing of this document and some of the delegates were unhappy with it. Many delegations vowed not to endorse the

Constitution, unless a Bill of Rights was added, because they wanted to protect the people from the possibility of a tyrannical, overreaching federal government. Does this sound familiar?

After the Constitution was completed, and the delegates left, Benjamin Franklin was asked by a woman outside the hall what had been wrought? Franklin answered: "Madame, a republic, if you can keep it." Then, he chuckled and walked away. When any type of movement begins, there is always a common goal amongst the participants. There is also a common goal held by the leaders of any movement. Sometimes these goals and objectives coincide, but in most cases, the leaders have a separate agenda, unknown to the rest of the people in the movement. There is the publicly avowed common objective and the leaders' own private goals. We have always told people, and history certainly bears this out, that the people must be extremely diligent concerning the motives and actions of their own leaders. When people have fought so hard and so long to achieve a noble objective, it is not wise of them to let their leaders decide what is best for the people, because in most situations, those decisions are made for the best interests of the leaders and not for those of the people. People have slowly learned over time that freedom requires eternal vigilance. Without that, all the hard work, sacrifice and effort expended to achieve any objective can quickly be lost.

As we said earlier, many of the states openly declared that they would not ratify the Constitution unless a Bill of Rights was added. Many leaders at what became the Constitutional Convention had openly opposed a Bill of Rights. Significant among them were George Washington, Alexander Hamilton, who was Washington's Adjutant General, and John Jay, who became the first Supreme Court Chief Justice. You might wonder why these notables opposed a Bill of Rights for the people who so bravely fought the Revolution in order to obtain and secure their God-given rights and freedom. After much pressure by the states and the people, the first Ten Amendments to the Constitution were added as The Bill of Rights in 1791.

In the very beginning of this article, we stated that a new vision of freedom came upon the world when America gained her independence and her Constitution was established. The forming of this document came about through divergent interests of all types and different objectives. With the Bill of Rights added, our Constitution, despite some shortcomings, is the finest egalitarian document ever created by mankind for the governance of a nation by the people of that nation. This was the first time in all of history that this experiment was ever attempted. No similar document has existed in the history of mankind, so this, indeed, was a first for humanity. The Constitution put the political power in the hands of the people through their oversight and supervision of government, thus, making America a self-governing nation. Again, this type of popular political power never existed before throughout history, and the fact that it was created in this way is absolutely monumental and more especially given the times in which it was structured.

Human society has always had its leaders and its followers. The overwhelming majority of mankind is comprised of followers who simply obey and do whatever the leaders want and demand, without question or challenge. It is extremely unfortunate for all of us that the American people of that time did not take their constitutional responsibilities seriously, thus, did not exercise their supervisory and oversight authority over government. This is especially troubling, since the very people who fought the Revolution did so to achieve freedom, independence and justice. The Constitution guaranteed these to them, yet the people did not accept those guarantees, in fact, shirked them, and never in the history of American society have they ever exercised their political power by overseeing and supervising their own government. The document provided everything the people wanted, but the people ignored what was given to them, and those who created the Constitution knew that the people never would exercise their political authority, because they put their trust in those they believed to be "their betters" to govern fairly. Remember the reference to what Ben Franklin said in answer to the question as to what had been wrought? The American people failed to keep their constitutional republic and the true leadership and true power took supreme advantage of that failure, then, just as has always been done in America and is being done now.

True freedom is a rare state of being enjoyed and known by only the few who are willing to work to achieve and keep it. The American people were given that rare opportunity, which few people on this planet have ever gotten, yet they were not wise enough to cherish it and protect it. Jesus came, in part to tell the truth, create freedom for the people and let the true law live. His mission was to help all of mankind. The leaders of His time could immediately see that he was a threat to their power, and, tragically, the people were not bright enough to understand what Jesus said and who He truly was. This man who came to help the people and restore the truth to mankind died miserably upon a cross and the people He came to help spat upon Him. In the same way, the American people have spat upon their Constitution and foolishly spurned their own responsibilities to achieve and protect their own freedom by and through the power and authority of the Constitution. This was a tragic mistake by the people then, and it is a tragic mistake by the American people, right now.

Our Constitution provides everything that the American people want and need to correct and stop the unconstitutional criminality that is rampant throughout all governments in this country, federal, state and local. The people can achieve true freedom, independence and justice by the proper and lawful use of this document, but the American people still refuse to do so, as did their predecessors. The people who fought the Revolution were of a different ilk from the people of today, yet even those hardy, brave souls allowed themselves to be duped by their own leaders into trusting them to govern justly and wisely, so refused to accept and exercise the authority placed in them by the Constitution. Today's American people never fought a revolution, yet they still refuse to use their political authority, just as their forefathers did. The American people obey all the unconstitutional "laws", fight all the unconstitutional wars and pay all the unconstitutional taxes, without comment, question or objection—except in very rare instances. Just like our forefathers, we failed to see the ultimate requirement for freedom, which is eternal vigilance.

The Declaration of Independence urges all Americans to oppose all enemies of the Republic, both foreign and domestic. If we take a sincere, dedicated, objective, rational and reasonable view of the practices and activities of the American government, since the beginning, and especially since the War of Northern Aggression, then we can easily deduce that virtually all presidents, all congresses, all politicians, federal, state and local, with some exceptions, are the domestic enemies of which Thomas Jefferson spoke. Observation is very important and, further, the reasons behind what we observe are vital, if we to understand what we see. One can view a painting, but not really see it or understand it. Americans do not see anything, when it comes to politics, except what they want to see, because their own government has programmed them to see exactly that. At the present time in America, what remains of our constitutional republic is either on shaky ground or non-existent, and this happened because the American people observed nothing. The same thing happened when our predecessors observed nothing after the Constitution was created.

In today's America, we have approximately 93 million or more Americans, who are able-bodied and want to work, out of work. 43 million or more Americans live in poverty and are dependent upon food stamps and welfare to exist. Not only factories, but whole industries, have left this country and gone overseas for tax breaks and cheap labor, so they can make larger profits. After George Washington and Alexander Hamilton created the first private central bank in this country, known as the Bank of the United States, completely in violation of all constitutional requirements, America was at the mercy of a central bank, and in one way or another, has been ever since. These central banks, especially the Federal Reserve, have created booms and busts, recessions and depressions, all of which have thrust deep blows into the economic welfare of the people and America, herself. The depression that started in 2007 was one of the worst we have ever had and we are still not out of it, no matter what anyone says. The fraudulent foreclosure crisis, deliberately created, by which bankers made fortunes bundling and selling notes to investors, cost many millions of people not only their homes, but everything they had acquired and had put into their homes for years. This was an American tragedy of epic proportions. Instead of congress helping out the American people who suffered under this contrived tragedy, congress and the Fed bailed out the criminal banks and corporations who caused the problems to the tune of 39 trillion dollars, all at the expense of the American people. All of this and much, much more was done right in front of the American people, in clear sight, yet they did absolutely nothing to stop it and made no objections to the carnage that took place. Politicians get away with whatever they want, take the American people for whatever they have, and then jail them for minor, trivial "offenses". This will not stop until the American people finally awaken to reality and accept their responsibility to oversee government and correct it when it errs.

America has fought a silent war against Communism for a very, very long time—at least, that is the proffered view by government. In reality, America has adopted the tenets of Communism by accepting and implementing the planks of the Communist Manifesto, imposing its policies and objectives, and has done so in ever increasing amounts since the War of Northern Aggression. From that horrible, savage, unnecessary, unjustified, barbaric war, every president, every congress and virtually all federal, state and local politicians have proposed, implemented and furthered Communist programs throughout America. It would appear that these "public servants" who do so are Communists; if not, why would a true American public servant, who loves and respects America and our founding documents, ever propose, implement and support Communist policies and programs? The answer is obvious. He would not. Despite this, American public servants have inundated America with Communist programs and have done so, in the open, right before the eyes and ears of the American people. Again, the American people have not observed and have not taken the responsibility to oversee and supervise government. In the Bible, Hosea, Chapter 4, Verse 6, states "My people perish for lack of knowledge." Americans should read and heed these words.

If a true, loyal public officer, who honors his oath and upholds the Constitution(s) would not implement Communist policies and programs throughout this nation, then, the real question is, who does? Obviously, that answer is congress, government bureaucrats, the administration of the time, and the true backers of Communism, namely the Zionists, the bankers and the New World Order. While some of these leaders are definitely Communists, whether they admit it or not, others may not be. If non-Communist leaders still implement Communism, does it truly matter whether they are Communists, or not? The bottom line is still the bottom line, no matter how one gets there. If these so-called non-Communist leaders follow the dictates of Communism, the bankers, the Zionists and the New World Order, against the best interests of the people whom they theoretically serve, then, it should be pretty obvious to any reasonably intelligent, objective American that these so-called non-Communist leaders do not represent you, the American people, but represent a diabolical political enemy of all freedom-loving people. Those leaders who are actual Communists insanely follow the dictates of a ruthless, barbaric, cruel political ideology that has savagely killed hundreds of millions of people, mostly their own, in order to gain political power, and in the process, totally ruined the countries they ruled and the lives of all who lived therein.

Many people naively believe that Communism would lead to an egalitarian society, but they are very sadly mistaken. If we look at what Communist regimes have done throughout the world and to their own people, as stated above, this type of political rule is despotic, heinous, crushes creativity and individuality, leaves no freedom, whatsoever, and breaks the spirit of the people. In the alternative, if the true believer wants to create an egalitarian society, what better way exists for the people to do this than the Constitution of the United States of America? This document was intended to place the power of government in the hands of the people, so that the people could create, through the machinery of government, under the people's supervision, the type of government and society the people want. The Constitution authorizes the people all the power they want and need to create the greatest egalitarian society this world has ever seen or known. This power is embodied within the document, itself, yet those who claim to crave an egalitarian society, constantly turn to Communism, because most of them have no understanding, whatsoever, that they are serving a private, capitalistic agenda, disguised as a humanitarian movement intended to equalize the divide between the people and the rulers. History has clearly proven otherwise. As we have said before, in Communist countries it is Communism for the people, but fascism and capitalism for the rulers.

President Trump ran on a platform position and has continued to state since he was elected, that he is returning the political power back to the American people, where it belongs. The real question here is whether the people have the wisdom and understanding to accept that power, use it as it is intended and restore constitutional governance to this country, or let the Communist State/New World Order continue. If we look at what the American people have done to oppose the excesses of government, to reinstate constitutional governance, to hold public officers to the strict constitutional mandates imposed upon them by and through their oaths, and to remove errant public officers from office, pursuant to the self-executing Sections 3 & 4 of the 14th Amendment, an objective observer can see that the American people, as a society, have done nothing to achieve these righteous ends. A betting man says he can determine the future based upon the past, which is quite logical, because people and the societies they compose tend to do the same things over and over and over again. President Trump is a miracle for the American people, whether they understand this or not, and he is the first non-Communist or non-Communist leaning president that we have had for a very long time. He can show them the way, but the question is whether the people will follow him, accept the challenge and assume the responsibilities required of people who live in a truly self-governing nation.

As we said before, our Constitution holds within it everything the people need to use it lawfully and effectively, as was intended long ago, to stop the blatant, unconstitutional criminal actions routinely committed by government, to hold criminal politicians accountable and liable for their actions and to restore real constitutional governance to this nation. Just as Jesus showed the people the way, the Constitution shows the way to true freedom, independence and justice for the people and for America, herself. Now, as in the aftermath of the Revolution, it is firmly up to the people. Let us all pray that the American people are up to this noble task.

I thank Jack and Margy Flynn for allowing the inclusion of their very enlightening article and hope that it motivates every American to stand against tyranny and traitors.

Many of us fail to understand our God-given rights and often wonder why some individuals working for an out-of-control government agency can overstep the boundaries of their position of employment. Overzealous federal agents are often found to be rogue in their actions, and our standing up to tyranny can create quite a liability for those outlaw agents.

People need to educate themselves about current and past events because history tends to repetitively show patterns of atrocious behavior performed by governments against their own citizens.

As an example, people should look at the Bush family and their true family business—war. As you have read, some of the Bush family war crimes are detailed in George Bush: The Unauthorized Biography. There is no justice when the Bushes or the Clintons are placed above the law and not held responsible for their crimes.

We all know the Constitution and federal laws limit public officials' actions, but the final responsibility falls to the people to ensure such obvious criminality is appropriately punished. There has to be a way to sue a former president or secretary of state. If anyone knows the manner to pursue claims against the above-mentioned, please let me know, and perhaps the people can obtain justice.

God knows the government is not doing its job of holding criminal government officials accountable for their actions. Are the bloody unconstitutional desires of any families or groups more important than the lives of three hundred million Americans? We are sanctioning by our silence the betrayal of our nation and the traditions that far too many soldiers died protecting!

Has anyone ever investigated the actual contents of a bill passed by the corporate Congress and signed by the president of the US Corporation? It really is a bill in the sense that the people have to pay for it. That is the product of all legislation: a bill that is simply more debt for the American people.

People are the liable party for the politicians' incredibly wasteful monetary spending created via legislation. Bills passed into law include projects and programs that Americans are ultimately required to fund through ever-growing and burdensome taxation schemes, which never end, unless ended by the people's protest and redress of the government.

The US Corporation has no way of making income, other than stealing it from its citizens. The US Corporation, in direct opposition to its Constitution, demands that corporations registered under the various secretary of state offices engage in the collection of taxes on behalf of the state and federal governments. Corporate employers take money from people's salaries knowing there is no law requiring them to do such a thing and pay income taxes. Again, Aaron Russo's film, *America: Freedom to Fascism*, available at freedomtofascism.com, provides provides more information regarding what tax obligations each of us may or may not have under the actual law.

Although mentioned before, because of its importance and because millions of Americans have pressing IRS problems, I will mention it again. For one of the most interesting discussions I have found regarding one's liability or lack thereof to pay taxes, check out takefromcaesar.com and David Myrland's informative video, Key to the Code / One True Master of American Tax Law.

Always be careful when you poke any giant, especially the IRS; you had better know what you are doing or start learning as fast as you can because the IRS does not fool around in these types of matters.

The US Corporation produces nothing but death and destruction through military strife and errant US foreign policy. Nowhere in the US Constitution does it demand that America initiate military action as the world's enforcer against foreign enemies because of perceived or invented "threats to national security." US military actions and foreign relations ought to comply with the Constitution and not put the US military in the position of being the world's military enforcer on behalf of the international private bankers.

The United States is supposed to provide for the general welfare of the American people. If the general welfare of the American people was adequately being protected, the country and the world would be a more peaceful and harmonious place. The US government, with its ridiculous foreign policy, is making America a more dangerous place to live. When America kills millions of foreigners, there are millions more foreigners who become angry and want retribution.

When we analyze many of the government-created, media-disseminated terrorist acts—designed by intelligence agencies—we quickly realize that false-flag attacks are being regularly introduced to remove and restrict the rights and freedoms of the people. Whenever terrorist attacks are committed around the globe, including here in America, chances are the CIA, the Mossad, MI6, or other intelligence agencies from around the world had a hand in orchestrating the bloody acts. Terror manufactured daily by these intelligence groups is conducted to sway public opinion to accept the restrictions being put in place, restrictions that exchange freedom and liberty for the security and preservation of what remains of the American way of life.

We can never really believe the information reported regarding the war on terror because it is really a war on all the people.

It is a sad state of affairs when the once-glorious United States of America, which has abandoned its original Constitution, has now become a slave to its creditors; the United States quickly controls any group or invades any country that rebels against the interests of the international bankers. By forsaking the Constitution, the United States has become the host of the parasitic Federal Reserve and the international banking cabal, which are currently engaged in destroying the US and the world's economies to satiate their gluttonous desire for world domination.

The US government, self-enslaved by the international private bankers, is so hard up for its next financial fix that it will do anything to get funds. This includes invading any country under the direction of the private bankers and killing millions without remorse or even the slightest amount of honest-to-goodness reflection.

Most oppressive and tyrannical rulers lead a cowed and afraid society until a cataclysmic shift of intellect occurs, and then the peasants usually invite the tyrants to their own bloodbaths and lynchings.

Has anyone noticed that today's functioning of the federal government is in direct opposition to the intent described in the US Constitution? The government has abandoned its care of the general welfare of the citizenry, pledging its allegiance to the private bankers. To return to America the right to control and regulate its own money is above all else the most important and fundamental right, which will return stability to the American economy and its military and therein bring peace and harmony throughout the world.

Every public official who is not working for the dismantlement of the Federal Reserve System is theoretically a traitor and in violation of his or her oath of office. Oaths of office, taken by public officials, demand they uphold the US Constitution. When public officials are dealing with money that is privately issued at interest, it is in direct violation of Article 1, Section 10, Clause 1 of the US Constitution, which states:

> No State shall enter into any Treaty, Alliance, or Confederation; grant Letters of Marque and Reprisal; coin Money; emit Bills of Credit; **make any Thing but gold and silver Coin a Tender in Payment of Debts**; pass any Bill of Attainder, ex post facto Law, or Law impairing the Obligation of Contracts, or grant any Title of Nobility[emphasis added].

It appears that all our politicians, judges, prosecutors, and police officers are in violation of their oaths of office whenever they unconstitutionally demand a payment in anything other than gold or silver, as succinctly explained in the above constitutional clause. Are we supposed to comply with an unconstitutional order or demand by a court or other agency?

Nowhere is Congress authorized to allow a group of foreign bankers to regulate the value of US money.

Article 1, Section 8, clauses 5 and 6 state:

> Congress shall have the power to . . . coin money, regulate the value thereof, and of foreign coin, and fix the standard of weights and measures;

> To provide for the punishment of counterfeiting the securities and current coin of the United States.

When politicians pass bills that extract even more funds from the people through a scheme of privately issued and inflatable fiat money and a private taxation system, they are in direct violation of the Constitution and the oaths they swore to uphold.

Mother used to contend, "Just because everyone's doing it, doesn't make it right!"

There are no provisions in the US Constitution for the federal government to purchase its money from the Federal Reserve or direct Congress to treasonously forfeit control of its money supply and financially enslave every American.

Without reservation, it can be irrevocably stated that the most destructive action any country can undertake is forfeiting control of its money creation to a private-party outside government control. In the late hours of December 23, 1913, this is exactly what occurred, as the Federal Reserve Act was unconstitutionally passed, empowering an unconscionable criminal cabal.

HONORABLE LOUIS T. MCFADDEN

One of America's greatest heroes who fought for the people's freedom was the Honorable Louis T. McFadden. He served in the US House of Representatives from 1915 to 1935. He weighed in on the government's selling-out the American people by giving control of the country's money to the privately owned Federal Reserve. McFadden's historical speeches, and his astonishing exposure of the Federal Reserve System, are as important and true today as they were circa 1934.

The compilation of McFadden's speeches below, regarding the Federal Reserve Corporation, are reprinted here for your review and with the permission of the 1978 Arizona Caucus Club. I thank them for their patriotic preservation of such a precious piece of American history.

> On May 23, 1933, McFadden brought formal charges against the Board of Governors of the Federal Reserve Bank, the Comptroller of the Currency, and the Secretary of the US Treasury for numerous criminal acts, including but not limited to conspiracy, fraud, unlawful conversion, and treason. The petition for Articles of Impeachment was thereafter referred to the Judiciary Committee and has yet to be acted upon.

Congressman McFadden's Speech On the Federal Reserve Corporation

Quotations from several speeches made on the Floor of the House of Representatives by the Honorable Louis T. Mc-Fadden of Pennsylvania. Mr. McFadden, due to his having served as Chairman of the Banking and Currency Committee for more than 10 years, was the best posted man on these matters in America and was in a position to speak with authority of the vast ramifications of this gigantic private credit monopoly. As Representative of a State which was among the first to declare its freedom from foreign money tyrants it is fitting that Pennsylvania, the cradle of liberty, be again given the credit for producing a son that was not afraid to hurl defiance in the face of the money-bund. Whereas Mr. McFadden was elected to the high office on both the Democratic and Republican tickets, there can be no accusation of partisanship lodged against him. Because these speeches are set out in full in the Congressional Record, they carry weight that no amount of condemnation on the part of private individuals could hope to carry.

The Federal Reserve—A Corrupt Institution

Mr. Chairman, we have in this Country one of the most corrupt institutions the world has ever known. I refer to the Federal Reserve Board and the Federal Reserve Banks, hereinafter called the Fed. The Fed has cheated the Government of these United States and the people of the United States out of enough money to pay the Nation's debt. The depredations and iniquities of the Fed have cost enough money to pay the National debt several times over.

This evil institution has impoverished and ruined the people of these United States, has bankrupted itself, and has practically bankrupted our Government. It has done this through the defects of the law under which it operates, through the maladministration of that law by the Fed and through the corrupt practices of the moneyed vultures who control it.

Some people think that the Federal Reserve Banks are United States Government institutions. They are private monopolies which prey upon the people of these United States for the benefit of themselves and their foreign customers; foreign and domestic speculators and swindlers; and rich and predatory money lender. In that dark crew of financial pirates there are those who would cut a man's throat to get a dollar out of his pocket; there are those who send money into states to buy votes to control our legislatures; there are those who maintain international propaganda for the purpose of deceiving us into granting of new concessions which will permit them to cover up their past misdeeds and set again in motion their gigantic train of crime.

These twelve private credit monopolies were deceitfully and disloyally foisted upon this Country by the bankers who came here from Europe and repaid us our hospitality by undermining our American institutions. Those bankers took money out of this Country to finance Japan in a war against Russia. They created a reign of terror in Russia with our money in order to help that war along. They instigated the separate peace between Germany and Russia, and thus drove a wedge between the allies in World War. They financed Trotsky's passage from New York to Russia so that he might assist in the destruction of the Russian Empire. They fomented and instigated the Russian Revolution, and placed a large fund of American dollars at Trotsky's disposal in one of their branch banks in Sweden so that through him Russian homes might be thoroughly broken up and Russian children flung far and wide from their natural protectors. They have since begun breaking up of American homes and the dispersal of American children. Mr. Chairman, there should be no partisanship in matters concerning banking and currency affairs in this Country, and I do not speak with any.

In 1912 the National Monetary Association under the chairmanship of the late Senator Nelson W. Aldrich made a report and presented a vicious bill called the National Reserve Association bill. This bill is usually spoken of as the Aldrich bill. Senator Aldrich did not write the Aldrich bill. He was the tool, if not the accomplice, of the European bankers who for nearly twenty years had been scheming to set up a central bank in this Country and who in 1912 has spent and were continuing to spend vast sums of money to accomplish their purpose.

We were opposed to the Aldrich plan for a central bank. The men who rule the Democratic Party then promised the people that if they were returned to power there would be no central bank established here while they held the reins of government. Thirteen months later that promise was broken, and the Wilson administration, under the tutelage of those sinister Wall Street figures who stood behind Colonel House, established here in our free Country the worm-eaten monarchical institution of the "King's Bank" to control us from the top downward, and from the cradle to the grave.

The Federal Reserve Bank destroyed our old and characteristic way of doing business. It discriminated against our 1-name commercial paper, the finest in the world, and it set up the antiquated 2-name paper, which is the present curse of this Country and which wrecked every country which has ever given it scope; it fastened down upon the Country the very tyranny from which the framers of the Constitution sough to save us.

President Jackson's Time

One of the greatest battles for the preservation of this Republic was fought out here in Jackson's time; when the second Bank of the United States, founded on the same false principles of those which are here exemplified in the Fed was hurled out of existence. After that, in 1837, the Country was warned against the dangers that might ensue if the predatory interests after being cast out should come back in disguise and unite themselves to the Executive and through him acquire control of the Government. That is what the predatory interests did when they came back in the livery of hypocrisy and under false pretenses obtained the passage of the Fed.

The danger that the Country was warned against came upon us and is shown in the long train of horrors attendant upon the affairs of the traitorous and dishonest Fed. Look around you when you leave this Chamber and you will see evidences of it in all sides. This is an era of misery and for the conditions that caused that misery, the Fed are fully liable. This is an era of financed crime and in the financing of crime the Fed does not play the part of a disinterested spectator.

It has been said that the draughts man who was employed to write the text of the Aldrich bill because that had been drawn up by lawyers, by acceptance bankers of European origin in New York. It was a copy, in general a translation of the statues of the Reichsbank and other European central banks. One-half million dollars was spent on the part of the propaganda organized by these bankers for the purpose of misleading public opinion and giving Congress the impression that there was an overwhelming popular demand for it and the kind of currency that goes with it, namely, an asset currency based on human debts and obligations. Dr. H. Parker Willis had been employed by Wall Street and propagandists, and when the Aldrich measure failed—he obtained employment with Carter Glass, to assist in drawing the banking bill for the Wilson administration. He appropriated the text of the Aldrich bill. There is no secret about it. The test of the Federal Reserve Act was tainted from the first.

A few days before the bill came to a vote, Senator Henry Cabot Lodge, of Massachusetts, wrote to Senator John W. Weeks as follows:

New York City,
December 17, 1913

My Dear Senator Weeks:

Throughout my public life I have supported all measures designed to take the Government out of the banking business. This bill puts the Government into the banking business as never before in our history The powers vested in the Federal Reserve Board seem to me highly dangerous especially where there is political control of the Board. I should be sorry to hold stock in a bank subject to such dominations. The bill as it stands seems to me to open the way to a vast inflation of the currency. I had hoped to support this bill, but I cannot vote for it cause it seems to me to contain features and to rest upon principles in the highest degree menacing to our prosperity, to stability in business, and to the general welfare of the people of the United States.

Very Truly Yours,
Henry Cabot Lodge.

In eighteen years that have passed since Senator Lodge wrote that letter of warning all of his predictions have come true. The Government is in the banking business as never before. Against its will it has been made the backer of horse thieves and card sharps, bootlegger's smugglers, speculators, and swindlers in all parts of the world. Through the Fed the riffraff of every country is operating on the public credit of the United States Government.

The Great Depression

Meanwhile and on account of it, we ourselves are in the midst of the greatest depression we have ever known. From the Atlantic to the Pacific, our Country has been ravaged and laid waste by the evil practices of the Fed and the interests which control them. At no time in our history, has the general welfare of the people been at a lower level or the minds of the people so full of despair.

Recently in one of our States, 60,000 dwelling houses and farms were brought under the hammer in a single day. 71,000 houses and farms in Oakland County, Michigan, were sold and their erstwhile owners dispossessed. The people who have thus been driven out are the wastage of the Fed. They are the victims of the Fed. Their children are the new slaves of the auction blocks in the revival of the institution of human slavery.

The Scheme of the Feds

In 1913, before the Senate Banking and Currency Committee, Mr. Alexander Lassen made the following statement: The whole scheme of the Fed with its commercial paper is an impractical, cumbersome machinery—is simply a cover to secure the privilege of issuing money, and to evade payment of as much tax upon circulation as possible and then control the issue and maintain, instead of reducing interest rates. It will prove to the advantage of the few and the detriment of the people. It will mean continued shortage of actual money and further extension of credits, for when there is a shortage of money people have to borrow to their cost.

A few days before the Fed passed, Senator Root denounced the Fed as an outrage on our liberties. He predicted: "Long before we wake up from our dream of prosperity through an inflated currency, our gold—which alone could have kept us from catastrophe—will have vanished and no rate of interest will tempt it to return."

If ever a prophecy came true, that one did.

The Fed became law the day before Christmas Eve, in the year 1913, and shortly afterwards, the German International bankers, Kuhn, Loeb and Co. sent one of their partners here to run it.

The Fed Note is essentially unsound. It is the worst currency and the most dangerous that this Country has ever known. When the proponents of the act saw that the Democratic doctrine would not permit them to let the proposed banks issue the new currency as bank notes, they should have stopped at that. They should not have foisted that kind of currency, namely, an asset currency, on the United States Government. They should not have made the Government [liable on the private] debts of individuals and corporations, and, least of all, on the private debts of foreigners.

As Kemerer says: "The Fed Notes, therefore, in form, have some of the qualities of Government paper money, but in substance, are almost a pure asset currency possessing a Government guarantee against which contingency the Government has made no provision whatever."

Hon. L.J. Hill, a former member of the House, said, and truly: "They are obligations of the Government for which the United States received nothing and for the payment of which at any time, it assumes the responsibility: looking to the Fed to recoup itself."

If this United States is to redeem the Fed Notes, when the General Public finds it costs to deliver this paper to the Fed, and if the Government has made no provisions for redeeming them, the first element of unsoundness is not far to seek.

Before the Banking and Currency Committee, when the bill was under discussion Mr. Crozier of Cincinnati said: "The imperial power of elasticity of the public currency is wielded exclusively by the central corporations owned by the banks. This is a life and death power over all local banks and all business. It can be used to create or destroy prosperity, to ward off or cause stringencies and panics. By making money artificially scarce, interest rates throughout the Country can be arbitrarily raised and the bank tax on all business and cost of living increased for the profit of the banks owning these regional central banks, and without the slightest benefit to the people. The 12 Corporations together cover the whole country and monopolize and use for private gain— every dollar of the public currency and all public revenue of the United States. Not a dollar can be put into circulation among the people by their Government, without the consent of and on terms fixed by these 12 private money trusts."

In defiance of this and all other warnings, the proponents of the Fed created the 12 private credit corporations and gave them an absolute monopoly of the currency of these United States—not of the Fed Notes alone—but of all other currency! The Fed Act providing ways and means by which the gold and general currency in the hands of the American people could be obtained by the Fed in exchange for Fed Notes—which are not money—but mere promises to pay.

Since the evil day when this was done, the initial monopoly has been extended by vicious amendments to the Fed and by the unlawful and treasonable practices of the Fed.

Money for the Scottish Distillers

Mr. Chairman, if a Scottish distiller wishes to send a cargo of Scotch whiskey to these United States, he can draw his bill against the purchasing bootlegger in dollars and after the bootlegger has accepted it by writing his name across the face of it, the Scotch distiller can send that bill to the nefarious open discount market in New York City where the Fed will buy it and use it as collateral for a new issue of Fed Notes. Thus the Government of these United States pay the Scotch distiller for the whiskey before it is shipped, and if it is lost on the way, or if the Coast Guard seizes it and destroys it, the Fed simply write off the loss and the government never recovers the money that was paid to the Scotch distiller.

While we are attempting to enforce prohibition here, the Fed are in the distillery business in Europe and paying bootlegger bills with public credit of these United States.

Mr. Chairman, by the same process, they compel our Government to pay the German brewer for his beer. Why should the Fed be permitted to finance the brewing industry in Germany either in this way or as they do by compelling small and fearful United States Banks to take stock in the Isenbeck Brewery and in the German Bank for brewing industries? Mr. Chairman, if Dynamite Nobel of Germany, wishes to sell dynamite in Japan to use in Manchuria or elsewhere, it can draw its bill against the Japanese customers in dollars and send that bill to the nefarious open discount market in New York City where the Fed will buy it and use it as collateral for a new issue of Fed Notes—while at the same time the Fed will be helping Dynamite Nobel by stuffing its stock into the United States banking system.

Why should we send our representatives to the disarmament conference at Geneva—while the Fed is making our Government pay Japanese debts to German Munitions makers?

Mr. Chairman, if a German wishes to raise a crop of beans and sell them to a Japanese customer, he can draw a bill against his prospective Japanese customer in dollars and have it purchased by the Fed and get the money out of this

Country at the expense of the American people before he has even planted the beans in the ground.

Mr. Chairman, if a German in Germany, wishes to export goods to South America, or any other Country, he can draw his bill against his customers and send it to these United States and get the money out of this Country before he ships, or even manufactures the goods.

Mr. Chairman, why should the currency of these United States be issued on the strength of German Beer? Why should it be issued on the crop of unplanted beans to be grown in Chili for Japanese consumption? Why should these United States be compelled to issue many billions of dollars every year to pay the debts of one foreigner to another foreigner? Was it for this that our National Bank depositors had their money taken out of our banks and shipped abroad? Was it for this that they had to lose it? Why should the public credit of these United States and likewise money belonging to our National Bank depositors be used to support foreign brewers, narcotic drug vendors, whiskey distillers, wig makers, human hair merchants, Chilean bean growers, to finance the munitions factories of Germany and Soviet Russia?

The United States Has Been Ransacked

The United States has been ransacked and pillaged. Our structures have been gutted and only the walls are left standing. While being perpetrated, everything the world would rake up to sell us was brought in here at our expense by the Fed until our markets were swamped with unneeded and unwanted imported goods priced far above their value and make to equal the dollar volume of our honest exports, and to kill or reduce our favorite balance of trade. As Agents of the foreign central banks, the Fed try by every means in their power to reduce our favorable balance of trade. They act for their foreign principal and they accept fees from foreigners for acting against the best interests of these United States. Naturally there has been great competition among foreigners for the favors of the Fed.

What we need to do is to send the reserves of our National Banks home to the people who earned and produced them and who still own them and to the banks which were compelled to surrender them to predatory interests.

Mr. Chairman, there is nothing like the Fed pool of confiscated bank deposits in the world. It is a public trough of American wealth in which the foreigners claim rights, equal to or greater than Americans. The Fed are the agents of the foreign central banks. They use our bank depositors' money for the benefit of their foreign principals. They barter the public credit of the United States Government and hire it out to foreigners at a profit to themselves.

All this is done at the expense of the United States Government, and at a sickening loss to the American people. Only our great wealth enabled us to stand the drain of it as long as we did.

We need to destroy the Fed wherein our national reserves are impounded for the benefit of the foreigners. We need to save America for Americans.

Spurious Securities

Mr. Chairman, when you hold a $10.00 Fed Note in your hand, you are holding a piece of paper which sooner or later is going to cost the United States Government $10.00 in gold (unless the Government is obliged to go off the gold standard). It is based on limburger cheese (reported to be in foreign warehouses) or in cans purported to contain peas (but may contain salt water instead), or horse meat, illicit drugs, bootleggers fancies, rags and bones from Soviet Russia (of which these United States imported over a million dollars worth last year), on wines whiskey, natural gas, goat and dog fur, garlic on the string, and Bombay ducks.

If you like to have paper money—which is secured by such commodities—you have it in Fed Note. If you desire to obtain the thing of value upon which this paper currency is based, that is, the limburger cheese, the whiskey, the illicit drugs, or any of the other staples—you will have a very hard time finding them.

Many of these worshipful commodities are in foreign Countries. Are you going to Germany to inspect her warehouses to see if the specified things of value are there? I think more, I do not think that you would find them there if you did go.

On April 27, 1932, the Fed outfit sent $750,000 belonging to American bank depositors in gold to Germany. A week later another $300,000 in gold was shipped to Germany. About the middle of May $12,000,000 in gold was shipped to Germany by the Fed. Almost every week there is a shipment of gold to Germany. These shipments are not made for profit on the exchange since the German marks are below parity with the dollar.

Mr. Chairman, I believe that the National Bank depositors of these United States have a right to know what the Fed are doing with their money. There are millions of National Bank depositors in the Country who do not know that a percentage of every dollar they deposit in a Member Bank of the Fed goes automatically to American Agents of the foreign banks and that all their deposits can be paid away to foreigners without their knowledge or consent by the crooked machinery of the Fed and the questionable practices of the Fed.

[Editorial Note- Problem with next paragraph in original] Mr. Chairman, the American people should be told the truth by their servants in office. In 1930, we had over a half billion dollars outstanding daily to finance foreign goods stored in or shipped between several billion dollars. What goods are these on which the Fed yearly pledges several billions of dollars? In its yearly total, this item amounts to several billions of dollars of the public credit of these United States?

What goods are those which are hidden in European and Asiatic stores have not been seen by any officer of our Government but which are being financed on the public credit of the United States Government? What goods are those upon which the United States Government is being obligated by the Fed to issue Fed Notes to the extent of several billions of dollars a year?

The Bankers' Acceptance Racket

The Fed have been International Banks from the beginning, with these United States as their enforced banker and supplier of currency. But it is none the less extraordinary to see these twelve private credit monopolies, buying the debts of foreigners against foreigners, in all parts of the world and asking the Government of these United States for new issues of Fed notes in exchange for them.

The magnitude of the acceptance racket as it has been developed by the Fed, their foreign correspondents, and the predatory European born bankers, who set up the Fed here and taught your own, by and of pirates, how to loot the people: I say the magnitude of this racket is estimated to be in the neighborhood of 9,000,000,000 per year. In the past ten years it is said to have amounted to $90,000,000,000.00. In my opinion it has amounted to several times that much. Coupled to this you have to the extent of billions of dollars, the gambling in the United States securities, which takes place in the same open discount market —a gambling on which the Fed is now spending $100,000,000.00 per week.

Fed Notes are taken from the U.S. Government in unlimited quantities. Is it strange that the burden of supplying these immense sums of money to the gambling fraternity has at last proved too heavy for the American people to endure? Would it not be a national [calamity to] again bind down this burden on the backs of the American people and by means of a long rawhide whip of the credit masters, compel them to enter another seventeen years of slavery?

They are trying to do that now. They are trying to take $100,000,000.00 of the public credit of the United States every week, in addition to all their other seizures and they are sending that money to the nefarious open market in a desperate gamble to reestablish their graft as a going concern.

They are putting the United States Government in debt to the extent of $100,000,000 a week, and with the money they are buying our Government securities for themselves and their foreign principals. Our people are disgusted with the experiences of the Fed. The Fed is not producing a loaf of bread, a yard of cloth, a bushel of corn, or a pile of cordwood by its check-kiting operations in the money market.

Mr. Speaker, on the 13th of January of this year I addressed the House on the subject of the Reconstruction Finance Corporation. In the course of my remarks I made the following statement: In 1928 the member banks of the Fed borrowed $60,598,690,000.00 from the Fed on their fifteen-day promissory notes. Think of it, sixty billion dollars payable on demand in gold in the course of one single year. The actual amount of such obligations called for six times as much monetary gold as there is in the world. Such transactions represent a grant in the course of one single year of about $7,000,000 to every member of the Fed.

Is it any wonder that American labor which ultimately pays the cost of all banking operations of this Country has at last proved unequal to the task of supplying this huge total of cash and credit for the benefit of the stock market manipulators and foreign swindlers?

In 1933 the Fed presented the staggering amount of $60,598,690,000 to its member banks at the expense of the wage earners and tax payers of these United States. In 1929, the year of the stock market crash, the Fed advanced $58,000,000,000 to member banks.

In 1930 while the speculating banks were getting out of the stock market at the expense of the general public, the Fed advanced them $13,022,782,000. This shows that when the banks were gambling on the public credit of these United States as represented by the Fed currency they were subsidized to any amount they required by the Fed. When the swindle began to fall, the bankers knew it in advance and withdrew from the market. They got out with whole skins —and left the people of these United States to pay the piper.

My friend from Kansas, Mr. McGugin, has stated that he thought the Fed lent money on rediscounting. So they do, but they lend comparatively little that way. The real discounting that they do has been called a mere penny in the slot business. It is too slow for genuine high flyers. They discourage it. They prefer to subsidize their favorite banks by making them $60,000,000,000 advances and they prefer to acquire assistance in the notorious open discount market in New York, where they can use it to control the price of stocks and bonds on the exchanges.

For every dollar they advanced on discounts in 1928, they lent $33.00 to their favorite banks for whom they do a business of several billion dollars income tax on their profits to these United States.

The John Law Swindle

This is the John Law swindle over again. The theft of Teapot Dome was trifling compared to it. What King ever robbed his subject to such an extent as the Fed has robbed us? Is it any wonder that there have been lately ninety cases of starvation in one of the New York hospitals? Is there any wonder that the children are being abandoned?

The government and the people of these United States have been swindled by swindlers deluxe to whom the acquisition of American or a parcel of Fed Notes presented no more difficulty than the drawing up of a worthless acceptance in a Country not subject to the laws of these United States, by sharpers [swindlers] not subject to the jurisdiction of these United States, sharpers with strong banking "fence" on this side of the water, a "fence" acting as a receiver of a worthless paper coming from abroad, endorsing it and getting the currency out of the Fed for it as quickly as possible exchanging that currency for gold and in turn transmitting the gold to its foreign confederates.

Ivan Kreuger, the Match King

Such were the exploits of Ivan Kreuger, Mr. Hoover's friend, and his rotten Wall Street bankers. Every dollar of the billions Kreuger and his gang drew out of this Country on acceptances was drawn from the government and the people of the United States through the Fed. The credit of the United States Government was peddled to him by the Fed for their own private gain. That is what the Fed has been doing for many years.

They have been peddling the credit of this Government and the [signature of this] Government to the swindlers and speculators of all nations. That is what happens when a Country forsakes its Constitution and gives its sovereignty over the public currency to private interests. Give them the flag and they will sell it.

The nature of Kreuger's organized swindle and the bankrupt condition of Kreuger's combine was known here last June when Hoover sought to exempt Kreuger's loan to Germany of $125,000,000 from the operation of the Hoover Moratorium. The bankrupt condition of Kreuger's swindle was known here last summer when $30,000,000 was taken from the American taxpayers by certain bankers in New York for the ostensible purpose of permitting Kreuger to make a loan to Colombia. Colombia never saw that money.

The nature of Kreuger's swindle was known here in January when he visited his friend, Mr. Hoover, at the White House. It was known here in March before he went to Paris and committed suicide.

Mr. Chairman, I think the people of the United States are entitled to know how many billions of dollars were placed at the disposal of Kreuger and his gigantic combine by the Fed, and to know how much of our Government currency was issued and lost in the financing of that great swindle in the years during which the Fed took care of Kreuger's requirements.

A few days ago, the President of the United States with a white face and shaking hands, went before the Senate on behalf of the moneyed interests and asked the Senate to levy a tax on the people so that foreigners might know that these United States would pay its debt to them.

Most Americans thought it was the other way around. What does these United States owe foreigners? When and by whom was the debt incurred? It was incurred by the Fed, when they peddled the signature of the Government to foreigners—for a price. It is what the United States Government has to pay to redeem the obligations of the Fed.

Thieves Go Scot Free

Are you going to let these thieves get off scot free? Is there one law for the looter who drives up to the door of the United States Treasury in his limousine and another for the United States Veterans who are sleeping on the floor of a dilapidated house on the outskirts of Washington?

The Baltimore and Ohio Railroad is here asking for a large loan from the people, and the wage earners and the taxpayers of these United States. It is begging for a handout from the Government. It is standing, cap in hand, at the door of the R.F.C. [Reconstruction Finance Corporation] where all the jackals have gathered to the feast. It is asking for money that was raised from the people by taxation and wants this money of the poor for the benefit of Kuhn, Loeb and Co., the German International Bankers.

Is there one law for the Baltimore and Ohio Railroad and another for the hungry veterans it threw off its freight cars the other day? Is there one law for sleek and prosperous swindlers who call themselves bankers and another law for the soldiers who defended the flag? The R.F.C. is taking over these worthless securities from the Investment Trusts with United States Treasury money at the expense of the American taxpayer and the wage earner.

It will take twenty years to redeem our Government. Twenty years of penal servitude to pay off the gambling debts of the traitorous Fed and to vast flood of American wages and savings, bank deposits, and the United States Government credit which the Fed exported out of this country to their foreign principals.

The Fed lately conducted an anti-hoarding campaign here. They took that extra money which they had persuaded the American people to put into the banks—they sent it to Europe—along with the rest. In the last several months, they have sent $1,300,000,000 in gold to their foreign employers, their foreign masters, and every dollar of that gold belonged to the people of these United States and was unlawfully taken from them.

Fiat Money

Mr. Chairman, within the limits of the time allowed me, I cannot enter into a particularized discussion of the Fed. I have singled out the Fed currency for a few remarks because there has lately been some talk here of "fiat money." What kind of money is being pumped into the open discount market and through it into foreign channels and stock exchanges? Mr. Mills of the Treasury has spoken here of his horror of the printing presses and his horror of dishonest money. He has no horror of dishonest money. If he had, he would be no party to the present gambling of the Fed in the nefarious open discount market of New York, a market in which the sellers are represented by 10 discount corporations owned and organized by the very banks which own and control the Fed.

Fiat money, indeed!

What Mr. Mills is fighting for is the preservation, whole and entire, of the banker's monopoly of all the currency of the United States Government.

Mr. Chairman, last December, I introduced a resolution here asking for an examination and an audit of the Fed and all related matters. If the House sees fit to make such an investigation, the people of these United States will obtain information of great value. This is a Government of the people, by the people, for the people. Consequently, nothing should be concealed from the people. The man who deceives the people is a traitor to these United States.

The man who knows or suspects that a crime has been committed and who conceals and covers up that crime is an accessory to it. Mr. Speaker, it is a monstrous thing for this great nation of people to have its destinies presided over by a traitorous government board acting in secret concert with international usurers.

Every effort has been made by the Fed to conceal its powers —but the truth is—the Fed has usurped the Government. It controls everything here and it controls all of our foreign relations. It makes and breaks governments at will.

No man and no body of men is more entrenched in power than the arrogant credit monopoly which operated the Fed. What National Government has permitted the Fed to steal from the people should now be restored to the people. The people have a valid claim against the Fed. If that claim is enforced the Americans will not need to stand in the bread line, or to suffer and die of starvation in the streets. Women will be saved, families will be kept together, and American children will not be dispersed and abandoned.

Here is a Fed Note. Immense numbers of the notes are now held abroad. I am told that they amount to upwards of a billion dollars. They constitute a claim against our Government and likewise a claim against our peoples' money to the extent of $1,300,000,000 which has within the last few months been shipped abroad to redeem Fed Notes and to pay other gambling debts of the traitorous Fed. The greater part of our money stock has been shipped to other lands.

Why should we promise to pay the debts of foreigners to foreigners? Why should the Fed be permitted to finance our competitors in all parts of the world? Do you know why the tariff was raised? It was raised to shut out the flood of Fed Goods pouring in here from every quarter of the globe—cheap goods, produced by cheaply paid foreign labor, on un-limited supplies of money and credit sent out of this Country by the dishonest and unscrupulous Fed.

The Fed are spending $100,000,000 a week buying govern-ment securities in the open market and are making a great bid for foreign business. They are trying to make rates so at-tractive that the human hair merchants and the distillers and other business entities in foreign land will come here and hire more of the public credit of the United States Govern-ment to pay the Fed outfit for getting it for them.

World Enslavement Planned

Mr. Chairman, when the Fed was passed, the people of these United States did not perceive that a world system was being set up here which would make the savings of the American school teacher available to a narcotic—drug vendor in Aca-pulco. They did not perceive that these United States was to be lowered to the position of a coolie country which has nothing but raw material and heart, that Russia was des-tined to supply the man power and that this country was to supply the financial power to an "international superstate". A superstate controlled by international bankers, and inter-national industrialists acting together to enslave the world for their own pleasure.

The people of these United States are being greatly wronged. They have been driven from their employments. They have been dispossessed from their homes. They have been evicted from their rented quarters. They have lost their children. They have been left to suffer and die for lack of shelter, food, clothing and medicine.

The wealth of these United States and the working capital have been taken away from them and has either been locked in the vaults of certain banks and the great corporations or exported to foreign countries for the benefit of the foreign customers of these banks and corporations. So far as the people of the United States are concerned, the cupboard is bare.

It is true that the warehouses and coal yards and grain elevators are full, but these are padlocked, and the great banks and corporations hold the keys.

The sack of these United States by the Fed is the greatest crime in history.

Mr. Chairman, a serious situation confronts the House of Representatives today. We are trustees of the people and the rights of the people are being taken away from them. Through the Fed the people are losing the rights guaranteed to them by the Constitution. Their property has been taken from them without due process of law. Mr. Chairman, common decency requires us to examine the public accounts of the Government and see what crimes against the public welfare have been committed.

What is needed here is a return to the Constitution of these United States.

The old struggle that was fought out here in Jackson's time must be fought all over again. The independent United States Treasury should be reestablished and the Government should keep its own money under lock and key in the building the people provided for that purpose.

Asset currency, the devise of the swindler, should be done away with. The Fed should be abolished and the State boundaries should be respected. Bank reserves should be kept within the boundaries of the States whose people own them, and this reserve money of the people should be protected so that the International Bankers and acceptance bankers and discount dealers cannot draw it away from them.

The Fed should be repealed, and the Fed Banks, having violated their charters, should be liquidated immediately. Faithless Government officials who have violated their oaths of office should be impeached and brought to trial.

Unless this is done by us, I predict, that the American people, outraged, pillaged, insulted and betrayed as they are in their own land, will rise in their wrath, and will sweep the money changers out of the temple.

Mr. Chairman, the United States is bankrupt: It has been bankrupted by the corrupt and dishonest Fed. It has repudiated its debts to its own citizens. Its chief foreign creditor is Great Britain, and a British bailiff has been at the White House and the British Agents are in the United States Treasury making inventory arranging terms of liquidations!

Great Britain, Partner in Blackmail

Mr. Chairman, the Fed has offered to collect the British claims in full from the American public by trickery and corruption, if Great Britain will help to conceal its crimes. The British are shielding their agents, the Fed, because they do not wish that system of robbery to be destroyed here. They wish it to continue for their benefit! By means of it, Great Britain has become the financial mistress of the world. She has regained the position she occupied before the World War.

For several years she has been a silent partner in the business of the Fed. Under threat of blackmail, or by their bribery, or by their native treachery to the people of the United States, the officials in charge of the Fed unwisely gave Great Britain immense gold loans running into hundreds of millions of dollars. They did this against the law! Those gold loans were not single transactions. They gave Great Britain a borrowing power in the United States of billions. She squeezed billions out of this Country by means of her control of the Fed.

As soon as the Hoover Moratorium was announced, Great Britain moved to consolidate her gains. After the treacherous signing away of American rights at the 7- power conference at London in July, 1931, which put the Fed under the control of the Bank of International Settlements, Great Britain began to tighten the hangman's noose around the neck of the United States.

She abandoned the gold standard and embarked on a campaign of buying up the claims of foreigners against the Fed in all parts of the world. She has now sent her bailiff, Ramsey MacDonald, here to get her war debt to this country canceled. But she has a club in her hands! She has title to the gambling debts which the corrupt and dishonest Fed incurred abroad.

Ramsey MacDonald, the labor party deserter, has come here to compel the President to sign on the dotted line, and that is what Roosevelt is about to do! Roosevelt will endeavor to conceal the nature of his action from the American people. But he will obey the International Bankers and transfer the war debt that Great Britain should pay to the American people, to the shoulders of the American taxpayers.

Mr. Chairman, the bank holiday in the several States was brought about by the corrupt and dishonest Fed. These institutions manipulated money and credit, and caused the States to order bank holidays.

These holidays were frame-ups! They were dress rehearsals for the national bank holiday which Franklin D. Roosevelt promised Sir Ramsey MacDonald that he would declare.

There was no national emergency here when Franklin D. Roosevelt took office excepting the bankruptcy of the Fed— a bankruptcy which has been going on under cover for several years and which has been concealed from the people so that the people would continue to permit their bank deposits and their bank reserves and their gold and the funds of the United States Treasury to be impounded in these bankrupt institutions.

Under cover, the predatory International Bankers have been stealthily transferring the burden of the Fed debts to the people's Treasury and to the people themselves. They stole the farms and the homes of the United States to pay for their thievery! That is the only national emergency that there has been here since the depression began.

The week before the bank holiday was declared in New York State, the deposits in the New York savings banks were greater than the withdrawals. There were no runs on New York Banks. There was no need of a bank holiday in New York, or of a national holiday.

Roosevelt and the International Bankers

Roosevelt did what the International Bankers ordered him to do!

Do not deceive yourself, Mr. Chairman, or permit yourself to be deceived by others into the belief that Roosevelt's dictatorship is in any way intended to benefit the people of the United States: he is preparing to sign on the dotted line! He is preparing to cancel the war debts by fraud!

He is preparing to internationalize this Country and to destroy our Constitution itself in order to keep the Fed intact as a money institution for foreigners. Mr. Chairman, I see no reason why citizens of the United States should be terrorized into surrendering their property to the International Bankers who own and control the Fed. The statement that gold would be taken from its lawful owners if they did not voluntarily surrender it, to private interests, show that there is an anarchist in our Government.

The statement that it is necessary for the people to give their gold—the only real money—to the banks in order to protect the currency is a statement of calculated dishonesty!

By his unlawful usurpation of power on the night of March 5, 1933, and by his proclamation, which in my opinion was in violation of the Constitution of the United States, Roosevelt divorced the currency of the United States from gold, and the United States currency is no longer protected by gold. It is therefore sheer dishonesty to say that the people's gold is needed to protect the currency.

Roosevelt ordered the people to give their gold to private interests—that is, to banks, and he took control of the banks so that all the gold and gold values in them, or given into them, might be handed over to the predatory International Bankers who own and control the Fed.

Roosevelt cast his lot with the usurers. He agreed to save the corrupt and dishonest at the expense of the people of the United States.

He took advantage of the people's confusion and weariness and spread the dragnet over the United States to capture everything of value that was left in it. He made a great haul for the International Bankers.

The Prime Minister of England came here for money! He came here to collect cash!

He came here with Fed Currency and other claims against the Fed which England had bought up in all parts of the world. And he has presented them for redemption in gold.

Mr. Chairman, I am in favor of compelling the Fed to pay their own debts. I see no reason why the general public should be forced to pay the gambling debts of the International Bankers.

Roosevelt Seizes the Gold

By his action in closing the banks of the United States, Roosevelt seized the gold value of forty billion or more of bank deposits in the United States banks. Those deposits were deposits of gold values. By his action he has rendered them payable to the depositors in paper only, if payable at all, and the paper money he proposes to pay out to bank depositors and to the people generally in lieu of their hard earned gold values in itself, and being based on nothing into which the people can convert it the said paper money is of negligible value altogether.

It is the money of slaves, not of free men. If the people of the United States permit it to be imposed upon them at the will of their credit masters, the next step in their downward progress will be their acceptance of orders on Company stores for what they eat and wear. Their case will be similar to that of starving coal miners. They, too, will be paid with orders on Company stores for food and clothing, both of indifferent quality and be forced to live in Company—owned houses from which they may be evicted at the drop of a hat. More of them will be forced into conscript labor camps under supervision.

At noon on the 4th of March, 1933, FDR with his hand on the Bible, took an oath to preserve, protect and defend the Constitution of the U.S. At midnight on the 5th of March, 1933, he confiscated the property of American citizens. He took the currency of the United States standard of value. He repudiated the internal debt of the Government to its own citizens. He destroyed the value of the American dollar. He released, or endeavored to release, the Fed from their contractual liability to redeem Fed currency in gold or lawful money on parity with gold. He depreciated the value of the national currency.

The people of the U.S. are now using unredeemable paper slips for money. The Treasury cannot redeem that paper in gold or silver. The gold and silver of the Treasury has unlawfully been given to the corrupt and dishonest Fed. And the Administration has since had the effrontery to raid the country for more gold for the private interests by telling our patriotic citizens that their gold is needed to protect the currency.

It is not being used to protect the currency! It is being used to protect the corrupt and dishonest Fed.

The directors of these institutions have committed criminal offense against the United States Government, including the offense of making false entries on their books, and the still more serious offense of unlawfully abstracting funds from the United States Treasury! Roosevelt's gold raid is intended to help them out of the pit they dug for themselves when they gambled away the wealth and savings of the American people.

Dictatorship

The International Bankers set up a dictatorship here because they wanted a dictator who would protect them. They wanted a dictator who would protect them. They wanted a dictator who would issue a proclamation giving the Fed an absolute and unconditional release from their special currency in gold, or lawful money of any Fed Bank.

Has Roosevelt relieved any other class of debtors in this country from the necessity of paying their debts? Has he made a proclamation telling the farmers that they need not pay their mortgages? Has he made a proclamation to the effect that mothers of starving children need not pay their milk bills? Has he made a proclamation relieving householders from the necessity of paying rent?

Roosevelt's Two Kinds of Laws

Not he! He has issued one kind of proclamation only, and that is a proclamation to relieve international bankers and the foreign debtors of the United States Government.

Mr. Chairman, the gold in the banks of this country belongs to the American people who have paper money contracts for it in the form of national currency. If the Fed cannot keep their contracts with United States citizens to redeem their paper money in gold, or lawful money, then the Fed must be taken over by the United States Government and their officers must be put on trial.

There must be a day of reckoning. If the Fed have looted the Treasury so that the Treasury cannot redeem the United States currency for which it is liable in gold, then the Fed must be driven out of the Treasury.

Mr. Chairman, a gold certificate is a warehouse receipt for gold in the Treasury, and the man who has a gold certificate is the actual owner of a corresponding amount of gold stacked in the Treasury subject to his order.

Now comes Roosevelt who seeks to render the money of the United States worthless by unlawfully declaring that it may No Longer be converted into gold at the will of the holder.

Roosevelt's next haul for the International Bankers was the reduction in the pay of all Federal employees.

Next in order are the veterans of all wars, many of whom are aged and inform, and other sick and disabled. These men had their lives adjusted for them by acts of Congress determining the amounts of the pensions, and, while it is meant that every citizen should sacrifice himself for the good of the United States, I see no reason why those poor people, these aged Civil War Veterans and war widows and half-starved veterans of the World War, should be compelled to give up their pensions for the financial benefit of the International vultures who have looted the Treasury, bankrupted the country and traitorously delivered the United States to a foreign foe.

There are many ways of raising revenue that are better than that barbaric act of injustice.

Why not collect from the Fed the amount they owe the U.S. Treasury in interest on all the Fed currency they have taken from the Government? That would put billions of dollars into the U.S. Treasury.

If FDR is as honest as he pretends to be, he will have that done immediately. And in addition, why not compel the Fed to disclose their profits and to pay the Government its share?

Until this is done, it is rank dishonesty to talk of maintaining the credit of the U.S. Government.

My own salary as a member of Congress has been reduced, and while I am willing to give my part of it that has been taken away from me to the U.S. Government, I regret that the U.S. has suffered itself to be brought so low by the vultures and crooks who are operating the roulette wheels and faro tables in the Fed, that is now obliged to throw itself on the mercy of its legislators and charwomen, its clerks, and it poor pensioners and to take money out of our pockets to make good the defalcations of the International Bankers who were placed in control of the Treasury and given the monopoly of U.S. Currency by the misbegotten Fed.

I am well aware that the International Bankers, who drive up to the door of the United States Treasury in their limousines, look down with scorn upon members of Congress because we work for so little, while they draw millions a year. The difference is that we earn, or try to earn, what we get—and they steal the greater part of their takings.

Enemies of the People They Rob

I do not like to see vivisections performed on human beings. I do not like to see the American people used for experimental purposes by the credit masters of the United States. They predicted among themselves that they would be able to produce a condition here in which American citizens would be completely humbled and left starving and penniless in the streets.

The fact that they made that assertion while they were fomenting their conspiracy against the United States that they like to see a human being, especially an American, stumbling from hunger when he walks.

Something should be done about it, they say. Five-cent meals, or something! But FDR will not permit the House of Representatives to investigate the condition of the Fed. FDR will not do that. He has certain International Bankers to serve. They not look to him as the man Higher Up who will protect them from the just wrath of an outraged people.

The International Bankers have always hated our pensioners. A man with a small pension is a ward of the Government. He is not dependent upon them for a salary or wages. They cannot control him. They do not like him. It gave them great pleasure, therefore, to slash the veterans.

But FDR will never do anything to embarrass his financial supporters. He will cover up the crimes of the Fed.

Before he was elected, Mr. Roosevelt advocated a return to the earlier practices of the Fed, thus admitting its corruptness. The Democratic platform advocated a change in the personnel of the Fed. These were campaign bait. As a prominent Democrat lately remarked to me; "There is no new deal. The same old crowd is in control."

The claims of foreign creditors of the Fed have no validity in law. The foreign creditors were the receivers—and the willing receivers - of stolen goods! They have received through their banking fences immense amounts of currency, and that currency was unlawfully taken from the United States Treasury by the Fed.

England discovered the irregularities of the Fed quite early in its operations and through fear, apparently, the Fed have for years suffered themselves to be blackmailed and dragooning England to share in the business of the Fed.

The Fed have unlawfully taken many millions of dollars of the public credit of the United States and have given it to foreign sellers on the security of the Debt paper of foreign buyers in purely foreign transactions, and when the foreign buyers refused to meet their obligations and the Fed saw no honest way of getting the stolen goods back into their possession, they decided by control of the executive to make the American people pay their losses!

Conspiracy of War Debts

They likewise entered into a conspiracy to deprive the people of the U.S. of their title to the war debts and not being able to do that in the way they intended, they are now engaged in an effort to debase the American dollar so that foreign governments will have their debts to this country cut in two, and then by means of other vicious underhanded arrangements, they propose to remit the remainder.

So far as the U.S. is concerned, the gambling counters have no legal standing. The U.S. Treasury cannot be compelled to make good the gambling ventures of the corrupt and dishonest Fed. Still less should the bank deposits of the U.S. be used for that purpose. Still less should the national currency have been made irredeemable in gold so that the gold which was massed and stored to redeem the currency for American citizens may be used to pay the gambling debts of the Fed for England's benefit. The American people should have their gold in their own possession where it cannot be held under secret agreement for any foreign control bank, or World Bank, or foreign nation. Our own citizens have the prior claim to it. The paper [money men] have in their possession deserves redemption far more than U.S. currency and credit which was stolen from the U.S. Treasury and bootlegged abroad.

Why should the foreigners be made preferred creditors of the bankrupt U.S.? Why should the U.S. be treated as bankrupt at all? This Government has immense sums due it from the Fed. The directors of these institutions are men of great wealth. Why should the guilty escape the consequences of their misdeeds? Why should the people of these U.S. surrender the value of their gold bank deposits to pay off the gambling debts of these bankers? Why should Roosevelt promise foreigners that the U.S. will play the part of a good neighbor, "meeting its obligations"?

Let the Fed meet their own obligations.

Every member of the Fed should be compelled to disgorge, and every acceptance banker and every discount corporation which has made illegal profits by means of public credit unlawfully bootlegged out of the U.S. Treasury and hired out by the crooks and vultures of the Fed should be compelled to disgorge.

Federal Reserve Pays No Taxes

Gambling debts due to foreign receivers of stolen goods should not be paid by sacrificing our title to our war debts, the assets of the U.S. Treasury—which belong to all the people of the U.S. and which it is our duty to preserve inviolate in the people's treasury.

The U.S. Treasury cannot be made liable for them. The Fed currency must be redeemed by the Fed banks or else these Fed banks must be liquidated.

We know from assertions made here by the Hon. John N. Garner, Vice-President of the U.S. that there is a condition in the [United States such] would cause American citizens, if they knew what it was, to lose all confidence in their government.

That is a condition that Roosevelt will not have investigated. He has brought with him from Wall Street, James Warburg, the son of Paul M. Warburg. Mr. Warburg, alien born, and the son of an alien who did not become naturalized here until several years after this Warburg's birth, is a son of a former partner of Kuhn, Loeb and Co., a grandson of another partner, a nephew of a former partner, and a nephew of a present partner.

He holds no office in our Government, but I am told that he is in daily attendance at the Treasury, and that he has private quarters there! In other words, Mr. Chairman, Kuhn, Loeb and Company now has control and occupies the U.S. Treasury.

Preferred Treatment for Foreigners

The text of the executive order which seems to place an embargo on shipments of gold permits the Secretary of the Treasury, a former director of the corrupt, to issue licenses at his discretion for the export of gold coin, or bullion, earmarked or held in trust for a recognized foreign government or foreign central bank for international settlement. Now, Mr. Chairman, if gold held in trust for those foreign institutions may be sent to them, I see no reason why gold held in trust for Americans, as evidenced by their gold certificates and other currency issued by the U.S. Government, should not be paid to them. I think that American citizens should be entitled to treatment at least as good as that which the person is extending to foreign governments, foreign central banks, and the bank of International Settlements. I think a veteran of the world war, with a $20.00 gold certificate, is at least as much entitled to receive his own gold for it as any international banker in the city of New York or London.

By the terms of this executive order, gold may be exported if it is actually required, for the fulfillment of any contract entered into prior to the date of this order by an applicant who, in obedience to the executive order of April 5, 1933, has delivered gold coin, gold bullion, or gold certificates. This means that gold may be exported to pay the obligations abroad of the Fed which were incurred prior to the date of the order, namely, April 20, 1933.

If a European Bank should send 100,000,000 dollars in Fed currency to a bank in this country for redemption, that bank could easily ship gold to Europe in exchange for that currency. Such Fed currency would represent "contracts" entered into prior to the date of the order. If the Bank of International Settlements or any other foreign bank holding any of the present gambling debt paper of the Fed should draw a draft for the settlement of such obligation, gold would be shipped to them because the debt contract would have been entered into prior to the date of order.

Crimes and Criminals

Mr. Speaker, I rise to a question of constitutional privilege.

Whereas, I charge . . . Eugene Meyer, Roy A. Young, Edmund Platt, Eugene B. Black, Adolph Casper Miller, Charles S. Hamlin, George R. James, Andrew W. Mellon, Ogden L. Mills, William H. Woo, W. Poole, J.F.T. O'Connor, members of the Federal Reserve Board; F. H. Curtis, J.H. Chane, R.L. Austin, George De Camp, L.B. Williams, W.W. Hoxton, Oscar Newton, E.M. Stevens, J.S. Wood, J.N. Payton, M.L. McClure, C.C. Walsh, Isaac B. Newton, Federal Reserve Agents, jointly and severally, with violations of the Constitution and laws of the United States, and whereas I charge them with having taken funds from the U.S Treasury which were not appropriated by the Congress of the United States, and I charge them with having unlawfully taken over $80,000,000,000 from the U.S. Government in the year 1928, the said unlawful taking consisting of the unlawful creation of claims against the U.S. Treasury to the extent of over $80,000,000,000 in the year 1928; and I charge them with similar thefts committed in 1929, 1930, 1931, 1932 and 1933, and in years previous to 1928, amounting to billions of dollars; and

Whereas I charge them, jointly and severally with having unlawfully created claims against the U.S. Treasury by unlawfully placing U.S. Government credit in specific amounts to the credit of foreign governments and foreign central banks of issue; private interests and commercial and private banks of the U.S. and foreign countries, and branches of foreign banks doing business in the U.S., to the extent of billions of dollars; and with having made unlawful contracts in the name of the U.S. Government and the U.S. Treasury; and with having made false entries on books of account; and

Whereas I charge them jointly and severally, with having taken Fed Notes from the U.S. Treasury and with having put Fed Notes into circulation without obeying the mandatory provision of the Fed Act which requires the Fed Board to fix an interest rate on all issues of Fed Notes supplied to Fed Banks, the interest resulting therefrom to be paid by the Fed Banks to the government of the U.S. for the use of the Fed Notes, and I charge them of having defrauded the U.S. Government and the people of the U.S. of billions of dollars by the commission of this crime, and

Whereas I charge them, jointly and severally, with having purchased U.S. Government securities with U.S. Government credit unlawfully taken and with having sold the said U.S. Government securities back to the people of the U.S. for gold or gold values and with having again purchased U.S. Government securities with U.S. Government credit unlawfully taken and with having again sold the said U.S. Government security for gold or gold values, and I charge them with having defrauded the U.S. Government and the people of the U.S. by this rotary process; and

Whereas I charge them, jointly and severally, with having unlawfully negotiated U.S. Government securities, upon which the Government liability was extinguished, as collateral security for Fed Notes and with having substituted such securities for gold which was being held as collateral security for Fed Notes, and with having by the process defrauded the U.S. Government and the people of the U.S., and I charge

them with the theft of all the gold and currency they obtained by this process; and

Whereas I charge them, jointly and severally, with having
unlawfully issued Fed currency on false, worthless and fictitious acceptances and other circulating evidence of debt, and
with having made unlawful advances of Fed currency, and
with having unlawfully permitted renewals of acceptances
and renewals of other circulating evidences of debt, and
with having permitted acceptance bankers and discount
dealer corporations and other private bankers to violate the
banking laws of the U.S.; and

Whereas I charge them, jointly and severally, with having
conspired to have evidences of debt to the extent of
$1,000,000,000 artificially created at the end of February,
1933, and early in March 1933, and with having made unlawful issues and advances of Fed currency on the security of
said artificially created evidences of debt for a sinister purpose, and with having assisted in the execution of said sinister purpose; and

Whereas I charge them, jointly and severally, with having
brought about the repudiation of the currency obligations of
the Fed Banks to the people of the U.S. and with having
conspired to obtain a release for the Fed Board and the Fed
Banks from their contractual liability to redeem all Fed currency in gold or lawful money at the Fed Bank and with
having defrauded the holders of Fed currency, and with
having conspired to have the debts and losses of the Fed
Board and the Fed Banks unlawfully transferred to the Government and the people of the U.S., and

Whereas I charge them, jointly and severally, with having
unlawfully substituted Fed currency and other irredeemable
paper currency for gold in the hands of the people after the
decision to repudiate the Fed currency and the national cur-

rency was made known to them, and with thus having obtained money under false pretenses; and

Whereas I charge them, jointly and severally, with having brought about a repudiation of the notes of the U.S. in order that the gold value of the said currency might be given to private interests, foreign governments, foreign central banks of issues, and the Bank of International Settlements, and the people of the U.S. to be left without gold or lawful money and with no currency other than a paper currency irredeemable in gold, and I charge them with having done this for the benefit of private interests, foreign governments, foreign central banks of issue, and the bank of International Settlements; and

Whereas I charge them, jointly and severally, with conniving with the Edge Law banks, and other Edge Law institutions, accepting banks, and discount corporations, foreign central banks of issue, foreign commercial banks, foreign corporations, and foreign individuals with funds unlawfully taken from the U.S. Treasury; and I charge them with having unlawfully permitted and made possible "new financing" for foreigners at the expense of the U.S. Treasury to the extent of billions of dollars and with having unlawfully permitted and made possible the bringing into the United States of immense quantities of foreign securities, created in foreign countries for export to the U.S. and with having unlawfully permitted the said foreign securities to be imported into the U.S. instead of gold, which was lawfully due to the U.S. on trade balances and otherwise, and with having lawfully permitted and facilitated the sale of the said foreign securities in the U.S., and

Whereas I charge them, jointly and severally, with having unlawfully exported U.S. coins and currency for a sinister purpose, and with having deprived the people of the U.S. of their lawful medium of exchange, and I charge them with having arbitrarily and unlawfully reduced the amount of money and currency in circulation in the U.S. to the lowest rate per capita in the history of the Government, so that the great mass of the people have been left without a sufficient medium of exchange, and I charge them with concealment and evasion in refusing to make known the amount of U.S. money in coins and paper currency exported and the amount remaining in the U.S. as a result of which refusal the Congress of the U.S. is unable to ascertain where the U.S. coins and issues of currency are at the present time, and what amount of U.S. currency is now held abroad; and

Whereas I charge them, jointly and severally, with having arbitrarily and unlawfully raised and lowered the rates of money and with having arbitrarily increased and diminished the volume of currency in circulation for the benefit of private interests at the expense of the Government and the people of the U.S. and with having unlawfully manipulated money rates, wages, salaries and property values both real and personal, in the U.S. by unlawful operations in the open discount market and by resale and repurchase agreements unsanctioned by law, and

Whereas I charge them jointly and severally, with having brought about the decline in prices on the New York Stock Exchange and other exchanges in October, 1929, by unlawful manipulation of money rates and the volume of U.S. money and currency in circulation: by theft of funds from the U.S. Treasury by gambling in acceptances and U.S. Government securities; by service rendered to foreign and domestic speculators and politicians, and by unlawful sale of U.S. gold reserves abroad, and

Whereas the unconstitutional inflation law imbedded in the so-called Farm Relief Act by which the Fed Banks are given permission to buy U.S. Government securities to the extent of $3,000,000,000 and to drew forth currency from the people's Treasury to the extent of $3,000,000,000 is likely to result in connivance on the part of said accused with others in the purchase by the Fed of the U.S. Government securities to the extent of $3,000,000,000 with U.S. Government's own credit unlawfully taken, it being obvious that the Fed do no not [sic] intend to pay anything of value to the U.S. Government for the said U.S. Government securities no provision for payment in gold or lawful money appearing in the so-called Farm Relief bill—and the U.S. Government will thus be placed in a position of conferring a gift of $3,000,000,000 in the U.S. Government securities on the Fed to enable them to pay more on their bad debts to foreign governments, foreign central banks of issue, private interests, and private and commercial banks, both foreign and domestic, and the Bank of International Settlements, and

Whereas the U.S. Government will thus go into debt to the extent of $3,000,000,000 and will then have an additional claim of $3,000,000,000 in currency unlawfully created against it and whereas no private interest should be permitted to buy U.S. Government securities with the Government's own credit unlawfully taken and whereas currency should not be issued for the benefit of said private interest or any interests on U.S. Government securities so acquired, and whereas it has been publicly stated and not denied that the inflation amendment of the Farm Relief Act is the matter of benefit which was secured by Ramsey MacDonald, the Prime Minister of Great Britain, upon the occasion of his latest visit to the U.S. Treasury, and whereas there is grave danger that the accused will employ the provision creating U.S. Government securities to the extent of $3,000,000,000 and three millions in currency to be issuable thereupon for the benefit of themselves and their foreign principals, and that they will convert the currency so obtained to the uses of Great Britain by secret arrangements with the Bank of England of which they are the agents, and for which they maintain an account and perform services at the expense of the U.S. Treasury, and that they will likewise confer benefits upon the Bank of International Settlements for which they maintain an account and perform services at the expense of the U.S. Treasury; and

Whereas I charge them, jointly and severally, with having concealed the insolvency of the Fed and with having failed to report the insolvency of the Fed to the Congress and with having conspired to have the said insolvent institutions continue in operation, and with having permitted the said insolvent institutions to receive U.S. Government funds and other deposits, and with having permitted them to exercise control over the gold reserves of the U.S. and with having permitted them to transfer upward of $100,000,000,000 of their debts and losses to the general public and the Government of the U.S., and with having permitted foreign debts of the Fed to be paid with the property, the savings, the wages, and the salaries of the people of the U.S. and with the farms and the homes of the American people, and whereas I charge them with forcing the bad debts of the Fed upon the general public covertly and dishonestly and with taking the general wealth and savings of the people of the U.S. under false pretenses, to pay the debts of the Fed to foreigners; and

Whereas I charge them, jointly and severally, with violations of the Fed Act and other laws; with maladministration of the evasions of the Fed Law and other laws; and with having unlawfully failed to report violations of law on the part of the Fed Banks which, if known, would have caused the Fed Banks to lose their charters, and

Whereas I charge them, jointly and severally, with failure to protect and maintain the gold reserves and the gold stock and gold coinage of the U.S. and with having sold the gold reserves of the U.S to foreign Governments, foreign central banks of issue, foreign commercial and private banks, and other foreign institutions and individuals at a profit to themselves, and I charge them with having sold gold reserves of the U.S. so that between 1924 and 1928 the U.S. gained no gold on net account but suffered a decline in its percentage of central gold reserves from the 45.9 percent in 1924 to 37.5 percent in 1928 notwithstanding the fact that the U.S. had a favorable balance of trade throughout that period, and

Whereas I charge them, jointly and severally, with having conspired to concentrate U.S. Government securities and thus the national debt of the U.S. in the hands of foreigners and international money lenders and with having conspired to transfer to foreigners and international money lenders title to and control of the financial resources of the U.S.; and

Whereas I charge them, jointly and severally, with having fictitiously paid installments on the national debt with Government credit unlawfully taken; and

Whereas I charge them, jointly and severally, with the loss of the U.S. Government funds entrusted to their care; and

Whereas I charge them, jointly and severally, with having destroyed independent banks in the U.S. and with having thereby caused losses amounting to billions of dollars to the said banks, and to the general public of the U.S., and

Whereas I charge them, jointly and severally, with the failure to furnish true reports of the business operations and the true conditions of the Fed to the Congress and the people, and having furnished false and misleading reports to the congress of the U.S., and

Whereas I charge them, jointly and severally, with having published false and misleading propaganda intended to deceive the American people and to cause the U.S. to lose its independence; and

Whereas I charge them, jointly and severally, with unlawfully allowing Great Britain to share in the profits of the Fed at the expense of the Government and the people of the U.S.; and

Whereas I charge them, jointly and severally, with having entered into secret agreements and illegal transactions with Montague Norman, Governor of the Bank of England; and

Whereas I charge them, jointly and severally, with swindling the U.S. Treasury and the people of the U.S. in pretending to have received payment from Great Britain of the amount due on the British war debt to the U.S. in December, 1932; and

Whereas I charge them, jointly and severally, with having conspired with their foreign principals and others to defraud the U.S. Government and to prevent the people of the U.S. from receiving payment of the war debts due to the U.S. from foreign nations; and

Whereas I charge them, jointly and severally, with having robbed the U.S Government and the people of the U.S. by their theft and sale of the gold reserves of the U.S. and other unlawful transactions created a deficit in the U.S. Treasury, which has necessitated to a large extent the destruction of our national defense and the reduction of the U.S. Army and the U.S. Navy and other branches of the national defense; and

Whereas I charge them, jointly and severally, of having reduced the U.S. from a first class power to one that is dependent, and with having reduced the U.S. from a rich and powerful nation to one that is internationally poor; and

Whereas I charge them, jointly and severally, with the crime of having treasonable conspired and acted against the peace and security of the U.S. and with having treasonable conspired to destroy constitutional Government in the U.S.

Resolve, That the Committee on the Judiciary is authorized and directed as a whole or by subcommittee, to investigate the official conduct of the Fed agents to determine whether, in the opinion of the said committee, they have been guilty of any high crime or misdemeanor which in the contemplation the Constitution requires the interposition of the Constitutional powers of the House. Such Committee shall report its finding to the House, together with such resolution or resolutions of impeachment or other recommendations as it deems proper.

For the purpose of this resolution the Committee is authorized to sit and act during the present Congress at such times and places in the District of Columbia or elsewhere, whether or not the House is sitting, has recessed or has adjourned, to hold such clerical, stenographic, and other assistants, to require of such witnesses and the production of such books, papers, and documents, to take such testimony, to have such printing and binding done, and to make such expenditures as it deems necessary.

After some discussion and upon the motion of Mr. Byrns, the resolution and charge were referred to the Committee on the Judiciary.

Attacks on McFadden's Life Reported

Commenting on Former Congressman Louis T. McFadden's "heart-failure sudden-death" on Oct. 3, 1936, after a dose of "intestinal flu," [an article by publicist and economist Robert Edward Edmondson in] Pelley's Weekly of October 14 said:

> Now that this sterling American patriot has made the Passing, it can be revealed that not long after his public utterance against the encroaching powers of Judah, it became known among his intimates that he

had suffered two attacks against his life. The first attack came in the form of two revolver shots fired at
him from ambush as he was alighting from a cab in
front of one of the Capital hotels. Fortunately both
shots missed him, the bullets burying themselves in
the structure of the cab.

He became violently ill after partaking of food at a
political banquet at Washington. His life was only
saved from what was subsequently announced as a
poisoning by the presence of a physician friend at the
banquet, who at once procured a stomach pump and
subjected the Congressman to emergency treatment.

President Andrew Jackson stated in reference to the bankers
at the start of his administration, "You are a den of vipers
and thieves. I intend to rout you out, and by the Eternal
God, I will rout you out."

Many could argue that there lived no greater advocate for human
rights than Honorable McFadden. His relentless work was dedicated to
providing America a free and equitable monetary system, therein liber-
ating all Americans from the very oppressive financial tyranny imposed
upon them by immoral bankers.

It is a sad commentary when one reads of McFadden's courage and integrity and compares this great man to today's sycophant politicians, who
cower to the bankers, thereby betraying the faith and trust of the American people.

When one looks at the insane policies the government adopts to pay
the interest on the debt supposedly owed by the American people to the
Federal Reserve—the biggest criminal enterprise in history—one soon
realizes that the US monetary system has been doomed to failure from its
inception. Today there is no fixing America's corrupt and debase monetary system. The only remedy for the US economy is to cease functioning under the Federal Reserve System and create an honest and
constitutional system using real money.

Mathematically, the Federal Reserve System has already reached the
point of no return, and there is no chance of monetary recovery or even

sustainability of the currency, unless radical restructuring of the system occurs. The United States has a similar balance sheet as Greece had when it recently collapsed, specifically in regard to its ratio of debt to total gross domestic production. Greece's debt is mostly the result of socialistic entitlement programs. The United States is granted more leniency than Greece by the bankers in return for the US militarily enforcing the banks' interests.

Congress is supposed to investigate any crimes of US presidents, keep the checks and balances of government in place, and ensure no branch of government usurps more power than it is allowed under the Constitution.

How can Congress protect the people when it criminally commits so many blatant breeches against the Constitution itself by allowing the Federal Reserve to monopolize US currency? How, then, is it possible for Congress to exercise any type of checks and balances over the US presidents or any other entity? For the most part, checks and balances within the federal government are an antiquated notion, undetectable, and nearly extinct today. Asking the Congress to investigate unconstitutional activities within government is like requesting a snake to walk upright; it is simply does not happen.

Look at the despicable investigation and conclusions that were drawn by FBI Director Comey regarding Hillary Clinton and her allegedly criminal handling of top-secret information. Many say it is blatantly obvious that she has treasonously acted against the interests of the United States, and it is disgusting that the director turned a blind eye to her crimes and turned his back on the American people. Despicable, the whole thing is just despicable.

Congress is so corrupt that its members do not dare to investigate and broadcast the rampant criminality and treasonous acts regularly occurring against the American people for fear that the many skeletons in Congress's closets will start to rattle back to life. Most politicians have dark secrets in their past, making them prey and fair game of the bankers' blackmail and extortion rackets.

Congress has never been the same since president of the Confederacy, Jefferson Davis, and the South parted ways with the tarnished Union just prior to the US Civil War. Upon the South's protest and leaving the US Congress, the mutation and transformation of the US government from a de jure government into a de facto government, or private corporation, soon became a reality.

Congress from that point forward no longer had concern for the American people; its responsibility converted to overseeing the US bankruptcy. The sole purpose and allegiance of US politicians were transferred away from the people and directed toward protecting the interests of the US corporate shareholders.

For a fascinating and revealing look at the US Civil War from a righteous and southern point of view, read The Un-Civil War: Shattering the Historical Myths, authored by Leonard M. Scruggs and is available on Amazon at amazon.com/Civil-War-Shattering-Historical-Myths/dp/098 343560X.

On occasion, we are blessed with individuals that look outside themselves and contribute to correcting, as best they can, whatever situation they deem in need of correction and improvement, to make this planet a more habitable environment for humanity. James Traficant Jr. was such a great man. I had the pleasure of discussing many of the injustices that plague our society with this fearless freedom fighter and am honored to call him a friend.

Traficant is truly an American hero. He had the courage to speak on the floor of Congress and inform the American people of the US bankruptcy and the mounting troubles facing this nation. Shortly after delivering the speech below, he was imprisoned for seven and a half years. Traficant had an abundance of integrity and an unconditional love for the people of this country. His character was unassailable; he walked tall and worked tirelessly to abolish the tyrannical Federal Reserve System and Internal Revenue Service.

His untimely and suspicious death has led many to conjecture that he was murdered at the hands of the banking elite. You can hear a fascinating and implicating interview with James Traficant and the prodigious Alex Jones at youtube.com/watch?v=gKrlTfMMncM in which they discuss the foreign special interests that control and run the United States. Here is another video given just prior to his death, James Traficant's Last Public Speech, which is viewed at youtube.com/watch?v=pY 7n-KFmU7o.

Whenever you get the chance, thank the long-time radio host Alex Jones for his great work. He is an incredible man who constantly fights for the rights and freedoms of every American. He would be included as one of the modern-day Founding Fathers. If you want to hear the truth regarding the events of the day and not the baloney disseminated by the mass media, you should tune into Jones's always revealing daily radio show at infowars.com and prisonplanet.com.

Prior to his being railroaded and imprisoned, US Congressman Traficant openly and defiantly discussed the bankruptcy of the United States in a speech recorded in the United States Congressional Record on March 17, 1993, Vol. 33, page H-1303, Speaker-Rep. James Traficant Jr. (Ohio) addressing the House of Representatives:

James Traficant's US Bankruptcy Speech

Mr. Speaker, we are here now in chapter 11. Members of Congress are official trustees presiding over the greatest reorganization of any Bankrupt entity in world history, the U.S. Government. We are setting forth hopefully, a blueprint for our future. There are some who say it is a coroner's report that will lead to our demise.

It is an established fact that the United States Federal Government has been dissolved by the Emergency Banking Act, March 9, 1933, 48 Stat. 1, Public Law 89-719; declared by President Roosevelt, being bankrupt and insolvent. H.J.R. 192, 73rd Congress m session June 5, 1933—Joint Resolution To Suspend The Gold Standard and Abrogate The Gold Clause dissolved the Sovereign Authority of the United States and the official capacities of all United States Governmental Offices, Officers, and Departments and is further evidence that the United States Federal Government exists today in name only.

The receivers of the United States Bankruptcy are the International Bankers, via the United Nations, the World Bank and the International Monetary Fund. All United States Offices, Officials, and Departments are now operating within a de facto status in name only under Emergency War Powers. With the Constitutional Republican form of Government now dissolved, the receivers of the Bankruptcy have adopted a new form of government for the United States. This new form of government is known as a Democracy, being an established Socialist/Communist order under a new governor for America. This act was instituted and established by transferring and/or placing the Office of the Secretary of Treasury to that of the Governor of the International Monetary Fund. Public Law 94-564, page 8, Section H.R. 13955 reads in part: "The U.S. Secretary of Treasury receives no compensation for representing the United States."

Gold and silver were such a powerful money during the founding of the united states of America, that the Founding Fathers declared that only gold or silver coins can be "money" in America. Since gold and silver coinage were heavy and inconvenient for a lot of transactions, they were stored in banks and a claim check was issued as a money substitute. People traded their coupons as money, or "currency." Currency is not money, but a money substitute. Redeemable currency must promise to pay a dollar equivalent in gold or silver money. Federal Reserve Notes (FRNs) make no such promises, and are not "money." A Federal Reserve Note is a debt obligation of the federal United States government, not "money." The federal United States government and the U.S. Congress were not and have never been authorized by the Constitution for the united states of America to issue currency of any kind, but only lawful money, gold and silver coin.

It is essential that we comprehend the distinction between real money and paper money substitute. One cannot get rich by accumulating money substitutes, one can only get deeper into debt. We the People no longer have any "money." Most Americans have not been paid any "money" for a very long time, perhaps not in their entire life. Now do you comprehend why you feel broke? Now, do you understand why you are "bankrupt," along with the rest of the country?

Federal Reserve Notes (FRNs) are unsigned checks written on a closed account. FRNs are an inflatable paper system designed to create debt through inflation (devaluation of currency). Whenever there is an increase of the supply of a money substitute in the economy without a corresponding increase in the gold and silver backing, inflation occurs.

Inflation is an invisible form of taxation that irresponsible governments inflict on their citizens. The Federal Reserve Bank who controls the supply and movement of FRNs has everybody fooled. They have access to an unlimited supply of FRNs, paying only for the printing costs of what they need. FRNs are nothing more than promissory notes for U.S. Treasury securities (T-Bills)—a promise to pay the debt to the Federal Reserve Bank.

There is a fundamental difference between "paying" and "discharging" a debt. To pay a debt, you must pay with value or substance (i.e. gold, silver, barter or a commodity). With FRNs, you can only discharge a debt. You cannot pay a debt with a debt currency system. You cannot service a debt with a currency that has no backing in value or substance. No contract in Common law is valid unless it involves an exchange of "good & valuable consideration." Unpayable debt transfers power and control to the sovereign power structure that has no interest in money, law, equity or justice because they have so much wealth already.

Their lust is for power and control. Since the inception of central banking, they have controlled the fates of nations.

The Federal Reserve System is based on the Canon law and the principles of sovereignty protected in the Constitution and the Bill of Rights. In fact, the international bankers used a "Canon Law Trust" as their model, adding stock and naming it a "Joint Stock Trust." The U.S. Congress had passed a law making it illegal for any legal "person" to duplicate a "Joint Stock Trust" in 1873. The Federal Reserve Act was legislated post-facto (to 1870), although post-facto laws are strictly forbidden by the Constitution. [1:9:3]

The Federal Reserve System is a sovereign power structure separate and distinct from the federal United States government. The Federal Reserve is a maritime lender, and/or maritime insurance underwriter to the federal United States operating exclusively under Admiralty/Maritime law. The lender or underwriter bears the risks, and the Maritime law compelling specific performance in paying the interest, or premiums are the same.

Assets of the debtor can also be hypothecated (to pledge something as a security without taking possession of it) as security by the lender or underwriter. The Federal Reserve Act stipulated that the interest on the debt was to be paid in gold. There was no stipulation in the Federal Reserve Act for ever paying the principle.

Prior to 1913, most Americans owned clear, allodial title to property, free and clear of any liens or mortgages until the Federal Reserve Act (of 1913) "Hypothecated" all property within the federal United States to the Board of Governors of the Federal Reserve—in which the Trustees (stockholders) held legal title. The U.S. citizen (tenant, franchisee) was registered as a "beneficiary" of the trust via his/her birth certificate. In 1933, the federal United States hypothecated all of the present and future properties, assets and labor of their "subjects," the 14th Amendment U.S. citizen, to the Federal Reserve System.

In return, the Federal Reserve System agreed to extend the federal United States corporation all the credit "money substitute" it needed. Like any other debtor, the federal United States government had to assign collateral and security to their creditors as a condition of the loan. Since the federal

United States didn't have any assets, they assigned the private property of their "economic slaves", the U.S. citizens as collateral against the unpayable federal debt. They also pledged the unincorporated federal territories, national parks forests, birth certificates, and nonprofit organizations, as collateral against the federal debt. All has already been transferred as payment to the international bankers.

Unwittingly, America has returned to its pre-American Revolution, feudal roots whereby all land is held by a sovereign and the common people had no rights to hold allodial title to property. Once again, We the People are the tenants and sharecroppers renting our own property from a Sovereign in the guise of the Federal Reserve Bank. We the people have exchanged one master for another.

This has been going on for over eighty years without the "informed knowledge" of the American people, without a voice protesting loud enough. Now it's easy to grasp why America is fundamentally bankrupt.

Why don't more people own their properties outright?

Why are 90% of Americans mortgaged to the hilt and have little or no assets after all debts and liabilities have been paid? Why does it feel like you are working harder and harder and getting less and less?

We are reaping what has been sown, and the results of our harvest is a painful bankruptcy, and a foreclosure on American property, precious liberties, and a way of life. Few of our elected representatives in Washington, D.C. have dared to tell the truth. The federal United States is bankrupt. Our children will inherit this unpayable debt, and the tyranny to enforce paying it.

America has become completely bankrupt in world leadership, financial credit and its reputation for courage, vision and human rights. This is an undeclared economic war, bankruptcy, and economic slavery of the most corrupt order! Wake up America! Take back your Country.

I thank the reverent US Congressman James Traficant Jr. from Ohio for the courageous life he lived, always serving and helping his fellow man. His contributions to history will be appreciated for generations to come.

After serving six months in prison on trumped-up charges of racketeering, for allegedly accepting bribes, and for tax evasion, Traficant was offered a deal for immediate release from prison on the condition he admit guilt to the charges that were used to railroad him. He thought his honor and integrity were more important than his new federal address and refused all offers made by the Justice Department. He spent the next seven years in prison.

Traficant died under very suspicious circumstances on September 27, 2014. While driving his yard tractor on the flat land of his small farm, he supposedly had a heart attack and overturned it, pinning himself underneath the tractor causing his suffocation. His death occurred under very dubious circumstances, and many believe foul play was definitely involved in his demise.

This secret of US bankruptcy, let out of the bag by Traficant on the floor of the House of Representatives, is unknown to most Americans, and the government is more than content in keeping it that way. Once we realize that the politicians are purely interested in lining their own pockets, we can see the insincerity constantly voiced by American politicians and the duplicity in most of their actions.

Our corrupt, unworkable, and unsustainable monetary system exists today because of the American people's unfaltering and unquestioning compliance and acceptance. What happens when the American people wake up and remove their allegiance from a system that is bankrupting Americans and enriching foreigners?

As a nation, we cannot justify a monetary policy enforced at the cost of a veteran's arm, leg, or life.

Do not kid yourself and believe that many of the so-called terrorist attacks are anything except intelligence operations (psych ops), performed under the direction of the international intelligence agencies to protect the interests of the banks.

Anyone can easily understand the fact that robbery and criminality exist at the end of a gun barrel, but the US government is much more devious at hiding its theft and the fleecing of America behind the obfuscating curtain of the status quo. The government has been duping Americans since 1913, and this is becoming all too prevalent, all too well known to not be responsibly addressed by the leaders of this world. More important, the abuse of the American people by their government needs to be immediately addressed by the American people. Americans get what we deserve, and if we sit silently, we will get the most corrupt criminal regime of a government, the kind that we see in a banana republic third-world country. Blatant criminality is running rampart in the US government, and the people are doing literally nothing to bring the criminals to justice.

In the old days, in countries far away, treasonous politicians were hanged in public view. Great Britain enjoyed festive public hangings, and many thieves and killers would gasp in the breeze as the onlookers cheered with exuberance and glee!

Remember, regarding government immorality, if we remain silent, we accept and acquiesce. If we sit by and do nothing at the expense of our brothers and sisters, we damage ourselves more than any outside influence possibly could. Silence equates to death, just as intelligent reason equates to life; this pattern or equation has been repeatedly exemplified as being true in all societies that have preceded this one.

The gig is up. The people are sick and tired of being financially abused by disgusting politicians who have sold themselves for the trinkets of the international bankers. We are sick and tired of working to pay a debt that we never were part of creating and are not responsible to pay in any manner. The people are sick and tired of being slaves under the current system of Federal Reserve Feudalism.

The US government is no longer tied to the original Constitution and operates solely as a corporation that extracts funds from the American populace by coercing the people to pay corrupt bankers via the IRS. This is the mechanism used to enslave Americans and all the people of the world. The people are living under financial tyranny imposed by lawyers, cloaked in two-thousand-dollar suits, with evil intentions disguised by legal mumbo-jumbo that the average person does not comprehend.

Today's corrupt political system will not correct itself. Politicians are the beneficiaries of today's corrupt criminal system and the ones that created America's debased system of government that is intensely contrary to the intentions of the Founding Fathers. There is a legal axiom that states, "What starts twisted ends twisted," and the Federal Reserve System is one of the most twisted institutions ever devised and implemented by men that are sworn to and worship Satan.

One cannot correct a broken leg by simply asking the person to continue to walk farther and faster on it. By continuing to walk on a broken leg, the person will see the leg only get worse. The US Corporation cannot fix itself, nor does it have a desire to fix itself. When politicians are being bought and sold like prostitutes, the people are the ones who get screwed. The Federal Reserve was created and governed by short-sighted criminal minds bent on utilizing the monetary system for domination over all humankind.

The Federal Reserve's owners and directors understand that the US monetary system is irreparable and should be immediately abandoned. Mathematically, it can only get worse and worse since there is no built-in corrective mechanism to adjust the imbalances within the Fed.

The Federal Reserve is incompetently attempting to correct a broken system by implementing drastically unsuccessful financial measures like quantitative easing, which is as stupid as buying your own debt. This is one of the many ridiculous and laughable attempts to plug the leaking holes in America's sinking economic ship. With insatiable greed, the international bankers are not going to be satisfied until they control the entire world, everyone, and everything in it.

The US monetary system is built and directly mirrors the insanity of world domination and enslavement conceived by the original and demented founders of the Federal Reserve. They are obsessed with the death and destruction of humanity.

Depraved bankers want to have dominion over all people and every aspect of their lives. What people are witnessing today is simply another step toward world domination, human degradation, and planetary enslavement.

The Constitution was designed to limit the powers of the government and prevent the usurpation of governmental powers by individuals and groups of individuals for their own private benefit. When the government is covertly overthrown, there are no provisions in the Constitution to deal with such an occurrence—other than rebellion and a complete do-over. The only things that stop government corruption are people who are aware enough to care for and defend their freedom.

Americans must take action or suffer the consequences of our country's collective cowardice. Tyranny exists when the populace becomes apathetic toward their government and, worse, the people are disrespecting their priceless freedom and those Americans who died to protect it. The Constitution cannot do anything by itself; the people must act to protect their rights and liberties if they care to keep them; if not, our rights shall be forfeited, perhaps forever.

By ignoring the Constitution, those in power operate unencumbered without rules or limitations. Politicians take their orders from economic dictators of the Federal Reserve, who use bribery and coercion to forward their preordained agenda of enslavement upon the masses.

Without upholding the Constitution and limiting the actions of the government, the people will be financially bled to abject poverty. The nexus of the banking cartels, which own everything, decide the financial fate of this nation and this planet, unless the people stand together against such vast global tyranny.

Do people really want to continue down this road of tyrannical financial suppression? Do people want to have a treasonous government that cares less about them than the wicked and malicious desires of the bankers?

The Founding Fathers conceived and created the US government to provide basic services that were impractical for the individual states to provide. The federal government was intentionally designed to remain small, mostly govern itself, and not interfere in the lives of the people.

A most important function to prevent the financial takeover of the US government was the delineation under the Constitution that gold and silver were the only permitted forms of money. The Founding Fathers devised the use of redeemable money to safeguard and protect Americans from tyrannical foreign banks. The politicians were supposed to hold responsible and press charges against treasonous politicians who sold out the American people to the foreign owners of the Federal Reserve System.

Lincoln and his cronies changed the government into a corporation, which provided the opportunity for insincere, unethical, and treacherous psychotics to gain control of the government and ultimately the American people.

Those who control the Federal Reserve have not relinquished one inch of that control since its inception. We the people must demand our rights, or we will wake one day and wonder why we have let our rights and property be taken from us and our posterity. History is full of examples of people demanding their rights from tyrants, usually in the form of revolutions, which often end with the oppressors of the people hanging at the end of a rope.

It is the responsibility of every American to conceive of and implement a method to regain control of our government and our rights while acting free of hatred and violence.

What would occur if the people demanded that the United States officially declare itself bankrupt and expel all foreign banking interests? Americans need to force their politicians to fall back into alignment with the procedures and guidelines enumerated in the US Constitution. For politicians to do otherwise is to partake in treasonous and seditious crimes against the people of the United States.

Will we either stand and demand liberty and freedom or ignore our responsibility to humankind? Our actions determine our fate and the fate of all succeeding generations. We hold in our hands the keys to liberty and, at the same time, the shackles of enslavement.

History shows us that people must stand up for themselves while they still have an opportunity—before it is too late. Time is running out, and if we fail to resist tyranny and oppression, our children will never know the heavenly taste of freedom and liberty. For humankind, it is better to stand and die demanding what is right than to capitulate and live another instant on our knees as slaves.

Wake up America, for the future never sleeps. The fate of future generations depends on what we do here and now to uplift and benefit our fellow man and, ultimately, society.

Do not let the lamp of liberty be extinguished during our lives and on our watch, but rather, let the lamp of liberty illuminate the way for all humanity to enjoy.

CHAPTER 14

Courts, Police, and Prisons

No one truly knows a nation until one has been inside its jails. A nation should not be judged by how it treats its highest citizens but its lowest ones.

— NELSON MANDELA

There is a higher court than courts of justice and that is the court of conscience. It supersedes all other courts.

— MAHATMA GANDHI

I learned that courage was not the absence of fear but the triumph over it. The brave man is not he who does not feel afraid but he who conquers that fear.

— NELSON MANDELA

Two men looked out from prison bars. One saw the mud, the other saw stars.

— DALE CARNEGIE

Do not judge me by my success, judge me by how many times I fell down and got back up again.

— NELSON MANDELA

This is a court of law, young man, not a court of justice.

— OLIVER WENDELL HOLMES JR.

For to be free is not merely to cast off one's chains, but to live in a way that respects and enhances the freedom of others.

— NELSON MANDELA

If I had written all the truth I knew for the past ten years, about 600 people—including me—would be rotting in prison cells from Rio to Seattle today. Absolute truth is a very rare and dangerous commodity in the context of the professional journalism.

– HUNTER S. THOMPSON

Overcoming poverty is not a task of charity; it is an act of justice. Like slavery and Apartheid, poverty is not natural. It is man-made and it can be overcome and eradicated by the actions of human beings. Sometimes it falls on a generation to be great. YOU can be that great generation. Let your greatness blossom.

– NELSON MANDELA

When you go into court, you are putting your fate into the hands of twelve people who weren't smart enough to get out of jury duty.

– NORM CROSBY

You never really know your fellow man until you are imprisoned with him.

– NELSON MANDELA

On average, drug prisoners spend more time in federal prison than rapists, who often get out on early release because of the overcrowding in prison caused by the Drug War.

– MICHAEL BADNARIK

As I walked out the door toward my freedom, I knew that if I did not leave all the anger, hatred and bitterness behind that I would still be in prison.

– NELSON MANDELA

Human progress is neither automatic nor inevitable. Every step toward the goal of justice requires sacrifice, suffering, and struggle; the tireless exertions and passionate concern of dedicated individuals.

– MARTIN LUTHER KING

THE CALIBER OR ADVANCEMENT LEVEL of any society is measured by its equitable dispensation of uniform justice, or the lack of it. Justice functions to remedy the transgressions committed against members of society without having to resort to violence in order to attain adequate remedy and relief. The true purpose of the justice system is to exert outside control over individuals within a society who fail to monitor and regulate their own behavior in a manner conducive with the harmonious functioning of all other members of society.

When individuals fail to act in accord with the norms of society, the judicial system institutes outside corrective actions to preserve the peace and tranquility of society. In America's society, this function has been monopolized by the court system.

Without really understanding the various mechanizations of the legal and penal systems and their true purposes and propensities for profit and pain, it is difficult to conceive the existence of such a vile and punitive prison system that is too often void of rehabilitation.

The court system does not intend to deliver rehabilitative and therapeutic processes on behalf of inmates; instead, the system acts in a punitive manner without long-term concerns in mind for each individual's rehabilitation and re-absorption into free society. Failure to rehabilitate the criminal members of society is a failure to rehabilitate and improve the society itself. Reintroducing a person into society who has not been adequately rehabilitated and has not had a sincere change of thought and character results in fractionally debasing society with this person's reentry; he or she is an example of a social liability, created by America's penal system.

American recidivism rates are appallingly high, with some estimates saying over two-thirds of those released from prison are again arrested and over 50 percent are re-incarcerated.

There are over two million people in prison in the United States, and yet America is supposedly the land of the free. There are over eight million people involved with the corrections, probation, and prison industries in America, which is more than all other nations of the world combined. Statistics indicate that in the United States, during an average year, over thirteen million people spend time in jail.

The racial profile of convicts varies drastically from that of the overall population. There are seven times as many blacks and three times as many Hispanics incarcerated in America's prisons as there are whites.

Vera.org has in-depth reports on America's prison system that really capture the warped demographic and rehabilitation problems, which need to be addressed in a manner more conducive to preparing a guest of our prison systems to function productively once released. Additionally, we need to ensure prisoners' ability to financially support themselves in the real world upon release, as gainful employment helps a person to live within the bounds of the law. Society is damaged when insufficiently rehabilitated criminals are released and then perpetrate more crimes against the community. Who is satisfied with the antiquated penal system of America that allows prisoners to become educated only in the latest criminal techniques taught by other prisoners?

Over 90 percent of all US prisoners are released from incarceration without receiving the rehabilitation one would expect from a system that costs taxpayers over sixty billion dollars a year. Should there be minimal educational standards or requirements demanded of prisoners in order for them to receive early released from prison? There should be, at a minimum, vocational training programs that provide prisoners the opportunity to gain a trade that will assist them in earning a decent living once released from incarceration.

If requirements were established in which prisoners had to receive the equivalent of a year of college education or technical training for every year they spent in prison, society would be releasing prisoners with far better qualities and higher skill sets that are useful in adapting to life outside prison.

Jails and prisons should be places where extreme emphasis is placed on education, for without education, rehabilitation is unattainable. Education is the ingredient or therapy that is missing in the development of most people that are incarcerated.

If a person's education level increases, upon release from prison, he or she is better able to re-assimilate into society; therefore, recidivism rates would crash, and the dignity of the inmate would finally be restored. Inmates, after all, are people.

Imagine if prisoners were required to study for at least eight hours per day while in prison; think how educated they would be after studying for a ten-year term. Prisons would be releasing astrophysicists and advanced computer scientists and people that could get really good jobs. Do you think all that studying would lower recidivism rates?

Obviously, those with an insufficient academic background would be tutored to insure that there would be a high level of improvement in the character of the individuals before they are released from prison.

Across America there are such low standards regarding the types of rehabilitation offered to prisoners. Where is the training to assist them to become anything more than desperate criminals upon release? There are many difficulties placed upon prisoners who have been incarcerated for several years and typically leave prison functionally illiterate.

Penniless and without prospects for employment, newly released ex-cons rejoin their dysfunctional families and friends.

A released prisoner who is broke with no job prospects, is poorly educated, and has no means of transportation is likely to commit crimes in order to eat and survive. The odds of recidivism are very high under these overwhelming circumstances because there is not an adequate support system in place to assist ex-convicts in obtaining sufficient employment to provide for the basics of food, clothing, and shelter once released. More than this, felons have a record that follows them for the rest of their lives. Who wants to hire a felon?

There is a solution to our failing prison system, and it is comprised of alternative programs that treat offenders as human beings, not sub-humans. The Academy of Training Skills (ATS) in Louisiana (aattss.com) is a successful program that accepts for rehabilitation, first time, nonviolent felons who would have otherwise been sentenced to a stint in state prison. Very importantly, the individuals that attend the academy in lieu of prison and finish the eighteen-month rehabilitative program do not have their criminal records permanently marked as a felon.

The residents of ATS are required to work a forty-hour week and pay for their own room and board, relieving the state of the financial burden of housing inmates in overly crowded and very costly state-run prison systems. Furthermore, education plays a pivotal role in rehabilitation, and ATS mandates that all residents of ATS must learn a trade before being released back into society.

Additionally, the residents at ATS are certified in a trade that prepares them for assimilation into society, which is what most prisoners and every person needs in order to live a life free of crime. According to its website, the Academy of Training Skills offers several certified training programs including general hazard awareness, hazardous waste worker, hydroblasting, rigging, hazardous waste supervisor, safety training course, medical records, emergency response technicians, process safety management, certified welding courses, and much more. Watch the academy's life-changing video at youtube.comwatch?v=CfByTQ7fH4s For the complete list of training that is available, please visit aattss.com/training.php.

The Academy of Training Skills is a vanguard of the prison industry for producing significant prisoner rehabilitation and the reduction of recidivism rates. The recidivism rates for aattss.com graduates are well below the national average.

The National Institute of Justice reports the following national statistics on recidivism (nij.gov/topics/corrections/recidivism/Pages/welcome.aspx). The Bureau of Justice has found the following rates of recidivism in a study that tracked 404,638 prisoners, in thirty states, after their release from prison in 2005. The researchers found that:

- within three years of release, about two-thirds (67.8 percent) of released prisoners were rearrested;
- within five years of release, about three-quarters (76.6 percent) of released prisoners were rearrested;
- of those prisoners who were rearrested, more than half (56.7 percent) were arrested by the end of the first year.

Property offenders were the most likely to be rearrested with 82.1 percent of released property offenders rearrested for a new crime, compared with 76.9 percent of drug offenders, 73.6 percent of public order offenders, and 71.3 percent of violent offenders.

As mentioned, one of the primary reasons for high recidivism rates is that many ex-convicts do not possess adequate skills to support themselves once released. The ATS offers a modern model that encourages rehabilitation through education and counseling. These are the keys to correcting the alarming recidivism rates we find in traditional prison establishments.

Another major difference is the environment at the Academy for Training Skills. Compared to most state prisons, there is an incredible amount of care and respect that a resident of ATS receives from the staff and the other participants in the program.

Poor and often indifferent treatment is all too common in too many incarceration facilities; this creates a bleak and hopeless environment making rehabilitation barely possible.

Additionally, released residents from ATS often have accumulated several thousand dollars in savings, which those that successfully finish the program use to reestablish themselves in the community, paying for rent and transportation—compared to the average ex-convict who leaves jail with only pennies in his pocket.

Another exciting benefit for a graduate from ATS, compared to the newly released ex-convict from prison, is that the ATS graduate is already far ahead because he or she is able to continue working at the position of employment obtained while training at ATS. Rather than rotting away in a cell or learning the latest in criminality, which is abundantly available at most prisons, residents at ATS are in a type of working environment that allows them to live a structured and productive lifestyle, hence creating a pattern of stability that contributes to their reentry into unsupervised society.

Since the Academy of Training Skills deals with people who have not committed violent crimes, one may contend that it is easier to rehabilitate such individuals. However, traditional prisons are filled with violent and nonviolent criminals alike who want rehabilitation more than anything. Indeed, a majority of America's prisoners are incarcerated for nonviolent crimes according to the Justice Policy Institute (justicepolicy.org).

There are over a million nonviolent offenders locked away in America's prison systems. A large portion of these people are there for possessing marijuana or cocaine or other minor drug-related charges. Unfortunate as it is, nonviolent prisoners are sometimes placed in the company of murderers and rapists, hardened criminals who are perhaps not as easily rehabilitated.

Often in prisons, there is a separation of the different types of offenders, and those with nonviolent tendencies should be given the opportunity to lead lives that are more productive by attaining increased education and viable employment prior to their release into society. This is the least that we can do for people.

The courts work hand in hand with the police, who work hand in hand with the prison system, and these businesses are booming in America. On a visit to any city across this great land, you will notice that the courthouse is often one of the largest buildings in the city, and the very tallest is usually a bank.

There is a secondary business model, which we will shortly discuss, germane to the court and prison systems. Although one would suspect these institutions cost the government billions to operate annually, the exact opposite is true. Prison and the warehousing of people is a very profitable business. Crime does pay, and it pays very well, just not for defendants.

Virtually every document in the police, court, and prison systems requires a signature of the person completing it. As an example, when a traffic citation is issued, the police officer signs the ticket and then has the violator sign it as well or risk being arrested. The violator signs the ticket, and the ticket then becomes a type of negotiable or security instrument under the Uniform Commercial Code. The court clerk bundles these tickets in the same manner that the bankers bundle house mortgages and sells them in the financial markets. Everything, including tickets, indictments, arraignments, warrants, and court orders issued by a judge, is monetized as security instruments. This profits many members of the criminal justice system and fattens the already burgeoning retirement accounts of our public servants.

For sheriffs and judges in rural areas in which the sheriff often owns a piece of the local prison and operates it, there are often financial incentives that help keep the jails at full capacity.

While adjudicating from the bench, judges have an incentive to protect and contribute to their own Judicial Retirement Funds. Impartiality and fairness in courtrooms are things of the past. How can a judge be impartial, when a good portion of the monies received by the court is added to the Judicial Retirement Fund of the judges? See the Retirement System of Alabama at rsa-al.gov as an example.

Below is a tragic story regarding the horrible treatment of several children at the hands of corrupt judges in Wilkes-Barre, Pennsylvania. Wikipedia reports self-dealing crimes in the "Kids for Cash Scandal" at en.wikipedia.org/wiki/Kids_for_cash_scandal and is included below:

The "Kids for Cash Scandal" unfolded in 2008 over judicial kickbacks at the Luzerne County Court of Common Pleas in Wilkes-Barre,

Pennsylvania. Two judges, President Judge Mark Ciavarella and Senior Judge Michael Conahan, were accused of accepting money from Robert Mericle, builder of two private, for-profit youth centers for the detention of juveniles, in return for contracting with the facilities and imposing harsh adjudications on juveniles brought before their courts to increase the number of residents in the centers.

For example, Ciavarella adjudicated children to extended stays in youth centers for offenses as minimal as mocking a principal on Myspace, trespassing in a vacant building, or shoplifting DVDs from Walmart. Ciavarella and Conahan pled guilty on February 13, 2009, pursuant to a plea agreement to federal charges of honest services, fraud and conspiracy to defraud the United States (failing to report income to the Internal Revenue Service, known as tax evasion) in connection with receiving $2.6 million in payments from managers at PA Child Care in Pittston Township and its sister company Western PA Child Care in Butler County. The plea agreement was later voided by a federal judge who was dissatisfied with the post-plea conduct of the defendants, and the two judges charged, subsequently withdrew their guilty pleas which raises the possibility of a criminal trial.

For more information, it is highly recommend you watch the harrowing documentary Kids For Cash (youtube.com/watch?v=mVzSe2T Q3d0).

Here is how the secondary business model of the prison system works and is where the real money in the prison system is made when a person is incarcerated. Upon being booked, fingerprinted, and photographed, the prison registers new convicts and their unique Social Security numbers on bonds and other security instruments. These bonds or security instruments need to be collateralized, and that is where the prisoner participates in the transaction. For each of the bonds and security instruments that are created at the time of incarceration, the prisoner is warehoused for the duration of his or her sentence as the actual collateral for the security instruments that are generated upon the inmate's arrival.

The security instruments are created, backed, and guaranteed by the prisoner and his or her being warehoused as the collateral for those same security instruments. Human collateral provides the public correctional system the means to adjust the accounting records of the nation and its public debt. When the court creates and issues securities and other financial instruments, there is a person that guarantees that security; that is the defendant and the soon-to-be convict.

The amount of time inmates are sentenced is the term of the security instrument associated with each particular inmate's record and crime. If a convict is incarcerated for murder, the county that incarcerates the murderer makes approximately four million dollars in negotiable security instruments, and the federal government may make up to forty million dollars for selling that same negotiable security instrument to the Chinese government.

In a police station, courthouse, jail, or prison, every piece of paper a person signs that contains his or her social security number has a monetary amount attached and associated with it. Those signed papers become negotiable instruments, which are sold on the financial markets. You can learn more regarding Social Security numbers and other very interesting information regarding the government's monetary machinations, intentionally hidden from the ordinary person at iamsomedude.com.

Today's monetization of the prison system provides billions, maybe even trillions, to city, county, state, and federal governments. The negotiable instruments created upon a prisoner's arrest and incarceration are traded by some of the most popular financial brokerage firms on Wall Street.

All police departments, courthouses, and prisons are private and not public corporations having their own specific Dun and Bradstreet credit ratings. As a result of prison privatization, there is a monetary incentive in America to lock up people for the slightest infractions, which years ago would be punished with a slap on the wrist. This is one of the reasons that there are far too many people incarcerated for minor drug charges within the American prison system. Get the facts at drugwarfacts.org.

More enlightening information about the US government and its friends profiting from the tragic suffering caused by human trafficking and enslaving incarceration is available on Sara Flounders's website (warwith outvictory.com), which contains the article "Pentagon and Slave Labor in U.S. Prisons," printed below with Sara's gracious permission. It certainly pulls back the curtain and clarifies any ambiguity or confusion that may exist regarding America's for-profit incarceration system and the depths to which it has deteriorated.

Pentagon and Slave Labor in U.S. Prisons

Prisoners earning 23 cents an hour in U.S. federal prisons are manufacturing high-tech electronic components for Patriot Advanced Capability 3 missiles, launchers for TOW (Tube-launched, Optically tracked, Wire-guided) anti-tank missiles, and other guided missile systems. A March article by journalist and financial researcher, Justin Rohrlich, of World in Review is worth a closer look at the full implications of this ominous development and can be read at minyanville.com

The expanding use of prison industries which pay slave wages as a way to increase profits for giant military corporations is a frontal attack on the rights of all workers.

Prison labor with no union protection, overtime pay, vacation days, pensions, benefits, health and safety protection, or Social Security withholding also makes complex components for McDonnell Douglas/ Boeing's F-15 fighter aircraft, the General Dynamics/Lockheed Martin F-16, and Bell/Textron's Cobra helicopter. Prison labor produces night-vision goggles, body armor, camouflage uniforms, radio and communication devices, and lighting systems and components for 30-mm to 300-mm battleship anti-aircraft guns, along with land mine sweepers and electro-optical equipment for the BAE Systems Bradley Fighting Vehicles' laser rangefinder. Prisoners recycle toxic electronic equipment and overhaul military vehicles.

Labor in federal prisons is contracted out by UNICOR, previously known as Federal Prison Industries, a quasi-public, for-profit corporation run by the Bureau of Prisons. In 14 prison factories, more than 3,000 prisoners manufacture electronic equipment for land, sea and airborne communication. UNICOR is now the U.S. government's 39th largest contractor, with 110 factories at 79 federal penitentiaries.

The majority of UNICOR's products and services are on contract to orders from the Department of Defense. Giant multinational corporations purchase parts assembled at some of the lowest labor rates in the world, then resell the finished weapons components at the highest rates of profit. For example, Lockheed Martin and Raytheon Corporation subcontract components then assemble and sell advanced weapons systems to the Pentagon.

Increased Profits, Unhealthy Workplaces

However, the Pentagon is not the only buyer. U.S. corporations are the world's largest arms dealers, while weapons and aircraft are the largest U.S. export. The U.S. State Department, Department of Defense and diplomats pressure NATO members and dependent countries around the world into multibillion-dollar weapons purchases that generate further corporate profits, often leaving many countries mired in enormous debt.

But the fact that the capitalist state has found yet another way to drastically undercut union workers' wages and ensure still higher profits to military corporations—whose weapons wreak such havoc around the world—is an ominous development.

According to CNN Money, the U.S. highly skilled and well-paid "aerospace workforce has shrunk by 40 percent in the past 20 years. Like many other industries, the defense sector has been quietly outsourcing production (and jobs) to cheaper labor markets overseas." (Feb. 24) It seems that with prison labor, these jobs are also being outsourced domestically.

Meanwhile, dividends and options to a handful of top stockholders and CEO compensation packages at top military corporations exceed the total payment of wages to the more than 23,000 imprisoned workers who produce UNICOR parts.

The prison work is often dangerous, toxic and unprotected. At FCI Victorville, a federal prison located at an old US airbase located in California, prisoners clean, overhaul and reassemble tanks and military vehicles returned from combat and coated in toxic spent ammunition, depleted uranium dust and chemicals.

A federal lawsuit by prisoners, food service workers, and family members at FCI Marianna, a minimum security women's prison in Florida, cited that toxic dust containing lead, cadmium, mercury and arsenic poisoned those who worked at UNICOR's computer and electronic recycling factory.

Prisoners there worked covered in dust without safety equipment, protective gear, air filtration or masks. The suit explained that the toxic dust caused severe damage to nervous and reproductive systems, lung damage, bone disease, kidney failure, blood clots, cancers, anxiety, headaches, fatigue, memory lapses, skin lesions, and circulatory and respiratory problems. This is one of eight federal prison recycling facilities —employing 1,200 prisoners—run by UNICOR.

After years of complaints the Justice Department's Office of the Inspector General and the Federal Occupational Health Service concurred in October 2008 that UNICOR has jeopardized the lives and safety of untold numbers of prisoners and staff. (Prison Legal News, Feb. 17, 2009)

RACISM & U.S. PRISONS

The U.S. imprisons more people per capita than any country in the world. With less than 5 percent of the world population, the U.S. imprisons more than 25 percent of all people imprisoned in the world.

There are more than 2.3 million prisoners in federal, state and local prisons in the U.S. Twice as many people are under probation and parole. Many tens of thousands of other prisoners include undocumented immigrants facing deportation, prisoners awaiting sentencing and youthful offenders in categories considered reform or detention.

The racism that pervades every aspect of life in capitalist society— from jobs, income and housing to education and opportunity—is most brutally reflected by who is caught up in the U.S. prison system.

More than 60 percent of U.S. prisoners are people of color. Seventy percent of those sentenced under the three strikes law in California— which requires mandatory sentences of 25 years to life after three felony convictions—are people of color. Nationally, 39 percent of African-American men in their 20s are in prison, on probation or on parole. The U.S. imprisons more people than South Africa did under apartheid. (Linn Washington, "Incarceration Nation")

The U.S. prison population is not only the largest in the world—it is relentlessly growing. The U.S. prison population is more than five times what it was 30 years ago.

In 1980, when Ronald Reagan became president, there were 400,000 prisoners in the U.S. Today the number exceeds 2.3 million. In California the prison population soared from 23,264 in 1980 to 170,000 in 2010. The Pennsylvania prison population climbed from 8,243 to 51,487 in those same years. There are now more African-American men in prison, on probation or on parole than were enslaved in 1850, before the Civil War began, according to Law Professor Michelle Alexander in the book "The New Jim Crow: Mass Incarceration in the Age of Color-blindness."

Today a staggering 1-in-100 adults in the U.S. are living behind bars. But this crime, which breaks families and destroys lives, is not evenly distributed. In major urban areas one-half of Black men have criminal records. This means life-long, legalized discrimination in student loans, financial assistance, access to public housing, mortgages, the right to vote and, of course, the possibility of being hired for a job.

STATE PRISONS CONTRACTING SLAVE LABOR

It is not only federal prisons that contract out prison labor to top corporations. State prisons that used forced prison labor in plantations, laundries and highway chain gangs increasingly seek to sell prison labor to corporations trolling the globe in search of the cheapest possible labor.

One agency asks: "Are you experiencing high employee turnover? Worried about the costs of employee benefits? Unhappy with out-of-state or offshore suppliers? Getting hit by overseas competition? Having trouble motivating your workforce? Thinking about expansion space? Then Washington State Department of Corrections Private Sector Partnerships is for you." (educate-yourself.org, July 25, 2005)

Major corporations profiting from the slave labor of prisoners include Motorola, Compaq, Honeywell, Microsoft, Boeing, Revlon, Chevron, TWA, Victoria's Secret and Eddie Bauer.

IBM, Texas Instruments and Dell get circuit boards made by Texas prisoners. Tennessee inmates sew jeans for Kmart and JCPenney. Tens of thousands of youth flipping hamburgers for minimum wages at McDonald's wear uniforms sewn by prison workers, who are forced to work for much less.

In California, as in many states, prisoners who refuse to work are moved to disciplinary housing and lose canteen privileges as well as "good time" credit, which slices hard time off their sentences.

Systematic abuse, beatings, prolonged isolation and sensory deprivation, and lack of medical care make U.S. prison conditions among the worst in the world. Ironically, working under grueling conditions for pennies an hour is treated as a "perk" for good behavior.

In December, Georgia inmates went on strike and refused to leave their cells at six prisons for more than a week. In one of the largest prison protests in U.S. history, prisoners spoke of being forced to work seven days a week for no pay. Prisoners were beaten if they refused to work.

PRIVATE PRISONS FOR PROFIT

In the ruthless search to maximize profits and grab hold of every possible source of income, almost every public agency and social service is being outsourced to private for-profit contractors.

In the U.S. military this means there are now more private contractors and mercenaries in Iraq and Afghanistan than there are U.S. or NATO soldiers.

In cities and states across the U.S., hospitals, medical care facilities, schools, cafeterias, road maintenance, water supply services, sewage departments, sanitation, airports and tens of thousands of social programs that receive public funding are being contracted out to for-profit corporations. Anything publicly owned and paid for by generations of past workers' taxes—from libraries to concert halls and parks—is being sold or leased at fire sale prices.

All this is motivated and lobbied for by right-wing think tanks like that set up by Koch Industries and their owners, Charles and David Koch, as a way to cut costs, lower wages and pensions, and undercut public service unions.

The most gruesome privatizations are the hundreds of for-profit prisons being established.

The inmate population in private for-profit prisons tripled between 1987 and 2007. By 2007 there were 264 such prison facilities, housing almost 99,000 adult prisoners. (house.leg.state.mn.us, Feb. 24, 2009) Companies operating such facilities include the Corrections Corporation of America, the GEO Group Inc. and Community Education Centers.

Prison bonds provide a lucrative return for capitalist investors such as Merrill-Lynch, Shearson Lehman, American Express and Allstate. Prisoners are traded from one state to another based on the most profitable arrangements.

MILITARISM AND PRISONS

Hand in hand with the military-industrial complex, U.S. imperialism has created a massive prison-industrial complex that generates billions of dollars annually for businesses and industries profiting from mass incarceration.

For decades workers in the U.S. have been assured that they also benefit from imperialist looting by the giant multinational corporations. But today more than half the federal budget is absorbed by the costs of maintaining the military machine and the corporations who are guaranteed profits for equipping the Pentagon. That is the only budget category in federal spending that is guaranteed to increase by at least 5 percent a year —at a time when every social program is being cut to the bone.

The sheer economic weight of militarism seeps into the fabric of society at every level. It fuels racism and reaction. The political influence of the Pentagon and the giant military and oil corporations—with their thousands of high-paid lobbyists, media pundits and network of links into every police force in the country—fuels growing repression and an expanding prison population.

The military, oil and banking conglomerates, interlinked with the police and prisons, have a stranglehold on the U.S. capitalist economy and reins of political power, regardless of who is president or what political party is in office. The very survival of these global corporations is based on immediate maximization of profits. They are driven to seize every resource and source of potential profits.

Thoroughly rational solutions are proposed whenever the human and economic cost of militarism and repression is discussed. The billions spent for war and fantastically destructive weapons systems could provide five to seven times more jobs if spent on desperately needed social services, education and rebuilding essential infrastructure. Or it could provide free university education, considering the fact that it costs far more to imprison people than to educate them.

Why aren't such reasonable solutions ever chosen? Because, military contracts generate far larger guaranteed profits to the military and the oil industries, which have a decisive influence on the U.S. economy.

The prison-industrial complex—including the prison system, prison labor, private prisons, police and repressive apparatus, and their continuing expansion—are a greater source of profit and are reinforced by the climate of racism and reaction. Most rational and socially useful solutions are not considered viable options.

Thank you, Sara Flounders. For more insightful information regarding the link between America's prisons and the Pentagon, I strongly recommend Sara's enlightening book, War Without Victory: The Pentagon's Achilles Heel (available at warwithoutvictory.com).

Again, crime does pay, just not for the convict. It pays for the criminals who run and own the prison system. For additional information detailing and concerning the bonding and warehousing of prisoners, please Google "prison industrial complex" and you will be amazed to find the level of barbarity with which we treat our fellow Americans.

The courts have become administrative tribunals that no longer are concerned with justice; their sole motivation is commerce and profit. The courts are sub-corporations of the federal government, as verified by the court's Dun and Bradstreet credit rating. Corporation records of virtually all courthouses can be viewed at each secretary of state's website.

Justice (just us) is no longer dispensed through law but through the color of law. If you are so unfortunate to find yourself in court, realize it is a private club and you are the special guest, or as some call it, the sacrifice of the day!

All legal representatives of the court belong to the American Bar Association. Attorneys are the enforcers and ultimate initiators of untold misery across America and beyond her shores.

Attorneys have special privileges and are not required to register with the state as other professions are required to do. One hundred seventy-four different occupations are licensed and regulated by the state of California (careeronestop.org); this covers practically ever profession, except attorneys. Attorneys are not licensed by any state in the union. This leads one to speculate, "Why do attorneys have special privileges compared to non-attorneys?"

Attorneys do not take an oath to uphold the rights and best interest of their clients. Attorneys take an oath to be loyal first and foremost to the courts, and concern for protecting the rights of their clients is a secondary or tertiary interest. Attorneys are first and foremost required to demean themselves to the courts wherein they practice. Below is the oath that attorneys swear to uphold and abide by in Florida.

Oath of Admission to the Florida Bar

I do solemnly swear:

I will support the Constitution of the United States and the Constitution of the State of Florida;

I will maintain the respect due to courts of justice and judicial officers;

I will not counsel or maintain any suit or proceedings which shall appear to me to be unjust, nor any defense except such as I believe to be honestly debatable under the law of the land;

I will employ for the purpose of maintaining the causes confided to me such means only as are consistent with truth and honor, and will never seek to mislead the judge or jury by any artifice or false statement of fact or law;

I will maintain the confidence and preserve inviolate the secrets of my clients, and will accept no compensation in connection with their business except from them or with their knowledge and approval;

To opposing parties and their counsel, I pledge fairness, integrity, and civility, not only in court, but also in all written and oral communications;

I will abstain from all offensive personality and advance no fact prejudicial to the honor or reputation of a party or witness, unless required by the justice of the cause with which I am charged;

I will never reject, from any consideration personal to myself, the cause of the defenseless or oppressed, or delay anyone's cause for lucre or malice. So help me God.

Since they are unlicensed, lawyers are therefore foreign agents and not subject to the rules and regulations of the state in which they practice and which other corporations and their employees are required to follow. Attorneys sanction and govern themselves—talk about the fox guarding the hen house!

Attorneys are esquires, which is a British title of nobility. Therefore, all attorneys are constitutionally prohibited from practicing in a court of law, unless of course, they are registered under the Foreign Agents Registration Act. I have yet to meet an attorney or judge that is properly registered under the Foreign Agents Registration Act. Visit fara.gov for more information.

The courts' main impetus is dispensing the type of justice that returns the most money and profit for the highly corrupt court system, especially for the attorneys and the judges. How can one be expected to receive a fair trial if the judge, police officer, bailiff, and prosecutor all work for the state that is prosecuting an individual?

All the above-mentioned persons have retirement plans, which can influence the outcomes of many cases.

The justice system in America has become a system of the rich, for the rich, and by the rich, and at the expense of everyone else. An example of this is no more obvious than with judges who adjudicate on thousands of IRS cases and only seldom adjudicate in favor of the taxpayer. How can people expect judges to do anything other than rule in favor of the outcome that produces the most revenue for their court-funded retirement plans? Something like over 99.7 percent of tax cases are judged in favor of the government and against the taxpayer. Give us a break!

If one is unfortunate enough to find himself or herself named as a defendant in a criminal case, this often requires one to spend minimally tens of thousands of dollars to hire even the most obtuse of attorneys who often provide an inadequate defense. Everyone in the court system wants to be paid, and the legal adjudications and final decisions usually side with those who can afford to pay the most money into the system.

If one is poor and hires a public defendant, the person might as well kiss his or her ass goodbye. How much does it cost to hire the dream team of attorneys in order to defend oneself from a government that has unlimited resources?

The scales of justice no longer weigh only evidence. In too many cases, the scales of justice are weighed down with currency. First, the plaintiff drops down a lot of money for experts to testify during the discovery process. Then, the defendant must pay experts to testify against the evidence presented by the plaintiff's experts, and it can go on and on for quite some time and with considerable expense. More often than not, whoever piles the most money on the scales of justice prevails with a decision in his or her favor.

For your own edification and understanding of legal procedures, I highly recommend **everyone study the law as thoroughly as possible.** One of the most convenient methods for doing this without having to pay for law school is to study Jurisdictionary, which lays out the procedural aspects of lawsuits and teaches clients to defend or prosecute a law-suit by themselves, or pro se. Jurisdictionary is a remarkable value, and I recommend acquiring the complete course, which includes the tools needed to win in court without hiring an attorney.

Even if you decide to hire an attorney to prosecute or defend a law-suit, it is advisable to have a thorough understanding of the law in order to ensure you get your money's worth from your attorney. Some attor-neys are, after all, consummate liars and have barely any integrity. To be unfamiliar with the legal system and its intricacies is perilous to one's fu-ture. It is never too early to prepare to defend your life and freedom in a courtroom.

To reiterate, another great link for legal information on statutes and codes is law.cornell.edu/. Additionally, there is also findlaw.com, and for those with greater appetites for knowledge, visit James Publishing to add almost everything you need for your personal law library. Be certain as well to build a collection of legal dictionaries for your library to conceptu-ally grasp and understand legal terms and definitions used within the legal system. For the history buffs among us, you can access for free Bouvier's Law Dictionary, revised sixth edition, 1856, courtesy of constitution.org/bouv/bouvier.htm. Teamlaw.net also provides incredible information and forums that highly assist in learning, understanding, and applying the law in different situations.

It is incredible from an etymological perspective to see how the usage of words has changed and evolved over the years. These resources are in-valuable in studying the law. It is imperative that we all do our part by standing up and demanding the proper political administration of this great nation. Standing up for one's rights in America can involve a court case or two; therefore, it only makes sense to know the law in our liti-gious society.

Law is the tangled web that the government uses to control its citi-zens. All of us must learn the law and apply it when injustice occurs in order to stand up for our rights and the rights of our fellow citizens. We need to stand our ground, hold the government accountable for its trans-gressions, and stop fearing the government. We must put the govern-ment in its rightful place under the control of the populace, and humankind will again be free.

Many people are dismayed when government officials or corporate executives act in an objectionable and criminal manner, as allegedly did

BP's executives who negligently wreaked havoc on the Gulf of Mexico. We are appalled when nothing happens after calamities strike and wonder what is the government's proper role in protecting Americans and the entire nation, especially in states of emergency?

We the people are the government. We are the last resort, solely and wholly responsible for holding corporate government crooks' feet to the prosecutorial fire. We have been extraordinarily lazy and remiss in our patriotic duty to the point that if we fail to stand for something today by taking a more active and responsible role in making the world a better place, then very soon the world may exponentially deteriorate out of control, and at that point it may be much more difficult for us to make a difference on behalf of humanity. The United States does not have an unlimited amount of time to address problems like the economy and the exponential deterioration of the environment, which steadily approach the point of no return; some skeptics believe we have already passed that nebulous point.

Some people claim that a successful method employed to handle government criminals is to sue them in court and have them removed from their office for violations of their oaths of office. Many claim that the judges will not dispense justice fairly, but once there are thousands of people filing lawsuits and crooked and criminal judges are removed for treason and sedition, the people will prevail. Another method to consider is that treason and sedition are to be immediately reported to a federal judge once you become aware of such information, in accordance with 18 USC 2332, Misprison of Treason, which states:

Whoever, owing allegiance to the United States and having knowledge of the commission of any treason against them, conceals and does not, as soon as may be, disclose and make known the same to the President or to some judge of the United States, or to the governor or to some judge or justice of a particular State, is guilty of misprision of treason and shall be fined under this title or imprisoned not more than seven years, or both.

Additionally, 18 USC 4 Misprision of Felony reads:

Whoever, having knowledge of the actual commission of a felony cognizable by a court of the United States, conceals and does not as soon as possible make known the same to some judge or other person in civil or military authority under the United States, shall be fined under this title or imprisoned not more than three years, or both.

To all federal judges that are reading this book, you are hereby notified that the author is herein officially informing you that Hillary Clinton has allegedly committed treason and several felonies against the United States in her use of a private email server and her subsequent failure to properly handle, store, and protect classified, top-secret, and above top-secret information of the United States. It is likely that ex-US Attorney General Loretta E. Lynch, FBI Director Comey, ex-President Bill Clinton, and others are involved and have committed misprision of treason and misprision of felony against the United States.

Should judges decide not to apply the law, then the next judge to hear the appeal may be a little more open and accepting of the facts and sanction the treasonous acts of the lower court.

Citizens receive justice only if they demand it. The problem is that everyone is waiting for the other fellow to stand up for our liberties. In order to be free, we must stand up and demand freedom for ourselves first and then for others. To our deepest core, we must never bow to oppression and evil in its slightest or mightiest form.

In the days of the Founding Fathers, it was considered abominable not to know and understand the law. It was part of every good education to have a strong foundation in law and to be able to stand up for oneself and others in a court of law.

Americans have allowed a slithering class of unethical men and women to monopolize the legal field to the detriment of society. The citizens, in order to combat such an evil force of traitorous attorneys, need to build an army of hundreds of thousands of people who are knowledgeable in law and able to defend themselves once under attack. Americans are constantly under attack in nearly every aspect of their lives. It is time to change that and to relentlessly stand up to our oppressors.

If 2 percent of everyone that received a speeding ticket stood up and contested it, the courts would be so busy that the police would stop giving out tickets. There is additional advice for those interested in contesting traffic citations at takefromcaesar.com. Once there and you read the mission statement, enter WEvGov and visit the motor vehicle code link.

The legal profession has intentionally occluded the subject of law by incorporating all kinds of fanciful legalese and mumbo jumbo. With the help of a good law dictionary and some tenacity and perseverance, we can all become well versed in legal matters and understand the fundamental principles involved with obtaining justice under America's usurped and perverted legal system.

Yes, the court system has been usurped by the attorneys of the American Bar Association, which is anything but American; oddly enough, the American Bar Association's headquarters are located in the City of London Corporation.

It is fundamental that one use a good law dictionary while studying law because the only way to understand any subject is to fully and conceptually understand the words of that subject. Like any subject, the law is learned one word at a time. We cannot and should not back down from any intellectual challenge, including understanding the law, as there are those who use esoteric knowledge, which encapsulates the law, to enslave others.

To fail to learn the law is to fail to learn our remedy and redress of transgressions committed by the government against the people. To fail to learn the law is to relegate ourselves to the camp of the weak and defenseless.

We have all sat in the corner for too long and allowed tyrants to expand their oppressive control to the detriment and extinction of our freedoms; the only solution is organizing and using the law to obtain justice, where goodness always prevails over evilness. We need to become educated in the law to understand the injustices that are occurring in the world and then to have the knowledge, coupled with a high level of integrity, to pursue and obtain justice for ourselves and for our fellow man.

One of the most classic, philosophical, and fundamental books to gain a better understanding of the philosophy of law is Frédéric Bastiat's The Law, which can be read at bastiat.org/en/the_law.html#SECTION_ G001. Brilliant Bastiat provides a refreshing perspective of the law that allows one to grasp the true sense of justice, which is seldom found in today's courthouses.

It is going to take a concerted effort from each of us to stand against tyranny and injustice. Look at what tragically happened when the people united against tyranny in the Bundy Standoff in Nevada at en.wiki pedia.org/wiki/Bundy_standoff

The Bundy cowboys allegedly committed felonies by protesting on government land. Their contention and protest questioned what right the corporate government has under the Constitution to claim land belonging to the people of the United States as federal property through an illegal and unconstitutional manner.

These cowboys are true American heroes and patriots. We should and can support the Bundys and go to their defense by donating at bundy ranch.blogspot.com.

To cower in the face of tyranny and lick the boots of one's oppressor is tantamount to fastening prison doors tightly behind us as we crawl through life, frightened to lift our heads too high and be noticed.

We need to become capable people who demand the protection of our personal and our family's rights and the future rights and liberties of this nation and ultimately the world. We have this brief time to exercise our God-given talents and abilities to combat the ever-encroaching suppressive policies and tendencies implemented by our crooked politicians. To fail to stand and demand the freedom we deserve enslaves all future generations. Our inaction today equates to a tomorrow filled with tyrannically induced misery and perpetual slavery; our actions define us and our collective future more than anything else does.

Tomorrow and for the next ten thousand tomorrows, will we say we stood our ground and fought for freedom, or will we regret our pathetic inaction and forever fasten our self-imposed shackles of slavery?

It is always better to die tearing off one's shackles than to live another moment as a slave. The choice is ours; we must decide accordingly.

And no matter what, love—for love lifts and empowers all humanity.

CHAPTER 15

War Is the Problem

The unexamined life is not worth living.

– PLATO

The supreme art of war is to subdue the enemy without fighting.

– SUN TZU

Military men are just dumb stupid animals to be used as pawns in foreign policy.

– HENRY KISSINGER

He who marches to music in rank and file has already earned my contempt. He has been given a large brain by mistake, since for him the spinal cord would suffice. This disgrace to civilization should be done away with at once. Heroism at command, senseless brutality, deplorable love-of-country stance, how violently I hate all this, how despicable and ignoble war is; I would rather be torn to shreds than be part of so base an action! It is my conviction that killing under the cloak of war is nothing but an act of murder.

– ALBERT EINSTEIN.

We shall defend our island, whatever the cost may be, we shall fight on the beaches, we shall fight on the landing grounds, we shall fight in the fields and in the streets, we shall fight in the hills; we shall never surrender.

– WINSTON CHURCHILL

Our enemies are innovative and resourceful, and so are we. They never stop thinking of new ways to harm our country and our people, and neither do we.

– GEORGE W. BUSH

Voice or no voice, the people can always be brought to do the bidding of the leaders. That is easy. All you have to do is to tell them they are being attacked, and denounce the pacifists for lack of patriotism and exposing the country to danger. It works the same in any country.

– HERMANN GOERING

You cannot simultaneously prevent and prepare for war.

– ALBERT EINSTEIN

I am not afraid of any army of lions led by a sheep; I am afraid of an army of sheep led by a lion.

– ALEXANDER THE GREAT

The two most powerful warriors are patience and time.

– LEO TOLSTOY

All wars are fought for the sake of getting money.

– PLATO

The cost of freedom is always high, but Americans have always paid it. And one path we shall never choose, and that is the path of surrender, or submission.

– JOHN F. KENNEDY

ON BOTH THE DOMESTIC AND INTERNATIONAL SCENE, bankers and weapon suppliers are the only winners in the game of war. Throughout history, they have been an ongoing plague against humanity. One small and insane sector of humanity is determined to profit from the horrific suffering and degradation it continually creates through war. Behind the scenes, the unseen hands of the bankers politically incite death and destruction on an international and monstrous scale. Within their insane minds, bankers believe, the more war the better. War merchants are psychotic people aimed at destroying the human race in exchange for the almighty dollar and some kind of twisted and maniacal control over the people.

Murder by governments is so common there are several interesting words for its variations. Government murder is called either politicide, the gradual extermination of a political enemy, or democide, the government's murder of its own people, ranging from a single government-committed homicide up to and including mass murder and genocide. The fact that these words exist in the world's dictionaries is an unfortunate commentary regarding the state of humanity, which is ruled by the political psychopaths who are destroying the quality of life on this planet by the implementation of archaic, demoralizing, and devastating wartorn international policies.

It is difficult to believe that a select group of immoral and nefarious banking families actively endeavors to destroy humanity for military profits and their disgustingly demented agenda. They do this as a living, as a job, as a legal business venture. Can you imagine waking up every morning and thinking, *Whom shall I kill today?*

We need to protect ourselves and eliminate this plague of miscreants who misuse military force against society for the sole purpose of profit and to enforce the oppressive policies and agenda of the banks. As a civilization, we should strive to preserve the human species, while holding accountable those who ply their trade in the creation of wars and the proliferation of death, all around the world.

This is not the first call to stop senseless wars. Even someone as dumb as Einstein was adamantly against war. To get a better understanding of Einstein's antithetical perspective of war, we can research the results of war at en.wikipedia.org/wiki/List_of_wars_and_disasters_by_death_toll. There, you can read about too many wars in which millions of people were murdered or, more accurately, hundreds of millions were sacrificed to secure the banks' interests. In total, approximately 360 million people were killed in these unnecessary wars.

Three hundred sixty million is more than the current population of the United States. That is a lot of death and destruction associated with warfare. We will live in an uncivilized society until we declare all war as unacceptable and intolerable. Military conflict is innately uncivilized and ultimately destructive; it does not assist a culture to aspire to reaching greater heights in reality and in association with our fellow man.

Wikipedia lists eighty-one bloody wars in which under a million people were slaughtered. The total death toll of these minor but calamitous wars was more than eleven million people. These figures are highly conservative, and comprehensive, detailed reports should be compiled to assist in the correcting of this abhorrent commentary of our hijacked world, hijacked under the leadership of psychotic and inhumane rulers.

The most heinous crimes of man are performed as acts of war. Human brutality is never executed more efficiently than on the battlefield or more devastatingly than under the cover of the US battle flag. Without an ounce of dissention, the military pawns, our loving soldiers, unwittingly enforce the heinous dictates of the international private banks and kill as though the enemy were void of and never imbued with human life, rights, or dignity.

Stop the hate, baby—stop the hate.

For centuries, military conflict has been purportedly initiated to resolve disputes among different factions of the world's population. Saner avenues of redressing international conflicts are thrust aside in order to pursue and obtain military profits regardless of the cost in human lives and limbs.

The actual financing of war is the most profitable aspect of all the various war-related business sectors. Bank financing is used by just about every corporation that produces war armaments. The big money for the banks results from financing the warring countries that buy the death-inflicting weapons that are solely used for conducting war.

The financiers of death eagerly loan exorbitant fortunes for wars' goods and services with the intention of financially crippling both countries involved in the conflict.

The financiers of death understand that if there were no companies making munitions, there could be no war profits. The armament companies are but a cog in the bankers' wheel of financial and earthly ruin.

It is interesting that many aspects of the military-industrial complex have been privatized in a manner that simply diverts the government's military gravy train into the pockets of political cronies at the expense of taxpayers. This is social welfare for the rich and is made possible by whoring lobbyists and corrupt politicians, whose unscrupulously treacherous betrayal of the American people occurs behind the closed doors of smoke-filled rooms and amid the sound of shuffling suitcases stuffed with cash. Play ball or go home!

The highest financial cost of war is the never exhaustible interest that must be paid by the warring countries to finance the incalculable and never-ending expenses of war. If we outlawed the financing of all wars, war products, and war activities, we would soon see a drastic decline of the number, frequency, and duration of wars around the globe.

Because of its importance and spot-on intelligence, the following article is included in its entirety thanks to the author, Michael Rivero. For your convenience you can enjoy and share his video, All Wars Are Bankers' Wars, at youtube.com/watch?v=5hfEBupAeo4.

Rivero's great article evidences that the bankers' bloodied hands are often unseen as the primary force responsible for all of today's wars, as well as the majority of terrorist acts.

ALL WARS ARE BANKERS' WARS!

Banking was conceived in iniquity and was born in sin. The Bankers own the Earth. Take it away from them. But leave them the power to create deposits, and with the flick of a pen they will create enough deposits to buy it back again. However, take it away from them, and all the fortunes like mine will disappear, and they ought to disappear, for this world would be a happier and better world to live in. But if you wish to remain slaves of the Bankers and pay for the cost of your own slavery, let them continue to create deposits.

– SIR JOSIAH STAMP
PRESIDENT OF THE BANK OF ENGLAND IN THE 1920'S,
THE SECOND RICHEST MAN IN BRITAIN.

I know many people have a great deal of difficulty comprehending just how many wars are started for no other purpose than to force private central banks onto nations so let me share a few examples so that you understand why the US Government is mired in so many wars against so many foreign nations. There is ample precedent for this.

The United States fought the American Revolution primarily over King George III's Currency Act which forced the colonists to conduct their business using printed bank notes borrowed from the Bank of England at interest.

The bank hath benefit of interest on all moneys which it creates out of nothing.

– WILLIAM PATERSON,
FOUNDER OF THE BANK OF ENGLAND IN 1694.

After the revolution the United States adopted a radically different economic system in which the government issued its own value-based money so that private banks like the Bank of England were not siphoning off the wealth of the people through interest-bearing bank notes.

The refusal of King George 3rd to allow the colonies to operate an honest money system, which freed the ordinary man from the clutches of the money manipulators, was probably the prime cause of the revolution.

– BENJAMIN FRANKLIN, FOUNDING FATHER.

Following the revolution the US Government actually took steps to keep the bankers out of the new government!

Any person holding any office or any stock in any institution in the nature of a bank for issuing or discounting bills or notes payable to bearer or order, cannot be a member of the House whilst he holds such office or stock.

– THIRD CONGRESS OF THE UNITED STATES SENATE,
23RD DECEMBER, 1793, SIGNED BY THE
PRESIDENT GEORGE WASHINGTON.

THE FIRST BANK OF THE UNITED STATES

But bankers are nothing if not dedicated to their schemes to acquire wealth, and they know full well how easy it is to corrupt a nation's leaders.

— MAYER AMSCHEL ROTHSCHILD

Just one year after Mayer Amschel Rothschild had uttered his infamous "Let me issue and control a nation's money and I care not who makes the laws", the bankers succeeded in setting up a new Private Central Bank called the First Bank of the United States, largely through the efforts of the Rothschild's chief US supporter, Alexander Hamilton.

Founded in 1791 by the end of its twenty year charter the First Bank of the United States had almost ruined the nation's economy while enriching the bankers. Congress refused to renew the charter and signaled their intention to go back to a state-issued, value-based currency on which the people paid no interest at all to any banker. This resulted in a threat from Nathan Mayer Rothschild against the United States Government, "Either the application for renewal of the charter is granted, or the United States will find itself involved in a most disastrous war." Congress still refused to renew the charter for the First Bank of the United States whereupon Nathan Mayer Rothschild railed, "Teach those impudent Americans a lesson! Bring them back to colonial status!" The British Prime Minister at the time, Spencer Perceval was adamantly opposed to war with the United States primarily because the majority of England's military might was occupied with the ongoing Napoleonic Wars. Spencer Perceval was concerned that Britain might not prevail in a new American war, a concern shared by many in the British Government. Then Spencer Perceval was assassinated, the only British Prime Minister to be assassinated in office, and replaced by Robert Jenkinson, the 2nd Earl of Liverpool, who was fully supportive of a war to recapture the colonies.

If my sons did not want wars, there would be none.

— GUTLE SCHNAPER,
WIFE OF MAYER AMSCHEL ROTHSCHILD
AND MOTHER OF HIS FIVE SONS.

Financed at virtually no interest by the Rothschild controlled Bank of England, Britain then provoked the war of 1812 to re-colonize the United States and force them back into slavery of the Bank of England, or to plunge the United States into so much debt they would be forced to accept a new private central bank.

The plan worked. Even though the War of 1812 was won by the United States, Congress was forced to grant a new charter for yet another private bank issuing public currency as loans at interest, the Second Bank of the United States. Once again, private bankers were in control of the nation's money supply and cared not who made the laws or how many British and American soldier had to die for it.

President Andrew Jackson and the Second Bank of the United States

Once again the nation was plunged into debt, unemployment, and poverty by the predations of the private central bank, and in 1832 Andrew Jackson successfully campaigned for his second term as President under the slogan, "Jackson And No Bank!" True to his word, Jackson succeeds in blocking the renewal of the charter for the Second Bank of the United States.

"Gentlemen! I too have been a close observer of the doings of the Bank of the United States. I have had men watching you for a long time, and am convinced that you have used the funds of the bank to speculate in the breadstuffs of the country. When you won, you divided the profits amongst you, and when you lost, you charged it to the bank. You tell me that if I take the deposits from the bank and annul its charter I shall ruin ten thousand families. That may be true, gentlemen, but that is your sin! Should I let you go on, you will ruin fifty thousand families, and that would be my sin! You are a den of vipers and thieves. I have determined to rout you out!" Andrew Jackson shortly before ending the charter of the Second Bank of the United States. From the original minutes of the Philadelphia committee of citizens sent to meet with President Jackson (February 1834), according to *Andrew Jackson and the Bank of the United States* (1928) by Stan v. Henkels. Geneva Gazette, October 2, 1833.

Shortly after President Jackson (the only American President to actually pay off the National Debt) ended the Second Bank of the United States, there was an attempted assassination, which failed when both pistols used by the assassin, Richard Lawrence, failed to fire. Lawrence later said that with Jackson dead, "Money would be more plentiful."

PRESIDENT ZACHERY TAYLOR

President Zachery Taylor opposed the creation of a new Private Central Bank because of the historical abuses of the First and Second Banks of the United States.

> *The idea of a national bank is dead and will not be revived in my time.*
>
> – ZACHERY TAYLOR.

Taylor died on July 9th 1850 after eating a bowl of cherries and milk rumored to have been poisoned. The symptoms he displayed are consistent with acute arsenic poisoning.

PRESIDENT JAMES BUCHANAN

President James Buchanan also opposed a private central bank. During the panic of 1857 he attempted to set limits on banks issuing more loans than they had actual funds and to require all issued bank notes to be backed by Federal Government assets. He was poisoned with arsenic and survived, although 38 other people at the dinner died.

The public school is as subservient to the bankers' wishes to keep certain history from you, just as the corporate media is subservient to Monsanto's wishes to keep the dangers of GMOs from you, and the global warming cult's wishes to conceal from you that the Earth has actually been cooling for the last 16 years. Thus it should come as little surprise that much of the real reasons for the events of the Civil War are not well known to the average American.

The few who understand the system will either by so interested in its profits or be so dependent upon its favours that there will be no opposition from that class, while on the other hand, the great body of people, mentally incapable of comprehending the tremendous advantage that capital derives from the system, will bear its burdens without complaint, and perhaps without even suspecting that the system is inimical to their interests.

– ROTHSCHILD BROTHERS OF LONDON
WRITING TO ASSOCIATES IN NEW YORK, 1863.

PRESIDENT LINCOLN

When the confederacy seceded from the United States, the bankers once again saw the opportunity for a rich harvest of debt and offered to fund Lincoln's efforts to bring the south back into the union, but at 30% interest. Lincoln remarked that he would not free the black man by en-slaving the white man to the bankers and using his authority as President, issued a new government currency, the greenback. This was a direct threat to the wealth and power of the central bankers, who quickly responded.

If this mischievous financial policy, which has its origin in North America, shall become endurated down to a fixture, then that Government will furnish its own money without cost. It will pay off debts and be without debt. It will have all the money necessary to carry on its commerce. It will become prosperous without precedent in the history of the world. The brains and wealth of all countries will go to North America. That country must be destroyed or it will destroy every monarchy on the globe.

– THE LONDON TIMES RESPONDING TO LINCOLN'S DECISION TO
ISSUE GOVERNMENT GREENBACKS TO FINANCE THE CIVIL WAR
RATHER THAN AGREE TO PRIVATE BANKER'S LOANS AT 30% INTEREST.

In 1872 New York bankers sent a letter to every bank in the United States urging them to fund newspapers that opposed government-issued money (Lincoln's Greenbacks).

> *Dear Sir: It is advisable to do all in your power to sustain such prominent daily and weekly newspapers...as will oppose the issuing of greenbacks paper money and that you also withhold patronage or favors from all applicants who are not willing to oppose the Government issue of money. Let the government issue the coin and the banks issue the paper money of the country... [T]o restore to circulation the Government issue of money, will be to provide the people with money, and will therefore seriously affect your profit as bankers and lenders.*
> – TRIUMPHANT PLUTOCRACY; THE STORY OF THE AMERICAN PUBLIC LIFE FROM 1870 TO 1920, BY LYNN WHEELER

> *It will not do to allow the greenback, as it is called, to circulate as money any length of time, as we cannot control that.*
> – TRIUMPHANT PLUTOCRACY; THE STORY OF THE AMERICAN PUBLIC LIFE FROM 1870 TO 1920, BY LYNN WHEELER

> *Slavery is likely to be abolished by the war power, and chattel slavery destroyed. This, I and my European friends are in favor of, for slavery is but the owning of labor and carries with it the care for the laborer, while the European plan, led on by England, is for Capita to control labor by controlling the wages. THIS CAN BE DONE BY CONTROLLING THE MONEY.*
> – TRIUMPHANT PLUTOCRACY; THE STORY OF THE AMERICAN PUBLIC LIFE FROM 1870 TO 1920, BY LYNN WHEELER

Goaded by the private bankers, much of Europe supported the Confederacy against the Union with the expectation that victory over Lincoln would mean the end of the Greenback. France and Britain considered an outright attack on the United States to aid the confederacy, but were held at bay by Russia which had just ended the serfdom system and had a state-controlled central bank, similar to the system the United States had been founded on.

Tsar Alexander II of Russia, prevented France and Britain from invading the United States during the civil war.

Left free of European intervention the Union won the war, and Lincoln announced his intention to go on issuing greenbacks. Following Lincoln's assassination, the Greenbacks were pulled from circulation and the American people forced to go back to an economy based on bank notes borrowed at interest from the private bankers. Tsar Alexander II, who authorized Russian military assistance to Lincoln, was subsequently the victim of multiple attempts on his life in 1866, 1879 and 1880, until his assassination in 1881.

With the end of Lincoln's Greenbacks, the US could no longer create its own interest free money and was manipulated during the term of President Rutherford B. Hayes into borrowing from the Rothschild's banking system in 1878, restoring to the Rothschild's control of the US economy they lost under Andrew Jackson.

> Messrs. Rothschild & Sons to Mr. Sherman.
> [Cable message.]
> April 12, 1878
> Hon. John H Sherman,
> Secretary of the Treasury, Washington D.C.:
> Very pleased we have entered into relations again
> with the American Government.
> Shall do our best to make the business successful.
> ROTHSCHILDS.

President James Garfield

James A. Garfield was elected President in 1880 on a platform of government control of the money supply.

> *The Chief duty of the National Government in connection with the currency of the country is to coin money and declare its value. Grave doubts have been entertained whether Congress is authorized by the Constitution to make any form of paper money legal tender. The present value of United States notes has been sustained by the necessity of war, but such paper should depend for*

its valuable and currency upon its convenience in use and its prompt redemption in coin at the will of the holder, and not upon its compulsory circulation. These notes are not money, but promises to pay money. If the holders demand it, the promises should be kept.

– JAMES GARFIELD

By the experience of commercial nations in all ages it has been found that gold and silver afford the only safe foundation for a monetary system. Confusion has recently been created by variations in the relative value of the two metals but I confidently believe that arrangements can be made between the leading commercial nations which will secure the general use of both metals. Congress should provide that the compulsory coinage of silver now required by law may not disturb our monetary system by driving either metal out of circulation. If possible, such an adjustment should be made that the purchasing power of every coined dollar will be exactly equal to its debt-paying power in all the markets of the world.

– JAMES GARFIELD

He who controls the money supply of a nation controls the nation.

– JAMES GARFIELD

Garfield was shot on July 2, 1881 and died of his wounds several weeks later. Chester A. Arthur succeeded Garfield as President.

PRESIDENT WILLIAM MCKINLEY

In 1896, William McKinley was elected President in the middle of a depression-driven debate over gold-backed government currencies and a balanced government budget which would free the public from accumulating debt.

Our financial system needs some revision; our money is all good now, but its value must not further be threatened. It should all be put upon an enduring basis, not subject to easy attack, nor its stability to doubt or dispute. Our currency should continue under the supervision of the Government. The several forms of our paper money offer, in my judgment, a constant embarrassment to the Government and a safe balance in the Treasury.

– WILLIAM MCKINLEY

McKinley was shot by an out-of-work anarchist on September 14, 1901, in Buffalo, NY, succumbing to his wounds a few days later. He was succeeded in office by Theodore Roosevelt.

THE ALDRICH PLAN

In 1910, Senator Nelson Aldrich, Frank Vanderlip of National City (Citibank), Henry Davison of Morgan Bank, and Paul Warburg of the Kuhn, Loeb Investment House met secretly on Jekyll Island, Georgia, to formulate a plan for a US central bank, and created the Aldrich Plan, which called for a system of fifteen regional central banks, openly and directly controlled by Wall Street commercial banks. These banks would have the legal ability to create money out of thin air and represented an attempt to create a new Bank of the United States. Public reaction was swift.

Due to the intense public opposition to the Aldrich Plan, the measure was defeated in the House of Representatives in 1912. One year later the bankers would be back!

THE THIRD BANK OF THE UNITED STATES, AKA THE FEDERAL RESERVE

Following the defeat of the Aldrich Plan, in 1912, the Private Central Bankers of Europe, in particular the Rothschilds of Great Britain and the Warburgs of Germany, met with their American financial collaborators once again on Jekyll Island, Georgia to form a new banking cartel with the express purpose of forcing the United States to accept a private central bank, with the aim of placing complete control of the United States money supply once again under the control of private bankers. Owing to hostility over the previous banks, the name was changed from the Third

Bank of the United States to "The Federal Reserve" system in order to grant the new bank a quasi-governmental image, but in fact it is a privately owned bank, no more "Federal" than Federal Express.

The Federal Reserve is neither "Federal" nor does it have any actual "Reserves" creating money out of thin air. Watch Greenspan discuss its power over the US at youtube.com/watch?v=fDu0Pm4PcoM&feature=player_embedded.

In 2012, The Federal Reserve attempted to rebuff a Freedom of Information Lawsuit by Bloomberg News on the grounds that as a private banking corporation and not actually a part of the government, the Freedom of Information Act did not apply to the "trade secret" operations of the Federal Reserve.

> *When you or I write a check, there must be sufficient funds in our account to cover the check, but when the Federal Reserve writes a check, there is no bank deposit on which that check is drawn. When the Federal Reserve writes a check, it is creating money.*
>
> – FROM THE BOSTON FEDERAL RESERVE BANK PAMPHLET, "PUTTING IT SIMPLY"

> *Neither paper currency nor deposits have value as commodities. Intrinsically, a 'dollar' bill is just a piece of paper. Deposits are merely book entries.*
>
> – "MODERN MONEY MECHANICS WORKBOOK"

Federal Reserve of Chicago, 1975.

> *I am afraid the ordinary citizen will not like to be told that the banks can and do create money. And they who control the credit of the nation direct the policy of Governments and hold in the hollow of their hand the destiny of the people.*
>
> – REGINA MCKENNA AS CHAIRMAN OF THE MIDLAND BANK ADDRESSING STOCKHOLDERS IN 1924.

> *States, most especially the large hegemonic ones such as the United States and Great Britain are controlled by the international central banking systems working through secret agree-*

*ments at the Bank for International Settlements (BIS), and op-
erating through national central banks (such as the Bank of
England and the Federal Reserve)... The same international
banking cartel that controls the United States previously controlled Great Britain and held it up as the international
hegemon. When the British order faded, and was replaced by
the United States, the US ran the global economy. However, the
same interests are served. States will be used and discarded at
will by the international banking cartel, they are simply tools.*

– ANDREW GAVIN MARSHALL

THE SIXTEENTH AMENDMENT AND INCOME TAX

1913 proved to be a transformative year for the nation's economy,
first with the passage of the 16th "income tax" Amendment and the false
claim that it had been ratified.

*I think if you were to go back and try to find and review the
ratification of the 16th Amendment, which was the internal
revenue, the income tax, I think if you went back and examined that carefully, you would find that a sufficient number of
states never ratified that amendment.*

– US DISTRICT COURT JUDGE JAMES C FOX,
SULLIVAN V. UNITED STATES, 2003.

Later that same year apparently unwilling to risk another questionable
amendment, Congress passed the Federal Reserve Act over Christmas
holiday December 23, 1913, while members of Congress opposed to the
measure were at home. This was a very underhanded deal, as the Constitution explicitly vests Congress with the authority to issue the public
currency, does not authorize its delegation, and thus should have required a new Amendment to transfer that authority to a private bank.
But pass it Congress did, and President Woodrow Wilson signed it as he
promised the bankers he would in exchange for generous campaign contributions.

PRESIDENT WOODROW WILSON

Woodrow Wilson later regretted that decision.

> *I am a most unhappy man. I have unwittingly ruined my country. A great industrial nation is now controlled by its system of credit. We are no longer a government by free opinion, no longer a government by conviction and the vote of the majority, but a government by the opinion and duress of a small group of dominant men.*
>
> – WOODROW WILSON 1919

THOMAS EDISON

Thomas Edison, arguably the most brilliant man of the age, was aware of the fraud of private central banks.

> *People who will not turn a shovel full of dirt on the project nor contribute a pound of material, will collect more money from the United States than will the People who supply all the materials and do all the work. This is the terrible thing about interest …But here is the point: If a nation can issue a dollar bond it can issue a dollar bill. The element that makes the bond good makes the bill good also. The difference between the bond and the bill is that the bond lets the money broker collect twice the amount of the bond and an additional 20%. Whereas the currency, the honest sort provided by the Constitution, pays nobody but those who contribute in some useful way. It is absurd to say our Country can issue bonds and cannot issue currency. Both are promises to pay, but one fattens the usurer and the other helps the People. If the currency issued by the People were no good, then the bonds would be no good, either. It is a terrible situation when the Government, to insure the National Wealth, must go in debt and submit to ruinous interest charges at the hands of men who control the fictitious value of gold.*
>
> – THOMAS A. EDISON

THE WAR TO END ALL WARS – WORLD WAR ONE

The next year World War One started, and it is important to remember that prior to the creation of the Federal Reserve, there was no such thing as a world war.

World War One started between Austria-Hungary and Serbia with the assassination of Archduke Ferdinand.

Although the war started between Austria-Hungary and Serbia, it quickly shifted to focus on Germany whose industrial capacity was seen as an economic threat to Great Britain who saw the decline of the British Pound as a result of too much emphasis on financial activities to the neglect of agriculture, industrial development, and infrastructure not unlike the present day United States. Although pre-war Germany had a private central bank, it was heavily restricted and inflation kept to reasonable levels. Under government control, investment was guaranteed to internal economic development, and Germany was seen as a major power. So, in the media of the day, Germany was portrayed as the prime opponent of World War One and not just defeated, but its industrial base flattened. Following the Treaty of Versailles, Germany was ordered to pay the war costs of all the participating nations even though Germany had not actually started the war. This amounted to three times the value of all Germany itself. Germany's private central bank, to whom Germany had gone deeply into debt to pay the costs of the war, broke free of government control, and massive inflation followed mostly triggered by currency speculators, permanently trapping the German people in endless debt.

WORLD WAR TWO

When the Weimar Republic collapsed economically, it opened the door for the National Socialists to take power. Their first financial move was to issue their own state currency which was not borrowed from private central bankers. Freed from having to pay interest on the money in circulation, Germany blossomed and quickly began to rebuild its industry. The media called it "The German Miracle." TIME magazine lionized Hitler for the amazing improvement in life for the German people and the explosion of German industry, and even named him TIME Magazine's Man of the Year in 1938.

Once again Germany's industrial output became a threat to Great Britain.

Should Germany merchandise (do business) again in the next 50 years we have led this war (WWI) in vain.
— WINSTON CHURCHILL IN THE TIMES (1919).

We will force this war upon Hitler, if he wants it or not.
— WINSTON CHURCHILL (1936 BROADCAST).

Germany becomes too powerful. We have to crush it.
— WINSTON CHURCHILL (NOVEMBER 1936 SPEAKING TO US- GENERAL ROBERT E. WOOD).

This war is an English war and its goal is the destruction of Germany.
— WINSTON CHURCHILL (AUTUMN 1939 BROADCAST.)

Germany's state issued value-based currency was also a direct threat to the wealth and power of the private central banks, and as early as 1933 they started to organize a global boycott against Germany to strangle this upstart ruler who thought he could break free of private central bankers!

As had been the case in World War One, Great Britain and other nations threatened by Germany's economic power looked for an excuse to go to war, and as public anger in Germany grew over the boycott Hitler foolishly gave them that excuse. Years later, in a spirit of candor, the real reasons for that war were made clear.

The war wasn't only about abolishing fascism, but to conquer sales markets. We could have, if we intended so, prevented this war from breaking out without doing one shot, but we didn't want to.
— WINSTON CHURCHILL TO TRUMAN (FULTON, USA MARCH 1946)

*Germany's unforgivable crime before World War II was its at-
tempt to loosen its economy out of the world trade system and to
build up an independent exchange system from which the world-
finance couldn't profit anymore... We butchered the wrong pig.*
– WINSTON CHURCHILL (THE SECOND WORLD WAR - BERN, 1960)

MARINE CORPS MAJOR GENERAL SMEDLEY BUTLER

As a side note, we need to step back before World War Two and recall
Marine Major General Smedley Butler. In 1933, Wall Street bankers and
financiers had bankrolled the successful coups by both Hitler and Mus-
solini. Brown Brothers Harriman in New York was financing Hitler right
up to the day war was declared with Germany. And they decided that a
fascist dictatorship in the United States based on the one in Italy would
be far better for their business interests than Roosevelt's "New Deal"
which threatened massive wealth redistribution to recapitalize the
working and middle class of America. So the Wall Street tycoons re-
cruited General Butler to lead the overthrow of the US Governments
and install a "Secretary of General Affairs" who would be answerable to
Wall Street and not the people, would crush social unrest and shut down
all labor unions. General Butler pretended to go along with the scheme
but then exposed the plot to Congress. Congress then as now in the
pocket of the Wall Street bankers refused to act. When Roosevelt learned
of the planned coup, he demanded the arrest of the plotters, but the
plotters simply reminded Roosevelt that if any one of them were sent to
prison, their friends on Wall Street would deliberately collapse the still-
fragile economy and blame Roosevelt for it. Roosevelt was thus unable to
act until the start of WWII at which time he prosecuted many of the
plotters under the Trading With The Enemy Act. The congressional
minutes into the coup were finally declassified in 1967, but rumors of
the attempted coup became the inspiration for the movie, Seven Days in
May but with the true financial villains erased from the script.

I spent 33 years and four months in active military service as a
member of our country's most agile military force, the Marine Corps. I
served in all commissioned ranks from second lieutenant to Major General. And during that period I spent more of my time being a high–class

muscle man for Big Business, for Wall Street and for the bankers. In short, I was a racketeer, a gangster for capitalism.

> *I suspected I was just a part of a racket at the time. Now I am sure of it. Like all members of the military profession I never had an original thought until I left the service. My mental faculties remained in suspended animation while I obeyed the orders of the higher-ups. This is typical; with everyone in the military service. Thus I helped make Mexico and especially Tampico safe for American interests in 1914. I helped make Haiti and Cuba a decent place for the National City Bank boys to collect revenues in. I helped in the raping of half a dozen Central American republics for the benefit of Wall Street. The record for racketeering is long. I helped purify Nicaragua for the international banking house of Brown Brothers in 1909-1912. I bought light to the Dominican Republic for American sugar interests in 1916. In China in 1927, I helped see to it that the Standard Oil went its way unmolested. During those years, I had, as the boys in the back room would say, a swell racket. I was rewarded with honors, medals and promotion. Looking back on it, I feel I might have given Al Capone a few hints. The best he could do was to operate his racket in three city districts. I operated on three continents.*
>
> – GENERAL SMEDLEY BUTLER, FORMER
> US MARINE CORPS COMMANDANT, 1935

THE HONORABLE LOUIS T. MCFADDEN
US CONGRESSMAN

Louis T. McFadden was a member of the House of Representatives in the twenties and thirties. He was the chair of the House Banking and Currency Committee during the twenties. He used his position in Congress occasionally to crusade against the Federal Reserve.

> *Mr. Chairman, we have in this country one of the most corrupt institutions the world has ever known. I refer to the Federal Reserve Board and the Federal Reserve Banks. The Federal Reserve*

> Board, a Government board, has cheated the Government of
> the United States out of enough money to pay the national debt.
> The depredations and the iniquities of the Federal Reserve
> Board and the Federal reserve banks acting together have cost
> this country enough money to pay the national debt several
> times over. This evil institution has impoverished and ruined
> the people of the United States; has bankrupted itself, and has
> practically bankrupted our Government. It has done this
> through defects of the law under which it operates, through the
> maladministration of that law by the Federal Reserve Board
> and through the corrupt practices of the moneyed vultures who
> control it.
>
> – LOUIS T. MCFADDEN, JUNE 10, 1932

At one point McFadden started impeachment proceedings against the entire board of the federal reserve. Not too surprisingly, there were three attempts on McFadden's life, one shooting and two poisonings, the second of which was successful. Although still officially declared as heart failure, newspapers of the time reported ...

Now that this sterling American patriot has made the Passing, it can be revealed that not long after his public utterance against the encroaching powers of Judah, it became known among his intimates that he had suffered two attacks against his life. The first attack came in the form of two revolver shots fired at him from ambush as he was alighting from a cab in front of one of the Capital hotels. Fortunately both shots missed him, the bullets burying themselves in the structure of the cab.

He became violently ill after partaking of food at a political banquet at Washington. His life was only saved from what was subsequently announced as a poisoning by the presence of a physician friend at the banquet, who at once procured a stomach pump and subjected the Congressman to emergency treatment.

PRESIDENT JOHN F. KENNEDY

As President, John F. Kennedy understood the predatory nature of private central banking. He understood why Andrew Jackson fought so hard to end the Second Bank of the United States. So Kennedy wrote and signed Executive Order 11110 which ordered the US Treasury to issue a new public currency, the United States Note.

Kennedy's United States Notes were not borrowed from the Federal Reserve but created by the US Government and backed by the silver stockpiles held by the US Government. It represented a return to the system of economics the Unites States had been founded on and was perfectly legal for Kennedy to do. All told, some four and one half billion dollars went into public circulation, eroding interest payments to the Federal Reserve and loosening their control over the nation. Five months later John F. Kennedy was assassinated in Dallas, Texas and the United States Notes pulled from circulation and destroyed except for samples held by collectors. See youtube.com/watch?v=OXHyFUXvGAk [Author's note: if you look closely while watching this video, at the fifty-five-second mark, you should be able to see what appears to be the driver of the limousine shooting our dear President Kennedy. So much for Lee Harvey Oswald and the lone assassin theory!]

JOHN J. MCCLOY

John J. McCloy, President of the Chase Manhattan Bank and President of the World Bank, was named to the Warren Commission, presumably to make certain the banking dimensions behind the assassination were concealed from the public.

After a decade and a half of what future history will most certainly describe as World War Three, we need to examine the financial dimensions behind wars.

BRETTON WOODS RESORT, NEW HAMPSHIRE

Toward the end of World War Two when it became obvious that the allies were going to win and dictate the post war environment, the major world economic powers met in Bretton Woods, a luxury resort in New Hampshire, in July of 1944 and hammered out the Bretton Woods agreement for international finance. The British Pound lost its position as the global trade and reserve currency to the US dollar (part of the price demanded by Roosevelt in exchange for the US entry into the war).

Absent the economic advantages of being the world's "go-to" currency, Britain was forced to nationalize the Bank of England in 1946. The Bretton Woods Agreement, ratified in 1945, in addition to making the dollar the global reserve and trade currency, obligated the signatory nations to tie their currencies to the dollar. The nations that ratified Bretton Woods did so on two conditions. The first was that the Federal Reserve would refrain from over-printing the dollars as a means to loot real products and produce from other nations in exchange for ink and paper, basically an imperial tax. That assurance was backed up by the second requirement, which was that the US dollar would always be convertible to gold at $35 per ounce.

The Federal Reserve, being a private bank and not answerable to the US Government, did start over printing paper dollars, and much of the perceived prosperity of the 1950's and 1960's was the result of foreign nation's obligations to accept the paper notes as being worth gold at the rate of $35 an ounce. Then in 1970, France looked at the huge pile of paper notes sitting in their vaults, for which real French products like wine and cheese had been traded, and notified the United States government that they would exercise their option under Bretton Woods to return the paper notes for gold at the $35 per ounce exchange rate. The United States had nowhere near the gold to redeem the paper notes, so on August 15th, 1971 Richard Nixon "temporarily" suspended the gold convertibility of the US Federal Reserve Notes.

PRESIDENT RICHARD NIXON

Later termed the "Nixon Shock" this move effectively ended the Bretton Woods agreement and many global currencies started to delink from the US dollar.

Worse, since the United States had collateralized their loans with the nation's gold reserves, it quickly became apparent that the US Government did not in fact have enough gold to cover the outstanding debts. Foreign nations began to get very nervous about their loans to the US and understandably were reluctant to loan any additional money to the United States without some form of collateral. So Richard Nixon started the environmental movement, with the EPA and its various programs such as "wilderness zones", "Road-less areas", "Hermitage rivers", 'Wetlands", all of which took vast areas of public lands and made them off limits to the American people who were technically the owners of those lands. But Nixon had little concern for the environment and the real purpose of this land grab under the guise of the environment was to pledge those pristine lands and their vast mineral resources as collateral on the national debt. The plethora of different programs was simply to conceal the true scale of how much American land was being pledged to foreign lenders as collateral on the government's debts, eventually almost 25% of the nation itself. All of this is illegal as the Enclave Clause of the Constitution limits the Federal Government to owning the land under Federal Government buildings and military bases, and that Enclave Clause was written into the Constitution by the Founding Fathers to specifically to prevent the Federal Government simply seizing the land belonging to the people to sell off, pledge as collateral, or rent!

With open lands for collateral already in short supply, the US Government embarked on a new program to shore up the sagging international demand for the dollar. The United States approached the world's oil producing nations, mostly in the Middle East, and offered them a deal. In exchange for only selling their oil for dollars, the United States would guarantee the military safety of those oil-rich nations. The oil rich nations would agree to spend and invest their US paper dollars inside the United States in particular in US Treasury Bonds redeemable through future generations of US taxpayers. The concept was labeled the "petrodollar." In effect, the US no longer able to back the dollar with gold, was now backing it with oil, other people's oil. And that necessity to keep control over those oil nations to prop up the dollar has shaped America's foreign policy in the region since.

But as America's manufacturing and agriculture declined, the oil producing nations faced a dilemma. Those piles of US Federal Reserve notes were not able to purchase much from the United States because the United States had little other than real estate anyone wanted to buy. Europe's cars and aircraft were superior and less costly, while experiments with GMO food crops led to nations refusing to buy US food exports. Israel's constant belligerence against its neighbors caused them to wonder if the US could actually keep their end of the petrodollar arrangement. Oil producing nations started to talk of selling their oil for whatever currency the purchasers chose to use.

SADDAM HUSSEIN AND THE LIE OF IRAQ'S NUCLEAR WEAPONS

Iraq already hostile to the United States policy shift following Desert Storm demanded the right to sell their oil for Euros in 2000 and in 2002, the United Nations agreed to allow it under the "Oil for Food Program" instituted following Desert Storm. One year later the United States re-invaded Iraq under the lie of Saddam's nuclear weapons, lynched Saddam Hussein, and placed Iraq's oil back on the world market only for dollars.

The clear US policy shift following 9/11 away from being an impartial broker of peace in the Middle East to one of unquestioned support for Israel's aggression only further eroded confidence in the Petrodollar deal and even more oil producing nations started openly talking of oil trade for other global currencies.

GADDAFI AND THE GOLD DINAR

Over in Libya Muammar Gaddafi had instituted a state-owned central bank and a value based trade currency, the Gold Dinar.

Gaddafi announced that Libya's oil was for sale, but only for the Gold Dinar. Other African nations seeing the rise of the Gold Dinar and the Euro as the US dollar continued its inflation-driven decline flocked to the new Libyan currency for trade. This move had the potential to seriously undermine the global hegemony of the dollar. French President Nicolas Sarkozy reportedly went so far as to call Libya a "threat" to the financial security of the world. So the United States invaded Libya, brutally murdered Qaddafi the object lesson of Saddam's lynching, not being enough of a message, imposed a private central bank, and returned Libya's oil output to dollars only. The gold that was to have been made into the Gold Dinars is as of last report unaccounted for.

Subsequently, General Wesley Clark blows the whistle on US plans to conquer the oil-rich Middle East.

According to General Wesley Clark, the master plan for the "dollarification" of the world's oil nations included seven targets: Iraq, Syria, Lebanon, Libya, Somalia, Sudan, and Iran. Venezuela which dared to sell their oil to China for the Yuan is a late addition. What is notable about the original seven nations targeted by the US is that none of them are members of the Bank of International Settlements, the private central bankers', private central bank, located in Switzerland. This meant that these nations were deciding for themselves how to run their nations' economies, rather than submit to the international private banks.

Now the bankers' gun sights are on Iran, which dares to have a government central bank and sell their oil for whatever currency they choose. The war agenda is, as always, to force Iran's oil to be sold for dollars and to force them to accept a privately owned central bank. Malaysia, one of the few remaining nations without a Rothschild central bank, is now being invaded by a force claimed to be "Al Qaeda" and has suffered numerous suspicious losses of its passenger jets.

With the death of President Hugo Chavez, plans to impose a US and banker friendly regime on Venezuela are clearly being implemented.

SO JUST WHERE IS THE GOLD?

The German government recently asked for the return of some of their gold bullion from the Bank of France and the New York Federal Reserve. France has said it will take 5 years to return Germany's gold. The United States has said they will need 8 years to return Germany's gold. This suggests strongly that the Bank of France and the NY Federal Reserve have used the deposited gold for other purposes, most likely to cover gold futures contracts used to artificially suppress the price of gold to keep investors in the equities markets, and the Central Banks are scrambling to find new gold to cover the shortfall and prevent a gold run. So it is inevitable that suddenly France invades Mali, ostensibly to combat Al Qaeda, with the US joining in. Mali just happens to be one of the world's largest gold producers with gold accounting for 80 percent of Mali exports. War for the bankers does not get more obvious than that!

Mexico has demanded a physical audit of their gold bullion stored in the Bank of England, and along with Venezuela's vast oil reserves (larger than Saudi Arabia), Venezuela's gold mines are a prize lusted after by all the Central Banks that played fast and loose with other peoples' gold bullion. So we can expect regime change if not outright invasion soon.

CAN A BANK FORECLOSE ON YOUR HOUSE IF THEY HAVE PROVIDED NOTHING OF REAL VALUE IN THE MORTGAGE?

A little remembered footnote in banking history occurred in December 1968. A bank was moving to foreclose on a house, and the homeowner decided to fight the foreclosure in court, arguing that contract law requires two contracting parties to agree to swap two items of value, legally called the "consideration." In the case of First National Bank of Montgomery vs. Jerome Daly, Daly argued that since the bank simply wrote a number in a ledger to create the loaned money out of thin air, there was no real value and therefore no legally binding consideration. The lawyers for the bank admitted that this is how the bank works. They create money out of thin air as a ledger or computer entry, which you must repay with your labor. And there was no law in 1968 that specifically gave banks the legal right to do that. Daly argued that because there was no equal consideration, the mortgage was null and void and the attempt to foreclose invalid. The jury agreed! So did Judge Mahoney, who resisted demands to over-rule the jury in favor of the bank, and wrote a simple straightforward decision that stated that there was no question that the mortgage contract was void because the claim that the bank simply made up the money out of thin air was not disputed by the bank itself.

Judge Mahoney was murdered with poison less than six months later, and the lawyer representing Daly was debarred. The decision in favor of Daly was then nullified on procedural grounds and the entire matter forgotten!

YOU ARE BRAINWASHED!

You have been raised by a public school system and media that constantly assures you that the reasons for all these wars and assassinations are many and varied. The US claims to bring democracy to the conquered lands (they haven't; the usual result of a US overthrow is the imposition of a dictatorship, such and the 1953 CIA overthrow of Iran's democratically elected government of Mohammad Mosaddegh and the imposition of the Shah, or the 1973 CIA overthrow of Chile's democratically elected government of President Salvador Allende, and the imposition of Augusto Pinochet), or to save a people from a cruel oppressor, revenge for 9-11, or that tired worn-out catch all excuse for invasion, weapons of mass destruction. Assassinations are always passed off as "crazy lone nuts" to obscure the real agenda.

The real agenda is simple. It is enslavement of the people by creation of a false sense of obligation. That obligation is false because the Private Central Banking system, by design, always creates more debt than money with which to pay the debt. Private Central Banking is not science, it is a religion; a set of arbitrary rules created to benefit the priesthood, meaning the owners of the Private Central Bank. The fraud persists, with often lethal results, because the people are tricked into believing that this is the way life is supposed to be and no alternative exists or should be dreamt of. The same was true of two earlier systems of enslavement, Rule by Divine Right and Slavery, both systems built to trick people into obedience, and both now recognized by modern civilization as illegitimate. Now we are entering a time in human history where we will recognize that rule by debt, or rule by Private Central Bankers issuing the public currency as a loan at interest, is equally illegitimate. It only works as long as people allow themselves to believe that this is the way life is supposed to be.

But understand this above all, Private Central Banks do not exist to serve the people, the community, or the nation. Private Central Banks exist to serve their owners, to make them rich beyond the dreams of Midas all for the cost of ink, paper, and the right to bribe the right officials.

Behind all these wars, all these assassinations, the hundred million deaths from all the wars lies a single policy of dictatorship. The private central bankers allow rulers to rule only on the condition that the people of a nation be enslaved to the private central banks. Failing that, said ruler will be killed, and their nation invaded by those other nations enslaved to private central banks.

The so-called "clash of civilizations" we read about on the corporate media is really a war between banking systems, with the private central bankers forcing themselves onto the rest of the world, no matter how many millions must die for it.

Indeed the constant hate-mongering against Muslims lies in a simple fact. Like the ancient Christians (prior to the Knights Templars private banking system), Muslims forbid usury, or the lending of money at interest. And that is the reason our government and media insist they must be killed or converted. They refuse to submit to currencies issued at interest. They refuse to be debt slaves.

So off to war your children go, to spill their blood for the money-junkies' gold. We barely survived the last two world wars. In the nuclear/bio weapon age, are the private central bankers willing to risk incinerating the whole planet just to feed their greed?

Apparently so.

This brings us to the current situation in the Ukraine, Russia, and China.

The European Union had been courting the government of the Ukraine to merge with the EU, and more to the point, entangled their economy with the private owned European Central Bank. The government of the Ukraine was considering the move, but had made no commitments. Part of their concern lay with the conditions in other EU nations enslaved to the ECB [European Central Bank], notably Cyprus, Greece, Spain, and Italy. So they were properly cautious. Then Russia stepped in with a better deal and the Ukraine, exercising the basic choice all consumers have to choose the best product at the best price, dropped the EU and announced they were going to go with Russia's offer. It was at that point that agents provocateurs flooded into the Ukraine, covertly funded by intelligence agency fronts like CANVAS and USAID, stirring up trouble, while the western media proclaimed this was a popular revolution. Snipers shot at people and this violence was blamed on then-President Yanukobivh. However a leaked recording of a phone call between the EU's Catherine Ashton and Estonia's Foreign Minister Urmas Paet has confirmed the snipers were working for the overthrow plotters, not the Ukrainian government. Urmas Paet has confirmed the authenticity of that phone call.

This is a classic pattern of covert overthrow we have seen many times before. Since the end of WW2, the US has covertly tried to overthrow the governments of 56 nations, succeeding 25 times. Examples include the 1953 overthrow of Iran's elected government of Mohammed Mossadegh and the imposition of the Shah, the 1973 overthrow of Chile's elected government of Salvador Allende and the imposition of the Pinochet dictatorship, and, of course, the current overthrow of Ukraine's elected government of Yanukovich and the imposition of the current unelected government which is already gutting the Ukraine's wealth to hand to the western bankers.

Brazil, Russia, China, and South Africa have formed a parallel financial system called BRICS, scheduled to officially launch on January 1, 2015. As of this writing some 80 nations are ready to trade with BRICS in transactions that do not involve the US dollar. Despite US economic warfare against both Russia and China, the Ruble and Yuan are seen as more attractive for international trade and banking than the US dollar, hence, the US attempt to fan the Ukraine crisis into war with Russia and attempts to provoke North Korea as a back door to war with China.

Flag waving propaganda aside, all modern wars by and for the private bankers are fought and bled for by third parties unaware of the true reason they are expected to gracefully be killed and crippled. The process is quite simple. As soon as the Private Central Bank issues its currency as a loan at interest, the public are forced deeper and deeper into debt. When the people are reluctant to borrow any more, that is when the Keynesian economists demand the government borrow more to keep the pyramid scheme working. When both the people and the government refuse to borrow any more, that is when wars are started, to plunge everyone even deeper into debt to pay for the war, then after the war to borrow more to rebuild. When the war is over, the people have about the same as they did before the war except the graveyards are far larger and everyone is in debt to the private bankers for the next century. This is why Brown Brothers Harriman in New York was funding the rise of Hitler.

As long as Private Central Banks are allowed to exist, inevitably as night follows day there will be poverty, hopelessness, and millions of deaths in endless World Wars. Until the Earth itself is sacrificed in flames to Mammon.

The path to true peace on Earth lies in the abolishment of all private central banking everywhere and a return to the state-issued value-based currencies that allow nations and people to become prosperous.

"Banks do not have an obligation to promote the public good."
ALEXANDER DIELIUS, CEO,
GERMANY, AUSTRIAN, EASTERN EUROPE GOLDMAN SACHS, 2010

"I am just a banker doing God's work."
– LLOYD BLANKFEIN, CEO, GOLDMAN SACHS, 2009.

Below is dialogue from the movie The International (2009) starring Clive Owen.

Q: But why is the bank committing so much of its capital and resources to the sale of these missiles?

A: It's a test. Small arms are the only weapons used in 99% of the world's conflicts. And no one has the capacity to manufacture them faster and cheaper than China. What Scarsin is attempting to do is to make the IBBC the exclusive broker of Chinese small arms to the third world. . . . this is the gateway transaction

Q: You have billions of dollars invested simply to be a broker. There can't be that much profit for them?

A: Nah! This is not about making profit from weapon sales. It's about control.

Q: Control the flow of weapons, control the conflict?

A: Noooo, no, no, the IBBC is a bank. Their objective isn't to control the conflict; it's to control the debt that the conflict produces. You see, the real value of a conflict, the true value, is in the debt that it creates. You control the debt, you control everything. You find this upsetting, yes? But this is the very essence of the banking industry. To make us all, whether we be nations or individuals, slaves to debt.

The International Link: youtube.com/watch?fea ture =player_embed ded&v=2B_SxGmSJP0

Thank you very much, Michael Rivero, for this historical encapsulation. Enjoy all his great articles and videos that are available at whatreallyhappened.com.

The truth can often quickly appear obvious when a dark and hidden secret is brought to light. Resorting to military means to resolve international disagreements has been the downfall of humankind throughout the ages. In order to establish a safer, more tranquil world, we need to eliminate all military skirmishes and further escalations from the face of the planet. The reasons why wars are fought have eluded man for centuries and yet have been clearly and concisely herein explained.

We have to ask ourselves is military conduct ever the answer that helps ameliorate international disagreements, and if it is the answer, then we can incontrovertibly conclude that it is the wrong answer!

If we believe the solution to an international problem involves killing others, then that solution is inept and could hardly be considered a sane and viable solution. Killing a single human being could be considered an unacceptable solution for all international problems. Solutions to international problems that involve the mass murder of others are likely developed with the idea of profit in mind. People who create such deficient ideas fail to solve international problems and only make them worse. This is how we can spot a criminal; the area he or she influences and has responsibility over deteriorates and gets worse.

It does not matter whether we are fighting as terrorists or freedom fighters; when we kill our fellow man, regardless of religious proclivity, we lose our religious affiliation before the first bullet ever leaves the chamber. Killing is wrong, whether it is done with military bombs or in the classrooms, in a nightclub or at the office Christmas party; none is justifiable. Nations and people short of ideas need to stop using bullets to solve problems.

All lives matter, and murder is wrong, no matter the participants' hue. Killing is killing, and like the imbalanced racial statistics we find in American prisons, one is more likely to be murdered the darker one's color.

As an aside, Democrats always campaign with hate-filled screams that are intended to incite the nation's racial bias and prejudice. Newly elected Democrats have historically turned their backs on their black constituents, sadly abandoning a large portion of the black community to a second-class life filled with unemployment, crime, and despair.

It is about time that the black community wakes up and stops supporting the same ineffective politicians that are not uplifting the black community but are actively oppressing it.

If we ever elect someone like the criminal Hillary Clinton as president, the corruption, degradation, and separation of Americans, which has been escalated by Obama and the press, will only get worse. Not only blacks but all Americans will suffer because of the growing racial and bigoted environment constantly being created by horribly ineffective domestic policies, while the racial flames of discontent are broadcast by the press and bellowed by desperate politicians. America cannot blame one party more than the other, which is why party loyalty is such a terrible joke that is being played on the American people. Republicans have not fared better when it comes to soiling our nation with uninvited and unprovoked war.

The actions of the Bush family instigated the largest escalation of American hatred this world has ever seen. Let's take a ride down memory lane if you like.

Allegedly, unscrupulous charlatans, like Senator Prescott Bush and his family, profited from loans given to Adolf Hitler to finance Nazi Germany. In the very revealing book, George Bush: The Unauthorized Biography by Webster G. Tarpley and Anton Chaitkin (available for you, for free, at tarpley.net/online-books/george-bush-the-unauthorized-biography/), the authors discuss the financing of Hitler's Germany using Wall Street banks and a host of other clandestine activities. This book thoroughly examines the military profits the Bush family received from pig iron contracts (pig iron is the raw material used to make nuts and bolts) in return for Prescott Bush's help in securing financing for Hitler's mighty military machine.

Blood money is indeed very profitable, and many believe similar unconscionable financial practices continue to thrive today in and around the Bush family.

Tarpley and Chaitkin's book further explains the Bush family's involvement with the illegal drug industry and Bush Sr.'s clandestine career as the head of the CIA.

It is difficult to fathom the lack of decency inherent in the Bush family; they possess such a strong predilection toward war and criminality. They profit from the same wars that they start, fund, and propagate.

We should punish war crimes and acts of moral turpitude according to the amount of human and earthly devastation they create. It is essential that we bring criminal war charges against the principal agents of the international private banking families who create, fund, and prolong virtually all wars.

Many wonder about the friendship between the Bush and the bin Laden families, as well as their mutual business interests. Is such a relationship treasonous to the United States? How can it be that the Bush family, who seem to be very good friends with the bin Laden family, can conduct business with members of the same family who supposedly blew up the World Trade Center?

Surprising or not, there has been no investigation into the financial trades and activities of the Carlyle Group, a defense and financial banking conglomerate with whom Bush Sr. has had a working and very profitable relationship. It is conjectured that Bush Sr. raked in billions and more, negotiating defense contracts during the time his malleable son was the president of the United States.

Think of it. George W. is starting World War III, and his daddy is profiting hand over fist. Regarding the different wars in the Middle East, many believe that the Bush family acted treasonously against the United States and that they are as corrupt and debased a family as one could ever imagine.

In all likelihood, Bush Sr. was calling all the shots when George W. was the president. Did the father line his family and his cronies' coffers by pooling resources from billionaires around the world and making timely investments in military-armament manufacturing companies prior to George W.'s initiating WWIII with preemptive strikes against Iraq? Most people believe this to be the case, and if history is prone to repeating, the smart money is on the Bushes making billions in undeserved profits and capitalizing on every future military debacle in the Middle East and around the globe.

When it comes to sucking off the government gravy train, the Clintons are rookies; the Bushes are the real pros. Think of it. How much of the six trillions spent in the Middle East ended up in the Bushes' bank accounts? Probably more than you and I could ever spend.

We need an outsider, a man of the people to run this country the way it is supposed to be run. Americans need to join forces and take back this country from the criminals that have usurped the government.

Donald Trump may provide the option of a legitimate political outsider, and for sure, he is a very successful self-starter. He intends to unite the entire country, black, white, brown, yellow, and red. Trump is far from the bigoted racist the media and Democrats portray him as.

When it comes to military murder for hire, we need to eliminate the problem; the problem is the lust for money and the insatiable greed of a minute fraction of a percentage of the world's population who unconscionably profit from the many wars they all too eagerly plan and orchestrate. There are virtually twelve banking families that are militarily destroying this world, making it unsuitable for human habitation.

When we follow the money, we soon discover ISIS could not even survive without the total cooperation and assistance from government-sanctioned banking institutions.

Why are the banks not intercepting the funds that ISIS receives for selling their oil to Turkey and other Persian Gulf nations? The banks are actually conspirators and complicit in supporting and assisting the war crimes of ISIS. Without ISIS being able to move its funds through corrupt banks, it would not be able to sell its oil, acquire food, munitions, and other staples needed to fight the war, and wreak havoc around the world. Bankers that assist the terrorists by moving and transferring funds should be indicted and tried for war crimes against humanity. Those that assist the terrorists financially are essentially terrorists themselves.

Funds that are stolen from the American people by the IRS, in cahoots with the federal government, go to the same twelve families that own the Federal Reserve and are responsible for all the military murder and blowback murders we are starting to see in America.

We kill them, they kill us; they kill us, we kill them; we kill them, they kill us . . . no matter how you say it, it sounds quite ridiculous and elementary in logic and karma.

The world would greatly benefit by stopping the outlandish and never-enough payments that have been stolen from the people of the United States by the Federal Reserve. We operate in a debt economy, a fanciful world of commerce, because there is no actual money; there are only debt instruments.

The world needs to reboot the international monetary system by declaring gold and silver as the legal tender for all transactions, as the state of Utah did on May 30, 2011.

Also, there should be an international banking amnesty declared, and from that point forward, all countries would control the issuance of their own money, which has to be redeemable for substances of value, such as gold or silver. All countries would control their own financial destinies by controlling the creation and regulation of their own valuable money. Thus, none would be subject to financial enslavement and manipulation by a foreign banking cartel.

The United States could send its powerful military to collect all the gold and wealth that has been stolen by the international banking families and return it to its rightful owners, the American people. We need to get a grip as a nation and as citizens of the world.

The people need to gain control of the bankruptcy of the United States and not allow Congress to continue to destroy the American people by legislating never-ending wars. The world's politicians are bought and sold by the international bankers, and their loyalties have long been against the people. Politicians do not mind sending far too many of our greatest young men and women into harm's way to be brutally slaughtered while upholding and solidifying the interests of the banks.

We need to abolish from the face of the world economy all privately controlled currencies. By using a privately controlled currency, the nation is condemning its people to an economic hell, whose fire is fueled with the lives and freedom of the young and still to come.

Not only is the use of private currency debilitating to the world's economy and the standard of living of every American; it also enslaves everyone that touches it. All of us subject to such an incredibly unfair and rigged system need to demand the abolishment and banishment of the fiat banking system, the most heinous monetary system ever designed to intentionally injure and enslave virtually every member of society.

Our planet is at constant war, not solely because of the perverted actions of the bankers and politicians; we acquiesce and empower war with our apathy and our silence. Let us silently acquiesce no more.

CHAPTER 16

Reverberations of War

One believes things because one has been conditioned to believe them.

– ALDOUS HUXLEY

When I despair, I remember that all through history the way of Truth and Love has always won. There have been tyrants and murderers and for a time they can seem invincible, but in the end they always fall. Think of it, always.

– MAHATMA GANDHI

In the end, we will remember not the words of our enemies, but the silence of our friends.

– MARTIN LUTHER KING JR.

History will have to record that the greatest tragedy of this period of social transition was not the strident clamor of the bad people, but the appalling silence of the good people.

– MARTIN LUTHER KING JR.

The ultimate tragedy is not the oppression and cruelty by the bad people, but the silence over that by the good people.

– MARTIN LUTHER KING JR.

I do not think the measure of a civilization is how tall its buildings of concrete are, but rather how well its people have learned to relate to their environment and fellow man.

– SUN BEAR OF THE CHIPPEWA TRIBE

The critical point is that the Constitution places the right of silence beyond the reach of the government.
— WILLIAM O. DOUGLAS

Silence can only be equated with fraud where there is a legal or moral duty to speak or where an inquiry left unanswered would be intentionally misleading.
— UNITED STATES V. NICHOLAS J. TWEEL

Never be bullied into silence. Never allow yourself to be made a victim. Accept no one's definition of your life; define yourself.
— HARVEY FIERSTEIN

We are not human beings on a spiritual journey. We are spiritual beings on a human journey.
— STEPHEN COVEY

Chronic remorse, as all the moralists are agreed, is a most undesirable sentiment. If you have behaved badly, repent, make what amends you can and address yourself to the task of behaving better next time. On no account brood over your wrongdoing. Rolling in the muck is not the best way of getting clean.
— ALDOUS HUXLEY

NOW WE UNDERSTAND that the insatiable pursuit of profits is the common thread in all wars and the catastrophic sufferings of this planet. The attainment of world peace seems more likely when we boil the war problem down to its simplicity. If we eliminate financing and profiting from war, then we eliminate war.

In an economic system where money is backed by metal of value and substance, as opposed to the fiat currency of the Federal Reserve Note, it becomes readily apparent that any country entertaining war over diplomacy quickly understands that to participate in war is essentially the same thing as declaring the imminent and self-imposed bankruptcy of such a shortsighted country. A war economy can only be temporarily sustained until members of the economy no longer have the inclination, ability, or willingness to endure the oppressive debt that inevitably results from participation in wars.

It is simply a matter of choice. Do we continue with a psychotic and unworkable central banking system, or do we evolve into a nation that demands to have legitimate and redeemable money under the control of the US government?

Once people realize such a small segment of society (less than 0.000000001 percent of the world's population) is financially and culturally destroying the rest of society, it becomes easier to handle the situation and improve the political harmonics of the world. Further, the inflationary problems in which the economy becomes embroiled are solved simply by establishing a monetary system based on value and substance and removing all forms of interest associated with bank loans. This is done only when the control of the money is rightfully protected and placed in the hands of the public, under the direction of an ethical and moral government and not in the hands of an abusive private group of psychopathic shysters, lawyers, and bankers.

Today bankers are similar to slave owners prior to the Civil War era. The slave masters' whips and physical duress have been replaced by mortgages and loans that bear outlandish interest. Although we are free to leave the plantation, we remain enslaved, as the chains of interest are long and have no limit. There is no acceptable level of slavery. We must abolish it in its root form, freeing and uplifting members of society from financial tyranny toward independence, wherein concepts like liberty and freedom again become attainable assets.

A guiding religious belief of Muslims in the Middle East is that no person can participate in a loan of money that has an interest payment associated with it. Without spiritually tarnishing themselves, no followers of the Prophet Muhammad can lend or borrow money if there is an interest payment associated with the loan; it does not matter if the Muslim is the lender or the borrower. The Muslims have known for many centuries that financial slavery is enforced by men, onto the world's population, through the mechanism of debt. This philosophy held by Muslims, of not lending or borrowing money at interest, is contrary to the international bankers' twisted philosophies and intentions.

Why do you think we are supposedly warring with ISIS? Do you think that the fact that the United States has killed millions of people in the Middle East has anything thing to do with the violence we are now experiencing around the world? What is the bottom line or reason we are at war with people from the Middle East? Who said oil?

The reason for war is not oil, or we would have taken it when we left Iraq. The only reason for war is to provide profit and control to the international banks.

Regarding America's national security, why is it important to the United States what Middle Easterners do to each other? How do we as a nation justify the US military's actions that have provoked hatred from millions upon millions of people in the Middle East and almost everywhere else around the globe? Americans often fail to realize that the actions of our government, killing millions of defenseless people under the guise of protecting national security, are creating millions of enemies that want to exact retribution and revenge against us.

It is time for America to rethink and reformulate its foreign and domestic policies to align with the concepts of decency and love, wherein America's role is to safeguard and care for the people of this world and not kill them for corporate profit.

Throughout the history of this great nation, never have we witnessed such a debacle of communication and diplomatic failures as those that occurred under the Bush and Obama administrations. Constant debacles of foreign policy resulted in the hatred of Americans and our way of life by millions of people from around the world.

Muslims, who see so obviously the financial enslavement caused through participation in a private money system of debt, laugh at the ignorance of oblivious Americans who proclaim to live in the land of the free, when actually Americans are living in the home of the financial slave. Muslims, especially those highly educated in the Quran and the Islamic faith, see the blatant deception of the American people, a deception many Americans are unable to detect. Very few Americans even know that the Federal Reserve's interest charges are responsible for fastening the shackles that bind the hands and feet of all Americans.

Most Muslims do not hate Americans. They hate that Americans allow an evil financial and banking system to exist, which destroys and enslaves the world's population and incites endless war.

Americans are a proud people and ought to fight for themselves, their families, and this great country in order to protect the freedom and liberty they enjoy. We cannot be satisfied with the actions of the US military to enforce a corrupt and criminal banking system against a billion Muslims, who are fervently against the unsustainable, private, and for-profit international banking system.

America needs to create a different banking system that comports with the intention and direction of the US Constitution, which benefits all the people and happens to align with the beliefs of Muslims and their religious teachings of Islam regarding interest on loans.

Radical Islam extremists will exist as long as enslaving banking practices are forced upon the Middle East in general and members of the Islamic faith in particular. Until Americans rid the world of private banking, a karmic repercussion of opposition and hatred will fester throughout the world. This is apparent and not difficult to understand.

The United States needs to control its own money once and for all, and this will start to quell the massive distrust and unrest that are prevalent throughout the world. When the bankers' influence is removed from warfare, there will be an automatic uplifting of the planet in which a general amnesty can be given to all nations, thus permitting the global reimplementation of sustainable banking and monetary practices that are not dependent on the US military for their continuation and unwanted enforcement.

There are over seven billion people on this planet whose demands for a fair monetary system are not being met, jeopardizing the sustainability and continuation of this world. By changing the focus of defense contractors into something aimed at improving this world for everyone, the world will immediately improve and raise its scope of economic production, leading to the creation of products that improve the human experience. We can start with solutions for adequate food, clean water, and clean air. That should keep us busy for a while; see wakeenlabs.com.

Without reservation, Obama sank to any depth, absent even a hint of remorse. He executed the most insane policies regarding the nation's healthcare, its military, and its foreign policy, intended not for the benefit of the American people but for their destruction.

Obama's policies were in full alignment, contributed to, and supported radical Islamic terrorists. It appears that Obama is not a bumbling incompetent but, rather, a devious and calculating man with a proclivity to destroy the United States and the American way of life from the top down and from the inside out. These claims can be substantiated when we examine Obama's inviting unknown and fraudulently documented Syrian refugees into the United States.

In addition to the harmful immigration policies of Obama, virtually every decision made by Obama facilitated more suffering and more death to Americans. We must examine his intention in inviting Syrian refugees, including members of ISIS, into the United States without the ability to vet adequately these potentially dangerous individuals. If one considers Obama's immigration policies regarding the Syrian refugees, one would swear that Obama was surreptitiously conducting his own private jihad against Americans.

Let us not even imagine the amount of terror only a small number of jihadists can inflict on unsuspecting Americans. Still, Obama essentially said, "Come on in refugees! We don't know who you are, but come on in anyhow!"

Now you tell me, is Obama a moron and a babbling incompetent, or was he hell-bent on destroying America and its Christian traditions? I reckon the latter. Giving one hundred fifty billion dollars to Iranians who want to kill Americans indicates Obama is a radical jihadist himself with anti-American sentiments as his guiding principles, which affected most every decision he made.

Obama dealt in subterfuge, as do all traitors. He hid his many crimes behind the racism of society and its perpetual strife.

For an interesting perspective regarding Obama's Muslim heritage, beliefs, and practices in his own words, you can watch "Obama Admits he's a Muslim" at youtube.com/watch?v=tCAffMSWSzY. It is quite a revelatory video and fully substantiates that the people of the United States have been duped by Obama, allegedly a covert operative and Islamic jihadist.

On a different front, we can see interesting parallels by comparing various perspectives regarding the debacle in the Middle East and the American Revolutionary War.

The colonialists considered the patriots to be freedom fighters, while the British considered the patriots to be traitors against England. The patriots considered the British to be terrorists in their demand and enforcement that the colonists use only British money in place of the colonial script used until the early 1770s. This aspect of history is preserved by our friends at Wikipedia (en.wikipedia.org/wiki/Early_American_currency).

In the Middle East, many people consider members of ISIS to be freedom fighters, attempting to free themselves from the international private bankers' aggression and domination. At the same time, the American media covers the situation without discussion of the Federal Reserve's financial demands and actions that have caused the retribution and violence we are experiencing on America's shores.

Diplomatically, we need to reach real solutions that allow respect and fraternity to blossom, replacing the animosity and hatred generated and conducted on a daily basis by many of the world's intelligence agencies. Intelligence agencies are designed to assist and direct the public to accept the ongoing agenda of the banking elite and to conduct unending psychological operations necessary to usher in irreparable damage to society.

The international bankers' debilitating effects encompass every sector of society. Its pain is felt everywhere we look. Shortages and poverty are the hallmark of the banking villains.

Today, the average citizen is wiser and better comprehends the criminal nature of the suppressive economic systems in place that are used to enslave humankind. Virtually all humanity is under the thumb of the oppressive regime of the international private banking families.

Many of the Muslim states are in the middle of turmoil and conflict, fighting the oppressive bankers for their financial freedom, because Middle Easterners refuse to become part of the Bank for International Settlements. The worldwide banking oppression is never covered in the media, which focuses, instead, on a never-ending religious battle of radical Islamic terrorists versus Christianity and their opposing ways of life. Let's at least examine the actual problems and start discussing the real causes of unrest in the Middle East and around the world. Perhaps, then, we can create better solutions than the ones that involve guns and bombs.

Unfortunately—or fortunately, depending upon how you view it—the financial systems are crumbling right before our very eyes. Thank God, as this gives us an opportunity to create a better financial system where international bankers do not devastatingly subjugate the masses and continuously create suffering and death through horrific wars.

Americans know in their hearts that their beloved country is conducting itself improperly and immorally by instigating military conflicts to defend and enforce the interests of the bankers. Nevertheless, Americans are the ones that silently condone the brutality that is being exported from America's shores.

It has fallen upon us to be the ones who can change America's brutal exports from military products and killing machines to something a little nicer, like products that deal in peace and love. We need to develop products and systems that improve life for members of the human society, not products and systems that kill our fellow man by the millions. We should export products that reflect the goodness of the American people.

American products, which we need to once again export in massive quantities, will be better received if those products help people and are constructive and not destructive in character. The American economy once again will flourish if we regulate and bring to a conclusion the manufacture of all military products and the financing of all wars.

Defense contractors would soon shift their manufacturing output from military-related products to helpful products that lift the standard of living around the world.

Imagine if the American economy focused on solving real world problems like starvation and sanitation-related disease. America could develop products that provide water for a thirsty world, food for the hungry, and shelter for the downtrodden and homeless.

The military-industrial complex, in order to survive, would have to stop being evil and start doing good things for the world. Demanding that corporations make products that help instead of harm humanity is a good step in the right direction.

If we create and manufacture helpful things, the world naturally becomes a better place. If we manufacture weapons of human destruction, the world naturally becomes worse. When we manufacture helpful products and perform friendly gestures, the world evolves to a higher plane.

To manufacture harmful products is to ensure the world becomes a worse place. It is a natural consequence of events. According to the laws of karma, you get what you give. This applies to countries as well; countries import what they export. If a country continues to export killing machines and death, it will obviously import the same. Should America continue to export death, we will inevitably make our own lands more dangerous as a result. To expect anything else would be contrary to reality and empirical facts.

The sickest aspect of all this armament-producing, military-financing, evil cabal is that these people are working diligently to create death in all parts of the world. This is a very small percentage of the people, and they need to be stopped immediately to prevent further escalation of the destruction, extermination, and potential extinction of humankind.

The US military should do what it is sworn and supposed to do and that is to protect the people and the Constitution. The United States should start a campaign to round up the traitors of humankind and have them face public trial for their dreadfully heinous crimes and violations against humanity. When we discover who exactly is responsible for the degradation and enslavement of mankind, then we—if we cherish and want to preserve our dignity and hope for the generations to come—must voice our intolerance and act in accordance with the dictates of our personal responsibility level.

Everyone should work to make the world a better place. Our action is needed as the impetus or catalyst necessary to initiate world change and evolution of the species to a higher level or harmonic that approaches peace and tranquility.

To do nothing is to consent to the direction of this world that a few bankers have chosen for the rest of humanity. To do something positive is to help reverse the destructive path that humankind has chosen to take. Taking positive action raises the world to a new level of freedom and caring for ourselves and our fellow man and woman. By individually and collectively standing up, citizens can and will reverse the denigration that humankind is now suffering and start to finally build a world that is safe and tranquil for all to enjoy.

We neither need nor want continual military strife; therefore, let us demand continual peace.

We have, by our thunderous silence and ubiquitous apathy, allowed our society to fall prey to the credit monsters that seek only the enslavement and destruction of humanity. We, in our silence and disorganization, tacitly lick the boots crushing the throats of our children, grandchildren, and all generations that follow.

We have built what appears an inescapable financial prison, constructed with the bricks of an oppressive monetary system that pins one tiny group's success and profit against the remainder of humanity's ensured peril and loss. Once people understand the components of the financial enslavement game and who the responsible players are, we can restructure the monetary systems to transform the economy and society into a civilization that reflects the goodness of humanity. Finally, the world will stop reflecting the evilness and hatred of the sordid bankers and start reflecting the goodness and love of the people. The world and every member of society will start to heal.

Recreating a fair economic model using real money is the only solution to the financial slavery inherent in our unjust monetary system. By correcting and rebuilding the outdated and collapsing feudal monetary system, we will automatically rid the world of almost all future irresolvable dilemmas that precipitate the initiation of military conflicts. Corrupt bankers can fund international conflicts only by using a corrupt monetary system, wherein the banks are permitted to endlessly create credit.

A country using real and redeemable money would shortly collapse into bankruptcy after stupidly and aggressively spending its nation's wealth on costly military goods and services. Countries using redeemable money share a built-in deterrent to war and must avoid conflict at all cost; for any country that risks its financial stability for something as stupid as war is a financially suicidal country.

On the contrary, a country using fiat money provides an incentive for corrupt and malevolent bankers who want nothing more than to send a country financially over the edge and turn it into a bankrupt nation. A profit motive can only be associated with wars if there is a fiat money system in use because, with a legitimate money system in use, war will lead quickly to the bankruptcy and financial enslavement of the battling people.

Any country that uses redeemable and valuable money has no financial motive to entertain or participate in war, as conducting war will inevitably result in its bankruptcy, both moral and financial.

A guaranteed method of preventing and removing the financial incentives to create and conduct war is simple; eliminating all fiat money systems will eliminate virtually all wars.

US defense spending exceeds all other governmental spending combined, excluding, of course, the payment of interest on the national debt. To continue using fiat currency is financial and military suicide for any country. As predictable as gravity and as a result of military expenditures, the United States is financially collapsing while you are reading this book.

As history has recorded thousands of times and again, every society that has ever used a fiat currency has completely and devastatingly collapsed. Every world empire has collapsed as defense spending became economically unsustainable in proportion to the gross production or manufacturing output of the empire.

Simple mathematics reveals that once a nation's debt becomes over-burdening and the tax rate becomes too high, it becomes unsustainable for such a nation to continue to pay its national debt. At some point, it becomes obvious that the nation's people become slaves to the debt.

Food and other necessities become impossible to purchase as ever-increasing inflation rates make fiat money worthless. Hyperinflation is usually followed by a revolution, as empty stomachs are the ultimate incentive that quickly inspires revolt and change. This is what happened in Syria; the cost of food escalated to incredible levels, and the people quickly revolted. Now look at the mess; welcome to the Arab Spring, courtesy of Hillary Clinton.

Americans are wise enough to read the writing on the wall and not wait until the valueless Federal Reserve Notes collapse, taking with them the economy and what remains of the low standard of living found too commonly across America. Proactively, we need to organize and demand a new, fair, and ethical money system with a dollar backed by value.

There is a funny thing about peace; it is produced automatically when militarily derived solutions to international disagreements and hatred are no longer tolerated. If decent people dedicate themselves to assisting in the preservation of humanity and uplifting this society, we cannot help but create a better world.

Where do the soldiers get armaments to use when a majority of both sides of the conflict is hungry, penniless, and homeless? Armaments are sold over our silent objections, an unheard silence that permits government officials to legislate ongoing global strife and genocide.

When billions of dollars of weaponry arrive in Baghdad for distribution to US forces and only a fraction of the weapons arrives at the proper destination and in the hands of US forces, we must identify who is ripping off the country and selling the missing weapons to Middle Eastern enemies of the United States. American weaponry and armored vehicles are being used to arm, support, and sustain the enemies of the United States.

Government policies are often insane. In many warring countries, there is not enough food to feed the people, yet the warlords are driving brand-new Jeeps with .50-caliber machine guns mounted to the top of their vehicles. Foreign heads of state usually steal a majority of the American foreign aid earmarked for their countries while the people living under such a criminal regime usually receive only a small fraction of the hundreds of billions of dollars annually distributed.

If the human race plans to free itself and its posterity from the stranglehold of the bankers, we must unite to address and eliminate financial slavery and the slaughter of our brothers and sisters through systematically created wars and military conflicts. How can we stand by and allow one more bullet to shatter the skull of an innocent while knowing that the only reason for this inhumane barbarity is to raise the profits of the entertainment-financial-industrial-medical-military-technical complex?

Through whatever measures are necessary, we the people must insist and create a peace-industrial complex. The transference of the economic output of America needs to shift from a war-based to a peace-based economy. Failure to do this is to invite the destruction of society while welcoming and assisting the installment of a New World Order that is full of criminality and class warfare run amuck.

Instead of corporations creating "defense" products, corporations need to produce products that are closely aligned with the overall needs and desires of the human race; corporations need to build products that uplift the people and better the condition of the world.

The vast majority of people in this world would much rather see peace and tranquility than conflict and disharmony. Our silence, coupled with an apathetic inability to demand a better quality of life for ourselves and our children, ensures that the war- or military-based economy that we currently live under thrives and grows until there is nothing and no one left to kill.

For the sake of society, it is time to rectify an evil system developed in greed and secrecy. It is time to evolve toward a monetary system that uplifts society and leads to harmonious international relations. Let's get with the program and abolish banker-imposed slavery. This is the twenty-first century, not the sixteenth century.

Overhauling the corrupt and tyrannical banking system used in the United States is the first step in moving this society toward a higher plateau where men and women free themselves from the world's most oppressive financial group of psychotics this planet has ever seen.

Yo ho, yo ho, financial slavery has got to go! Yo ho, yo ho, financial slavery has got to go! That is what protesters should chant, as the corrupt banking system is the real problem plaguing every country in this world and increasingly spawning protest rallies and unrest across the land. It is time for Americans to smarten up. How much more are we going to take?

When the Muslims stand up to the bankers' financial system of usury, outlawed not only in the Quran but also in the Christians' Holy Bible, they are portrayed as terrorists. In essence, Middle Easterners are fighting for their financial right not to be a slave. They know that modern-day slavery is constructed using fiat money and loans that carry interest.

When America started the Iraq War under George W. Bush's doctrine of preemptive strike, American troops were not treated as liberators, as predicted by Dick Cheney, and never will be. American troops were treated by Iraqis only as the invaders they were. Imagine if the Arab nations decided it was time to kill a few million Americans by dropping countless bombs on the United States. We would expect that Americans would be very upset, want to get even, and extract revenge for their family and friends that were bombed!

Remember when King George III told the thirteen Colonies that they were no longer allowed to use colonial script and were forced by England to cease its issuance, the colonists revolted. According to the English history books, the colonists were terrorists, and America was a land built by traitors to England and King George III. Revolting colonists knew their lives were in danger, for they were about to begin fighting the world's greatest army, which enforced the oppressive policies of England's banks and their fiat currency. The colonists still risked it all to build a better life for themselves and future generations of Americans.

American revolutionaries considered themselves patriots and freedom fighters while the English considered the Americans terrorists, who should be hung for committing treason against the Crown. Patriots care about the important things in life, including freedom, liberty, and religion.

Never forget that we get the government we deserve. By not standing up for our fellow Americans and ourselves, we remain on our knees and kiss the ring of the banking tyrants.

Many believe war to be a solution to an insurmountable set of circumstances, which haphazardly occur, as the winds of fate blow in a hostile and unpredictable manner. This is never the case. Wars are calculated and conceived just as business ventures are. After all, wars are incredibly profitable business ventures of the wealthy.

Although often unexamined, the reasons promulgated by politicians for creating wars are never the real causes of the war and never justify the vast human carnage and suffering that result from war.

George W. Bush's unconscionable decision to thrust the world into war has changed the direction of humanity for the worse. This decision, planned well before the events of 9/11, was designed to profit the special interests and the Bush family. The Bush family's disgraceful predilection for war has caused the deaths of millions and created profits in the trillions.

Catastrophic effects upon the entire population occur as a result of the direct exposure to the horrific perils of war, including exposure to radioactive materials contained in the remnants of depleted uranium shells fired from tanks and planes into the enemies' homes and other buildings. These radioactive toxins leave millions suffering in agony and the environment withering in pain. Throughout the Middle East, babies are being born with horrific abnormalities, and the state demands parents slaughter their deformed babies soon after birth and are forbidden to raise such abominations of human DNA.

Leo Tolstoy claims, "Government is an association of men who do violence to the rest of us." That sentiment is never truer than in war. This fact is evidenced by a world that is at perpetual war. Wars conducted to resolve an irresolvable dilemma are presented and sold to the public under the guise of protecting national security. For many years, wars failed to resolve the fictitious national security problems that they were initiated to solve. During war, profits just keep adding up—right along with the death toll.

Politicians and bankers throughout history have exhibited a bloodcurdling desire for war and its prolongation to reap incredible financial rewards, no matter the consequences.

Even having limited intelligence, two people involved in a conflict should be able to settle their differences and obtain a better outcome without engaging in warfare. With all the intelligent people in Washington, DC, it seem peculiar that America resorts to war to handle national security issues, when by participating in war, we are actually destroying and lessening the nation's security.

If Americans want to be safe at home, we must stop being the biggest bully of the world. Are we that blind that we fail to see the harm we are perpetrating as the top warring nation of the world? Do we stop to imagine the inevitable karmic consequences of our often-unexamined military actions of brutality against our fellow man?

Why has humankind not evolved to a higher level of intelligence to resolve conflicts with other nations in a more peaceful manner than resorting to warfare?

The fate of the world is anything but unchangeable. War relentlessly extinguishes the dreams and lives of all Earth's inhabitants. Time is running out, but it is not too late to change the path this civilization is travelling and to elevate humanity.

If people choose to be intolerant of anyone or anything, let it be war and war-profiteers.

Most all of us have not been living up to our innate, God-given potential. With a resilient effort, we can modify the monetary systems of the world into fair and just systems that can only lead to a better society where peace and trust flourish.

The devastation and loss of the war-torn youths' lives and limbs are somehow deemed acceptable collateral losses, necessary for the good of our nation and its security. To abandon the welfare of the citizens and irresponsibly subject the nation's youth to the perils of war is despicable in every respect.

The missing limbs, the ruined minds, and the radioactive bodies of the wounded warriors all seem unimportant and secondary to the intentions of those who feed on military conflict and make trillions in profits. The pain, the suffering, and the futility of war—considered inconsequential and written off as the cost of doing business by the ruthless war profiteers—are known in the hearts of every soldier and their families. National suffering and tragedy are often hidden behind the patriotic speeches of politicians while our minds are unwittingly brainwashed to the point where we fail to see the inhumanity in every aspect of war.

The purported cause of wars is never the actual reason for wars. Wars are simply fought for profit, but the government promotes to the public false reasons and fabricated stories for the cause of wars, encouraging mothers and fathers to send little Johnny and Jamie off to their deaths or an even more agonizing life.

The media, one of the intelligence arms of the bankers, serve war to the American people on a platter of patriotism, with a side of hogwash and a topping of nonsense.

Today the created and fabricated enemy is ISIS. Let us ponder: did the Mossad or the CIA or a combination of both create ISIS? It does not even matter in the slightest because many intelligence agencies are indistinguishable in purpose and work hand in hand achieving the most dastardly of terroristic deeds.

Very little is known about the Mossad. Although some might doubt this, cautiously I will brave to tell you that according to historical accounts, ISIS stands for Israeli Secret Intelligence Service. All one has to do is Google Israeli Secret Intelligence Service, and there is plenty to read about a criminal Jewish network that supports the bankers' intentions and are responsible for orchestrating virtually all wars and terrorist acts in the Middle East and throughout the world. Most all the international bankers are Zionists and share their arrogant philosophy and lack of concern for the human race.

This sort of information proves useful when trying to understand which parties benefit from having Christians slaughter millions of Muslims and vice versa. If the Christians are killing the Muslims and the Muslims are killing the Christians, what group benefits? The radical Zionist extremists benefit.

Radical Zionist extremists are not all Jewish people but only a small evil group of warmongers that happen to hide cowardly behind the Jewish religion and population.

This information should not be construed as anti-Semitic; rather, it is meant to be simply accurate and unbiased. Too often, the Jewish people are confused with the radical Zionist extremists, and any attack against hateful and destructive Zionists is usually labeled as anti-Semitic in nature by the media.

Lumping the entire Jewish population with the extreme Zionist movement is like lumping all Muslims with radical Islamic extremists. Nothing could be further from the truth.

Many believe that a small group of depraved Zionists is totally to blame for orchestrating and contributing to the upset in the Middle East. To enlighten ourselves further, information regarding radical Zionism should be studied in depth. For further clarification of these claims, please read "Judaism and Zionism Are Not the Same Thing" available at nkusa.org/aboutus/zionism/judaism_isnot_zionism.cfm.

The above article by Jews Against Zionism expounds, "The truth is that the Jewish faith and Zionism are two very different philosophies. They are as opposite as day and night."

For years, radical Zionist extremists have been hiding behind the good people of the Jewish religion and committing the most heinous crimes imaginable, including the events of 9/11. Their network is well established; their crimes are hidden; their enemy is the rest of humanity.

Anyone brave enough to speak against the Zionists will be immediately and loudly touted by the press as an anti-Semitic, a bigot, and a racist. The media will fabricate and zealously spread ad hominem attacks against the character of any person who dares discuss the Zionists' crimes against humanity. The media constantly resort to insinuating and fabricating claims of conspiracy theories and lunacy against anyone that speaks ill of Zionists.

People must decide that this world, and everyone who lives in it, is worth helping and defending. No one group of people is better than the others; to disagree would be an admission of prejudice. Wars are conducted under the false belief that one group's imagined superiority means their needs and rights are more important than the needs and rights of another group who are perceived as inferior.

Instead of being on the path of constant world war, America should be on the path of creation and striving to make improvements in the human condition, not destroying it. The corrupt media conglomerates and their lack of ethical leadership have involved Americans in military conflicts with many foreign countries. Sadly, we are also at war with one another under the cloak of racism. In our floundering and unstable country, the last thing the races should ever do is attack one another.

We can look at America as it approaches extremely unjust racial and class warfare and wonder how we can soothe the media-induced societal inflammation. Bankers and their minions create different factions to incite and commit violence against other factions of the population, usually utilizing the services of a third-party intelligence agency and camouflaged by news agencies that promote and establish news cycles of attacking and degrading various segments of society on a continual basis.

In the past years, there has been an escalation of racial tensions in America, propagated by the media to incite animosity among different groups and different colored people, black, white, brown, yellow, and red.

It is apparent that the leading criminal element of the Black Lives Matter group is being financed by billionaire liberals with a proclivity to embrace socialistic and communistic agendas. These seditious billionaires have been hiring agent provocateurs to demonstrate and inflame the public. The agent provocateurs use the other Black Lives Matter demonstrators as foolish tools to assist in unwittingly ushering into existence the billionaires' agenda and the further demise and decimation of the black community.

The Democratic Party uses the black community to get elected but cares little about improving the plight of the inner cities. If the Democrats cared, there would not be the dire conditions that exist today in our inner cities.

After abandoning the Republican Party—the party of Lincoln—to vote for John F. Kennedy in the sixties, black Americans have ever since been supporting criminal politicians under the Democratic Party. Where has it gotten them? Again, watch the movie *Hillary's America: the Secret History of the Democratic Party*. This movie explains, in frightening horror, the terrible treatment of blacks at the hands of the Democratic Party.

Washington politicians betrayed and abandoned any concern for the black community decades ago. Has anyone noticed how the black communities of the major cities have dilapidated into urban killing fields, which results from little to no financial opportunity? Few politicians have worked to improve the plight of inner-city blacks. Crime rates are through the roof, murders are at an all-time high, and safety, at an all-time low in many neighborhoods, is a relic of the past.

There has been an ongoing campaign designed to keep the black communities down by destroying the quality and level of public education within those communities. Drugs, violence, and degradation have overstayed their welcome, and there were no real solutions put forth by the Democrats to revive our poor and murderous inner cities.

As an example, Chicago is becoming a lawless jungle where thousands of blacks are murdered in cold blood by one another. That means thousands of murderers are now in jail and thousands of families are permanently traumatized.

The time has come for a big change in order to improve the black community and bring it out of the ghetto and into the American Dream. Blacks should wake up, abandon the Democratic Party, and emancipate themselves from poverty and crime. The Democratic Party is largely responsible for the deplorable conditions affecting our inner cities and the black community. The education in many inner cities is deplorable, and employment opportunities are nearly nonexistent.

What have the Democrats, who have been governing our inner cities for the past seventy years, been doing for the black community?

It is time for a change. Blacks have rights too! Black lives do matter—as much as every other life matters. Blacks have been deprived and subjugated to a life of shortage and strife. With the unemployment of black youth exceeding 55 percent, is there any wonder why we find more crime in black communities than elsewhere?

Wherever there are government welfare and a lack of gainful employment opportunities, there are corollary high rates of crime. Without employment opportunities, inner-city crime becomes the only available opportunity or avenue to achieve financial stability and wealth within much of the suffering black community.

To obtain improvement and uplifting of the city's forgotten communities, we all need to remove our partisan blinders and stop supporting criminal politicians who only widen the gap of inequality between not only the races but also the classes.

Instead of heading toward a media-incited race war in America, the entirety of the oppressed population, regardless of color, should put its differences aside, join forces, and finally resolve the class warfare that has been oppressing the world for centuries. It's the politicians and bankers against everyone else.

Regardless of skin hue, the betterment of the citizenry is the least concern of politicians in a democratic system. Political racism is not black or white; regardless of color, we are the ones the politicians are against, the remainder of the non-politically connected American people! It is simply the same old class warfare. The interests of the bankers and politicians versus the interests of the masses are fundamentally being exploited across America. It is class warfare between the rich and the poor.

For years, the Democrats and the Republicans have wanted the different races to be quarrelling with one another. Racial unrest keeps the public's focus off the career criminal politicians that are adversely affecting everyone, no matter our race, sex, or religion.

The Democratic Party's platform is based on the Machiavellian principle of divide and conquer. The blacks and the very poor are the pawns that Democrats use as the societal catalyst to incite animosity and unrest among the different races.

Bankers aim to mutually enslave all people, regardless of race. The bankers' biggest fear is that blacks, whites, browns, yellows, and reds will soon unite and with solidarity overthrow the world's ruling criminal class.

Racism is a tool of bankers and politicians to keep the people harboring animosity toward one another while distracting the population from identifying the planet's true slave masters. As long as the races are angry and staring each other down, we are not staring down the correct origin of our society's number one enemy and enslaver of the American people. It is up to all the people to unite and overthrow our common oppressors.

If humanity does not replace the cyclical pattern of international psychosis, manifested as hatred and warfare, then everyone on Earth will perish for our lack of perseverance in the protection of humankind and for our failure as stewards of humanity, society, and this world.

Our stewardship of the Earth up to this point has been absent any real attempt to inject order and sanity into an insane world. A shoulder-to-shoulder, organized effort would be enough to tip the scales of injustice and barbarity and, at the same time, provide a safer environment for the evolution of the world's future generations into a kinder, gentler people.

All conflict is resolvable through communication, yet communication is the exact tool perverted by the governments and media to justify the necessity of war and the indiscriminate sacrifice of millions of lives. The media internationally disseminate inaccurate information to antagonize the various races and classes of the population. They spread fictitious and fanciful stories to justify debased military actions against manufactured enemies.

For people to evolve to a higher spiritual level of existence, humanity needs to abolish war from the face of the planet. War holds the earth's harmonics prisoner, preventing the evolution of man to higher and higher states of existence.

On a spiritual level, the mechanism that dooms humanity to hate and perpetual war is similar to the mechanism that repeatedly condemns humanity to act like crabs in a bucket. A group of crabs placed in a bucket will always prevent the other more ambitious crabs from climbing out of the bucket. This innate mechanism imprisons all the crabs within an otherwise easily escapable bucket. As the ambitious crabs start to scale the walls of the bucket, those crabs lower in the bucket grab and pull the escaping crabs back into the depths of the bucket.

As a society, people monitor, govern, and prevent themselves and others from escaping the desolation and despair of an insane world into higher realms of human existence.

Crabs are their own worst enemy and continually sabotage their neighbors. We are different from crabs, yet their actions are incredibly reflective of the human predicament!

To protect special interests, ambitious people that escape the "human bucket of thought" and bring better ideas to humanity suffer attack, libel, and persecution. Check virtually any religious or historical text regarding revolutionary ideas, including those by thinkers like Moses, Jesus, Galileo, da Vinci, Abraham Lincoln, John F. Kennedy, Robert Kennedy, Martin Luther King Jr., and Malcolm X. It is amazing the number of courageous and honorable people that have spoken out against oppressive tyranny throughout history and have paid the ultimate price as a result.

Getting back to war and our acquiescence of it, whether we are discussing a real or fabricated enemy, war is the least reasonable and most illogical action a civilization can allow and undertake in its foreign affairs. Continual warfare is destroying the environment so quickly that humankind's inevitable extermination is approaching at a breakneck pace should we fail to change the course of humanity. Uranium-238 has a half-life of 4.5 billion years, which leads us to understand the damage that radioactive rounds, fired from tanks, can cause to the environment, eventually making the world uninhabitable for all living organisms The only logical prognostication of a world involved in constant war is the ultimate destruction and death of such a world.

To think that by initiating war we are creating a solution to a problem is an absurd perspective. Warfare, by its very nature, is humanity's most destructive activity and has no place in the affairs of a civilized people, but somehow, we unconscionably tolerate war.

The harmonic of war is so debased and beneath the decency of the human race that all nations need to outlaw it. No longer can people sit by as governments enlist the youth of the world to fight wars for the almighty dollar.

Now is the time to replace our failing fiat currency system with a stable money system backed by production and intrinsic value, not the might of the US military. Every society in modern civilization that has over-financed and over-extended the reach of its military has economically imploded with the ferocity of an atom bomb.

The greatest psychos in this world are responsible for creating the greatest damage. War damages virtually everything and everyone it contacts and can no longer be tolerated by a sane society that strives for improvement. The most criminal element of society can be identified as that element that aims to cause the most harm and destruction to others.

Most rational people believe there is no justifying war. To justify war would be to define and categorize humankind as incapable of solving its problems without resorting to violence and equate the intellectual functioning of man and woman to that of the birds of the air, the fish of the sea, and the beasts of the land.

Imagine if international and military roles were the reverse. If American families were being bombed out of existence by a foreign military power, would Americans sit by, suffer incalculable losses, and not want revenge? Would we be classified as terrorists for standing up for our fellow compatriots, taking up arms, and fighting against the outright oppressors of America?

America can build a better world, one in which death is not the number one US export to the rest of the world. America and the world deserve better.

America was loved abroad when it had a manufacturing base that made products that people around the world enjoyed. Foreigners revered America when its products were thoroughly enjoyed around the world because superior goods were made in the land of the free and the home of the brave. Outstanding products were stamped with our national insignia "Made in the U.S.A." America was very respected around the world. America was selling its never-ending supply of good old-fashioned American ingenuity, which was built into every American-made product. The products were of such high quality that the whole world was buying everything as fast as the United States could make it!

Today America makes next to nothing. The majority of what America exports are a deplorable amount of military products that produce only death and destruction. This is what America has sadly become in the eyes of the world, a military merchant of death.

The US government seems to consider wounded veterans simply as government liabilities, expenses to be paid by the taxpayers. Should disabled US veterans seek remuneration from corporations that manufacture weapons and profit from war? Armaments corporations should be required to pay to support those injured in battle by their very destructive products. Defense contractors should be required to set aside a portion of gross revenue for the care of our American military heroes, our veterans.

What would happen if an injured soldier sued an armaments company for injuries sustained in battle? Would the jury find the armaments company liable for causing bodily injury?

Dead-peasant life insurance policies are procured for every US soldier, and upon injury or death of a soldier, an insurance claim is paid to offset the government's loss of the soldier's life or disability. Soldiers are classified as the property of the good old USA. Our soldiers are valued as a commodity and considered nothing more than a financial asset of the US government, monetized and insured as the government sees fit.

We should no longer tolerate war or those who promote and profit from such barbarity. All human effort needs to be aimed at improving the spirituality of humankind and aligning the actions of the sexes and the various races to promote the goodness of humankind and the achievement of a saner planet.

Imagine if civilization designed its laws to support the creation, enlightenment, and improvement of humankind. Ponder a world where war profiteers, and the other merchants of death, are outlaws and appropriately punished. Conceive of uplifting humanity to a level where love and peace govern international political affairs and war becomes a relic of the past. Such a civilization is no more a fantasy or some imagined environment than the one we are living in today.

In today's poorly governed and administrated world, there is an ever-present intent to create constant upset, strife, and war. That is why there is war somewhere on this planet at any given time. If we remove profit from the equation, there is no remaining incentive or reason to create war and not resolve problems intelligently and amicably.

Politicians should act like adults, reclaim the power from the banks, and prosecute international bankers as the true enemies of humanity that they are.

Murder has become socially acceptable under the guise of patriotism and duty for one's country. This society has become numb to the killing that occurs across the planet, justified and authorized under the guise of national security.

Uniforms do not exonerate any barbaric transgressions against one's fellow man. The killing of a person is not a minor matter. When the uniforms come off and soldiers get on their knees and pray, it may be difficult to justify to themselves, and more importantly to their Creator, the wrongs committed under the name of patriotism.

Politicians who choose to represent the United States should be held to the highest levels of ethics, morality, and honor as they act on behalf of this great nation. In cases where politicians deviate from the instilled ideals and beliefs that we love our neighbors and do what is right for our country, their deviant acts diminish and tarnish not only the offending politicians' integrity level but also our country's cumulative integrity level.

It is a karma thing. Karma happens on a personal level, as well as a national level; there is no dodging it. We are all responsible for our actions, and these actions accumulate to comprise the quality of life within America and its reputation, which is felt by people from all nations.

Military conflict keeps the combined wavelengths, or the harmonic, of this planet at such a low level or frequency that the evolution and the spiritual uplifting of the species are virtually impossible—unless and until we abolish war. We need to eliminate war, and then we will witness a revitalization of the greatest qualities of humanity as civilization blossoms for the betterment of all. Man will rise in quality and character when there is a sane environment and we implement safeguards to protect and ensure the survival of humanity.

When we decide to remove the conflicts of war from the face of this planet, we will vastly improve as a species in a plethora of ways. Improvement and the raising of the intelligence of humankind is what the international bankers fear the most—the evolution of the species to a higher, more intelligent, and more caring level. Bankers fear the peasants will pull back the curtain on human slavery and finally demand liberation and abolition from financial bondage.

Protecting and uplifting the society should be the objectives of every piece of legislation and every policy that is developed and implemented by government. Today, political legislation and policy are designed to profit one sector of society at the expense of the remainder of society; this is what creates antagonism against police, politicians, and government.

The society suffers hatred and racism because of horribly unworkable policies instituted by politicians that unfairly affect the different races. These policies segregate the black, brown, yellow, and red races to lives of poverty and criminality at a much higher rate than that which affects whites. All races are suffering in today's global economy that was intentionally created to destroy and enslave virtually everyone.

Many up-and-coming members of society are diligently enhancing themselves intellectually, and it behooves each of us to spend more time studying and obtaining occupational and other certifications that are necessary in this society in order to improve our income level, station, and lifestyle. Studying and anything else done to enhance ourselves, in order to better serve our fellow man, are activities that should be effusively undertaken.

Whenever people move in the direction of assisting others, they are assisting in the creation of a better world with happier people in it. Whenever the opportunity presents itself—and it presents itself every second of every day—we must help one another as much as possible, and the world will immediately begin to improve. Helping others is the only way to make the world a better place to live.

Every religion describes and instructs us of our duty to humanity, "Do unto others as you would have them do unto you." When we help someone else, we are improving the world around us. Therefore, within the act itself of helping another, we are essentially creating and ensuring a better world for ourselves.

There are two classes of people—those that live to serve others and those that live to be served. There are those that help others, and there are those that help themselves. In reality, you truly help yourself by helping others.

The most valuable people help others; the greatest leaders serve humanity.

If we silently stand by while our brothers and sisters are murdered, we are by default guilty because we are sanctioning our neighbors' spilled blood with our deafening silence. It is as though, by our thunderous silence, we consent to pulling the trigger and releasing the sniper's bullet, adding another corpse to the death toll of the government's politicide.

We all need to say enough is enough and work in the direction of realizing and obtaining peace in America's domestic and foreign relations.

Are people so naïve that they believe their government's military actions overseas are not going to come home to roost? Regardless of Americans' justification of the US government's killing of several million people in the name of national security, these deadly actions are going to have ramifications felt here in the United States and other parts of Western civilization. Actually, they already are being felt. Paris, San Bernardino, California, Orlando, Florida, and too many other communities to name have suffered mass shootings and terror, conducted at the hands of radical Islam extremists or even more nefarious characters.

Reverberations felt from war affect every aspect of life—materially, emotionally, and spiritually. We need to protect the world's inhabitants by establishing positive dialog that develops the methods and necessary procedures to improve the world and make it more habitable for all. Political policies, designed to readily rid the whole world of its omnipresent oppression, need nevertheless to be immediately implemented to radically reverse the decay and deterioration of our one and only wonderful world.

What kind of world are Americans creating? Our distance from other parts of the world does not extricate us from our moral responsibility as a nation to guarantee our proper and loving treatment of the rest of humanity. The distance from where our country's actions take place does not lessen the crimes that this nation is committing. Moreover, distance does not prevent karma from extracting its rightly deserved retribution in return for our international offenses. Karma works like a boomerang; what we do to others comes back to us, sometimes a hundred times over.

Why do we sit deafly ignoring the calls for justice and the cries of a dying world? Has our acceptance of an unacceptable world been induced by the misdirected edicts of the media conglomerates and their mesmerizing technology?

Now is the time for all good men to unite with the intention to improve our surroundings and relations with all the nations of the world.

We cannot be satisfied with a world corrupted by a miniscule sliver of the population that has the intention to destroy all that is good and cherished by humankind. It is a sin, far beyond our ability to justly punish, to allow this glorious world to slip into oblivion through the blood-soaked hands of demented war profiteers.

From now till the end of time, the blood of veterans of every country need not spill; it is up to Americans to safeguard the world in order that decency and respect among all people can multiply and flourish. We should strive to create a world in which humankind can obtain higher heights and holier ambitions, thus improving the living conditions for all humanity. There should be a roof over every head and a meal in every fridge—and everyone should have a fridge—even in the most remote parts of abandoned Africa.

The government and media's marketing campaigns hypnotize the masses into a state in which it is okay to die for a country and, even worse, it is okay to kill a fabricated and manufactured enemy created by the media.

Any act done to another that we would personally regret being done to ourselves should never be undertaken by a government that is supposed to be the reflection and embodied representation of the people. Every American needs to demand a higher level of integrity and decency in the handling of America's foreign affairs. Around the world, when we as a nation imbue love, we get love in return; when we imbue hate, we get hate in return.

Veterans, who know they were lied to and who have killed others in battle, understand the relentless remorse resulting from taking a life un-deservingly. We cannot ignore our past transgressions against our fellow man and avoid the accompanying pain, depression, and remorse so often felt by those who take aim and fire upon their brothers and sisters during warfare and other situations where we have harmed another.

Many soldiers experience post-traumatic stress disorder (PTSD) when they realize that they have unjustifiably killed or hurt another while serving their country. Once back in the United States after their tour of duty or retired from military service, it is not so simple to justify an act as terrible as killing another human being. Everyone suffers karmic consequences. No uniform, no gang, no philosophy, no religion, nothing at all mitigates murder or makes it acceptable to decent people.

Soldiers who get PTSD are often the most decent members of society and may have incredible difficulty reckoning and justifying their personal actions performed on the battlefield on behalf of the country they love and for which they have sincerely sacrificed.

The burden, upset, and sadness we all carry are a result of the harmful transactions or sins we have committed against others. Our remorse, depression, and melancholy are only lessened and replaced by other positive actions we undertake to improve the lives of our fellow man. We must offset the damage caused by the negative actions and transgressions we have committed against humanity. If we have hurt others, it only makes sense that we repair that damage by performing actions that improve the lives of others. We all need to take more responsibility in our lives and help others all the time—especially when we start to feel bad about the horrible things we have done.

Don't sit in a room smoking or taking pills till your head gets numb. Get out and help!

To bathe in the mud of the past harmful actions we have committed is not a good way to cleanse ourselves of our sins. We cleanse ourselves by praying to our Creator for forgiveness, by forgiving ourselves for our destructive acts, and by making amends as much as possible to those we have negatively affected and harmed.

If we have killed, then we make amends in the best way that we can. We must do our best to build a better world in order that others will not have to repeat the heinous actions that we as a nation undertook without proper knowledge, evaluation, and judgment of the situation.

To fail to evolve as individuals and as a species is to guarantee our extinction. Our present actions determine our future; so let us act like angels to assure that humankind minimally has a future. Let us behave as individuals and as nations in a manner that improves the image of humanity. Let us be an example of decency and love among people, reflective of our Creator, no matter what or who we believe that to be.

Moreover, let us all work to improve the lives of those around us and through our actions build a better world. Let us do this to make amends to the people we have harmed.

If you are looking for a way to improve the world, 911andtheworld today.com was created to organize concerned citizens of the world and to improve and safeguard the world in a number of areas that desperately need improvement. Please join 911andtheworldtoday.com and help build a better world. It is time for us to speak up and have the people's voice finally be heard. Let the good people unite and fight the true terrorists of this planet.

As age works its magic, the once-youthful and once-exuberant soldier may have realizations that the marketing campaign, which the government and media used to sell the war, was riddled with lies and the real reasons for the war were never revealed for public examination or evaluation. The real reasons for war are much more sinister, debased, and never spoken of or reported in the evening news. The truth of the matter is that today there are some unconscionable war criminals, who create war in order for their companies and shareholders to make money. Sick and depraved bankers are the root of all evil on this planet. They are the cause and perpetrators of all war. They are traitors against the world's population; they are traitors against every one of us!

The guilt and sorrow that accompanies harming and killing others is not lessened by pharmaceuticals. Alcohol and marijuana will not quiet the voice of our conscience. People cannot lessen their personal guilt without taking responsibility for those they have harmed. No sedative extinguishes the pain we carry and our personal suffering that result from offending our fellow man. In this universe, if we send out hate, we receive back hate; when the emittance is love, we receive the same wavelength or better!

The empty feeling we get in our hearts from betraying our fellow man vanishes only when we forgive ourselves. It is prudent and cleansing for all of us to forgive ourselves and our neighbors for the regrettable acts of hatred that we have committed that have injured and damaged our fellow man. Only with forgiveness of self and others, coupled with action to ameliorate, amend, and repair the damage we have caused, can we escape the past transgressions we have committed against others. Relief is available for all the secret and deeply buried crimes we have committed; however, that relief will never be found hiding in a bottle of pills or spilling tears in our beers at a local gin joint. Personal redemption is achieved only through personal efforts to help others; for by helping others, we help ourselves.

Relief from guilt and suffering occurs when we restore our personal worth by contributing positively to improve the world and serve our brothers and sisters. When the world's population is committed to improving things for their fellow man and woman, the world will evolve to a higher level of decency and spirituality.

With our intention and actions aimed at reversing the evil we have committed and replacing it with kindness toward others, we grow as individuals because our actions improve our relationships with our fellow man. By helping others, we become less ostracized and introverted; by focusing on helping others, we become extroverted and removed from our imagined and often self-fabricated problems. Emotional upset only exists in the past; therefore if our attention is directed in the present and future toward helping others, we will diminish the amount of personal turmoil that affects virtually all of us.

Precious life is boundless in perspective and beauty; no matter what damage we have done, when we help others we contribute to life's beauty; we contribute to life. Our only real escape from the reverberations and suffering that we have brought upon ourselves by committing harmful and hurtful transgressions against others is to firstly forgive ourselves and then reverse that bad karma and mojo by helping to uplift our brothers and sisters in humanity.

There should be orientation programs for veterans to assist them with their readjustment into society. Imagine if there were programs where veterans were given the chance to help heroin addicts and assist them to overcome their heroin addictions and problems. This or other altruistic programs would surely contribute to assisting our soldiers to lead more fulfilling lives, rather than casting them away in a dark room with a handful of pills, a life of despondency, and the very real possibility of early termination.

We develop and evolve, both as individuals and as a species, through each decision that we individually make every instant of our lives. To make better decisions is to build a better world and a better life for ourselves. There is no higher purpose than to decide to make the world a better place for others. We make the world we live in, and we make it as a result of our decisions. This is great news because if we don't like our current lives, we can change our decisions and that will change our lives. Life appears to be the result of all our past decisions. That means, in order to have a better life in the future, we need to start making better decisions in the present.

By assisting our fellow man, we are able to recover from the evil we have committed. Nothing but our best effort can save us from our past acts and actions that have contributed to the damage of another. It matters not whether our transgressions were blatantly committed or silently condoned; if we hurt someone, it reverberates back and hurts us.

Pain is a stubborn thing. It heals from within, often in a corollary relationship to every good deed we do for others. No amount of toxins in the brain can quiet the screams of our conscience. The only true answer is that love trumps all; just ask yourself or Mother Theresa.

Recall how you felt after the last time you were mean to someone you love, and then recall how you felt the last time you helped someone; there is quite a drastic difference in those feelings. Now multiply that by ten thousand deeds and ask yourself which would you rather commit, deeds that help or deeds that hurt.

We lift ourselves by uplifting our fellow man. The fact that we all have created some devastating and horrific atrocities in this world simply indicates the capability we possess to do wonderful things in this world. By eliminating our evil actions and focusing our objectives on assisting others and creating a better world, we can use more of our personal ability and power to create positive effects in the world. This is how we will build a better world—by each of us doing our part to help others, one good deed piled upon another.

We have all done bad things. We must forgive ourselves, and if our future actions help others and improve the world, we and the world have no choice but to elevate to a higher plane of existence. The world that we experience is a culmination and aggregation of everyone's individual decisions and actions. The result is our common reality. Our decisions and actions are part of the world's magical equation and result in the spiritual manifestation of the world that we all continuously share.

If you are not happy with the world, change your input and the output automatically changes. As mentioned above, for more absolutely incredible information regarding this world's aggregate universe, watch Mark Passio's Natural Law: the Real Law of Attraction at youtube.com/watch?v=Z8Rbj-lPwi4. The universe gives us everything that we ask for, so ask for many great things, for a beautiful civilization, and for peace on Earth. Ask for many great experiences, for heavenly blessings, and for amazing stuff for everyone. It is better to ask for an abundance of things, rather than not ask for and not have enough!

You might want to read It's Time to Align: The Most Powerful Self-Help Book Ever Written, available at balboapress.com/bookstore/book detail.aspx?bookid=SKU-000965931.

Years ago, America was highly revered in the hearts and minds of people from around the world. They would come to America from distant lands, overcoming many obstacles, to obtain their piece of the American Dream. Legend had it that the streets were paved with gold, as were the hearts of Americans.

Transitioning from a war-based to a peace-based economy that uplifts instead of destroys humanity is preferable and in the long term more beneficial for the corporations and the entire civilization.

We need to speak up and demand that politicians and corporations stop acting criminally and start acting sanely, contributing to the improvement of humankind and not its extinction. The choice is ours. Either we speak up and change things, or we silently acquiesce to the destruction of humankind and this beautiful planet.

It starts with us. Our actions and decisions of today determine the quality of our tomorrows. Pick a purpose for your life that does the most good for everyone, and go with it. There is an abundance of opportunity to improve the world; you can even invent your own!

Govern yourself and decide accordingly!

CHAPTER 17

Rebuilding a Broken World

The main thing that I learned about conspiracy theory, is that conspiracy theorists believe in a conspiracy because that is more comforting. The truth of the world is that it is actually chaotic. The truth is that it is not the Illuminati, or the Jewish Banking Conspiracy, or the Gray Alien Theory. The truth is far more frightening. Nobody is in control. The world is rudderless...

– ALAN MOORE

Bilderberg's modus operandi reinforced in his mind the complexity of the global hierarchy. He didn't know if Omega controlled the Bilderberg Group or vice versa, but the situation reminded him that no matter how much anyone thought they knew about the New World Order elite, there were always higher levels in the plethora of secret societies and shadow organizations that ruled the planet."

– JAMES MORCAN

Before aligning the body to the future, the mind has to straighten out from the impairment of religion.

– DAVID L. LLOYD

I believe that in this new world that we live in, we often have a responsibility, you know, to actually go beyond the "thou shalt nots"—that is, the not harming others—and say we can help others and we should be helping others.

– PETER SINGER

How wonderful it is that nobody need wait a single moment before starting to improve the world.

– ANNE FRANK

Never doubt that a small group of thoughtful, committed, citizens can change the world. Indeed, it is the only thing that ever has.

— MARGARET MEAD

Marcia Wilson was a good example of Omega's core strategy for creating a New World Order. It involved placing their people, or moles, in positions of power within the CIA, the NSA, the Pentagon, the White House and global organizations like the UN, the IMF and the World Bank. This enabled Omega to pull some of the strings of these organizations and to direct American, and world politics, to an extent.

— JAMES MORCAN

Throughout history it has been the inaction of those who could have acted; the indifference of those who should have known better; the silence of the voice of justice when it mattered most; that have made it possible for evil to triumph.

— HAILE SELASSIE

NOW MORE THAN EVER IN ITS HISTORY, the world is in need of improvement. Instead of having a majority of the world's so-called defense industries focused on products that murder, we can create international objectives of providing electricity and infrastructure to the many parts of the world as needed, starting with the United States. As any advanced civilization would, we can begin to focus our efforts on producing products that improve the habitat for humanity, as Jimmy Carter would say.

Imagine a world where the media broadcast real news, instead of the degraded stories it does today. Imagine media that broadcast the improvements created internationally that lift this deranged planet out of its bloody dark ages of war and into its light ages of peace and prosperity.

Detroit sits abandoned, crushed from unemployment and poverty. Perhaps retooling its factories to make high-speed rail systems connecting North and South America would be a worthwhile infrastructure project and the starting point to transform the world from a war-based to a peace-based economy.

Look at the vast improvements that we can implement throughout Africa and other third-world countries and economies. There, people are starving and living in the dark ages of the twenty-first century; literally hundreds of millions of Africans have no electricity. What would happen if the world focused on providing power for Africa?

There is a lot more money in the business of improving the planet than there is in destroying it; therefore, it only makes sense to initiate programs that improve the world and benefit humankind.

Let us examine our broken world in more detail, and then we can see where our efforts to rebuild the world will make more sense.

If we continue with a world economy based on war, we will eventually run out of resources needed to support life. If we continue with death-based military initiatives, we will inevitably reap what we sow, which is inevitably more death.

The world economies are going to need massive infrastructure projects to assist in transitioning from a war-based economy to a peace-based economy. At the same time, the world is going to need to develop a new monetary system that replaces today's overburdening and collapsing monetary system with a more stabilizing and sustainable one. America needs an effective monetary system that the bankers cannot covertly place under their control and use to enslave the people. History has demonstrated that such a monetary system uses real money, which is redeemable for metals of substance, and not the fiat currencies that are in use today.

The following is an excerpt from President Eisenhower's farewell address to the nation on January 17, 1961. Visit youtube.com/watch?v=CWiIYW_fBfY to watch the entire speech. It portends the dangers of an unchecked military-industrial complex resulting from a lack of oversight and the treasonous actions of corrupt and unethical politicians.

> *Until the latest of our world conflicts, the United States had no armaments industry. American makers of plowshares could, with time and as required, make swords as well. But now we can no longer risk emergency improvisation of national defense; we have been compelled to create a permanent armaments industry of vast proportions. Added to this, three and a half million men and women are directly engaged in the defense*

establishment. We annually spend on military security more than the net income of all United States corporations.

This conjunction of an immense military establishment and a large arms industry is new in the American experience. The total influence—economic, political, and even spiritual—is felt in every city, every State House, every office of the Federal Government. We recognize the imperative need for this development. Yet we must not fail to comprehend its grave implications. Our toil, resources and livelihood are all involved; so is the very structure of our society.

In the councils of government, we must guard against the acquisition of unwarranted influence, whether sought or unsought, by the military-industrial complex. The potential for the disastrous rise of misplaced power exists and will persist.

We must never let the weight of this combination endanger our liberties or democratic processes. We should take nothing for granted. Only an alert and knowledgeable citizenry can compel the proper meshing of the huge industrial and military machinery of defense with our peaceful methods and goals, so that security and liberty may prosper together.

Written by speechwriters Malcolm Moos and Ralph Williams, the importance of Eisenhower's sentiments, imparted in this foreboding speech, should not be underestimated or relegated as an unimportant piece of history. The above admonition, so eloquently spoken by President Eisenhower—a true and great patriot of our nation, has gone by the wayside and unheeded by most Americans, resulting in an often distracted and inactive citizenry that is perceived as too preoccupied to care.

The lack of citizens' inspection and monitoring of the government to perform at a higher and more ethical production level has allowed the special interests that now own the government to implement wars at their own whims.

The government should demand that defense contractors transition from solely manufacturing armaments to introducing and producing other non-military type products that benefit humankind. An example would include products and new technologies that remediate and improve the world's water and air supplies. There is no shortage of products that need to be created to repair the damage we have caused to the environment.

Imagine if the military-industrial complex dedicated itself to ridding the world of starvation. There are over two billion people starving right now. This is a horrible commentary and indictment against humankind, demonstrating our incredible lack of stewardship for the less fortunate and hungry.

Is this the best we can do for starving people in the twenty-first century, or as the incomparable Jack Nicholson (as Melvin Udall in As Good as It Gets) insightfully queried, "What if this is as good as it gets?" Come on people; we have to at least raise the bar a bit; we would be doing way better if only a billion people were starving at any given time. Imagine if none of us was starving; then imagine the magnitude of insanity and the improper priorities that lead to such abject conditions. Priorities change; only then our actions change.

If the destructive armament products that contribute to killing the world's population were eventually replaced with products that assisted in raising the character of the world's population, we would witness society's rehabilitation simply as a result of transitioning from a war-based economy to a peace-based economy. The decision and succeeding actions to change from a war-based to a peace-based economy would bring about more benefit to mankind than the world has seen in the previous ten thousand years.

Life-empowering projects of significant magnitude could replace the demand for the military-industrial complex's deadly products. The direction of the world would be changed from the destructive road humankind has been unquestionably marching down for the past thousands of years to a new road filled with optimism, opportunity, and an abundance of accord and consideration. This is how we will change the world.

Imagine a world in which all corporate intentions are aligned with the survival and enhancement of the human condition and the restoration of the environment to its pristine condition. If the governments of the world aligned their intentions with the well-being of humanity, as well as the preservation of the planet, imagine how much the world would change for the positive.

If all scientists currently working to develop the next best-killing device decided to transition their efforts toward peaceful products, the world would automatically improve because the people are introducing positivity into the environment. Before you know it, outer-space travel could become a real possibility. Should humanity fail to conquer space, the advancements realized during such an attempt would certainly revolutionize many fields of science here on Earth.

Most people would be glad to fly across the world in a matter of minutes, instead of days! This is the kind of research that the world should be undertaking. And when you think about it, where is the flying car and the jet pack?

Speed-of-light devices and undreamed-of technologies could impel us to greater heights of scientific understanding, thereby transitioning the world's employment toward the peaceful-industrial complex, which is designed to evolve and uplift the population.

We do not even have to go that far scientifically; we have all the science we need today to make the world a better place. We need players. We could bring a higher standard of living to the many different parts of the world, which do not have even the minimal necessities of food, water, and adequate shelter. We could develop agricultural and other economically enriching programs that would ultimately benefit billions of people and help them to overcome the abject poverty so unnecessarily endured around the world.

A small segment of society works not for the creation and uplifting of humankind, but rather, it works doggedly for the destruction and elimination of humankind. These twisted individuals, bent on global domination, believe that most of the Earth's human population would simply be better off dead than alive. They are doing their best to ensure the rapid demise of humankind and its virtual extinction.

We should not sit idle as the largest genocide in the history of this planet continues. We are witnessing the genocide of our species, a genocide that has been designed and engineered to systematically shorten the lifespan of the population and is aimed at reducing the species' capability to reproduce. By failing to defend the air we breathe, the water we drink, and the food we eat, we are signing the death warrants of every species and everyone we hold near and dear.

If we care to live, we must act—as a small sliver of the population is hell-bent on the destruction of humankind. This small group is facilitating a push to exterminate the human population in accordance with the dictates carved on the Georgia Guidestones located in Elbert County, Georgia.

These large stones, secretly erected under the darkness of night by an unknown group, ominously bespeak a genocidal message. According to the website radioliberty.com/stones.htm, the following is carved in eight different languages on these stones:

- Maintain humanity under 500,000,000 in perpetual balance with nature.
- Guide reproduction wisely—improving fitness and diversity.
- Unite humanity with a living new language.
- Rule passion—faith—tradition—and all things with tempered reason.
- Protect people and nations with fair laws and just courts.
- Let all nations rule internally resolving external disputes in a world court.
- Avoid petty laws and useless officials.
- Balance personal rights with social duties.
- Prize truth—beauty—love—seeking harmony with the infinite.
- Be not a cancer on the earth—Leave room for nature— Leave room for nature.

We must not sit by silently as the extinction of our species is treacherously engineered; we must take a stand to preserve our dignity and our right to live. For more information pertaining to the Georgia Guidestones, en.wikipedia.org/wiki/Georgia_Guidestones divulges the perverted intention of those intending to reduce the population from seven billion to a more controllable level of five hundred million. This heinous genocide against humankind is currently being implemented by organizations such as the United Nations, the World Health Organization, and the International Monetary Fund.

Ted Turner is one of the many advocates of population control. The method he would like to see implemented is to control the birth rate by limiting parents to one child per family, as they do in China. Still others seem to be a little more proactive in reducing the world's population by injecting chemical pollutants into our air, water, and food. Another way to achieve population elimination and population control is to introduce fabricated viruses, created under the direction of the World Health Organization, and have those viruses proliferate to the four corners of the world.

In 1947, the World Health Organization created the Zika virus, or ATCC VR-84, using genetically modified mosquitoes. The Zika virus and its international patents are reportedly owned by the Rockefeller Foundation and can be investigated at collective-evolution.com/2016/02/04/1947-rockefeller-patent-shows-origins-of-zika-virus-and-what-about-those-genetically-modified-mosquitoes/. This disease causes birth defects in infants and is considered by many as a strategic biological weapon used for population reduction.

Studies show that Zika may survive in the vaginal tract of infected women, and this was brought to light in an article by the Daily Mail at dailymail.co.uk/wires/afp/article-3758702/Zika-persist-vaginal-tract-study.html. More recently, it has been reported that Zika may be transmitted through tears and sweat. See washingtonpost.com/news/to-your-health/wp/2016/09/13/zika-virus-may-spread-through-bodily-fluids-study-finds/.

The above articles came to my attention after visiting DrudgeReport.com, which is owned by one of America's revered freedom fighters, Matt Drudge. DrudgeReport.com contains a vast number of well-organized and enlightening articles. I thank Drudge for his extraordinary humanitarian work and enlightening website. I highly recommend you avail yourself of the abundantly interesting information contained on his site and spend your free time there studying and educating yourself. That will certainly be time well spent.

Many other viruses are being spread using long chemical trails, or "chemtrails," which are released from the exhaust of jet airliners in criss-cross patterns in the sky. Poisonous fumes intentionally introduced to destroy the environment and the population, chemtrails can be fifty to one hundred miles long.

Chemtrails are different from the normal concentration trails, and if you look to the sky, you can tell which jets are releasing the different types of trails. The small exhaust trails, which disappear very quickly after being expelled from the jet's exhaust, are concentration trails. After being released from a jet's exhaust, chemtrails remain noticeable in the sky for several hours. Chemtrails remain for several days, losing their shape, wafting and cohering into clouds. Watch the documentary What in the World Are They Spraying? at youtube.com/watch?v=jf0khstYDLA.

Many of us can remember back in the 1970s and 1980s when the sky was actually blue and the exhaust from all jet airliners would quickly disappear, once the exhaust was expelled from the engines.

Today we can look to the sky and see crisscross patterns covering the sky, the result of having toxic chemtrails aggressively sprayed upon us from many jets' engines. On a clear day, you can often see a patchwork of toxicity being sprayed over America's sprawling cityscapes.

George W. Bush had a role in providing us with chemtrails, and you can read about this traitor of humanity and anything else you want to know about chemtrails at chemtrailsplanet.net/tag/george-w-bush. Thanks, George W.; with friends like you, who needs enemies?

Watch an incredibly informative short video, Chemtrail Cowboy, at google.com/#q=chem+trail+cowboy. For more in-depth information, check out the following: Chemtrails Confirmed by William Thomas (facebook.com/pages/Chemtrails-Confirmed-by-William-Thomas/244156038955106) and the Earth Island Journal (earthisland.org/journal/index.php/eij/article/stolen_skies_the_chemtrail_mystery), which expose the truth regarding chemtrails and the dangers to every American citizen who is being chemically sprayed and poisoned on a daily basis.

Health problems resulting from chemtrails include sterility, chronic fatigue, Alzheimer's, numerous respiratory and coronary diseases, and other serious neurological imbalances that are being manifest through numerous other symptoms. If you ever wonder why the health of the nation is deteriorating at such an alarming rate and the incidents of cancer and other unwanted health conditions are skyrocketing, just go outside and see all the chemicals that are regularly being sprayed in the skies and ingested by our lungs. Life seems hard enough without some lunatics poisoning the human population via chemtrails, but that is exactly what is happening; it is complete lunacy and designed madness.

There are movies, documentaries, and scientific papers explaining the deadly pollutants contained in chemtrails that are continually sprayed over the entire country. Still, we wonder why politicians are doing nothing to protect the citizens and the air from being sprayed on a daily basis with noxious toxins and carcinogenic chemicals that are extermi-

nating the human race. To the elite, the human population is as unwanted as fire ants. Just like fire ants, we are being sprayed with toxins
by inhuman exterminators who fly in the sky. Can the people and the
environment get any relief, any help from the politicians who are allowing all types of poison and death to befall us?

An arrogant, demented, and evil group has decided that the rest of
the world's population does not have the right to live. In cases where a
morally defunct group intentionally destroys the air, water, and food that
people consume, we have no option than to investigate, identify, and
prevent that group from creating further destruction. Since members of
that group are the enemies of the human race, they should be rounded
up by the military, tried in court for committing treasonous war crimes
against the general population, and held accountable as the court sees fit.

Some believe that those who commit such atrocious acts against humanity and the environment should be prosecuted and punished for
committing mass murder and genocide. We must outlaw the introduction of medical and toxic wastes into the skies, which ultimately fall
from the Earth's atmosphere and are ingested into the lungs of us all.
What is the appropriate punishment for those who participate in genocide by destroying nature, the ecosystem, and the means for the human
race to get what it needs to consume in order to survive?

Historically, the US government has poisoned, deceived, and enslaved
Americans. War has been declared against the American people by the
United States. If you do not believe it, check out the Trading with the
Enemy Act of 1917 at the following site: law.cornell.edu/uscode/html/
uscode50a/usc_sup_05_50_10_sq1_20_sq1.html.

War plainly contributes to reducing the world population in accordance with the tenets of the globalists' desires. Thus, let there be war!
What most Americans do not comprehend is that the government is
fighting a war against its own people, first and foremost, to protect the
illegal bankers' monopoly and the accompanying human enslavement
they covet.

Many hypothesize that the reason for war is to bring rebellious countries under the control of the banks. What do we really know about
Saddam Hussein, Osama bin Laden, or any country's leaders who were
originally America's friends, CIA operatives, and its allies before they
were assassinated or killed by the United States?

Bin Laden was once a US ally, a CIA asset working to protect Afghanistan's poppy fields against Russia. Bin Laden was instrumental in leading the Afghans against the Russians in the Soviet-Afghan War from December of 1979 to February of 1989. During this time, bin Laden was referred to as a "freedom fighter" by the Afghans, the United States, and the world at large.

During that time, bin Laden battled Russia with armaments procured from US weapons manufacturers. When all this fighting was occurring between Afghanistan and Russia, the bin Laden family in Saudi Arabia was busy doing construction projects and other huge deals with the Bush family. These families are very close; the Bushes and the bin Ladens even used to take family vacations together. This revelation turns the stomachs of many Americans.

Several American leaders are very familiar with the evil dictators who are US allies one day and US enemies the next. Most Americans only know what CNN, Fox News, or One American News Network (OANN) tells them. Many citizens have not considered what is happening internationally and simply repeat the stories broadcast on the nightly news, provided courtesy of the Associated Press and United Press International.

One day the US approved and appointed the dictator of Iraq, Saddam Hussein, to his position and power; then the next thing you know, all the news stations declared him to be the worst leader in the world, terrorizing and exterminating his own people. Suddenly, this justifies attacking and killing Saddam Hussein, along with millions of innocent Iraqis.

At the commencement of the first Gulf War in August of 1990, Operation Desert Storm, General Schwarzkopf announced simultaneously on the major news networks something to the effect that Saddam Hussein was an evil and despicable man who had to be stopped from invading Kuwait. George H. W. Bush was the most fierce and determined proponent of initiating the war, while he spun a yarn claiming that Hussein posed a threat to the US national security and had to be attacked.

This is so removed from the truth. It is refreshing to read some truth at the historical and popular sites of American freedom fighter and legendary talk show host Alex Jones of prisonplanet.com and infowars.com. One of the many fascinating articles, "Flash Back: How the CIA Found and Groomed Saddam," can be read at prisonplanet.com/how_the_cia_found_and_groomed_saddam.html.

Saddam Hussein was a CIA operative and groomed to follow the orders of the American administrations that controlled his overall actions in the Middle East.

Why and how did Hussein pose a threat to US national security? There is enough oil here in the United States to last two hundred more years with gasoline prices fixed at $1.50 a gallon by simply opening the currently capped wells located on the northern slope of Alaska. Learn more from oil insider Lindsey Williams in his video and informative book, The Energy Non-Crises (youtube.com/watch?v=CZFO1tq5OeI).

With cars that run on water and carburetors that can power vehicles to run at 300 mpg, why was it a matter of US national security when Iraq invaded Kuwait? It is quite enlightening to discover that Saddam Hussein was double-crossed by Bush, as provided by another great humanitarian and freedom fighter, Jeff Rense, at rense.com/general45/overth.htm.

It did not bother a majority of Americans when Kuwait was invaded, but it sure bothered US President Bush Sr. He and his family, with the support of the CIA, had extensive interests in the oil business, including holdings in Zapata Oil. An aptly named article, "The United States of Oil" (globalresearch.ca/articles/CAV111A.html) sheds light on the oil industry and how it controlled the Bush administrations.

As the infamous Dracula might say, "Black oil is never worth the spilling of red blood."

History reveals that many fabricated enemies of the United States have committed one grave sin in common: they print their own money in direct conflict to the interests of the International Monetary Fund. The way to free Americans from the clutches of the bankers is to provide an economy that operates using real money under the control of the United States of America.

Iraq is a perfect example of the methods used by the international bankers to garner control of a country's currency and steal all its wealth. Iraq's new constitution, drafted soon after it was conquered by the US military, ensures that the Bank for International Settlements' dictates and interests are respected and its fiat currency is exclusively used from that day forward in Iraq's economy. The Central Bank of Iraq previously operated directly as an independent and sovereign bank under the control of the independent and sovereign country of Iraq. Since being democratized at the end of American guns, Iraq's money is now under the control and dictates of the international private bankers who control the Bank for International Settlements.

After Hussein's demise and the reorganization of Iraq, the Central Bank of Iraq, now a member of the Bank of International Settlements, reports the following:

> *Following the deposition of Saddam Hussein in the 2003 invasion of Iraq, the Iraqi Governing Council and the Office for Reconstruction and Humanitarian Assistance began printing more Saddam dinar notes as a stopgap measure to maintain the money supply until new currency could be introduced.*

> *The Banking Law was issued September 19, 2003. The law brings Iraq's legal framework for banking in line with international standards, and seeks to promote confidence in the banking system by establishing a safe, sound, competitive and accessible banking system.*

> *Between October 15, 2003 and January 15, 2004, the Coalition Provisional Authority issued new Iraqi dinar coins and notes, with the notes printed using modern anti-forgery techniques, to 'create a single unified currency that is used throughout all of Iraq and will also make money more convenient to use in people's everyday lives. Old banknotes were exchanged for new at a one-to-one rate, except for the Swiss dinars, which were exchanged at a rate of 150 new dinars for one Swiss dinar.*

> *The Central Bank of Iraq was established as Iraq's independent central bank by the Central Bank of Iraq Law of March 6, 2004.*

> *The bank is in charge of: 1) Maintaining price stability 2) Implementing monetary policy (including exchange rate policies), 3) Managing Foreign Reserves, 4) Issuing and managing the currency, 5) Regulating the banking sector for promoting a competitive and stable financial system.*

Perhaps it was "independently established" according to the Central Bank Law of March 6, 2004, but the Central Bank of Iraq is listed as a member of the Bank of International Settlements and functions in accord with the tenets, guidelines, and regulations of the Bank of International Settlements (bis.org/country/iq.htm). From that time forward, Iraq has been using the fiat currency prescribed and approved by the Bank for International Settlements. It is obvious that the autonomy of the financial system of Iraq has been transferred to the international bankers by agreeing to such an acceptable fiat form of currency, backed by nothing and controllable by the foreign international bankers under the direction and authority of the Bank for International Settlements.

Iraq got itself the best democracy that money could buy and that the United States would militarily enforce. The United States picked politicians that would control and administrate Iraq in accordance with the dictates of the bankers. The bankers' interests and dictates are enforced by the mighty US military to ensure the protection of alleged US national security interests, which happens to be the same thing as the security interests of the Bank for International Settlements.

The Iraqi Constitution in Article 100 theoretically separates and distinguishes control of Iraq's monetary creation and supply from the Central Bank of Iraq to independent entities responsible for its monitoring and oversight. Below are those functions that occur within the bank. Since the Central Bank of Iraq is a member of the Bank for International Settlements, the BIS fundamentally regulates and dictates the Central Bank of Iraq's overall functionality.

ARTICLE 100

First: The Central Bank of Iraq, Board of Supreme Audit, Communication and Media Commission, and the Endowment Commissions are financially and administratively independent institutions. A law shall regulate the work of each of these institutions [emphasis added].

Second: The Central Bank of Iraq is responsible before the Council of Representatives. The Board of Supreme Audit and the Communication and Media Commission shall be attached to the Council of Representatives.

Third: The Endowment Commissions shall be attached to the Council of Ministers.

The above is an example of the typical regime change that is established by the bankers after sovereign countries such as Iraq, Syria, and Libya are destroyed by the US intervention and upheaval. Iraqis were given a new constitution for their country, and the articles of that document detail the particular arrangement of Iraq's monetary policy as being under the direction of the Bank for International Settlements through the Central Bank of Iraq. This arrangement is similar to the Federal Reserve System that controls the currency used by the United States. If the BIS or any exterior agency, other than the country itself, controls a country's currency or its debt, the resources of the country are going to be collateralized and taken for payment for that nation's debt and its exponentially accruing interest payments that become due to the bankers. The collateralized resources include virtually everything of recordable value above and below ground in the conquered land of the bankrupt country.

This is the process of and reason for regime change that occurs very often across the globe. Whenever a sovereign country fails to use the fiat currency that unjustly enriches the private banking families, the BIS will sic the US military on that country to enforce the bankers' wishes and implement their enslaving fiat currency.

Eventually the overly burdensome national debt, combined with astronomical accruements of interest, as is becoming the case within the US economy, will exceed a major portion of the production levels of the nation thereby creating an inability of its citizens to pay the interest of the enormous national debt, therein ensuring the nation's inevitable bankruptcy to the foreign private banking interests.

This is the method used by banks to essentially own all the country's assets upon bankruptcy. Once the bankruptcy occurs, the international private bankers take possession of the country's pledged assets such as the mineral-rich US national parks that were assigned by the United States to the international banking families. This fraudulent scheme has gone on long enough. Today the bankruptcy of insolvent nations should honestly be voided, contested, addressed, and relinquished to free the people from unbearable duress implemented under the corrupt and collapsing banking and taxation systems. Bankruptcy is the unavoidable legal repercussion of membership in the Bank for International Settlements. Almost every country in the world, and virtually every country under the BIS, is now bankrupt because of the astronomical debt owed to the international private bankers.

All bankrupt nations should be declared as such and dealt with accordingly, using amicable diplomacy and restructuring the bankrupt country's monetary system incorporating a real, unassailable dollar.

It is utmost in importance that nations reestablish themselves by retaking control of their original sovereignty and, true to their heritage, exercise once again their inherent national rights, responsibilities, and duties of controlling their nation's money. This especially includes the all-important rights pertaining to the creation, control, and production of a nation's money supply; for stability's sake, money should be backed by gold and silver—which are designed and destined to be impervious to attack by warped foreign private bankers.

The international bankers, who have abused the entire population and absconded with the wealth of the world, should be prosecuted under the International Criminal Court, the same justice system used to prosecute war criminals for horrific crimes against humanity. The bankers are responsible for the deaths of hundreds of millions, the intentional starvation of billions, and the financial suffering and enslavement of the rest of the population. They should pay the ultimate price. Society will be better off without psychopathic, felonious, and murderous criminals who are abusing and enslaving every one of us from birth till death.

To be economically stable, a country's money system should be designed to protect the consumers' interests over the interests of the banks. When the economy is rigged in favor of one particular class of people, as the present world economy is rigged in favor of the bankers, the interests of the consumers are ignored. Consumers in economies thusly designed inevitably forfeit all their wealth to the banking class through taxation and interest payments of the nation's debt.

To correct the collapsing US currency, the people, not the private bankers, must replace the private Federal Reserve System with a monetary system stabilized by substance and value, as succinctly directed in the US Constitution.

As a result of the massive and fraudulent debt owed by almost every country, any New World Order agenda that the bankers attempt to institute internationally will be initiated economically by bringing the nations of the world to their financial knees.

America is no longer a country where the people are represented by the politicians; rather, politicians represent the international bankers and corporate interests, senior to and regardless of the interests and well-being of the people.

When we examine war in a purely financial manner, it is easy to deduce that the corporations that provide armaments and war-consulting services to the US government are being very profitably subsidized. In essence, a corporate welfare relationship exists in which trillions of dollars of unnecessary orders for goods and services are being paid for by the government to a select group of government cronies and defense contractors. This is a method of reallocating the funds from the citizens of warring nations to the banking special interests and war profiteers. Government welfare for the rich affects the economy like a blood-starved vampire that sucks the life out of its victims in order to stay alive.

Without this military-industrial-complex welfare program for rich war-profiteers, the defense contracting corporations would either go bankrupt or retool and build peaceful products that this society desperately needs.

Enough is enough, and it is time we start a new world free from the tyranny created under such an unethical international banking system. We will be free if we decide and work to be. Only if we create an acceptable world that serves the people will humanity rise to greater heights and be able to solve the problems that have plagued humanity for millennia.

It's Our Responsibility

America's responsibilities are clearly laid out in the writings of the Founding Fathers. Where is it written in the founding documents that it is the responsibility of the United States to become involved in wars with countries overseas, like fighting ISIS in Iraq? It is not the responsibility of the United States to police and enforce its will, or the will of the international bankers, against a multitude of countries around the world.

On behalf of whose interest was the United States really fighting when it preemptively attacked Iraq, a country that committed no aggressive act of war against the United States or any other country? The interests of the banking globalists are being enforced when the politicians send American soldiers onto foreign soil. The banking globalists benefit from the United States deploying troops overseas to force weaker countries to accept the Bank of International Settlements' offer to exclusively use its fiat money; as they say, this is an offer that you can't refuse.

In Iraq, hundreds of thousands of troops have been subject to all kinds of harrowing experiences while protecting and enforcing the interests of the globalists. The press protects the bankers' interests and intent by denying the public the benefit of examination and inspection of the bankers' affairs, no matter the cost in human tragedy, often measured in bloodied bodies and broken dreams.

When will we, as members of humankind, smarten up and stop sending incredibly talented and wonderful soldiers to fight the bankers' wars? This is not an illuminated New World Order; these are the same old-world mercenaries and guns for hire that have been around for centuries.

The insanity and the fighting of war is not the appropriate manifestation of a healthy and sane human mind or civilization. Imagine if we visited a planet where one sector of the civilization was continually at war with another sector. We would consider it a crazy planet.

Imagine a body that is at continual war with itself. The prognosis for such a body would be grave. The same could be said about a world at constant war with itself. If we continue annihilating each other in this insane, warlike manner, how long do you think humanity can continue down this destructive path until we cross the point of no return and usher in the inevitable extinction of humankind?

A human mind or civilization properly functioning would provide solutions to global problems that result in the implementation of policies that incorporate and strive to achieve the best for humanity. How stupid is it that people with intelligence, far greater than that possessed by the beasts of the jungle, resort to violence resort to violence in order to settle their differences? When was the last time you saw two dogs negotiating for a bone?

We should diplomatically work for harmonious improvements in society by protecting and ensuring the liberties and freedoms of the people, including the fundamental right of all nations to self-govern.

It is time to say to the traitorous nincompoop politicians "enough is enough!" We have had it with war and the politicians that create it! It is time to indict those inbred bastards that aid and abet in the creation of wars and the murder of our soldiers for bloody profit.

Recently, the Islamic extremists are reportedly to blame for inciting the United States into war, and this excuse has become transparent, untenable, and unjustifiable when examined under the light of truth. We cannot continue to hold the population of the world hostage under the antiquated charade of war.

The gig is up, and the people have figured out that the reason for war is to protect the banking, defense, and other so-called national security interests. War is used to protect the international private bankers' fiat currencies and to seize control of a particular nation's assets.

If there is going to be positive change made in this world, it is going to be made by the people and not the politicians. The politicians are the ones that created the rigged system that we call America. The people are up against a well-organized and powerful enemy.

It is a fallacy to conclude that the military-industrial complex is comprised of philanthropic institutions exercising charitable activities endeavoring to benefit humankind in all its facets. In actuality, the military-industrial complex is comprised of organizations whose chief mission is the extermination of the human race for profit.

Then there are the war-mongering defense organizations and corporations that have mission statements that might read something like, "Corporately we shall create turmoil utilizing the various governmental factions throughout the world, which we control through financial pressures and rewards. This allows for the implementation, deployment, and eventual disposal of destructive weaponry designed to extinguish life, while providing maximum profit for our government-funded, war-profiteering manufacturers, brokers, and agents. Furthermore, the population is to be deceived into believing that the United States is accomplishing and providing beneficial improvements for the countries that are being destroyed under the pretense of spreading democracy. And above all, we must never divulge our little secret that all wars are fought to provide profits to the international bankers who finance the opposing nations and their opposing military-industrial complexes."

There is likely to be an escalation in the frequency of government-created terrorist actions against the people in order that more of the peoples' liberties and freedoms can be bartered in exchange for so-called security. There is no security in America, other than that which we provide for ourselves. An armed citizenry is a secure citizenry.

Immediately after the attacks on 9/11, both present and former politicians, including Gary Hart and Dan Quayle, spoke of limiting citizens' rights in exchange for security. Both men happen to be members of the Council of Foreign Relations and the Trilateral Commission. Both are philosophically globalist and have the elimination of individual nations' sovereignty and the enslavement of its citizens as top priorities. These traitors are part of the old guard and have to go.

The intent of the above-mentioned treasonous groups is not to benefit the masses but to eliminate them, so that the elite can rule the world. This sounds like something one would hear in elementary schoolyards or see in black-and-white movies. Instead, those who control the banking industry, and subsequently the entirety of industry, are responsible for the worldwide psychosis we find ourselves living within today.

If achieved—although never accomplished in history—global domination would be the result of one of two methods. The first would be a gradual erosion of the rights and liberties of citizens until they awake one day as unsuspecting slaves with no recourse from an engrained and over-dominating system of enslavement. Elitists are attempting to implement this method in the United States today by passing legislation that strips citizens of their rights as free people and removes the people's rights of self-determinism by instituting oppressive governmental regulations that adversely affect virtually every aspect of the American way of life. Google "NDAA conspiracy" and see for yourself.

The second method would be one of military force should the first course of action take too long or meet with too much resistance. Many people feel that a government would never use military force against its own citizens. This fallacy is laid to rest once one looks at the many dictators and fascists throughout history who have employed such very means against their constituents. Stalin and his famous psychopathic quote come to mind, "Death is the solution to all problems. No man—no problem."

Many military men and women are more aware of these oppressive facts than most Americans who have never served in the armed forces. As the globalists attempt to extend their domination, it will be interesting to see if military personnel will obey an illegal order that harms the American people. Others wonder if the US military will go as far as to allow foreign troops to round up, control, and detain Americans. Most believe the US military will always hold steadfast with its loyalty to protect American lives!

Many current and former military and police personnel are involving themselves with organizations such as Oath Keepers (oathkeepers.org), which organizes well-intentioned Americans who have taken an oath to uphold the US Constitution. Oath Keepers is a phenomenal and caring organization that all Americans can be proud of and should support. The Oath Keepers are speaking up and breaking the silence of oppression by pledging not to enforce ten illegal orders against the American people. They are as follows:

1. We will NOT obey any order to disarm the American people.

2. We will NOT obey any order to conduct warrantless searches of the American people, their homes, vehicles, papers or effects—such as warrantless house-to-house searches for weapons or persons.

3. We will NOT obey any order to detain American citizens as "unlawful enemy combatants" or to subject them to trial by military tribunal.

4. We will NOT obey orders to impose martial law or a "state of emergency" on a state, or to enter with force into a state, without the express consent and invitation of that state's legislature and governor.

5. We will NOT obey orders to invade and subjugate any state that asserts its sovereignty and declares the national government to be in violation of the compact by which that state entered the Union.

6. We will NOT obey any order to blockade American cities, thus turning them into giant concentration camps.

7. We will NOT obey any order to force American citizenry into any form of detention camps under any pretext.

8. We will NOT obey orders to assist or support the use of any foreign troops on US soil against the American people to "keep the peace" or to "maintain control" during any emergency, or under any other pretext. We will consider such use of foreign troops against our people to be an invasion and an act of war.

9. We will NOT obey any orders to confiscate the property of the American people, including food and other essential supplies, under any emergency pretext whatsoever.

10. We will NOT obey orders which infringe on the right of the people to free speech, to peaceably assemble, and to petition their government for a redress of grievances.

I recommend that we all join and support Oath Keepers, and please spread the word.

The globalists' plan of world domination has a chance to be achieved only by pinning the police and military against the people. It is better to have the police and the military working to enforce the rights of the people, rather than enforce the dictates of a few twisted and evil people who are hell-bent on global destruction and domination.

Will we stand and protect our God-given rights, or will our posterity be doomed for eternity because we pathetically kneel like broken slaves? Our actions are the keys to the next generation's worldly inheritance; our actions will decide if our progeny's shackles will be forever locked in oppression and misery or if they will be born free, as man and woman are destined to be.

We can no longer remain silent. Our duty to all humanity necessitates our immediate action. To ensure a healthy future, we need to peacefully resist government oppression and to stand and be heard as a people that strive for righteousness and liberation.

Silence and ignorance are more than enough to cause citizens of a nation to lose all their rights and freedoms. This has happened countless times throughout history. When good people silently condone the murderous actions of their government, it is not long until those murderous actions are aimed internally at the general populace or a segment of that nation's populace.

It is up to the people and the people alone to design and rebuild our broken world, one wherein humankind is free to aspire to higher heights and sunnier days. Our responsibility as a member of the civilized world is to ensure at all costs and to unequivocally demand that the rights and dignity of all people are staunchly protected.

Whether we like it or not, the public shapes the type of world order we live in, approving or protesting its quality and character. If we do nothing and accept the New World Order that is being offered, we will be condemned to misery and death as the Earth hurls towards a hell so ferocious that its very concept exceeds the limits of imagination.

If we stand shoulder to shoulder and perform our innate human duties as caretakers of this planet and society and demand to have a planet where the survival of humankind is utmost in the minds of the people and unwaveringly protected by world leaders, we as an entire species might just avoid obliteration this time around. It is really up to us to create our own New World Order; we can call it the People's World Order and establish it in a manner that contributes and enhances human existence while continually working towards creating heaven on Earth.

We live in an ongoing battle between good and evil that is occurring every moment on this planet. The people can no longer sit on the sidelines and place bets upon which side will win. It is time we get into the game and pick a side. The good or light side is playing for life and creation, while the bad or dark side is playing for death and destruction.

We can tell the intentions of a person or a group's actions based on a simple test: is the action performed to empower or disempower another person or group? Are actions designed to enable or disable, to enhance or destroy, to uplift or squash? As far as individuals and societies are concerned, the former categories above give reign to heaven, and the latter can go to hell. All actions regarding war are in the latter category of evil-based intentions and therefore against the best interest of the human race. As a minimal standard, governments should be restricted to operating only in the first category of actions that empower rather than disempower the people.

This is also how we can and should choose our friends; our friends empower and contribute to our survival and our lives, as we do theirs. People that do not have your best interest in mind are far from friends.

Actions committed by government officials are actually treasonous in nature if they disempower the people. Actions that disempower the people lead to the enslavement of the people. Once the enforcement of such debilitating evil-based actions are levied against the will of the people, a negative karmic reaction is likely to occur. Actions of disempowerment will lead to the degradation and eventual destruction of the people, and that is something that we should never silently accept.

To build the People's World Order, we must demand and guarantee all actions performed by any government are actions designed to empower the people, all people. This will inevitably lead to a saner society if and only if we demand and receive such uplifting actions and policies from our leaders.

The world becomes an accumulation, or more exactly an agglomeration, of the acts that we all commit individually and collectively. These acts affect us and our fellow human beings and ultimately form the content and quality of society. If our actions are destructive, humanity will decay into the lowest form of degradation and enslavement conceivable. Humanity will be made to endure a life of misery, a life foreign to the free. If our actions are empowering to everyone, Earth will heal itself, and humanity will propel to new heights. Society will blossom; peace and love will ubiquitously reign.

The psychosis that we are experiencing on an international level is a result of committing acts that disempower large segments of the population. A natural negative phenomenon or karmic reaction will occur and manifest itself once a disempowering action is committed against another person or group. By compounding our crimes and producing a majority of disempowering actions against others, the population will inevitably decline into a state of hell, not unlike what we are currently experiencing, only with accelerating frequency and devastation.

As a species, our only chance at survival is to do the opposite of what the dark operators who are destroying civilization are doing; we should seek the light.

By creating the People's World Order, which is based on empowering actions, the world will be able to grow and reach new heights, where the lamb can lie down with the lion and the Muslim can dance with the Jew.

Otherwise, we will have a world where the superior ruling class will demand subservience and obeisance from all the people.

The choice is always ours. Whether we like it or not, we will get either a suppressive New World Order or an empowering People's World Order. Our inaction and negative actions will bring a living hell for humankind; only our positive actions will usher in a living heaven.

We all have a chance, but more than that, we have an innate responsibility to make this world a better place. Let us create a better world where men and women have rights to live and can evolve to a higher plane of existence. We need to create a world where love replaces hatred, kindness vanquishes violence, and all people are able to enjoy fully our God-given freedom and liberties.

We are up against an unethical and powerful group that owns all the money, as well as all the militaries of the world. Still we must stand, for true strength and power reside in the righteous. The oppressors of humanity have been organizing and plotting their treachery for centuries. Still we must stand; our steadfast defiance will mightily and rapidly conquer the wicked and vile.

In order to preserve and improve society as we know it, we need to choose life and empowerment. Let us make a People's World Order that is befitting the children of God; the world disorder that we currently experience has been created by Satan and his helpers. Fundamentally, we are all responsible for the condition of this planet and society at large. It does not help to blame another for our actions or the lack of them.

We determine what road this world will travel into the future. Help preserve humanity from those Satanists who choose to assist in the obliteration of the species.

Let time record that we accepted the challenge to improve the world we inherited. The measure and quality of a generation is the condition of the world it leaves behind for its younglings. For the unborn billions to come, let us leave a beautiful and heavenly world and not a hellish nightmare.

With your help, we can make a difference. Speak up and be heard. The world is counting on us, especially on you. Make us proud!

CHAPTER 18

Religious Philosophies Exposed

Evil is powerless if the good are unafraid.

> – RONALD REAGAN

Our race is the Master Race. We are divine gods on this planet. We are as different from the inferior races as they are from insects. In fact, compared to our race, other races are beasts and animals, cattle at best. Other races are considered as human excrement. Our destiny is to rule over the inferior races. Our earthly kingdom will be ruled by our leader with a rod of iron. The masses will lick our feet and serve us as our slaves.

> – MENACHEM BEGIN

America needs to understand Islam because this is the one religion that erases from its society the race problem. Throughout my travels in the Muslim world, I have met, talked to, even eaten with people who in America would have been considered 'white' but the 'white' attitude had been removed from their minds by the religion of Islam.

> – MALCOLM X

We stand today at a unique and extraordinary moment. The crisis in the Persian Gulf, as grave as it is, also offers a rare opportunity to move toward an historic period of cooperation. Out of these troubled times, our fifth objective—a new world order—can emerge: a new era—freer from the threat of terror, stronger in the pursuit of justice, and more secure in the quest for peace.

An era in which the nations of the world, East and West, North and South, can prosper and live in harmony. A hundred gener-

ations have searched for this elusive path to peace, while a thousand wars raged across the span of human endeavor. Today that new world is struggling to be born, a world quite different from the one we've known. A world where the rule of law supplants the rule of the jungle. A world in which nations recognize the shared responsibility for freedom and justice. A world where the strong respect the rights of the weak. This is the vision that I shared with President Gorbachev in Helsinki. He and other leaders from Europe, the Gulf, and around the world understand that how we manage this crisis today could shape the future for generations to come.

– GEORGE H. W. BUSH

[It is] certain that we stand in the defining hour. Half way around the world we are engaged in a great struggle in the skies and on the seas and sands. We know why we're there. We are Americans; part of something larger than ourselves. For two centuries we've done the hard work of freedom and tonight we lead the world in facing down a threat to decency and humanity. What is at stake is more than one small country. It is a big idea a new world order, where diverse nations, are drawn together in common cause, to achieve the universal aspirations of mankind. Peace and security, freedom and the rule of law, such is a world worthy of our struggle and worthy of our children's future.

– GEORGE H. W. BUSH

We have before us the opportunity to forge for ourselves and for future generations a new world order. A world where the rule of law, not the law of the jungle, governs the conduct of nations. When we are successful, and we will be, we have a real chance at this new world order. An order in which a creditable United Nations, can use its "peace keeping" role to fulfill the promise and vision of the U.N.'s founders.

– GEORGE H. W. BUSH

If the American people were to ever find out what we have done, they would chase us down the street and lynch us.
— GEORGE H. W. BUSH

The invisible Money Power is working to control and enslave mankind. It financed Communism, Fascism, Marxism, Zionism, Socialism. All of these are directed to making the United States a member of a World Government.
— AMERICAN MERCURY MAGAZINE

The drive of the Rockefellers and their allies is to create a one world government, combining super-capitalism and Communism under the same tent, all under their control. . . . Do I mean conspiracy? Yes I do. I am convinced there is such a plot, international in scope, generations old in planning, and incredibly evil in intent.
— LAWRENCE PATTON MCDONALD

Today America would be outraged if U.N. troops entered Los Angeles to restore order; tomorrow they will be grateful! This is especially true if they were told that there were an outside threat from beyond, whether real or promulgated, that threatened our very existence. It is then that all people of the world will plead to deliver them from this evil. The one thing every man fears is the unknown. When presented with this scenario, individual rights will be willingly relinquished for the guarantee of their well-being granted to them by the World Government.
— HENRY KISSINGER

OF PARTICULAR INTEREST in the above quotations are George H. W. Bush's State of the Union addresses foretelling of the coming New World Order. Watching him speak just might make the hair on the back of your neck stand up. It is rather peculiar that, of all days available in a calendar year, Bush Sr. gave two State of the Union speeches—one on September 11, 1990, and the other on September 11, 1991. Was this indicative of his knowing the significance of that date years before the horrific events occurred on September 11, 2001? Were Bush's September 11 State of the Union speeches just coincidences, or were they an obvious foretelling of the diabolic events to come? The odds of delivering two ominous State of the Union addresses on September 11, 1990 and 1991, are over one in a billion. When you calculate the other coincidental factors related to September 11, the coincidental odds well exceed one in a trillion.

It is also rather strange that the Pentagon's construction began on September 11, 1941. Is this simply another coincidence, or is there more to this date than meets the eye?

Leading numerologists and black magic occultists have theories that can be found all over the Internet, but these theories are many times censored and disabled by YouTube and Google.

Were the bankers and warmongers planning the World Trade Center disaster years and years in advance? Of course they were! The elite conduct their planning in spans of centuries, not years.

Many of us have heard of the New World Order, but what really is it? According to Menachem Begin, the Zionists should be ruling the world with an iron rod and the slaves should be licking the leaders' feet. Begin's perverted viewpoint is a glimpse into the vast, demented, and bigoted religious and racial philosophies of rabid hatred and contempt, which inflict those who aim to dominate humankind. Imagine a world leader that considers most of the world's population to be on par with human excrement as Begin so boldly decreed. Was this dude a sick puppy or what?

Begin's quote is not indicative of all Jewish people's opinions of their fellow man, but Begin's opinion is common among what is called radical Zionists, who believe the human race, except themselves, is beneath the level of animals. Their philosophies are beyond insane! Their attitudes plainly display a portion of the philosophical insanity that we are dealing with in the Middle East.

The globalists that plan to control the population of the world through the creation of their New World Order are interested in further controlling the lives of those subjected to such a global system of domination. If the implementers of the new world government have their way, health, finances, spirituality, education, and virtually every aspect of our lives will be monitored and controlled. Our lives already are highly monitored and controlled. Thanks to Edward Snowden—who many consider an American hero—we can read in the government's own words about the CIA's abundantly abusive intrusion of and over-reaching surveillance into our lives.

Snowden deserves an unconditional pardon by the president and to be returned to the United States as a hero. He has suffered more than enough for blowing the whistle on a corrupt and overreaching American government.

There is no doubt that there needs to be changes made in the world, changes that incorporate the improvement of social and moral values that contribute to the improvement of the domestic and international state of affairs, which limit the military interaction of the United States with other nations. These changes ought to provide a safer environment that contributes to the uplifting of humanity. Let us not accept or tolerate changes that subjugate the population under an abusive and corrupt ruling class.

Today, as World War III continues under the guise of a religious war, the bankers and their intelligence agents are pitting Muslims against Christians and orchestrating the violence and terrorist acts we see around the globe. George W. Bush started World War III shortly after September 11, 2001, taking steps to implement the New World Order his father discussed in those two speeches previously mentioned.

In case you have not noticed, currently, we are living in a New World Order and fighting our third world war. This is it folks; the new world is already here; it actually arrives every fraction of every second. The world's rulers are providing us constant and endless war in which Christians are killing Muslims and Muslims are killing Christians.

Radical as each group is, there are opposing fundamental philosophies possessed by each side of the conflict, which preceded all the terroristic killings and the truckloads of bad will harbored by both sides.

Besides the obvious fundamental philosophical differences possessed by the extremists on both sides of the fighting, there are many more similarities than there are differences between the battling Middle Eastern and American cultures. These cultures are comprised of billions of not-so crazy people who are looking for peaceful solutions to the terror that is happening more and more often, both here in the United States and around the world.

A large majority of all cultures are comprised of good-hearted human beings, doing their best to get through the day. Most people know deep in their hearts that the human race is not as evil as what is portrayed on the nightly news and that we as a species should be able to sanely address the international problems we all face as a united force for good.

Only a small group, which continually orchestrates the terroristic actions on both sides, is causing the destruction that we are seeing on a more frequent basis. Watch Muslim Invaders !!! The Shocking Truth. UK, Germany, Sweden, America, Denmark etc. at youtube.com/watch? v=ido8bW5bAes.

With no other choice, the remaining force of good people is left to correct the situation caused by the bankers and must unite to responsibly harness the unstoppable force for good possessed by humanity. Today, the force for good is the silent majority, a super-large but nevertheless silent majority, lacking only organization and voice to achieve our goals of a peaceful planet, free from war and all the insanity associated with such a banal affront to mankind.

The Holy Scriptures of both Middle Eastern Muslims and US Christians—the Quran and the Bible, respectively—forbid the existence of the world's current private international banking monopoly, in which loans are made with an associated interest payment. Christianity forbids usury, as portrayed in the temple when Jesus Christ angrily overturned the tables of the moneychangers and threw them out on their asses.

Some often forgotten and overlooked verses of the Bible explain Christianity's beliefs regarding the loaning of money for interest. Refraining from such loans is seldom practiced in Judeo-Christian culture, and it is no wonder most Americans find themselves in terrible financial condition.

America has turned its back on God and on its people. America has become a country with a fiat monetary system, built in accordance with the intent of Satan and aiming to solidify the enslavement of man. For the benefit of the country and the protection of man's freedom, a return to the intelligent use of real money is in order.

Perhaps if the United States returns to its heavenly intent, treats others as they would like to be treated, and functions as an ambassador of God instead of Satan, then the lion shall have the opportunity to lie down with the lamb. The Muslims and the Christians will finally unite and bring to light the underlying party, which remains hidden behind the scenes and is responsible for the continuation of terror and warfare throughout the world.

In the meantime, the following are taken from the Holy Bible, used with the permission of God and the nice folks from the King James Bible. The Bible is an incredible gift, one with which many of us might enjoy reacquainting ourselves. Its eternal tenets and teachings may commensurately provide assistance to our personal, spiritual, and national enlightenment and resurrection, assisting and directing us to help and empower our fellow man.

Exodus 22:25 (King James Version): If thou lend money to any of my people that is poor by thee, thou shalt not be to him as an usurer, neither shalt thou lay upon him usury.

Deuteronomy 23: 19–20 (KJV) Thou shalt not lend upon usury to thy brother; usury of money, usury of victuals, usury of any thing that is lent upon usury: Unto a stranger thou mayest lend upon usury; but unto thy brother thou shalt not lend upon usury: that the LORD thy God may bless thee in all that thou settest thine hand to in the land whither thou goest to possess it.

Ezekiel 18:13 (KJV): Hath given forth upon usury, and hath taken increase: shall he then live? He shall not live: he hath done all these abominations; he shall surely die; his blood shall be upon him.

Leviticus 25:35–37 (KJV): And if thy brother be waxen poor, and fallen in decay with thee; then thou shalt relieve him: yea, though he be a stranger, or a sojourner; that he may live with thee. Take thou no usury of him, or increase: but fear thy God; that thy brother may live with thee. Thou shalt not give him thy money upon usury, not lend him thy victuals for increase.

Ezekiel 22:12 (KJV): In thee have they taken gifts to shed blood; thou hast taken usury and increase, and thou hast greedily gained of thy neighbors by extortion, and hast forgotten me, saith the Lord God.

Ezekiel 18:8 (KJV): He that hath not given forth upon usury, neither hath taken any increase, that hath withdrawn his hand from iniquity, hath executed true judgment between man and man,

Luke 6:35 (KJV): But love ye your enemies, and do good, and lend, hoping for nothing again; and your reward shall be great, and ye shall be the children of the Highest: for he is kind unto the unthankful and **to** the evil.

Proverbs 22:7 (KJV): The rich ruleth over the poor, and the borrower is servant to the lender.

Ezekiel 18:17 (KJV): **That** hath taken off his hand from the poor, **that** hath not received usury nor increase, hath executed my judgments, hath walked in my statutes; he shall not die for the iniquity of his father, he shall surely live.

Proverbs 28:8 (KJV): He that by usury and unjust gain increaseth his substance, he shall gather it for him that will pity the poor.

Psalms 15:5 (KJV): **He that** putteth not out his money to usury, nor taketh reward against the innocent. He that doeth these **things** shall never be moved.

Psalms 112:5–6 (KJV): A good man sheweth favour, and lendeth: he will guide his affairs with discretion. Surely he shall not be moved for ever: the righteous shall be in everlasting remembrance.

Nehemiah 5:1–13 (KJV): And there was a great cry of the people and of their wives against their brethren the Jews. For there were that said, We, our sons, and our daughters, many: therefore we take up corn for them, that we may eat, and live. Some also there were that said, We have mortgaged our lands, vineyards, and houses, that we might buy corn, because of the dearth. There were also that said, We have borrowed money for the king's tribute, and that upon our lands and vineyards. Yet now our flesh is as the flesh of our brethren, our children as their children: and, lo, we bring into bondage our sons and our daughters to be servants, and some of our daughters are brought unto bondage already: neither is it in our power to redeem them; for other men have our lands and vineyards. And I was very angry when I heard their cry and these words. Then I consulted with myself, and I rebuked the nobles, and the rulers, and said unto them, Ye exact usury, every one of his brother. And I set a great assembly against them. And I said unto them, We after our ability have redeemed our brethren the Jews, which were sold unto the heathen; and will ye even sell your brethren? or shall they be sold unto us? Then held they their peace, and found nothing to answer. Also I said, It is not good that ye do: ought ye not to walk in the fear of our God because of the reproach of the heathen our enemies? I likewise, and my brethren, and my servants, might exact of them money and corn: I pray you, let us leave off this usury. Restore, I pray you, to them, even this day, their lands, their vineyards, their olive yards, and their houses, also the hundredth part of the money, and of the corn, the wine, and the oil, that ye exact of them. Then said they, We will restore them, and will require nothing of them; so will we do as thou sayest. Then I called the priests, and took an oath of them, that they should do according to this promise. Also I shook my lap, and said, So God shake out every man from his house, and from his labour, that performeth not this promise, even thus be he shaken out, and emptied. And all the congregation said, Amen, and praised the LORD. And the people did according to this promise.

Jeremiah 15:10 (KJV): Woe is me, my mother, that thou hast borne me a man of strife and a man of contention to the whole earth! I have neither lent on usury, nor men have lent to me on usury; **yet** every one of them doth curse me.

Luke 11:46 (KJV): And he said, Woe unto you also, **ye** lawyers! for ye lade men with burdens grievous to be borne, and ye yourselves touch not the burdens with one of your fingers. Woe unto you!

Psalms 15:1–5 (KJV): A Psalm of David. LORD, who shall abide in thy tabernacle? who shall dwell in thy holy hill? He that walketh uprightly, and worketh righteousness, and speaketh the truth in his heart. He that backbiteth not with his tongue, nor doeth evil to his neighbour, nor taketh up a reproach against his neighbour. In whose eyes a vile person is contemned; but he honoureth them that fear the LORD. He that sweareth to *his own* hurt, and changeth not. *He that* putteth not out his money to usury, nor taketh reward against the innocent. He that doeth these *things* shall never be moved.

Luke 6:38 (KJV): Give, and it shall be given unto you; good measure, pressed down, and shaken together, and running over, shall men give into your bosom. For with the same measure that ye mete withal it shall be measured to you again.

Isaiah 1:2–5 (KJV): Hear, O heavens, and give ear, O earth: for the LORD hath spoken, I have nourished and brought up children, and they have rebelled against me. The ox knoweth his owner, and the ass his master's crib: **but** Israel doth not know, my people doth not consider. Ah sinful nation, a people laden with iniquity, a seed of evildoers, children that are corrupters: they have forsaken the LORD, they have provoked the Holy One of Israel unto anger, they are gone away backward. Why should ye be stricken any more? ye will revolt more and more: the whole head is sick, and the whole heart faint.

Great thanks again to the folks at KingJamesBibleOnline.org for its permission to include the above biblical passages.

This is not an attempt to Bible thump, but the United States is supposed to be a nation founded upon Christian values. Yet the United States ignores and trespasses upon the rest of humankind by violating Holy Scripture and supporting planetary usury imposed by the participation and enforcement of the bankers' enslaving policies.

President Reagan weighed in regarding the nation, its philosophical guiding principles, and its relationship to a higher deity:

> *America needs God more than God needs America. If we ever forget that we are One Nation Under God, then we will be a Nation gone under. . . . Without God, there is no virtue, because there's no prompting of the conscience. Without God, we are mired in the material, that flat world tells us only what the senses perceive. Without God, there is a coarsening of the society. And without God, democracy will not and cannot long endure. If we ever forget that we're one nation under God, then we will be a nation gone under.*

President Reagan went so far as to declare the importance of God's words and their effect on the United States. On February 3, 1983, Reagan crafted Proclamation 5018, The Year of the Bible, 1983 (presidency.ucsb.edu/ws/?pid=40728). It reads as follows:

> *Of the many influences that have shaped the United States of America into a distinctive Nation and people, none may be said to be more fundamental and enduring than the Bible.*
>
> *Deep religious beliefs stemming from the Old and New Testaments of the Bible inspired many of the early settlers of our country, providing them with the strength, character, convictions, and faith necessary to withstand great hardship and danger in the frontier of a new and rugged land. These shared beliefs helped forge a sense of common purpose among the widely dispersed colonies—a sense of community which laid the foundation for the spirit of nationhood that was to develop in later decades.*

The Bible and its teachings helped form the basis for the Founding Fathers' abiding belief in the inalienable rights of the individual, rights which they found implicit in the Bible's teachings of the inherent worth and dignity of each individual. This same sense of man patterned the convictions of those who framed the English system of law, inherited by our own Nation, as well as the ideals set forth in the Declaration of Independence and the US Constitution.

For centuries the Bible's emphasis on compassion and love for our neighbor has inspired institutional and governmental expressions of benevolent outreach such as private charity, the establishment of schools and hospitals, and the abolition of slavery.

Many of our greatest national leaders-among them Presidents Washington, Jackson, Lincoln, and Wilson—have recognized the influence of the Bible on our country's development. The plainspoken Andrew Jackson referred to the Bible as no less than "the rock on which our Republic rests." Today our beloved America and indeed, the world, is facing a decade of enormous challenge. As a people, we may well be tested as we have seldom, if ever, been tested before. We will need resources of spirit even more than resources of technology, education, and armaments. There could be no more fitting moment than now to reflect with gratitude, humility, and urgency upon the wisdom revealed to us in the writing that Abraham Lincoln called "the best gift God has ever given to man ... But for it we could not know right from wrong."

The Congress of the United States, in recognition of the unique contributions of the Bible, in shaping the history and character of this Nation and so many of its citizens, has by Senate Joint Resolution 165 authorized and requested the President to designate the year 1983 as the 'Year of the Bible.'

Now, Therefore, I, Ronald Reagan, President of the United States of America, in recognition of the contributions and influ-

ence of the Bible on our Republic and our people, do hereby proclaim 1983 the Year of the Bible in the United States. I encourage all citizens, each in his or her own way, to reexamine and rediscover its priceless and timeless message.

In Witness Whereof, I have hereunto set my hand this third day of February, in the year of our Lord nineteen hundred and eighty-three, and of the Independence of the United States of America the two hundred and seventh.

That day the above proclamation was officially signed by President Reagan.

Reagan's proclamation is reflective of the original intent of the Founding Fathers and their adherence to protecting the people's freedoms at the formation of a nation that would make the Creator proud.

Look at the barbarity that the United States incites through foreign affairs. Examining one's heart, one finds it intolerable to continue with a New World Order that permits war and government-sanctioned mass murder and politicide. Reversing the negative energy that the United States is exporting is the first change that needs to occur in America's foreign policy in order that we as a nation can start walking down the road to moral recovery.

The New World Order that we are currently living under is a terrible world order. Those responsible need to be rounded up and incarcerated for committing treason against the people of the world at large. It is unfathomable that a world order exists where blowing up the World Trade Center, preemptively attacking foreign nations, and creating a world filled with violence and terrorism is acceptable to anyone, except to the vilest segment of society.

The design of the current New World Order is to enslave the people through taxation and financial oppression. For centuries, the oppression and plight humankind has experienced is simply more of the same—a small minority of rich, inbred heathens steals from the rest of society.

The current New World Order religiously operates a corrupt central banking system in order to subjugate the people of all sovereign nations and financially cripple the ability of those nations to direct and guide their own destiny. The free will of a vast number of the world's nations has been replaced by the dictates of the international bankers.

The New World Order obviously already exists—since the planet already has a corrupt world banking system that negates the sovereignty and financial control of individual countries and replaces those nations' sovereign control with US appointed democracies and despotic dictatorships in accordance with the agenda of the Bank for International Settlements.

National independent banking systems are simply camouflaged under the disguise of what appears to be different nations' independent monetary systems, when in fact the world's monetary systems are virtually all controlled by the Bank for International Settlements or the World Bank, take your pick as they are virtually one and the same.

We Americans had a sinister New World Order thrust upon us years ago while we were sleeping and not being diligent in the slightest way. If we want our freedom, we need to demand it and take it back now! We, as a country, need to work hard to be successful in reclaiming our collective future; the enemy never sleeps.

Every terrorist action that the media reports and broadcasts is done to further the agenda of those who are pulling the monetary strings on this planet. A majority of the news, whether in newspapers, on the radio, or on television, is designed to strategically deprive the rights of the people and strengthen the power and criminal stranglehold that the rulers have around the throats of the people. The media's job is nothing more than a brainwashing presentation of the type of world that is to come, the one that people should start agreeing with completely. The design of the media is to win and control the minds of the masses in order that there will be no disagreement or resistance to the enslavement of humanity and the further ushering in of the elite's New World Order.

The psychological operations and tools used by the media are more advanced than one would imagine. After all, war is not for the faint of heart; this is a war for the minds and souls of the public and the elite's tyrannical control of the future.

The world is in a constant battle between good and evil. Which side we choose determines our fate and future.

When politicians vote on bills before they even possess or read them, then even the most intellectually challenged person knows there is something very wrong in Washington, DC, and upon reflection, something awfully wrong with our society. By our inaction and apathy, we choose to have a world atrociously filled with gruesome events far below the dignity of the human race; yet this debased world has persisted for millennia with very little change or protest from the people.

In the present New World Order, Washington works under the direction of the City of London, whose directions and orders, some say, are received from the Vatican. The intention of those behind the New World Order is to have all the countries of the world join under a despotic ruling class that appears hell-bent on eliminating and sacrificing a good portion of the human race.

We as a nation are responsible for our apathy, inaction, and tacit approval of a crazy new world government, one that compulsively wars against the people of the world. The people of this nation are responsible for everything that happens to us as a nation and what happens to the world. Our actions are important and vital to changing the direction of this dying planet.

We are the ones who will bear the suffering that all this warfare and mayhem is causing. Will Americans be complicit and be known throughout posterity as the country that betrayed the liberties and freedom of the world's people and thus turned us all into slaves of the New World Order? Another possibility exists; we smarten up and fix this very misdirected and poorly governed land, instead of letting it slip into oblivion. The answer lies in the actions performed, or not, by each one of us. Every one of us has a personal stake in this earthly game; our cards were dealt at birth.

The New World Order is being run by the most extreme radical Zionists of the world for their own selfish interests. They work tirelessly against the rest of humanity, whom the bigoted Zionists refer to as goyim (Hebrew for non-Jews). The goyim are obviously viewed as inferior to Jewish people, according to radical Zionist extremists like Menachem Begin, who stated, "Other races are considered as human excrement." This pretty much covers the philosophical viewpoint that the prejudicial, racist, and radical Zionist extremists have towards the remainder of humanity that is not Jewish.

The crazy radical Zionists extremists, who are responsible for creating and implementing the New World Order, number less than ten thousand. They have virtually nothing in common with the average Jew, who does not harbor such disdain regarding the other races. Most of the radical Zionist extremists fervently assist the international bankers in implementing the bankers' corrupt and immoral agenda, regardless of the cost in human lives and misery.

To understand better the depth of hatred the radical Zionist extremists possess toward the other races, check out The Protocols of the Learned Elders of Zion available at biblebelievers.org.au/przion1.htm. It is a must-read for everyone, and it just so happens to be printed in William Cooper's Behold a Pale Horse. This great book is highly recommended and forever indexed in the chronicles of humanity's struggle for freedom and the patriot movement in America.

Israel, the US number one ally in the Middle East, receives approximately twenty-five thousand dollars of American aid and other financial support for every Israeli man, woman, and child. Why does the United States consider Israel its number one ally? More importantly, why is anyone that questions the US-Israeli relationship too often met with disdain and ridicule, often wrongly labeled as anti-Semitic and having his or her reputation disparaged and dragged through the mud by the media?

In discussions with Middle Easterners, many inevitably conclude that the so-called suicide bombings, car bombings, and other deadly acts occur directly under the direction of the CIA or Israel's Secret Intelligence Service, which is often referred to as the Mossad. Many Middle Easterners believe that terrorist attacks in their region are committed not by radical Islamic extremists but by intelligence agencies and their network of associates that criminally profit from such explosive events. Many Middle Easterners believe the terroristic killings are being committed by agent provocateurs, which, as we know, are defined by Wikipedia as "a secret agent hired to incite suspected persons to commit some illegal action, outbreak, civil unrest, etc., that will make them liable to punishment." Many people believe those responsible for the destruction of the World Trade Center, the Morrow Building in Oklahoma, the July 7, 2005 train bombings in London, and so on and so on, were agent provocateurs working for the US CIA, Israeli Mossad, or England's secret intelligence service, the notorious MI6.

Many reports confirm that agent provocateurs of the same intelligence agencies are responsible for the mass shootings, car bombings, decapitations, and other horrific terroristic acts we regularly see in the media. These devious intelligence agencies then blame it on targeted and innocent parties whom the United States later attacks.

Tactics of agent provocateurs can further be witnessed in the assassinations of heads of state, done in order to quickly motivate and implement a regime change in a specific country with the newly appointed regime being much more compatible with the interests of the United States.

The agent provocateurs will commit all sorts of atrocities, including blowing up trains in London, and blame it on radical Islamic extremists. This leads one to question, "How did the Mossad know the London bombings were going to happen?" The answer to this question is in the article by the same name, written by Michael Rivero and available at whatreallyhappened.com/WRHARTICLES/london_mossad.html. Rivero's informative site is definitely worth voraciously studying.

Upon examination of the New World Order, we discover there is an interwoven network, commonly referred to as the "Establishment" or "Deep State," a group, or better yet a cabal, brushed aside as quickly as mentally possible and usually without adequate evaluation. The Establishment and its secret government survive from one presidential administration to the next without interruption or detection. Only recently has the truth of the Establishment, and how it derives and maintains its power over the American people, started to become somewhat known and identified.

Any whisper in the media regarding this Jewish or, rather, Zionist criminal network, which has infiltrated the federal government and exerts international Mafia-like control over the goyim's population, is brushed quickly aside to save such whispers from scrutiny and examination by the public.

Every race and religion has its own network of affiliates and associations that are supportive of their biases, beliefs, and customs. The whites have groups and allegiances; the blacks do too, as do the Hindus, the Buddhists, the Japanese, and Jews. All races and religions have networks; however, one group has special privileges that allow for its seamless integration into the federal government in order to control and influence US policies more than all the other special interest groups combined.

There is a Zionist criminal network so vast that it controls all the governments that are worth controlling and has the resources of these same very governments under its issuance, control, and disposal. All the neat stuff, the science stuff, the advanced technologies developed under black ops trillion-dollar research and development budgets—all of it has fallen into wrong and dirty hands. This is a very important point when one considers the technology that was necessary to vaporize most of the World Trade Center towers. All that toxic dust did not occur as a result of one floor of concrete collapsing onto the next floor below it and so on and so on.

There is an overwhelming number of videos one can watch that attempts to explain the truth of what actually happened that day and proves the government portrayed myths to be as fanciful as they are. A few eye-openers to watch are 911 Truth New Bombshell Video (youtube.com/watch?v=GIFk5wAuHQY), 25 Hard Facts About 9/11 (available at youtube.com/watch?v=5H2wr0khnJA), and Loose Change, a film about September 11 available at loosechange911.com. These videos are all well worth the visit.

No discussion regarding the Establishment's role in 9/11 is complete without examination of Dr. Judy Wood's research and the exposing of advanced vaporizing technologies that were at work on 9/11 turning the buildings into dust. Her excellent video can be watched at DrJudy-Wood.com and explains the government-controlled, advanced demolition technology that was used to vaporize the World Trade Center towers.

Dr. Wood's video, describing Tesla's directed free-energy technology used to vaporize and neatly bring down the buildings, guarantees that the only group that could possibly be responsible for demolishing the World Trade Center towers was a government or a group working within and/or controlling a government that has access to this advanced Tesla technology. A group of box-cutter wielding Saudis lack the ability to vaporize matter. Only governments like the United States and Israel possess advanced technologies that can splatter molecular cohesion, which is necessary to turn concrete and steel into dust.

As we delve deeper into this nightmare, it is astonishing to discover that many of the US government's top officials have dual citizenship, both in the United States and Israel. In essence, many of these duplicitous officials are spies and traitors against the United States and at the hire of the Israeli government and its intelligence networks. The allegiance and loyalty of these US-Israeli citizens, who hold powerful positions in the US government, is demonstrably in favor of Israel and against the interests of the United States of America. Every raging Zionist criminal extremist who is acting in a manner against the interests of people of the United States and for the benefit of Israel needs to be rounded up, tried for his or her crimes, incarcerated, and barred forever from holding public office in the United States.

I have nothing against Jews. I married a Jew. I have a problem with demented Zionists that commit genocide in order to satisfy their blood-soaked desires.

The radical Zionist criminal network that I am discussing is exposed and substantiated in the incredibly informative and earth-shattering video—probably the most important of all the videos mentioned in this book—9/11 Missing Links. For your edification, you can view his awesome video at 911missinglinks.com. Spread the word; this video is incredibly important!

In addition, 9/11 Missing Links provides a very keen and enlightening insight to the clandestine Israeli Secret Intelligence Service and the role Israel's radical Zionist criminal network played in orchestrating the events of 9/11 and many other so-called terrorist attacks. The video 9/11 Missing Links explains how the vast Zionist criminal network infiltrated and usurped the US government to achieve the aims of Israel and the implementation of the New World Order.

I believe the point has been adequately stressed that all the videos referenced in this book, and especially this last one, should be studied several times for greater understanding of the events of September 11, 2001. The 9/11 Missing Links video evidences in detail how a radical Zionist criminal network of extremists has infiltrated the US government at its highest levels and is creating government policy for the benefit of Israel. This is obviously treasonous and very damaging to the people of the United States. This Zionist criminal network is referred to by media as the Deep State or Establishment.

Israel is the only country in the world in which a person can have a dual citizenship, with a passport issued by both Israel and the United States, and obtain employment at the highest levels of the US government. It is horrific that the United States allows foreigners, with an obvious agenda of implementing Israeli Zionist policies of hatred towards Arabs and Muslims, to use the resources of the United States to further Israel's international goals and aspirations of world domination.

A group of radical extremist Zionists works within the US government toward the complete destruction of the United States. Many might find these allegations to be unfounded, but upon deeper examination, there can be no other conclusion intelligently drawn, especially and obviously when considering the intentions, actions, and crimes committed at the highest levels of the US government.

Barack Obama gave to Iran over 150 billion dollars and the most sweetheart nuclear deal that Iran could ever ask for in a million years. Obama also traitorously gave over 1.7 billion in untraceable cash to Iran, which is destined to finance future terroristic acts.

To be fair to Obama, neither John Kerry nor Hillary Clinton exclusively negotiated the Iranian nuclear deal. Allegedly, Wendy Sherman negotiated much of the Iranian deal. Here's a little info about Sherman. She was born to a prominent Jewish family and loyal to Zionists' interests. With Sherman in charge of negotiating such a great deal for Iran, it allows for the proliferation of endless future terrorism throughout the Middle East by tendering 150 billion dollars to a mad regime interested in destroying America and Americans. This should satisfy the Zionists' Satanic plans to keep the US military busy killing Muslims for the next several decades.

By providing this huge payment to Iran, this further allows for even more slaughter of Muslims and Christians over the next decades, ultimately leading to the expansion of Israel's borders when they walk in and take over the rubble, rare earth metals, and oil that underlie a war-torn and decimated Middle East.

This is the objective of the New World Order extremists—to increase lighting the fires of discontent in the Middle East and the world at large for the benefit of the Zionist criminal network and their international banking interests.

The Zionist criminal network has access to all of America's and Israel's latest and most advanced technology that was used in the demolition of the World Trade Center towers.

These Zionists orchestrate virtually every aspect of the world we see around us. This network has treasonously taken control of America's entertainment-financial-industrial-medical-military-technical complex. They invade and permeate all facets of American politics and provide all the experts that you see corroborating all the malarkey that the media spews regarding war and terror.

Let us consider the relationship of the Zionist criminal network and the US government. The press and politicians declared that Obama is incompetent, but this is far from true. He accomplished everything that he intended—by loyally and feverishly doing his part to destroy the United States, its economy, and the Christian values it imbues. He pushed the United States to the point of financial obliteration and bankruptcy by doubling the national debt, which is well over twenty trillion dollars. He created a healthcare plan that is doomed to destroy the medical industry in 2017. He signed executive orders infringing upon the Second Amendment and eviscerating the US Constitution along with the rights and livelihoods of most all Americans.

Obama appeared to be a very competent person bent on destroying the United States in accordance with the tenets of radical Islamist extremists. Obama's actions exemplified the anatomy of a traitor, as he worked diligently to usher in a New World Order. His New World Order was designed to let the jihadists spread their caliphate and civil unrest across America and the rest of the civilized world. This is obvious when we observe Obama's policies and actions permitting tens of thousands of Syrian refugees, who cannot be properly vetted, to immigrate into the United States. Obama spread the seeds of discontent and a terroristic caliphate across the Middle East, as well as across the United States. He should be charged for his crimes, along with the rest of the traitors that assist the Zionist criminal network, for it is one of the most dangerous plagues inflicting humanity.

Every calculated decision that Obama approved has led to the detriment of the people of the United States and the destruction of the financial stability of the US economy. Executive orders were created to paralyze the US population, and those executive orders are to be implemented during times of crisis and states of emergencies, including terror attacks, a financial collapse of the economy, and/or civil unrest. Simply Google "Obama executive orders," and there is overwhelming data substantiating this claim; you might want to Google "Obama executive orders conspiracy" and have even more fun.

Evidently, there was a struggle within the US government between two parties that were not elected by the people. On the one side, you had the interests of the radical Islamic extremists supported by Obama, and on the other side were the radical Jews, or more politically correct, the Zionist criminal extremists who control the federal government from within, in allegiance with the international bankers' all-encompassing monetary interests. The radical Zionist extremists are interested in having the US military destroy the Islamic way of life and exterminate, via genocide, ISIS and its money made of gold from the face of the planet. Along with the death of ISIS, the Zionist criminal network is also rooting for the death of any money systems that use redeemable money, backed by silver and gold, in their economies.

Does anyone in America still believe that nineteen Saudi Arabians with box cutters were responsible for the events of 9/11? Does anyone still believe that a plane full of Bostonians and another plane full of New Yorkers would allow three or four 150-pound Saudis to overthrow a flight crew and take control of the aircraft using only box cutters? The hijackers might slice one or two flight attendants' throats before all havoc would ensue. Angry Bostonians and New Yorkers would quickly beat to a pulp and likely kill any hijackers the very instant a flight attendant was killed. If the alleged hijackers harmed even one hair on a flight attendant's head, the throats of those Saudi hijackers would have been sliced with their own box cutters by the hands of American heroes.

Unfortunately, the sad truth is that those planes were brought down with remote control technology, and there was nothing the passengers on board could do about it! Some surmise the original planes were crashed into the ocean a thousand miles off shore.

Did you ever watch Wag the Dog, a 1997 comedic film starring Anne Heche, Robert De Niro, and Dustin Hoffman?

Does anyone still believe that the World Trade Center buildings somehow miraculously collapsed and vaporized into their own footprints without the assistance of detonation and demolition experts and using Tesla's state-of-the-art energy disintegration technology?

Not one other skyscraper in the world, either before or since 9/11, has ever collapsed because of fire, and there have been a lot of fires in high-rises; just Google it. Uncontrolled fire cannot melt steel sufficiently to create a weakness necessary to precipitate a collapse, especially such a perfect collapse like the one that sent the two World Trade Center buildings, all 1,368 feet of them, straight down into their own footprints. By professional demolition standards, this was an extraordinary accomplishment, a masterful demolition!

That is like dropping a building that is four and a half football fields high exactly into its own footprint while simultaneously vaporizing most of the concrete, steel, office equipment, and two jumbo airliners on the way down. This was quite a magic trick, one done right before our very eyes!

Give me a break. The towers were expertly demolished with precision, killing almost three thousand innocent people and shattering even more families.

Is there anyone who believes that the Patriot Act—allegedly authored by radical Zionist extremist Michael Chertoff, secretary of Homeland Security during the George W. Bush administration, which was planned well in advance according to Jennifer Van Bergen's article, "**The USA PATRIOT Act Was Planned Before 9/11**"—was passed to make America safer from terrorism? In fact, the Patriot Act stripped Americans of their constitutional rights; read Jennifer's article at ratical.org/ratville/CAH/index.html.

Fingers of the media are pointing to the radical Islamic extremists as being the perpetrators of terrorist acts without having any real evidence. There is never a news story by the media about Israel, the Mossad, and the role they play in spreading and inciting international terrorism. Why does half the population know the dirt regarding the Mossad yet the American media remain mute and will never dare report anything implicating the Mossad in world terrorism? The media are afraid to mention anything derogatory about the Mossad or the involvement of the world's intelligence agencies, which lurk in the shadows of virtually every terrorist attack.

Israeli Secret Intelligence Service (ISIS), or the Mossad as it is commonly called, has a motto that states, "By way of deception, thou shalt do war." Think of what kind of subversive group has a motto that debased; these are sick people. This is exactly how the Mossad operates today, generating war throughout the world. The Mossad is the hidden intelligence arm of the Zionist banking cabal, which controls the US government and its foreign policy and orchestrates from behind the scenes all wars across the globe.

Most Middle Eastern people do not believe that the terrorists decapitating Americans are Islamic extremists or radicals; they think they are the Mossad and the CIA. Many skeptics have strong suspicions that a large majority of the brutal terrorist atrocities are committed under the direction of clandestine intelligence agencies acting behind the scene. Many Middle Easterners consider those who commit such heinous murders simply as murderers and believe murderers have forfeited all religious affiliation and association.

Throughout history, the majority of false-flag operations have been conducted by intelligence agencies that are controlled by special interests, inciting the population to demand war and the destruction of a false and fabricated enemy. The media know this is historically true yet never mention it to their audiences. Can anyone recall any negative stories about Israel being spread by the media? Israel controls and is admired in the media and portrayed as the perfect place and the perfect country filled with perfect people. They are also portrayed as a poor, victimized country needing sympathy and help as they are always being picked on by the mean old Arabs. Any television anchor that speaks out and mentions anything contrary to the interests of Israel usually ends up unemployed or worse.

Israel is constantly provoking and involved in war. It seems Israel is always involved with and making profits off war.

The Honorable James Traficant suspiciously died after he exposed the corruption between AIPAC (American Israeli Public Affairs Committee) and US politicians. Traficant broadcast how AIPAC was controlling Washington, DC, and the politicians that were supposed to be working for you and me. This major special interest controls US policy and the politicians that legislate it. You can watch James Traficant on Alex Jones Tv 1/5: AIPAC Runs America's Foreign Policy at youtube.com/watch? v=gKrlTfMMncM.

Can you imagine the nightly news constantly reporting stories in which the religious beliefs of the perpetrators of heinous crimes and terrorist acts were described as radical Christian extremists, radical Protestant extremists, radical Jewish extremism, or any other contrived epithets?

People who murder are murderers, plain and simple. Terrorists are not of any religious affiliation because religious affiliation is shattered and disavowed when a religious follower murders another human being. Radical jihad extremists that murder their fellow man are not members of the Islamic faith but are demented in their beliefs and attitudes toward their fellow man. A religion that sanctions the murder of another human being is not a religion designed to uplift and benefit the human race and the entirety of society.

To solve the radical Islamic extremists' attacks requires identifying the people that actually sponsor and implement such attacks from behind the scenes and hidden from view of the public. We must follow the trail of blood money and expose the real culprits who are responsible for implementing international policies that allow extremists the opportunity to savagely kill and torment the innocent.

The sanctioning of murder and genocide by the special interests remains obscured from the public, and as we know, the media never report the special interests' connection to and the real reasons for war and terror. The media, wholly bent on assisting in the formation of the New World Order, fabricate and embellish as they are told by their masters each story designed to further the world-oppressors' domination over humankind.

A religion that condones murder, in any form, is not a religion formed in the likeness of a loving God or Prophet but a religion that follows the works and intentions of Satan. Satan alone would revel in the catastrophic devastation occurring in the Middle East. Those who create such chaos and havoc are his agents.

There continuously have been religious wars for the last few millennia, and the odd thing about it is that no one is catching on. It is the same thing repeatedly, and you would reckon people would finally conclude that enough is enough. The people of a country embattled in a religious war usually do not start or continue religious wars; traitorous leaders of such war-torn countries are the ones that typically profit from the wars they initiate and fight. When we stop and think about it, how is resorting to war to solve a problem a good idea? What limited mental factors go into the calculation that if we start killing people things will get better? In many ways, this is incredibly retarded. Computations that involve killing people are insane and more than anything else under the sun, moon, and heavenly stars are usually motivated by greed and power.

Wars typically profit and benefit the ruling class over the ignorant fighting factions. The New World Order in place today is just another version of the same old story of religious warfare, which has existed throughout the ages. In feudal times, kings declared wars, which were fought by the unsuspecting serfs, the common folk. The kings profited; the serfs died.

The New World Order is being ushered in under the guise of an insurmountable and unsolvable international scene filled and constructed with terror and conflict. The actions and inactions of the politicians who work for the international bankers are aligned with the intention of assisting the arrival and implementation of a stronger and far more oppressive New World Order upon humanity.

Much of the US media report only one side of the war story to the American public, the side the international bankers want Americans to hear. The media do not mention the destroyed lives of American families who are left in a wake of untold suffering, as the United States continues its unnecessary war against Arabs. The media never publish the actual death rates, nor do the media mention the millions of people who are killed who had nothing to do with Ground Zero and the destruction of the World Trade Center.

The United States immediately retaliated against the Afghans when most of the hijackers were actually Saudi Arabian. Bush Jr. said in a presidential debate with Kerry that he would invade Iraq and get Saddam Hussein; this was over a year before September 11, 2001. George W. Bush and his daddy probably made hundreds of billions from starting the third world war, a war that will never end, unless we the people end it.

Why do the media not call out George W. Bush, his father, and their radical Zionist extremist friends as the warmongers they are, responsible for countless deaths in the Middle East? The Bush family assisted Hitler in his rise to power. What won't that corrupt family do? And still the feckless media remain silent.

When Obama delivered 150 billion dollars to Iran, the world's largest sponsor of terrorism, it is done with the intention of keeping the world in constant war and unrest in order to usher in the New World Order. Where was the media digging in and exposing Obama as the traitor he is? When millions of refugees are admitted to European countries, including tens of thousands of ISIS sympathizers or worse, it is not accidently done; it is intentionally done to create strife and unrest.

This Trojan horse is but one item on the agenda of the oppressors making it more possible to foist upon the population a New World Order that will be presented as a solution to all the world's problems, problems created by the same folks that will present the same inhuman solution. Where is the media informing the American people? Media, you traitors to humankind, do your job and protect the people's freedoms and liberties.

The New World Order is growing like a malignant cancer right under our noses. It is being disguised as an unsolvable religious conflict, sprinkled with war, terrorism, and political incompetence. Whenever we see war, we should understand that it is not a natural state of affairs, but it is a contrived state, specifically initiated by a clandestine group with a private agenda and the ultimate purpose of suppressing humankind under the rule and compass of the Zionist criminal network that controls the Bank for International Settlements.

Wars are declared as religious wars when, in fact, wars hardly ever have anything to do with religion. Religion has conveniently been used to obfuscate the true profit motives for wars. Now religion is being used to hide the fact that the New World Order proponents are molding this world and are militarily exterminating any and all their enemies who do not fall in alignment with their twisted and oppressive-banking philosophy.

The New World Order and its design and implementation by the criminal radical Zionist extremists will consist of a world filled with outbreaks of continual violence, terrorism, and war until, eventually, the people get fed up and have had enough of the violence, terrorism, and war. The New World Order crowd hopes a frantic population, frustrated and afraid, will accept any proffered global solutions that make the violence, terrorism, and war go away.

It is extremely important for humankind to understand exactly which groups of deviants are responsible for the current state of affairs and a majority of the terrorist bombings and killings. The identity of humanity's enemies needs to be broadly disseminated, and society ought to prosecute and segregate those responsible for causing the world's wars and render them powerless and unable to further disturb and destroy the world at large.

The world is full of pain and suffering only because a group of individuals is going around causing pain and suffering. Imagine the world and international affairs as a schoolyard with children happily playing. Normally, children in a playground get along pretty well, and the overall ambience of the playground is peaceful. In an average playground, many games are played, and everyone has a great time. The playground, full of lots of random activity, is nevertheless a somewhat stable and loving environment.

When we introduce a bully into the playground, there is an immediate breakdown of the quality of the environment. When a brute starts bullying the children, the children panic and run to escape the bully. The adults need to keep the bully from disturbing the children and the cheerful environment.

This world needs some adult supervision to keep the bullies in line and away from the general population. Segregation and separation are the instant remedies to the bullying that is occurring these days around the world. The international scene we are experiencing today is fixable; we just need to get rid of the bullies and their bad attitudes.

We should simply ask ourselves, "Who really benefits from the Christians and the Muslims wiping each other off the face of the planet?" When we discover this, we will discover the actual enemies of humanity. Once we have identified the bad characters in world affairs, we will then be able to right the ship of the United States and the world. There needs to be a complete removal from positions in the government of all persons with foreign allegiances to Israel or any other country for that matter. This especially includes every single traitor that is working for the federal government and possesses US and Israeli dual citizenship.

Mossad, or the Israeli Secret Intelligence Service (ISIS), and its agent provocateurs constantly commit atrocious crimes against humanity. This is a small gang of radical Zionists terrorists, who think like Begin and consider goyim, or non-Jews, to be human excrement. This type of debased thinking is far beyond the comprehension of most Westerners, as well as most Jews, as most decent people find such an attitude deplorable, unacceptable, and prejudiced beyond the pale.

Many Zionists consider themselves the chosen people of God, and perhaps this attitude of arrogance theoretically indemnifies them from guilt and remorse for their wicked actions against humanity. Nothing could be further from the truth.

To have a world leader such as Begin, and many others that share the goal of a New World Order, so determined to rule over the rest of the world and desperately wanting to have the population lick the feet of their anointed leaders is beyond the imaginations of most moral people. The Middle East is in shambles because we have not accurately identified exactly who is profiting and who is ultimately responsible for the mayhem in that desolate and dying part of the world.

It is a destructive policy in which extremists—Christian, Muslim, Jew, or any other political body, religion, and/or race—have an agenda to enslave the rest of humanity. Those that aim to destructively control humanity are in essence the true enemies of humankind, and they need to be dealt with accordingly. There are war crimes being committed harming every member of society, and it is time to purge the evil from government and from society as a whole. Many people have had enough with the old guard of this planet. Many believe that an instant filing of charges for war crimes against the appropriate people would immediately improve the chaotic situation that currently exists in the Middle East.

The Bible weighs in against those that worship death and destruction in Revelation 2:9, as it warns, "I know your works, tribulation, and poverty (but you are rich); and I know the blasphemy of those who say they are Jews and are not, but are a synagogue of Satan." The true enemies of humanity are not the Jews but the demented Zionist psychopaths who are hiding and camouflaging themselves behind the Jewish religion. The demented Zionist psychopaths hide and cower under the Jewish religion to camouflage their hateful acts and for protection from exposure and prosecution for their war crimes.

In fact, when we evaluate the multitude of atrocities that have occurred throughout history, which have been blamed on different religions, we quickly realize there is virtually no religion that has the upper hand in killing of our fellow man. When a religion turns violent against the world and attempts to rule the world, it is usually a small schism or segment of that religious group that has gone off the rails, intending to harm humankind.

Catholics come to mind and the unforgettable Spanish Inquisition that started in 1232 and ended with the last execution occurring in 1826. Countless were killed under the guise of Christianity, although Pope Gregory and his successors are generally not remembered and recorded in history for such a thorough religious cleansing. In retrospect, the inquisition was really a turf war to expand the Catholic Church's real estate holdings, under the cloak of a religious war.

"Religious cleansing" is defined in Wikipedia as "a euphemism for a form of religious persecution in which members of a religious population are subjected to imprisonment, expulsion, forced conversion or death by a majority to achieve religious homogeneity in majority-controlled territory." This is what is occurring in the Middle East today and has become the standard operating procedure of the New World Order. The Zionists are the ones behind the curtain, pulling the levers to keep Americans killing Muslims.

Only a small network of corrupt and evil radical Zionist extremists—a very small number compared to the good and decent Jews of the world who coexist and love their fellow man—are working tirelessly to expand their control over the remainder of the population while ushering in their demented vision of a New World Order. The Israeli Secret Intelligence Service with its super-advanced technology and highly trained personnel has infiltrated not only the US government but also most of the world's top governments. Control the government; control the people.

The Israeli Secret Intelligence Service abuses its stolen power to the detriment of the masses to assist in achieving its demented aims. Finally, the holy Zionist leader will be able to have his feet licked by the lower-class humans or animals as they refer to the rest of us. The United States has become the war tool of the Israeli Secret Intelligence Service, which directs from the shadows the evilness of war, as it controls the plight of this planet.

Read the fascinating book By Way of Deception: The Making and Unmaking of a Mossad Officer, the true story of a former case officer and his thrilling experiences working in and extricating himself from the Israeli Mossad, by Victor Ostrovsky. Before you roll your eyes in disbelief, remember the Mossad's slogan, "By way of **deception**, thou shalt do war." The deception is over now. Let us eradicate the evil Zionists that control and wield power over the US government and the rest of the world's population.

For those that want to cry foul and yell "anti-Semite" or other disparaging epithets, this is not an attack on the Jewish people. Instead, this is an exposure of a tiny segment of the Jewish population, which hides behind organizations like the Anti-Defamation League (ADL), the B'nai B'rith, and too many other Jewish organizations and Zionist-controlled think tanks to name.

Please visit en.wikipedia.org/wiki/Category:Jewish_organizations for a list of an extensive network of over one hundred Jewish organizations. These organizations are vast and have membership rolls and affiliations in the hundreds of thousands, even the millions. These are very wealthy and powerful organizations. Throughout history, the Zionist cowards, who have steadily worked toward the destruction of civilization and the reduction of the population of the world, hide and obfuscate their actions by accusing anyone that divulges the tightly knit criminal Zionist network as being anti-Semitic and prejudiced against all Jews.

Imagine if Charles Manson was referred to by the media as a radical Christian extremist. How long would that be tolerated? Definitely considered a nut job, he was found guilty of conspiracy to commit murder of seven people. To call Manson a radical Christian extremist is racist toward the entire Christian religion. Is it religious racism every time a news anchor calls someone an extremist this or an extremist that?

The Anti-Defamation League, to be true to the credo on its website recruitment page, indicates its mission is to "stand with ADL to fight anti-Semitism and all forms of bigotry, defend democratic ideals and protect civil rights for all." Is that occurring when the media attack the Islamic people and associate their religion with radical extremists? After all, just like Jews, Arabs are Semites.

Could you imagine the uproar if the media called the likes of Bugsy Siegel, Monk Eastman, Harry Horowitz, Herman Rosenthal, Arnold Rosenthal, Meyer Lansky, Mickey Cohen, Dutch Schultz, or the other Jewish criminals of the twentieth century names like radical Jew extremists? Imagine if, in every newscast and television program discussing the history of the Jewish-American Mafia, these criminals were referred to in such derogatory terms.

It appears that the Anti-Defamation League has redefined the word "anti-Semitic" as hatred against Jews and Israel, when in actuality Semitic is defined by the Oxford Dictionary as the following:

1. Relating to or denoting a family of languages that include Hebrew, Arabic, and Aramaic and certain ancient languages such as Phoenician and Akkadian, constituting the main subgroup of the Afro-Asiatic family subgroup.

2. Relating to the peoples who speak the Semitic languages, especially Hebrew and Arabic [emphasis added].

The Jewish people have co-opted the term anti-Semite to mean hostile to Jews when it was first created to mean hostility or hatred for all Semites, which in addition includes Arabs. Apparently, the Anti-Defamation League has turned its back on the Arabic people and is mainly concerned with protecting only the interests of the Jews and the secret criminal Zionist network, which is determined to overthrow and has already to a large degree overthrown many governments of the world.

For a summary of the peculiar etymology of the word "anti-Semitic," visit en.wikipedia.org/wiki/Antisemitism#Etymology and notice how the word was changed over time to exclude non-Jewish Semites. Now the term "anti-Semite" applies only to actions or prejudicial statements cast exclusively against Jews and not Arabs.

On the Anti-Defamation League's website, the ADL refers to domestic terrorists as "Domestic Islamic Extremists." Nowhere does the ADL mention anything on its website regarding "domestic Jewish extremists" or the Zionist criminal network responsible for the deaths of millions, or would that be anti-Semitic and not politically correct?

Everything that is happening in the Middle East is in accordance with the desires of the same old people who are marshaling in the New World Order, including members of the Trilateral Commission and the Council on Foreign Relations. It is not surprising that many of these organizations' members also possess dual citizenship in both Israel and the United States. They intend to create so much terror, chaos, and killing that the remaining people of Earth will gladly accept, then invite, and even beg for a New World Order to stop all the insanity.

All along, the very same people are the ones responsible for creating all the terror and violence against humanity. We need to abolish and hold accountable for their crimes those groups that believe in and actively work toward one class's superiority over the remainder of the population, for this is slavery in its basic form. We need to abolish those groups whose primary aim is to implement a world dominated by a few self-selected Zionists at the cost and harm to the remaining seven billion of us.

One of the first items on the New World Order's agenda is to eradicate over 90 percent of the entire population, and although this might appear a colossal project in itself, this objective may be closer than many imagine. Simply look at the level of toxicity in our air, water, and food. Then, consider the biological warfare being conducted, including the different biological weapons being released into the world's population like the AIDS virus in the 1980s and, not to be outdone, today's Zika virus, which destroys babies in the womb and could decimate millions and even billions of babies in the future.

It will be firmly and conclusively established that the Zika virus, like the AIDS virus, was intentionally designed as a biological weapon by the World Health Organization to largely reduce the population of the planet in perfect agreement with the foreboding population-reduction plans written on the Georgia Guidestones.

Is it coincidence that the Olympics, which draw people from around the world, were held in Brazil—Zika central? Brazil has the highest concentration of Zika in the world. How did that happen?

For more information regarding the intentional spreading of Zika by the world's foremost health organizations you can visit Wikipedia at en.wikipedia.org/wiki/2015%E2%80%9316_Zika_ virus_epidemic.

On another front regarding biological and electronic types of warfare, voluminous reports indicate that sterility is caused by the use of cell phones, medications, and sterilization chemicals found in tap water. In this case, reducing 90 percent of the population will occur over the next couple of generations without the need for an outright and obvious genocide, militarily orchestrated in plain and obvious view. Plausible deniability is the avenue taken by America's duplicitous politicians and the world's true rulers.

However, do not expect the continuous intelligence, military, and terrorist actions (really the same thing from different perspectives) to end anytime soon. The ongoing and seemingly disconnected series of violent terrorist attacks, which are being portrayed as individual and random assaults and used by the media to create constant distractions to keep the people from discovering the true enemies of humankind, are sometimes planned years and even decades prior to their date of execution. Many family-owned European business conglomerations make and orchestrate plans using a two-hundred-year timetable. Why should the Zionist criminal network utilize a timetable any shorter to plan the overthrow and domination of the world?

No group, religion, or race is any more important than any other group, religion, or race. The real bigots of this world are those that believe they are born superior to the rest of the races and the rest of us.

Americans have been subject to an entire disinformation brainwashing campaign that has continued for several decades regarding Islam and Muslim beliefs. It is time to study these beliefs and compare them to what the media have been reporting. We cannot be satisfied with what the nightly news teaches us about such beliefs. Remember, Satan can interpret scriptures, and it is up to us to study the different religions and to see for ourselves the tenets that the various faiths hold as truth. Searching is a component of understanding; without it, learning is impossible. Seek and ye shall find; therefore, if ye do not seek, ye will not find.

It is time Americans studied Islam for themselves. Many religious scholars believe there are philosophical similarities among Christian and Islamic beliefs that provide a common direction for man to live at a higher plane of existence. There are more similarities among the Eastern and Western religious beliefs than most people realize. If people focus on the positive aspects of any belief system, they will be taking strides in a proper and saner direction to better understand and, with that understanding, better resolve world disputes in ways other than through warfare.

Many believe that much of the hatred toward America, evidenced by that whole "death to America" chant, is the result of somewhat recent political policies that include dropping extensive amounts of explosives on a mostly innocent Middle Eastern population. The US government has killed millions of people in the Middle East. Some conclude that the terroristic violence we are currently seeing today in Europe and the United States is the result of, or blowback from, the havoc and death we earlier created.

Playing a big part in causing international unrest and violence are the hateful doctrines brainwashed into the minds of young children throughout many parts of the Middle East under the guise of religion and education. We must eliminate the teaching of hate, no matter where it is done or who is teaching it.

One thing is for sure: the radicalized and extreme white, Anglo-Saxon Christians are not strangers to genocide; throughout history, they have actively participated in much human slaughter. Those New World Order proponents behind the scenes would like to see World War III come to an end, as the conflict with the Native Americans ended with the annihilation and decimation of a people and their way of life.

Today we are experiencing a more covert but comparably vicious genocidal militaristic model being implemented upon Muslims and the Muslim way of life. In times of international conflict, the opponent is portrayed in the media as a savage people beneath the care, dignity, and ideals of decent Americans. The idea of an inferior enemy is broadcast continuously to keep the concept in Americans' heads that killing the enemy is acceptable and right for our one great and especially blessed nation under God. Evidently, in the minds of many Americans, God doesn't mind the murder of our fellow man—as long as the one doing the murdering is wearing a US military uniform while flying Old Glory on high, and the one being murdered is a turban-wearing motherfucker wanting to die.

The United States has the highest proclivity to start wars and possesses more militaristic inclination and weaponry than any other nation. It is imperative to investigate this fact to better understand the role the United States plays as the enforcing military arm of the international bankers, who are developing the New World Order. That is why the United States is continually at war.

Whenever there is a problem with the loan sharking contracts of the international bankers, the US military is the one called in to break legs and have the borrowing country pay an un-payable amount of interest.

I wonder who will bomb America when we can no longer make our interest payments to the Federal Reserve and the international bankers. We need to address and investigate the insane militaristic actions of the United States, the world's monetary system, and its relation to a world continuously at war. We have to connect the dots. It is not too hard to figure out why we live in a world where one section of the world is at war with another, as ominously foretold in George Orwell's classic book, 1984.

The current New World Order would like the American population to be so ignorant that they are unable to evaluate what is actually occurring around them. Those profiting from warfare fear disclosure of their devious actions and would rather keep them unknown to the public. Scurrilous war-profiteering criminals prefer hiding behind a tangled web of confusion, constructed and camouflaged by the media, rather than being open, in plain sight, and under the scrutiny of the public's gaze.

To improve international relations, the people of the world need to unite and find an attainable solution to war. In the meanwhile, the only way to win a war is simply not to fight it.

To rightfully give equal time to extol the life-changing virtues available in the scriptures of Islam, it is imperative to note that when a person of Islamic faith steps outside the bounds of Islam and defies decent behavior, as outlined by the Prophet Mohammed, then that person is considered a sinner.

The actions of a sinner are not representative of an entire religion. Sinners, through their sins, have disassociated themselves from Allah.

The life and sayings of Prophet Mohammed convey a broad range of sentiments and examples to help live in peace with oneself and one's neighbors.

To get a better understanding of the people who are being killed and a truer understanding of Islamic beliefs, one can and should examine the words of the Islamic Prophet Mohammed. Below are what most Muslims truly believe and practice.

Like any other religious practitioners, most Muslims are great people who should not be harmed but should be helped.

The following quotations are from The Profound Teachings of the Prophet Mohammad and are tendered to give the reader a better understanding of the decency and goodness possessed by the majority of Muslims. For our own edification, let us acquaint ourselves and generously ponder the beautiful and very insightful words and teachings of the Prophet Mohammed.

Spirituality: Wealth does not come from having great riches; [true] wealth is contentment of the soul.

Cognizance: The similitude of the one who contemplates his Lord versus the one who does not is that of the living versus the dead.

Sincerity: Actions will be judged according to their intentions.

Mercy: Show mercy to those on earth so that He who is in heaven will have mercy on you.

Gentleness: Whoever is deprived of gentleness is deprived of all good.

Forgiveness: Whoever suffers an injury done to him and forgives [the person responsible], Allah will raise his status to a higher degree and remove one of his sins.

Virtue: Do not be people without minds of your own, saying that if others treat you well you will treat them well, and that if they do wrong, you will do wrong. Instead, accustom yourselves to do good if people do good and not to do wrong if they do evil to you.

Justice: The most virtuous jihad is when one speaks a word of truth before an unjust ruler.

Civility: The Muslim does not slander, curse, speak obscenely, or speak rudely.

Honesty: Honesty leads to righteousness, and righteousness leads to Paradise. A man remains honest and concerned about honesty until he is recorded as an honest man with Allah. Lying leads to sinfulness and sinfulness leads to the Fire. A man keeps lying and remains partial to lies until he is recorded as a liar with Allah.

Tolerance: Once, the Prophet was seated at some place in Madinah, along with his companions. During this time a funeral procession passed by. On seeing this, the Prophet stood up. One of his companions remarked that the funeral was that of a Jew. The Prophet replied, "Was he not a human being?"

A disbelieving Bedouin urinated in the mosque, and the people rushed to beat him. Allah's Apostle ordered them to leave him alone, let him finish, and pour water over the place where he has passed urine. The Prophet then explained to the Bedouin calmly, "This is a place of worship, in it is the worship of God and the reading of Qur'an." After the Bedouin had left, the Prophet then said to his companion, "You have been sent to make things easy [for the people], and you have not been sent to make things difficult for them."

Equality: There is no superiority for an Arab over a non-Arab, nor for a non-Arab over an Arab, nor for a fair-skinned person over a person with dark skin, nor for a dark-skinned person over a person with fair skin. Whoever is more pious and God-fearing is more deserving of honor.

Gratitude: Contemplate those who have less than you and not those who have more than you, lest you belittle the favors of Allah conferred upon you.

Simplicity: What is little but sufficient, is better than that which is abundant but causes heedlessness.

Humility: God has revealed to me that you must be humble, so that no one oppresses another and boasts over another.

Generosity: The food of two people is enough for three, and the food of three people is enough for four.

Appreciation: Whoever does not thank people [for their favors] has not thanked Allah [properly], Mighty and Glorious is He!

Calmness: Calmness and determination is from Allah and haste is from Satan.

Patience: No one can give a better or more abundant gift than patience.

Perseverance: There is no clement person who has not stumbled, nor is there a wise person who possesses no experience.

Nonjudgment: Do not search for [the faults of others] for if anyone searches for [others'] faults, God will search for his.

Self-criticism: Blessed is he who preoccupies himself with his own defects rather than those of others.

Advice: Make things easy for people, and do not make them difficult and cheer people up and do not drive them away.

Moderation: The religion [of Islam] is easy. No one ever made it difficult without its becoming too much for him. So avoid extremes and strike a balance; do the best you can and be cheerful, and seek Allah's help [prayer] in the morning, and evening, and part of the night.

Charity: Charity is due upon every joint of a person on every day that the sun rises. Administering justice between two people is an act of charity; and to help a man concerning his riding beast by helping him onto it or lifting his luggage onto it is an act of charity; a good word is charity; and every step which you take to prayer is charity; and removing that which is harmful from the road is charity.

Community: The believer is not the one who eats his fill when the neighbor beside him is hungry.

Affability: The believer is one who is sociable [with others], and there is no benefit in one who is not sociable [with others] nor in one who is not met sociably [by them].

Business Ethics: A truthful and trustworthy merchant will be in the company of the prophets, the very truthful, and the martyrs.

Employment: Pay the laborer his due before his sweat dries.

Leadership: On a journey, the leader of the group is their servant.

Reliability: He who does not keep his trusts lacks in faith, and he who does not keep his agreements lacks in religion.

Accountability: The burden of proof is upon the plaintiff, and the taking of oath is upon the defendant.

Responsibility: Each one of you is a guardian and is responsible for what he is entrusted with.

Morality: The most perfect of the believers in faith are the best of them in moral excellence, and the best of you are the kindest to their wives.

Nobility: None but a noble man treats women in an honorable manner, and none but an ignoble treats women disgracefully.

Unity: Believers are like a single person; if his eye is in pain, his whole body pains, and if his head is in pain, his whole body pains.

Family: The best of you is the one who is best to his own family, and I am the best of you toward my family. He is not one of us who does not show mercy to our little ones and respect to our elders.

Efficiency: There are two blessings that many people fail to make the most of: good health and free time.

Education: Seeking knowledge is a religious obligation for every Muslim [male or female].

Inquiry: The cure for ignorance is to question.

Vigilance: A believer is not stung from the same hole twice.

Discipline: The wise one is he who has subdued his lower self and had prepared for what follows death. And the foolish one is he who has placed his lower self in pursuance or its desires and has vain hopes about Allah.

Modesty: Modesty is part of faith.

Beauty: Allah is beautiful and loves beauty.

Hygiene: Purity and cleanliness are part of faith.

Diet: There is no vessel worse for the son of Adam to fill than his stomach. A few morsels are sufficient for him. If he is to consume, more than a third is for his food, a third for his drink and a third for his air.

Nature: If a Muslim plants a seedling or cultivates a field, whenever a bird, a human, or an animal eats of it, it will be counted as a charity.

Animals: Anyone who kills even a sparrow for no reason [should know that] it will cry aloud to Allah on the Day of the Resurrection, saying, "O my Lord! So-and-so killed me just for fun; he killed me for no reason!"

I was once riding a difficult [slow moving] camel so I kept hitting it. When the Prophet saw me, he said: "Be gentle, for gentleness adorns everything in which it is found, and its absence leaves everything tainted."

CHAPTER 19

The People's World Order

Each one of them is one in a million. They number six thousand on a planet of six billion. They run our governments, our largest corporations, the powerhouses of international finance, the media, world religions, and, from the shadows, the world's most dangerous criminal and terrorist organizations. They are the global super-class, and they are shaping the history of our time.

— DAVID ROTHKOPF

Some even believe we are part of a secret cabal working against the best interests of the United States, characterizing my family and me as 'internationalists' and of conspiring with others around the world to build a more integrated global political and economic structure, one world, if you will. If that is the charge, I stand guilty, and I am proud of it.

— DAVID ROCKEFELLER

It would seem that men and women need a common motivation, namely a common adversary, to organize and act together in the vacuum such as motivation seemed to have ceased to exist or have yet to be found. The need for enemies seems to be a common historical factor. . . . Bring the divided nation together to face an outside enemy, either a real one or else one IN-VENTED for the purpose. . . . Democracy will be made to seem responsible for the lagging economy, the scarcity and uncertainties. The very concept of democracy could then be brought into question and allow for the seizure of power.

In searching for a new enemy to unite us, we came up with the idea that pollution, the threat of global warming, water short-ages, famine and the like would fit the bill. The real enemy [of the elites and their minions] then is humanity itself.

– THE FIRST GLOBAL REVOLUTION
(PUBLISHED BY THE CLUB OF ROME)

A world government can intervene militarily in the internal af-fairs of any nation when it disapproves of their activities.

– KOFI ANNAN

America will never be destroyed from the outside. If we falter and lose our freedoms, it will be because we destroyed ourselves.

– ABRAHAM LINCOLN

IT IS IN THE BEST INTEREST OF HUMANITY that we retire the current New World Order and implement the People's World Order. The rights of the people shall be protected and enhanced in the People's World Order, and any groups that attempt to subvert the rights of the people shall be rightly deemed enemies of the people.

Regardless of the mountains of evidence, many seem to believe that the implementation of a tyrannical New World Order is not really de-sired by those who run the planet. After weighing the evidence, it soon becomes apparent that those in power would like to have unlimited worldly power and control, unimpeded by trivial things such as outdated countries, their constitutions, and laws.

As mentioned, The Rockefeller File, by Gary Allen (educate-your-self.org/ga/RFcontents.shtml), is perhaps one of the most important books of recent history. It was one of the first conspiracy books ever written and concludes that in order to merge the United States and Russia into a New World Order, the US standard of living has to be pulled down to the level of Russia's standard of living. In order to make this merger acceptable to Americans, since the 1960s, the plan has been to destroy the manufacturing base of America to the point that the United States becomes a third-world country.

Systematically, America's trade relations, its borders, and the Amer-ican way of life have been under attack by politicians that have slowly implemented policies intended to destroy the culture of America and its repute around the world. Since the implementation of such destructive foreign policies, the merger of America with its North American neighbors is an important step in the consolidation of the world's countries.

George W. Bush has initiated the amalgamation of North America by signing the Security and Prosperity Partnership of North America (wnd.com/2006/06/36586/). In Orwell's 1984, the Newspeak language that politicians use whenever they name any legislation or treaty, including the Security and Prosperity Partnership of North America (SPP), represents the opposite of what the legislation or treaty does in reality. In Newspeak, hot is cold and black is white.

The SPP stands out as a dangerous and unconstitutional agreement that is not in the best interests of the United States as a sovereign country. This partnership was entered on March 23, 2005, in Waco, Texas, by Paul Martin, prime minister of Canada; Vincent Fox, president of Mexico; and George W. Bush.

Of virtually all the news anchors, practically the only one who spoke in opposition to the Security and Prosperity Partnership of North America was Lou Dobbs, and he was highly criticized and attacked, as one would imagine, by the media establishment. Dobbs was rightfully livid as he reported on the treasonous agreement. He is a commendable man of the people and a friend to every American.

Many consider Bush Jr. a traitor to the United States for, among other things, his participating in and signing the SPP without the consensus of Congress.

It is apparent that the creation of a North American union is now accomplished. The amero is the proposed currency that is to be implemented upon the destruction of the Federal Reserve currency in use today. The amero is North America's future currency; it is North America's equivalent of the euro. This is just another step towards the New World Order that needs to be exposed in order to inform the masses of the deviant direction this country has taken.

It is up to every person to contribute to the creation of the People's World Order and to enhance the rights of the people and imbue society with greatness and God's blessings. The People's World Order is inimical to the New World Order, which is designed by Satan and implemented by the elite with the destruction of humankind foremost in their malevolent minds and intent.

The People's World Order that we are forming would require sovereign nations to create their own independent mode of money redeemable for gold or silver. The primary reason we are experiencing such international turmoil is a direct result of utilizing an unsustainable economic and monetary system.

The establishment of sustainable monetary and banking systems, in conjunction with the establishment of sound monetary policies that incorporate the use of real money, is imperative if we are to graduate to creating the People's World Order, which consists of a world without war and the abounding insanity that curses this nuthouse of a planet.

Redeemable money is necessary to level the playing field not only among the various countries but also among the different classes of people. Only by establishing fair and equitable monetary and banking systems do the people of the world have any opportunity for peace, growth, and evolution as a species.

By implementing sane monetary and banking systems, the value of any country will be determined by the creativity, intelligence, and ingenuity of its people in direct proportion to the products it produces and sells, rather than determined by banking corporations manipulating the different currencies of the world through the criminal mechanisms inherent in today's inequitable monetary and banking systems.

As citizens unite to build the People's New World Order, individuals will again have rights and be treated with decency. The people must implement sane policies that empower humanity and solve the challenges facing this world. By incorporating policies that promote the survival and enhancement of humanity, we will raise the harmonic of the planet, automatically eradicating humankind's destructive tendencies and repetitive cycles of disastrous and violent behavior, ongoing for the past couple millennia or more. By removing financial oppression, humanity and civilization will evolve to a higher plateau, and sanity will prevail over lunacy.

Using redeemable money will usher in a new period of prosperity for the entire country and for the entire world. Therefore, it is up to every American not to stand by but to stand up, participate, and demand a better world.

Very important to the People's World Order is another aspect of the economy that is vital to the prosperity of the United States, and that is international trade or, rather, the imbalances of international trade. If the people fail to demand more favorable trade relations with foreign nations, then we are guilty of abandoning a future filled with prosperity. Furthermore, we may feel we have betrayed the American Dream and the ideals that make America great. America must recapture its manufacturing base that was stolen by unfavorable trade deals like GATT and NAFTA. These abysmal trade agreements are still responsible for decimating the US economy and shipping America's manufacturing base overseas.

Some people may scoff at the notion that America is becoming a third-world country, but the sad fact is that America has already become a third-world country. As of early 2015, the Supplemental Nutrition Assistance Program, or food stamps, had over forty-six million recipients or beneficiaries, which comprise over 15 percent of the US population. That is a significant number and is indicative of the alarming number of Americans that are suffering in poverty without hope or opportunity for a better life. This will stop under the People's World Order because we will insist on trade deals that benefit the American workers and not destroy the American way of life.

The food stamp statistics reflect the types of horrible trade and general economic policies that were implemented by the bought-and-paid-for politicians under the direction of the globalists.

Under the People's World Order, citizens cannot stand by silently and fail to demand term restrictions and the instant removal of politicians who are in the pockets of the bankers. Politicians should only be allowed to self-fund or raise money from the electorate, and the amount of money raised by any politician should be limited to an appropriate and agreed-upon amount. This would allow less of an advantage to the very rich and those who have sold their souls to the devil. By limiting the amount that can be spent on elections, a common person could actually run and become the president of the United States.

Instead of having billionaires and corporations through Citizens United controlling US elections, we should limit their participation in politics. Corporations now run the government in a fascist manner without consideration of the interests of the American people; they are only interested in profits for their stockholders. For information regarding Citizens United and billionaires exercising financial control over political campaigns, please visit uscommonsense.org/research/citizens-united/.

The policies of the US government have already bankrupted this country. The people, as a nation, need to demand more from themselves and more from their elected officials. If we are satisfied with mediocrity in America, then we will be looked upon with disdain by the rest of civilized people. Without addressing these matters, the United States will ultimately be ostracized and left to drift into oblivion and despair, unable to compete with the rest of the world.

America is a nation of great people. We have had enough and are not going to drift silently into the darkness of night. We, as a nation, would rather stand and fight than see the greatest country in the world reduced to a footnote in the annals of world history.

However, violence is unnecessary in reforming this planet into something great again; the people are a strong and powerful force for good and justice.

Brazil, Russia, India, China, South Africa—commonly abbreviated as BRICS—and many other nations are creating strategic trade alliances that exclude the use of the Federal Reserve Note and the US petrodollar. In essence, because the US national debt is colossal, far beyond the capability of the US citizenry to satisfy it, the BRICS international alliance is preparing for an international economy that does not include the United States. The other countries know that the United States is the largest debtor in the world and is soon destined to be a third-world, bankrupt country.

The ramifications of horribly negotiated strategic trading alliances are leaving Americans doomed to economic isolation and contraction. Without a unified effort to change the policies and direction of today's New World Order, which is devised to destroy America, Americans are doomed to inherit the current New World Order. This will ultimately leave the United States in shambles.

With over twenty trillion dollars' worth of federal debt and many tens of trillions of entitlements, there is no way that US citizens can pay the tax needed to satisfy the US national debt. The escalation of the amount of benefits and entitlements owed is exponentially growing in order to pay for the over ten thousand baby boomers who are reaching retirement age every day. As a result, taxing of Americans must accelerate in direct proportion to the escalation of the number of elderly people receiving federally mandated entitlements. Because of this, it is very urgent that citizens act to establish economic policies that are realistic in nature and not detrimental to the upcoming generations.

If left unabated by citizens' inaction, the country will likely implement some drastic measures in order to be able to balance its books. This will create a situation much like the one recently experienced in Greece. The IMF has confiscated many of the valuable properties of Greece to collateralize its debt. This includes the Greek seaports, airports, and the most valuable real estate that the country has to offer.

The Greek politicians that chose to renegotiate with the international bankers decided to betray the Greek citizens and remain enslaved to the European Central Bank. A sane, properly negotiated solution on behalf of the Greek citizens would have been to negate, terminate, and eradicate their national debt because the country acquired this debt under fraudulent circumstances.

Americans need to implement a sane monetary policy to avert the largest financial debacle the world has ever seen. If the United States continues with its current monetary policy, a worldwide economic collapse will allow New World Order proponents to accelerate their plans toward achieving their diabolic goals.

To create a world in which people can enjoy themselves and thrive, we must realize that the government, under the direction of the international banks, implements devastating monetary policies that allow for immense pillaging of the middle class's wealth, thereby allocating the people's funds to the very richest segment of society. This pillaging of the middle class's wealth is done quite effectively through the acquisitions of military armaments and supplies and other government purchases that increase the national debt. Welfare for the rich is easily illustrated through defense contracts and the purchase of armaments from a very small group of unconscionable manufacturers with intimate and clandestine government relations. This betrayal of the American people will immediately cease under the People's World Order.

The US government has lost creditability because it has mismanaged the affairs of the US economy for many decades. The US economy is designed to allow monetary theft from the public at large. At some point, the economic scales of the nation's debt and its gross domestic production will not balance. The United States will inevitably collapse under the theft of the national debt.

Today in order to avoid the highest corporate tax rates of all the countries in the world, companies are fleeing America like rats from a sinking ship. To do business in America today is to assure a loss tomorrow, unless and until the people insist that the US monetary and taxation systems are changed to more ethical and just systems that assist the economy and the people to prosper. That is how life is supposed to be.

There is no need for all the financial stress Americans face on a daily basis. It occurs only because we are using a monetary system conceived in hell and dishonestly and deceptively foisted upon the nation by agents of Satan himself.

The oppressive mechanisms inherent in the Federal Reserve System or any other privately owned fiat currency is not going to be rectified by simply increasing the magnitude of the government's taxation. This simply leads to the people laboring immense amounts to pay ever-increasing taxes for an imaginary debt created by a hellacious criminal banking and taxing cabal.

In America, people who disapprove of the criminal tax systems are branded as criminals and tax protesters, when the criminals are those that institute unfair economic conditions making flourishing in America almost impossible. Life will be a breeze, compared to what we are now experiencing in America's bleak economy, once we extricate ourselves from the chains and shackles that have been thrown upon us by the bankers and their contemptible corruption.

In economics, one can mathematically derive the point where the people are unable to pay the nation's debt, and that is the point where the bankruptcy of the nation becomes obvious to just about everyone. Currently, the United States is so upside down in its financial affairs that the country's only logical course of corrective action is to default on the national debt, which has been bogus from its inception, and quit paying our hard-earned wages to extorting criminals.

Since the nation's debt was contracted and accumulated under fraudulent circumstances, the debt can therefore be adjudicated as void and invalid, cancelled and nonexistent, under the legal axiom, "No one should profit from fraud." Therefore, all financial and monetary policies undertaken to build a better world order need to insist on the negation and forgiveness of all countries' debts owed to international private bankers. By simultaneously cancelling and forgiving a nation's debts, countries will avoid bankruptcy and receive amnesty once they design and provide an in-house monetary system based on redeemable money.

Another prudent step to take in reversing the economic damage created by the world bankers is to return all gold, silver, and all other assets taken by the bankers and return it to the people, either voluntarily or under the orders enforced by America's great fighting men and women in the US armed forces. Every service member is sworn to protect America from all enemies, both foreign and domestic. America's armed forces should round up, arrest, and prosecute the international bankers for their crimes against society and protect the American people and the billions suffering in deplorable conditions and abject poverty because of the evils of using fiat money and a corrupt banking system.

Twelve families control all the wealth of this planet, and three hundred million Americans sit silently as the financial noose tightens around our necks and the necks of our children. Let us take back what is rightfully ours as a nation—our money and our dignity.

How ridiculous is a monetary system when there is no actual money of value, only debt instruments created out of thin air and conceived to enslave everyone under the bankers?

Once people understand that all countries under the rule of the BIS are precariously susceptible to hyperinflation, as Brazil experienced with its three- and four-digit inflation rates that were accelerating out of control from 1980 to 1984, they soon come to realize that drastic monetary change is in order. When we see the alternative, it becomes apparent that financial restructuring is the only sane course of action for all countries that are currently using worthless fiat currencies. The fundamental economic indicators comparing a nation's debt to its GDP currently foretell that America is quickly approaching similarly perilous economic conditions as those experienced by Brazil just prior to 1980 when its inflation began to skyrocket.

Watch out, America. Our turn is soon, unless we care to do something about it. Let us fix our country; our country is very broken but not beyond repair. Our country is burdened by a highly destructive monetary system that imprisons and enslaves everything and everyone it touches; let us replace it for a monetary system that empowers the people and not the bankers.

The corruption of government and its rulers has run its course. The people of every nation have had more than enough government-sponsored and government-subsidized terror and warfare. To continue on this path is to commit treason against all humankind.

One way or the other, either the New World Order or the People's World Order will come to fruition. It is best if the next world order is designed by and for the people and not the corporations. Today, US corporations' interests are treated far superior to the interests of US citizens. This is wrong on so many levels that one becomes inclined to examine the standard of justice delivered in the nation's court systems to discover how this is allowed to continue.

How corrupt are the courts that intend to usher humanity into permanent shackles of enslavement? How can judges adjudicate against the interests of the population and in support of a criminal banking apparatus, administratively instituted to support and benefit the international bankers and corporations over the interests and benefit of the American people? How can the judges sleep knowing they are ruling in favor of the enslavement of the population? Every tax case, as well as every foreclosure case, adjudicated against an American citizen and in favor of foreign bankers is an act of treason.

One can steal only so much, for only so long, before the populace wakes up and says enough is enough! The people understand the consequences of the country's reaching the point of having an unserviceable debt. The nation's debt is the exact amount of money that the international bankers have ripped off from all of us—as well as our children, our grandchildren, and their progeny.

The monetary point of no return or recovery was experienced in the recent collapses of Iceland, Argentina, Greece, Ukraine, and many other countries. The United States, unwavering in its course, is soon to follow in their footsteps and collapse.

The US resolution for bankruptcy, like all other problems facing incompetent politicians, is to throw more money at the problem and simply kick the proverbial can down the road. This avoidance tactic works only for so long, and then becomes a national calamity. Once the market is flooded with too many dollars, those dollars inevitably become unacceptable to other nations, corporations, and individuals.

Throwing money at the problem was the method the US government used to assist the "too big to fail" banks and insurance companies. The problem is that many countries, banks, and insurance companies have already failed. In William Engdahl's interview, US Won't Recover for at

Least 15 Years (youtube.com/watch?v=SmWQxNKOD7U&NR=1), he explains what actually caused the collapse of Greece. In Gods of Money, Engdahl further discusses the actions of the international financiers, who engage in covert economic warfare to gain control over various populations. In a best-case scenario, he believes that the US economy will not recover for at least a decade and that it may take fifteen years or it may never recover.

Max Keiser discussed the Greek economic crisis and the financial predators on Athens's international radio on March 8 and 17, 2010. Keiser's insights can be heard in this short interview (Brasschecktv.com/page/846.html) where he exposes the treasonous actions of financial pirates bent on destroying one nation after another.

Additionally, I highly recommend studying at Brasschecktv.com, as it has an incredible library of informative videos that you should find very interesting to view regarding what the Establishment calls "conspiracy theories." Unfortunately, upon review, many of the ominous predictions of the New World Order discussed on Brasscheck.tv have come true.

Greece suffered the plight of doing business with private bankers and learned one cannot stave off the inevitability of bankruptcy by throwing citizens' money at the problem. Other countries like Japan tried throwing money at its economic crisis in the 1980s, and its economy is just starting to rebound to the level it was at before the beginning of its economic crisis. Japan's economy still has not improved to its previous level of viability or sustainability, even though the government threw hundreds of billions of yen at the problem to stimulate its economy. Although this action of throwing money at the problem was very unsuccessful for the Japanese economy, it is nevertheless exactly what Obama did, which resulted in unsuccessfully delivering an economic recovery or a vitalized US economy.

Obama spent ten trillion dollars in eight years. Where is the improvement to the US economy? Many suspect that money was diverted to political cronies and crooks.

Any incomplete economic restructuring that continues to use fiat money creates only a larger problem further down the line. That is the "kick the can down the road" principle that the United States is employing to handle the instability of the American economy to no avail. The United States is never going to be able to pay the debt owed to the international bankers, and a major restructuring of the monetary system needs to be addressed on a global level, which will result in bettering the world economy, and in the process, raising the standard of living of all people.

If it is impossible for the United States to satisfy the national debt, then what practical reason could there be for the nation to continue down this monetary path of financial fantasy and wishful thinking by continuing to pay an unpayable debt?

Interest payments to the international bankers do not include paying the value of the principal amount that was theoretically borrowed. In reality, the international bankers never loaned the United States anything of value. In a transaction, if nothing of value changes hands, the transaction is and always remains invalid. The folks at the Federal Reserve have never lent a penny of value to the United States; they have only conned and defrauded the American people.

Americans can never be free as long as they are financial slaves to the world's banking cartel. Black, white, brown, yellow, or red—race does not matter; we are all slaves to the banking industry. Remember, after all, the Federal Reserve is a group that has special, magical powers to create fanciful US debt out of thin air. This firmly demonstrates that there is a special class that has procured a financial advantage over the rest of society, and this is the reason for the financial slavery that binds and bonds all Americans. This financial slavery is a sad commentary on America and its once-great and free people.

Only we the people can revitalize this world so that the important people, the masses, win. Our actions and our actions alone determine if we will finally liberate ourselves from the shackles that have been thrown upon the people of this great land. "Out with the bankers!" will be the next battle cry.

Only a monetary system that provides the population with an equitable form of money can endure. Real money frees the society; it also ensures the financial prosperity for those that use it. Why are Americans forced to pay for the use of private-fiat money when the United States can print its own real money for next to nothing?

Throughout history, those nations that reclaim their right to control and use real money have established economies that flourish, while those that use fiat money eventually and inevitably perish. There is nothing new in today's system of monetary enslavement where a wealthy ruling class of people possesses an advantage over the remainder of the people.

Most people understand this injustice, and yet there still exists actual slavery for millions around the world (en.wikipedia.org/wiki/History_of_slavery) and financial slavery for billions.

As humanity moves forward, it becomes imperative that under the People's World Order there can be no private banking systems allowed, as these are designed and destined to enslave humankind. The People's World Order is going to need to create an equitable banking system where the rights of humankind prevail in accordance with the foundational tenets of America, as originally conceived under its constitutional government, designed to protect the rights, liberties, and freedoms of all.

The right of the United States to control its own money should be vigilantly protected and, if need be, enforced by public hangings should any future group attempt to monetarily and treasonously subvert the United States and the American people. We have had quite enough continuous war, death, and terrorism!

Cabaltimes.com has an interesting article regarding the impetus of the Federal Reserve, its continual propagation of war, and its operational and philosophical differences compared with the Bank of Canada—"The Federal Reserve as an Instrument of War" at cabaltimes.com/2011/01/08/the-federal-reserve-as-an-instrument-of-war.

If we want a free and harmonious world, we have to demand that the wicked and unscrupulous Federal Reserve System is the first organization to be banished from the face of the earth.

As we return to our roots and build the People's World Order with peace and tranquility in mind, our primary objective regarding a stable monetary system is to ensure that redeemable money is recognized as legal tender for all transactions. A legal tender redeemable for value is almost unassailable by oppressive bankers, which by the way is why the Founding Fathers insisted and, even more so, demanded it to be the only type of money permitted in the US economy.

In order to free ourselves from the system's monetary enslavement that exists today, it is imperative that we usher in the return of an equitable and just monetary system as outlined by the Founding Fathers in the US Constitution, Article 1, Section 8, Clauses 5 and 6, which read:

Congress shall have power . . .

To coin Money, regulate the Value thereof, and of foreign Coin, and fix the Standard of Weights and Measures;

To provide for the Punishment of counterfeiting the Securities and current Coin of the United States

Furthermore, Article 1, Section 10, Clause 1 reads:

No State shall enter into any Treaty, Alliance, or Confederation; grant Letters of Marque and Reprisal; coin Money; emit Bills of Credit; **make any Thing but gold and silver Coin a Tender in Payment of Debts**; pass any Bill of Attainder, ex post facto Law, or Law impairing the Obligation of Contracts, or grant any Title of Nobility [emphasis added].

The Founding Fathers understood the fundamental principle and importance of protecting our nation's inherent rights—especially its right to control its own destiny by controlling its own redeemable money.

Americans fought the American Revolutionary War and the War of 1812 to protect our nation's right to control its money and not pay astronomical interest to corrupt foreign bankers. The Founding Fathers did not approve or provide in the US Constitution any provisions for private bankers to control the money of the United States. The Bank of North America, followed by the First and Second Banks of the United States, all of which were private banks and all of which had their charters revoked, were created to enslave the masses, and eventually were dissolved by ethical politicians.

The War of 1812 was a direct retaliation and result of the failure of the First Bank of the United States to have its charter renewed by the US government in 1811.

There has been an ongoing war for control of the money system, longer than there has been a United States. There have also been four attempts to overthrow the United States by privatizing the banking system. As previously mentioned, these are detailed in The Coming Battle: A Complete History of the National Banking Money Power in the United States by America-loving patriot M. W. Walbert. This fascinating book discusses the various attempts of private bankers to monetarily overthrow the US government by instituting other private national banks similar to the Federal Reserve System. Walbert's book discusses the courageous politicians of the time, who took a stand, represented their fellow citizens at all costs, and revoked the foreign-owned bank's charter, returning control of the nation's money supply back into the hands of Congress.

As discussed previously in All Wars Are Bankers' Wars, many politicians opposing the private banks were assassinated for their efforts. An example of an American politician that stood his ground and fought for the financial rights of his fellow citizens is President Jackson. When asked of his greatest accomplishment while in office he replied, "I killed the bank." Of course, Jackson was speaking of the Second Bank of the United States, which he so strongly opposed.

He knew full well the consequences and retaliation the private bankers would mount against his opposition. Jackson considered the defeat of the Second Bank of the United States, the cancellation of its charter, and his returning the country's rights to control and regulate its own interest-free money back to the people—with whom the power correctly resides—among his greatest accomplishments.

In biographybase.com/biography/Jackson_Andrew.html, Jackson's positions are explained, which includes the reasons he believed private banking was not only unconstitutional but also monetarily destructive to the financial destiny of the country. Jackson realized the importance of the country's ability to self-govern and to self-direct the destiny of this great nation. He knew that a country forfeiting control of its money also forfeited its liberty and destiny.

President Jackson was a tenacious man who stood up to the omnipresent evils that existed as a result of the establishment of the Second Bank of the United States, which is tyrannically embodied today as the Federal Reserve System. Jackson bravely fought the New World Order of banking throughout his administration and won.

Many politicians of that time valued honor above their personal financial enrichment. Today, as it was in those days, great wealth is offered to every federal politician in exchange for selling his or her constituency down the river by agreeing wholeheartedly to further the aims of the international private bankers.

Politicians who represented the people during those times found it an abomination that a private banking cabal would endeavor to usurp the US government, a government that provided the greatest opportunity of freedom available to mankind anywhere in the world.

Today's politicians have not only abandoned their duty of representing the people, but they have also united with private banking factions intent on usurping the God-given rights and freedoms outlined in the Constitution, thereby becoming active participants in treasonously enslaving the population.

Consider the presidential election of 2016 and the efforts of the banking and political establishment, which are one and the same, to defeat Donald Trump. The media and that faction of the Republican Party that is controlled by the Establishment with spokesmen like Ted Cruz, Jeb Bush, Marco Rubio, Lindsey Graham, John McCain, and other haters aggressively attacked Trump in an attempt to prevent him from cleaning up the cesspool of special interests that control the US government. It appears that those politicians that attacked Trump and attempted to divide the Republican Party were working as whores on behalf of the Establishment. Most of the above-mentioned politicians have failed to honor the pledge that they signed to support the presidential nominee of the Republican Party, who happened to be Donald Trump.

Grandpa used to say, "A person either is honest or is not. There's no gray area." A person whose word means nothing is deplorable and likely a criminal character with little to no integrity. Grandpa spoke the truth, for there is no compromise regarding integrity.

What people refer to as the Republican establishment or the Democratic establishment can be alternatively construed as fanciful; there is only one establishment, and it controls all political parties. This is why Republican sore losers and members of the Establishment like Jeb Bush attempted to destroy Trump and his chances to become the president with the hopes of having Clinton, allegedly the consummate establishment whore, winning the presidency. Virtually anyone that is still breathing knows that Clinton is bought and paid for by the special interests. She cares not about the needs of the people, but only about her and Bill's selfish interests.

There will continue to be greater efforts to induce Americans to forfeit their sovereignty and to participate in the New World Order.

People should never allow their freedoms to be taken from them. Any New World Order serving the private banking interests will only profit the few at the cost of the many. The world's unjust monetary system provides incredible profits and benefits to the special class of disgustingly corrupt bankers while preventing the rest of humanity from economically flourishing and prospering.

The facade that the New World Order presents to the population of the world is significantly different from the aims it secretly harbors. The financial enslavement by the bankers is the mechanism that is being utilized to bring down the standard of living of the world's nations in order that the different counties of the world will then be incentivized to merge into a totalitarian world state.

People will receive the New World Order that they demand. If we allow the bankers to utilize monetary enslavement methods to strip our freedoms, then we agree and fasten our own shackles of enslavement. It is up to each one of us to do our part to bring about the People's World Order, a world order we can be proud of, as it protects the freedoms of the masses and the sovereignty of all nations.

What we do here and now seals our fate and the fate of those to come. Our actions have to consist of more than being a lowly spectator. It is our duty as Americans to participate and stand against tyranny and to demand our rights by realizing our responsibilities. Without responsibilities, there are no rights; you are as free as you are responsible.

Generations from now, as the population either laments or delights in regard to the freedoms of society, people will know if our generation performed our duty to liberate mankind or if we failed. Do not think that we are fighting this battle for only ourselves. We are fighting for all humankind and future generations.

The People's World Order should ensure that the hungry cries of billions do not go unheard and uncared for but, instead, that compassion and the necessary economic infrastructure is created to uplift the devastating conditions of abject poverty that exist virtually everywhere today.

Abject poverty can be eliminated with organized programs that utilize internationally available natural resources. We can produce cooperative organizations that focus on improving the circumstances of the abject poor of this world by instituting proven agricultural models to uplift such devastated societies.

Poverty is the byproduct of poor organizational skills. Poverty is not a fixed and unchangeable condition, unless we agree it is fixed and unchangeable. Poverty can be eradicated by improving educational, administrative, and organizational skills that permit a group to utilize its resources to create exchangeable products with the outside world.

Successful economic agricultural models to eradicate starvation can be implemented in order to create farming communities that are able to feed many people. Such a feat is not that tough to pull off. Check out and support the good works of Farm Africa at farmafrica.org and Heifer International at heifer.org.

The reason abject poverty exists in the world today is that there is an interest in keeping people oppressed and desperately trying to scratch out a living. Why should much of the world's population not even have the simple necessities one needs to live, even water? Water.org is a fantastic program that provides clean drinking water to millions of deprived Africans.

I especially recommend that you read about and support the Buy a Lady a Drink campaign that Stella Artois has created in conjunction with water.org to bring water to millions of thirsty people, people that are dying because there is no drinkable water. Go buy a lady a drink is at stellaartois.com/en_us/buy-a-lady-a-drink.html. My wife regularly buys these attractive chalices, and with each purchase, a woman is given access to clean drinking water for five years. It's a win-win all around!

According to Stella Artois's website, almost seven hundred million people, more women and children than men, do not have access to clean drinking water. In five years, Buy a Lady a Drink has provided over three hundred thousand people with clean drinking water for five years. How wonderful is it that for every beautiful limited-edition chalice that you buy, water.org provides access to clean water for a woman living in an undeveloped country for five years?

We can all support these kinds of great efforts to provide food, water, and really dignity to humanity.

Many of us are constantly deluded into believing that the sufferings of humankind do not influence us on any level. This is untrue; we are all affected by the overall condition of this planet.

If we fast for a day or two, we can start to ponder what it would be like to die from starvation, dehydration, and hypothermia. The experience might deeply move us when we realize that on a daily basis over two billion people are starving to death. Two billion people are dying from a lack of food, water, and shelter. This statistic demonstrates the incompetence that humanity and the world's governments are applying to very important issues like starvation under the existing New World Order.

Surely, we can do better in the People's World Order. We can work internationally to solve the biggest problems facing humanity. We can work to establish policies that concentrate on removing abject poverty and starvation from the face of the planet allowing all a chance for dignity and life.

Instead of having a war on terrorism or drugs, let us play a game that rids the world of the suffering that plagues humanity. If we all put our heads, shoulders, and wallets together, we should be able to finally eradicate the evils of this world.

The eradication of starvation is right at the top of the People's World Order agenda.

Remember, hard work is the lubricant in the engine of success. Let us build the People's World Order, a better world order where future generations will examine our humanitarian actions and say that our generation took the responsibility and had the guts to stand up and change the world for the better. How long can we ignore the world's problems? Starvation and enslavement are no longer the world's problems; they are yours and mine. Your help is needed to build the People's World Order; furthermore, your assistance and contribution is fervently requested.

Let us all do our part to safeguard the world from the private bankers and their New World Order! Let us build the People's World Order. Let us build a world we can be proud of, where all people can live in harmony and rise to new heights. As a society, we need to strive to attain new heights of human intellect, which combine to allow humankind to create saner international relations and policies that are designed to provide peace, freedom, and honesty for all.

CHAPTER 20

America's Leading Role
in Societal Evolution

My dream is of a place and a time where America will once again be seen as the last best hope of earth.

— ABRAHAM LINCOLN

America was not built on fear. America was built on courage, on imagination and an unbeatable determination to do the job at hand.

— HARRY S. TRUMAN

Our flag honors those who fought to protect it, and is a reminder of the sacrifice of our nation's founders and heroes. As the ultimate icon of America's storied history, the Stars and Stripes represents the very best of this nation.

— JOE BARTON

I believe that freedom of speech and freedom of religion go hand-in-hand in America.

— KIRK CAMERON

America's fighting men and women sacrificed much to ensure that our great nation stays free. We owe a debt of gratitude to the soldiers that have paid the ultimate price for this cause, as well as those who are blessed enough to return from the battlefield unscathed.

— ALLEN BOYD

The things that will destroy America are prosperity-at-any-price, peace-at-any-price, safety-first instead of duty-first, the love of soft living, and the get-rich-quick theory of life.

– THEODORE ROOSEVELT

Here in America we are descended in blood and in spirit from revolutionists and rebels-men and women who dare to dissent from accepted doctrine. As their heirs, may we never confuse honest dissent with disloyal subversion.

– DWIGHT D. EISENHOWER

America is moving forward and gaining strength. We have been tested, and we have proven ourselves to be a tough, resilient and resourceful nation.

– BILL FRIST

The Constitution doesn't guarantee happiness, only the pursuit of it. You have to catch up with it yourself.

– BENJAMIN FRANKLIN

THERE COMES A TIME IN EVERY CIVILIZATION when those who are oppressed rise against their oppressors. History reports various revolutions and the brutal manner in which oppressors are rounded up by those they have oppressed, who in turn enjoy dispensing a form of fleeting justice solely found at the end of a rope. There is usually an abundance of violence associated with political revolutions, and those who start revolutions, if they live, usually become the leaders of the post-revolution nation.

Instead of a violent revolution, there is another method to employ that assists in creating social and political improvements. Evolution of the species and improving the awareness and intelligence of the individual members of society will result in the citizens demanding improved professional administration of the society's governments by political leaders competent to create policies more intelligently designed to raise and enlighten the consciousness of humanity. Raising of awareness and intelligence increases the odds of preserving humanity as a species; for failing to increase the awareness and intelligence of a species often results in the demise and extinction of such a retarded species.

Preservation and propagation of the human species are the primary elements that should be examined to determine the effectiveness of those who create and implement policies that affect the people en masse. If the policies implemented negatively affect the survival capabilities of the human species as a whole, then that policy should be modified to promote the continuation and support of all people that comprise society.

It is vital that people dedicate their lives to improving the politically instituted policies, which negatively affect us all. Evil prevails when decent people do nothing.

America has reached the point of no return. The politicians have given control of the country to the enemies of the people. The enemies of humanity have used their power to suppress the populace with tyrannical taxation and other legislative methods designed to transfer any remaining freedoms citizens possess into the hands of a global government bent on the destruction of humanity.

The US government has overstepped its bounds to such a degree that it is now attempting to dictate how citizens live every aspect of their lives starting in the cradle and ending in the grave. Government infringes upon our rights by dictating what kind of doctors and medical treatment we can seek, what kinds of cars we can buy and how fast we can drive them, whom we can marry, how our children are raised, and what kinds of structures we can build on land that we supposedly have purchased.

Anyone who cares to investigate the US government can see it long ago changed its allegiance from its constituents to its controlling corporate donors, who are the financial dictators of politicians and the policies of the world.

It is time we hold criminal politicians accountable. People have suffered under the duress of these financial dictators and political maniacs long enough and have had more than enough of their self-serving crimes.

It is time that all Americans swear to uphold and perform their civic duty and reinvigorate America and the American spirit. The greatness that America represents needs to be magnified and promoted a hundred times over. Americans have been complacent and have allowed the American Dream to become tarnished to the point of its becoming the American Nightmare.

As America leads, the world follows. The great people of America have led the world with technical advancements that have greatly improved the world. Our once-prominent manufacturing base was the envy of the world, and we have let it become exported to other countries around the globe.

America has degraded to such an extent that it primarily exports war and death, and in response, the rest of the world has no option but to re-ciprocate in kind. When America exports technology that improves the human condition, the world will also respond in kind.

This is one of the keys to elevating the condition of the world. This philosophy is covered in many religions under the golden rule, "Do unto others as you would have them do unto you," and the Bible tells us, "You reap what you sow."

It is time America returns to being the world's moral and ethical leader, stops exporting bombs and bullets, and starts exporting products that are needed and wanted by the rest of the world.

If Americans are hell-bent on killing others, as evidenced by the deadly military actions we conduct around the world, do you think others will be hell-bent on killing Americans?

There is much room for improvement in this world, and America needs to be the guiding light utilizing the vast talents of the American people to create such improvement. The focus of US foreign policy needs to be shifted to feeding and improving the lives of the people of the world instead killing them. Programs that provide food, water, and shelter and improve the world's infrastructure should be immediately ini-tiated to ameliorate poverty and starvation.

If America spent the six trillion dollars on programs that improved the human condition around the world, instead of fighting in Iraq and Afghanistan, the world would be a much nicer place to live.

Hundreds of millions, if not billions, of people around the world equate the United States and its incredibly efficient killing machine with Satan. The United States is hated wherever its military men and women drop a bomb or pull a trigger. Fractured families, displaced and de-stroyed by America's military conquests, are very likely to retaliate and dedicate their lives to killing Americans.

America leads the world, and when it goes around instituting politi-cide, we can expect nothing less in return for ourselves. Upon examining the quality of the air, food, and water in the United States, one can only conclude that the government is currently exterminating the US popula-tion. When sterilization agents are legislatively mandated into municipal water systems, the result is the intended reduction and elimination of the species. Americans are being killed without the use of guns and bullets; we are being chemically exterminated like a colony of unwanted bugs.

Americans are tired of the oppressive elements within their government and the treasonous politicians who miserably fail to rid the government of both foreign and domestic enemies. Even though the politicians are sworn to uphold the Constitution, it is amazing how many treasonous actions they commit and how many of them, on a daily basis, become enemies of the nation.

There are still dedicated politicians who sincerely fight for the well-being of the people. Those ethical politicians are admired by the masses very much but are seldom adequately acknowledged and appreciated for their loyal service to the country and its citizens.

Then there are treasonous politicians. Consider the Iran deal negotiated under the leadership of the secretaries of state, Clinton and Kerry. What kind of signal are we sending to the world when we give over 150 billion dollars to Iran, the largest sponsor of international terrorism? What do the people of the world think of the American government when they see our politicians destroying our world?

Did the president approve this deal to incite massive upset and violence in the Middle East? You bet he did. Was the president—who is of Muslim faith—using his political power to further a religious war among Americans, Arabs, and the Jews? Yes, unequivocally, he is guilty as charged.

Obama's actions, which the press promoted as the result of incompetency, were performed treacherously and treasonously to escalate the hatred between Muslims, Christians, and Jews. His actions were calculated to cause as much damage as possible to the stability of America's international relations.

Consider Obama's acceptance of Syrian refugees—thousands of whom we were unable to vet. This infiltration by Syrian refugees happened at an alarming rate. We can easily conclude that Obama's surreptitious actions were covertly designed to destroy America. It appears Obama is simply a traitor to the American people and should be treated accordingly.

It is not that the people of the world despise governments, but rather, the people cry out for proper, just, and ethical governments. Americans deplore their tyrannical form of private governance, which robs from the poor and gives to the rich.

If we fail to stand up to the tyranny in America, any rights the people still possess will vanish.

America's position and its reputation in the world is a reflection of the actions that it undertakes to bring peace and tranquility to the rest of the world. During the 1940s, 1950s, and 1960s, the United States was the envy of the world because it produced products that were exported and enjoyed internationally.

The GATT and NAFTA agreements shipped much of America's manufacturing base to foreign countries like China, Japan, Mexico, India, Vietnam, and too many others to list. Treasonous politicians intentionally implemented these trade agreements to lower Americans' standard of living and destroy this once-great nation.

When America lost most of its manufacturing base, it turned to increasing the last vestiges of industry left in the United States; it vastly increased military spending and production. When America focuses on making and exporting military weaponry and using it to maim and kill our fellows, America becomes Satan to the rest of the world, and the repute of this once glorious nation tanks.

If a foreign country were bombing your neighborhood, you might quickly learn to despise and hate that enemy with the same disdain as Satan. When foreigners literally chant, "Death to America," it is not because the United States is exporting love and kindness. Foreigners do not hate America because it is performing good acts and loving deeds around the world; they do not hate the United States because of America's high standard of living. People hate Americans because we bomb the hell out of them! Do not be fooled for an instant.

America needs to take inventory of all the great industries it has created and lost to overseas markets throughout its history. It would behoove America to reinvigorate its manufacturing base and start making products that bring third-world countries into the twenty-first century.

As the world's superpower, America could benefit greatly if it focused on uplifting the people of this world and not destroying them. Think of the harmonizing effect the United States could have internationally if we decide to create a world that empowers and uplifts all people from the hardships that most of the world's population endures. Imagine if the US built and exported products that raised the standard of living of people everywhere around the globe.

Starvation should no longer exist on this planet, and if Americans simply focused as a nation to eradicate starvation, we would be playing a more proper role as the superpower that America really is and should be.

America needs to lead with strength, but moreover, America needs to lead with compassion and intelligence. America should stop being a military superpower with a military-based economy and start making products that are useful and helpful to humankind. If the United States significantly penalizes corporations that make military weapons, this would persuade those corporations to retool and devise products that are more reflective of the goodwill and nature of the American people.

Defense contractors and the products and services they deliver should be heavily taxed. There should be a corollary taxation policy; industries that create damage should be more heavily taxed than all other areas or sectors of the economy.

America has to make a choice. Should the United States continue to irresponsibly deploy American troops and remain the world's largest military merchant of chaos, or should America make the world a better place? If we all do nothing and ignore the problem, it could result in this nuclear age in the complete destruction and annihilation of humanity and the world as we know it.

Time has proven throughout history that war is the wrong road to travel. America is better than this; it is time we start behaving accordingly. To sit by and do nothing is to condone the actions of psychotic leaders who have usurped the government for their own devious means and profits. It is time for Americans to demand more of their leaders and country.

Since the George W. Bush administration, there has been an ongoing public relations campaign to destroy the goodwill and repute of America. Many of us thought that no one could damage the repute of the United States any further than George W. Bush, but boy, were we wrong.

Under Obama and Secretary Clinton, the repute of America was tarnished like never before, as our nation was pimped out like a skanky prostitute to the highest bidder. Shame on the Justice and State Departments and shame on the FBI! The subordinates of Lynch, Clinton, and Comey are potentially just as treasonous for their inaction by not demanding the removal of their bosses. For there to be justice, the attorneys at the Justice and State Departments and the FBI need to do whatever it takes to initiate proceedings to remove any and all corrupt bosses and/or employees from their positions of federal employment and charge them as the traitors they are—traitors against the people of the United States.

It is time we grow up as a country and a civilization and become the ethical leader that America was born to be! As they say, for the past several decades or more, America has played the role of the world's police officer. It is time for America to play the role of the world's peace officer and become a conduit of empowerment around the world. Let our country be recognized as the ultimate force for good that this planet has ever seen. By bringing peace and prosperity, may we silence the thunderous and unwanted chants of "death to America."

CHAPTER 21

Organize or We All Die

There is more power in unity than division.
— EMANUEL CLEAVER

One of the main tasks of theology is to find words that do not divide but unite, that do not create conflict but unity, that do not hurt but heal.
— HENRI NOUWEN

Look out into the universe and contemplate the glory of God. Observe the stars, millions of them, twinkling in the night sky, all with a message of unity, part of the very nature of God.
— SAI BABA

The very first lesson I learnt from the Qur'an was the message of unity and peace.
— CAT STEVENS

Unity can only be manifested by the Binary. Unity itself and the idea of Unity are already two.
— BUDDHA

Our Christian conviction is that Christ is also the messiah of Israel. Certainly it is in the hands of God how and when the unification of Jews and Christians into the people of God will take place.
— POPE BENEDICT XVI

Unity is strength . . . when there is teamwork and collaboration, wonderful things can be achieved.
— MATTIE STEPANEK

Where there is unity there is always victory.

– PUBLILIUS SYRUS

Even if a unity of faith is not possible, a unity of life is.

– HANS URS VON BALTHASAR

Unity teaches us that unity is strength and cautions us to sub-merge and overcome our differences in the quest for common goals, to strive with all our combined strength for the path to true African brotherhood and unity.

– HAILE SELASSIE

The essence of the beautiful is unity in variety.

– FELIX MENDELSSOHN

Talent perceives differences; genius, unity.

– WILLIAM BUTLER YEATS

World Peace Day is envisioned to become a moment of global unity. It is up to each and every one of us to make this a reality.

– JEREMY GILLEY

Our flag is not just one of many political points of view. Rather, the flag is a symbol of our national unity.

– ADRIAN CRONAUER

THROUGHOUT HISTORY, there has run a common thread of suppression by a small segment of the population that collects its energies and profits from the masses. These devious people know the importance of proper planning and execution against an unsuspecting populace.

The elite's greatest fear is that the population will turn off its sports channels and decide to do something about the insidious ploy continually perpetrated against Americans and all people from around the world. Distraction after bloody distraction is thrust upon Americans by the media with the sole intention of preventing us from investigating for ourselves what the special interests are actually doing to the population of the planet to satisfy their insatiable lust for power.

The major purposes of this book are to release the world from the grip of a tiny cabal of evil oppressors, to facilitate and assist Americans to regain their rights, and to return the US government's power back to the American people. This transformation should be conducted in a peaceful movement by intellectually elevating the masses and collectively returning the current corporate fascist form of the US government back to a republic, as established by and in accordance with the intentions of the Founding Fathers' Constitution.

Americans do not want, neither should we have, a foreign policy of globalism. It is not the job of the United States to police the world. Americans are sick and tired of being abused and having our best young men and women maimed and killed in battles that have nothing to do with American interests. We are tired of fighting wars for corporations.

Americans no longer want to be harbingers of death and war; Americans want to be harbingers of light and peace. Americans are a good people, and the actions of the government need to reflect that goodness.

Today the actions of the US government are reflective of what one would expect from a class of psychopaths who are determined to inflict harm as severely, as often, and to as many innocent people as possible. The world needs to replace the terrorist movement by forming a responsible class of citizens to reformulate our world to reflect the goodness of the brotherhood and sisterhood of humanity. Rather than writing "brotherhood and sisterhood," we can coin the word "humanhood" meaning the rank, level, or quality of the collective well-being of the species and society.

Humanhood also encapsulates the relation of humanity and its care and stewardship of the environment, including other various ecological manifestations such as the quality of the air, water, and different micro and macro habitats of the world.

We need to curb the power possessed by the demented political segment of this society and direct that power into the hands of more capable individuals and groups that have good intentions in their hearts. The creation of a group of united citizens from each country should have a say, if not all the say, in the direction that this world shall head.

The worldwide government corruption and oppression that civilization has been living under for centuries have failed miserably. It is time that the people demand loyal and not treasonous service from their public servants. Traitors, once discovered, need to be punished to the full extent of the law. Treason is a crime that most direly affects the people of a nation.

To honor our fallen friends of 9/11 and their families, 911truthbetold.com is a site that is dedicated to bringing peace to this world. We need to have a more intelligent and effective group that truly wants and diligently works for positive change in this world, change that rightfully benefits the people and not the miniscule special ruling class. We especially welcome you to join and be the force for good that this world needs, and please encourage your friends to join us. Your suggestions, your input, and your help are appreciated more than anything you can imagine. Be the spokesperson for the billions that have no voice.

More quickly than one would think, as an organized force, we can create positive change in the different topics discussed in this book that are destroying our world. Help bring about the change you have always imagined possible to this forsaken world. If left uninterrupted, our world is frantically racing towards oblivion. Be the positive interruption on behalf of and for the sake of humanity.

As you recall, many of the world's national and state capitals have reflection pools, which symbolically suggest that people get the quality of government that they deserve. The government is a reflection of the people. Americans are looking into their nation's reflection pools and expressing their dissatisfaction in the performance of those who govern them. More than that, we are realizing our own dissatisfaction of our own actions and failure to demand betterment for this world. Now is the time to do something about all the pain, suffering, and injustice that plagues humanity in a world designed and controlled by psychopaths.

Instead of implementing destructive American foreign policies, the government should create policies and relations that soothe and bring comfort to the world's population. America cannot continue to justify its ongoing international killing spree or continue to approve of and carry on with the barbarity we constantly see in the Middle East and around the world.

Since the inception of nuclear weapons, to continue to participate in world war is an insane act of demented governments and a people bent on genocide and national suicide.

Those who work in government service must be especially diligent in rounding up the bad apples that are destroying the world. Anyone who assists the treasonous parties working on behalf of the private bankers needs to be tried, convicted, and punished for treason or at least as an accessory to treason against the United States. It should not matter if one's relative was the president; in America, no one is supposed to be above the law.

It is up to the people to clean up a corrupt and criminal government. Following is a lawful tool that can be used for that purpose. It is a necessary step to clean house in order to institute a moral and effective representative government. Without removing the basket of criminal traitors from within the US government, any actions to implement an honest and forthright government will be fought by those that are benefiting from an abundance of corruption and criminality that exists within the US government.

The US government has a history of being as laughable a puppet government as the corrupt government appointed in Iraq by the globalists. There are a few heroes who resist the puppet government and are conducting congressional oversight hearings and investigation, thereby attempting to bring integrity back to the function of the federal government.

Under Federal law 18 USC 2381, treason is defined as follows:

Whoever, owing allegiance to the United States, levies war against them or adheres to their enemies, giving them aid and comfort within the United States or elsewhere, is guilty of treason and shall suffer death, or shall be imprisoned not less than five years and fined under this title but not less than $10,000; and shall be incapable of holding any office under the United States.

Do government and military employees ever question what they are doing and the orders they carry out during the course of their employment? If a government supervisor demands that his subordinate perform an action that is unconstitutional, does the subordinate worker have an avenue of reporting the treasonous act and not immediately becoming an accessory to that act of national betrayal? We should ask the Justice Department and the FBI if the federal government whistleblower programs really provide any protection for those that expose the real criminals hidden within the government.

Only by every American demanding that all government employees behave in accordance with the US Constitution and follow the laws of the land will this country turn around, start to recover, and elevate to a higher plane of existence. Any group is only as strong and valuable as it believes in and upholds justice and ethics. Professionals have a code of integrity and decency that the criminal cannot imagine; there is neither honor among thieves nor decency among traitors.

If the members of a team do not insist their teammates, and even the coach, act in a manner that is best for the team, one can almost immediately conclude that is going to be a losing team. Players on a winning team insist that all teammates contribute towards the best interests and goals of the team. They ardently protect, zealously prevent, and fervently repel anything that is the least bit harmful toward the interests and aspirations of the team. Once the team discovers that a player or coach is working against the best interests of the team, as quickly as can be arranged, that person is fired or traded to an opposing team.

The United States considers treason an incredibly damaging crime and includes death as a punishment for treasonous violations. During the 1800s, although not always recorded in the pages of history, once committers of treasonous acts against society were discovered, usually their hangings were quick to follow. More often than you can imagine, cowboys would hang a judge or politician who got too big for his britches and acted against the people he was supposed to serve.

The United States, if properly operated and administrated in accordance with the original tenets established in the Constitution, should be a government that serves the people who created it and not the bankers who stole it.

The bankers stole something very important to this world; they stole the good ole USA and everything the American Dream represents. It is time to take our country back! If we fail to take back America, which is rightfully ours, then we have forfeited something more valuable than all our dreams.

In all likelihood, this is humanity's last chance to remove the bankers' noose from around the necks of the people. Sadly but true, if we don't throw the bankers' noose off our necks now, the noose will likely be too tight for our children to free themselves in the future. For our sake and our children's sake, there is nothing more important than for us to leave this world a better place than we found it.

For far too long, Americans have allowed hoodlums and scumbags to run this country, and the world for that matter, for their own selfish profits and at a cost of hundreds of millions of lives that they have harmed with indescribable heartbreak and injury. To allow the Establishment's deranged management of the usurped United States to continue is to allow the scourge of the earth to operate unchecked and unobstructed and leaving only human carnage in its wake. Human carnage is the telltale indicator and the Establishment's trademark of death.

The world's children will inherit the world we leave upon our deaths. Americans need to unite and bring their power to Washington and demand that the US government create and institute policies designed for the good of the planet and, most importantly, the benefit of humankind. When Americans stand up to global oppression, the lobbying powers of corporations that buy politicians will quickly wither into a relic of the past. With outrageous and clamoring cries of the American people to restore the federal government back to an empowering constitutional government, we can work together and build a better world for our progeny and theirs.

To honor all the great men and women who have died in service to America, we should restore the ideals that make America the greatest nation ever conceived by man. Once again, America and its unconquerable people will be recognized as the land of opportunity. America will once again possess an especially glorious beacon of love, protecting and imbuing the entire world with the light of the ages.

America's return to a great nation will occur when the people stand and demand a return to the true principles of the Constitution. America's republic was conceived to liberate man from the tyrannical rule of England. Now, centuries later, Americans are no longer free but ruled by the same foreign English bankers. Americans and the world at large are no longer self-governed but governed by a nefarious cult, who possess unlimited wealth and viciousness.

Abraham Lincoln's Gettysburg Address (November 19, 1863) decreed that America's fallen did not die in vain but died to preserve the freedoms and liberties available only in America (interestingly, there are four copies of Lincoln's Gettysburg Address, which can be compared at the following link, abrahamlincolnonline.org/lincoln/speeches/gettysburg.htm

Four score and seven years ago our fathers brought forth on this continent a new nation conceived in liberty and dedicated to the proposition that all men are created equal.

Now we are engaged in a great civil war testing whether that nation or any nation so conceived and so dedicated can long endure. We are met on a great battlefield of that war. We have come to dedicate a portion of that field as a final resting place for those who here gave their lives that that nation might live. It is altogether fitting and proper that we should do this.

But in a larger sense we cannot dedicate, we cannot consecrate, we cannot hallow this ground. The brave men, living and dead who struggled here have consecrated it far above our poor power to add or detract. The world will little note nor long remember what we say here, but it can never forget what they did here. It is for us the living rather to be dedicated here to the unfinished work, which they who fought here have thus far so nobly advanced. It is rather for us to be here dedicated to the great task remaining before us. That from these honored dead we take increased devotion to that cause for which they gave the last full measure of devotion. That we here highly resolve that these dead shall not have died in vain. That this nation, under God, shall have a new birth of freedom. And that government of the people, by the people, for the people shall not perish from the earth.

What are we doing? Are we going to disappoint all Americans that have come before us, our countless American ancestors who sacrificed and died in order that we can enjoy all the liberties this great land provides? Although those in power believe they are the only ones capable of directing this nation, the American people must regain control of this great nation. It is every American's responsibility to ensure that not another drop of our veterans' blood spills for the bankers' shiny coins. American troops need to be commanded to fight for the American people and not the interests of the financial and corporate elites.

American resolve is an undervalued commodity that is bred into every American's DNA and permeates to the depths of our souls and the bottom of our hearts; we will not sit silently as the life of our nation is strangled away right before the eyes of the American people. We will rise with great resolve, relinquish power from undeserving and incompetent criminals, and return our nation's power back to the people.

The goal of the elite is to reduce the population by over six and a half billion people, thereby making the population manageable by the self-proclaimed murderous elite. The elite are already marching ahead with their very achievable goal of exterminating a majority of humankind. That is one reason why warfare is so very popular among the so-called elite; it aligns with their goals of vastly reducing the world's population.

Throughout history, evil people have organized to forward their goals and objectives, often with assistance from governments, while good and decent people have simply gone on living their individual lives to the best of their ability, unaware that such devious plans are in the works to eradicate their freedoms. Centuries ago, evildoers and connivers organized to rule society and fulfill their interests, while the masses have to this day failed to organize and the people's interests remain ignored.

The elite number only a paltry and pathetic seven thousand of the seven billion people living in the world; this is a small fraction of the overall population—one in a million. Most of the population practice goodness and kindness in daily actions, while the elite commit the most anti-social and horrendous acts without a speck of compunction or remorse.

Organized, civic-minded people need to continually and diligently monitor government activities and implement independent civilian checks and balances to remove organized evil from the US government. The people need to create their own legal community that fights for the people's rights over politicians' rights and eradicates corruption from within the walls of government.

The most effective method to manage the masses is to prevent us from discovering that we are being scientifically and systematically monitored and manipulated, attacked and abused, and infected and injured for the entirety of our lives.

Keeping the masses unaware of the master's iron fist, often wrapped in a velvet glove, is the primary method used by the elite to prevent their overthrow from power. This is the composition and aim of the matrix we find ourselves trapped within, a matrix that keeps humanity confused and ignorant of who exactly makes society function as poorly as it does. To overcome the matrix, our life's work must include improving the actual condition of this world. Only our contributions to others—whom we have helped and what we have contributed to improving the world for humanity—may be the only things remembered upon and after our passing.

The biggest fear of the so-called elite is that common people will unite and take back what is rightfully ours.

Our rights and freedoms that are gifts from the Creator have been replaced by privileges extended by a superior class of tyrants with drudgery, hardships, and suffering the universal result. We cannot continue to allow a miniscule group of unethical politicians under the guise of an infallible state to regulate our lives into bondage and slavery.

The United States of America was founded to eliminate taxation without representation and has deviated as far as humanly imaginable from that original tenet. Now there is no representation of the people, only taxation and abuse of the people. Taxation is only necessary because Americans have been hoodwinked by the Federal Reserve into believing we owe a national debt that was created through criminality and fraud. Americans must stop honoring the despicable and dishonorable agreements crafted and implemented fraudulently by criminals at the Federal Reserve.

Most people would do fine controlling their own lives and survive much better if they did not give over half their hard-earned money to the government. By being good citizens, remaining silent, and paying taxes, Americans are financing not only their own personal enslavement but also the enslavement of future generations.

The time to wake up is now, before it is too late. The elite have dug a hole of such gigantic proportions that returning our government to its original republic may seem difficult, if not virtually impossible. History is being forgotten and deleted at such a fast rate that future generations will have no idea of the basic fundamental doctrines, beliefs, and ideals that the United States was founded upon and proudly represents.

Americans must unify as a people and a nation, join their strengths, and do their best to improve the world to the point where Americans will be able to pass unto their posterity a world that reflects humanity's greatness, not a debased image of humanity that prevails and results from insanity and selfishness. Americans must form a unified and concentrated effort to rectify the insanity that the people, our parents, and our grandparents have allowed to pass as an excuse for the US government.

Americans need to clean house and get the US government under the people's control as originally designed. First, in order to obtain a saner world that we can all be proud of, we must reorganize the US government and its criminal monetary and banking systems. By eliminating these criminal elements from the US government, we will see immediate improvements in foreign policies, and the rest of the world will join under the new moral and ethical leadership of the United States. In turn, other nations will rise and uplift their country and their part of the world. Americans need to work with one another and, in cooperation with the rest of the world, build a better world. This is achievable by implementing saner and more effective policies designed to empower the people of the world, not destroy them.

We can no longer permit detrimental international planning by a small cabal to damage and exterminate the masses. Outdated Zionist methods of war and population control need to be replaced by more creative and evolutionary programs that contribute to the expansion and benefit of the masses.

Transformation of the economy from a war-based economy to a peace-based economy should be the number one item on corporate America's to-do list. Talk about a revolutionary idea. Imagine a world filled with an overflowing abundance of compassion and love; imagine a world where all America's goods and services are singularly designed to raise the people's standard of living.

Billions of people are in need of water on this planet, while others have wealth that exceeds the annual gross domestic production of many smaller nations. This is not a cry for socialism, merely a pleading for decency and equity for all.

Theft is highly rewarded in a corrupt political system such as America's, but soon it will be punished very aggressively, therein deterring future politicians from committing criminal acts. We need to hold politicians to the highest ethical and moral standards because their actions affect the populace at large. No longer will people tolerate self-serving politicians; they should be jailed as anyone else would be for committing such heinous acts against the people and certainly for traitorous acts against our country.

Americans must organize and demand that their government acts to prevent further catastrophes and terrorist acts, which in turn will lead to more stringent laws being passed, which will further usurp the citizens' rights and freedoms. It is your responsibility—yes, the responsibility of you, the reader, and not exclusively the responsibility of some other leader—to wake up and organize as many of your family, friends, associates, and followers and friends on Twitter and Facebook; it is up to each of us to promote a positive message of national reform and pride.

Please prevent the total annihilation of humankind, and do your best to uplift and empower the condition of humanity. Your actions as an individual and as a member of the human race are requested, for without dedicated individuals and actions, we shall all perish.

Thousands of groups individually fight and protest injustices that are usually thrust upon the people by the government. Unification of these groups into a collective and powerful juggernaut will assist in speedily removing the criminal rulers of the world.

Billions of people want to achieve freedom from oppression, and many consider it one of the highest priorities in their lives and the lives of their children. The biggest fear of the elite is that people will stand together and form a colossal and indivisible force for good against the elite's microscopic force for evil.

One needs only to think of all the psychological operations implemented by our oppressors to keep the various groups from uniting. Many on television continually play the racist card, pinning blacks against whites against browns against yellows against reds. The democratic media especially use the race card every day to keep different races, religions, and segments of the world's population hating one another.

As long as those in power keep the masses hating and fighting each other, the rulers hope that the American people will be too busy and distracted to discover the atrocious crimes that the bankers and politicians are continually committing against each of us. The greatest fear of the world's rulers is that the races will put their differences aside and finally attack the real problems facing and oppressing all Americans.

American society is filled with choices that continually distract the people and keep them busy choosing one thing over another. Should I go with the Big Mac or the Whopper? Should I live in the country or the city? Jeans or shorts? White or black? Chinese or Japanese? Red Sox or Yankees? Blonde or brunette? Democratic or Republican? Fox or CNN?

The choices presented are unlimited and can often create animosity and anger amongst different sectors of society. Have you ever worn a visiting team's jersey to a Steelers' football game? It is incredible how infuriated Steelers fans get when they see team jerseys that are not Pittsburg Steelers' colors—the black and yellow of bumblebees.

Religious factions are constantly played one against another in the hopes of keeping the religious segment of society from organizing, discovering, and extracting the actual cancer from our society that is unfairly killing us all.

People must start embracing the differences among the masses and focusing their intentions and actions on publicly ousting those that are working against the masses by pinning one group of people against another. Americans need to start tarring and feathering traitors of this once great country. This will instill into the elite's twisted minds that the people will no longer overlook and tolerate heinous and barbarous actions in the land of the free and the home of the brave.

It behooves us all to work on the home of the brave part, instead of just singing about it. Let us help the nation stand up to government-imposed enslavement that is fortified by humanity's oppressors. We have to stop complaining and start doing what is right in order to regain our liberty and our dignity.

Throughout history, only zealous and organized groups have successfully been able to confront the evil people that control this planet. The first step in reversing the harmful and enslaving effects of the bankers is to organize and become an effective force for good over whatever evil they contrive.

It cannot be overstated: the well-intentioned people of the world must organize and work for peaceful solutions for the human condition, or surely as a species, we shall perish. Well-intentioned people must organize, or we all die!

CHAPTER 22

Gun Control: The Magic Pill

*Firearms are second only to the Constitution in importance;
they are the people's liberty teeth.*

– GEORGE WASHINGTON

*The strongest reason for the people to retain the right to keep
and bear arms is as a last resort to protect themselves against
tyranny in government.*

– THOMAS JEFFERSON

*A gun is no more dangerous than a cricket bat in the hands of a
madman.*

– PRINCE PHILLIP

*There are hundreds of millions of gun owners in this country,
and not one of them will have an accident today. The only
misuse of guns comes in environments where there are drugs, alcohol, bad parents, and undisciplined children. Period.*

– TED NUGENT

*Our votes must go together with our guns. After all, any vote
we shall have shall have been the product of the gun. The gun
which produces the vote should remain its security officer—its
guarantor. The people's votes and the people's guns are always
inseparable.*

– ROBERT MUGABE

*All you need for happiness is a good gun, a good horse and a
good wife.*

– DANIEL BOONE

One man with a gun can control one hundred without one.

— VLADIMIR LENIN

I come bearing an olive branch in one hand, and the freedom fighter's gun in the other. Do not let the olive branch fall from my hand.

— YASSER ARAFAT

You can have all the gun control laws in the country, but if you don't enforce them, people are going to find a way to protect themselves. We need to realize that bad people are doing bad things with these weapons. It's not the law-abiding citizen; it's not the person who uses it as a hobby.

— MICHAEL STEELE

I have a very strict gun control policy: if there's a gun around, I want to be in control of it.

— CLINT EASTWOOD

If it's lawful to have a rifle club to kill pheasants, it should be just as lawful to have one to kill wolves or dogs that are being sicked on little black babies. In fact, it's constitutional. Article Number Two of the Constitution guarantees the right of every citizen to own a rifle or a shot gun.

— MALCOLM X

Any unarmed people are slaves, or are subject to slavery at any given moment.

— HUEY P. NEWTON

THOMAS JEFFERSON UNDERSTOOD the need for the American population to keep tabs on the federal government perhaps better than most of his comrades. He realized that trusting a government that has the ability to expand and infringe on the rights of its citizens would lead to the government tyranny we are experiencing today. Jefferson believed that the federal government should be strictly bound by the tenets of the Constitution and that sovereign people were charged with the responsibility of ensuring that the government remained limited and bound in its power and function.

The Founding Fathers devised the US Constitution to delineate exactly what the federal government could do, thereby limiting its role, responsibilities, and sphere of influence. The Founding Fathers intended the federal government's function to be limited to a small number of activities, including conducting a census, controlling and coining currency, raising taxes utilizing duties and tariffs on imports, and sustaining a navy to protect the country from foreign invasion.

The Tenth Amendment provides a covenant that restricts the federal government: "The powers not delegated to the United States by the Constitution, nor prohibited by it to the States, are reserved to the States respectively, or to the people." This amendment was to protect the states and the people from an overly exuberant and ever-expanding federal government, inclined to usurp the rights and freedom of the people as put forth and delineated under the Constitution.

The federal government has participated and continues to participate in thousands of activities that are prohibited by the Constitution. These include, but are not limited to, the functions of the EPA, IRS, FDA, and other humongous bureaucratic entities with letters designating unconstitutional infringements. The federal government has overstepped its constitutional responsibility in so many different ways that it is difficult to understand completely what its duties actually are, unless one studies the Constitution and notes the federal government's limitations.

Liberties and rights are given by God and are unalienable. The federal government now makes it a privilege, and therefore a taxable activity, for Americans to participate in activities that actually fall under "life, liberty, and the pursuit of happiness" as detailed in one of the most eloquently written documents ever crafted, the Declaration of Independence.

People have failed miserably in restraining the federal government from becoming tyrannical in its overly zealous participation in so many activities.

To allow the people to take a stand and defend themselves from all forms of tyranny, the Founding Fathers thought it was imperative that the people retain the right to keep and bear arms, and this right shall not be infringed. Only a government that intends to harm its constituents finds it necessary to infringe on the right of the people to bear arms and the ability of the people to protect their rights and themselves from government abuse.

There is very limited evidence that shows terrorism exists on any level, other than what has been promulgated by the federal government. Watch the movie Fabled Enemies, directed by Jason Bermas and produced by Alex Jones, at topdocumentaryfilms.com/fabled-enemies/. It explains the federal government's incentive and, more specifically, the military-industrial complex's creation of enemies, whether real or fabricated, for the purpose of conducting wars for profit while concurrently limiting the understanding, rights, and freedoms of the American populace.

Recall the days immediately following 9/11. There was an avalanche of politicians instructing a frightened American population that the solution to this disaster was for Americans to give up some of their God-given rights so that the government could better protect the people and provide security. Hitler used this type of propaganda when he was disarming the population of Germany.

When people make claims that the government will protect us, the pathetic thing to consider is that there is neither protection nor any security that can be provided for any of us by another. Walk around any large city or small town, and examine the environment as a terrorist would. Walk down Park Avenue in New York and try to find the security that is supposedly being provided by the government. There is no security. A person can walk into virtually any mall, supermarket, theater, or store and take it over with the most minimal of weapons.

The snipers in Washington, DC, are a perfect example that there is no security, as two poorly organized people were able to create fear and havoc for weeks in a major city. Were they operatives of the government? Check out Programmed To Kill/Satanic Cover-Up Part 57 (The Washington DC Snipers - John Allen Muhammad) at youtube.com/watch?v=a9vyAn1F4AA.

Any perception that the government can provide security for all its citizens should be scrutinized closely and dismissed for the farce that it is. As one walks down the street, it is easy to see there is a lack of security against attacks orchestrated by insane and bad actors.

Governments are the terrorists. Governments kill more people than all the other fabricated terrorist groups combined. All wars and actions that lead to war are designed to terrorize the people of the world. People cannot allow governments to put them in the mindset of fear. The governments of the world trade exclusively in fear and deception to retain their power. Most interaction with the government is based upon fear and intimidation used against citizens to garner their cooperation and compliance. The government's final redress is to throw uncooperative and non-complying citizens in jail or simply do away with them.

The Founding Fathers knew the depths that government tyranny can degenerate into as it strips away the rights and liberties of its citizens. The Founding Fathers' foresight provided protective measures in the US Constitution and the Bill of Rights. The Second Amendment is only twenty-seven words long and reads, "A well regulated Militia being necessary to the security of a free State, the right of the people to keep and bear arms shall not be infringed."

The states were not satisfied with the limitations and deficiencies of the Constitution, so many were reluctant to participate and accept the Constitution until the Bill of Rights was added to grant more protection to the citizenry from a potentially abusive federal government. It is amazing how important the Founding Fathers believed it to be to protect our rights to keep and bear arms, which supports our right of self-protection from an abusive federal government.

Paramount to all rights, the right of self-protection, once denied, expedites the forfeiture of all the individuals' remaining rights.

When certain bad actors infiltrate the government on behalf of the Establishment, the government no longer functions in the best interests of the citizenry at large but, instead, functions to line the pockets of those who have corrupted it.

Once the people become aware of the injustices and criminality of such a debased government, the government usually attempts to devise stricter methods of protecting its special interests over the interests of the people. If a populace is unarmed, it is all the better and much easier for a corrupt and criminal government to continue to exact control over the populace unabated. The prejudicial favoring of the ruling class over the remainder of the population usually includes restrictive policies that eventually lead the people to revolt. Stalin and many other dictators used gun control as their favorite method to weaken the population's ability to resist government intrusion and tyranny.

In order to prevent a revolt against corrupt and usurped governments, those leaders, who have wrongly seized power against the will of the people, fervently implement gun-control programs and laws regulating, restricting, and often prohibiting the carrying, selling, and owning of firearms. Gun-control laws make the masses unable to resist any government abuse, coercion, or violence perpetrated against the people.

Dictators often use gun control as a method of weakening the defenses of the populace before the government attempts its final takeover and domination of the people. We have witnessed this scenario in several different examples throughout history, yet the result is always the same; an unarmed populace is unable to defend itself. This makes it easy for tyrannical governments to dominate and abuse their unarmed populace.

The single reason for gun control is to lessen the ability of law-abiding citizens to protect themselves and their families against an out-of-control government.

The restriction of ammunition, the restriction of gun ownership, and the restriction of carrying firearms weaken the rights of the people to protect themselves from a government that perceives the people as an adversarial citizenry. Restrictions on and depletion of ammo are two of the more interesting topics that governments use to tear down the defenses of an angry population.

The government can obviously limit the sale and distribution of ammunition simply by buying more than the manufactures can make. This results in the citizens' firearms becoming useful only as a club or a stick, and in cases like this, there is typically insufficient amounts of ammunition and firepower to support a rebellion. If you value your freedom or what is left of it these days in America, do not just buy guns; buy ammo, lots and lots of ammo!

Throughout history, we see governments, through agent provocateurs, inciting one faction of the population against another. Simply put, the black team is agitated against the white team, and members of the brown team are played equally against both. The different races are attacking each other and creating racial schisms and rifts as witnessed today within the agitated Black Lives Matter movement.

During race wars, the different factions of society become so busy attacking and shooting each other that they use up all their ammo and then the government comes in and cleans up what is left of the rebellious undesirables. Governments typically use their legislative power to eliminate the threat of civil rebellion by implementing gun control laws that restrict the ownership and use of firearms. The Second Amendment unequivocally protects our right to keep and bear arms and is constantly infringed upon by the unscrupulous US government. Such infringement could only be orchestrated by a government that has an interest in weakening the ability of the population to protect itself by putting up an armed resistance against such a corrupt and tyrannical government.

Wherever one is in the world, one can be assured that a government is an unethical and tyrannical government if it constantly works to deprive its citizens from arming and protecting themselves.

The government owns all the powerful weapons. It definitely outguns the population, but those that are in charge of the military know that the beloved military men and women in the armed forces would find it almost impossible to attack their own population. Instead, some speculate that many governments plan to use foreign troops, provided through the UN, to quash their own populations.

By not allowing the government to infringe upon our Second Amendment rights, we can all sleep a little more soundly knowing that the last defense against a tyrannical government is a well-armed populace. An abundantly armed American population is the only force that prevents the US government from fully oppressing the people. Additionally, America's well-armed populace is definitely a significant deterrent to potential foreign invaders.

The next time a disturbed person on prescription drugs walks into a movie theatre to extract some imagined revenge, an armed audience should fill the lunatic with lead.

Americans have rights because we have guns. If we ever forfeit our guns, we will forfeit our liberty and perish at the hands of insane and oppressive government criminals.

Lock and load, America; lock and load!

CHAPTER 23

Human Farming

The time is near at hand which must determine whether Americans are to be free men or slaves.

         – GEORGE WASHINGTON

The genius of any slave system is found in the dynamics which isolate slaves from each other, obscure the reality of a common condition, and make united rebellion against the oppressor inconceivable.

         – ANDREA DWORKIN

The danger of the past was that men became slaves. The danger about the future is that man may become robots.

         – ERICH FROMM

Disobedience is the true foundation of liberty. The obedient must be slaves.

         – HENRY DAVID THOREAU

The real names of our people were destroyed during slavery. The last name of my forefathers was taken from them when they were brought to America and made slaves, and then the name of the slave master was given, which we refuse; we reject that name today and refuse it. I never acknowledge it whatsoever.

         – MALCOLM X

I freed a thousand slaves. I could have freed a thousand more if only they knew they were slaves.

         – HARRIET TUBMAN

It only stands to reason that where there's sacrifice, there's someone collecting the sacrificial offerings. Where there's service, there is someone being served. The man who speaks to you of sacrifice is speaking of slaves and masters, and intends to be the master.

– Ayn Rand

I have a dream that one day on the red hills of Georgia, the sons of former slaves and the sons of former slave owners will be able to sit together at the table of brotherhood.

– Martin Luther King Jr.

I believe that the human race has developed a form of collective schizophrenia in which we are not only slaves to this imposed thought behavior, but we are also the police force of it.

– David Icke

Those who will not reason are bigots, those who cannot, are fools, and those who dare not are slaves.

– Lord Byron

AN INTERESTING COMMONALITY of our lives is that we are deceived by our senses regarding the true nature of reality. Our senses are only capable of inputting and discerning a fraction of the information around us. This is analogous to being able to see only the bull's eye of a mile-wide target. To clarify further, a dog whistle is a perfect example of the deception our senses continually play on us. When it is blown, its sound is imperceptible to the human ear. The range of its wavelengths is simply too short to cause the average human eardrum to vibrate. Dogs' eardrums, having a finer membrane, vibrate more intensely making hearing the dog whistle simple for canines.

Other senses are just as limited and unreliable as the sense of hearing. When one looks down the length of railroad tracks, one perceives an intersection of the tracks, while in reality the tracks never meet. One's sense of taste and touch are found equally deceptive and unreliable.

Whenever two people examine a singular event from different points of view, they see two different aspects of the same event. When one sees a concert in a theater, the vantage point of those seated in front of the stage is different from that of those seated backstage.

The reliability in reporting facts has a great deal to do with one's point of view and many other factors, such as keenness of mind, lucidity of thought, and educational level. Every witness of a car accident has a different story that he or she tells to the police who investigate the accident.

The major media outlets present biased stories in order to prevent real understanding by the average US citizen who is indoctrinated by the public schools, which are under the control of the Department of Education in Washington, DC. The reality portrayed by the media inundates the viewing audience with information intended to shape the psyche of the viewer and to change it according to the whims of the group that controls the media.

William Casey, director of the CIA in 1981, succinctly commented regarding the media, "We'll know our disinformation program is complete when everything the American public believes is false." Programming of the masses is very effective and implemented to cause more than a change in purchasing habits; the media programs the masses in order to change the guiding and overall viewpoints of the society.

The media's entire job is to ensure the masses never discover the truth of their enslavement on the plantation of human farming we call America. If people discover in the morning the lengths that those in control have continually undertaken to enslave the population, there would be mayhem and revolution before sunset.

Most of us fail to examine the amount of effort and energy that the media regularly exert and thrust upon us to keep our psyches in such a state that we accept human slavery or human farming as a normal part of life. False information, believed without examination, can be more damaging to personal and intellectual freedom than virtually anything else.

To break from our self-imposed enslavement mentality, we must examine the chains that bind us. People lock themselves down, just as the master wants them to do, better than anyone else possibly could. By examining the false and unexamined beliefs we possess, only then is it possible for us to free ourselves from our self-imposed mental slavery that binds our lives more than we care to realize.

When free thinkers attempt to inform others of a new discovery, the free thinkers often are met with disdain, and their ideas are usually attacked and rebuffed. This book and its concepts may be highly ridiculed by the powers-that-be, the slave masters and their minions, simply because it informs people that there is a higher plane of human existence, far above the plane of human existence we currently experience in our daily lives. People may scoff at the idea of slavery as an existing condition today because in their minds Lincoln emancipated the slaves. Upon examining the US Constitution, one discovers that the Thirteenth Amendment outlawed slavery and involuntary servitude; however, Americans are still far from free.

Amendment 13—Slavery Abolished, Ratified 12/6/1865:

1. Neither slavery nor involuntary servitude, except as a punishment for crime whereof the party shall have been duly convicted, shall exist within the United States, or any place subject to their jurisdiction.

2. Congress shall have power to enforce this article by appropriate legislation.

The Thirteenth Amendment theoretically abolishes involuntary servitude. If that is the case, then why do citizens toil from January to July to pay taxes in one form or another? Unjust taxation needs to be abolished, as the power to tax is the power to enslave.

The Thirteenth Amendment only discusses involuntary servitude and does not discuss voluntary servitude, which is implemented on a daily basis because of the legal agreements people have signed with the federal government. Many do not believe they are in essence slaves to the Social Security and other government agreements, but for most Americans, employment and taxation are conducted under and using the slaves' Social Security numbers.

Think of the absurdity of the national debt, which is what the IRS is contracted to collect. One asks, where on Earth did a group of bankers get the twenty trillion dollars to loan to the United States? Did it just magically appear? They made this money out of thin air to enslave the population through income tax.

Slavery never truly ended when Lincoln presented his Emancipation Proclamation to the nation on January 1, 1863, almost 150 years ago. Coincidentally, it took effect on the most important day of the year for a slave, April 15, the same date that lives on in infamy, being the day when the slaves' IRS tax returns are due.

Regardless of a person's race, slavery still exists. Today, virtually every person in the world is a voluntary slave of his or her government and its imprisoning system of taxation.

One thinks of a slave as an African American who labored for the slave master on America's plantations under conditions filled with duress and relentless punishment. The slave produced goods and services and was paid with only the necessities of food, clothing, and shelter. If the slave acted up, the master or his foreman would punish and often whip the slave to keep him in line and producing for the benefit of the master.

We can define "slavery" as a state that exists when the fruits of one's labor are not exclusively the property of the worker. When the master takes a part of the value or all the value derived from one's labor, we have entered into a state of slavery. If an American worker receives a paycheck in which income and other taxes are removed, prior to the worker even receiving it, the value of the worker's labor is divided between the IRS (the slave master) and the American working slave. The slave is not entitled to all the fruit of his or her labor under the slave system that is enforced by the IRS.

On a worldwide scale, we can consider America as living and working under a form of occupational slavery resulting from unjust taxation. This employment and taxation system is equivalent to human farming. Humans, under the Federal Reserve System and the Internal Revenue Service, are slaves who toil and split their paychecks with banking criminals who get something for nothing. We know it is all fake money, magically created by the superior banking class out of thin air; yet for all American workers, a dollar represents a unit of labor because we have to work for our paychecks and cannot mystically create currency out of thin air.

Most countries currently implement this form of human farming, an effective and modern form in which the slaves believe themselves to be free. After all, people do not look like slaves. They wear no shackles. They do not get whipped or beaten when they don't work; they just get fired and likely become homeless. American slaves are not singing Negro spirituals in the fields as they labor picking cotton. People get to choose their occupations, so they believe they must be free.

Nothing is further from truth. People are no longer tethered to the plantation; rather, working under the income tax scheme, the entire nation, better yet, the entire world becomes the plantation. We are all slaves under today's system of human farming, which is enforced by the Internal Revenue Service's diabolic taxation schemes.

Our plight of human farming and enslavement is never revealed on the nightly news. Everything one views on television is created to keep us distracted from the fact that we are slaves.

The best slaves are the deluded ones who believe they are free. They work the hardest for their masters, all the time oblivious to their station as slaves.

America is the pinnacle of slavery. The United States has one of the highest tax rates in the world, and Americans are supposed to live in the land of the free! In America, the slaves believe they are free but somehow ignore the fact that much of the funds they are owed for their labor is taken by the master in one form of tax or another. Money is taken from our paychecks before we are even paid, whether we like it or not.

Today's free-range slavery was popularized during the Industrial Revolution for the purpose of extending the reach of the slave masters; this new form of slavery ensured the masters would benefit from free-range slavery on a global scale. Human farming and its free-range slavery eliminate the expenses incurred by plantations to minimally feed, clothe, shelter, and maintain their slaves. Under free-range slavery, the slave owner no longer has to maintain the slaves.

Free-range slavery is a much more efficient and streamlined version of slavery that is currently implemented around the world. Free-range slaves are the best kind of slaves to own. A free-range slave believes in his or her heart that he or she is free. A slave that is oblivious to his or her station in life and cannot even feel the invisible shackles and chains imprisoning him or her is unlikely to revolt and flee the plantation.

After the slaves were freed, blacks joined the ranks of the other immigrants of America and sought employment, often in less-than-desirable conditions, to say the least. Irish, Italians, and many others worked in factories and mines for pennies a day. Company stores and company housing became a fixture upon the industrial landscape; the employees lived in these company houses and were forced to purchase their provisions in company stores, owned by the same companies for whom they worked.

To further trap the slaves, these abused laborers were often paid with company script instead of dollars. This company script was only exchangeable for provisions sold in the company store or used to purchase lodging in the company's houses.

The problem was that, once employed, the slaves never got ahead because the corporate design was to recover all the company script given to the employees as pay. This was a vicious cycle of enslavement often used in labor-intensive industries such as coalmining and farming. The hopeless immigrants opted to participate in this system of corporate slavery rather than experience abject poverty and starvation as the result of unemployment.

Starvation is the most basic motivating factor for any human. When the option exists between eating as a slave or starving as a free man, when hungry enough, most believe that the former presents a better strategy than the latter. Others, understanding the perils encountered from abandoning their self-integrity, would rather stand and starve than kneel and eat.

The international bankers make their living off human farming and enslaving the rest of humanity. This is the most profitable enterprise on the planet. One can imagine the vast fortunes that are harvested from owning a large percentage of all human labor worldwide. In today's model of human farming, humans are considered and treated about the same as livestock.

To further understand human farming and human ownership, I urge you to watch the following movies that detail the present-day slavery mechanics used to control and enslave the masses: The Story of Your Enslavement (youtube.com/watch?v=Xbp6umQT58A) and The Handbook of Human Ownership—A Manual for New Tax Farmers (youtube.com/watch?v=k67_imEHTPE). Also watch the video, The Horror of American Slavery, detailing the inhumane brutality that African slaves endured at youtube.com/watch?v=cXrRyyzpue4&t=2087s. I highly recommend you visit the Lest We Forget Slave Museum in Philadelphia and view its website at lwfsm.com.

These videos are important for better understanding today's world, which is filled with oppression that each of us endures for our entire lives. Just think what kind of a world our posterity will inherit should we fail to break the shackles of human farming and slavery.

Few understand how extremely profitable it is to enslave the masses and simply live off what the masses generate. Throughout history, there has never been a more efficient or more sinister manner of enslaving the people than the present covert system of human farming and enslavement.

Americans believe they are free. They even sing about how free they are in the "Star Spangled Banner," ending the first verse with the line "O'er the land of the free and the home of the brave." How can people be free in the United States when they pay outlandish taxes?

The plantation owners now own all the countries in the world. There is no way to escape captivity by moving from one country to another or from one plantation to another. There needs to be another strategy implemented in order to escape tyranny. In order to escape tyranny, one must confront and stand up against tyranny. Many insights on how to stand up for oneself are explained at onefreemanswar.com. Although there are no guarantees in life, this site contains some extremely interesting information that can purportedly be used to defend oneself from government-imposed tyranny.

On a different note, much of the information we find on the Internet is "for educational purposes only," so buyer beware with all your purchases. If I had the tens of thousands of dollars spent in search of my personal freedom, I would be a much richer man. Many bad investments taught me a lesson about the "pay" in "patriots." The problem with buying one's freedom on the Internet is that one's freedom only comes from within. Many people better than I have landed themselves in jail for standing up against tyranny, while others are incarcerated for following their lawyer's bad advice. Be careful; it is a tough world out there.

Many a doubting Thomas may be skeptical that slavery still exists because of the privileges that the governments of the world dole out to their slaves, such as driving licenses or incorporating a business. People were born free, and now they need to ask the government permission to do this and to do that. People are snookered into believing they are free because they choose the blue car over the red car or the bigger boat over the faster one. People are slaves as long as they involuntarily and begrudgingly give the government much of their hard-earned pay.

The enslavers of humanity, with the hopes of increasing the overall production of the free-range slaves, allow their slaves to pick their own employment and occupation. In the graduated income tax model of the IRS, as one's production increases, his or her tax rate also increases; therefore, it is beneficial for the master to allow the slaves to choose a profession in which the slaves will excel. This creates additional tax revenue for the master.

Any appearance that the government wants a person to be happy or healthy or wise is simply propagated to camouflage the true and devious purpose of the government to enslave the people. The reason that the government takes care of its people is to insure that the slaves will be more productive and yield more to their master.

The IRS steals from citizens of the United States on behalf of foreign banking interests. The amount of money that the IRS extorts from citizens makes the Mafia look like a bunch of rookies by comparison. No insult is meant to the Mafia by comparing it to the true expert of organized crime, the IRS. Not only is the IRS organized crime; it is also government sanctioned and supported against the freedoms and liberties of the people. The IRS is the whipping or enforcement arm of the world's slave masters.

Who would ever have the audacity to call themselves free while slaving to pay taxes for over six months of the year? Every day, from January to midsummer, Americans arise at dawn, drink their imported coffee with a quick breakfast, and head to the eight-to-five plantation.

Americans live in a country where its citizens pretend to be free, pretend to be happy, and pretend to be brave. America is no longer as great as it used to be. When conceived, the United States was the greatest country in the world, but since its usurpation and overthrow, it singularly serves the needs of the enslavers of the people; one can hardly call that a great country.

People actively participate in their own slavery, many fully unaware of the Social Security chains that bind them to their often-unnoticed and too-seldom-protested shackles of slavery. Many Americans begrudgingly agree to the terms of enslavement not even knowing what they are, since they often are heard bragging, "We live in the greatest country in the world." I wonder if the inhabitants of many other countries thusly brag.

The United States of America has unlimited room for improvement. Many claim it is already the greatest country in the world, but it could be so much better. We citizens simply need to demand more from our government and free ourselves from our enslavers and the human farming system. This should be the top priority of every concerned American.

Once we peel back the many layers of the onion called the American society, we can conclude that the United States has not graduated or evolved from serfdom and slavery into a free society but has morphed into a cancerous and covert form of human free-range farming. We live in a society where the slave master's whip has been replaced with over-taxation, unemployment, and the ever-present threat of homelessness.

The human farm does not generate pro-survival solutions to problems; it generates only solutions that result in disabilities, usually tending toward death and destruction, rather than tending toward life and construction. In human farming, all humans are considered subjects or animals to be exploited. All legal decisions and laws are written in favor of the human farmers against the interests of the people.

Our enslavement is essential to those select few who have decided to capitalize on everyone else by creating and implementing human farming. Human farming is the current methodology used in the progression of oppressing the people as slaves of the elite.

Through the use of disinformation, deceitful campaigns, and outright lies, slavery is accepted in the minds of the people and rarely questioned.

The following is repeated here because of its importance. By examining the different governmental departments and viewing their function in the exact opposite way from what their names suggest, one quickly discovers some of the major elements that are utilized to keep people down. The government is the instrumental tool used to maintain and enforce today's system of human farming.

The Department of Agriculture allows farmers to use petroleum-based fertilizers that often make people sick. The FDA allows foods to be grown and eaten that are not really foods but are genetically altered products similar to food, and no one knows exactly what effects such genetically altered foodstuffs may ultimately have on the body.

The Internal Revenue Service is neither internal to nor a service provided on behalf of the people of the United States. Actually, it provides the worst kind of service one could imagine. The Internal Revenue Service is the private collection agency of the foreign-owned corporation called the Federal Reserve System, and it operates traitorously to the US Constitution and the taxing intent of the Founding Fathers of the United States.

The corrupt Federal Reserve neither is federal nor has reserves. Without the Federal Reserve System, there would be absolutely no need for today's IRS.

The Department of Energy has suppressed new energy technologies for decades such as a 300 mpg carburetor that adapts to gasoline-powered engines, water-powered engines, advanced solar technologies, and many other technologies that compete with the petroleum business and the almighty petrodollar.

The Drug Enforcement Agency, with its decades-long war on drugs, has only stopped the drug trafficking entrepreneurs who compete against the Establishment's drug traffickers, who work for the elite's families, including the Bush family and other lowlifes spawned from the CIA.

The Department of the Interior allows mining and forestry to strip natural resources at alarming rates, often severely damaging the environment. The Berkeley Pit located in Butte, Montana, and thousands of other mines remain toxic dumps after the copper and other precious metals are depleted (en.wikipedia.org/wiki/Berkeley_Pit).

The list goes on and on, but the common denominator of the regulatory departments is that, if any individual or any group starts to get too powerful and threaten the monopoly of those in charge of human farming, then a government agency will be able to crush that group or individual and bring it back under control.

The different departments act like crabs in a bucket. Anyone that attempts to escape the human farm is attacked by one or more of the above agencies until he or she is brought in line and placed back on the plantation.

The various government agencies work on behalf of the human farmers by enforcing violations of one or more of the millions of federal laws and regulations that are weighing down and destroying the United States of America with the intention of controlling any dissidents or rebels protesting the enslaving conditions of the farm.

The government destroys any self-starting individuals it wants by using litigation that the government can always afford to conduct, while individuals rarely have enough money to protect themselves from the unlimited litigious resources of the government. Never mind individuals; many companies cannot afford to litigate against the federal government and must settle, rather than bear the costly expense of going to trial and unjustly enriching immoral attorneys.

The government knows this and even makes many innocent defendants accept a plea agreement for a three-year prison stay or go to trial and face a thirty-year sentence. What would you do facing this quite gloomy option?

Litigation and incarceration are ultimately the devices implemented by the government to keep all the slaves in line on the plantation. Too many people have experienced injustices regarding the government and the way it attacks those who try to break away and free themselves from the flock.

One example is that of the great auto designer John DeLorean. He had ambitions to build an automobile of which all Americans could be proud. DeLorean's story is similar to and reminiscent of the story of Preston Tucker, founder of the Tucker Corporation of the late 1940s.

Both men were going to introduce better automobiles than Detroit was manufacturing. Both men were going to infringe on the markets of the Big Three automobile producers. Both men had made it through the initial startup and prototype aspect of their businesses when the government in cahoots with the special interests pulled the rug out from under their corporate feet. These two examples illuminate, all too well, the destructive forces that the government will undertake to ensure that the special interests are cared for at the expense of not only free enterprise but also plain and simple decency.

Many people that dare expose the human farmers are often done away with and never heard from again. Consider what the media has done to stop Donald Trump or anyone else that threatens the exposure, dismantling, and obliteration of the special interests' control over its slaves, and you will understand the self-preservation methods employed at all costs by the human farmers in order to retain their control over the populace.

The media lambasts President Trump at any opportunity, fails to report the truth, and unjustifiably assails his character. Anyone with half a brain realizes you do not accomplish all Trump's business successes without being a man of substantial character and outstanding mental acumen. His business statistics speak louder than the media's lies, and millions supported him as their choice for president. Americans have had it with this system of human farming, and with any luck, President Trump can dismantle the oppressive system of free-range slavery that has taken centuries to build, but I doubt it and hope to be proven wrong.

Human farming will exist as long as the people contribute to and support its existence. The plantation will exist until people organize and outlaw private banking. By ignoring the situation and contributing to a government systematically designed to enslave the people, we are choosing to live on a slave plantation rather than standing and fighting for freedom and the American way.

It is time our oppressors hear our voices and the freedom cry of our dying nation. Americans can no longer sit idle and comfortable in their shackles and watch as humanity languishes under incredible oppression. All that is decent regarding humanity is at stake.

The entire future of this planet depends on the actions that each of us performs to free humanity from an existence of degradation and insanity imposed by twelve oppressive banking families.

Attainment of a nation's freedom is garnered on a personal basis by first demanding justice in our own lives and then demanding justice on a societal level. We must disdain and fight the injustice and inequality that the richest members of society enforce on the rest of the populace. There is no dignity in living a life of servitude.

We have smelled the manure of human farming for far too long a time, and now we must act to remove the stench from the shores of America. Only by standing against all terror created by the banks can Americans become free again in accordance with our inherent birthrights. America is the land of the free if and only if it is the home of the brave.

The government will never guarantee Americans' God-given rights; such rights are guaranteed only by our courage and diligent defiance of tyranny. We are the only guarantors of our rights. Any God-given rights possessed by any Americans were fought for and ultimately ensured by the sacrifice of better people than you or I.

If Americans sit around and do nothing to regain their freedom from the internationally imposed banking tyranny, then America will have a future of suffering unparalleled in the annals of history. It is one of the saddest commentaries to see apathetic and dejected Americans sitting around ignoring their future fates, as their rights and their country are being flushed down the toilet. Our inaction is tantamount to our tacit agreement and approval of our own slavery and the slavery of all to come.

Regarding our nation and our freedoms, we have reached the point of no return. Our actions alone determine the quality of our future. Now is the time for good men to organize against terror and finally liberate all humanity from the clutches of evil. There is never a better time than now to decree our emancipation and to free ourselves from the treacherous slavery we all share on this human plantation.

Remember, as individuals we reap what we sow, and if we are too afraid to stand against our own tyrannical government, then how can we expect to live free? America remains a great land as long as its citizens demand proper performance of their government. Should the citizens fail to demand proper performance of their government, the country will disintegrate into a debauched system of criminality, like the government we obviously now have in America.

We can no longer let our government's debauchery create harm to the rest of the world, for if we do, history will record us as the ultimate betrayers of all future generations.

It is time that America cleans up the plantation and overthrows its masters. It is time that Americans do more than sit around and wait for the criminal politicians to correct a criminal system that they themselves have built and legislated into existence.

If we are going to farm anything, let us farm for our freedom. To put the United States back on track and free it from oppressive tyranny, Americans need to demand and institute a government-controlled monetary system. That is the first and most important step in freeing American slaves from the slave plantation named the United States of America.

It is up to us to restore freedom for humankind and for future generations—now that is worth cultivating!

CHAPTER 24

Our Emancipation

The flag that was the symbol of slavery on the high seas for a long time was not the Confederate battle flag; it was sadly the Stars and Stripes.

– ALAN KEYES

Dictatorship naturally arises out of democracy, and the most aggravated form of tyranny and slavery out of the most extreme liberty.

– PLATO

If you allow one single germ, one single seed of slavery to remain in the soil of America . . . that germ will spring up, that noxious weed will thrive and again stifle the growth, wither the leaves, blast the flowers and poison the fair fruits of freedom.

– ERNESTINE ROSE

Emancipate yourselves from mental slavery, none but ourselves can free our minds!

– MARCUS GARVEY

Some people try to get you out of slavery for you to be their slave.

– MIKE TYSON

No pen can give an adequate description of the all-pervading corruption produced by slavery.

– HARRIET ANN JACOBS

Racism, xenophobia and unfair discrimination have spawned slavery when human beings have bought and sold and owned and branded fellow human beings as if they were so many beasts of burden.

— DESMOND TUTU

As legal slavery passed, we entered into a permanent period of unemployment and underemployment from which we have yet to emerge.

— JULIAN BOND

Most men today cannot conceive of a freedom that does not involve somebody's slavery.

— W. E. B. DU BOIS

The last four or five hundred years of European contact with Africa produced a body of literature that presented Africa in a very bad light and Africans in very lurid terms. The reason for this had to do with the need to justify the slave trade and slavery.

— CHINUA ACHEBE

All the miseries and evils which men suffer from vice, crime, ambition, injustice, oppression, slavery and war proceed from their despising or neglecting the precepts contained in the Bible.

— NOAH WEBSTER

Elimination of illiteracy is as serious an issue to our history as the abolition of slavery.

— MAYA ANGELO

THROUGHOUT HISTORY, a small and most evil-intentioned segment of society has united and organized to join forces to subjugate the remainder of the planet's population. It is evident that this small segment of society that is vying to control the entire population, while sparing no measure or effort, has implemented special public relations campaigns to assist in obfuscating from the public the true intentions and actions of the indisputable and unchallenged rulers of this world.

During the era of imperial rule, the public relations campaign to control the people consisted partly in the belief and promulgation of the notion that the king and queen were created more favorably by God than the rest of humanity and were therefore chosen to be the leaders of those more unfavorably created by God, their imperial subjects. People in their ignorance believed that God inherently bestowed upon the king special qualities that made the king and his family superior to the subjects of his rule.

It is quite impressive that the subjects of the king believed such fanciful public relation campaigns, wherein one bloodline of the world was purportedly superior to all other bloodlines. For centuries under imperial rule, kings, lords, and lieutenants pillaged the people through taxation and terror. Fancy titles of nobility allowed for abuses to occur across the land without repercussion or impediment. Nothing was off limits. The cowed serfs paid incredible taxes and even allowed the king's lords to partake in sexual relations with the serfs' disinclined and protesting brides on their wedding night, under the covenant of jus primae noctis.

Today one looks back at feudal times as an era of brutality and oppression. A small, organized group of thieves and murderers, disguised as nobility with fanciful titles and power, oppressed and subjugated the ignorant masses. Millions of people lived at the barest levels of survival, while the king and his friends ate the thickest and juiciest steaks and washed them down with the finest wines. Meanwhile, the peasants scrounged for their next morsels to eat.

Uprisings of the serfs were barely organized and were squelched quickly by the lord's very organized and heavily armed soldiers. Empires, passed down through birthright, lasted for centuries.

On occasion, conflicts that overthrew and replaced a king were rebellions undertaken by a strong and organized minority of the people. Often an outside army removed the ruling nobility from power by force, and the conquering army would install its new breed of imperial rule. In this case, the first ruling family that had an inside track with the Almighty was replaced by the second and conquering ruling family, which evidently was held in even higher esteem by God.

Little has changed since the days nobility governed the ignorant masses under imperial rule. Instead of wearing a crown and robe and carrying a scepter, the kings today remain hidden and out of sight of the public. The crown's agents, however, wear just as elaborate costumes and uniforms today, which indicate their professional duties. Police wear uniforms, judges wear robes, and the agents wear fashionable haberdashery and dark suits purchased at Men's Wearhouse.

The function and methods of today's government are almost identical to the tyrannical, imperial rule dispensed by kings throughout history. The objective of the current governments' actions regarding the people is to allow the masses to enjoy little more than the basics of food, clothing, and shelter. Anything more than that is heavily taxed, which keeps the masses in a controllable and predictable state. The object of the oppressors is to keep the masses so incredibly busy scraping out a living that the people never examine their lives and realize how much easier it would be to live without having oppressive government policies imposed upon them.

When one considers the international economic scene, it readily becomes apparent that the United States, particularly the Department of the Treasury, has a real big problem. Americans owe foreign bankers more than all other nations on Earth combined. Over twenty trillion dollars of debt is a big problem. This is the same amount that Americans are demanded to pay in order to obtain their financial freedom from the Federal Reserve. Freedom is not free, but it sure doesn't cost twenty trillion dollars.

Before you know it, the Federal Reserve debt will be thirty trillion dollars unless we initiate a drastic change of course. This was why the thought of President Trump dreadfully frightens the Establishment. He claimed to be able to reduce the deficit to zero in eight years.

I do not know where he thinks he will get the money because, if we were able to pay off the national debt, there would be no Federal Reserve Notes left in circulation for Americans to use. We need to immediately default, cancel, and eliminate the debt and the US monetary system, not attempt to pay an unpayable debt. The international bankers prefer to keep nations heavily indebted and to continue to tax and control its duped citizens.

Twenty trillion dollars exemplifies a glaring deficiency in the competency and management skills of the political leaders of the United States. This creates financial depravation of the American people, all because some crooked politicians decided the most economically prudent course of action would be to use and invite fiat money and the government-sanctioned enslavement of the American people.

The fact that Americans have traded their old form of slavery under imperial rule to a newer form of slavery, or human farming, called monetary (financial or bank) rule, is seldom examined or discussed. When one compares his or her life today against the lives of those who lived under a tyrannical king a couple of centuries ago, one quickly notices that things have not come that far, regarding the uplifting and liberation of humankind across the planet. We have traded one form of slavery for another form; we have traded the imperially imposed feudal system for a more highly technical and advanced electronic form of free-range human farming under monetary rule.

After all these years, it boils down to the fact that humans have traded agricultural slavery for the modern free-range slavery; the primary difference is that under today's free-range slavery we are allowed to choose our profession and provide for our own maintenance and upkeep.

Monetary rule is a system so controlling in our lives that, without it, life might seem sometimes imponderable. Every transaction, every communication, everything we can imagine is highly monitored and scrutinized to ensure there are no attempts to liberate and emancipate the slaves.

In today's form of free-range slavery, the people are governed and ruled by legislation, which is enforced by the police state. Under a state of emergency, the United States has declared us all enemies of the nation and is treating us accordingly. When people discover that the imperial rule of a few hundred years ago has been replaced by today's monetary rule that is solely responsible for creating the oppressive conditions of human farming, they quickly grasp the actual mechanisms of modern enslavement.

Once the mechanisms of human farming and enslavement are discovered and understood, individuals will automatically work harder to free themselves from government bondage and take a lot more responsibility to help all humanity break the chains of enslavement and the degradation that currently prevails.

Americans cannot leave the fixing of the world's problems to the politicians because we know they are the ones responsible for legislating human farming and the many associated problems of society that we now face.

Americans cannot throw bad money after more bad money in a hopeless and futile attempt to pay a national debt that is mathematically impossible to pay. Americans must expend efforts to create redeemable money in order to free ourselves from our monetary enslavement.

People must intentionally avoid the offered distractions that prevent them from examining and understanding the predicaments the world faces today because of incompetent and often very despicable criminal politicians.

America did not become a nation with a twenty-trillion-dollar debt by accident. Every dollar of the national debt represents a dollar of labor stolen from the American people. The international bankers magically create the national debt out of thin air. Yet we are required to pay it back with our labor consisting of our blood, sweat, and tears. This does not seem at all equitable; to be fair, we should be able to pay the national debt back with money that we create out of thin air. If the debt is magically created out of thin air, then let us wave a magic wand and cancel that same debt.

It is up to well-intentioned individuals to band together in order to correct the direction and philosophy of today's US corporate government. The only interest a corporation has is to financially flourish and remunerate its shareholders. The government is no different; it is a government or, rather, a corporation designed to survive at all costs and cares not for the interests of the people or the planet but cares only for the interests of its shareholders.

By financially destroying the economy of America, the government gains more control over the people. It is therefore pertinent for the repair of this nation that the populace unites now before all our resources are robbed by a desperate government that cannot even pay its own bills.

A massive financial calamity is certain to occur within the next few years or sooner; this is a foregone conclusion when the national debt is examined logically through the eyes of a mathematician. The only thing a misguided, untended, and withering economy like ours can possibly do without intervention is to die.

Any delay in uniting the American people will only allow the system to economically decay further, as this nation speeds hastily into an unrecognizable third-world country.

One should support a responsible and representative form of government that works on behalf of all the people and not a select group of corrupt bankers. If every American were to unite in thought and withdraw financial support from the corrupt US government, it would soon crumble under its own weight of reckless spending.

Unfortunately, the government is likely to cease operation on its own accord, as the government's outlandish operational costs are becoming beyond the capacity of the citizens to finance. The only power that the government receives is that which the people provide.

The practice of organizing the people has had tremendous success in the different revolutionary movements recorded throughout history. Today, people have the ability to organize at the speed of light, using the Internet and all the social media available to them.

The Machiavellian divide-and-conquer techniques used by oppressive governments can no longer effectively prevent the populace from uniting and demanding a more responsible and representative form of government that considers the interests of all people above anything else. A government that does otherwise and serves the special interests is a compromised and corrupt organization, benefiting only those who receive the government's monstrous largesse in the form of military and other government contracts.

There are hundreds of millions of like-minded people scattered across America that want to improve the quality of life in the United States and the world at large. They are all making a small positive change in the winning back of America. We need to organize quickly before the oppressors control all the resources of this great land.

One of the primary initiatives that we can undertake to improve the world is to gather all the groups of like-minded people under one umbrella to efficiently combat the powerful bankers who are hell-bent on destroying this country and our families before we dare organize and stand against such blatant financial tyranny and enslavement.

By uniting, we can afford ourselves a chance to peacefully remove the oppression that too many of us regularly endure. We the people, all the people, are needed to make a difference. Our actions alone and not the actions of the state and its flunky politicians determine the direction of this society. By saying nothing, we are requesting nothing. With our deafening silence, there is no demand or insistence for the improvement of our society, and that simply allows the criminals to run amuck and continue to destroy the place. Only by rising up and being heard will we be able to improve our society and implement sane, pro-survival policies that elevate humanity and the environment; only then will humanity finally have a chance to live in peace and brotherly love.

We are responsible for the government we get. All Americans should participate and demand that the government rise to a more acceptable level of decency and provide for the needs of the people above all else.

The Founding Fathers demanded there be government control and issuance of the nation's redeemable money when they conceived the United States of America and its Constitution. Once bankers usurped the country and took control of the nation's money, there was not enough of an outcry from the people demanding that control of the nation's money be immediately returned to the government for the protection of the people.

We are the fortunate ones that can cry out for justice and equity and finally be heard! It is time we demand the US government regain control of the nation's money from the Federal Reserve. By revoking the Federal Reserve's charter and returning the control of the nation's money back to the US government and the people, where it rightly belongs, we immediately emancipate the American people from the tyranny, terrorism, and enslavement created by foreign bankers.

While we are at it, now seems an appropriate time to take back America's out-of-control kleptocratic government and return it to the people by removing all corrupt politicians from the government. Americans need to clean house and get the criminals out of the government and into the prisons that they seem so fond and eager to fill.

Americans allowed a small banking group of criminals to usurp the Capitol and the White House by abandoning our duties and responsibilities as Americans. It is time that citizens unite, stand together, and fulfill our responsibilities to our great nation in honor of those that have suffered and died fighting to preserve our rights and freedom. By uniting, we will rekindle the flames of liberty and once again provide humankind with the greatest nation the world has ever seen. Again, America is the land of the free only for as long as it is the home of the brave. Let us be brave and do our part in the earthly battle between good and evil. Our measure and value as a person are determined by our effectiveness in battling this ubiquitous evil and are the reason we are all here on Earth. We are facing the ultimate test and the ultimate evil. Greatness shall prevail as it always does.

Let us take back America and make it a shining example of a nation where freedom reigns forever.

It is not going to be an easy contest to wrestle control of the government from the avaricious and bloody hands of those in power and to reestablish the government in accordance with the writings of the Founding Fathers. We all must do our part as Americans and guarantee for our children and theirs that the lamp of liberty shall burn brightly, that freedom shall reign, and that the good-hearted shall prevail over the evildoers who bathe in tyranny and injustice.

One thing is guaranteed: complete obliteration of this civilization will occur should the good people fail to fight the good fight against the monetary enslavers of humankind. There are no "do overs" in the fight between good and evil. You either stand up for your freedom or kneel down and kiss the boots of your master.

It is imperative we do what is right in the eyes of our Creator. As stewards of this planet, it is imperative we fulfill our duty to uplift humanity and emancipate the people, or humanity as we know it shall surely perish.

The current financial irregularities of the government alone will lead to an unavoidable financial catastrophe unprecedented in modern history. Imagine the chaos when the bankrupt US government is no longer able to pay its employees; think of the consequences. It is better to act now, while there is still an occasion and ability to act, than to hold our peace and forever suffer as silent slaves.

America's economy, based on the reallocation of wealth from the middle class to the rich, will inevitably result in the rich owning everything, while the middle class joins the ranks of the impoverished and America is recorded as a third-world country in the footnotes of world history.

We the people are up against a colossal banking organization that owns our government lock, stock, and barrel. The people's only course of action is to unite and remove the criminals that have infiltrated our government and render them powerless and penniless. Without unification of the people, the government will simply continue to roll over us as individuals.

By organizing all the separate freedom-fighting groups, we can form a coalition of the people and quickly attain the freedoms that our ancestors died protecting for our benefit and enjoyment.

As a free society, our objectives should minimally include the reestablishment of America's republic—its true form of government. We need to return to having a government of, by, and for the people.

Americans need a government that cares for them, instead of an adversarial government that destroys them. We need a government designed to improve Americans' standard of living and create a peaceful and tranquil society where warfare and hate do not dominate but love and prosperity do.

We Americans have been remiss in our duties to protect the republic Ben Franklin and other fine men created. Now, it is up to us, America's current generation of citizens and the last guardians of the republic, to take a stand and demand that we all live in a country where the government reflects the goodness and decency of the people and not simply the interests of the corporations.

Without organizing, the people are allowing themselves to be steamrolled by the government at every turn of the road. The people of this Earth can survive only if everyone truly becomes a member of an efficient and organized group that stands against oppression. Let us form a coordinated effort to organize the majority of Americans who no longer tolerate being members of a society where people have merely the privileges of slaves and enjoy none of the rights bestowed by God upon free men and women. Let us recapture our human rights and dignity from all who deny us these fundamental essentials.

As individuals unite as a formidable force, we need to recover our God-given rights and stand up as a nation for our lives, our liberties, and our pursuits of happiness, free from governmental oppression and monetary enslavement.

Today we stand alone. We have no Abraham Lincoln to free us. We must emancipate ourselves or suffer indefinitely as slaves. Why should over three hundred million people allow a few thousand psychopaths to deprive us of our rights? Why should we be forced to bow and pay tribute to a group of demented bankers who regard the people as being less than the excrement produced by the beasts of the field?

The degraded state of humanity results from unethical and abusive politicians under the direction of their monetary rulers. There are no accidents; the monetary rulers execute their intentions and objectives every minute of every day.

The shackles of the bankers' brand of slavery are forever tightening around our throats. Let us rip our chains off while we still have the chance and the strength.

There is terror and abject suffering in this world because the monetary rulers create, invite, and propagate it. None of the universal vices of this planet—starvation, crime, terror, and war—are being solved by the monetary rulers. Instead, those universal vices are being implemented and expanded in accordance with the sick and twisted agenda of the bankers.

The time has come for us to take stock as human beings and form an organized strategy that will correct the path of our civilization, the path that we have allowed politicians to take us down for the past few centuries. We have had enough of government-imposed treachery and suffering.

Without actions to restore America's monetary system, our children and their children will live in oppressive servitude that we can barely comprehend or want to imagine. If one thinks that it is difficult to survive in America today, one just needs to consider what it will be like once the Federal Reserve currency fails and the United States enters a depression, the likes of which make the Great Depression seem like a walk in the park.

Inaction by the people will lead to an unseen catastrophe for this nation. If we fail to act, future generations will hold us liable for extinguishing the brightest light of liberty ever to shine in this world. Whether the future of this planet becomes a version of heaven or hell will be determined by whether we undertake to improve our society or sit and watch as it decays before our very eyes. What we do today determines a big part of our tomorrow and all our tomorrows to come.

There is no escape, no turning one's head away from the colossal calamity that stares us smack in the face. There is nothing worse for us to do than to do nothing. It is always better to act until you succeed, rather than to not act and surely fail.

A slave is someone who does not question his or her oppressor and willingly complies with unjust demands that diminish one's own liberties and freedoms. Rather than standing against any and all tyranny that imposes unjust demands, a slave cowardly capitulates and often silently assents to forfeit his or her rights and, ultimately, his or her dignity. As the unexamined life is not worth living, a life accepting oppression and enslavement is a life void of self-actualization and the fulfillment of one's human destiny.

Americans were not born slaves; we were legislated into slaves. Let us change the criminal banking legislation and rid the world of the financial tyranny that is typically enforced at the wrong end of a gun.

For centuries, America has been revered the world over as the greatest of nations, a hopeful and promising land where the American Dream flourishes, a land where the rights, liberties, and freedoms of the people are enjoyed and protected from tyrannical infringement by the government.

As Americans, we do not have an abundance of time in which we can regain our freedom. We either act now or accept the consequences of inaction. The future of this great nation and the entire planet depends upon what each one of us does here and now to build a better world. Let us not let ourselves down, let us not let America down, and let us not let down our brothers and sisters from around the world.

Americans are not quitters, and we certainly are not going to quit on the freedoms and rights of the human race. Americans have allowed ourselves to turn on each other like crabs in a bucket, our individual actions preventing our nation and our world from evolving to a higher plane. Together we can inform, educate, and help our fellow man to unite and work to return America to its status as the world's greatest beacon of light, hope, and love. By earnestly improving America, we can and will elevate the entire world.

Start today; do something right now that makes a positive difference in all your future actions; make a decision and a commitment to help humanity. Live as a free person lives. Join and support groups that have a mission to improve the human condition, and get to work. Work for the betterment of others in all your actions; make the world a better place. Join us at 911andtheworldtoday.com and make a difference we can be proud of.

I once heard that if we ask the universe, "How much time should we spend making this world a better place?" the universe will indubitably answer, "Spend it all. There's really nothing better to do. If you want to feel better about yourself, help another."

In this world, we all share a united and universal battle for our freedom. We are all counting on each other, and we are especially counting on you. We look forward to hearing good things from you,